PRINCIPLES

OF

CIVIL PROCEDURE

Second Edition

By

Kevin M. Clermont

Flanagan Professor of Law,
Cornell University

CONCISE HORNBOOK SERIES®

Mat #40709199

Concise Hornbook Series, WESTLAW, and West Group are trademarks registered in the U.S. Patent and Trademark Office.

Printed in the United States of America

ISBN: 978–0–314–19050–5

TEXT IS PRINTED ON 10% POST CONSUMER RECYCLED PAPER

Summary of Contents

Table of Contents

PRINCIPLES
OF
CIVIL PROCEDURE
Second Edition

*

Chapter 1

INTRODUCTION*

Table of Sections

§ 1.1 Civil Procedure Analyzed

A. Approaches to Civil Procedure

The topic of civil procedure concerns the societal processes for handling disputes of a noncriminal sort. But that rough definition tends to subordinate the importance of the subject by casting it as merely adjectival law. Procedure is important in its own right as an integral part of a system of justice; moreover, as the machinery of the legal system, procedure implements substantive law and, in so doing, inevitably affects substantive law in profound ways. As Felix Frankfurter put it, "I am not one of those who think that procedure is just folderol or noxious moss. Procedure—the fair, orderly and deliberative method by which claims are to be litigated—goes to the very substance of law."[1] Or, "The history of liberty has largely been the history of observance of procedural safeguards."[2]

---

* Actually, I would like to begin by thanking my summer research assistant, Sara Coelho '06, for her superb work on this book.

1. Cook v. Cook, 342 U.S. 126, 133 (1951) (Frankfurter, J., dissenting) (annulment of marriage case).

2. McNabb v. United States, 318 U.S. 332, 347 (1943) (Frankfurter, J.); see also Shaughnessy v. United States ex rel. Mezei, 345 U.S. 206, 224 (1953)

(Jackson, J., dissenting) ("Only the untaught layman or the charlatan lawyer can answer that procedures matter not. Procedural fairness and regularity are of the indispensable essence of liberty. Severe substantive laws can be endured if they are fairly and impartially applied. Indeed, if put to the choice, one might well prefer to live under Soviet substantive law applied in good faith by our common-law procedures than under our

1

Of course, the civil side of law is extraordinarily significant. Civil procedure is too—even as a subject of instruction in law school. Every lawyer of any sort can profit from a sophisticated knowledge of civil procedure, just as any law student can make much more sense of his or her other courses through an attentive study of civil procedure.

Facing down tides of disbelief, I have observed many times that for most students the course in civil procedure turns out to be not only an important subject but also the most pleasant surprise of the first year of law school. Civil procedure provides a series of revelations: it is not a how-to-do-it course, but is instead a course centered on a number of engrossing problems; it does not limit itself to the tactical mechanics of litigation, but extends to fundamental issues lurking at the fringes and in the interstices of those mechanics; it involves more than mere rules, as it plunges to problematic policies and then down to the profundities of needs, values, and ultimate goals lying below; and it conveys much information, but it addresses the unanswerable as well. The subject matter is quite foreign to the lay person and is not simple, but that provides challenge. In short, the systematic study of civil procedure should turn out to be interesting, new, challenging—and fun.

Nonetheless, teaching civil procedure is not easy. Where to start the course? The chief difficulty in breaking down civil procedure for systematic study is that interdependencies so dominate and characterize the subject. To understand anything the student must understand everything. The difficulty of access has prompted teachers to blaze many different approaches into this seamless web. Most approaches share this basic method: first to present the whole subject in survey fashion, then to study a series of fundamental problems of procedure, and finally to return to the whole subject by way of conclusion; the opening analytical orientation enables and facilitates the subsequent in-depth study of major problems that will illuminate that initial overview, while the study of major problems ultimately lays the groundwork for the closing synthesis. But within this standard method, or any other method, teachers have found room for a nearly infinite variety of emphasis and perspective. Still, their common goal is to build up to a solid grasp of civil procedure as a whole.

substantive law enforced by Soviet procedural practices."); Joint Anti–Fascist Refugee Comm. v. McGrath, 341 U.S. 123, 179 (1951) (Douglas, J., concurring) ("It is procedure that spells much of the difference between rule by law and rule by whim or caprice. Steadfast adherence to strict procedural safeguards is our main assurance that there will be equal justice under law.").

Georges Braque, Man with a Guitar (1911)

B. Approach of This Book

This book tries to break down the subject of civil procedure along the standard lines: a brief orientation and a lengthier overview, followed by a close inspection of major procedural problems, and then some reflections in conclusion. This book's selection of four problems (governing law, authority to adjudicate, former adjudication, and complex litigation) appropriately aims at informing students about the legal system under which they live: (1) one in which the federal and state relation is key, (2) one in which allocation of authority among the states is key, (3) one in which the separation of powers between the judiciary and other branches is key, and (4) one in which the capacity of the judiciary to adapt in handling new kinds of cases is key. Selection of all four of these problems is all the more appropriate because today they arise in an increasingly complex and globalized setting, and so they remain fresh and important. Hence, these four are tending increasingly to become the standard in civil procedure courses.

Chapter One of this book, sketching **introductory considerations**, provides a general *orientation* in the whole subject of civil procedure, by analytically breaking the subject down into comprehensible units. It also kicks off the study of the subject with a survey of its *history*.

Chapter Two, an overview of the **stages of litigation**, completes the introduction to civil procedure by tracing, at a considerably more detailed level, the six steps from commencing a lawsuit in some trial court to completing the final appeal in the highest available appellate court: *forum* selection, *pretrial* practice, *settlement* process, *trial* practice, *judgment* entry, and *appeal* practice. These mechanics of litigation appear to the untutored as the totality of procedure, but in fact many proceduralists and many procedure courses are mainly devoted instead to the four major problems lurking around these mechanics. Nevertheless, exploring the mechanics at the outset serves to give a structure to the subject of civil procedure.

Chapter Three, on **governing law**, examines a question that pervades the overview and deserves systematic treatment: when should a court choose to apply the law of some sovereign other than its own? This poses problems of interstate and international *choice of law* and also problems involving the *Erie* doctrine that concerns the choice between federal and state law.

Chapter Four, on **authority to adjudicate**, treats a major problem of civil procedure that arises at the start of the overview. There, it was assumed that the plaintiff had properly selected a court with authority to adjudicate. In fact, that preliminary step can be a most difficult and significant one. It involves satisfying three threshold requirements: *subject-matter jurisdiction, territorial authority to adjudicate*, and *notice*. Moreover, these requirements entail consideration of such subsumed matters as state and federal court systems, territorial jurisdiction, venue, and service of process.

Chapter Five, on **former adjudication**, studies a question that arises at the end of the overview: what impact does a previously rendered adjudication have in subsequent litigation? This question primarily entails problems of res judicata, a doctrine that pursues finality in its specification of the effects to be given a judgment, the judicial branch's end-product.

Chapter Six, on **complex litigation**, investigates the restrictions on which claims and parties the litigants must or may join in their lawsuit. In the overview, it was generally assumed that a single plaintiff was suing a single defendant on a single claim. In practice, much more complex *multiclaim* and *multiparty* lawsuits enjoy ever-increasing frequency and importance.

Chapter Seven, conveying **concluding considerations**, symmetrically begins with a glance at the *future* of civil procedure and closes with a *synthesis* of the subject that tries to reassemble the analyzed units into a comprehensible whole. Just as the focus of the initial chapter of this book on civil procedure had to be on breaking down the whole for systematic study, final review should seek the big picture by reconsidering the whole. For you art history majors who have wandered into law school, we will have then completed the procession from analytical to synthetic cubism. Picasso showed how much clearer everything will become.

Pablo Picasso, Harlequin with Violin (1918)

§ 1.2   History of Civil Procedure

Perhaps no single vantage point better reveals the subject of civil procedure than the historical one.[3] Although there is a constant danger of oversimplification in any historical study, the lessons can be incredibly illuminating. As I shall try to show as a broad example, a peculiar Anglo–Saxon and Norman society produced a certain procedural system, and that procedural system determined our procedural law of today and, more surprisingly, shaped our current substantive law as well.

A.   English Roots

Our legal system can be fairly clearly traced back to roots in the English system of a millennium ago.[4] One can safely be rather indefinite about the length of these roots because of the surprising

---

3. See generally Daniel R. Coquillette, The Anglo–American Legal Heritage (2d ed. 2004); John Maxcy Zane, The Story of Law (Charles J. Reid, Jr., ed., 2d ed. 1998).

4. See generally J.H. Baker, An Introduction to English Legal History (4th ed. 2002) (best treatment); Frederick G. Kempin, Jr., Historical Introduction to Anglo–American Law in a Nutshell (3d

ed. 1990) (simplified treatment); The Oxford History of the Laws of England (John Baker gen. ed., 2003–) (to be eventually twelve volumes treating the subject chronologically); Katherine Topulos, English Legal History Research Guide, http://www.law.duke.edu/lib/research guides/englishlegal.html (general bibliography).

legal continuity over the centuries—from the Anglo–Saxon invasions in the 400s, which wiped Roman law clean from the Briton slate, through the Viking and then Norman invasions and until the latter 1100s, when England's common law began to flower.[5] In other words, one can be safely indefinite about the beginning date, and just say that our legal system began developing sometime during that long continuous period after 410, when the Romans abandoned Britain with dramatic effect.

During that long period, various institutions served the function of courts. Some of these embodied centralized royal authority. Far more important, at that time, were the local authorities, who wielded most of the judicial power. This is the era of overlapping legal systems. The early story of procedure is in large part the story of the eventual displacement of local by royal authority. So let me begin at the local level in late Anglo–Saxon times.

The **local courts** comprised communal and feudal courts. As to the communal courts, the basic organizational unit was the hundred, notionally containing one hundred families of freemen. A freeman was a male who was not a villein—that is, not a serf who held land as a tenant at will of his lord, who owed often an uncertain amount of agricultural services to the lord, and who could not enforce any rights against the lord. A varying number of hundreds constituted the shires, or counties.

Once a month, each hundred held a moot, or assembly, at which the freemen would discuss local business, both administrative and judicial. This body was fully competent in matters criminal and civil. It is quite a stretch, however, to call this body a court. There were no trained judges or lawyers applying the law or keeping any records; instead, these were public meetings transacting public business in accordance with local custom. The hundred's assembly handled the more judicial matters not by reasoned decisionmaking, but by pushing settlement or by appealing to the supernatural. The simple purpose was to channel and discourage the urge toward violent self-help and blood-feud. The typical remedy was a fine such as wergeld, or blood-money in an amount dependent on the injured victim's social station.

Twice a year the shire's royally appointed chief official, at first the ealdorman and later the reeve (shire-reeve or sheriff), convened an assembly of the more important freemen of the shire. The shire's assembly proceeded in the same manner as the hundred's. Indeed, it had no hierarchical relationship with the hundred, although presumably it handled the more important disputes.

5. See Hunt Janin, Medieval Justice 64–73 (2004).

Similarly, a confusing welter of other decentralized and nonspecialized local authorities, such as borough assemblies, acting more as meetings than as courts, helped dispose of the rest of the nation's judicial-type business.

As to the feudal courts, they were a natural outgrowth of the prevailing feudal system, although they grew in importance after the Norman Conquest. At a time when violence was rife, the smaller had to seek protection from the greater, in the exchange becoming tenants of the latter. The lord handled civil disputes between his tenants in so-called seignorial courts. The lord might also exercise criminal jurisdiction, by special grant from the king, in so-called franchise courts. These private feudal courts dispensed a brand of justice that involved the individual lord's view of the case, unlike the communal courts' purer resort to custom.

Such was the legal system of those days. It might seem undeveloped to our eyes, but imagine the conditions.[6] England was a rough and wild land, with a small dispersed population. Travel was difficult, with roads long unrepaired and most rivers unbridged. Land was all-important, being not only necessary for subsistence but also the chief determinant of status. Agriculture was the chief activity, and little trade went on. Disputes centered on land, with injuries to person and property being a growing concern, but with contract disputes being few and simple. A primitive legal system sufficed.

Nevertheless, a **royal court** existed too. After all, the king was not an insignificant figure for that time, as Alfred the Great had converted a bunch of tribes into almost a real kingdom in part of England way back in the late 800s, and Canute had created a national kingship from 1018. Still, the English king had less power than we today are apt to imagine, and he had to remain constantly on the move throughout the kingdom to preserve it. So English government was quite decentralized, although much less so than the rest of Europe at that time.

Over the centuries, the kings had begun to concern themselves with justice, and indeed to appear as its fountainhead. They precociously used writs, which were formally written royal orders directed to particular official persons, to confer or define jurisdiction. And the seed of the later royal courts existed in the king's council of wise men, or the witan as it was then called. First, the witan served as a feudal court for tenants-in-chief, who were the king's top supporters holding their land directly from him. Second, it acted on occasion as a court of last resort for ordinary litigants in cases of failure of justice in the local courts. Third, the witan concerned

6. See Robert Lacey & Danny Danziger, The Year 1000: What Life Was   Like at the Turn of the First Millennium: An Englishman's World (1999).

itself with the steadily lengthening list of matters of special interest to the king, namely, the criminal pleas of the crown and especially acts done with force and arms breaching the king's peace. But the peace that the king had a special interest in preserving, so that a crime against that peace offended the king directly, was then far from having its ultimately all-encompassing scope, being limited to certain persons (such as those within a peace given by the king's own hand), certain places (such as the four great highways of England), and certain times (his coronation and the three annual festivals).

As to the substantive law underlying the whole local and royal process, it was mainly diverse customs, albeit the customs of powerful rather than ordinary people. In addition, kings had granted some special privileges and had compiled dooms, or codes. But these codes were quite limited in effect. They were incomplete, which presented no theoretical or practical problem because local customs underlay them. Much of the codes consisted of homilies, or good-sounding but empty admonitions. The codes might also regulate administration of justice and sometimes treat novel matters, and they did fix the amount of blood-money payable for various offenses. But the rest of their substance declared and clarified bits of local customs rather than displaced them wholesale. Although the codes thus did provide a little uniformity, lots of theoretical and practical room for variation persisted in the communal traditions. The point here is that, in any real sense, there was no legislation and no king's law. Substantive law was custom.

In another sense, there was no substantive law at all in legal proceedings. Formulaic claim met opaque denial, which was subjected to some supernatural test like ordeal. Such a legal system can generate rules as to procedure and remedies, but not substantive law, which simply has no role to play. Substantive issues arise only if the procedure is sophisticated enough for parties to take positions and for an adjudicator to have to weigh them. The point is "that early lawsuits settle disputes without raising questions of substantive law and that progress depends upon procedural changes which allow such questions to emerge."[7] It was only much later in the royal courts, after 1300, that more specific pleading began posing legal questions for the judges and also that the development of the jury prompted jurors' desire for instruction on the law. Then, the bearing of facts on some notion of substantive law started receiving attention and discussion.

Onto this Anglo–Saxon scene came the Normans. Legal historians formerly tended to stress the impact of the Norman Conquest of England in 1066, but in reality it was a small deal legally, albeit

7. S.F.C. Milsom, A Natural History of the Common Law 2 (2003).

a traumatic one politically and socially.[8] William the Conqueror claimed a lawful right to the English throne, under a succession promised by his relative Edward the Confessor. Although William came to a governmental and legal system basically similar to that of Normandy, he kept England and Normandy separate. One of his first acts after the Conquest was to promise the English that they could keep their laws, pronouncing that "you be worthy of all the laws that you were worthy of in the time of King Edward." The principal legal effects of the Conquest were a strengthened set of feudal courts and a stronger monarchy with a true gift for administration.

Once these long roots of our legal system were entrenched, England's common law—here in the sense of law common to all of England, as opposed to local custom—developed rapidly from the latter 1100s. Over the ensuing centuries, England's common law fundamentally divided into "common law" and "equity," which were two distinct systems of justice with different (1) origins, (2) courts, (3) procedure, (4) remedies, (5) substance, and (6) problems. I shall now describe these six features for each of the two systems, before turning to the process of reform that brings us down to today's law.

1. Common Law

The system of common law was the older of the two. Its eventual marker was that its courts offered trial by jury, but gave relief only in the form of money damages or recovery of possession pursuant to a rigid regime of substantive law.

a. Origins

In the 1100s the English kings started to expand their judicial influence by drawing on their traditional prerogative powers, such as the power to keep the king's peace. Royal attention at first focused on criminal and land cases, but later expanded to other types of disputes. Significantly, royal justice was a vast improvement over its competitors. Ultimately, the central royal system of common law came to dominate the judicial scene.

A principal technique in this expansion of royal powers was the issuance of writs, certain of which had the effect of bringing cases before the king and his councillors, or the curia regis as it was now called. Why was there a reliance on writs, and how did this reliance create the central role for the **writ system** in the development of the common law?

---

8. See David Howarth, 1066: The Year of the Conquest (1977).

In the jurisdictional contest between the local courts and the royal authority exercised by the curia regis, the latter was exercising what was in theory exceptional jurisdiction to provide justice not in the ordinary course. Therefore, the litigant had to kickstart the king's court into action, doing so by getting the king to grant specially the favor of royal justice. This grant usually came in the shape of a writ, written in Latin on parchment with the king's seal attached.[9] The officer in charge of writs was the chancellor, who was the handler of the king's written business and the keeper of the Great Seal of England. The plaintiff went to the chancellor to seek the particular writ that fit his case. The chancellor's staff, or Chancery, issued the writ for a fee. The writs that operated as a pass into the royal court, and thereby originated the proceeding, were called original writs. In such a writ the king ordered the local sheriff to get things going, the sheriff noted his action on the writ itself, and then he returned it to the court. The action was then rolling in the royal court.

Under Henry II in the latter 1100s, two general sorts of original writ existed for civil matters. First, the oldest writs were merely executive commands, often to the sheriff, to take some specified action. From them developed the praecipe writs, which told the sheriff to command (*praecipe*) someone to do right as demanded or else come into the king's court to explain the refusal. The prototype—the so-called writ of right—lay for invoking royal oversight of feudal courts' decisions on right to land. This approach built on the king's special and obvious interest in rectifying contempt of his precepts. As these writs dealt with matters of eternal "right," such as feudal tenure, the common law handled them solemnly and slowly.

Second, Henry II developed the possessory assizes, such as novel disseisin and mort d'ancestor, to deal with the wrong of dispossession of land by one's lord without due process. Later, but from similar roots, the ostensurus quare writs emerged to tell the sheriff directly to make the defendant appear in the king's court and show why (*ostensurus quare*) he had committed an alleged wrongdoing of some other sort. This general approach built on the king's peace idea that had already conquered all important criminal cases. These writs dealt with a mere "wrong," or past events generically called trespasses on the civil side, so the common law handled them a good deal more expeditiously than the praecipe writs. Of course, plaintiffs preferred the more expeditious ostensurus quare writs (like trespass and its bountiful progeny), which came as well to offer jury trial as the mode of proof and money

---

9. See David Mellinkoff, The Language of the Law (1963) (legal use of Latin, Law French, and English).

damages as the usual type of remedy, to the older praecipe writs (like covenant, debt, and detinue).

As new needs emerged, the chancellor drafted new types of original writ. But in the 1200s, in reaction to the expanding royal power that had by then conquered all of criminal law and much of civil law, the feudal lords managed to put constraints on the chancellor's inventiveness. This produced a closed set of original writs issued as a matter "of course," such as covenant, debt, and detinue as well as trespass and the other early ostensurus quare writs of ejectment and replevin, each covering a specific grievance of an ordinary sort.

The lords' success was temporary. By the 1300s the common law had begun growing again, but it now did so by the royal courts' approval of stretching and fictionalizing the established writs' fairly fixed wording to reach such matters as trespass on the case, trover, special assumpsit, and general assumpsit.

The irony here was that these writs, developed for very practical jurisdictional reasons, later became the intellectual framework of the law. The prominent role of the royal writs as the common law's framework is shown by a glance at England's very first legal treatise.[10] It dates from around 1188 and is questionably attributed to Ranulf de Glanvill, Henry II's chief officer, who held the old office of justiciar. Already the royal court was busy enough to justify a treatise based solely on its workings. More tellingly, this treatise's organization was predominantly a compilation of almost eighty writs and the associated procedures peculiar to each. Thus, the treatise's rules centered on procedure. Procedure was what a man who was learned in law had learned. And procedure turned on writs. There was no such thing as procedure at law, but rather there was procedure for an action of debt or whatever.

Within the confines of each type of writ the substantive law eventually grew up to create a "form of action," growing independently of the substantive law within every other type of writ and associated form of action. In the long run, the substantive law grew, as the royal courts' rulings on party pleadings and jury instructions, deciding whether a remedy lay but with no great substantive scheme in mind, slowly specified elements and defenses for the particular form of action.

10. The Treatise on the Laws and Customs of the Realm of England Com-   monly Called Glanvill (G.D.G. Hall ed. & trans., 1965).

HENRY II ATTEMPTS TO
INVENT THE COMMON LAW

Copyright © 1996, Stephen Morillo

Why Was Henry II So Important?

The great leap forward occurred under Henry II, who reigned from 1154 to 1189. He was the son of the Count of Anjou and William's granddaughter, with two decades of debilitating civil war necessary for him to reach the throne and thus to found the Plantagenet dynasty. He succeeded in shoring up royal authority at home. Abroad, through warfare and through marriage to Eleanor of Aquitaine—which were seemingly not that different (see the movie. The Lion in Winter (1968))—he extended his rule from Ireland to the Pyrenees.

His greatest and most lasting contribution, however, was to the law. Most of his motives were indirect. He acted to limit the power of the lords and sheriffs, and he sought the money that came from administering courts. But also he wished to promote order in his realm and especially to provide justice. He took seriously his role as the fountainhead of justice. In actuality, although he did not intend to displace or absorb the local courts, or to create the common law, that was the eventual consequence of his actions. "To put it another way, if Henry II walked into your law office [today], you could easily explain your professional world to him in terms of developments from, or reactions to, thirteenth-century ideas." Daniel R. Coquillette, The Anglo-American Legal Heritage 55 (2d ed. 2004).

The outcome of his initiatives was that by 1300 the royal courts and their common law had triumphed in the battle for supremacy, even though the local courts continued to conduct much judicial business for decades to come. The kings did not manage this triumph by fiat. The persons who used the courts wanted a new system. Suitors preferred the royal courts' brand of justice, and thus these courts quickly became the origin for almost all litigation. Indeed, the triumph was decisive enough that the common law was already showing signs of closing off and some rigidity by 1300.

Henry II was able to play such a key part in legal history because he was an exceptional person. He was a man of action and learning, impetuous and charming, of splendid physique and overwhelming will. However, his temper and other negative aspects of his temperament got him involved in the 1170 murder in the cathedral of his chancellor and archbishop, Thomas à Becket. These two old friends had fallen out in a dispute over jurisdiction, namely, whether royal or ecclesiastical courts would try "criminous clerks," or clergy accused of crime. (See the movie Becket (1964).)

That infamous and disastrous event brings to the fore the relation of the common law to canon and Roman law. The renewed canon law systematized by the monk Gratian, and the academic revival of Roman law upon

> the rediscovery of Justinian's Digest, swept from Italy through Europe in the 1100s and 1200s to create the civil-law system that still prevails there. These developments had undeniably significant effects in England too, but they did not overwhelm the common law. Why not? Largely because the common law had gotten such an early and strong start under Henry II. He immunized his island's precocious legal system from foreign invasion. And so by "a breath-taking twist of fate," today our considerable part of the world lives under the common law, not the civil law. J.H. Baker. An Introduction to English Legal History 28 (4th ed. 2002).

b. Courts

Early on, the curia regis handled the royal judicial work while traveling about with the king and otherwise governing the country. As that workload increased, the fairly natural innovation was division of labor and specialization, a trend encouraged by the king's frequent journeys abroad to tend to the empire. So, the curia regis first spawned a knot of trained jurists, and later a set of **three royal courts** centrally located but with their delegates delivering **itinerant justice** by traveling on circuits throughout the country—just as the successor to the curia regis, the King's Council, would still later produce the legislative and executive branches and other organs of the country's government. Here I shall relate the evolution of that judiciary.

The royal treasury provided the initial display of this tendency to spin off departments. The impracticality of the treasury following the king was evident by the beginning of the 1100s. The barons who managed the treasury therefore settled into a large palace just west of London near a monastery, or minster. At Westminster Palace they did their accounting on a large checkered tablecloth, which served as a money counting board. Their department consequently became known as the Exchequer.

Meanwhile, Henry II played an active judicial role, often sitting as a judge in his traveling court. But he was especially often absent from the realm, producing an acute problem for the administration of justice. So in 1178, he detached five judges from his entourage to hear cases regularly in the banquet hall of Westminster Palace. The tribunal started to keep records in the form of plea rolls.[11]

When King John, the youngest son of Henry II, tried to bring all litigation before his traveling court once again, those persons who had come to enjoy the advantages of a stationary court protested strongly. The result was the provision in chapter 17 of the Magna Carta in 1215 by which King John promised to maintain in a certain place the hearing of common pleas (which were actions against other subjects as opposed to actions involving the king):

---

11. See Baker, supra note 4, at 18–20, 175–94, 196–97 (court reports and legal treatises).

"Common Pleas shall not follow our court, but shall be held in some certain place." So courts remained at Westminster throughout the tumultuous course of English history. Indeed, one Chief Justice of Common Pleas in the 1660s supposedly refused to move his court a few feet back from the drafty north door, because he viewed any move from the "certain place" as violative of Magna Carta.

Out of this judicial activity at Westminster there slowly evolved a recognizable court for hearing common pleas. It began to keep separate records in 1234, and it acquired a chief justice in 1272. This court—eventually known variously as the Bench, the Place, the Common Bench, or the *Court of Common Pleas*—made most of the common law. It had considerable collateral impact as well. First, for this court a small corps of professional advocates developed, expert in the art of pleading. They soon generated standards governing how others might acquire their title of serjeant-at-law and thus gain admission to their restricted ranks. The serjeant was truly an officer of the court, appearing in court to assist the judges even when the serjeant himself had no cases being heard. Second, the office of judge changed. The early judges tended to be knights or more often clerics, because knights came from the king's entourage and because clerics could read and write. Later the king appointed judges from the ranks of serjeants. Third, this professional bench and bar helped to complexify the legal system. That complexity necessitated study prior to admission to the bar. Thus emerged medieval law students in the form of legal apprentices studying in the nearby Inns of Court and building a sense of independent professional identity.

Still, the curia regis had continued to handle a fair amount of judicial business. But this increasingly specialized business required specialists as decisionmakers. Another true court separated from the curia regis to meet this need. It kept its own records from 1234, and it received a chief justice as early as 1268. It did not always follow the king, although it did retain a close association with him. By a slow formation process, the *Court of King's Bench* became a fully independent court settled in Westminster. It long showed its roots in its official name, "The Justices of our Lord the King Assigned to Hold Pleas before the King Himself," and in the form of its writs, fictionally returnable "before the lord king wheresoever he should be in England." It eventually showed its grandeur in its chief justice's holding the title of Chief Justice of England—and in its conducting some of the most famous trials in English history, such as the one in 1535 condemning Henry VIII's chancellor Thomas More to death for refusing to recognize royal supremacy over the church.[12] The King's Bench had jurisdiction over criminal cases. On the civil side, it at first handled actions involving the king's interest, but by various maneuvers over the centuries it tremendously expanded its jurisdiction to hear personal common pleas, although not the real or mixed actions for the specific recovery of property. Such jurisdictional competition among the royal courts impelled some of the key procedural and substantive reforms. And the King's Bench ended up the busiest by far of the common law's courts.

Finally, the Exchequer, as the department of the treasury, had always had exclusive jurisdiction to decide revenue questions in the course of its functions. But it found ways to handle more ordinary cases. For instance, the writ of quo minus allowed a creditor to invoke its jurisdiction to enforce a mere private debt, on the ground that the king had an interest in any unpaid debt by which the creditor was less able (*quo minus*) to satisfy his tax liabilities to the king. By such clever maneuvers, the Exchequer of Pleas augmented its judicial business until it became a true court exercising a jurisdiction that extended to personal common pleas. It attained coequal status with the two other courts by act of Queen Elizabeth I in 1579. However, the *Court of Exchequer* retained its peculiarities—its judges were even called barons—so that it never played quite the role of the other two courts.

Thus, eventually these three bodies had developed into true courts sitting at Westminster. But by then, the jurisdictions of the three superior courts of common law had begun to overlap so extensively as to make their continued coexistence rather confusing. Yet their competition for business fostered innovation and long kept the lid on abuses.

Of course, royal justice could not completely localize its operation at Westminster. Litigants, and the needed jurors from the locality where the cause arose, could not always travel there. So, the royal courts relied on a scheme of itinerant justice to handle cases around the country. From the beginning the Norman kings regularly sent out high commissioners, later called the eyre, to inquire into the administration of the counties and to entertain cases, their visitations becoming normalized over six judicial circuits under Henry II from 1174. Between the regularized eyres, more ad hoc judicial commissions traveled the country, in fact taking over the task of itinerant justice upon the abolition of the unpopular eyre in the early 1300s. With time, the commissioner was more and more likely to be a judge from any one of the three common-law courts.

12. See John Guy, The Tudor Age, in The Oxford History of Britain 257, 282 (Kenneth O. Morgan ed., rev. ed. 1999).

Then the central courts integrated those itinerant institutions into royal justice by developing the nisi prius system. The nisi prius system entailed the plaintiff's commencing an action at Westminster. A writ would then order the sheriff of the county where the action arose to send jurors to Westminster, unless before (*nisi prius*) the rather distant trial date a traveling judge appeared in order to hold court in that county. As he always arrived before the set trial date, the traveling judge would conduct the trial locally and report the outcome to Westminster for entry of judgment. Thus, the king's justice became available throughout the realm, in increasingly regularized fashion.

Westminster Hall

Why Was Westminster Hall So Important?

Westminster Hall, the palace banquet hall, was the home of the three common-law courts until they moved to the Royal Courts of Justice on the Strand in 1882. The magnificent Westminster Hall, built by the year 1099 and remodeled in the late 1300s, was a then-astonishing 239.25 feet long, 67.5 feet wide, and 92 feet high. Being a center of political life, it hosted such events as the coronation banquets, at which the King's Champion would ride his horse into the hall and symbolically challenge anyone to dispute the succession. It was the venue for state trials, including the trial of Thomas More. Most gloriously, it was the forum where the common law developed. Today it remains a wonder, attached to the Houses of Parliament and still in occasional use for ceremonial functions.

As in the reprinted drawing from the year 1738, one entered Westminster Hall by the great north door. On the left of the far wall you can see the

Court of King's Bench, separated by a flight of stairs from the Court of Chancery. On the near right wall, you can see the Court of Common Pleas. Nearer still on that wall was a passageway to a large chamber where the Court of Exchequer sat. A "bar," at which counsel stood, separated each court from the greater room. Inside the bar was a large table covered with a green cloth (or a checkered cloth in the Exchequer), at which the court officials kept records. The judges sat on a high bench against the wall, under tapestries bearing the royal arms.

On both sides of the hall were shops rented to booksellers and clothiers. Food vendors circulated noisily among the milling populace. The result was a racket mixed confusingly with court proceedings. A visitor, around the time of the drawing, reported being "surprised to see in the same place, men on the one side with baubles and toys, and the other taken up with the fear of judgement, on which depends their inevitable destiny. In this shop are sold ribbons and gloves, towels and commodes by word of mouth; in another shop lands and tenements are disposed of by decree. On your left hand you hear a nimble-tongued painted seamstress, with her charming treble invite you to buy some of her nicknacks; and on your right a deep-mouthed cryer demanding impossibilities: that silence be kept among women and lawyers." Patrick Cormack, Westminster Palace & Parliament 18 (1981).

c. Procedure

The writ system shaped the law. Generally, the plaintiff established jurisdiction by obtaining a writ, and he had to pick the correct writ for his grievance. Each writ eventually generated its own form of action, with a distinctive procedural (and remedial) law, as well as a distinctive substantive law. For our purposes, a critical feature of the procedural law was the **pleading system**.

The particular writ dictated the requirements of the pleadings (which comprised the ping-pong of declaration, demurrer or plea, replication, rejoinder, surrejoinder, rebutter, surrebutter, etc.). The techniques of pleading changed with time. Early on, pleading was oral in Law French. Lawyers told their stories informally in a "counte" (from the French word for a story) and a specific defense, tentatively feeling their way toward joinder of issue with the advice of the judges. But in the 1400s pleadings became written, in the 1500s binding, and in the 1600s highly technical.

Pleading in theory worked for the good. "[P]leading is the honorable, commendable and profitable part of the law, and by good desert it is so. For cases arise by chance, and are many times intricate, confused and obscured, and are cast into form, and made evident, clear and easie, both to Judge and jury (which are the arbitrators of all causes) by good and fair pleading. So that this is the principal art of law, for pleading is not talking; and therefore it is required that pleading be true; that is, the goodness and virtue of pleading; and that it be certain and single, and that is the beauty and grace of pleading."[13] Nevertheless, pleading in practice degenerated into a baleful game of skill.[14]

13. Slade v. Drake, 80 Eng. Rep. 439, 440 (C.P. 1618) (Hobart, C.J.).

The pleadings were supposed to produce on each count a single issue of law or fact. If that issue was legal, the whole court of four or five judges decided it in banc. If factual, the court sent it out to be heard before a single judge on circuit sitting with a local jury at nisi prius; testimony was oral, but this efficiency was offset by the limitation that kept the parties themselves from testifying because they were interested witnesses; a jury decided the factual dispute; and, at least later in history, legal issues were allowed to return after trial to the in banc court at Westminster.

Pleading was a critical link between procedure and substance. Pleading produced questions of law for the judges, such as which circumstances must exist to constitute a trespass or a defense thereto. The result was the development of substantive law.

Why Was the Mode of Proof So Important?

A major reason for suitors' preferring the royal courts was that those courts employed a superior method of proof. The story here is the development of jury trial. "This is the procedure, far more rational than battle, or ordeal, or wager of law, which the king's court has at its command when it begins to bid against the communal and feudal courts." F.W. Maitland, The Forms of Action at Common Law 19 (1936).

The local courts, when faced with contradiction, had long used trial by ordeal or by oath. The plaintiff had to establish a prima facie case, albeit merely by oaths in very general terms. The defendant next swore the truth of his position, again in very general terms. The court would then require the defendant either to undergo an ordeal or to bring in oath-helpers in support of his oath. The court did not second-guess the ordeal or dissect the oaths, and of course there was no cross-examination.

Trial by ordeal was an ancient mode in criminal cases. A fair number of types of ordeal existed, but in England most involved fire or water. The precise ordeal depended on the defendant's status and the alleged offense. For example, freemen usually underwent the ordeal of hot iron. The accused fasted for three days. At the most solemn moment of a mass, the priest exhorted the accused to confess if guilty. The recalcitrant accused had to carry one or three pounds of burning iron in the form of a bar over a distance of three or nine feet, depending on the offense. Bandages went on the hand for three days. Finally, inspection: if the hand was clean, the accused was innocent, but if infected, guilty. The ordeal of cold water entailed dunking the bound defendant in a blessed pond: the guilty floated, but the water received the innocent who was promptly pulled out. Obviously, trial by ordeal heavily involved the Church. This involvement led to disquiet and eventually to the discredit of trial by ordeal. Finally, in 1215, the Lateran Council forbade clergy from participating in ordeals and thus completed their demise.

Trial by oath, or so-called wager of law, was the principal form of proof in civil cases, as well as in some early criminal cases. The defendant had to bring in eleven of his neighbors to swear that his oath was "clean." These oath-helpers, or compurgators, swore as to the defendant's general credibility, not as to the specific facts of the case. They had to recite precisely. "The

---

14. See Benjamin J. Shipman, Handbook of Common–Law Pleading (3d ed. 1923).

oath that [defendant] hath sworn is true, so help me God and the saints." The outcome lay solely with the compurgators. Under this method the local courts never had to go behind the oaths and get into the facts, nor did they have to develop and refine a substantive law. The royal courts temporarily adopted the old modes of proof, but continued to use trial by oath regularly in certain of the older forms of action until about 1600, thereby contributing to the unpopularity among suitors of those older forms of action. Formal abolition of wager of law awaited 1833. This method surely worked better during religious times in small communities than during later years at Westminster where the defendant could rent compurgators at a modest rate.

The Normans apparently introduced into England trial by battle, for use in some civil and criminal cases. The battle determined the case's outcome, so the court served only as umpire. In civil cases, hired champions, who in fiction were contradictory witnesses, fought to the point of exhausted submission. In criminal cases, accuser and accused fought, usually to the death. Never too common or trusted, trial by battle fell off in use almost completely during the 1200s.

These methods of conflict-resolution seem primitive to us, but remember their context. Early on, they served more the purposes of religious and social resolution than truth-finding. But even as truth-finding mechanisms, they may have worked better than we would guess. The participants were God-fearing persons who fully expected a sign from above and who would not lightly risk damnation by lying. Less obviously, but more importantly, the adjudicator likely chose and manipulated the mode of proof to facilitate the right outcome. The system was not wholly irrational. As already suggested, however, these methods kept the courts from working with the facts or with the substantive law. For those courts, procedure was all.

The various inadequacies of the old modes of proof left the royal courts and their litigants yearning for a new way. But it was not tolerable for the judge to usurp the divine role of finding truth. Instead, the slightly less upsetting new way—trial by jury—drew on ancient antecedents from throughout northern Europe. In England the jury was at first a group of local people summoned by public official to give upon oath their true word, or verdict, on some question put to them. That question might be a matter of administration, or it might have arisen in litigation. It might involve naming the landowners in the district, such as the inquests contributing to the historic Domesday Book compiled under William the Conqueror to ascertain title to land on the grand scale of the whole realm. It might involve identifying the suspects of crime, this jury of accusation evolving into the grand jury. Or it might involve deciding who had the greater right to a disputed piece of land, as this jury called the assize did in the actions called the possessory assizes under Henry II. This new method of trial was fundamentally innovative, in that it actually passed on the merits. But the twelve men only "recognized" the facts on the basis of what they knew or could find out on their own, and they were subject to judicial interrogation. Because of their witness-like function, the jurors necessarily came from the locality where the cause arose.

The trial jury was thus on its way to displace the older modes of proof. As its use increased, spreading to the criminal law and then to the new family of trespass writs during the 1200s, its character changed. In the 1300s, rules of sequestration and unanimity arose: from the moment of the jurors' oath until their verdict, the jury was shielded from outside contact; decision became a collective adjudication, no longer permitted by majority vote. In the 1400s, the jury ceased being a group of witnesses and began to develop into a representative and impartial group to hear evidence. The royal courts, with their nisi prius system to try cases locally, were now effectively employing modern trial by jury.

The consequences of the rise of jury trial were profound. Its single-episode trial and its orality critically shaped procedure. But it deeply affected substance too. It slowly forced the separation of questions of law from questions of fact. The lay jury by its very existence, and the general verdict by its predominant use, then forced the judges to formulate substantive law when instructing the jurors on matters of law. And in order to pose precisely the questions of fact to the jurors, pleading became a fine art at the core of the lawyers' job and developed further as the other instrument for producing substantive law.

d. Remedies

Under the mature common law, if the plaintiff succeeded, the court gave relief as an order that "plaintiff do recover" money damages, or sometimes that plaintiff do recover possession of land (ejectment) or a chattel (replevin). A legal judgment, then, is not an order to the defendant. It is up to the plaintiff to enforce the judgment. The plaintiff must get the sheriff to execute the judgment. Just like today.

e. Substance

Each form of action generated its own substantive law—for example, the sketchy law of trespass that grew up within the writ of trespass. Outside the particular form invoked, there was in effect no law. Thus, pigeonholed procedure shaped substance, and the limit on the number of procedural pigeonholes limited the range of substantive law. The range of law slowly expanded and its contents grew, first property law and then tort and finally contract, evolving by procedural stratagems and incremental rulings in particular cases. The law intuitively served society's pragmatic needs for regulation. But that law was not truly seen as a system, one viewable from above and subject to wide and intentional change by legislation or otherwise.

Thus, English substantive law remained rather undeveloped until very late. Indeed, the English common law's long-standing fragmentation may be the reason behind its historical unattractiveness to outsiders: no other country has ever adopted it voluntarily, except after it infiltrated as an accompaniment to English emigrants.

The major step toward coherent systematization had to await Judge William Blackstone's complacent lectures to young lay gentlemen at Oxford that began in 1753. His self-satisfied effort toward systematization ironically was to expose the common law to criticism and soon to legislative reform.

f. Problems

Early on, the common law sank into rigidity and narrowness. To mitigate this development, fictionalized thinking became rampant. The consequently uncertain boundaries on the forms of action caused all sorts of difficulties. The whole system inevitably came to exalt hideous technicality. In sum, the above-described inadequacies of wooden procedure, limited remedies, and bounded substantive law were all too evident.

2. Equity

The system of equity arose to overcome the growing inadequacies of the common law. Equity's eventual marker was that its courts did not conduct jury trials, but did give relief in the form of ordering the defendant to do or not to do something pursuant to a relatively dynamic substantive law.

a. Origins

The law courts had employed considerable ingenuity in accommodating the forms of action to changing needs. Nevertheless the formulary system was essentially a rigid one. It is unknowable whether it would have collapsed under the pressures of a vastly complexified society if it had stood alone to meet the blows of time. The fact that the formulary system continued well into the 1800s seems attributable in part to the birth and side-by-side existence of a complementary system of justice known as equity.

All along the king and his councillors had continued to act on direct petition to remedy injustice. The origins of equity lay there. Early petitions appealed to pity. The petitioner related that by reason of his poverty or illness, or the wealth and power of his adversary, he was unable to get a remedy in the ordinary course of law. Petitioners were not complaining, or not so much complaining, about the remedial or substantive rules of the common law, but rather about the defects in its procedures or its officials. Later petitions more obviously complained about the woodenness of the common law's substantive law. The petitioner sought to avoid the law's tendency to suffer hardship in his case rather than create an exception to its rule.

b. Courts

Early on, the petitions were addressed to the King's Council for action, with the chancellor shepherding the petitions along. In the 1300s litigants came to petition more frequently in order to circumvent the inadequacies of the common law, in effect creating the separate system of equity. The Council was ever busier, so that around 1350 it took to referring the more routine petitions to the chancellor for action, with instructions to him that increasingly contained only the simple directive to proceed appropriately. By 1400, petitioners were addressing directly the chancellor, who soon thereafter started issuing decrees in his own name. Here were the makings of a new court. Eventually, a recognizable Court of Chancery arose around the chancellor and his staff. It was to be the most notable of the various courts of equity (others included the conciliar courts such as the Star Chamber).

Why did this new jurisdiction fall to the chancellor? The answer lies in administrative convenience. He was a more and more important official on the Council, as well as the one most constantly in attendance. He was usually both a cleric and a lawyer. Moreover, he was already associated with the administration of justice. He had a large and well-organized staff of clerks, who had lots of experience issuing original and other writs, and who would have to get involved anyway in enforcing any remedies issued in response to the petition. Chancery indeed already exercised a common-law jurisdiction—called its Latin side because of its record-keeping language—a jurisdiction consisting largely of cases based on the king's feudal rights and duties. In sum, it was natural for the chancellor to handle cases within this new extraordinary jurisdiction—the so-called English side of Chancery.

c. Procedure

This system of equity was not pinned to any forms of action and had its own procedure. Equitable procedure vastly differed from legal procedure. At first, it was quite informal and streamlined. After examining the narrative of the petition, the chancellor might issue a writ of subpoena ordering the adversary to answer.

The pleadings initially were oral, but eventually almost everything was in writing. Pleadings (bill, answer, etc.) became long and detailed documents. The answer would respond to each of the particular charges of the bill. The chancellor would interrogate the witnesses in writing under oath, and he would seek discovery of other evidence. All testimony was written, but equity had the advantage of being able to compel a party's written testimony and thus to examine his conscience, unlike law where the parties were not competent as witnesses. On the complete dossier, the chancellor, not a jury, would decide, although he could refer disputed facts on an advisory basis to a common-law jury.

The chancellor's individualized decision emerged from the facts and from conscience, rather than from any new general rule. He thus exercised a jurisprudence based on the fair exception. The chancellor did not keep records of most of his decisions, and there was no reliance on precedent. Nevertheless, the chancellor was not acting in conflict with the law, but instead was facilitating and hence reinforcing its operation. The law court could strictly adhere to its rules without having to worry about the hard cases, because equity existed to make exceptions. Moreover, the chancellor's case-focused process ensured that he was not creating general rules in contradiction of the common law.

This arrangement meant that a defendant in a law action might be obliged to "go across the hall" for an injunction staying the law action, doing so where he had some matter that ought to defeat the action and that would be recognized by the chancellor but not by law. So, if a plaintiff brought a contract action "at law," the defendant might have a defense cognizable only in equity, such as mutual mistake. In that situation, the law-defendant would immediately sue "in equity," say, for reformation. The equity court would as a matter of course temporarily enjoin the law-plaintiff from pursuing his law action, and then would try the equitable issues. If the law-defendant prevailed on those issues, the law action would be permanently enjoined. If not, the law action would be allowed to resume. This complicated scenario followed from the law/equity bifurcation, although later some of the equitable doctrines, such as fraud, became cognizable as defenses at law as well and so simplified the scenario.

Analogously, a plaintiff desiring both legal and equitable remedies would have to bring separate actions. These two systems of justice were indeed separate, and thus legal and equitable causes were not joinable. However, in equity, at the plaintiff's request, the equity court had discretion to retain jurisdiction in order to pass on additional or sometimes even alternative legal relief under the so-called clean-up doctrine. For example, when equity took jurisdiction to grant specific performance of a contract, it might go on to give damages for delay in performance or past breach. All of this, of course, greatly affects today's jury right.

Other differences existed between legal and equitable procedure. On the one hand, an action at law was basically a contest between two and only two adversary sides (although there might be more than one party on each side), in which one side would eventually get a single judgment against the other. Even well into the 1800s, law narrowly restricted joinder of causes and the types of counterclaims that it would allow in an action. On the other hand, equity dealt with litigation of a much more complex character. Not only was it more liberal in allowing claims and counterclaims, but also it allowed multisided controversies (interpleader, for example, is an equity contrivance) that involved considerable complication of a suit's party-structure. When a number of parties were before it, equity would grant whatever relief appeared necessary among the parties; for example, one plaintiff might emerge with a decree against a co-plaintiff. In sum, many of the modern statutes and rules regulating complex litigation trace to equity practice.

As to appeal, in any modern sense it was unknown in the old days. Indeed, early on there was no appeal process of any sort. At common law, there was eventually a very limited, complicated, illogical, and changing scheme for review of legal decisions, characteristically only after final judgment, if the decision appeared on the bare record. Review came by writ of error in some court of error, which in the later historical period was the newly created Court of Exchequer Chamber. Finally, the writ of error procedure was killed off in 1852, and legislation thereafter introduced the appeal to law. In equity, meanwhile, there had long been a fairly complicated but changing scheme for appellate review by rehearing of both interlocutory and final decisions. Review in the later period was generally from any lower deciding official to the chancellor and thence to the House of Lords. In sum, our system of appeal today may actually be more a creature of equity, although many of the limitations on appeal, such as the final decision rule, come from common law.

d. Remedies

Traditionally, any equitable remedy would operate personally. Relief was typically a direct personal order to do or not to do something, which order might be conditional and was modifiable. It was enforceable by contempt. The most distinctive remedies were injunctions and orders of specific performance. But equity offered other remedies such as discovery, accounting, administration of estates, receivership, reformation, and rescission.

Courts of equity took the view that even if the remedy at law was inadequate, the grant of an equitable remedy still lay in the sound judicial discretion of the court. Thus the court might deny equitable relief because the plaintiff had driven an unconscionable bargain and so had the "unclean hands" abhorred by maxim, or because equitable relief would cause undue hardship to the defendant or third persons or cause detriment to the public interest, or because the court's overseeing and administering the decree would be impracticable or too difficult.

e. Substance

Equity interceded, in the chancellor's discretion, when the common law was inadequate. Early on, equity served primarily to overcome the procedural inadequacies of the common law, sometimes with a dose of arrogance. Jealous of its turf, the common law successfully strove through politics to prevent such intrusions by equity.

But by then equity had begun to create its own distinctive remedies and substantive law in order to overcome omissions and defects in the scope of the common law—for example, the equitable doctrines concerning uses and trusts, accident, mistake, and fraud. This advance intensified the conflict between law and equity. In the 1600s Parliament and the common law engaged in titanic struggles against equity and the Crown. The battlefields were cases in which a law court gave judgment, and then equity reopened the case and ultimately enjoined further proceedings at law. The spirit of law's attack on equity can be partly sensed in the sneer of lawyer and historian John Selden around 1650 that "Equity is a Roguish thing: for Law we have a measure, know what to trust to; Equity is according to the Conscience of him that is Chancellor, and as that is larger or narrower, so is Equity. 'Tis all one as if they should make the Standard for the measure we call a Foot, a Chancellor's Foot; what an uncertain Measure would be this."[15] Yet Chancery prevailed in these struggles, becoming entitled to the last word in case of conflict.

To prevail, however, equity surrendered its rationale of exercising the royal prerogative. And it recognized an obligation to treat like cases alike. It was no longer the king's delegate extraordinarily dispensing justice case-by-case, but a regular court of constant resort separately applying its general principles called maxims (such as "Equity regards substance rather than form," or "He who seeks equity must do equity"[16]) and even applying rules that it largely adopted from the common law ("Equity follows the law"). Equity no longer simply "did equity," but instead acted only within its fixed jurisdictional bounds. A reporting system started to embody the output. Equity was even following stare decisis by 1700. As a consequence of all these developments, Chancery received an increasing flood of cases. Equity went on to evolve a highly developed, regularized, and distinctive body of doctrine, within a jurisdiction restricted to acting when the common-law system was procedurally, remedially, or substantively inadequate.[17] The effects of these developments on today's law remain enormous.

The distance traveled from equity's origins was unwittingly revealed by Lord Chancellor Eldon, the greatest chancellor but an arch-conservative who resisted every effort at reform: "Nothing would inflict on me greater pain, in quitting this place, than the

---

15. See Table Talk of John Selden 43 (Frederick Pollock ed., 1927).

16. But cf. Eugene Volokh, Lost Maxims of Equity, 52 J. Legal Educ. 619 (2002) (e.g., "Equity abhors a nudnik").

17. See Henry L. McClintock, Handbook of the Principles of Equity (2d ed. 1948).

recollection that I had done any thing to justify the reproach that the equity of this Court varies like the Chancellor's foot."[18]

f. Problems

By the 1800s equitable procedure bogged down, becoming incredibly cumbersome and expensive. As to remedies and substance too, equity exhibited all the rigidities of a mature judicial system. Matters in Chancery were by then out of hand. The delay, expense, and corruption had become legendary. What had originated as an equitable cure for law's inadequacies ended up worse than the disease. Moreover, equity and the common law overlapped to an uncertain degree, adding confusion to the inefficiency of having two imperfectly meshed systems of justice. Reform was a pressing need.

3. Reform

Filled with revulsion at Blackstone's laudation of the common law, Jeremy Bentham (1748–1832), a law-trained philosopher, conducted for many years a bitter but brilliant attack on English law both substantive and procedural, pushing legislative reform. In England procedural reform on a substantial scale began in the 1830s, culminating in the final dissolution of the forms of action and in the merger of law and equity by the Judicature Act of 1873.

Effective reforms in pleading both at law and in equity lay in legislation from the 1850s onward. Parties became competent to testify at law by legislation dating from 1851. Legislation accomplished the reform of Chancery practice in large part, although practice orders issued by several chancellors played a part. Among many reforms in equity, radically transforming the outlandish procedures lampooned by Dickens in *Bleak House* (1852–1853), was the allowance in 1852 of oral testimony in open court in lieu of the cumbersome depositions.

All these reforms called for a reconstitution of the courts, which the Judicature Act and later legislation effected. At present there is in England a Supreme Court of Judicature into which have been merged the three superior courts of law, the Court of Chancery, the Court of Exchequer Chamber, and certain other courts. The Supreme Court has a general branch, the High Court of Justice (in turn divided administratively into three divisions: Queen's Bench Division, Chancery Division, and Family Division); a special criminal branch, the Crown Court; and an appellate branch, the Court of Appeal. The court of highest appeal is still the House of

---

18. Gee v. Pritchard, 36 Eng. Rep. 670, 674 (Ch. 1818).

Lords, but its jurisdiction is due to shift in October 2009 to a new Supreme Court of the United Kingdom.

A significant feature of the Judicature Act remains to be mentioned. It gave the judges wide rulemaking powers over procedure. Either House of Parliament might secure an annulment of a rule by resolution, and Parliament of course might enact any procedural legislation on its own initiative.

B. State Developments

The American states basically followed the English model until the code reforms of the 1800s.[19]

1. Early Period

In the early colonial period in this country, conditions of life were simple as compared to those in England. There was no real need for a sophisticated legal system, and there were very few lawyers to make such a system work if there had been one. So the colonies combined local innovations with rudimentary English imports to create a legal system suitable for their simple life.

The colonial law courts administered a sort of homespun justice based on English law, presumably neither knowing nor caring whether they were doing the work of any one of the common-law courts (or of the chancellor) in the mother country, where the division of labor had long lost most of its rationale. Accordingly, the multiple common-law trial courts were sensibly united here. But with time English legal procedure came to enjoy an increasing influence, bringing along its forms of action and infamous technicality. In short, the United States eventually shared many of the problems of the English legal system.

Chancery almost missed being transplanted altogether. In addition, the lingering identification of equity courts with the Crown impeded their development. At first, the colonial officials administered a sort of layman's equity. As judicial equity slowly came to develop, it did so in greatly varying ways in the several colonies, and likewise after the colonies became states. In 1789, while some states had separate courts of equity (e.g., New York) and other states had courts with separate law and equity divisions or sides (e.g., Connecticut), there were several states where equity jurisdiction was either in a very primitive form or truly nonexistent. For an extreme example, Massachusetts courts did not have full equity

---

19. See generally Lawrence M. Friedman, A History of American Law 3–23, 79–104, 111–12, 279–308 (3d ed. 2005); Robert Wyness Millar, Civil Procedure of the Trial Court in Historical Perspective 39–42, 52–57 (1952).

jurisdiction until 1877. But all the states' equity work did grow with time, raising problems like England's that demanded reform.

2. Code Reform

The greatest procedural reform in American history has been the comprehensive code of civil procedure. The preeminent such code was the New York Code of Procedure of 1848, which revolutionized civil procedure. It was primarily the work of David Dudley Field (1805–1894), a prominent and prosperous trial lawyer, who valued certainty and believed procedure should serve substance. The Field Code abolished the forms of action and merged law and equity, resulting in "but one form of action" offering the full range of legal and equitable remedies and substantive law. For that unitary civil action, the Field Code simplified and reformed procedure, taking the best of law, equity, and more modern thinking.[20]

The New York Code embodied a number of other changes and reforms. It called for verified pleading of the facts constituting a cause of action; cut down the number of permissible pleadings to complaint, answer, reply, and demurrers; limited the use of demurrers; revised the old rules on joinder of causes of action; altered and made somewhat more pliant the rules as to joinder of, and relief against, parties to an action; reformed the rules governing permissible counterclaims (this came into the Code by an amendment in 1852); slightly liberalized the granting of pleading amendments and softened the consequences of variances between pleading and proof; set out a flexible system of provisional remedies; authorized limited discovery procedures; extended the jury right, but facilitated the waiver of jury trial; modernized the procedures on enforcement of judgments; and made the parties to some extent competent as witnesses. The New York Constitution had previously been amended to provide that "the testimony in equity cases shall be taken in like manner as in cases at law."

The Field Code swept through most of the states—including California, which produced in 1850 a code version that served in turn as a basis of codes in several Western states. The Code still constitutes the basis of the procedural law in a good number of states, especially the populous ones. There remain only a tiny handful of states that can be said still to show noticeable allegiance to the common-law practice, and their practices bear little resemblance to the pristine form of the classic common law. In the very few states where law and equity have not been merged in a unitary action, the consequences have been mitigated by provisions for easy

---

20. See Charles E. Clark, Handbook of the Law of Code Pleading (2d ed. 1947).

transfer from one division of the court system to the other. Finally, the Code served as one of the principal models for the Federal Rules of Civil Procedure, which most states have since used as the model for renewed procedural reform. The Federal Rules thus owe a great deal to the Field Code model, as naturally do the rules of the many states now patterned upon the Federal Rules. All this leaves some states with the Field Code or one of its variants, a few states in a sort of pre-code status subject to piecemeal reforms, and most states substantially in the Federal Rules camp.[21]

Over the years Field's Code, which was notably brief and simple, received unsympathetic treatment by the New York courts, and the legislature persisted in amending and enlarging it until it became a structure with incredible detail. The same thing happened to a number of state codes modeled on the Field Code. All this increased the need for renewed reform. The mode of more recent reform in the majority of states has been through legislation confiding rulemaking power in some form to the courts, most often by statutes similar to the soon-to-be-described Federal Rules Enabling Act. Some states, however, still choose to proceed directly by the enactment of a code by the legislature; and a few states make rules under merely the inherent power of the courts.

C. Federal Developments

The federal legal system followed traditional ways until the rules reform well into the 1900s.[22]

1. Early Period

The federal courts were established in 1789 by the first Congress. There were no separate law and equity courts. Instead, the same federal judges administered the two jurisdictions in quite separate law and equity sides of the trial court and according to separate procedures. Until 1938 law and equity were kept separate in the relatively conservative federal courts, subject to some remedial statutes allowing pleading amendments to transfer cases between the law and equity sides and allowing assertion of equitable defenses and counterclaims in actions at law.

21. See John B. Oakley & Arthur F. Coon, The Federal Rules in State Courts: A Survey of State Court Systems of Civil Procedure, 61 Wash. L. Rev. 1367 (1986); John B. Oakley, A Fresh Look at the Federal Rules in State Courts, 3 Nev. L.J. 354 (2003).

22. See generally Richard H. Fallon, Jr., Daniel J. Meltzer & David L. Shapi-

ro, Hart and Wechsler's The Federal Courts and the Federal System chs. I, VI–1 (5th ed. 2003); Erwin C. Surrency, History of the Federal Courts (2d ed. 2001); Charles Alan Wright & Mary Kay Kane, Law of Federal Courts §§ 1, 61–63 (6th ed. 2002).

To avoid "injurious clashing" with state courts, Congress required the federal courts' procedure in actions at law to conform to the procedure for like causes in the state where the particular federal court sat; under the Process Act of 1789 federal courts had to conform to the state procedure prevailing at some fixed date ("static conformity"), but under the Conformity Act of 1872 federal courts were to conform to the state procedure currently prevailing ("dynamic conformity"). The procedure at law in the federal district courts, being a reflection of state procedure, was thus disuniform from state to state. Yet, conformity being subject always to particular federal statutes regulating procedure and to various intractable elements deriving from the very nature of the federal judicial power, there existed many statutory and judge-made exceptions to conformity, and exceptions to exceptions, that further complicated this extraordinarily complex scheme.

Because equity was so stunted in such divergent degrees in the new states, Congress instructed the federal courts hearing suits in equity to follow generally the procedure of English equity, but Congress also gave the Supreme Court rulemaking power for such suits. Thus federal equity, not hampered by any conformity act, was uniform from the start. After 1822, the Court promulgated comprehensive sets of uniform rules on equitable procedure from time to time—including the progressive Equity Rules of 1912, which was to serve as another of the models for the Federal Rules of Civil Procedure. Incidentally, it was not until 1912 that the Court assimilated the method of taking testimony in federal equity suits to the method at law.

At any rate, in the good old days, a lawyer practicing in the state and federal courts of a particular locality must have mastered three systems of procedure: the state procedure (which might be unmerged and therefore comprise two procedures); the federal law-procedure (which was the state procedure in law actions but with a federal overlay); and the federal equity-procedure. A lawyer practicing in federal courts throughout the country (as a government lawyer, for example, might well do) had to beware of the state procedure at law (as modified by the federal overlay) for each state in which the lawyer appeared.

2. Rules Reform

Decades of pressure for reform culminated in the Rules Enabling Act of 1934 ("REA"),[23] which authorized uniting law and equity "so as to secure one form of civil action and procedure for

---

23. See Stephen B. Burbank, The Rules Enabling Act of 1934, 130 U. Pa. L. Rev. 1015 (1982).

both." The statute is now with some changes 28 U.S.C. §§ 2072–2074, which in its present form reads in part:

§ 2072.

(a) The Supreme Court shall have the power to prescribe general rules of practice and procedure and rules of evidence for cases in the United States district courts (including proceedings before magistrates thereof) and courts of appeals.

(b) Such rules shall not abridge, enlarge or modify any substantive right. All laws in conflict with such rules shall be of no further force or effect after such rules have taken effect.

* * * *

§ 2074.

(a) The Supreme Court shall transmit to the Congress not later than May 1 of the year in which a rule prescribed under section 2072 is to become effective a copy of the proposed rule. Such rule shall take effect no earlier than December 1 of the year in which such rule is so transmitted unless otherwise provided by law. * * *

Four years after the REA's enactment, a distinguished Advisory Committee had drafted and the Supreme Court had approved a set of Federal Rules of Civil Procedure, effective September 16, 1938. The key figure in the drafting process was Charles E. Clark (1889–1963), Yale Law School Dean and later Second Circuit Judge, who detested procedural rigidity as an impediment to like-minded judges' ability to work social reform. Those Rules merged law and equity and abandoned the idea of conformity to state procedure; Rule 2 thus provides: "There is one form of action—the civil action." For that civil action, the Rules further simplified and reformed procedure, to be marked by greatly simplified notice pleading, broad joinder, and extensive discovery.

Early on, the validity of the Rules was challenged unsuccessfully in *Sibbach v. Wilson & Co.*[24] The Supreme Court broadly interpreted the REA as authorizing rulemaking throughout but not beyond the realm of civil "procedure"—"the judicial process for enforcing rights and duties recognized by substantive law and for justly administering remedy and redress for disregard or infraction of them." Thus, the empowering first sentence of the REA restricted civil rulemaking to matters of procedure, broadly defined. The *Sibbach* Court apparently read the REA's second sentence concerning "substantive" rights as imposing no additional restriction on rulemaking, although some scholarly dispute persists on this point. Consequently, the Supreme Court has never invalidated a Federal Rule of Civil Procedure.

---

24.   312 U.S. 1, 14 (1941) (upholding validity of Fed. R. Civ. P. 35).

The success of the Federal Rules has been "quite phenomenal," creating "a uniform procedure that is flexible, simple, clear, and efficient" and that has had a tremendous impact on the development of procedure in other jurisdictions.[25] A less restrained commentator wrote that the Rules were "one of the greatest contributions to the free and unhampered administration of law and justice ever struck off by any group of men since the dawn of civilized law."[26] The Federal Rules of Civil Procedure made federal procedure the prime model of modern civil procedure within the United States.

Of course, perfection was not achieved, leading to significant sets of amendments from time to time, and also prompting fundamental questions such as whether the concise Rules are too open-textured and general or whether reform has gone too far toward producing a single form of action for procedurally or substantively different kinds of cases.

Currently, the advisory function with respect to the Supreme Court's rulemaking power under 28 U.S.C. § 2072 is entrusted to the Judicial Conference of the United States, a body of federal judges headed by the Chief Justice that has long been charged with improving the administration of federal courts. By legislation of 1958 amending 28 U.S.C. § 331, the Judicial Conference is directed to carry on a continuous study of the rules of practice prescribed by the Court for the inferior federal courts and to make recommendations to the Court. Under 28 U.S.C. § 2073, the Judicial Conference works through a standing committee, appointed by the Chief Justice, and advisory committees, also appointed by the Chief Justice, which report to the standing committee. There are now five advisory committees respectively for Civil, Criminal, Evidence, Bankruptcy, and Appellate Rules, each assisted by a reporter who is usually a law professor. The advisory committees draft new or amended rules with explanatory notes, circulate them under the aegis of the standing committee to the bench and bar and public for comment, rework the rules in the light of the comments, and transmit them to the standing committee. The standing committee in turn makes recommendations to the Judicial Conference, which finally advises the Court. At this point the specific procedure of 28 U.S.C. § 2074 takes over with respect to submission of the Rules to Congress.

This rulemaking machinery itself is currently very much under attack and reconsideration. Its contribution has been great, but some argue for radical change. Legislation rewriting the REA in 1988 helped to move the machinery out into public view. Persisting concerns center on process (e.g., lack of effective participatory

---

25. Wright & Kane, supra note 22, at 432.

26. B.H. Carey, In Favor of Uniformity, 3 F.R.D. 507, 507 (1944).

process), institutional structure (e.g., supersession clause of the REA that allows Rules to override statutes), and scope (e.g., dealing with subjects too important for rulemaking).[27] Moreover, since the 1970s, Congress has been reasserting its authority over the procedural arena, by rejecting some rules under its review and by directly enacting certain procedures.

What Is All This Talk About Procedure's Impact on Substance?

The grand theme of the historical development, which is the emergence of the unitary civil action, underlies three of the hottest topics in civil procedure today: fostering case management by activist judges who oversee and push individual cases through the process while they use their discretion to customize the applicable procedure; creating separate and different tracks for procedurally distinguishable kinds of cases; and molding different sets of procedures for the varying substantive claims. Perhaps the old systems generated such a revulsion that it pushed the reform of unification to an extreme, thereby causing the ills of modern procedure that today require renewed reform. A need to differentiate among cases persists—and so generates the three calls for intensifying the use of ad hoc case management, which may have gone too far already; for elaborating the tracking scheme, which already comprises alternative dispute resolution mechanisms and forms of complex litigation, by creating additional pigeonholes for, say, small federal claims; and for overtly tailoring procedural law to particular substantive fields, so that civil rights cases get treated differently from debt collection.

The significant insight offered by considering such reforms in a historical light concerns the effects of procedure on substance. One has a tendency to think of procedure and substance as separate realms, involving separate values and susceptible to separate reform. The natural thought is that society can rework the procedural regime in pursuit of the supposedly neutral values of fairness, efficiency, and accuracy independently of substantive values. But the truth is that changes in the procedural law inevitably impose effects, albeit indirect effects, on the substantive law. The best reason for studying the development of the unitary civil action—from common law to equity to reform—is to uncover this interaction between procedure and substance.

First, under the old common-law regime, procedure preceded substance, and then it shaped the substantive law through pleading decisions and jury instructions. Each body of substantive law independently grew up within a particular writ, substance so being "secreted in the interstices of procedure" and being largely nonexistent outside the writs. Henry Sumner Maine, Dissertations on Early Law and Custom 389 (New York, H. Holt 1883). "Nobody will gainsay the importance to an understanding of our common-law system of a knowledge of the essentials of the forms of action at common law, for as Maitland has truly said, 'The forms of action we have buried, but they still rule us from their graves.' They rule us, however, not as procedure but as substantive law ***." Arthur T. Vanderbilt, Cases and Other Materials on Modern Procedure and Judicial Administration 7 (1952). For example, our modern law of contract derived from the tort family of

---

27. See Winifred R. Brown, Federal Rulemaking: Problems and Possibilities (1981). But see Paul D. Carrington, The New Order in Judicial Rulemaking, 75 Judicature 161 (1991); cf. Robert G. Bone, The Process of Making Process: Court Rulemaking, Democratic Legitimacy, and Procedural Efficacy, 87 Geo. L.J. 887, 955 (1999) (justifying rulemaking as akin to common-law reasoning, as long as rulemaking centers on "inferring general principles from existing practice and choosing rules that implement those principles well in light of practice realities").

trespass, with plaintiffs invoking tort to get to a jury and thereby avoid the wager of law used in the old contract-type forms of action. That history of fuzzing the boundary between tort and contract has many reverberations down to today, including as examples our confusing law of unjust enrichment and the possibility of recovering punitive damages for tortious breach of contract.

Second, the ancient law/equity bifurcation profoundly affected the development of our substantive law. An example here is our traditional reliance generally on "liability rules" giving damages at law rather than "property rules" enforced by equitable injunctions and specific performance. Although this preference arose through equity's jurisdictional requirement that the legal remedy be inadequate, it has had widespread and arguably beneficial effects on our society's efficiency. See Gene R. Shreve, The Premature Burial of the Irreparable Injury Rule, 70 Tex. L. Rev. 1063 (1992).

Third, reform itself further revealed the effect of procedure on substance. The nineteenth-century creation of the modern procedural regime radically shoved substance into the foreground, leaving procedure as substance's handmaiden well in the background. Most obviously, the abolition of the forms of action led to gap-filling in the substantive law, a law that logically began to extend toward situations formerly falling between the write and otherwise began to follow the dictates of generalized reasoning. The merger of law and equity had profound effects too. Perhaps the two systems were meant to coexist, with equity generating needed reforms while law met settled expectations. Law without equity has the flaw of being too stringent, and equity without law has the flaw of being too discretionary. Current commentators complain that now both these flaws prevail. Compare Thomas O. Main, Traditional Equity and Contemporary Procedure, 78 Wash. L. Rev. 429 (2003), with Stephen N. Subrin, How Equity Conquered Common Law: The Federal Rules of Civil Procedure in Historical Perspective, 135 U. Pa. L. Rev. 909 (1987).

Think again of the three calls for case management, tracking, and substance-specific procedures. First, among countless more subtle changes induced by the historical progression, the "neutral" shift from a rule-based procedure to a discretion-dominated procedure has emboldened judges in the pursuit of social justice, but also rendered more elusive the protection of predefined rights. Second, the "neutral" shift from multitudinous forms to one form of action that could handle the biggest cases did disadvantage small plaintiffs with small grievances, thereby generating suggestions for a new tracking scheme. Third, the hottest of all debates in civil procedure today centers on whether procedural reformers should not only acknowledge the effects on substance but actually enhance them, rather than vainly trying to avoid them. Should reformers, for example, create detailed intervention rules to serve substantive values, so that interested groups have a duty to intervene in civil rights cases? In other words, should reformers abandon the ideal of transsubstantive rules of procedure that govern all sorts of cases, and instead shape substance-specific rules—creating what truly would be the new forms of action that would impose a peculiar procedure on each kind of substantive claim?

These debates lead to appreciating that procedural changes inevitably affect substantive law. Thus, procedural reforms implicate substantive values, perhaps in unintended ways but perhaps also in intentionally systematic ways. In either event, the effects of procedure cannot remain politically neutral.

Chapter 2

STAGES OF LITIGATION

Table of Sections

---

§ 2.1   Forum

A.   Authority to Adjudicate

The preliminary step for the plaintiff in commencing a lawsuit is to select a court with authority to hear and decide the case. First, commencing a lawsuit involves determining whether to sue in the state or the federal court system and, within the chosen system, selecting a trial court with *subject-matter jurisdiction*. That is, the court must have authority to adjudicate the type of controversy put before the court. Second, the plaintiff must further select a court having *territorial authority to adjudicate*. That is, there are limits on the court's authority to entertain litigation with nonlocal elements, and so the plaintiff must select a place of litigation that satisfies these restrictions of territorial jurisdiction and venue. Third, the persons whose interests are to be affected must receive adequate *notice*. For example, the defendant must be notified of the commencement of the lawsuit. These three basic threshold requirements will be given detailed treatment in Chapter Four, along with how to satisfy them and how to challenge whether they are indeed satisfied.

For most purposes of this Chapter Two, assume that the plaintiff has sued in a United States district court, which court has subject-matter jurisdiction because the case is within the federal question or diversity of citizenship provisions. Also assume that the plaintiff has selected a court with territorial authority to adjudicate—envisage perhaps a single plaintiff having brought a typical in personam and transitory action on a single claim against a single individual defendant in the federal district where the defendant is domiciled. Finally, assume that the defendant has received adequate notice of the lawsuit in accordance with Federal Rules of Civil Procedure 3 and 4.

The plaintiff registers his selection of court by filing a complaint with the clerk of the selected federal court. According to Rule 3, this "commences" the civil action.[1] Assume that the plaintiff has done so. Note that under the practice of some states, service of process is instead the act that is deemed to commence an action.

Service of process pursuant to Rule 4 formally asserts power over the defendant and officially notifies her that the plaintiff has commenced an action. Assume that a process server has served the defendant by handing her or her agent a copy of the summons and the complaint. Note that service and filing of subsequent papers in the action normally follow the simpler procedure of Rule 5.[2]

B. Federal Focus

Given the above assumptions, this Chapter Two will have a primary focus on the mechanics of federal procedure. Nevertheless, there will be occasional references to contrasting state practice, where appropriate.

A number of reasons make this choice of a federal focus the natural one. First, there is the need for some procedural model. In order to achieve economically an understanding of the subject of civil procedure, the student needs first to look at a single, complete,

---

1. See Fed. R. Civ. P. 5(d) (specifying how to file with the court).

2. See also id. 6(d) (giving three days' additional time to act after Rule 5 service by mail, by delivery to court clerk, or by consented means, in lieu of standard delivery by hand). See generally id. 6 (treating calculation of time periods).

concise procedural system. That model can later serve as a basis for comparison when dealing with other systems. Second, there is the importance of the federal model in particular. The federal judicial system is the single most important set of courts in the country, handling a considerable number of important cases and being a concern of every lawyer in the nation. Third, there is the success of the federal model. The procedural law followed in the federal courts is representative of the modern approach to procedure, being far from perfect but representing a vast improvement over more traditional models. Fourth, there is the influence of the federal model. Most states substantially adhere to the federal model, making study thereof widely practical.

§ 2.2   Pretrial

A.   Pleading Stage

In federal practice, the pleading stage is usually short in duration and seldom determinative in effect. That is, the pleading stage is relatively unimportant, in contrast to the situation prevailing under more traditional procedural systems.[3]

1.   General Rules

A number of policies and rules apply throughout the pleading stage in federal court. I shall discuss these before passing on to the individual pleading steps.

a.   *Purposes*

The primary purpose of federal pleadings has long been to give the adversary (and the court and the public) fair notice of the pleader's contentions. In *Conley v. Gibson*,[4] the Supreme Court discussed the need for *factual detail* in the complaint: "all the Rules require is 'a short and plain statement of the claim' that will give the defendant fair notice of what the plaintiff's claim is and the grounds upon which it rests." This purpose implies that there is little need for detailed statement in the pleadings. The complaint need not allege facts that constitute each of the substantive elements of a recognizable legal claim, as long as all those elements

---

3. See generally R. Lawrence Dessem, Pretrial Litigation ch. 4 (4th ed. 2007); Roger S. Haydock, David F. Herr & Jeffrey W. Stempel, Fundamentals of Pretrial Litigation § 3.2 (6th ed. 2007); J. Alexander Tanford, The Pretrial Process ch. 3 (2004); Charles Alan Wright &

Mary Kay Kane, Law of Federal Courts §§ 66–69A (6th ed. 2002).

4. 355 U.S. 41, 45–47 (1957). For the story of this case, see Emily Sherwin, The Story of Conley: Precedent by Accident, in Civil Procedure Stories 295 (Kevin M. Clermont ed., 2d ed. 2008).

are inferrable from the mention of some of the circumstances of the transaction on which the claim is based.[5] *Conley* also set out a very loose test of *legal sufficiency* of the complaint, looking to see if any legal claim existed that would be consistent with the words of the complaint. This test implies that there is no need for expressly legal content in the pleadings. A complaint need not identify any issues likely to be in dispute, as long as it encompasses a legal claim and does not contain allegations that actually defeat the plaintiff's claim.[6]

A favorite hypothetical used to criticize *Conley* involves a plaintiff's alleging simply that the defendant wronged him, in a specified amount. Some authorities say that *Conley*, applied literally, would approve such a complaint.[7] But that is incorrect, because it fails to distinguish between *Conley*'s two tests. Although such a bare complaint would satisfy *Conley*'s test for legal sufficiency, it fails *Conley*'s requirement of factual particularity.[8] The complaint does not give fair notice of the plaintiff's contentions. Moreover, judicially approving this complaint would surely send an undesirable message to future pleaders.

Such extreme cases aside, the overall simple mission of pleadings implies that there is little sense in spending time and money toiling or skirmishing over them. Contrast this so-called notice pleading with the older fact pleading and issue pleading. First, fact pleading is the code approach and requires more detail.[9] For example, a code complaint must state the facts constituting a cause of action. This might have benefits, but it also encourages senseless

5. See Dioguardi v. Durning, 139 F.2d 774 (2d Cir. 1944) (Clark, J.); Sierocinski v. E.I. Du Pont De Nemours & Co., 103 F.2d 843 (3d Cir. 1939); United States v. Bd. of Harbor Comm'rs, 73 F.R.D. 460 (D. Del. 1977); Bell v. Novick Transfer Co., 17 F.R.D. 279 (D. Md. 1955).

6. See Am. Nurses' Ass'n v. Illinois, 783 F.2d 716 (7th Cir. 1986) (Posner, J.) (reversing dismissal under Fed. R. Civ. P. 12(b)(6)); Kirksey v. R.J. Reynolds Tobacco Co., 168 F.3d 1039 (7th Cir. 1999) (Posner, J.) (affirming dismissal under Fed. R. Civ. P. 12(b)(6)); Garcia v. Hilton Hotels Int'l, Inc., 97 F. Supp. 5 (D.P.R. 1951); cf. Charles Alan Wright & Arthur R. Miller, Federal Practice and Procedure § 1226 (3d ed. 2004) (discussing dismissals based on defensive matter alleged in complaint).

7. E.g., Fleming James, Jr., Civil Procedure 86–87 (1965); Geoffrey C. Hazard, Jr., From Whom No Secrets Are Hid, 76 Tex. L. Rev. 1665, 1685 (1998) ("Conley v. Gibson turned Rule 8 on its head"; "compliance with Conley v. Gibson could consist simply of giving the names of the plaintiff and the defendant, and asking for judgment").

8. See Beanal v. Freeport–McMoran, Inc., 197 F.3d 161, 164 (5th Cir. 1999) ("a complaint, which contains a 'bare bones' allegation that a wrong occurred and which does not plead any of the facts giving rise to the injury, does not provide adequate notice"); Williams v. Lear Operations Corp., 73 F. Supp. 2d 1377, 1381 (N.D. Ga. 1999) ("lack of even a general description of the circumstances allegedly giving rise to a continuing tort violation by plaintiff is insufficient to satisfy the purpose of notice pleading and fails as a matter of law"); Shakespeare v. Wilson, 40 F.R.D. 500, 505 (S.D. Cal. 1966) ("Plaintiff in effect says no more than that she is entitled to relief because she desires relief.").

9. See supra § 1.2(B)(2).

battles over form—such as whether the pleader was being too specific by pleading "evidence" or too general by pleading "conclusions." Second, issue pleading was the common-law approach and expected the pleadings to produce a single contested issue of law or fact.[10] This asked too much of the pleading stage, which consequently became the center of legal attention, often ended up mired down in battles over technicalities, and provided the vehicle for monumental abuse.

Under modern pleading, most of the former functions of pleadings have been largely shifted forward into the stages of disclosure, discovery, pretrial conference, summary judgment, and trial. The motivating theory is that these later stages can more efficiently and fairly handle functions such as fully revealing facts and narrowing issues, and thus the whole system can better deliver a proper decision on the merits.

Yet federal pleadings are still sometimes asked to do significantly more than give notice, as evidenced by some courts' entertaining motion contests when a pleading suggests an absence of legal basis for claim or defense—usually by omission of some expected allegation—but does not actually defeat itself. For example, a contract complaint may suspiciously omit reference to consideration, or a tort complaint may suggest that the plaintiff is intending to seek recovery not on some traditional theory conceivably within the general allegations but on some innovative theory that goes beyond the law's current extent given the actual facts. The defendant naturally wants to nip the case in the bud, and the court might be inclined to go along with the effort in order to clear the docket.[11] In practice, however, such attempts to retain additional functions of pleadings most often seem counterproductive from the system's point of view.

Most recently, the Supreme Court itself created a new task for pleadings. In *Bell Atlantic Corp. v. Twombly*,[12] it imposed a plausi-

---

10. See supra § 1.2(A)(1)(c).

11. E.g., Case v. State Farm Mut. Auto. Ins. Co., 294 F.2d 676, 678 (5th Cir. 1961) ("What the courts have said does not mean that it is the duty of the trial court or the appellate court to create a claim which appellant has not spelled out in his pleading."); see Wright & Miller, supra note 6, §§ 1215–1216.

12. 127 S.Ct. 1955 (2007) (telephone and internet subscribers brought a class action against the telecommunications giants, claiming an illegal conspiracy in restraint of trade; under antitrust law, however, parallel and even consciously identical conduct unfavorable to compe-

tition is not illegal if it comprises only independent actions by competitors without any agreement; the complaint alleged parallel conduct in great detail, explaining how each company sought to inhibit upstarts in its own region and refrained from entering the other major companies' regions, but it alleged an agreement mainly in conclusory terms upon information and belief, because the plaintiffs had no proof yet in hand); see Dura Pharm., Inc. v. Broudo, 544 U.S. 336 (2005) (foreshadowing the new regime). But see A. Benjamin Spencer, Plausibility Pleading, 49 B.C. L. Rev. 431 (2008) (strongly criticizing the new

bility test on the pleading stage. The obvious concern in that complex antitrust case was with opening the door to the plaintiffs' expensive discovery. So, the Court ordered dismissal on a pre-answer motion, holding that the complaint failed to show to be plausible its allegation of the defendants' actual agreement to restrain trade. This move represented the Court's first unmistakable step backward from notice pleading. The Court did not step in the direction of simply reverting to a requirement of heightened detail in allegations, but instead it instituted a judicial inquiry into the pleading's convincingness. Such a move will prove momentous *if* it does not remain limited to antitrust cases and it is not cut back by the Court. For the time being, there is no movement to limit *Bell Atlantic* to antitrust cases, but the courts are having a terrible time figuring out how the plausibility test will work.[13] What exactly it means is clearly open to dispute, as is the wisdom of inventing with no forewarning or public discussion any sort of plausibility test on pleading, or of deciding factual disputes without suitable procedures even if under a low standard of proof.

Should Pleadings Do More Than Give Notice?

Why not get rid of pleading motions? One could propose abrogating the Rule 12(b)(6) motion for failure to state a claim, as well as the Rule 12(c) motion for judgment on the pleadings and the Rule 12(f) motion to strike an insufficient defense.

The argument in support would first address pleading motions that end up accomplishing nothing. It seems that this describes a solid majority of such motions, even many of those made in good faith. Apparently, many pleaders are quite capable of adequately stating an unfounded claim or defense, while others with a well-founded position might fail initially to follow the pleading Rules but with instruction can do so by amendment. Abolishing pleading battles would eliminate the abuse and waste involved in the unproductive motions made in such situations.

Now consider pleading motions that succeed in doing something but should not. Abolition would naturally cure this problem too. Rule 12 motions are an open invitation to force pleadings to perform functions that are better handled by the later stages of disclosure, discovery, pretrial conference, summary judgment, and trial. In particular, abolition would keep judges from subversively reviving fact pleading—whether the judges are doing so in order substantively to disfavor certain kinds of claims or litigants or simply to speed the process up, and whether they do so by demanding greater particularity or by requiring pleaders to proffer evidence.

---

regime). Although Rule 8 may now entail a plausibility test, it still does not impose a heightened pleading requirement that would demand factual detail for its own sake. See Swierkiewicz v. Sorema N.A., 534 U.S. 506 (2002) (employment discrimination claim); Leatherman v. Tarrant County Narcotics Intelligence & Coordination Unit, 507 U.S. 163 (1993) (civil rights claim).

13. See, e.g., Erickson v. Pardus, 127 S.Ct. 2197 (2007) (upholding conclusory civil rights complaint); In re Gilead Scis. Sec. Litig., 536 F.3d 1049 (9th Cir. 2008) (upholding securities fraud claim); Iqbal v. Hasty, 490 F.3d 143, 157–58 (2d Cir. 2007), cert. granted sub nom. Ashcroft v. Iqbal, 128 S.Ct. 2931 (2008).

Lastly the focus falls on pleading motions that serve a good function. Here other procedural devices can step in to deliver at least the same benefits as motions to dismiss on the pleadings. First, if the function to be served is notice, then Rule 12(e) is there for securing a more definite statement. It lies only where really needed, and it works without the cumbersomeness of dismissal and amendment. Better yet, discovery can provide the needed clarity. Second, if the function to be served is cutting off discovery by frivolous litigants, then a court could use a Rule 26(c) protective order to limit discovery. Perhaps big complex cases present a generic threat, but then a Rule amendment would be the preferred way to impose special pleading requirements, or directly to restrict early discovery, in certain kinds of cases. The Court's discovery of such a cure in the words of Rule 8 is a poor idea. Third, if instead the function to be served is disposition on the merits, then Rule 56's summary judgment is better tailored to ask the right questions and produce the right answers. It lies in simple form where the pleadings present an issue of law, and it continues to work even where an issue fades into one of fact underlying the pleadings. Moreover, reducing the redundancy of Rule 12(b)(6), (c), and (f) would clean up the Federal Rules, which would have its own rewards of fairness and efficiency.

In sum, abolishing pleading battles would finally pare pleading down to the sole proper function of giving fair notice of the pleader's contentions. Litigants should not be allowed to fight over, say, whether a contract complaint must state consideration, especially when there is freedom to amend and when there is a superior procedural mechanism for exploring both the legal need for proving consideration and its basis in actual fact— that is, let them fight over the adequacy of the actual claim, not the adequacy of its statement.

Probably the summary judgment Rule should undergo amendment to facilitate these challenges as to whether a need for trial exists, which challenges might come on the law or on the facts and in whole or in part. Indeed, summary judgment should perhaps undergo reconception as "summary adjudication," a broadened alternative to full-blown procedure. We do need a more effective way to test the *merits* of claims and defenses, but we can live henceforth without testing the *pleadings*. See generally Yoichiro Hamabe, Functions of Rule 12(b)(6) in the Federal Rules of Civil Procedure: A Categorization Approach, 15 Campbell L. Rev. 119 (1993).

b. Contents

The purposes of pleadings dictate their contents. Pleadings therefore should be simple, direct, and brief. Attacks on their contents should seldom succeed.

The burden of allegation dictates who pleads what. The plaintiff is required to assert his position on certain matters in order to raise those matters, while the defendant is required to assert her position on certain other matters in order to insert them into the case. This allocation of the burden of allegation for any particular kind of case accords with impulses of convenience, fairness, good policy, and apparent logic: which party has peculiar means of knowing the facts or superior access to evidence? which party is alleging the unusual? which side does the substantive law disfavor? Although that approach sounds vague, in practice the pleader can usually find clear guides as to the burden of allegation in court rules, form books, statutes, and precedents.

A prime example comes from the traditional regime of negligence and contributory negligence. On the one hand, the plaintiff in federal court must allege that the defendant's breach of duty caused him injury. The plaintiff need not assert that he himself was exercising due care. If the defendant wishes to prove that the plaintiff's negligence helped cause the accident, she must allege that the plaintiff was contributorily negligent. Indeed, if the plaintiff unnecessarily pleads his own due care, he may thereby inject the issue of contributory negligence into a case where it would otherwise not be in issue. The thought behind this allocation of the burden of allegation, albeit a questionable thought, is that analytically the plaintiff's due care is inherently a defensive matter and not part of the cause of action, which comprises what the defendant did wrong rather than what the plaintiff did right.[14] On the other hand, some states in the old days required the plaintiff to plead both the defendant's negligence and his own due care. So there is nothing inevitable about the burden of allegation.

Regarding those matters on which the pleader has the burden of allegation, he should refer only to what is relevant under the applicable law, by staying within the legal elements of those matters. His opponent will in effect merely deny or admit these allegations. The pleader should avoid redundant, immaterial, impertinent, or scandalous matter. Likewise, he should avoid alleging matters on which the opponent has the burden of allegation. Such irrelevancies will often be ignored, but sometimes they can put things in issue that would not otherwise be in issue, cure defects in the opponent's position, suggest defects in the pleader's position, tip the pleader's hand, box the pleader in later on, waste energy in pleading skirmishes, or require time and money later to correct.

As to fleshing out the elements by the pleader with the burden of allegation, the Federal Rules require little factual detail and no expressly legal content in pleadings. The pleader should indicate the elements of his claims or defenses by giving a somewhat particularized mention of their factual circumstances, but particularized only enough to give fair notice and establish plausibility. There is no call for pleading evidence. Too much detail can cause trouble for the pleader, just as irrelevancies do. The desired level of short and plain generality is suggested by Rule 8(d)(1) ("Each allegation must be simple, concise, and direct. No technical form is required.") and Rule 8(e) ("Pleadings must be construed so as to do justice.").

---

14. Cf. Gomez v. Toledo, 446 U.S. 635 (1980) (holding that qualified immunity is an affirmative defense); Ingraham v. United States, 808 F.2d 1075 (5th Cir. 1987) (holding that statutory cap on damages is an affirmative defense).

Therefore, the appropriate approach generally is lean pleading. However, to serve the notice-giving purpose of pleadings in certain special situations, Rule 9 does require somewhat greater factual particularity in raising the defense of lack of capacity to litigate, in pleading fraud or mistake, in denying performance or occurrence of a condition precedent, and in claiming special damage.[15] In the area of securities fraud, Congress has stepped in to enact a more demanding set of pleading requirements designed to curb the proliferation of suits.[16]

c. Form

The Appendix of Forms to the Federal Rules of Civil Procedure ("Federal Forms") contains illustrative documents that clarify the Rules' formal requirements.[17] Those requirements can be enforced by the opponent's motion invoking the applicable Rule, but they are rather lenient requirements.

As to captioning the pleading, Rule 10(a) requires every pleading to have a caption setting forth the court, the title of the action, the file number, and the kind of pleading.

As to paragraphing, Rule 10(b) provides that pleadings must be divided into "numbered paragraphs, each limited as far as practicable to a single set of circumstances." Such a qualified provision leaves paragraphing as a lenient requirement, suggesting only that the pleader should act as a reasonable person trying to be lucid.

As to separating counts and defenses, Rule 10(b) also provides that each claim "founded on a separate transaction or occurrence" and each defense other than a denial must be stated in a separate count or defense if "doing so would promote clarity." This qualification, of course, diminishes the mandatory nature of the Rule. Moreover, Rule 8(d)(2) permits two or more statements of the same claim or defense "either in a single count or defense or in separate ones." All this leaves the use of separate counts or defenses pretty much up to the pleader.[18]

As to signing the pleading, Rule 11 requires an attorney, or if there is no attorney then the party, to sign each pleading. The

---

15. See William M. Richman, Donald E. Lively & Patricia Mell, The Pleading of Fraud: Rhymes Without Reason, 60 S. Cal. L. Rev. 959 (1987). Compare Denny v. Barber, 576 F.2d 465 (2d Cir. 1978) (holding Fed. R. Civ. P. 9(b) not satisfied), with Denny v. Carey, 72 F.R.D. 574 (E.D. Pa. 1976) (holding Fed. R. Civ. P. 9(b) satisfied, on very similar facts).

16. Private Securities Litigation Reform Act, Pub. L. No. 104–67, tit. I,

§ 101(b), 109 Stat. 737, 747 (1995) (codified at 15 U.S.C. § 78u–4(b)); see Tellabs, Inc. v. Makor Issues & Rights, Ltd., 127 S.Ct. 2499 (2007) (construing "strong inference").

17. See Fed. R. Civ. P. 84 (stating purpose of Fed. Forms).

18. See also id. 18(a) (giving freedom to join claims).

signature certifies that to the best of the signer's knowledge, information, and belief formed after reasonable inquiry there is good ground in fact and law to support it and that it is not interposed for improper purpose. Violations of the Rule may be punished by sanctions. Rule 11 thus embodies a duty to investigate—a limited obligation to investigate facts readily accessible to the attorney or party and to look lightly into the law—and then an important albeit vague screening obligation based on the pleader's knowledge. This obligation to screen out frivolous cases offsets the easy entry into court that modern pleading would otherwise provide.[19]

As to verifying the pleading, Rule 11(a) does not require pleadings to be verified (i.e., sworn, or supported by an equivalent unsworn declaration),[20] although a few special federal provisions do require verification (e.g., Rule 23.1(b) requires a plaintiff's verification of the complaint in a shareholders' derivative action).[21] In contrast, some states widely require the formality of verified pleadings, despite its ineffectiveness.

Overall, the generally prevailing flexible federal model for pleading tries to avoid technical restrictions on the pleader's fully staking out a position. First, the Federal Rules liberally provide for multiclaim and multiparty litigation. Those provisions will be explored in Chapter Six. Second, a pleader may state his single or multiple claims or defenses "alternatively [either-or] or hypothetically [if-then]" and "regardless of consistency," as Rule 8(d) provides and other of the Rules imply.[22] This permissiveness allows someone who is not sure of the provable facts or the applicable law to proceed. He need not investigate the case fully, nor have a single legal theory of the pleadings. However, Rule 8(d) implicitly incorporates the pleading obligations of Rule 11.

On Rule 11 more generally, it applies to almost all papers in litigation,[23] and affects their substance as well as their form. Courts eventually took to applying its sanctions with such enthusiasm as to generate raging concerns about the possible undermining of modern pleading, the risk of uncivil harassment and satellite litigation, and the fear of a chilling effect on certain kinds of claims or

---

19. See, e.g., Christian v. Mattel, Inc., 286 F.3d 1118 (9th Cir. 2002) (failure to investigate facts); Walker v. Norwest Corp., 108 F.3d 158 (8th Cir. 1997) (failure to investigate law); Murphy v. Cuomo, 913 F. Supp. 671 (N.D.N.Y. 1996) (sanctions against lawyer); Heimbaugh v. City & County of San Francisco, 591 F. Supp. 1573 (N.D. Cal. 1984) (sanctions against pro se litigant).

20. See 28 U.S.C. § 1746.

21. See Surowitz v. Hilton Hotels Corp., 383 U.S. 363 (1966).

22. See, e.g., Henry v. Daytop Village, Inc., 42 F.3d 89 (2d Cir. 1994). For an illustration of such pleading, see Fed. Form 12.

23. But see Fed. R. Civ. P. 11(d), 26(g) (specially treating disclosure and discovery papers).

litigants and other deleterious effects on the attorney-client relationship. This controversy prompted toning down the Rule by amendment in 1993. That amendment attempted to refine the Rule while reducing the incidence of its application.[24] On the one hand, the new Rule seriously tries to reduce the burdens of Rule 11 practice. For example, according to Rule 11(c)(1), the court no longer "shall" but merely "may" impose an appropriate sanction. A more obvious attempt along these lines is the "safe harbor" provision of Rule 11(c)(2), giving twenty-one days to withdraw the paper after a separate motion challenging it. On the other hand, the 1993 version of the Rule somewhat broadens the scope of obligation under Rule 11. For example, the person's obligation now is a continuing duty: according to Rule 11(b), the certification is renewed whenever the person presents the paper to the court anew, as by later advocating its position.

d. Governing Law

Just as for most of the mechanics of civil procedure, federal law governs the mechanics of pleadings in any federal action, including diversity actions. That is, how to plead is answered by federal law. However, what ultimately constitutes claim and defense—the elements of claim and defense—is under the *Erie* doctrine governed by state law on state-created claims. Similarly, federal law governs the burden of allegation, but state law governs the burden of proof on issues to which state law applies. All this will be treated in Chapter Three.

2. Steps in Pleading Stage

Unlike the more traditional procedural models, modern pleading involves few steps: the plaintiff's complaint, the defendant's response in the form of motion and/or answer, and rather rarely the plaintiff's response in the form of motion, reply, and/or answer.

a. Complaint

What Does a Complaint Look Like?

A sample complaint for negligence can be composed
from Federal Forms 1, 2, 7, and 11:

---

24. See Hadges v. Yonkers Racing Corp., 48 F.3d 1320 (2d Cir. 1995) (reversing sanctions). But see Zuk v. E. Pa. Psychiatric Inst. of the Med. Coll. of Pa., 103 F.3d 294 (3d Cir. 1996) (affirming sanctions in questionable circumstances).

UNITED STATES DISTRICT COURT
FOR THE SOUTHERN DISTRICT OF NEW YORK

Civil Action No. _____

A. B., Plaintiff   )

        v.   )   *Complaint*

C. D., Defendant   )

     1. The plaintiff is a citizen of the State of Connecticut. The defendant is a citizen of the State of New York. The amount in controversy, without interest and costs, exceeds the sum or value specified by 28 U.S.C. § 1332.

     2. On March 1, 2009, in a public highway called Boylston Street in Boston, Massachusetts, the defendant negligently drove a motor vehicle against the plaintiff who was then crossing said highway.

     3. As a result, the plaintiff was physically injured, lost wages or income, suffered physical and mental pain, and incurred medical expenses of $1000.

     Therefore, the plaintiff demands judgment against the defendant for $200,000, plus costs.

Signed:

_____

Date

Attorney for Plaintiff

Printed Name: _____

Address: _____

Telephone number: _____

E-mail address: _____

The complaint informs the court and the defendant of the plaintiff's grievance and request for redress. As can be seen in the sample complaint for negligence, which is probably more detailed than strictly necessary, the body of a federal complaint consists of three basic parts.

The first basic part is an affirmative allegation of subject-matter jurisdiction. Rule 8(a)(1) requires "a short and plain statement of the grounds for the court's jurisdiction." The federal courts' approach to this requirement is generally pretty strict.[25] In state courts of general jurisdiction there is usually no need for such a paragraph on jurisdiction, but the federal requirement is typical of courts of limited jurisdiction.[26]

The heart of the complaint is the statement of claim, which appears as paragraphs 2 and 3 in the sample. Rule 8(a)(2) requires

25. But see 28 U.S.C. § 1653 (amendment of defective jurisdictional allegations); Fed. R. Civ. P. 21 (dropping of misjoined parties).

26. See infra § 4.1.

"a short and plain statement of the claim showing that the pleader is entitled to relief." States following more traditional procedural models might require much more elaborate pleading.

Finally, Rule 8(a)(3) requires "a demand for the relief sought, which may include relief in the alternative or different types of relief." However, this demand usually does not box the pleader in, because Rule 54(c) provides that every "final judgment should grant the relief to which each party is entitled, even if the party has not demanded that relief in its pleadings"—except that any "default judgment must not differ in kind from, or exceed in amount, what is demanded in the pleadings." Thus, the court is free to do justice, but cannot unfairly surprise a defaulting defendant.[27] In the various states, practices regarding demand for judgment range from enforcing strictly the demand to prohibiting a pleaded demand.

b. Motion and/or Answer

Under Rule 12(a), the defendant must respond, usually within twenty days after service of the summons and complaint upon her. Otherwise, the defendant risks losing by default under Rule 55. The defendant may present some or all of her responses by motion[28] or by answer.[29] Making a pre-answer motion extends the time to answer, according to Rule 12(a)(4).

This presentation scheme leaves considerable room for tactics on the part of the defendant, and so the system imposes a presentation and waiver scheme in an attempt to curb the delay, harassment, and surprise of pleading abuses. To avoid waiver of some of the responses, the defendant must observe carefully the complicated prescriptions of Rule 12.

Some possible responses by the defendant are obvious. She might want to contradict the complaint's factual allegations. It is natural to respond to an accusation by saying, "I deny that!" She can do so. She might also want to challenge the complaint's legal sufficiency. After all, the law does not remedy every sort of grievance. Imagine that the plaintiff is basically complaining about a social snub. The defendant would yearn to respond, "So what?" She can indeed do so by forwarding the defense called failure to state a claim. Or she might have some new matter that would defeat liability even if all that the plaintiff says is true and even if his allegations add up to a legally recognized claim. For example,

---

27. See Bail v. Cunningham Bros., 452 F.2d 182 (7th Cir. 1971).

28. For an illustration of a motion to dismiss, see Fed. Form 40. See also Fed. R. Civ. P. 7 (clarifying that a motion is technically not a pleading). For more on the mechanics of motions attacking pleadings, see id. 6(c)(2) (affidavits) and 43(c) (evidence).

29. For an illustration of an answer, see Fed. Form 30.

she might want to point out that the statute of limitations has expired, or to raise the matter of contributory negligence. The defendant wants to say in effect, "Here is something new to chew on." She can indeed do so by forwarding what is called an affirmative defense. The defendant can forward any or all of these responses. In actuality, many other sorts of response are available to the defendant, but Rule 12 forces the defendant to think about how to raise them without losing them. There are **five important groups** of responses, when grouped in terms of their *presentation* and *waiver*.

First, there are two types of so-called **objections**. Rule 12(e) allows the defendant to require the plaintiff to give "a more definite statement" if the complaint "is so vague or ambiguous that the party cannot reasonably prepare a response." Rule 12(f) allows the defendant to have the court strike from the complaint "any redundant, immaterial, impertinent, or scandalous matter" that causes her prejudice. These two rather uncommon and rarely successful objections are *presented* and disposed of by motion before answer. Normally, they are *waived* if the defendant omits them from her initial motion or if she answers.[30]

Second, there are the four so-called **disfavored defenses**, which are easily waived by procedural mistake. The defendant may try to defeat the claim off the merits by raising lack of territorial jurisdiction (Rule 12(b)(2)), improper venue (12(b)(3)), defects in the form of the summons (12(b)(4)), or defects in the manner of transmitting notice (12(b)(5)). These four threshold defenses will be discussed in Chapter Four, but for now observe that Rule 12(b) permits these defenses to be *presented* by pre-answer motion or by answer; and if any of these defenses is so raised, the judge (1) may, on the application of any party, hear and determine the defense in a pretrial proceeding or (2) may choose to defer the issue until trial in the interests of efficiency. Normally, the defenses are *waived* if the defendant omits them (1) from her initial motion (Rule 12(g) normally allows only one pre-answer motion under Rule 12) or (2) from the answer (including any amendment as a matter of course), whichever of these two papers the defendant serves first.[31]

Third, there are two types of **defenses on the merits**, which were both mentioned above. Rule 8(b) allows the defendant to deny some or all of the plaintiff's factual allegations: she may make "specific denials" of designated portions of the complaint or a "qualified general denial" that denies everything not expressly

---

30. See Fed. R. Civ. P. 12(e)-(g).

31. See id. 12(h)(1), (i); cf. Wright & Miller, supra note 6, §§ 1194, 1389, 1475 (discussing occasional judicial looseness in allowing amendment of motion, if movant seeks to amend promptly and in good faith and if opponent has not relied on original motion).

admitted, or she may sometimes resort to the usually improper "general denial" of the whole complaint; she can plead a denial not only by directly denying on the basis of knowledge, but also by denying "upon information and belief" or more frequently by merely stating that she is without "knowledge or information" sufficient to form a belief. Rule 8(c) allows the defendant to assert affirmative defenses, i.e., new matter that would legally avoid liability even if the plaintiff's allegations were factually and legally sound. These two defenses on the merits are properly *presented* by answer. Normally, they are *waived* if the defendant omits them from the answer, unless the answer is amended to include them.[32]

Fourth, there are the two so-called **favored defenses**, which are termed favored because they are less easily waived, but still a successful challenge on either ground often leads only to amendment of the complaint. Rule 12(b)(6) allows the defendant to challenge for "failure to state a claim upon which relief can be granted"; as explained above, this defense maintains that under the substantive law part or all of the complaint would result in no liability even if all the plaintiff's allegations were true; this is the usual avenue for challenging the legal sufficiency of the complaint, but under the lenient Federal Rules it should seldom succeed. Rule 12(b)(7) allows the defendant to challenge for "failure to join a [necessary or indispensable] party"; this defense will be discussed in Chapter Six. Rule 12(b) permits the defendant to raise these defenses by motion or by answer, which means that these defenses should be *presented* in the one pre-answer motion normally allowed under Rule 12(g), in the answer as amended, or in a post-answer motion for judgment on the pleadings or summary judgment; and if either of these defenses is so raised, the judge may, on the application of any party, hear and determine the defense in a pretrial proceeding or the judge may choose to defer the issue until trial. Normally, these defenses are *waived* if the defendant fails to raise them before the end of the trial.[33]

Fifth, there is the unique **subject-matter jurisdiction defense**. The issue of subject-matter jurisdiction, mentioned as a defense in Rule 12(b)(1), is treated with distinct solicitude in federal court. During the action, any party may challenge subject-matter jurisdiction at any time, and the court must ever be ready to

---

32. See Fed. R. Civ. P. 8(b)(6), 12(b); cf. Wright & Miller, supra note 6, § 1277 (discussing occasional judicial looseness in allowing defendant to raise affirmative defense by pre-answer motion); Rhynette Northcross Hurd, Note, The Propriety of Permitting Affirmative Defenses to Be Raised by Motions to Dismiss, 20 Mem. St. U. L. Rev. 411 (1990).

33. See Fed. R. Civ. P. 12(h)(2), (i); Coleman v. Frierson, 607 F. Supp. 1566 (N.D. Ill. 1985), aff'd sub nom. Coleman v. Smith, 814 F.2d 1142 (7th Cir. 1987) (finding waiver); cf. Madore v. Ingram Tank Ships, Inc., 732 F.2d 475, 480 (5th Cir. 1984) (holding that entry of judgment marks end of trial).

question its own subject-matter jurisdiction; and this defense may be *presented* in any fashion. Normally, this defense cannot be *waived*.[34]

c. Motion, Reply, and/or Answer

Unlike the common-law and code models, federal pleading in a two-party lawsuit usually stops with the answer. The limited mission of modern pleading has by then been accomplished. But there are two situations where there is the further step of the plaintiff's response.

First, assume that the defendant's answer includes defenses, but no counterclaims. Then there might be a motion or, rarely, a reply.

Usually within twenty days after service of the answer, the plaintiff may move under Rule 12(f) to strike "any redundant, immaterial, impertinent, or scandalous matter" that causes him prejudice. Such a motion is uncommon and very rarely succeeds. Also, Rule 12(f) permits the plaintiff to have the court strike from the answer "an insufficient defense." This poorly drafted provision is generally treated as authorizing a motion analogous to the defendant's 12(b)(6) motion.

Normally, the plaintiff neither must nor may reply to an answer containing only defenses. Instead, Rule 8(b)(6) provides that the answer's allegations are automatically taken to be "denied or avoided." However, the court may order a reply under Rule 7(a)(7) in the interests of clarification, most likely on the defendant's motion. In such a rare case, the plaintiff usually has twenty days after service of the court's order to respond under Rule 12(a)(1)(C): the plaintiff may in appropriate circumstances move under Rule 12(e) for a more definite statement, but should ultimately serve and file a reply denying or avoiding the new matter in the defendant's answer.

Second, assume that the defendant's answer contains one or more counterclaims, designated as such.[35] The plaintiff is then cast as a defendant with respect to the counterclaims. Under Rules 7(a)(3) and 12(a)(1)(B), the plaintiff must respond to the counterclaims, usually within twenty days after service of the defendant's answer. The response might be a motion and an answer.

The plaintiff may move under Rule 12 against the counterclaims, with this step being analogous to the defendant's motion against the complaint. Similarly, the plaintiff should ultimately

---

34. See Fed. R. Civ. P. 12(h)(3); infra § 4.4.

35. See infra § 6.2(A)(2), (B)(2) (treating counterclaims).

answer the counterclaims, with the pleading being analogous to the defendant's answer to the complaint.

3. Amendment of Pleadings

A hallmark of the federal pleading process is permitting amendments to the maximum extent consistent with the purposes of pleadings. Thus, a party can normally correct his pleading mistakes or amend on the basis of newly learned information. This is the realm of Rule 15.

a. Amendments as a Matter of Course

Under Rule 15(a)(1), a party can amend his pleading once without applying to the court for permission if he acts promptly. He can do this at any time "before being served with a responsive pleading." But if his pleading is one to which no responsive pleading is permitted, the party normally has only twenty days after serving his pleading.

For example, if P serves his complaint and D moves in response, and if thirty days later P wishes to amend in order to moot D's pending motion, then P can amend as a matter of course, because D has not yet responsively pleaded but only moved. But if P serves his complaint and D answers without counterclaiming, so that no responsive pleading by P is permitted, and if thirty days later D seeks to amend, then D must obtain leave of court or written consent of P, because the twenty-day period for amendments of course has expired.

b. Other Amendments

As just suggested, if a party cannot amend as a matter of course, the party must under Rule 15(a)(2) obtain the written consent of the adversary or move to obtain leave of court.

"The court should freely give leave when justice so requires."[36] The burden of persuasion will therefore be on the opponent of amendment. The court will discretionarily measure (1) the *prejudice* to the opponent's reliance interests that would be unavoidably caused by allowing the amendment and any *fault* of the movant in delaying, to see if together they exceed (2) the *prejudice* to the movant's interests in a full presentation of the merits that would be unavoidably caused by denying the amendment and any *fault* of the

---

36. Fed. R. Civ. P. 15(a)(2). Compare, e.g., Beeck v. Aquaslide 'N' Dive Corp., 562 F.2d 537 (8th Cir. 1977) (affirming allowance of amendment), with David v. Crompton & Knowles Corp., 58 F.R.D. 444 (E.D. Pa. 1973) (denying amendment because of delay).

opponent in inducing the delay—with the court also throwing onto the scales of this balance (3) the pertinent considerations of *public interest*, which usually favor amendment in the interests of rendering a single decision truly on the merits.

There are some hidden complexities in applying this otherwise typical balance of the equities. Only prejudice to the opponent's reliance interests goes onto the scales. After all, any amendment will cause prejudice to the opponent, as that is why the movant seeks to amend. The amendment may very well mean the difference between winning and losing. But all the court will count is prejudice to the opponent's reliance interests, which is disadvantage in a full presentation of the merits attributable to the movant's delay in seeking amendment. For example, because of the passage of time, the opponent may no longer be able to obtain evidence to meet the substance of the amendment. Furthermore, the court will count only such harm that is unavoidable harm, not harm that could be avoided by, say, granting a continuance. The court may grant leave to amend subject to conditions.

There is no time limit on seeking amendment, although by operation of the court's balance the chances of being allowed to amend usually decrease with the passage of time. Thus, a party can amend his pleading at or after trial. By so decreasing the significance of the pleadings, Rule 15 by itself largely solves the ancient problem of fatal "variance" between pleading and proof: the background necessary for understanding Rule 15 is the traditional but now outmoded axiom providing that a claim or defense can be sustained after trial only if its essentials had been pleaded in full and also only if it has been fully proved in conformity with those pleadings.

More specifically, Rule 15(b) treats the following two special situations of late amendments, which otherwise fall within the general scope of Rule 15(a). Rule 15(b) reads:

(1) *Based on an Objection at Trial.* If, at trial, a party objects that evidence is not within the issues raised in the pleadings, the court may permit the pleadings to be amended. The court should freely permit an amendment when doing so will aid in presenting the merits and the objecting party fails to satisfy the court that the evidence would prejudice that party's action or defense on the merits. The court may grant a continuance to enable the objecting party to meet the evidence.

(2) *For Issues Tried by Consent.* When an issue not raised by the pleadings is tried by the parties' express or implied consent, it must be treated in all respects as if raised in the pleadings. A party may move—at any time, even after judgment—to amend the pleadings to conform them to the evidence and to raise an unplead-

ed issue. But failure to amend does not affect the result of the trial of that issue.

First, Rule 15(b)(1) covers the special situation of an amendment to circumvent the opponent's successful objection to trial evidence on the ground that the proffered evidence is irrelevant under the pleadings.[37] This part of the Rule simply emphasizes that such a curative amendment is permissible under Rule 15(a)(2).

Second, Rule 15(b)(2) covers the different situation where the opponent failed to object fully to trial evidence that unambiguously went beyond the pleadings.[38] When issues have been so tried by express or implied consent, this part of the Rule specially provides that the pleadings later will be treated as if the original pleadings included those issues and further provides that the pleadings may even be actually so amended. Actual amendment to conform to evidence at trial would help, for example, to facilitate later application of res judicata.

In fact, by the courts' loose reading of consent, the two parts of Rule 15(b) combine to provide an unexpected punch. If a party objects to evidence as being outside the pleadings, but the court erroneously overrules that objection, and if the objector next either fails to request a continuance or litigates fully against the new matter, then the court will likely treat this as trial by consent, so obviating any reversible error in the original objection's overruling.

c. Relation Back of Amendments

Rule 15(c) addresses an amended pleading's effective date, which is primarily of importance for the statute of limitations. Under Rule 15(c)(1)(A), the amendment relates back if the applicable limitations law so provides.[39] Also, Rule 15(c)(1)(B) provides an alternative provision for relation back: the amendment relates back to the date of the original pleading if "the amendment asserts a claim or defense that arose out of the conduct, transaction, or occurrence set out—or attempted to be set out—in the original pleading,"[40] a test that is best read loosely to require only "a common core of operative facts";[41] however, under this provision,

---

37. Compare Robbins v. Jordan, 181 F.2d 793 (D.C. Cir. 1950) (allowing amendment), with Cox v. Fremont County Pub. Bldg. Auth., 415 F.2d 882 (10th Cir. 1969) (disallowing amendment).

38. See Brandon v. Holt, 469 U.S. 464 (1985); Wasik v. Borg, 423 F.2d 44 (2d Cir. 1970).

39. See, e.g., Saxton v. ACF Indus., Inc., 254 F.3d 959 (11th Cir. 2001) (hold-ing that this Fed. R. Civ. P. 15(c)(1)(A) relation back operates independently of the federal relation-back provision set out in the rest of Fed. R. Civ. P. 15(c)).

40. See, e.g., Blair v. Durham, 134 F.2d 729 (6th Cir. 1943); Bonerb v. Richard J. Caron Found., 159 F.R.D. 16 (W.D.N.Y. 1994).

41. Wright & Miller, supra note 6, § 1497. But see Marsh v. Coleman Co., Inc., 774 F. Supp. 608 (D. Kan. 1991)

the amendment relates back with respect to a changed party-defendant only if, in addition, that new party received timely notice of the misdirected lawsuit.[42]

d. Supplemental Pleadings

To be distinguished from an amended pleading is a supplemental pleading under Rule 15(d), which is a pleading "setting out any transaction, occurrence, or event that happened after the date of the pleading to be supplemented." Upon motion, the court may permit such a supplemental pleading.

B. Disclosure Stage

In 1993, amid much controversy, the rulemakers introduced a new stage called disclosure. In 2000, they had to cut it back. Now, parties must disclose, without awaiting a discovery request, only certain core information that elaborates on the pleaded facts.[43]

1. Purposes

Disclosure aims at achieving some savings in time and expense, and also at moderating litigants' adversary behavior in the pretrial phase. Parties find the core information useful in virtually all cases. The information is all discoverable anyway. Disclosure essentially makes this obvious discovery automatic, so that parties just hand over the information without awaiting a discovery request in the form of interrogatories.

2. Scope

According to Federal Rule 26(a), there are three distinct types of disclosure. However, the presiding judge by order or the parties by stipulation may alter these disclosure obligations.

First, there are the initial disclosures. Rule 26(a)(1)(A) requires disclosure, at the outset, of routine evidentiary and insurance matters that are reasonably available. These matters comprise (i) witnesses "likely to have discoverable information * * * that the disclosing party may use to support its claims or defenses, unless the use would be solely for impeachment," (ii) documents and things "that the disclosing party has in its possession, custody, or

---

(giving narrow reading to "transaction or occurrence").

42. See Fed. R. Civ. P. 15(c)(1)(C). Compare Singletary v. Pa. Dep't of Corr., 266 F.3d 186 (3d Cir. 2001), with

Worthington v. Wilson, 790 F. Supp. 829 (C.D. Ill. 1992) (following majority view), aff'd, 8 F.3d 1253 (7th Cir. 1993).

43. See generally Wright & Miller, supra note 6, §§ 2053–2054.

control and may use to support its claims or defenses, unless the use would be solely for impeachment," (iii) computation of claimed damages, and (iv) insurance agreements that might cover part or all of an eventual judgment. Rule 26(a)(1)(B) exempts certain special categories of cases from this requirement.

Second, there is the matter of expert information. Rule 26(a)(2) requires a party to disclose, at a specified time, the identity of any expert who may be called at trial. Most of these experts must also deliver a detailed report, which must include all opinions to be expressed and the underlying reasons, as well as details about qualifications, compensation, and previous experience as a witness.

Third, there are the pretrial disclosures. Rule 26(a)(3) requires disclosure, shortly before trial, of trial witness lists and the like regarding nonimpeachment evidence. In particular, the party must disclose trial exhibits, which allows airing evidentiary disputes in advance of trial.

3. Mechanics

Disclosure under the Federal Rules is meant to proceed in an atmosphere of cooperation. But under Rule 26(a)(4) all disclosures are to be in writing, signed, and served. Rule 26(g) requires an attorney, or if there is no attorney then the party, to sign each disclosure made under Rule 26(a)(1) or (3). The signature is a certification that to the best of the signer's knowledge, information, and belief formed after reasonable inquiry the disclosure is complete and correct as of the time it is made. Violations of the Rule are to be punished by sanctions.

A key feature of the disclosure and discovery schemes lies in Rule 26(f): very early on, the attorneys and unrepresented parties normally must confer to consider the case and the disclosures, as well as attempt to develop a proposed discovery plan and then submit a written report to the court along the lines of Federal Form 52. A duty to participate in good faith is enforceable under Rule 37(f). Under Rule 26(d)(1), discovery normally cannot proceed until this conference takes place.

The pretrial disclosures under Rule 26(a)(3) must be promptly filed with the court, but the other disclosures, like most discovery items, must not be filed until used in the proceeding.[44]

Rule 26(e)(1) says that a party is under a duty to supplement disclosures if the party learns that in some material respect the information disclosed is incomplete or incorrect, unless the other parties are aware of the additional information. A special duty to

---

44. See Fed. R. Civ. P. 5(d)(1) (specifying the filing obligation).

supplement with respect to expert information is set forth in Rule 26(e)(2).

In case of noncompliance, after conferring with the nondisclosing party, a party may move under Rule 37(a) to compel disclosure, along with appropriate sanctions.[45] Also, Rule 37(c)(1) independently provides that a party who without substantial justification fails to make a mandatory disclosure, unless such failure is harmless, is subject to appropriate sanctions, which will usually prohibit use of the nondisclosed evidence.

4. Problems

Overlaying a stage of disclosure on the current pretrial system of the Federal Rules would seem to increase costs, as well as produce more satellite litigation. In addition, disclosure seems to clash with parts of that pretrial system, especially tending to undermine modern pleading. Although scholarly attacks on disclosure have tended to exaggerate these costs, empirical research discouragingly demonstrates that initial disclosure under Rule 26(a)(1), at least, has little beneficial effect to offset the costs.

What Does Initial Disclosure Teach About the Rulemaking Process?

One of the most controversial pretrial reforms of recent times has been mandatory disclosure. This 1993 innovation required initial disclosure of unfavorable as well as favorable information relevant to disputed facts alleged with particularity in the pleadings. However, districts by local rule could alter these initial disclosure obligations, and almost half the districts opted out of the standard scheme by diminishing initial disclosure to some degree.

The federal rulemakers had credited as their inspiration in 1993 the anecdotal advocacy in two law review articles by Professor Wayne D. Brazil. The Adversary Character of Civil Discovery: A Critique and Prospects for Change, 31 Vand. L. Rev. 1348 (1978), and by Judge William W Schwarzer, The Federal Rules, the Adversary Process, and Discovery Reform, 50 U. Pitt. L. Rev. 703, 721–23 (1989). Critics counterargued that disclosure, in its routine operation and by the consequent disputes, would actually increase delays and expenses. Also, critics claimed that disclosure would counterproductively clash with the prevailing adversary system and with the Rules' notice pleading scheme. Note that mandatory disclosure applies even in the majority of cases where there is no discovery or at least no real dispute over discovery, and also in the many cases where disclosure would occur anyway on a voluntary basis between cooperative lawyers. After the rulemakers' introduction of disclosure, the unabating controversy prompted them finally to commission empirical studies, by both the Federal Judicial Center and the RAND Institute for Civil Justice.

The FJC reported a survey of 2000 attorneys involved in 1000 general civil cases terminated in 1996 that were likely to have some discovery activities, a survey with a 59% response rate. Most of the responding attorneys felt that initial disclosure had no effect on delay or fairness, but among those who detected effects more attorneys believed the effects to be

---

45. See, e.g., Comas v. United Tel. Co. of Kan., CIV.A. No. 94–2376–GTV, 1995 WL 476691 (D. Kan. Aug. 10, 1995).

positive than negative. Also, the survey found that respondents rarely reported fears of increased satellite litigation. Finally, by statistical analysis of its small sample of cases, the FJC found that the use of initial disclosure tended to shorten actual disposition time. See Thomas E. Willging, John Shapard, Donna Stienstra & Dean Miletich, Discovery and Disclosure Practice, Problems, and Proposals for Change: A Case-based National Survey of Counsel in Closed Federal Civil Cases (1997).

The RAND report used its pre-existing data to compare a small group of district courts with local rules requiring some type of disclosure during 1992–1993 to another small group with no such rules. The data included the attorneys' subjective measures of satisfaction and sense of fairness, as well as objective measures of attorneys' hours worked and case disposition time. RAND found no significant effect of disclosure on fairness sensed, hours worked, or disposition time. But mandatory disclosure did markedly lower attorney satisfaction. See James S. Kakalik, Deborah R. Hensler, Daniel McCaffrey, Marian Oshiro, Nicholas M. Pace & Mary E. Vaiana, Discovery Management: Further Analysis of the Civil Justice Reform Act Evaluation Data (1998).

In 2000, based on these two imperfect studies, the rulemakers amended Rule 26(a)(1) to prohibit the district courts from opting out of the initial disclosure requirements, to exempt eight specified categories of proceedings from initial disclosure, and, most importantly, to change the scope of the initial disclosures. Now, a party need only disclose witnesses, and documents and things in the party's custody or control, "that the disclosing party may use to support its claims or defenses."

A graduate student at Cornell Law School recognized the shortcomings of the two previous studies and then performed his own clever study of disclosure by using governmental data. Kuo-Chang Huang, Mandatory Disclosure: A Controversial Device with No Effects, 21 Pace L. Rev. 203 (2000). Among other statistical analyses, he "vertically" compared disposition time in the years before a district court required initial disclosure with disposition time after adoption of such disclosure. He also "horizontally" compared district courts that required initial disclosure with district courts that had opted out of such disclosure. By multivariate regression, Mr. Huang showed that adoption of initial disclosure tended slightly but significantly to slow down disposition. He concluded that because it has almost no other practical effects, this controversial device has no justification. Thus, the rulemakers in 2000 would have been better advised just to eliminate initial disclosure under Rule 26(a)(1). See generally Kevin M. Clermont & Theodore Eisenberg, Litigation Realities, 88 Cornell L. Rev. 119, 132–35 (2002).

C. Discovery Stage

The pivotal feature of the federal procedural system is a significant discovery stage, or rather its availability. Many federal cases do not involve any discovery, but its existence allows the de-emphasis on pleading and inevitably diminishes the trial's importance. Its extensiveness stands in marked contrast to discovery under more traditional procedural systems. In the old days, there were the three procedural stages of extensive pleadings, limited investigation done privately, and then a significant and often surprising trial; today, the model is modern pleading, extensive discovery by court authorization, and then an occasional trial unfolding predictably and orderly. It is the middle innovation of making available extensive discovery that has so changed what comes before and after it in the procedural sequence.[46]

A number of policies and provisions apply throughout the discovery stage in federal court. I shall discuss them first, before turning to specific discovery devices.

1. Purposes

Discovery allows a party to expand on the notice given by the pleadings and by any disclosures. He thereby can (1) clarify and narrow the issues and (2) investigate the facts and explore the evidence before trial. These two grand functions of discovery permit him to build his own case and feel out his opponent's case. Discovery can perform these functions better than elaborate pleadings and extensive disclosures would.

But should the procedural system so try to perform these two functions before trial? Other countries choose not to use discovery. The primary motive behind this country's pretrial airing of the case by discovery is to avoid an inaccurate or unfair outcome determined by the parties' differing capacities for pursuing private investigation and for surviving a blind trial. In addition, there is the motive of efficiency: discovery might facilitate settlement; it might even allow the tried case to proceed more efficiently, as the trial stage becomes more predictable and orderly (and dull).

2. Scope

The scope of discovery is very wide, according to Federal Rule 26(b). The same scope generally applies to all the various discovery devices, and under it a party may discover any matter that is "relevant" and that is "nonprivileged," according to Rule 26(b)(1).

As to relevance under Rule 26(b)(1), the discovering party is free to seek any matter that is "relevant to any party's claim or defense" under the pleadings.[47] Moreover, for "good cause" shown, the court may order discovery of any matter that is "relevant to the subject matter involved in the action" (and thus perhaps relevant only to unasserted but possible claims or defenses).[48] These two

---

46. See generally Wright & Kane, supra note 3, §§ 81–90.

47. See Christine L. Childers, Note, Keep on Pleading: The Co-existence of Notice Pleading and the New Scope of Discovery Standard of Federal Rule of Civil Procedure 26(b)(1), 36 Val. U. L. Rev. 677 (2002).

48. See Sanyo Laser Prods. Inc. v. Arista Records, Inc., 214 F.R.D. 496

(S.D. Ind. 2003); Hill v. Motel 6, 205 F.R.D. 490 (S.D. Ohio 2001) (finding no good cause for age-discrimination plaintiff's nationwide discovery, and so allowing discovery only as to geographic region supervised by regional vice president who made decision to terminate plaintiff). Compare Thomas D. Rowe, Jr., A Square Peg in a Round Hole? The 2000 Limitation on the Scope of Federal

nearly equivalent relevance standards are meant to be loose, encompassing all the issues possibly in the case and the evidence thereon.[49] Furthermore, the Rule says, "Relevant information need not be admissible at the trial if the discovery appears reasonably calculated to lead to the discovery of admissible evidence."[50] However, the party must seek to discover the matter for the reason that it bears on, or because it might reasonably lead to other matter that bears on, some issue that will or may be decided in the case.[51]

As to privilege under Rule 26(b)(1), the reference to privilege incorporates the evidentiary rules of privilege applicable at trial, such as the attorney-client privilege.[52]

There are other policies and provisions restricting the scope of discovery, some of which are expressed in the remainder of Rule 26(b). I turn to them now.

a. Work Product

Hickman v. Taylor[53] recognized an important, broad, and complex policy further limiting the scope of discovery in two ways: (1) materials that were prepared by or for a party or his representative in anticipation of any litigation or for any trial ("ordinary work product"), such as witness statements, can be discovered only upon a showing of substantial need and of inability without undue hardship to obtain the substantial equivalent;[54] and (2) mental

Civil Discovery, 69 Tenn. L. Rev. 13 (2001), with Christopher C. Frost, Note, The Sound and the Fury or the Sound of Silence: Evaluating the Pre–Amendment Predictions and Post–Amendment Effects of the Discovery Scope-narrowing Language in the 2000 Amendments to Federal Rule of Civil Procedure 26(b)(1), 37 Ga. L. Rev. 1039 (2003).

49. Compare Davis v. Precoat Metals, a Div. of Sequa Corp., No. 01 C 5689, 2002 WL 1759828 (N.D. Ill. July 29, 2002) (allowing racial-discrimination plaintiff to discover discrimination complaints by other employees of defendant), with Davis v. Ross, 107 F.R.D. 326 (S.D.N.Y. 1985) (not allowing defamation plaintiff to discover complaints by other employees of Diana Ross).

50. E.g., Lindberger v. Gen. Motors Corp., 56 F.R.D. 433 (W.D. Wis. 1972) (allowing discovery of inadmissible subsequent remedial measures).

51. See Oppenheimer Fund, Inc. v. Sanders, 437 U.S. 340 (1978) (Fed. R. Civ. P. 26(b)(1) does not authorize attempt to obtain class members' names

and addresses for purpose of sending class-action notice, as opposed to information bearing on a disputed issue).

52. E.g., Jaffee v. Redmond, 518 U.S. 1 (1996) (psychotherapist-patient privilege); Upjohn Co. v. United States, 449 U.S. 383 (1981) (attorney-client privilege); Butler v. Rigsby, Civ. Action No. 96–2453 Sec. "R" (5), 1998 WL 164857 (E.D. La. Apr. 7, 1998) (doctor-patient privilege); see Fed. R. Evid. 1101(c), 501.

53. 329 U.S. 495 (1947). For the story of this case, see Richard L. Marcus, The Story of Hickman: Preserving Adversarial Incentives While Embracing Broad Discovery, in Civil Procedure Stories 323 (Kevin M. Clermont ed., 2d ed. 2008). See also United States v. Nobles, 422 U.S. 225 (1975) (holding that doctrine continues to apply at trial but is subject to waiver).

54. E.g., Rackers v. Siegfried, 54 F.R.D. 24 (W.D. Mo. 1971) (insurance adjuster's papers); see Special Project, The Work Product Doctrine, 68 Cornell L. Rev. 760 (1983).

impressions, conclusions, opinions, or legal theories of the party's attorney or other representative concerning the litigation ("opinion work product") are even more strictly protected and indeed can perhaps never be discovered.[55]

Rule 26(b)(3) codifies *Hickman*'s broad policy for "tangible work product," except that the Rule permits any person to obtain his own statement without any special showing:

(A) *Documents and Tangible Things.* Ordinarily, a party may not discover documents and tangible things that are prepared in anticipation of litigation or for trial by or for another party or its representative (including the other party's attorney, consultant, surety, indemnitor, insurer, or agent). But, subject to Rule 26(b)(4), those materials may be discovered if:

(i) they are otherwise discoverable under Rule 26(b)(1); and

(ii) the party shows that it has substantial need for the materials to prepare its case and cannot, without undue hardship, obtain their substantial equivalent by other means.

(B) *Protection Against Disclosure.* If the court orders discovery of those materials, it must protect against disclosure of the mental impressions, conclusions, opinions, or legal theories of a party's attorney or other representative concerning the litigation.

(C) *Previous Statement.* Any party or other person may, on request and without the required showing, obtain the person's own previous statement about the action or its subject matter. If the request is refused, the person may move for a court order, and Rule 37(a)(5) applies to the award of expenses. A previous statement is either:

(i) a written statement that the person has signed or otherwise adopted or approved; or

(ii) a contemporaneous stenographic, mechanical, electrical, or other recording—or a transcription of it—that recites substantially verbatim the person's oral statement.

By omission, Rule 26(b)(3) leaves the rest of *Hickman* undisturbed for "intangible work product."[56] The messy legal process that

---

55. E.g., Duplan Corp. v. Moulinage et Retorderie de Chavanoz, 509 F.2d 730, 735 (4th Cir. 1974) ("Should an advocate's thoughts, theories, opinions, and impressions, collected and developed during pending litigation, become discoverable in connection with later litigation because they are thought to be relevant, our adversary system would clearly suffer."). But see Holmgren v. State Farm Mut. Auto. Ins. Co., 976 F.2d 573, 577 (9th Cir. 1992) ("opinion work product may be discovered and admitted when mental impressions are *at issue* in a case and the need for the material is compelling"). See generally Note, Protection of Opinion Work Product Under the Federal Rules of Civil Procedure, 64 Va. L. Rev. 333 (1978).

56. See Ford v. Philips Elecs. Instruments Co., 82 F.R.D. 359, 360 (E.D. Pa. 1979) ("Insofar as defendant's question attempted to elicit from the witness the

produced this mélange of precedent and Rule does nothing to simplify the subject.

How Does Partial Codification Work?

Hickman soundly divided the subject into ordinary and opinion work product. Rule 26(b)(3) surprisingly, irrelevantly, and apparently inadvertently divided the same world into tangible and intangible work product. The Rule implicitly recognized that both ordinary and opinion work product, which deserve different degrees of protection, could appear in documents and other tangible things, but the Rule left intangible work product to the prior and subsequent case law.

The critical insight into this regulatory scheme is partial codification. By this is meant that the Rule neither spans the whole subject of work product nor supplants all of the prior case law. As a codification, the Rule provides some answers, but only for questions arising within part of the doctrine. When a question arises outside the scope of the Rule, an approach that looks directly to the Rule for an answer is at best misleading.

Acquiring the insight of partial codification is but the first step of analysis. Then come fixing the realm of the Rule's coverage and concluding that within that realm the Rule preempts Hickman. At a first-level glance, the Rule authoritatively treats tangible work product. Within that realm, the Rule's protection might expand Hickman (perhaps, for example, regarding its wide range of persons other than lawyers whose efforts can create work product) or might contract Hickman (perhaps, for example, by its strictness as to the anticipation-of-litigation requirement). For questions involving tangible work product—such as when a party seeks to obtain a witness statement—authoritative answers derive from the Rule and not from Hickman. Obviously, a knowledge of Hickman's policies will inform a reading of the Rule. Nevertheless, interpreting a Rule presents a task jurisprudentially distinct from elaborating a case-law doctrine.

Outside the Rule, Hickman survives. There the challenge lies in resorting to that case's policy bases. For questions outside the reach of the Rule—such as when a party seeks the opposing counsel's opinion on some matter like a witness's credibility, or seeks by interrogatory only the substance of a witness statement as opposed to a copy of the statement—it is Hickman that is still authoritative. Of course, the Rule will exert some influence as an existing, parallel reading of Hickman. Nevertheless, elaborating work product on a sensitive case-by-case basis yields a nuanced doctrine without the "squared-off corners" produced by the rulemakers' words.

Next comes the challenge of recognizing that those aspects of Hickman that the Rule fails to handle will apply even to tangible work product (like application at trial or loss by waiver). Hickman thus expands or contracts the first-impression thrust of Rule 26(b)(3), with the protection extending to trial but disappearing by waiver even for tangible work product. See generally Kevin M. Clermont, Surveying Work Product, 68 Cornell L. Rev. 755 (1983).

Whether one is wrestling with *Hickman* or Rule 26(b)(3), work product is of immense practical importance, with the outcome of the case often turning on its discoverability. Moreover, this kind of material is commonly created by lawyers and others, so there is always a lot of it. The discoverability line that the courts draw is a

specific questions that plaintiff's counsel posed to him, or even the area of the case to which he directed the majority of his questions, it exceeds the permissible bounds of discovery and begins to infringe on plaintiff's counsel's evaluation of the case. However, insofar as it was directed to the substance of the witness' knowledge of relevant facts, it is clearly an acceptable line of inquiry.").

difficult one to discern. Consequently, work-product immunity is the most frequently litigated discovery issue.

More than the outcome of the case turns on discoverability of work product. Protecting work product, and hence encouraging full preparation and discouraging freeriding, is thought to be critical to the workings of the adversary system. However, its protection conflicts with discovery's policy of cooperatively laying one's cards on the table. One manifestation of the necessary compromise is the rule that protection does not extend to prevent normal discovery of raw facts that happen to be encased in undiscoverable work product.

Additionally, Rules 33(a)(2) and 36(a)(1) permit some inquiry into those opinions that come in the form of contentions, even though contentions are in the nature of work product. The idea is that it should be okay to ask one's opponent what he is suing for or what is her ground for defense. The discoverable contentions can be factual or can involve the application of law to fact, but one cannot ask for contentions of pure law.[57] Unlike Rule 26(b)'s wide application to all discovery devices, Rules 33(a)(2) and 36(a)(1) make a special extension to the scope of discovery that applies only to interrogatories and requests for admission, because these two devices effectively enable the opposing counsel to answer in writing at an appropriate time after reflection and even investigation.[58] Contention discovery can thereby deliver the specificity formerly provided by the pleadings. However, answers to interrogatories are not binding, which means that the answering party can use evidence that contradicts its answer to an interrogatory.[59] Contrastingly, admissions in response to Rule 36 requests are normally binding, so

---

57. See Booth Oil Site Admin. Group v. Safety-Kleen Corp., 194 F.R.D. 76 (W.D.N.Y. 2000) (admissions); Kendrick v. Sullivan, 125 F.R.D. 1 (D.D.C. 1989) (interrogatories); O'Brien v. Int'l Bhd. of Elec. Workers, 443 F. Supp. 1182 (N.D. Ga. 1977) (interrogatories). See generally Iain D. Johnston & Robert G. Johnston, Contention Interrogatories in Federal Court, 148 F.R.D. 441 (1993) (also briefly discussing admissions).

58. See In re Convergent Techs. Sec. Litig., 108 F.R.D. 328, 332 (N.D. Cal. 1985) (while delaying obligation to respond, the court observed: "Some people would classify as a contention interrogatory any question that asks another party to indicate *what* it contends. Some people would define contention interrogatories as embracing only questions that ask another party *whether* it makes some specified contention. Interrogato-

ries of this kind typically would begin with the phrase 'Do you contend that....' Another kind of question that some people put in the category 'contention interrogatory' asks an opposing party to state all the *facts* on which it *bases* some specified contention. Yet another form of this category of interrogatory asks an opponent to state all the *evidence* on which it *bases* some specified contention. Some contention interrogatories ask the responding party to take a position, and then to explain or defend that position, with respect to *how the law applies to facts*. A variation on this theme involves interrogatories that ask parties to spell out the *legal basis* for, or theory behind, some specified contention.").

59. See Freed v. Erie Lackawanna Ry., 445 F.2d 619 (6th Cir. 1971); cf. Fed. R. Civ. P. 26(e)(1) (duty to supplement).

that a discovering party who encounters a welcome contention by use of Rule 33(a)(2) might then try to pin the contending party down on the point via Rule 36(a)(1).

b. Expert Information

Rule 26(b)(4) overrides Rule 26(b)(3) to provide a special rule for discovery from experts, who play an ever-increasingly critical role in modern litigation. This Rule on expert information is fairly permissive in allowing regulated discovery regarding experts whom a party may call as expert witnesses at trial, including documents provided to or prepared by the experts.[60] But the Rule is much more restrictive with respect to discovery of facts known and opinions held by other experts who have been retained or specially employed in anticipation of litigation or preparation for trial.[61] The party obtaining discovery may be ordered to pay fees and expenses. This Rule's approach thus permits thorough trial preparation, while minimizing the risk of freeloading.

On the one hand, apparently subject to ordinary discovery is the identity of an expert in either category, as well as expert information not acquired or developed in anticipation of litigation or preparation for trial, including information acquired by an expert as an actor or viewer with respect to the events in suit.[62]

On the other hand, apparently immune from discovery are the identity of and the facts known and opinions held by a nontestifying expert who has acquired or developed his information in anticipation of litigation or preparation for trial, if that expert was not "retained or specially employed" by the opposing party for the particular case but only "informally consulted."[63]

---

60. See Herman v. Marine Midland Bank, 207 F.R.D. 26 (W.D.N.Y. 2002) (holding that defendant was entitled to discovery of alleged work product of attorney that plaintiff had shared with its expert); Michael J. O'Hara & Graham Mitenko, Scope of Discovery of an Expert's Work Product, J. Legal Econ., Fall 2000, at 37.

61. Compare Chiquita Int'l Ltd. v. M/V Bolero Reefer, 93 Civ. 0167 (LAP), 1994 WL 177785 (S.D.N.Y. May 6, 1994) (denying discovery from marine surveyor), with Thompson v. Haskell Co., No. 93–1327–Civ-J–20, 1994 WL 597252 (M.D. Fla. June 21, 1994) (allowing discovery of psychologist's report).

62. See Note, Discovery of Retained Nontestifying Experts' Identities Under the Federal Rules of Civil Procedure, 80 Mich. L. Rev. 513 (1982); David S. Day,

The Ordinary Witness Doctrine: Discovery of the Pre–Retention Knowledge of a Nonwitness Expert Under Federal Rule 26(b)(4)(B), 38 Ark. L. Rev. 763 (1985).

63. See Ager v. Jane C. Stormont Hosp. & Training School for Nurses, 622 F.2d 496, 501 (10th Cir. 1980) (defining informal consultation in terms of factors to "be considered: (1) the manner in which the consultation was initiated; (2) the nature, type and extent of information or material provided to, or determined by, the expert in connection with his review; (3) the duration and intensity of the consultative relationship; and, (4) the terms of the consultation, if any (e. g. payment, confidentiality of test data or opinions, etc.)"); In re Shell Oil Ref., 132 F.R.D. 437, clarified, 134 F.R.D. 148 (E.D. La. 1990) (a nontestifying regular employee of the opposing

c.　E–Discovery

Today's big discovery problem, beyond doubt, involves the discovery of electronically stored information. About 1995, the problem just exploded. Judicial efforts to cope became herculean, as did the lawyers' performance. Digital information certainly has its tricky facets, such as the dynamic and precarious form of its storage. But the central difficulty is simply its volume. Any statistic on volume will be hopelessly inaccurate tomorrow. Suffice it to say that already the vast majority of all information exists exclusively in digital form. Each day produces many billions of e-mails in this country alone.

The nature and volume of computer-based information mean that it will hold the key to winning or losing numberless cases, ranging from divorce suits to corporate megasuits. Regardless of its content, its sheer volume means that the parties' discovery requests and responses will often entail crushing effort and expense. Many specialized businesses have sprung up to supply e-discovery services to litigants. Moreover, the looming possibility of e-discovery has deeply affected business and personal practices. Appropriate here is mention of the increasingly common existence of "document retention policies." Finally, law practice has surely changed. Office lawyers as well as litigators spend much of their time anticipating, if not conducting, e-discovery.

Once litigation is on the horizon, efforts and expenses pick up. The lawyer must retain third-party computer experts, while taking steps to ensure the preservation of digital evidence by both the client and the opponent. Parties will engage in a fair amount of meeting and conferring, under Rules 16 and 26(f), about e-discovery. Discoverers will rely most heavily on Rule 33 interrogatories to acquire the necessary knowledge of the respondent's computer system, and then on requests for production under Rules 34 and 45 to get the actual computer-based information. Finally, the courts must wade in under Rules 26(c) and 37(a), all too often.[64]

The federal rulemakers started their serious study of this new problem in 2000. Meanwhile, courts gave ever increasing attention to the problem. Amendments worked through the rulemaking process to emerge in 2006 as new provisions on e-disclosure and e-discovery. Rules 16, 26, 33, 34, 37, and 45, among others, under-

---

party who is retained or specially employed for the case falls within Fed. R. Civ. P. 26(b)(4)(B)). See generally Wright & Miller, supra note 6, § 2033.

64. See generally W.E. Aubuchon Co. v. BeneFirst, LLC, 245 F.R.D. 38 (D.

Mass. 2007); Sharon D. Nelson, Bruce A. Olson & John W. Simek, The Electronic Evidence and Discovery Handbook (2006) (providing many useful, and lengthy, forms).

went amendment to codify the formerly disparate practices ordained by case law and local rules.

The changes promoted the discovery of "electronically stored information" to equal status with discovery of "documents" and "things," thereby lifting the necessity of conceptually squeezing the digital within the documentary. The changes also tried to refine the scope of e-discovery by encouraging the balancing of costs and benefits under Rules 33, 34, and 45. In particular, Rule 26(b)(2)(B) distinguishes digital material that is reasonably accessible from digital material that is not, with cost-shifting openly on the table for the latter. And the discovering party under Rule 34 or 45 can now designate the form of production, subject to the respondent's objection.

Meanwhile, changes to the conferencing procedures of Rules 16(b) and 26(f), by becoming information-technology sensitive, facilitate supervision of e-discovery by the court. Incidentally, while the Rules recognize the existence of a duty to preserve digital material imposed by common law, statute, regulation, or court order, Rule 37(e) maps a usually safe harbor for destruction of digital material as part of "the routine, good-faith operation of an electronic information system."

d. Other Restrictions

When the court intervenes in the discovery process, as explained below pursuant to a motion for a protective order under Rule 26(c) or for an order compelling discovery under Rule 37(a), it may limit or regulate discovery. On this case-by-case basis, it will vindicate implicit policies, such as the uncodified part of the work-product doctrine or policies emanating from the First Amendment, or, more frequently, it will seek to avoid annoyance, embarrassment, oppression, or undue burden or expense. This case-by-case approach, then, represents the real limit on discovery's scope. It is thus misleading to say that a party may discover any matter that is relevant and nonprivileged. The actuality is that a party generally may discover only matter that is relevant, nonprivileged, and otherwise within the specified bounds of all of Rule 26(b) and also that has not been ruled out of bounds by Rule 26(c)/37(a)-type judicial supervision.

One sees this real limit in all sorts of cases. When a court decides that the defendant cannot interrogate on the sexual history of a sexual-harassment plaintiff,[65] or when a court says that counsel

---

65. See Mitchell v. Hutchings, 116 F.R.D. 481 (D. Utah 1987) (allowing such discovery, but only for contempora- neous work-environment behavior); Herchenroeder v. Johns Hopkins Univ. Applied Physics Lab., 171 F.R.D. 179 (D.

cannot compel an answer to a question posed to a lay deponent because it is too legal in nature,[66] the court is drawing the line on this case-by-case basis. Likewise, when a court seeks to shield impeachment evidence from free discovery by first allowing deposition of the witness subject to impeachment, the court is utilizing Rule 26(c)/37(a)-type flexibility.[67]

3. Mechanics

a. General Provisions

Discovery under the Federal Rules is meant to work almost wholly by action of the parties, without intervention by the court.[68]

Just as for disclosures, Rule 26(g) requires an attorney, or if there is no attorney then the party, to sign each discovery request or response. The signature is a certification of reasonableness, with violations of the Rule to be punished by sanctions.[69]

Again, a key feature of the disclosure and discovery schemes lies in Rule 26(f): very early on, the attorneys and unrepresented parties normally must confer to consider the case and the disclosures, as well as attempt to develop a proposed discovery plan and then submit a written report to the court along the lines of Federal Form 52. A duty to participate in good faith is enforceable under Rule 37(f). Under Rule 26(d)(1), discovery normally cannot proceed until this conference takes place.

Despite the aim of a party-governed discovery process, anyone involved in the process should be able to invoke the court's assistance in a situation of need, in order to remedy either abuse or recalcitrance. Also, bear in mind that the court by order, or commonly the parties by a Rule 29 negotiated stipulation, may alter most of the discovery Rules.

Requests to Discover. A party may initiate any of the discovery devices without addressing the court—except where he seeks to invoke the broader relevance standard under Rule 26(b)(1); where

---

Md. 1997) (further subjecting such discovery to a confidentiality order); cf. Stalnaker v. Kmart Corp., No. CIV.A. 95-2444-GTV, 1996 WL 397563 (D. Kan. July 11, 1996) (limiting such discovery sought by plaintiff).

66. Compare Umphres v. Shell Oil Co., 15 Fed. R. Serv. 2d (Callaghan) 1116 (S.D. Tex. 1971) (denying discovery), with Brandenberg v. El Al Israel Airlines, 79 F.R.D. 543 (S.D.N.Y. 1978) (allowing discovery on slightly more factual questions).

67. See Edward H. Cooper, Work Product of the Rulesmakers, 53 Minn. L. Rev. 1269, 1314–18 (1969).

68. See Thompson v. Dep't of HUD, 199 F.R.D. 168 (D. Md. 2001) (ordering parties to consult further).

69. See St. Paul Reinsurance Co. v. Commercial Fin. Corp., 198 F.R.D. 508 (N.D. Iowa 2000) (requiring counsel within four months to write an article by himself explaining why it is improper to assert the objections that he asserted to discovery requests and submit the article to two bar journals).

he seeks discovery before the parties' conference under Rule 26(f); where under Rule 27 he seeks discovery before commencement of an action or pending appeal in order to perpetuate evidence; or where under Rule 35 he seeks a physical or mental examination.[70]

Discovery Responses. The respondent (1) may seek the court's protection, as can any party, (2) may simply refuse to comply, or (3) may comply with the request for discovery. If the discovering party is dissatisfied with the course followed, he may seek sanctions from the court. Thus, at the point of response, either side may choose to get the court involved. The burden of persuasion is normally on the person resisting discovery, regardless of who invokes the court's assistance. Such skirmishing for protective orders or sanctions takes place in the court in which the action is pending—except that with regard to a protective order as to a deposition, the skirmishing may take place in the court for the district where the deposition is to be taken; with regard to a order to compel discovery from a nonparty deponent, it must take place in the court for the district where the deposition is to be taken; and with regard to a subpoena, it must take place in the court from which the subpoena issued.

First, if the discovery response is to seek the court's protection, Rule 26(c)(1) allows the respondent or any party so to curb abuse by getting the court involved.[71] But the party or person must first confer with affected parties. Then the court may upon motion limit or regulate discovery "to protect a party or person from annoyance, embarrassment, oppression, or undue burden or expense."

The court has broad power to issue such a protective order, often shaping it discretionarily and flexibly to meet the problem at hand; indeed, the court may act on its own initiative under Rule 26(b)(2). Alternatively, the court may deny the motion and instead issue an order compelling discovery under Rule 26(c)(2).

Second, if the respondent instead refuses wholly or partly to comply with the request for discovery, the possibility of sanctions arises, which in fact entails a three-step process: conferring, order, and sanction. For the first step, when the discovering party meets such recalcitrance, he usually must confer with the recalcitrant party or person. For the second step, if conferring fails, he must go to court under Rule 37(a) to move for an order compelling discovery, unless the court has already entered an equivalent order (e.g., an order under Rule 35) or unless there has been a gross failure to

---

70. See also Fed. R. Civ. P. 30(a)(2), (d)(1), and 31(a)(2) on leave of court required for depositions of prisoners, excessive depositions, and lengthy depositions, and id. 33(a)(1) on leave of court required for excessive interrogatories.

71. See also id. 30(d)(3) (procedure for controlling oral depositions in progress).

respond that is directly sanctionable (i.e., a party's failure to appear for deposition, to serve any answers or objections to interrogatories, or to serve any written response to a request for inspection, or a person's failure to obey a subpoena, as provided in Rules 37(d) and 45(e)).[72] In ruling on a motion for an order compelling discovery, the court will decide whether discovery should be ordered or denied, and on what terms and conditions. For the third step, in case of further need for relief, the discovering party must go to the ordering court to obtain a sanction under Rule 37(b). Sanctions include having disputed facts treated as established, obtaining a dismissal or default, having failure to obey an order treated as contempt, or obtaining reimbursement of reasonable expenses.

Courts long restricted themselves to occasional and light remedial sanctions in the discovery process, but they now seem increasingly tough in imposing sanctions as deterrents.[73] On the one hand, a court will not order discovery or impose sanctions if the person, through no fault of his own, cannot comply. For example, the person may be subject to foreign law forbidding the revelation of the materials sought.[74] On the other hand, if the person is at fault, as where he intentionally destroyed evidence to prevent its discovery, the court may order discovery and ultimately impose sanctions. This approach parallels the spoliation doctrine, which allows a court to admit proof of the destruction of evidence.[75]

Third, upon satisfactory compliance with a request for discovery, a duty of supplementation arises. Rule 26(e)(1) says that the responding party is under a duty to supplement her response to an interrogatory, request for production, or request for admission if the party learns that the response is in some material respect incomplete or incorrect, unless the other parties are aware of the additional information. This Rule tries to limit the burden on the responding party and at the same time tries to protect the other parties from being seriously misled. Incidentally, the supplementa-

---

72. Cf. id. 36(a)(3), 37(c)(2) (sanctions for failure to admit).

73. E.g., Cine Forty–Second St. Theatre Corp. v. Allied Artists Pictures Corp., 602 F.2d 1062 (2d Cir. 1979); Poole v. Textron, Inc., 192 F.R.D. 494 (D. Md. 2000); see Roadway Express, Inc. v. Piper, 447 U.S. 752 (1980); Nat'l Hockey League v. Metro. Hockey Club, 427 U.S. 639 (1976).

74. See Société Internationale pour Participations Industrielles et Commerciales, S.A. v. Rogers, 357 U.S. 197 (1958) (holding dismissal with prejudice not warranted for failure to comply with order under Fed. R. Civ. P. 34 to produce Swiss banking records, where produc-

tion would subject party to criminal sanctions in Switzerland).

75. See Wright & Miller, supra note 6, § 5178 ("the spoliation cases could be read as a rule of procedure that punishes misconduct polluting the well of evidence by permitting the jury to consider such misconduct in adjudicating the substantive rights of the parties"); cf. Robert L. Tucker, The Flexible Doctrine of Spoliation of Evidence: Cause of Action, Defense, Evidentiary Presumption, and Discovery Sanction, 27 U. Tol. L. Rev. 67, 82–84 (1995) (relating spoliation to Fed. R. Civ. P. 37).

tion Rule's listing of requests for admission as being within the Rule could be a little confusing, given that such an admission is binding unless amended with judicial permission. But there are possible responses to such requests other than an admission, and these responses might need to be supplemented. In any event, to escape the binding effect of an admission the responding party cannot merely supplement but must seek to amend under Rule 36(b).[76]

As to the use of whatever discovery produces, the parties generally may use the products of discovery as evidence in the trial only so far as those products are admissible under the Federal Rules of Evidence—and generally the scope of admissibility is more restricted than the scope of discovery itself. However, the use of depositions, which are so like trial testimony, receives special treatment in Rule 32(a): the Rule specifies that the rules of evidence need only be applied as though "the deponent were present and testifying," provided that the use of the deposition falls within one of the situations listed in Rule 32(a)(2)-(4) or (6) and thus justifies this avoidance of the normal hearsay rule. When used, the products of discovery generally count only as evidence, to be weighed along with the other evidence.

Discovery Expenses. The expenses incurred in discovery can be enormous. Normally, they fall ultimately on the party who initially incurred them; for example, the discovering party pays the small cost of preparing interrogatories, and the responding party pays the huge cost of answering them. However, the court may eventually award certain, relatively insignificant discovery expenses as costs to the party who prevails in the lawsuit. More significantly, the Rules have ample provisions for shifting reasonable discovery expenses (including attorneys' fees) as a condition of approving discovery;[77] for ordering parties, deponents, or counsel to reimburse anyone's reasonable expenses incurred in successfully invoking the court's assistance in a discovery dispute or resisting such an attempt;[78] and for requiring reimbursement of reasonable expenses as a discovery sanction.[79]

b.   Specific Devices

The Federal Rules provide six major types of discovery devices. The litigator today must have a solid grasp of these varying discovery tools and their relative value.

---

76. See Asea, Inc. v. S. Pac. Transp. Co., 669 F.2d 1242, 1247 (9th Cir. 1981); Republic Sav. Bank v. United States, 57 Fed. Cl. 73, 75 (2003).

77. See, e.g., Fed. R. Civ. P. 26(c).

78. See, e.g., id. 37(a)(5).

79. See, e.g., id. 37(d)(3).

Unless otherwise ordered, the parties may use one or more of these devices repeatedly, and in any sequence or simultaneously according to Rule 26(d)(2). However, in the absence of leave of court or agreement of the parties, Rules 30(a)(2)(A) and 31(a)(2)(A) now limit each side to ten depositions and prohibit redeposing the same person; Rule 30(d)(1) similarly limits an oral deposition to one day of seven hours; and Rule 33(a)(1) similarly limits each party's interrogatories served on any one party to twenty-five, "including all discrete subparts."

Oral Depositions. A deposition by oral examination is a proceeding initiated by any party for taking anyone's testimony, in a private setting but otherwise similar to trial—with oral direct examination, cross-examination, and so on.[80] The party can have himself deposed, or depose any other party or any other person, which is, when you think about it, an extraordinary power to bestow on a private person.

In the usual case, leave of court is not needed to initiate the deposition procedure. The discovering party gives reasonable notice in writing to the other parties to the action, specifying the time and place of the deposition and naming the deponent. A nonparty deponent is officially summoned to appear at the deposition, and perhaps to bring and produce documents and other things, by the service upon him of a subpoena under Rule 45; a nonparty deponent can thus be compelled to appear for a deposition only within the geographical limits for a subpoena as set by Rule 45. If the deponent is a party, a subpoena need not be used, because the notice of examination itself suffices as a command, and the notice to a party deponent may be accompanied by a request under Rule 34 to produce documents and other things at the taking of the deposition; a party deponent can be noticed for a deposition anywhere, and so a party deponent must sometimes resort to a motion under Rule 26(c) for protection from an inconvenient deposition.

Typically, the actual oral deposition involves a sworn deponent, a reporter, and a bunch of lawyers sitting around a table in some lawyer's office. Unlike trial, there is no judge; there is only a presiding officer, who is described in Rule 28 and who has no judicial powers; therefore, Rules 30(c)(2) and 32(b) and (d) exist to provide a mechanism for preserving evidentiary objections. The idea is that the deponent should answer, under any appropriate objection, all questions, except the deponent may refuse to answer particular questions thought to fall outside the scope of discovery and to call for an answer that would infringe on privilege or otherwise be damaging or offensive.

80. See id. 30.

Largely because of all the attorneys' time involved, an oral deposition is very expensive. But there is no substitute for pinning down a respondent or reaping other fruits of oral testimony.

Written Depositions. A deposition by written questions resembles an oral deposition but with all the questions written out in advance.[81] The presiding officer simply reads the questions to the sworn deponent and has the responses recorded.

This inflexible device is seldom used, being markedly less effective than an oral deposition and markedly more expensive than employing interrogatories. But being less expensive to conduct than an oral deposition (because the attorneys need not be present for a written deposition), a deposition by written questions might be used where the device of interrogatories would suffice except that (1) it is unavailable because the desired respondent is a nonparty, (2) it is unsuited because the discovering party wants to specify a particular officer or agent to respond for a corporate party, or (3) it is unsatisfactory because the aim is to generate admissible testimony from a person who will be unavailable at trial.

Interrogatories. Interrogatories are simply written questions, each of which the responding party must answer in writing under oath, unless her attorney objects thereto with reasons in writing.[82] You should be able to imagine how easy it would be to ask the responding party, say, to list the details of every date she has been on since 1990, and how burdensome and intrusive it would be to respond. Rule 33(d) provides some protection from interrogatories directed to massive business records by allowing the responding party to invite the discovering party to inspect the records himself, and the court must be sensitive to abuse by other kinds of interrogatories.

Answers to interrogatories tend to be studied and artfully evasive, and they are nonbinding. But they very often provide a simple and inexpensive way either to clarify the issues, such as by seeking contentions ("State in what respect, if any, other than already set forth in the complaint, it is claimed that defendant acted in an unsafe or dangerous manner with respect to failing to maintain a proper lookout for plaintiff."), or to obtain evidence and leads to evidence, such as by asking for a list of eyewitnesses ("List the full names and addresses of all persons known to you or your counsel who have or claim to have relevant knowledge concerning this accident or the injuries alleged to have resulted from this accident.").[83]

81. See id. 31.

82. See id. 33.

83. See 3A Jay E. Grenig, West's Federal Forms—District Courts §§ 3497, 3500 (5th ed. 2002); see also supra text accompanying notes 57–59.

Production of Documents and Such. A written request to a party for production of any designated documents or other tangible things (or for entry upon land or other property) within that party's possession, custody, or control provides a route for the discovering party to inspect, copy, test, or sample them.[84] The responding party must serve a written response, either agreeing to comply or objecting with reasons. Similarly, a nonparty may be compelled to produce by subpoena under Rule 45.

The rulemakers have expanded the reach of this production Rule to reflect changing technology. The Rule now treats electronically stored information. The discovering party can designate the form of production, subject to the respondent's objection. So, the responding party may be required to translate into reasonably usable form. Often she will supply a print-out of computer data, but the court has flexible powers sufficient to assure the discovering party adequate information and at the same time to protect the responding party against undue burden or expense.[85]

Physical and Mental Examination. Upon motion and for "good cause" shown, the court in which the action is pending may order a physical or mental examination of any party or a person in the custody or under the legal control of any party (e.g., a party's minor child), if the physical or mental condition of the person to be examined is "in controversy."[86] Because of concerns of privacy and risks of serious abuse, the court should use special care in exercising its discretion to order an examination.[87]

Requests for Admission. A written request to a party to admit, for purposes of the pending action only, the truth of matters set forth in the request (including genuineness of described documents) can lead to admissions that are *conclusive* on the party who made the admission—unless later the court on motion permits withdrawal or amendment of admissions.[88] The responding party or her attorney must serve a written response, which will admit or deny each matter, explain why she cannot truthfully admit or deny it, or object thereto with reasons.

Any such admissions are like the specific pleadings under the old procedural regimes, except that they come at a much more appropriate time in the case. Indeed, they usually come late enough

---

84. See Fed. R. Civ. P. 34; see also Fed. Form 50.

85. See, e.g., N. Crossarm Co. v. Chem. Specialties, Inc., No. 03–C–415–C, 2004 WL 635606 (W.D. Wis. Mar. 3, 2004) (approving production of hard copy).

86. Fed. R. Civ. P. 35(a); see also id. 35(b) (exchange of reports of findings).

87. See Schlagenhauf v. Holder, 379 U.S. 104 (1964) (carefully allowing examination of defendant who has not put his own condition in issue); see also Sibbach v. Wilson & Co., 312 U.S. 1 (1941) (upholding validity of Fed. R. Civ. P. 35).

88. See Fed. R. Civ. P. 36; see also Fed. Form 51.

that courts are rather tough about amending them. One might say that the difficulty of amending pleaded positions, keeping constant the equities of the parties, increases along a spectrum like this: Rule 15(a)(1) amendment as a matter of course, Rule 15(b)(2) amendment to conform to evidence, Rule 15(a)(2) motion to amend during pretrial, Rule 15(b)(1) motion to amend over trial objection, and Rule 36(b) motion to amend admission during trial. Thus, although the format of this discovery device is rather inflexible and limited, it does offer a simple and inexpensive way to narrow the issues with binding effect.

How Do the Specific Discovery Devices Compare and Contrast?

	Oral Depositions	Written Depositions	Interrogatories	Production of Documents and Such	Physical and Mental Examination	Requests for Admission
Fed. R. Civ. P.	30	31	33	34	35	36
Availability	Any time, but Rule 27 requires order before action or pending appeal, and Rule 30(a)(2) and (d)(1) requires leave of court or stipulation for certain depositions	Any time, but Rule 27 requires order before action or pending appeal, and Rule 31(a)(2) requires leave of court or stipulation for certain depositions	Any time after filing complaint, but leave of court or stipulation required before Rule 26(f) conference or for more than 25 interrogatories	Any time, but leave of court or stipulation required before Rule 26(f) conference; for nonparties, see Rules 34(c) and 45; see also Rule 27	Any time, but only on court order; see also Rule 27	Any time after filing complaint, but leave of court or stipulation required before Rule 26(f) conference
Respondents	Any person, but use subpoena under Rule 45 for nonparties	Any person, but use subpoena under Rule 45 for nonparties	Parties (for nonparties, use deposition with subpoena)	Any person, but use subpoena under Rule 45 for nonparties	Parties and persons in custody of or under legal control of a party	Parties
Time Periods	Reasonable notice in writing to every other party; time required for review through delivery under Rule 30(e) and (f)	Notice, with written questions, to every other party; then 14 + 7 + 7 days for preparation of cross, redirect, and recross questions; time required for review through delivery	30 days after service of interrogatories to answer or object	30 days after service of request to agree or object; for nonparties, see Rules 34(c) and 45	Notice of motion to examinee and to every other party	30 days after service of request to answer or object

		under Rule 31(b) and (c)				
Special Advantages	Quickly invoked; opposing lawyer cannot actively assist deponent; discovering lawyer can flexibly react to answers given; other advantages of oral testimony	Advantageous only in very special circumstances	Inexpensive and simple to prepare; useful for clarifying issues and for obtaining evidence leads	Serves particular purposes	Serves particular purposes	Fairly inexpensive and simple to prepare; useful for narrowing issues with binding effect and thus for fleshing out pleadings
Special Disadvantages	Very expensive	Expensive, although attorneys need not attend deposition; cumbersome; other disadvantages of written interrogation	Can be used only against parties; corporate respondent can choose any officer or agent to answer; disadvantages of written interrogation	Can result in a pile of paper or data	Expensive	Inflexible format and limited purposes

4. Problems

Questions persist regarding the desirability of the federal model's extensive discovery, at least when one moves out of the abstract world of theory and into the real world of litigation. That is, doubts remain whether the promised benefits of discovery outweigh its actual costs. Surprise at trial might sometimes act as a promoter of truth, and the discovery weapon sometimes allows browbeating of the opponent. Certainly, the time and money involved can be staggering in a few cases.

Nevertheless, given that most people agree that discovery is (and should be) here to stay, perhaps the most effective control on its costs (and therefore the most fruitful avenue for reform) is more active but selective case-by-case supervision of discovery by the court. At any rate, this route has been the one followed in recent decades by a series of modest amendments to the discovery Rules.

D. Pretrial Conference

The federal procedural system requires a tool to help move the case through this whole pretrial process and toward the climactic trial, and also to focus the case after the skeletal pleading stage and the dispersive effects of disclosure and discovery. The modern tool for accomplishing this is the judicially (or parajudicially, by magistrate or master) supervised pretrial conference.[89]

Traditionally, a conference followed the loose pretrial procedure authorized by Federal Rule 16 in 1938. However, with scant empirical support, the 1983 and 1993 amendments radically expanded Rule 16 to provide for more conferences and to make the court's involvement therein a little more dictatorial in tone and structured in format and a lot more active in case management, thus rather basically and questionably affecting the role of the judge in the adversary system. Indicative of the change is the important new requirement in Rule 16(b) that in most cases, within about 100 days of commencement, the court after consultation must issue a "scheduling order" limiting the time for settling pleadings, filing motions, and completing discovery.

This evolution accurately suggests that the big question in connection with pretrial conferences is whether they are most effective and fair when they are voluntary and loose affairs or when the court adopts a highly directive role. For illustration, should the judge merely ask whether the parties have discussed settlement, and so get the topic of settlement on the table but otherwise let it be a natural by-product of conferring as the trial looms, or should the judge use the considerable powers of office to push settlement actively, helping to clear today's crowded docket but perhaps undermining the other missions of the pretrial conference and the impartial tone of office? There has in fact been a wide range of judicial practice regarding settlement, but recently there has been a noticeable shift toward activism. Since 1983, Rule 16(a)(5) and (c)(2)(I) expressly mentions settlement and the Advisory Committee's note thereon even suggests the possibility of convening a settlement conference. The Rule's new emphasis can only accelerate the shift toward activism.[90]

1. Purposes

A pretrial conference allows the court and the litigants to confer about the case, so moving it along to disposition and molding it for trial. Such a conference may lead to settlement. It should condense and shape the case, as by amending the pleadings, formulating and simplifying the issues, streamlining the proof, or handling any other of a wide variety of pretrial matters.

89. See generally Wright & Kane, supra note 3, § 91.

90. Compare Kothe v. Smith, 771 F.2d 667 (2d Cir. 1985), and Judith Resnik, Managerial Judges, 96 Harv. L. Rev. 374 (1982), with Steven Flanders, Blind Umpires—A Response to Professor Resnik, 35 Hastings L.J. 505 (1984).

2. Procedural Incidents

At any time after commencement of the action, the court in its discretion may direct the attorneys and unrepresented parties to appear before it for one or more pretrial conferences. The key feature (and perhaps the secret strength) of this procedure is that there is no uniform practice, but instead the practice varies from district to district, from judge to judge, and especially from case to case.

In the piddling case, the court may not hold any pretrial conference. In selected, more difficult cases—typically—the court will call one pretrial conference shortly before trial; local rules will require the litigants to engage in an extensive written exchange of views beforehand, and the litigants will have to attend the conference further to reveal fully and fairly their positions and plans; but that conference will properly tend—with some courts' practices in notable disagreement—to be otherwise voluntary in tone and relatively uncomplicated, informal, and nonbinding in format. In the "big case," the court today is likely to be much more active through a series of conferences, all being held on the record.

3. Order

After a pretrial conference, the court must enter a binding order reciting the action taken at the conference, although the order is amendable. An order following a final pretrial conference just before trial, however, is amendable "only to prevent manifest injustice" or, in other words, only if the movant can carry the *burden* of satisfying the elevated *standard* of clearly showing the injustice of denying the amendment.[91]

Finally, Rule 16(f) provides the sanctions for violation of the court's order or of the Rule.

E. Other Stages

Numerous other procedural steps can be taken in the pretrial period, the more important of which are described below. Do not slip into thinking that the various steps must all be taken or that they must always be taken in some fixed order.

---

91. Compare Walker v. Anderson Elec. Connectors, 944 F.2d 841 (11th Cir. 1991) (denying amendment), Shuber v. S.S. Kresge Co., 458 F.2d 1058 (3d Cir. 1972), McKey v. Fairbairn, 345 F.2d 739 (D.C. Cir. 1965), and Payne v. S.S. Nabob, 302 F.2d 803 (3d Cir. 1962), with Washington Hosp. Ctr. v. Cheeks, 394 F.2d 964, 965 (D.C. Cir. 1968) (allowing amendment), and Smith Contracting Corp. v. Trojan Constr. Co., 192 F.2d 234 (10th Cir. 1951).

1. Provisional Remedies

The claimant may seek temporary relief to protect himself from loss or injury while his action is pending. The point is to preserve, or sometimes to alter, the status quo in the short run, so that intervening events will not frustrate any final relief that may eventually be granted. There are two major kinds of such temporary relief.[92]

First, there is seizure of property. If the plaintiff seeks a money judgment, he has an interest in ensuring that the defendant's assets will still be there to satisfy any eventual judgment. Accordingly, the law provides security by way of seizure of the defendant's real or personal property at the outset of or during the lawsuit.

In federal court, Federal Rule 64 authorizes all pre-judgment seizure remedies available under the law of the state in which the district court is held, in the circumstances and manner provided by that law, except that any existing federal statute governs to the extent applicable. As a consequence, federal practice varies from state to state.

States provide for such remedies where circumstances suggest a sufficient need for security, as where the defendant has left the jurisdiction. States provide for such remedies in various manners, such as by "attachment" (legal process directing seizure of the defendant's property that is in the hands of the defendant) and "garnishment" (legal process subjecting to the plaintiff's claim the defendant's property that is in the hands of a third person, or "garnishee," or freezing a debt owed to the defendant by the garnishee). A typical example of a garnishable debt is the defendant's bank deposit: by the service of proper process upon the bank, the bank is warned not to pay the defendant the amount deposited and now garnished, but to hold it for application to the plaintiff's judgment if he should get one; the garnishment excuses the bank from paying the defendant; indeed, if the bank nevertheless does pay the defendant, it can be made to pay again to the successful plaintiff. Such remedies' drastic effects on the defendant can raise questions of fundamental fairness under the Due Process Clause.[93]

Second, there is injunctive relief. The plaintiff may have an immediate interest in making the defendant do or not do some act, in order to avoid frustrating any permanent relief. Accordingly, the court may grant interim injunctive relief—which binds the defendant and those persons in active concert or participation with her,

---

92. See generally Dan B. Dobbs, Dobbs Law of Remedies §§ 1.3, 2.11 (2d ed. 1993).

93. See infra § 4.3(B).

provided that the party or person to be bound has received actual notice of the court's action.[94] There are two kinds of this relief: temporary restraining order and preliminary injunction.

As to the temporary restraining order, or "t.r.o.," the court may grant a request for relief that is of very short duration, doing so without a hearing and sometimes even without advance notice to the defendant. The plaintiff may obtain such a temporary restraining order upon a showing of immediate irreparable harm. A temporary restraining order is typically a stopgap in expectation of a preliminary injunction, which differs in that it comes only after a hearing.

After notice and hearing, the court may grant a motion for a preliminary injunction, which can last until final judgment. Granting this discretionary remedy to prevent possible irreparable harm involves measuring the tilt toward interim relief in the *balance of the plaintiff's and the defendant's harms and the public interests*, with the required degree of tilt decreasing as the *likelihood of the plaintiff's ultimate success on the merits* increases.[95] "The court asks whether the plaintiff will be irreparably harmed if the preliminary injunction is denied (sometimes also whether the plaintiff has an adequate remedy at law), whether the harm to the plaintiff if the preliminary injunction is denied will exceed the harm to the defendant if it is granted, whether the plaintiff is reasonably likely to prevail at trial, and whether the public interest will be affected by granting or denying the injunction"—but ultimately the court balances and somehow combines these factors, granting or denying provisional relief in a more or less rigorous attempt to choose the path with lesser expected costs.[96]

Federal Rule 65 imposes typically severe limitations on these drastic forms of injunctive relief, such as by Rule 65(c)'s requiring any plaintiff other than the federal government to give security "in an amount that the court considers proper to pay the costs and damages sustained by any party found to have been wrongfully enjoined or restrained." The working of this security is a bit tricky. The court must require security, which comes usually in the form

94. See Robert C. Casad & Kevin M. Clermont, Res Judicata: A Handbook on Its Theory, Doctrine, and Practice 157–58 (2001).

95. See, e.g., Abbott Lab. v. Mead Johnson & Co., 971 F.2d 6, 11–12 (7th Cir. 1992) (applying the dominant sliding-scale approach described in text); cf. Sonesta Int'l Hotels Corp. v. Wellington Assocs., 483 F.2d 247, 250 (2d Cir. 1973) ("The settled rule is that a preliminary injunction should issue only upon a clear showing of either (1) probable success on the merits *and* possible irreparable injury, *or* (2) sufficiently serious questions going to the merits to make them a fair ground for litigation *and* a balance of hardships tipping decidedly toward the party requesting the preliminary relief."); William Inglis & Sons Baking Co. v. ITT Cont'l Baking Co., 526 F.2d 86 (9th Cir. 1976) (same).

96. Am. Hosp. Supply Corp. v. Hosp. Prods. Ltd., 780 F.2d 589, 593–94 (7th Cir. 1986); see infra § 7.1(A)(1) (law-and-economics formulation).

of a bond. However, it can, at least, discretionarily fix the amount at a nominal level for a poor but deserving plaintiff. The defendant who ultimately prevails on the propriety of injunctive relief, by any means from a full-blown trial down to a voluntary dismissal without her consent, can recover her actual economic losses resulting from obeying the wrongfully imposed injunction. She can ordinarily recover these losses up to the amount of the bond, but not beyond. This limitation follows from the proposition that the plaintiff is ordinarily not liable for the harm that the defendant suffers from litigation.

2. Summary Judgment and Other Steps That Avoid Trial

In addition to the motions attacking pleadings, which were discussed in connection with the pleading stage above, there are various other steps that may avoid trial. If a party cannot win by some such pretrial device, that party will want to settle. In most cases, trial is ultimately avoided in one of these ways. Trial is thus an event of vanishing occurrence.

a. Summary Judgment

This increasingly important tool for determining whether trial is necessary nicely complements the prevailing federal scheme of modern pleading and extensive discovery.[97] That is, providing for summary judgment is a good idea, especially in today's strained procedural system, as it allows weeding out those cases that do not require trial at all.

Of course, the system must avoid overuse of summary judgment that would undercut the right to trial. But overuse should not ensue as long as the standard for summary judgment is sufficiently tough. The prevailing standard seems tough enough, at least in theory, in that it will knock out cases only when one side is being unreasonable, i.e., irrational, in disputing the facts (or the application of a legal standard to the facts).[98] Admittedly, however, courts sometimes can be too eager to get rid of a case and so give summary judgment on a showing that seems too weak.[99]

---

97. See generally Edward J. Brunet & Martin H. Redish, Summary Judgment (3d ed. 2006); Wright & Kane, supra note 3, § 99.

98. Compare Jack H. Friedenthal, Cases on Summary Judgment: Has There Been a Material Change in Standards?, 63 Notre Dame L. Rev. 770 (1988), with Jeffrey W. Stempel, A Distorted Mirror: The Supreme Court's

Shimmering View of Summary Judgment, Directed Verdict, and the Adjudication Process, 49 Ohio St. L.J. 95 (1988).

99. See, e.g., Bias v. Advantage Int'l, Inc., 905 F.2d 1558 (D.C. Cir. 1990) (actively reconciling affidavits to avoid existence of genuine issue of fact); Am. Airlines v. Ulen, 186 F.2d 529 (D.C. Cir. 1949) (obscurely construing law to give

Availability. Federal Rule 56 is the governing provision. It makes the summary judgment device available broadly, in at least three ways.

First, either a claimant or a defending party may move. A defending party may move at any time, either before or after the pleadings close, as Rule 56(b) specifies. A claimant may move at any time after the defending party serves a summary judgment motion or after the expiration of 20 days following commencement of the action, as Rule 56(a) specifies.

Second, the motion may concern all of a claim or only some of its issues. Rule 56(d) expressly but somewhat grudgingly treats partial summary adjudication. Until recently, the courts have tended to frown on Rule 56(d), seeing it merely as a procedure that was ancillary to an ordinary motion for summary judgment on a whole claim or at least on liability under Rule 56(a), (b), or (c) and that had the purpose of salvaging something from the effort expended in denying such an ordinary summary judgment motion. But partial summary adjudication is also a good idea, and so it should become more common in the future.

Third, either the summary judgment motion may be made on the pleadings alone or it may be supported by affidavits, products of discovery, and other factual materials, all of which can be used to pierce the pleadings. The summary judgment procedure aims at revealing whether factual disputes truly exist so as to necessitate a trial. Just as the movant can support his motion, the opponent is free to submit affidavits, products of discovery, and other factual materials in opposition. The court may also consult materials in the case on file with the court. However, from all those materials, only information that would be admissible at trial is considered on a summary judgment motion, because the aim is only to see if trial is necessary and not to get to truth in some other sense.

Standard of Decision. Summary judgment will be given to a movant "entitled to judgment as a matter of law" if "there is no genuine issue" as to any fact that matters in the case.[100] Summary judgment thus allows the court to decide legal disputes, without trial, when there are no genuine and material factual disputes. The principal inquiry on the motion is whether factual disputes truly exist—never how to resolve factual disputes that do exist. If there is a genuine, i.e., triable, factual dispute, then the motion must be denied and trial awaited.

summary judgment of negligence per se); cf. Joe S. Cecil, Rebecca N. Eyre, Dean Miletich & David Rindskopf, A Quarter–Century of Summary Judgment Practice in Six Federal District Courts, 4 J. Empirical Legal Stud. 861 (2007) (finding increasing frequency of summary judgment grants).

100.   Fed. R. Civ. P. 56(c).

In determining whether there is a genuine issue as to any fact, the court construes all factual matters in the light reasonably most favorable to the party opposing the motion and then asks whether reasonable minds could differ as to the fact's existence.[101] That is, summary judgment can be granted if, looking only at all the evidence that is favorable to the opponent of the motion but not incredible and also at the unquestionable evidence that is favorable to the movant, the judge believes that a reasonable factfinder could not find for the opponent. Under this standard, disputes on the papers as to objective fact can sometimes be resolved by overwhelming evidence that removes all reasonable doubt, but disputes that turn on credibility cannot. Accordingly, it is easier to obtain summary judgment against the party who will bear at least the burden of production at trial, although even a party who will bear the burden of both production and persuasion at trial can sometimes properly obtain summary judgment with a sufficiently strong showing.[102]

Celotex Corp. v. Catrett[103] elaborated the burden of proof on the summary judgment motion itself. The movant ultimately has the burden of persuasion that summary judgment should be granted to him because no genuine issue exists and the substantive law favors him. However, if the movant supports his motion sufficiently to make a prima facie showing that summary judgment should be granted on the basis of what is then before the court, the opponent normally cannot rest upon her pleading but instead must produce a real response or suffer summary judgment.[104] So, if a defendant

---

101. See Anderson v. Liberty Lobby, Inc., 477 U.S. 242 (1986) (settling that for summary judgment essentially the same standard applies as the one used on the motion for judgment as a matter of law, which is discussed below, although the latter comes later on a fuller record; clarifying that on a summary judgment motion the judge must hypothesize a reasonable jury measuring the evidence against the applicable standard of proof, whether the standard be preponderance of the evidence or clear and convincing evidence or proof beyond a reasonable doubt, and thus an elevated standard of proof affects the availability of summary judgment; and seeming to reject any special summary judgment standard for state-of-mind or personal-knowledge cases); cf. Scott v. Harris, 127 S.Ct. 1769 (2007) (arguably lowering standard of proof to encourage summary judgment).

102. See infra § 2.4(A)(1) (treating burdens of proof at trial). Compare Lundeen v. Cordner, 354 F.2d 401, motion to amend denied, 356 F.2d 169 (8th Cir. 1966) (affirming summary judgment for burdened party based on uncontradicted and unimpeached testimony of impartial witness), with Cross v. United States, 336 F.2d 431 (2d Cir. 1964) (reversing summary judgment for burdened party because his showing rested on his own testimony), on remand, 250 F. Supp. 609 (S.D.N.Y. 1966) (finding at trial against burdened party).

103. 477 U.S. 317 (1986). For the story of this case, see David L. Shapiro, The Story of Celotex: The Role of Summary Judgment in the Administration of Civil Justice, in Civil Procedure Stories 359 (Kevin M. Clermont ed., 2d ed. 2008). See also Linda S. Mullenix, Summary Judgment: Taming the Beast of Burdens, 10 Am. J. Trial Advoc. 433, 464 (1987).

104. See, e.g., Houchens v. Am. Home Assurance Co., 927 F.2d 163 (4th Cir. 1991); Dyer v. MacDougall, 201 F.2d 265 (2d Cir. 1952); Alderman v. Balti-

moves by specifically describing the basis of the motion and demonstrating the absence of evidence in the record on an element of the plaintiff's claim on which the plaintiff will bear at least the burden of production at trial, the plaintiff normally cannot hold back her evidence but instead must respond to the motion by showing that there will be enough evidence on the element at trial to allow a reasonable factfinder to decide for the plaintiff.[105] But the burden of persuasion on the motion stays on the movant. This is what Rule 56(e)(2) means in providing:

> When a motion for summary judgment is properly made and supported, an opposing party may not rely merely on allegations or denials in its own pleading; rather, its response must—by affidavits or as otherwise provided in this rule—set out specific facts showing a genuine issue for trial. If the opposing party does not so respond, summary judgment should, if appropriate, be entered against that party.

On the one hand, the judge in actuality can almost always choose to deny a summary judgment motion and proceed to trial. The judicial role is, in reality, discretionary. The judge might indulge a disinclination to adjudicate on a summary basis by finding the motion to be not properly made, finding the time not right under Rule 56(f)'s provision allowing delay when the opponent needs time to assemble a response, or finding the facts in genuine controversy. In any event, because a denial of summary judgment is normally nonappealable and nonreviewable, the trial judge's refusal to adjudicate on a summary basis is normally not correctable.

On the other hand, the judge can grant summary judgment in favor of the party opposing the motion, or even so act sua sponte in the absence of a motion, if the party is fairly entitled thereto and the other party has received adequate notice.

Relation to Other Motions. Consider the difference between summary judgment and the motion for judgment on the pleadings. Rule 12(c) authorizes any party to move for judgment on the pleadings, after the pleadings are closed but within such time as not to delay the trial. The court will grant such judgment to a movant entitled to judgment under the law when the *pleaded facts* are read most favorably to the party opposing the motion. This device allows the movant to argue—on the basis of the opponent's view of the facts as shown by what the opponent's pleadings allege or admit, this being a collection of facts that the movant accepts for the purpose of the motion only—that the movant is entitled to

more & Ohio R.R., 113 F. Supp. 881 (S.D.W. Va. 1953).

105. See Nidds v. Schindler Elevator Corp., 113 F.3d 912 (9th Cir. 1996); Fri-

to–Lay, Inc. v. Willoughby, 863 F.2d 1029 (D.C. Cir. 1988).

judgment under the substantive law. That is, this device tests the legal sufficiency of the pleadings, but does not pierce those pleadings to get at the *underlying facts* as Rule 56 can. In brief, Rule 12(c) is a stunted version of Rule 56, available in only some of the many circumstances where summary judgment is available. In view of the many procedural advantages of Rule 56, the litigant should virtually never have reason to resort to the common-law relic embodied in Rule 12(c).

Contrariwise, the motion for judgment on the pleadings is quite similar both to the defendant's motion to dismiss under Rule 12(b)(6) for failure to state a claim and to the plaintiff's motion to strike under Rule 12(f) for failure to state a sufficient defense, which were discussed above in connection with the pleading stage. The major difference is timing. Indeed, the Rule 12(c) motion serves the purposes of these two motions when it later becomes available after the pleadings close, as Rule 12(h)(2)(B) makes clear. However, motions under Rule 12(c) and under Rule 12(f) may both be available at a given time, in which event the use of Rule 12(c) is technically proper if judgment on the whole claim is sought and the use of Rule 12(f) is technically proper if striking of fewer than all defenses to the claim is sought.

On a motion under Rule 12(b)(6), (f), or (c), if materials outside the pleadings are presented to and not excluded by the court, the motion is converted into a summary judgment motion, as Rule 12(d) makes clear.

b.　Other Steps That Avoid Trial

In addition to the above-discussed motions, there are four other steps that may avoid trial in federal court: voluntary dismissal, involuntary dismissal, default, and settlement.

A claimant generally may obtain voluntary dismissal of his action or claim by his filing a *notice of dismissal* early in the case, by all parties' signing a *stipulation of dismissal*, or by *court order* upon such terms and conditions as the court deems proper. Unless otherwise specified in the notice, stipulation, or order, any such dismissal is without prejudice to a new action—except that a notice of dismissal operates with prejudice when filed by a claimant who has in any federal or state court previously dismissed the same claim by notice of dismissal (the "two-dismissal" rule).[106]

A defending party may move for involuntary dismissal of an action or claim against her on the ground of the claimant's *failure to prosecute* or the claimant's *failure to comply* with a court order or

---

106.　See Fed. R. Civ. P. 41(a).

rule.[107] Also, the court may so act on its own initiative.[108] Unless otherwise specified by the court, any dismissal on such grounds is with prejudice to a new action under the law of res judicata.[109] There is only the slim hope of the claimant's obtaining relief from judgment under Rule 60(b).[110]

If a party against whom a claim for relief is asserted has *failed to plead or otherwise defend*, the claimant may (1) get the court clerk (or the judge pursuant to implicit powers) to enter a default, and then (2) get the judge (or the court clerk when the act is strictly ministerial) to enter a default judgment on the action or claim.[111] Also, the court may enter a default judgment for the defendant's *failure to comply* with a court order or rule.[112] Under Rule 55(c), by showing an appropriate balance of the parties' equities, the defendant may cure an entry of default or a default judgment.[113]

The parties may agree to a settlement, and then usher the action or claim out of court by one of the preceding routes or by entry of a consent judgment.[114]

3. Masters and Magistrate Judges

Another possible step in a lawsuit involves referring the case to a "parajudge," of which there are two kinds in the federal system.

The use of masters has ancient roots, and Federal Rule 53 now authorizes, limits, and regulates that use. Today the only kind of master is what was formerly termed a "special master," i.e., someone specially appointed by the district judge to help handle a particular action. The judge supposedly can appoint a master only upon the parties' consent or in complicated cases where there is exceptional need, and the master must assist rather than displace the judge. The judge gives the master specific assignments, often involving ascertainment of facts. Ultimately, the master files a report with the court, and the master's factual findings as well as his legal conclusions are normally subject to de novo review by the district judge. The master's compensation, fixed by the court, usually falls on the parties themselves upon terms directed by the court.

107. See id. 41(b).

108. See Link v. Wabash R.R., 370 U.S. 626 (1962).

109. See infra § 5.2(B)(4).

110. See Brandon v. Chicago Bd. of Educ., 143 F.3d 293 (7th Cir. 1998) (denying relief).

111. See Fed. R. Civ. P. 55.

112. See, e.g., id. 37(b)(2)(A)(vi).

113. Compare Shepard Claims Serv., Inc. v. William Darrah & Assocs., 796 F.2d 190 (6th Cir. 1986) (reversing refusal to relieve default under Fed. R. Civ. P. 55(c)), with Rogers v. Hartford Life & Accident Ins. Co., 167 F.3d 933 (5th Cir. 1999) (affirming refusal to relieve default judgment under Fed. R. Civ. P. 60(b)).

114. See infra § 2.3.

Congress created the corps of magistrates in 1968 and has since expanded their jurisdiction several times.[115] Magistrate judges are salaried judicial officers appointed for a term, a number being appointed for each district by the district judges of that district. In addition to a good deal of criminal work, magistrate judges exercise the following civil jurisdiction under 28 U.S.C. § 636:

(1) a district judge may designate a magistrate judge to serve as a special master;

(2) a district judge may designate a magistrate judge to hear and determine any so-called nondispositive pretrial matter, examples being some pleading motions and also discovery disputes and pretrial conferences; the judge will consider any party's objections to the magistrate's determination, setting aside any portion shown to be clearly erroneous or to be contrary to law;

(3) a district judge may designate a magistrate judge to conduct hearings, make proposed findings of fact, and recommend disposition with respect to a so-called dispositive pretrial matter, examples being motions for injunctive relief and for summary judgment; the judge must make a de novo determination (upon the record or after additional evidence) on those portions of the magistrate's findings and recommendation that any party objects to;

(4) upon consent of all the parties, the court clerk may refer to a specially designated magistrate judge all proceedings in any case, including trial of a jury or nonjury case and entry of judgment; appeal from the magistrate judge's judgment goes to the appropriate court of appeals; and

(5) district judges may assign to magistrate judges "such additional duties as are not inconsistent with the Constitution and laws of the United States."

Although this procedural innovation has enjoyed heavy use and proved generally successful, the broad extent of the magistrate judges' jurisdiction raises some unsettled constitutional questions of due process and separation of powers.[116]

§ 2.3 Settlement

Most lawsuits do not make it all the way through the above-described pretrial practice. Indeed, most disputes do not even

---

115. See 28 U.S.C. §§ 631–639; Fed. R. Civ. P. 72–73.

116. See Tim A. Baker, The Expanding Role of Magistrate Judges in the Federal Courts, 39 Val. U. L. Rev. 661 (2005); Linda J. Silberman, Judicial Adjuncts Revisited: The Proliferation of Ad Hoc Procedure, 137 U. Pa. L. Rev. 2131 (1989). But see Orsini v. Wallace, 913 F.2d 474, 477–79 (8th Cir. 1990) (upholding Federal Magistrates Act).

become lawsuits in the first place. Injured persons abandon or settle the overwhelming majority of grievances at some point along the line.

A useful image is the so-called grievance pyramid:

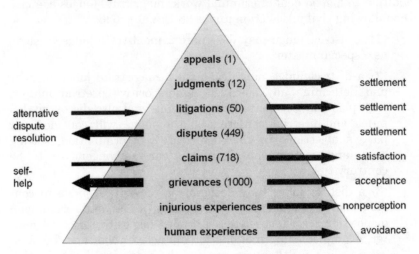

This image represents, as one progresses up the steps of the pyramid, how the whole realm of experiences narrows to disputes, a small subset that produces in turn those selected cases you study in law school. Infinite experiences produce countless disputes, which yield few cases. For example, only a small percentage of grievances ripen into claims, by the aggrieved's voicing the grievance to the injurer; most aggrieved persons accept their injury as part of life or just figure that there is no remedy available; tellingly, the theorists in this subject sometimes refer to acceptance as "lumping it." Similarly, most disputants never make it to a lawyer, much less to a courthouse. So this image of a pyramid suggests another image: in this book we have thus far focused on the tiny tip of a huge iceberg.

The slope of the sides of the pyramid is quite gentle. That is, a huge percentage of situations leaves the pyramid at each step upward. A survey of more than five thousand households indicated that during the previous three years just over a third of them had perceived one or more grievances of certain litigable types; 71.8% of those grievances produced a claim informally; 62.6% of those claims met an initial rebuff to produce a dispute; and 11.2% of those disputes resulted in filing a lawsuit.[117] Indeed, these percentages are exaggeratedly high, because the survey limited its inquiries to

117. See Richard E. Miller & Austin Sarat, Grievances, Claims, and Disputes: Assessing the Adversary Culture, 15 Law & Soc'y Rev. 525, 537 (1981); David M. Trubek, Austin Sarat, William L.F. Felstiner, Herbert M. Kritzer & Joel B. Grossman, The Costs of Ordinary Litigation, 31 UCLA L. Rev. 72, 86–87 (1983).

grievances involving $1000 or more. But even for such substantial grievances, litigation is by no means a knee-jerk or common reaction in the United States, as overall only about 5% of those grievances ultimately resulted in a court filing.

In the world of litigation at the top of the pyramid, the slope remains gentle. Of the relatively few filed cases, only a small percentage make it through the procedural system to a contested judgment. We can look at all the 271,753 federal civil cases terminated during fiscal year 2005. Of these, at least 67.7% were settled in one way or another; approximately 20.7% were adjudicated at the pretrial stage, as by a motion under Rule 12 or 56; about 1.3% were adjudicated at the trial stage; and the other 10.3% of the cases fell into other disposition method codes, predominantly remand or transfer to another court, whereby most result in an eventual settlement rather than a final adjudication.[118]

I can then combine these rough numbers with the visual presentation of the grievance pyramid. From the experiential infinitude, imagine that 1000 sizable grievances arise. This typical thousand will decrease to 718 claims, 449 disputes, 50 filed cases, 12 litigated judgments and 1 decided appeal. Thus, I advisedly described the pyramid's sides by saying that their slope is gentle.

From the viewpoint of the civil justice system, settlement is a critical need. Ours is a slow and expensive procedure. The system simply would not be able to adjudicate all cases filed.[119] We depend on the parties' finding alternatives to using the system. Accordingly, reformers are constantly seeking ways to increase the settlement rate, which is a loose term that measures the percentage of filed cases not resulting in contested judgments but instead leaving the sides of the grievance pyramid, whether by abandonment, concession, or privately negotiated settlement or by alternative dispute resolution such as arbitration, mediation, and conciliation.

Shifting from the viewpoint of the system to that of the disputants, settlement is also of critical importance. For them in the usual course, settlement *is* our system of justice. For their "trial" lawyers, negotiation of settlements—and pursuit of other alternatives to litigation—is what their profession primarily comprises.[120] Indeed, some theorists propose renaming litigation as "litigotiation."[121]

---

118. See Kevin M. Clermont, Litigation Realities Redux, 84 Notre Dame L. Rev. (forthcoming 2009) (explaining methodology).

119. See infra § 7.1(A)(3) (empirical studies of court congestion).

120. See infra § 7.1(A)(1) (law-and-economics formulation of settlement/litigation decision).

121. Marc Galanter, Worlds of Deals: Using Negotiation to Teach About Legal Process, 34 J. Legal Educ. 268, 268 (1984).

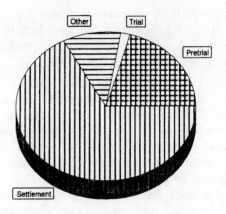

§ 2.4 Trial

A. Scenario

Eventually, a federal lawsuit that has survived the pretrial gantlet will come to trial under local calendar rules adopted pursuant to Federal Rule 40. In large part, trial practice is not laid down by the Federal Rules, but is instead confided to the discretion of the trial judge. Trial in federal court follows a relatively standard order by tradition. Trial practice is the special concern of such upperclass courses as Evidence and Trial Techniques.[122]

In federal and state court, there are jury trials as well as some nonjury or "bench" trials. The basic scenarios in these two kinds of trial are similar. Several aspects of the jury merit special attention, and so I shall discuss them first in the course of describing the six basic steps in the scenario. But at the end of the following treatment of each of the steps, I shall mention any unique features of nonjury trial.[123]

---

122. See generally Roger S. Haydock & John O. Sonsteng, Trial (3d ed. 2004).

123. See generally Wright & Kane, supra note 3, § 96.

A Local Court

Are Juries Really That Bad?

In Courts on Trial 123 (1949), Judge Jerome Frank pronounced: "To my mind a better instrument than the usual jury trial could scarcely be imagined for achieving uncertainty, capriciousness, lack of uniformity, disregard of the [law], and unpredictability of decisions." Such attitudes are widespread, and they are undoubtedly important in determining which cases the parties send to judge trial and which to the jury. But the basis in reality for these attitudes is problematic. Indeed, one of the more remarkable lessons that empirical study has to offer the law is that virtually no evidence exists to support the prevailing ingrained intuitions about juries as biased and incompetent, relative to judges.

In fact, existing evidence is to the contrary. Admittedly, not much effective empirical work exists on the quality of the jury's performance, and there is even less on juries' performance as compared to that of judges. Studies on broad questions regarding the jury are difficult to do, and correspondingly shaky to interpret. But the evidence, such as it is, consistently supports a view of the jury as generally unbiased and competent, or at least so compared to a judge. The fact that jury and judge show a high degree of agreement is better supported.

Research, for example, indicates that the strength of the trial evidence is the most important determinant of the verdict, not all those irrelevancies that everybody supposes prejudice the lay jurors. Evaluated over the run of cases, juries are good factfinders. More specifically, research does not support a view of the jury as overly generous on awards, frequently ignoring the law, or institutionally unable to handle complex cases. Related research suggests that a jury could even outperform a judge, because the judge is also human and because groups typically outperform individuals by virtue of superiority in such tasks as recall of facts and correction of errors.

The classic work in this area, Harry Kalven, Jr. & Hans Zeisel, The American Jury 63–64 (2d ed. 1971), addressed reliability (or the ability to treat like cases alike) rather than the validity (or correctness) of jury decisionmaking. Their questionnaires to presiding judges in some 4000 actual state and federal civil jury trials nationwide in the 1950s, asked them how they would decide those same cases, a decision supposedly formulated before the verdict but reported afterwards: this study yielded data showing a 78% agreement between judge and jury on liability. When judge and jury

> disagreed, they exhibited no distinct pattern other than the juries' very small tendency to favor plaintiffs relative to judges: the jury but not the judge found for the plaintiff in 12% of the cases, while the judge but not the jury found for the plaintiff in 10% of the cases.
>
> When compared to other human decisionmakers, this rate of agreement becomes more impressive than it first appears. The cases that reach trial are close cases. The 78% agreement rate is better than the rate of agreement on dichotomous decisions between scientists doing peer review, employment interviewers ranking applicants, and physicians diagnosing patients, and almost as good as the 79% or 80% rate of agreement between judges themselves making sentencing decisions on custody or no custody in an experimental setting. So even if theory plausibly suggests some judge/ jury differences—such as that juries, because of a need for compromise to produce a unanimous verdict, would tend to give plaintiffs more wins but less money—the significance of any such differences seems to fade in actuality. Apparently, judge trial and jury trial combine to deliver a decisionmaking system that is, at least in the technical sense, highly reliable. See generally Kevin M. Clermont & Theodore Eisenberg, Trial by Jury or Judge: Transcending Empiricism, 77 Cornell L. Rev. 1124 (1992).

1. Plaintiff's Case

At trial, the plaintiff ordinarily goes first. The plaintiff's attorney usually makes an *opening statement* to explain what the issues are and what he proposes to prove—an introductory road-map for his case. The defendant's attorney commonly follows with her own opening statement, although she sometimes can but seldom will choose to delay this until the beginning of the defendant's case.

The burden of proof dictates who must produce evidence and ultimately persuade the factfinder on which elements of the case. Burden of proof thus encompasses two concepts: burden of production and burden of persuasion. The **burden of production** might require either party at a given time during trial to produce evidence on an element or suffer the judge's adverse determination on that element. One party has the initial burden of production, but that burden may shift during the trial if that party produces very strong evidence. The **burden of persuasion** ultimately requires a certain party to persuade the factfinder of the truth of an element or suffer the factfinder's adverse determination on that element. The required degree of persuasion in a civil case is normally a "preponderance of the evidence," which requires only a showing of more-probable-than-not.[124]

Usually, but not always, both the initial burden of production and the burden of persuasion are on the party with the burden of allegation.[125] Here is an example: In a federal case for traditional negligence, the plaintiff need not plead his own due care. If the defendant carries the burden of allegation by pleading contributory

---

124. See infra § 7.1(A)(2), (B)(2) (treating standards of proof).

125. See supra § 2.1(A)(1)(b) (treating burden of allegation).

negligence under Rule 8(c)(1), the applicable state law will today put both of those burdens of proof on the defendant as well.

Formerly, however, some states allocated the initial burden of production and the burden of persuasion on this aspect of a negligence case to the plaintiff. If the defendant carried her burden of allegation, then at a jury trial the plaintiff would have to produce evidence of his own due care to avoid the judge's adverse judgment as a matter of law. Assuming that the plaintiff came forward with sufficient evidence to get to the jury and that the jury believed the evidence to be evenly balanced on this issue of due care, then the jury should find against the plaintiff, because he had the burden to persuade the jury by a preponderance of the evidence that he had exercised due care for his own safety.

It would also be erroneous to assume that the initial burden of production and the burden of persuasion necessarily are allocated to the same party. A familiar illustration to the contrary from the criminal law is the matter of the defendant's insanity: in some states the defendant must plead and initially present some evidence of insanity, but the prosecution must ultimately persuade the jury that the defendant was sane.

To prove the plaintiff's part of the case, which includes whatever elements that constitute the initial burden of production, the plaintiff's attorney calls his first witness, who is sworn and subjected to direct examination, cross-examination, and possibly redirect examination, recross-examination, and so on. This continues with other witnesses until the plaintiff's attorney rests his case.

The *rules of evidence* govern what the factfinder is hearing during this process. These rules include the basic requirement of relevance and the three principal exclusionary rules of incompetency, privilege, and hearsay. They also govern such matters as examination of witnesses and objections to evidence. In federal court, these rules are embodied in the Federal Rules of Evidence, a *statute* enacted in 1975.[126]

In a nonjury trial, the judge tends to apply the rules of evidence less strictly than the judge would in a jury trial. Indeed, if our system had no jury, our law of evidence would surely look quite different (and simpler).

2. Motions

In a jury trial, when the plaintiff rests, the defendant may move for **judgment as a matter of law** under Rule 50(a), former-

---

126. See generally Michael H. Graham, Handbook of Federal Evidence (6th ed. 2006); McCormick on Evidence (Kenneth S. Broun gen. ed., 6th ed. 2006).

ly called a directed verdict.[127] This can be granted if "a party has been fully heard on [a dispositive] issue during a jury trial and the court finds that a reasonable jury would not have a legally sufficient evidentiary basis to find for the party on that issue." Even if the defendant meets this standard, the judge can choose to deny the motion in order to let the trial proceed toward completion. The defendant waives no rights by so moving, and so can proceed with her evidence after denial of the motion. If she does proceed with her own evidence, however, she cannot raise on appeal the motion's denial, because as usual any midtrial decision on the state of the evidence is not reviewable.[128]

The standard of decision for judgment as a matter of law is extremely high: it allows granting only if, viewing the plaintiff's evidence in the light reasonably most favorable to the plaintiff, a reasonable jury could not find for the plaintiff. In hypothesizing the jury's function, the judge should draw all inferences in the plaintiff's favor to the limits of reasonableness, although this approach still requires discarding any of the plaintiff's evidence that is so incredible that a reasonable jury could not believe it. The granting judge then must think not merely that a verdict for the plaintiff would be wrong or even that it would be clearly wrong, but that it would be irrational.

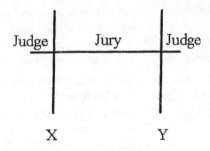

Imagine a single disputed issue of typical fact on which the plaintiff bears the initial burden of production and the burden of persuasion. Then imagine a grid representing the judge's disagreement with a potential verdict for the plaintiff, or equivalently the

---

127. See Galloway v. United States, 319 U.S. 372, 390, 394 (1943) (upholding constitutionality of directed verdict, because Seventh "Amendment did not bind the federal courts to the exact procedural incidents or details of jury trial according to the common law in 1791" but only to what was "essential"); cf. Walker v. N.M. & S.P.R. Co, 165 U.S. 593, 596 (1897) (upholding constitutionality of general verdict accompanied by interrogatories, because Seventh Amendment's "aim is not to preserve mere matters of form and procedure, but substance of right"); Fidelity & Deposit Co. of Md. v. United States, 187 U.S. 315 (1902) (upholding constitutionality of summary judgment).

128. See Wells v. State Farm Fire & Cas. Co., 993 F.2d 510 (5th Cir. 1993).

judge's view of probability of error in such a verdict, with disagreement or probability decreasing from one on the left to zero on the right.[129] It is important to realize that this diagram I have sketched represents the probability of jury error in finding that the disputed fact exists, not the judge's view of the evidential probability that the disputed fact exists. In other words, this diagram represents the judge's thought process in externally overseeing the jury that acts as factfinder, not the judge's thought process if the judge were finding facts. Alternatively stated, this diagram represents the burden of production, not the burden of persuasion.

The plaintiff in our imagined case starts at the left of the diagram. If he presents no evidence, the judge would ordinarily grant a motion for judgment as a matter of law against him. He is consequently bound to go forward with his evidence until he satisfies the judge that a reasonable jury would be warranted in finding for him. That is, he must get beyond line X to make a jury question of the imagined single issue of fact, doing so by presenting evidence. The plaintiff's getting to or beyond line X means that although the judge might still disagree with a verdict for the plaintiff, the judge thinks a reasonable jury could find that the plaintiff sustained his persuasion-burden, and therefore the judge will hold that the plaintiff sustained his production-burden. If the plaintiff does not get to line X, that means that the judge would so vehemently disagree with a verdict for the plaintiff as to consider the jury irrational, and so the judge can grant the motion for judgment as a matter of law. Line X, again, represents the judge's view on the limit of rationality in the jury's finding for the plaintiff, rather than the judge's view of the evidential probability that the disputed fact exists. For example, the judge might disbelieve all of the plaintiff's abundant evidence, but still acknowledge that a reasonable jury could believe it; the judge should then rule that the plaintiff has carried his production-burden, because a reasonable jury could conclude that the plaintiff sustained his persuasion-burden.

The diagram also helps to understand other concepts and special rules. A "permissive inference" (and res ipsa loquitur is one in the view of most courts) describes an inference that a jury is authorized but not required to draw from certain evidence in the nature of premise; in other words, the inference satisfies the plaintiff's production-burden by getting the case to line X, although not beyond line Y. A true "presumption" (such as the presumption against suicide as the cause of death) shifts the burden of produc-

---

129. See 9 John H. Wigmore, Evidence § 2487 (James H. Chadbourn rev. 1981); cf. John T. McNaughton, Burden of Production of Evidence: A Function of a Burden of Persuasion, 68 Harv. L. Rev. 1382 (1955) (offering alternative diagrams).

tion to the opponent after the introduction of the evidential premise; in other words, the presumption puts the case to the right of line Y and so requires the jury to find the presumed fact, unless the opponent introduces enough evidence to carry its production-burden and push the case at least back into the jury zone between Y and X.[130]

Among special rules, certain kinds of evidence will not satisfy an initial burden of production. To satisfy that burden, the burdened party cannot rely on the opponent's failure to testify,[131] on mere disbelief of the opponent's testimony,[132] or on demeanor evidence drawn from the opponent's testimony.[133] Similarly, naked statistical evidence will not satisfy the initial burden of production.[134] However, any of these kinds of evidence is perfectly proper to introduce as a supplement to positive and nonnumerical evidence that satisfies the initial burden of production.[135] The idea behind these special rules is that they are necessary to protect the notion of an initial burden of production, which serves to facilitate early termination of weak claims or defenses, to safeguard against irrational error, and to effectuate other process and outcome values. In the absence of these special rules, any burdened party could produce enough evidence to reach the jury, this evidence possibly being merely in the form of silence, disbelief, demeanor, or general statistics (such as that the defendant manufactured 60% of the supply of the injury-causing device of unknown provenance). Perhaps we harbor a special fear of the jury's mishandling of such evidence when undiluted by other admitted evidence and consequently rendering an unreasoned verdict for the proponent based either on prejudice without regard to the evidence or on undue deference to such bewildering evidence. To avoid such an outcome, and to ensure that the burden of production means something, the judge should require sufficient evidence of other kinds. Once the proponent clears that hurdle, the tribunal should give the feared evidence its probative effect.

In a nonjury trial, the defendant may move for **judgment on partial findings** under Rule 52(c). This can be granted if "a party has been fully heard on [a dispositive] issue during a nonjury trial and the court finds against the party on that issue." This standard

---

130. See Fed. R. Evid. 301.

131. See Stimpson v. Hunter, 125 N.E. 155 (Mass. 1919).

132. See Cruzan v. N.Y. Cent. & Hudson River R.R., 116 N.E. 879 (Mass. 1917).

133. See Dyer v. MacDougall, 201 F.2d 265 (2d Cir. 1952).

134. See Guenther v. Armstrong Rubber Co., 406 F.2d 1315, 1318 (3d Cir.

1969) (in a case where plaintiff had been injured by exploding tire, dictum that 75-to-80% chance it came from defendant manufacturer was not enough for case to go to jury).

135. See, e.g., Baxter v. Palmigiano, 425 U.S. 308, 316-20 (1976) (failure to testify).

of decision is easier to meet than the standard for a directed verdict, because here the defendant is merely asking the judge as factfinder for favorable findings without further proof, rather than asking the judge to intervene by withdrawing an extremely weak case from the jury as factfinder. That is, a judgment on partial findings means that the plaintiff has not quite persuaded the judge in a nonjury trial, while a judgment as a matter of law means that the plaintiff has not even produced enough evidence to reach the jury in a jury trial. It is much harder for the plaintiff to carry the persuasion-burden than the production-burden.

On a motion for judgment on partial findings, the defendant is asking the judge as factfinder in a nonjury trial whether she has to defend, i.e., whether the judge would find for her even without hearing her evidence because the plaintiff by his own evidence failed to carry his persuasion-burden. The judge applies no special tests or inferences, but instead objectively weighs the evidence so far introduced. To represent that weighing, we have to use a different diagram, one that represents the internal thought process of the factfinder. The grid now measures the judge's view of the evidential probability that the disputed fact exists, with probability increasing from 0% on the left to 100% on the right.

The plaintiff (π) in a nonjury trial of our imagined case again starts at the left. By presenting evidence, he must get beyond the midpoint to win. That is, he must show that it is more likely than not that the disputed fact exists. If after the plaintiff has given his best shot the judge thinks that he has not passed the 50%-line, then the judge can grant the motion for judgment on partial findings. Or the judge can choose to deny the motion in order to let the trial proceed toward completion. The defendant (Δ) waives no rights by so moving.

A necessary warning is that these diagrams serve merely as an impetus to thinking about these matters, rather than definitive statements thereon. For example, the diagram representing the burden of persuasion does not mean that a 50%-line exists in reality. The psychological truth is that equipoise is more of a fuzzy zone, or range of probabilities, than a line. Consequently, allocating the burden of persuasion affects many more cases than those in which the conflicting evidence results precisely in a dead heat.[136]

---

136. See United States ex rel. Bilyew v. Franzen, 686 F.2d 1238, 1248 (7th Cir.1982) (stressing importance of persuasion-burden and observing that "a judge or a jury can experience only a small, finite number of degrees of certainty * * *. Thus cases when the evidence * * * seem[s] in balance are not unique among some infinite variety of evidentiary balances, but instead are among a much smaller number of [ranges of] possibilities that may be perceived by the factfinder."); Kevin M. Clermont, Procedure's Magical Number Three: Psychological Bases for Standards of Decision, 72 Cornell L. Rev.

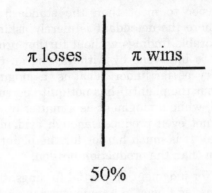

Finally, it is important to comprehend that the jury-trial and nonjury-trial motions entail very different standards of decision.[137] This follows inevitably from the judge's different roles on these two motions. On the former, the judge is patrolling the extreme outer limits of rationality on the factfinders' domain. On the latter, the judge is the factfinder and so can serve a more active function.

3. Defendant's Case

If the trial has not been short-circuited by the granting of such a motion, the defendant may present her part of the case, either trying to meet the plaintiff's contentions or trying to prove new matter on which the defendant has the initial burden of production.

In a nonjury trial, this step does not significantly differ from the scenario of a jury trial.

4. Motions

In a jury trial, when the defendant rests, the plaintiff may move for **judgment as a matter of law** under Rule 50(a). In terms of the above X–Y diagram, the moving plaintiff is contending that the case had progressed to the right of Y and stayed there even after the defendant's evidence, so that no reasonable jury could fail to find for the plaintiff. In other words, the plaintiff is contending that the production-burden had shifted to the defendant, even though the persuasion-burden stays on the plaintiff. If the plaintiff is correct as to this shift, then the defendant had to produce enough

1115, 1119 n.13, 1122 n.36, 1147–48 (1987).

137. See Hersch v. United States, 719 F.2d 873, 876–77 (6th Cir. 1983) (stressing difference between standards and observing: "A motion for a directed verdict under Rule 50(a), of course, in-

vokes a very different standard. The trial judge does not weigh the evidence. Rather, the judge views the evidence, and inferences therefrom in the light most favorable to the nonmoving party.").

evidence to get back into the jury zone from Y to X, where a reasonable jury could find either for the defendant or for the plaintiff in deciding whether the fact is more probable than not to exist.

If the plaintiff's motion is not granted, the plaintiff may then present *rebuttal evidence*, which should attempt to meet any new evidence presented by the defendant, as opposed to merely adding to the plaintiff's own evidence. Later, the defendant may present *rejoinder evidence*, and so on. These phases narrow down in focus, as each is normally limited to meeting new evidence from the prior phase. But whenever one side rests, the other side may move for judgment as a matter of law under Rule 50(a).

When both sides finally rest at the close of all the evidence, either side may move for judgment as a matter of law under Rule 50(a). As usual, this can be granted if, looking only at all the evidence that is favorable to the opponent of the motion but not incredible and also at the unquestionable evidence that is favorable to the movant, the judge believes that a reasonable jury could not find for the opponent.[138] If reasonable minds could differ on the evidence, the court must deny the motion.[139] By "unquestionable evidence," the standard of decision refers to evidence the jury would be unreasonable to disbelieve: looking at the totality of circumstances—including the nature of the evidence, interest of the witness, and possibility of additional impeachment and contradiction that was not offered—the inquiry is what evidence is the jury required to believe.[140]

Given a sufficiently strong body of evidence, even the party bearing the persuasion-burden can properly obtain judgment as a matter of law.[141] The same standard of decision applies to both parties' motions. Of course, judgment for the party with the persuasion-burden is less frequent than judgment against that party. But this follows from the fact that the proponent is unlikely to assemble enough unquestionable evidence to carry his burden overwhelmingly and thus to secure judgment as a matter of law, while the other

---

138. See, e.g., Pa. R.R. v. Chamberlain, 288 U.S. 333 (1933) (directed verdict against burdened plaintiff); Daniel J. Hartwig Assocs., Inc. v. Kanner, 913 F.2d 1213 (7th Cir. 1990) (directed verdict against burdened defendant).

139. See, e.g., Wilkerson v. McCarthy, 336 U.S. 53 (1949).

140. See Reeves v. Sanderson Plumbing Prods., Inc., 530 U.S. 133, 151 (2000) ("Thus, although the court should review the record as a whole, it must disregard all evidence favorable to the moving party that the jury is not required to believe. See Wright & Miller 299. That is, the court should give credence to the evidence favoring the nonmovant as well as that 'evidence supporting the moving party that is uncontradicted and unimpeached, at least to the extent that that evidence comes from disinterested witnesses.' Id., at 300."); Serv. Auto Supply Co. of P.R. v. Harte & Co., 533 F.2d 23 (1st Cir. 1976).

141. See, e.g., Chesapeake & O. Ry. v. Martin, 283 U.S. 209 (1931).

party need not have any unquestionable evidence in order to show that the proponent has failed to carry his burden and thus should suffer judgment as a matter of law. Moreover, it is harder for the proponent to *establish* something by excluding all other inferences than it is for the other party to show that the proponent *failed to establish* something. So, no difference in standard of decision is necessary to explain this difference in frequency of judgment as a matter of law.

After all, this one standard of decision makes sense, because judgment as a matter of law is no more than a safeguard against irrational behavior by the jury: the judge should envisage the thought process of properly functioning jurors when first filtering the evidence in the rational manner most favorable to the opponent of the motion and next viewing the resultant probabilities in like manner, with the judge doing all this in order to determine whether the jury could not rationally decide for the opponent.

In a nonjury trial, there can be motions for **judgment on partial findings** during this stage. This kind of motion entails the less demanding standard of decision appropriate to a judge acting as the factfinder.

5. Submission of Case

If the trial has still not been short-circuited, counsel usually make *closing arguments* that the evidence is on their side, with the plaintiff's attorney ordinarily speaking first and last. In a jury trial, after (and/or before) closing arguments, the judge gives oral *instructions* to the jury—the judge must determine and then instruct on the law,[142] may summarize the evidence on the contested factual issues, and may but most often does not comment on the evidence by expressing with restraint personal views on its weight and credibility.[143] Rule 51 allows counsel to submit beforehand written

---

142. See Markman v. Westview Instruments, Inc., 517 U.S. 370 (1996) (drawing law/fact line by historical and functional test); Feltner v. Columbia Pictures Television, Inc., 523 U.S. 340 (1998) (stressing history to give statutory damages under the Copyright Act to the jury); City of Monterey v. Del Monte Dunes at Monterey, Ltd., 526 U.S. 687 (1999) (stressing function to give takings issue to the jury); cf. Paul F. Kirgis, The Right to a Jury Decision on Questions of Fact Under the Seventh Amendment, 64 Ohio St. L.J. 1125, 1125 (2003) (looking to history to argue that under the Seventh Amendment "questions requiring inductive inferences about the transac-

tions or occurrences in dispute are 'fact' questions, which must be decided by the jury in appropriate cases"); Colleen P. Murphy, Integrating the Constitutional Authority of Civil and Criminal Juries, 61 Geo. Wash. L. Rev. 723, 754 (1993) (arguing that by text, precedent, and policy, Seventh Amendment's role here is to preserve the "essence" or "substance" of the jury).

143. Compare Virginian Ry. v. Armentrout, 166 F.2d 400, 407 (4th Cir. 1948) (reversal for "an argumentative presentation of the case which must necessarily have prejudiced defendant's cause"), with Trezza v. Dame, 370 F.2d 1006, 1009 (5th Cir. 1967) (comments

requests for specific instructions on the law; it also provides a procedure for specifically objecting, before the jury retires, to the judge's instructions.[144]

Then the jury retires to deliberate in isolation on a *verdict*, which will require deciding the contestable factual issues. The judge as a matter of discretion will have chosen the kind of verdict, which might be: (1) a general verdict, through which the jury simply finds in writing for the plaintiff or the defendant, in theory doing so by having applied the judge's instructions on the law to its own resolutions of the contestable factual issues; (2) a special verdict, "in the form of a special written finding on each issue of fact," under Rule 49(a); or (3) a general verdict accompanied by answers to "written questions on one or more issues of fact that the jury must decide," under Rule 49(b). The general verdict is the most common kind; the other two guide and constrain the jury and will better indicate what the jury decided, but might prevent the jury from doing "justice" by fiddling with the law and are so complicated to use that they require the detailed curative provisions of Rule 49.

If the jurors cannot agree on a verdict, the judge will eventually discharge the jury and later retry the case with a new jury. If the jury reaches a verdict, the verdict will be returned in open court with the jury present and then be recorded, and the jury will be discharged.

In a nonjury trial, in lieu of instructions and verdict, Rule 52(a)(1) requires that "the court must find the facts specially and state its conclusions of law separately." That is, unlike a jury, the judge is not allowed to speak as an oracle.[145]

6. Motions

After decision, judgment is normally entered in conformity therewith.[146] But other motions are still possible to change the outcome of the trial. In a jury trial, these motions are those for

leaving no doubt of judge's conclusion that defendant was negligent "came dangerously close to usurping the function of the jury" and "would have been better left unsaid," but were not prejudicial in light of the strong evidence and the instruction that jurors were free to disagree with judge). See generally Jack B. Weinstein, The Power and Duty of Federal Judges to Marshall and Comment on the Evidence in Jury Trials and Some Suggestions on Charging Juries, 118 F.R.D. 161 (1988).

144. See generally Wright & Kane, supra note 3, § 94.

145. See Dearborn Nat'l Cas. Co. v. Consumers Petroleum Co., 164 F.2d 332 (7th Cir. 1947) (reversing for further findings); Roberts v. Ross, 344 F.2d 747 (3d Cir. 1965) (reversing for inadequacy of findings); cf. Lansford-Coaldale Joint Water Auth. v. Tonolli Corp., 4 F.3d 1209, 1215 n.5 (3d Cir. 1993) (qualifying demandingness of Fed. R. Civ. P. 52(a)(1)).

146. See infra § 2.5.

judgment as a matter of law and for a new trial.[147]

First, as to judgment as a matter of law, Rule 50(b) authorizes a motion to have the adverse verdict and any judgment thereon set aside and to have judgment entered in the movant's favor, provided that the movant has filed this motion no later than ten days after entry of judgment and provided that the movant earlier had unsuccessfully moved for judgment as a matter of law under Rule 50(a).[148] This **renewed motion for judgment as a matter of law**, formerly called a motion for judgment notwithstanding the verdict and sometimes called a motion for judgment n.o.v. from its Latin name (*non obstante veredicto*), can be granted if the standard of decision for a directed verdict is met.[149] However, on a motion for judgment n.o.v., a judge who believes the n.o.v. standard is met can grant a new trial instead of a final judgment if that would better serve the ends of justice, as where the defect in the opponent's case was excusable and is curable.[150] In any event, if reasonable minds could differ, the court must deny the motion for judgment n.o.v.[151]

As just indicated, the standard of decision for granting the renewed motion for judgment as a matter of law is the same as for granting the motion for judgment as a matter of law, which was represented above in the X–Y diagram. Even though courts manage in their phrasing of standards to provide infinite variation between and within these various procedural devices, this standard for judgment as a matter of law is also the same as the one for granting the motion for summary judgment.[152] Still, despite the fact that these standards for the judge to *grant* the motion are all the same, the judge can choose to *deny* (or to decline to grant) the earlier motions. Therefore, the less-intrusive later motions, which also come on a fuller record, might be easier to sustain in actual practice.

Yet, why would a judge grant a renewed motion for judgment as a matter of law when the judge has, before submitting the case to the jury, denied the same party's motion for judgment as a matter of law? The judge has likely seen no more evidence in the

---

147. See generally Wright & Kane, supra note 3, § 95.

148. See Connie Alt, Note, Preservation of Judgment n.o.v. Motion Under Rule 50(b): Renewal of Directed Verdict Motion, 70 Iowa L. Rev. 269 (1984).

149. See, e.g., O'Connor v. Pa. R.R., 308 F.2d 911 (2d Cir. 1962) (affirming judgment n.o.v. against burdened party); Simblest v. Maynard, 427 F.2d 1 (2d Cir. 1970) (affirming judgment n.o.v. for burdened party).

150. See also Fed. R. Civ. P. 50(d) (allowing unsuccessful opponent of n.o.v. motion ten more days to move for a new trial in lieu of a final judgment).

151. See, e.g., Lavender v. Kurn, 327 U.S. 645 (1946); Norton v. Snapper Power Equip., 806 F.2d 1545 (11th Cir. 1987). But cf. Dixon v. Wal–Mart Stores, Inc., 330 F.3d 311 (5th Cir. 2003) (arguably overactive granting by appellate court).

152. See supra text accompanying note 101.

meantime, and the jury has since decided against the moving party. Will not the jury's verdict fortify the judge in his view supposedly expressed in denying the earlier motion? Well, consider a situation where the defendant moves for judgment as a matter of law in her favor at the close of all the evidence, and the judge inclines to the belief that the motion should be granted but he is not certain and wants time to reflect. Will he perhaps deny the motion, or refrain from granting it, and pass the case to the jury believing that the jury will probably find for the defendant, thus rendering it unnecessary to deal further with the difficulty posed by the motion for judgment as a matter of law? If the jury does find for the defendant, the judge has avoided the appearance of intruding into the sphere of the jury and obviated the appellate court's close scrutiny of judgment as a matter of law. But if the jury returns a verdict for the plaintiff, the judge may grant the defendant's renewed motion for judgment as a matter of law in accordance with his original inclination. Moreover, by having let the jury trial run its course, the judge has got a jury verdict recorded, thus possibly allowing reinstatement of the verdict and so avoiding the need for retrial in the event of a successful appeal of his decision to grant the motion.

Second, as to new trial, Rule 59(a) authorizes a motion to have the adverse verdict and any judgment thereon set aside and to hold a new trial, provided that the movant has filed this motion no later than ten days after entry of judgment. This **motion for a new trial** should be granted if the verdict (or its amount) is *against the weight of the evidence*, i.e., if, looking at all the evidence, the judge is clearly convinced that the jury was in error.[153] This standard is easier to meet than the standard for judgment as a matter of law, but not so easy as to authorize the judge freely to substitute his personal opinion for the jury's. That is, on a new-trial motion the federal judge should not ask himself whether the jury was wrong, nor whether it was irrational. Instead, looking at all the evidence, he should employ middle-level scrutiny and ask whether he is strongly convinced that the jury was in error. If so, he can send the case to a new trial as a double check, although normally he will not do so more than once. And, of course, he can order a new trial even when he has properly denied motions for judgment as a matter of law. Incidentally, the judge can grant a "partial new trial" if the verdict's infected issues are so distinct and separable from the rest of the case that retrial of them alone is possible without injustice.[154] And where a verdict goes against the weight of the evidence by awarding excessive damages to the plaintiff, the judge can grant a new trial on the terms that the plaintiff can avoid it by agreeing to

153. See Aetna Cas. & Sur. Co. v. Yeatts, 122 F.2d 350 (4th Cir. 1941).

154. See Gasoline Prods. Co. v. Champlin Ref. Co., 283 U.S. 494 (1931).

a "remittitur" of the damages,[155] which apparently should be in the amount by which the verdict exceeded the highest amount that would have survived a new-trial motion.[156]

Additionally, there are other entirely distinct grounds for a new trial, and these make new trial a common remedy. In particular, there can be a new trial on such grounds as non-harmless *error* by the judge or *misconduct* by the participants in the course of the trial, subject to the requirement that ordinarily there must have been an objection at the time of the error or misconduct.[157] There can also be a new trial on the ground of *newly discovered evidence*.[158] Indeed, Rule 59(a)(1)(A) authorizes a new trial upon motion wherever required to prevent injustice; and within the ten days a new trial can even be ordered on the court's own initiative, as Rule 59(d) specifies.

These additional grounds for a new trial are readily comprehensible. But it requires special attention to distinguish the motion for a new trial on the weight of the evidence ground from the renewed motion for judgment as a matter of law. The effects are obviously different, as the former results only in starting the trial over and not in a final judgment for the movant. The standard of decision for the motion for a new trial on the weight of the evidence ground could be represented by the X–Y diagram, if X and Y both shifted somewhat toward the center to become X′ and Y′. This shift indicates that the judge is more willing to intercede on the motion for a new trial, by granting one when the verdict for the opponent merely is clearly wrong as opposed to outright irrational. Thus, if the judge's view of the probability of jury error lies somewhere from X up to X′, but the jury has nevertheless found for the

155. See Suja A. Thomas, Re-examining the Constitutionality of Remittitur Under the Seventh Amendment, 64 Ohio St. L.J. 731 (2003); cf. Dimick v. Schiedt, 293 U.S. 474 (1935) (holding "additur" unconstitutional in federal court).

156. See Earl v. Bouchard Transp. Co., 917 F.2d 1320, 1330 (2d Cir. 1990) (holding that reduction of the verdict by remittitur should be "only to the maximum amount that would be upheld by the district court as not excessive"). But see Raske v. Raske, 92 F. Supp. 348, 352 (D. Minn. 1950) (remitting to the judge's view on amount of damages); Meissner v. Papas, 35 F. Supp. 676 (E.D. Wis. 1940), aff'd, 124 F.2d 720 (7th Cir. 1941) (remitting to the minimum amount that a jury could properly award).

157. See, e.g., Rojas v. Richardson, 703 F.2d 186 (invoking plain error doctrine to reverse for extremely improper closing argument), vacated, 713 F.2d 116 (5th Cir. 1983) (vacating reversal, upon supplemental record); Fed. R. Civ. P. 61 (treating harmless error).

158. See, e.g., Marshall's U.S. Auto Supply v. Cashman, 111 F.2d 140, 142 (10th Cir. 1940) ("A motion for new trial on the ground of newly discovered evidence must show that the evidence was discovered since the trial [and pertains to facts existing at the time of trial]; must show facts from which the court may infer reasonable diligence on the part of the movant; must show that the evidence is not merely cumulative or impeaching; must show that it is material; and must show that it is of such character that on a new trial such evidence will probably produce a different result.").

plaintiff, then the judge should correct the jury's clear error by granting the defendant's motion for a new trial, but the judge should deny the defendant's renewed motion for judgment as a matter of law.

These two "ten-day motions" for judgment as a matter of law and for a new trial may be and usually are made together, because the verdict-losing party will waive rights by failing to make any motions available. The four possible decisions on the two motions are treated in Rule 50(c) and (e):[159]

(1) Deny n.o.v.; Deny New Trial. This decision upholds judgment in accordance with the verdict.[160]

(2) Deny n.o.v.; Grant New Trial. This decision leads directly to a retrial.[161]

(3) Grant n.o.v.; Grant New Trial. This decision means that a judgment contrary to the verdict will be entered. The new-trial motion was decided conditionally. If the judgment is reversed on appeal, there will ordinarily be a new trial in accordance with the trial court's grant of a new trial, which was conditional on such reversal. In a case where the new-trial motion was on the ground of the weight of the evidence, the trial judge in so ruling was saying: "If I turn out to be wrong in granting judgment n.o.v., I would still believe that a new trial is proper because the verdict was at least against the weight of the evidence."[162]

(4) Grant n.o.v.; Deny New Trial. This decision means that a judgment contrary to the verdict will be entered. If that judgment is reversed on appeal, however, a judgment in accordance with the verdict will ordinarily be entered, given the trial court's conditional denial of a new trial. In a case where the new-trial motion was on the ground of the weight of the evidence, the trial judge would ordinarily grant a conditional new trial,[163] unless he was saying: "If I turn out to be wrong in granting judgment n.o.v. in the particular circumstances of this

---

159. See Montgomery Ward & Co. v. Duncan, 311 U.S. 243 (1940).

160. See, e.g., Dadurian v. Underwriters at Lloyd's, London, 787 F.2d 756 (1st Cir. 1986) (affirming denial of n.o.v., but questionably reversing denial of new trial on ground of weight of evidence); cf. Sears v. Pauly, 261 F.2d 304, 309 (1st Cir. 1958) ("It is only in a very unusual case that an appellate court would be justified in concluding that an abuse of discretion was committed by

the trial judge in refusing to grant a new trial on this ground.").

161. See, e.g., Pettingill v. Fuller, 107 F.2d 933 (2d Cir. 1939) (after retrial, reversing original grant of new trial on ground of misconduct of counsel).

162. See, e.g., Lind v. Schenley Indus. Inc., 278 F.2d 79 (3d Cir. 1960) (reversing both n.o.v. and grant of new trial).

163. See Marsh v. Ill. Cent. R.R., 175 F.2d 498 (5th Cir. 1949) (reversing both n.o.v. and denial of new trial).

case, then it must mean that I have been wrong about the legal contours of the case [for example, some supposed element of the claim turned out not to be an element]. Given the revised contours, I would believe that a new trial is improper [for example, because weak evidence on a point that turns out not to be a required element is no reason to overturn the verdict]."[164]

On that appellate review,[165] the court of appeals nondeferentially reviews a judgment n.o.v. as a decision of law; a new-trial grant on the weight of the evidence ground, as well as any new-trial decision on other grounds, is reviewed under the abuse of discretion standard; and a new-trial denial on the weight of the evidence ground, review that occurs after the trial judge and the sacrosanct jury concurred on the facts, is reviewed with the greatest deference under the clear abuse of discretion standard.[166]

In a nonjury trial, the roughly analogous ten-day motions are a motion to amend findings under Rule 52(b) and a motion for a new trial under Rule 59(a)(1)(B). But differences are as salient as similarities. For example, a new trial in a nonjury trial does not imply starting the trial over, but instead Rule 59(a)(2) provides:

> After a nonjury trial, the court may, on motion for a new trial, open the judgment if one has been entered, take additional testimony, amend findings of fact and conclusions of law or make new ones, and direct the entry of a new judgment.

B. Jury and Judge

164. See, e.g., Zimmerman v. Mathews Trucking Corp., 105 F. Supp. 57 (W.D. Ark. 1952), rev'd, 203 F.2d 864, modified, 205 F.2d 837 (8th Cir. 1953); Boulter v. Commercial Standard Ins. Co., 78 F. Supp. 895 (N.D. Cal. 1948), rev'd, 175 F.2d 763 (9th Cir. 1949).

165. See infra § 2.6.

166. See Fairmount Glass Works v. Cub Fork Coal Co., 287 U.S. 474, 483–84 (1933) (errors of law); Gasperini v. Ctr. for Humanities, Inc., 518 U.S. 415 (1996) (new-trial decisions); Ahern v. Scholz, 85 F.3d 774 (1st Cir. 1996) (denial of new trial); Kevin M. Clermont, Procedure's Magical Number Three: Psychological Bases for Standards of Decision, 72 Cornell L. Rev. 1115, 1133–34, 1155 (1987) ("I submit that a definite improvement would flow from recognizing only three review standards for decisions on new-trial motions. At one extreme, all issues currently classified as matters of law should still undergo review as such, with the appellate court asking whether it simply disagrees with the trial judge's decision and thus reversing only if it thinks error to be more likely than not. At the other extreme, on factual reconsideration the appellate court should reverse a denial of a motion on the ground that the verdict was against the weight of the evidence or that the verdict was excessive or inadequate only if it is almost certain that the trial judge erred. All other reviewable new-trial issues should receive customary middle-level scrutiny, by which the appellate court looks for clear or highly probable error."); infra § 7.1(A)(2) (law-and-psychology explanation); cf. Donovan v. Penn Shipping Co., 429 U.S. 648, 650 (1977) ("we now reaffirm the long-standing rule that a plaintiff in federal court, whether prosecuting a state or federal cause of action, may not appeal from a remittitur order he has accepted").

Many of the complications of trial practice result from the presence of a jury as the factfinder, and from its interaction with the judge.

1. Method of Trial by Jury

Traditionally a federal civil jury numbered *twelve* members—but now a federal district court may seat as few as six, who still deliver the requisite group deliberation and community representation that are the essential substance of the jury right, according to *Colgrove v. Battin*[167] and Federal Rule 48. Traditionally a federal civil jury's verdict had to be *unanimous*, but the parties could stipulate otherwise under Rule 48—the Rule still follows this approach to unanimity for federal civil trials, but significantly the Supreme Court has held in a series of cases that there is no constitutional impediment to decision by a substantial majority of the jury in state criminal trials.[168] To sum up, Rule 48 now provides:

> A jury must initially have at least 6 and no more than 12 members, and each juror must participate in the verdict unless excused under Rule 47(c). Unless the parties stipulate otherwise, the verdict must be unanimous and be returned by a jury of at least 6 members.

Today federal courts commonly impanel an eight-person civil jury, to insure against attrition below six during the trial by operation of Rule 47(c) ("During trial or deliberation, the court may excuse a juror for good cause."). Incidentally, state courts can do what they want regarding civil juries, because neither the Seventh Amendment nor Rule 48 applies to them.

Generally speaking as to jury practice, a panel of jurors is summoned from the body of citizens.[169] From this panel, the jurors for a particular civil trial are tentatively drawn by lot. These jurors are then subjected to a "voir dire" examination under Rule 47(a). Federal judges usually follow the more desirable practice of conducting this examination themselves, rather than leaving it to the attorneys. On the basis of the examination or other information, a party may challenge any individual juror or a panel of jurors "for

---

167. 413 U.S. 149 (1973). For the story of this case, see Jeffrey J. Rachlinski, The Story of Colgrove: Social Science on Trial, in Civil Procedure Stories 389 (Kevin M. Clermont ed., 2d ed. 2008). See also Ballew v. Georgia, 435 U.S. 223 (1978) (holding unconstitutional a five-person jury in a state criminal trial).

168. Apodaca v. Oregon, 406 U.S. 404 (1972) (approving 10–2 verdict); Johnson v. Louisiana, 406 U.S. 356 (1972) (approving 9–3 verdict). But cf. Burch v. Louisiana, 441 U.S. 130 (1979) (holding unconstitutional a 5–1 verdict).

169. See 28 U.S.C. §§ 1861–1869.

cause," with the court determining whether bias or other grounds for disqualification exist.[170] Also, an individual juror may be excluded by the exercise of one of either party's typically three "peremptory challenges" under 28 U.S.C. § 1870; the manner of exercising these largely arbitrary challenges is a matter of local rule or practice, although parties cannot use them on invidious bases such as race or gender.[171] By continuing this whole process, an impartial and qualified trial jury is eventually selected and then sworn.

A critical feature of trial practice is the interaction of judge and jury.[172] Following the common-law tradition, federal practice leans toward maximizing judicial control of the jury, through such powers as the trial judge's:

(1) prescribing much of trial practice as a matter of discretion;

(2) administering exclusionary and other rules of evidence;

(3) deciding issues of law;

(4) deciding judgment as a matter of law and new-trial motions;

(5) usually giving instructions after rather than before closing arguments;

(6) summarizing and commenting on the evidence; and

(7) sometimes using a special verdict or a general verdict with interrogatories.

However, federal judges often choose not to use all of these powers of control. Moreover, some states aggrandize the role of the jury vis-à-vis the judge and allow it freer rein, as by the common state prohibition of judicial comment on the evidence.

Meanwhile, a lot could be done to help the jurors function, especially in complex cases.[173] Federal judges have broad powers to act in any of the following ways:

(1) using the above-listed powers of control, existing but often dormant, in ways that aid the jury's functioning;

(2) letting the jurors ask written questions of the trial judge and, through the judge, of witnesses and counsel;

---

170. See Thompson v. Altheimer & Gray, 248 F.3d 621 (7th Cir. 2001).

171. See Edmonson v. Leesville Concrete Co., 500 U.S. 614 (1991) (race); J.E.B. v. Alabama ex rel. T.B., 511 U.S. 127 (1994) (gender).

172. See Pamela J. Stephens, Controlling the Civil Jury: Towards a Functional Model of Justification, 76 Ky. L.J. 81 (1988); Ann Woolhandler & Michael

G. Collins, The Article III Jury, 87 Va. L. Rev. 587 (2001).

173. See Saul M. Kassin & Lawrence S. Wrightsman, The American Jury on Trial: Psychological Perspectives (1988); Carrie P. Withey, Note, Court–Sanctioned Means of Improving Jury Competence in Complex Civil Litigation, 24 Ariz. L. Rev. 715 (1982).

(3) permitting the jurors to discuss the evidence among themselves during the trial;

(4) giving specific instructions at the outset and periodically throughout the trial;

(5) allowing the jurors to take notes during the trial;

(6) giving the retiring jury a copy or recording of the charge, perhaps along with a glossary, transcript, and written evidence; and

(7) using available psychological research to make instructions more understandable.

However, federal judges are not very active in using their considerable discretion so to act. And state judges are reluctant to depart from traditional ways.

2. Right to Trial by Jury

An important question is when trial by jury is allowed.[174] In federal court, there will be trial by jury on those issues that are contestable and factual[175] and:

(1) that are triable of right by a jury under the Seventh Amendment to the Federal Constitution, which provides in part that in "suits at common law, where the value in controversy shall exceed twenty dollars, the right of trial by jury shall be preserved" and hence which prohibits legislative and judicial infringement of a jury right within its scope;[176]

(2) that are triable of right by a jury under some federal statute, such as the Jones Act covering certain actions by seamen;[177] or

(3) on which the court, in its discretion with the express or implicit consent of both parties, orders a trial by jury under Federal Rule 39(c)(2).

Even if an issue does fall within one of the above-described three categories, it may still be tried by the judge as the result of either of two rules:

(1) There is a waiver of a constitutional or statutory right to trial by jury if *neither* party makes a timely written demand for

---

174. See generally Wright & Kane, supra note 3, § 92.

175. See supra note 142.

176. See Granfinanciera, S.A. v. Nordberg, 492 U.S. 33 (1989) (bankruptcy trustee's separate action to recover fraudulent monetary transfer; jury required by Seventh Amendment, notwithstanding federal statute); Pernell v. Southall Realty, 416 U.S. 363 (1974) (by implication) (repossession of real property; jury required by Seventh Amendment).

177.　46 U.S.C. § 30104.

trial by jury on the issue as provided in Rule 38(b)-(d), although the court in its discretion upon motion may relieve such waiver as provided in Rule 39(b) but sparingly does so.[178]

(2) The parties may consent to withdraw a demand for jury trial, as Rules 38(d) and 39(a)(1) provide.

So there are constitutional and statutory rights in the federal structure, as well as the equivalent possibility of jury trial by consent, but these rights can be waived or withdrawn. Note that allowance of trial by jury is determined on an issue-by-issue basis.

If an issue does not fall within one of the above-described three categories, it will be tried by the judge. That is, federal courts respect a complementary, albeit nonconstitutional, court-created right to trial by judge, which exists in the absence of contrary constitutional or statutory command.[179] However, the court, in its discretion upon motion or on its own initiative, may try any such issue with the assistance of an advisory jury under Rule 39(c)(1). This ancient device is not the same as a jury of right; the judge ultimately must decide the issue as in a nonjury trial under Rule 52(a)(1), and the judge may accept or reject the advisory jury's finding.[180]

The biggest uncertainty within this relatively clear federal structure arises in determining the scope of the Seventh Amendment's jury right. The starting point is the so-called historical test built on the idea that the Seventh Amendment preserves the common-law jury right prevailing in England in 1791, when the Seventh Amendment was adopted. First, the Seventh Amendment rather loosely preserves the wide array of procedural incidents of jury trial, such as the number of jurors, but only to the extent necessary to preserve the essential and not the form of common-law trial by jury: the modern federal jury need only operate substantially the same as the common-law jury.[181] Second, the Seventh Amendment goes on to provide that "no fact tried by a jury, shall be otherwise re-examined in any Court of the United States, than according to the rules of the common law": under this Re-examination Clause, federal courts today must find a historical antecedent to authorize any review, at the trial or appellate level, of a jury's factfinding, such as on a new-trial motion.[182] Third, the Seventh

---

178. See, e.g., Segal v. Am. Cas. Co. of Reading, Pa., 250 F. Supp. 936 (D. Md. 1966) (disallowing jury trial).

179. See Note, The Right to a Nonjury Trial, 74 Harv. L. Rev. 1176 (1961).

180. See supra § 1.2(A)(2)(c); Note, Practice and Potential of the Advisory Jury, 100 Harv. L. Rev. 1363 (1987).

181. See supra note 127 & text accompanying note 167.

182. See supra note 155; Debra Lyn Bassett, "I Lost at Trial—in the Court of Appeals!": The Expanding Power of the Federal Appellate Courts to Reexamine Facts, 38 Hous. L. Rev. 1129 (2001) (studying special historical constraints

Amendment's protection rather demandingly preserves the waivable right to go to a jury on all contestable factual issues that would have been triable to a common-law jury, as opposed to a chancellor sitting in equity: this law/equity line specifying the kinds of issues that must go to a jury today has indeed been the subject of expansive constitutional interpretation, as will now be explained.

The pure historical test generates many difficulties. Its application to the law/equity problem is especially difficult.[183] How are we to determine which contestable factual issues would have gone to a common-law jury in 1791? Few people now master legal history. Moreover, the law/equity line was not clearly delineated in 1791 and, indeed, was as always in the process of shifting over time. Furthermore, the procedural setting was then so different: on the one hand, many factors other than jury trial affected the old system's allocation of jurisdiction between law and equity and also the parties' choice of courts between law and equity, so it is strange now to make the single consequence of the jury right turn on what was then a many-factored decision; on the other hand, we have a procedural system today with law and equity merged and with very different procedures, so it is artificial now to recreate the decision between law and equity. It is very uncertain how the changed circumstances should be taken into account in recreating history— at the least, the cases now indicate that any historical judicial discretion in choosing to exercise law or equity jurisdiction should be exercised in light of modern realities. In short, the historical test perhaps should not and almost certainly cannot be applied in a pure form any longer, a situation that revives the tension between the popular reverence for the jury and the elitist distaste for the jury. So today, courts apply a modified historical test to the law/equity problem.

Today's initial inquiry is the historical one of whether a contestable factual issue arises in a case such that the issue would have been triable of right to a common-law jury, in which event there is a constitutional jury right thereon. Thus, there is a jury right if *P* sues *D* in a negligence action for damages, but not if *P* sues *D* in a suit for an injunction. History produces some special rules too, such as there being no jury right in actions against a sovereign.[184] Most

that should derive from Seventh Amendment's Re-examination Clause).

183. Compare Charles W. Wolfram, The Constitutional History of the Seventh Amendment, 57 Minn. L. Rev. 639 (1973) (broad view of Seventh Amendment's reach), with Martin H. Redish, Seventh Amendment Right to Jury Trial: A Study in the Irrationality of Ra-

tional Decision Making, 70 Nw. U. L. Rev. 486 (1975) (narrow view).

184. See Lehman v. Nakshian, 453 U.S. 156, 162 n.9 (1981) (treating Age Discrimination in Employment Act); Arango v. Guzman Travel Advisors, 761 F.2d 1527, 1531–35 (11th Cir. 1985) (treating Foreign Sovereign Immunities Act).

cases are easily handled under this historical approach, especially where the case presents a single claim for relief.

But in certain circumstances, the historical test undergoes modification. There are some tough cases in the gray area between the common-law and equity poles, especially where the historical approach is particularly difficult to apply, or leads to some sophisticated exception to the jury right, or is particularly ambivalent in outcome. Under the Supreme Court's decisions, the Seventh Amendment's protection currently tends to reach these gray cases, making it unclear just how much of the historical approach remains in the gray zone. Consider these five major problems:

(1) New Claims. Consider first a modern claim that did not exist in the old days. A federal court looks for a historical analogue in light of the nature of the new claim's right and remedy, and it gives a jury right whenever the common law plausibly supplied that analogue.[185] Recent cases lay special stress on the form of relief in the analogizing process, so that damages claims tend to be classified as legal.[186] Within this scheme, the legislature has some freedom to formulate a new cause of action so that it looks sufficiently foreign to the common law and hence falls on the nonjury side of the constitutional test;[187] the legislature may even abolish a common-law cause of action and replace it with something new of this sort that does not involve a jury trial.[188]

(2) Joinder of Legal and Equitable Claims. If the plaintiff seeks legal and equitable relief cumulatively (or if the plaintiff and the defendant by claim and by defense or counterclaim seek legal and equitable relief), a federal court allows both the plaintiff and the defendant a jury right on the legal issues. If an issue is common to the legal and equitable relief, the jury right includes having the jury rather than the judge first reach that issue with binding effect. The judicial tendency here is to

185. See Curtis v. Loether, 415 U.S. 189 (1974).

186. See Wooddell v. Int'l Bhd. of Elec. Workers, Local 71, 502 U.S. 93 (1991); Chauffeurs, Local No. 391 v. Terry, 494 U.S. 558 (1990); Tull v. United States, 481 U.S. 412 (1987).

187. Cf. Luria v. United States, 231 U.S. 9 (1913) (in statutory proceedings to cancel a certificate of citizenship, there was no jury right because right and remedy were essentially equitable).

188. Cf. Mountain Timber Co. v. Washington, 243 U.S. 219 (1917) (when the employee's right of action against the employer for negligence was replaced by statutes setting up a system of compensation for industrial injuries without regard to fault, there was no infringement of the jury right in providing for a commission to adjudicate factual disputes). As to the related notion that, where policy so motivates, Congress may simply entrust adjudicatory matters—but only those matters involving public rights—to an administrative agency for nonjury adjudication, see Atlas Roofing Co. v. Occupational Safety & Health Review Comm'n, 430 U.S. 442 (1977) (no jury required on government claim, before administrative agency, for civil penalties for employer's violation of OSHA).

ignore subtle historical distinctions—such as the discretionary clean-up doctrine and the old requirements of trying certain equitable issues first—that would limit the jury right of either party.[189]

(3) Alternative Remedies. If the plaintiff seeks legal and equitable remedies that are available only alternatively, the lower federal courts seem to give the plaintiff and the defendant a jury right on the legal and common issues. The tendency is to opt for this simple solution and thus to avoid the incredible complications of recreating this historical situation in a modern procedural setting.[190]

(4) Equitable Devices. If a party uses some procedural device that was previously available only in equity—such as interpleader, class action, shareholders' derivative action, intervention, or declaratory judgment—a federal court simply overlooks the device and gives a jury right on legal issues in the underlying claim. This practice might represent a dynamic view that the constitutionally protected realm of the common law has expanded to handle more kinds of cases than in 1791. Or this practice might represent a technique of viewing each issue in isolation, rather than in its contextual setting as part of a case. Either view obliterates the constraints of history.[191]

(5) Complex Cases. Some lower federal courts have taken the freewheeling modified historical test and turned it against the jury right, denying a jury right for highly complex but otherwise legal cases. It is currently a subject of dispute, but ultimately doubtful,[192] whether the Seventh Amendment's dictate can be circumvented on the ground of complexity, either because the issues thereby somehow become equitable[193] or because trial by an uncomprehending jury would violate due process.[194]

State jury practice is widely similar to federal, but it need not be. Very importantly, the Seventh Amendment is not incorporated

189. See Dairy Queen, Inc. v. Wood, 369 U.S. 469 (1962); Beacon Theatres, Inc. v. Westover, 359 U.S. 500 (1959); Amoco Oil Co. v. Torcomian, 722 F.2d 1099 (3d Cir. 1983).

190. See Johns Hopkins Univ. v. Hutton, 488 F.2d 912 (4th Cir. 1973).

191. See Ross v. Bernhard, 396 U.S. 531 (1970) (shareholders' derivative action; also offhandedly suggesting that whether an issue should go to a jury turns in part on the functionality of using a jury); Simler v. Conner, 372 U.S. 221 (1963) (declaratory judgment).

192. See SRI Int'l v. Matsushita Elec. Corp. of Am., 775 F.2d 1107, 1128–29 (Fed. Cir. 1985) (separate opinion); In re U.S. Fin. Sec. Litig., 609 F.2d 411 (9th Cir. 1979).

193. See In re Boise Cascade Sec. Litig., 420 F. Supp. 99 (W.D. Wash. 1976).

194. See In re Japanese Elec. Prods. Antitrust Litig., 631 F.2d 1069 (3d Cir. 1980).

or implicit in Fourteenth Amendment due process, hence does not apply to the states, and so does not constrain state civil trials. Indeed, the states generally have not followed the Supreme Court's modern expansion of the jury right. However, federal jury practice may occasionally apply in state courts under the reverse-*Erie* doctrine.[195] On the other hand, state jury practice should generally not apply in federal courts under the *Erie* doctrine.[196]

§ 2.5   Judgment

A.   Entry of Judgment

The outcome of litigation, reached with or without trial, finds expression in a judgment. More specifically, in federal court, Federal Rule 58 requires a *formal* and *prompt* expression of the outcome in a judgment. Federal Forms 70 and 71 give examples of a judgment—which should be simple and usually must be a separate document.

Various time periods (as for taking an appeal) begin running upon entry of this judgment. Entry can be accomplished in one of two ways: (1) on a simple verdict or decision, the court clerk promptly prepares, signs, and enters the judgment in the docket book, unless the judge otherwise orders; or (2) when the outcome is more complicated, the judge promptly approves the form of judgment, and then the court clerk enters it.

For correcting errors in the judgment, Rule 59(e) authorizes a motion to alter or amend the judgment, filed not later than 10 days after entry. Later relief from judgment may lie under Rule 60(b),[197] although insignificant mistakes can be corrected at any time under Rule 60(a).

B.   Kinds of Relief

Very important are the kinds of final relief that U.S. courts can give in their judgments.[198] There are the two principal categories of coercive and declaratory relief, as well as several subdivisions thereof, all of which may be given in a single lawsuit pursuant to the applicable substantive law. For explanatory purposes, assume that the plaintiff has sued the defendant on a single claim for relief.

---

195. See Dice v. Akron, C. & Y.R.R., 342 U.S. 359 (1952) (jury right in Federal Employers' Liability Act case); Norfolk & W. Ry. v. Liepelt, 444 U.S. 490 (1980) (jury instruction in FELA case).

196. See Simler v. Conner, 372 U.S. 221 (1963); Byrd v. Blue Ridge Rural Elec. Coop., 356 U.S. 525 (1958). But cf. Gasperini v. Ctr. for Humanities, Inc.,

518 U.S. 415 (1996) (applying state law to new-trial decision). See generally infra § 3.2.

197. See infra §§ 5.1(B), 5.7(B) on obtaining relief from judgment, as where a judgment was obtained by fraud.

198. See generally Dan B. Dobbs, Dobbs Law of Remedies (2d ed. 1993).

First, courts generally can give **coercive**, or active, relief that the government will enforce. The two great divisions of coercive remedies are substitutionary (giving money in lieu of in-kind relief) and specific (in-kind relief). These divisions roughly correspond to the relief formerly associated with common-law judgments and equity decrees respectively,[199] although today of course legal and equitable remedies can be given in combination by judgment. I shall indeed discuss remedies along the legal and equitable divide, because that division better sets up the following discussion on enforcement of judgment.

As to the *common law*, traditionally legal-type coercive relief, which comes in the form of an award to the prevailing party rather than an order to the losing party, appears in three major types:

(1) Damages. A court can award the plaintiff money damages, including (a) actual damages—as fixed by an out-of-pocket measure (an ordinary measure of damages for tort is the sum that will supposedly restore the plaintiff as nearly as possible to the position he would have been in had the defendant not committed the wrong), benefit-of-the-bargain measure (an ordinary measure of damages for breach of contract is the difference between what the plaintiff was promised and what he got), or restitutionary measure (a measure of damages used in some cases that prevents the defendant's unjust enrichment)— or, alternatively, nominal damages, which is a trifling sum given merely to recognize the plaintiff's legal right;[200] (b) punitive damages, which is designed to punish and deter or make an example of the defendant in some situations;[201] and (c) interest on damages, sometimes pre-judgment and always post-judgment.[202]

(2) Costs. A court normally awards costs to the prevailing party, either the plaintiff or the defendant, as part of any judgment. In federal court, Federal Rule 54(d)(1) and 28 U.S.C. § 1920 are the central provisions. Pursuant to them, costs are routinely taxed by the court clerk, whose determinations may upon motion be reviewed by the judge. Taxable costs usually include certain direct expenses incurred in conducting the litigation, such as fees of clerk and marshal, docket fees, some deposition expenses, statutory fees and disbursements for witnesses, and like items. Defining the bounds on such costs is a complicated and variable matter, but suffice it to say that

199. See supra § 1.2(A)(1)(d), (2)(d) on ancient remedies.

200. See, e.g., Carey v. Piphus, 435 U.S. 247 (1978) (nominal damages for denial of due process in absence of proof of actual damages).

201. See State Farm Mut. Auto. Ins. Co. v. Campbell, 538 U.S. 408 (2003) (due process limitation on punitive damages).

202. See 28 U.S.C. § 1961.

certainly not even all out-of-pocket expenses are reimbursed. Of crucial importance is the precept that costs in American courts (other than in Alaskan courts) ordinarily cannot include counsel fees, which are usually by far the biggest expense; however, this so-called American rule is subject to some significant exceptions, as particular statutes, court rules, and judicial doctrines call for reimbursement of attorney's fees.[203] In sum, although sometimes rather significant in absolute terms, costs typically represent only a small percentage of the total expenses of litigation, and each party normally ends up paying his own lawyer.

(3) Restoration of Property. A court can award the plaintiff the restoration of his real or personal property taken and wrongfully withheld by the defendant, as where the defendant has wrongfully appropriated the plaintiff's watch and retains it, or where the defendant has wrongfully entered upon the plaintiff's land and occupies it. This old kind of legal remedy is close in nature to equitable relief.

On the *equity* side itself, there is the traditionally equitable-type coercive relief by which a court can order the defendant to do or not to do something, as by an injunction or an order of specific performance. These discretionary remedies are available when the legal remedies are inadequate.[204]

Second, as to **declaratory** relief, courts generally can give passive relief that declares legal relationships.

Through the largely modern creation of actions for *declaratory judgment*, a court can directly declare the rights, duties, and other legal relations of the parties.[205] This was not always so. The traditional, restrictive view of the judicial process limited courts to coercive relief, such as an award of money damages or an injunction. Formerly, at common law and in equity, any judicial declarations of the rights and duties of parties were merely incidental to judgments ordering or denying some form of coercive relief, although there were some seeds of declaratory judgments in old equity practice. Indeed, the U.S. Supreme Court implied that a special barrier to declaratory relief lay in the Constitution's limiting the federal judicial power to cases and controversies in Article

---

203. See Alyeska Pipeline Serv. Co. v. Wilderness Soc'y, 421 U.S. 240 (1975); cf. Marek v. Chesny, 473 U.S. 1 (1985) (applying Fed. R. Civ. P. 68); infra § 7.1(A)(1) (law-and-economics analysis).

204. See, e.g., Walgreen Co. v. Sara Creek Prop. Co., 966 F.2d 273 (7th Cir.

1992) (injunction against mall's leasing to plaintiff's competitor); Smith v. W. Elec. Co., 643 S.W.2d 10 (Mo. Ct. App. 1982) (injunction against secondhand smoke in workplace).

205. See generally Wright & Kane, supra note 3, § 100.

III.[206] Nevertheless, a practical need for declaratory relief can readily arise when a dispute has not progressed far enough to authorize coercive relief or when an aggrieved opponent does not yet choose to seek coercive relief, but when the parties are already at each other's throat. For example, a party to a contract might justifiably want to determine whether certain behavior would be or is a breach. In the 1930s, the Supreme Court reversed its previous direction, encouraging and then upholding congressional enactment of the Federal Declaratory Judgment Act of 1934 ("DJA").[207]

Federal courts, therefore, can today give declaratory judgments consisting only of passive relief that does no more than define legal relations. A potential plaintiff or defendant may anticipatorily bring a federal action for a declaration of the rights, duties, and other legal relations of the parties. Federal subject-matter jurisdiction for the action must otherwise exist. And, as always, the dispute must be advanced enough to constitute an actual controversy that falls within the constitutional limits of Article III, in the sense that the private and public costs of not yet deciding exceed the public and private costs of immediately deciding. The declaratory remedy is then authorized and governed by the DJA and Rule 57. In sum, a federal court may in its discretion give a declaratory remedy in a case that has ripened beyond an abstract question into an actual controversy and that is otherwise within its jurisdiction.

A state court might be more restrictive or more permissive regarding declaratory relief than are the federal courts. Nearly every state has adopted a procedure to permit a declaration of legal relations of parties on specific facts unconnected with any coercive remedy. Indeed, in some states, a declaratory judgment in the nature of an advisory opinion may be obtained before any events that might constitute a violation of right or breach of duty have taken place. But in fact most states follow the federal approach regarding declaratory relief.

Bear in mind that declaratory relief may come other than in actions for declaratory judgment. The plaintiff could be seeking coercive relief, but the court's decision could incidentally have declaratory consequences. In fact, all judgments, most obviously many in rem judgments but also rather obviously any judgment for the defendant, have a *declaratory effect* like that of a declaratory judgment. These effects come about through the doctrine of res judicata.[208]

---

206. Willing v. Chicago Auditorium Ass'n, 277 U.S. 274 (1928).

207. 28 U.S.C. §§ 2201–2202; see Aetna Life Ins. Co. v. Haworth, 300 U.S. 227 (1937).

208. See generally infra § 5.1 on res judicata.

C. Enforcement of Judgment

Of great practical importance is the subject of enforcement of judgments. A lawyer may spend much time in such post-judgment activity. Devices must be available to ensure enforcement of judgments, but these tools must comport with the constitutional requirements of equal protection and due process.

The successful plaintiff (or any other prevailing party) seeks local enforcement in the court that rendered judgment for coercive relief.[209] Consider separately legal and equitable remedies.

Legal Coercive Relief. Legal-type coercive relief awards something to the plaintiff, but it is up to the plaintiff to enforce the judgment if the defendant does not voluntarily satisfy the judgment. The available mode of enforcement is cumbersome. The usual tool for enforcing a federal legal-type judgment is a "writ of execution," obtained from the court clerk and directing a marshal to seize literally or figuratively the defendant's property within the state.

Consider in particular the very common judgment for the payment of money. The initial step for the plaintiff is to identify and locate the defendant's assets. This sometimes requires extensive investigation. In connection with a federal judgment for the payment of money, Federal Rule 69(a)(2) specifically provides that the plaintiff may use the federal discovery devices or any state post-judgment discovery devices to identify and locate the defendant's assets.

The plaintiff is then in a position to invoke the force of government in order to obtain the relief to which the plaintiff has been found entitled. The applicable Rule 69(a)(1) states as a general matter that the procedure for enforcement of a judgment for money "must accord with the procedure of the state where the court is located," except that any existing federal statute governs to the extent applicable. That state law provides a maze of enforcement tools.[210] But Rule 69(a)(1) also provides: "A money judgment is enforced by a writ of execution, unless the court directs otherwise." So execution is the weapon to begin with, while complying with any restrictive terms of state law.[211]

---

209. See infra § 5.6 on interstate and international enforcement of judgments.

210. See, e.g., David D. Siegel, New York Practice ch. 18 (4th ed. 2005).

211. See Gabovitch v. Lundy, 584 F.2d 559, 561 n.3 (1st Cir. 1978) (in holding that judicial approval of writ

was required by the state's law, the court observed: "Although the forms of the process would, of course, be federal, the essential elements of state procedure for obtaining the writ must be followed."); cf. Yazoo & M.V.R. Co. v. City of Clarksdale, 257 U.S. 10 (1921) (execution sale should be held in federal court-

The court clerk will deliver the writ of execution to the marshal, and the plaintiff usually will tell the marshal about the identity and location of the defendant's property. Following state law, the marshal (or deputy marshal) typically will levy upon, or seize, so much of the defendant's nonexempt property within the state (state laws provide many and varied exemptions) as is necessary to pay the judgment—and will eventually sell that property if necessary, use the proceeds to cover the marshal's own fees and expenses and to satisfy the plaintiff's judgment, and then give any remainder to the defendant. Such execution extends even to authorizing the marshal to levy upon a debt owed the defendant by a third person.

Rule 69(a)(1) implies that if execution on a judgment for money is not fully successful, the judge may permit the plaintiff to use any additional enforcement devices that are available under state law, and which are termed "supplementary proceedings." For example, most states provide a means for compelling the defendant or a third person to appear before a judge to undergo sworn examination and for obtaining a court order that commands the person to take steps to satisfy the judgment. Such court orders include a turnover order and an installment payment order. Note that such orders are essentially equitable relief in aid of a legal judgment. Imprisonment for contempt under such a procedure has been upheld against constitutional attack, as long as the order is reasonably within the defendant's means.[212]

Enforcement of a judgment awarding restoration of property is ordinarily by writ of execution too. However, Rule 70(d) holds out the promise of equitable assistance in enforcing the order: "On application by a party who obtains a judgment or order for possession, the clerk must issue a writ of execution or assistance."

Why Do Federal Rules Adopt State Law Provisions?

We have seen that Rule 64 on provisional remedies and Rule 69 on final remedies adopt state law as federal procedural law, rather than formulating their own federal terms. We shall see other Federal Rules do the same, including Rules 4 and 17.

What are the reasons behind this practice? First, adopting state law eases the task of drafting the Federal Rules. It turns out that an area of law

---

house, not state courthouse); Wright & Miller, supra note 6, § 3012 ("Substantial compliance with the procedural provisions of the state statutes is sufficient.").

212. See Hicks ex rel. Feiock v. Feiock, 485 U.S. 624 (1988); Reeves v. Crownshield, 8 N.E.2d 283, 285 (N.Y. 1937) ("To compel the judgment debtor to obey the order of the court is not imprisonment for debt, but only impris-

onment for disobedience of an order with which he is able to comply. His refusal is contumacious conduct, the same as a refusal to obey any other lawful order of the court."); Richard E. James, Note, Putting Fear Back into the Law and Debtors Back into Prison: Reforming the Debtors' Prison System, 42 Washburn L.J. 143 (2002).

such as enforcement of judgments is a very complex thicket, which deals with matters like priority of liens that I have not even hinted at, and which states have slowly fashioned over time. The Rules could not feasibly cover all that area even if their drafters had wished to. Second, the federal courts by adopting the state scheme thereby achieve a law adapted to local conditions, which for some parts of law is critically important. Third, local lawyers, bankers, and a host of others are familiar with the state scheme and do not have to learn another. Fourth, creditors, debtors, and another host of others would find it difficult to plan their primary conduct given two diverging schemes, and they often rely on the features of one certain body of law being applied regardless of the court they get entangled with, an example being particular property's exemption from execution under state law. Fifth, by conforming to state law, the federal system incidentally manages to accommodate any state substantive interests implicit in their procedural law, such as the state's wanting to protect some kinds of judgment debtors.

That last reason might bring to mind the Erie doctrine to be examined in the next chapter. It is, however, important to understand that a Rule's across-the-board adoption of state procedure differs fundamentally from state law's selective application in federal court under the force of the Erie doctrine. The rulemakers could have written their own federal procedure but instead simply chose to adopt state law, not because of the federalism concerns of Erie but because of some or all of the above five reasons. That adoption covers all federal cases. In many of them, including cases based on purely federal causes of action, the state has no legitimate claim to have its procedural law applied in federal court under Erie; even for those completely federal cases in federal district courts, the rulemakers have dictated the adoption of state procedure. Moreover, unlike when Erie governs, a Rule like Rule 4(k) can mesh some uniform federal provisions with some variable adopted state provisions, and a Rule like Rule 17(b) can adopt an appropriate state's law rather than look inevitably to the state law that the forum state would apply.

Of course, counterarguments to the Rules' adopting state law exist. After all, the Federal Rules arrived in 1938 to replace the old Conformity Act, which in its broad adoption of state law did generally for procedure what Rule 69 does specifically for enforcement of money judgments. So, why do most Federal Rules resist adopting state law? First, the ease of drafting offered by adopting ready-made state law often results in difficulties of application. There is the obvious line to be drawn between state and federal law because of any proviso like Rule 69's "that a federal statute governs to the extent it applies" or because of any federal provisions specified by the rulemakers like Rule 69's preference for the writ of execution. Also, there is the line between complying substantially with the essentials of the adopted state law and conforming with federal practice on mere matters of form. An example: in a state where a plaintiff's lawyer can by himself issue the documents for execution, must the holder of a federal court judgment nevertheless go to the court clerk to get a writ of execution? The cases are split. The better answer may be to read the Rule's use of the word "writ" to require official issuance. The wise course for the lawyer surely would be to avoid future headaches in the litigation by going to the clerk. But no one knows the answer for sure. Second, the happy adaptation to local conditions means that there exists disuniformity in practice across the nation's federal courts. Third, national lawyers and entities have to learn and worry about all the local variations. Fourth, the content of some state provisions can be undesirable as a matter of policy, or even discriminatory or unfair, but unless the state provisions are unconstitutional or congressionally prohibited they will apply pursuant to their adoption by the Rule. Fifth, adoption of state law entails surrendering the opportunity to draft a Rule that furthers federal interests, so that in Rule 69 the federal government has sacrificed to some degree the federal interests in ensuring the efficacy of federal judgments and in controlling the federal use of force in the enforcement process.

Equitable Coercive Relief. Equitable-type coercive relief consists of a court order that operates directly upon the defendant. In case of disobedience, the court will usually enforce its order through contempt proceedings.

Contempt is a disregard or disobedience of public authority, such as a court order. There are two types of contempt proceedings, criminal and civil. The difference, it should be noted, is not necessarily in the nature of the contemptuous act but in the proceedings consequent thereto—the same contemptuous act might give rise to either or both types of proceedings. Distinguish the two as follows: Criminal contempt proceedings serve the interests of society by punishing and deterring deliberate disrespect of public authority; accordingly, the procedure is relatively protective of the defendant's rights, but an unconditional fine or a fixed jail term is the form of sanction. Civil contempt proceedings more directly help the party who would benefit from the contemnor's obedience; accordingly, the form of sanction is either (1) a compensatory payment from the contemnor to such party or (2) a conditional fine or imprisonment that need not be paid or further suffered by the contemnor if he obeys (thus the maxim that the contemnor "carries the keys of his prison in his own pocket"). In short, the design of criminal contempt proceedings is to punish and deter, and that of civil contempt proceedings is to compensate or compel.

Criminal contempt is not, strictly speaking, a means of enforcement of judgment, but the possibility of criminal contempt incidentally benefits the plaintiff by encouraging compliance with the judgment. Civil contempt, however, is a highly effective means of enforcement.

Among other enforcement tools, there are now some provisions for using legal enforcement techniques to enforce an equitable judgment. For example, Rule 70 provides, among other things, for enforcing a judgment ordering the defendant to do a specific act by the court's directing the act to be done by some other person appointed by the court. Note also that the above-discussed Rule 69(a)(1) applies to an equitable judgment ordering the defendant to pay money, thus making a writ of execution the usual tool for enforcement thereof.

§ 2.6 Appeal

A. Appealability

An "appealable" decision is one that can receive immediate appellate review. A party can take an appealable decision of a federal district court possibly through two levels of appellate review. State schemes are basically analogous.

First, there is an appeal to the appropriate court of appeals. The primary function of this appeal is *correctness review*, which mainly tries to satisfy a litigant's desire for the correct result and which implies the availability of at least one appeal of statutory right in some court in every case.

Second, there may be review by the Supreme Court. The primary function here is *institutional review*, which mainly tries to serve the systemic need for overview of the judicial branch's lawmaking and which implies largely discretionary review in a single court but only in important cases.

This scheme, although intuitive, is surprisingly contentious. Reform of many aspects of this scheme is always under consideration, right down to the level of whether there should be appeals at all.[213]

1. Routes to Court of Appeals

The basic jurisdictional rule, drawn from the common law, says that only final decisions of a federal district court are appealable to the court of appeals—but drawing on the tradition of equity, the courts and Congress have created a series of generally alternative exceptions that make some interlocutory decisions appealable.[214] The overriding aim is to strike an optimal balance, primarily between the general desire for the net efficiency of delaying appeal until the end of the case and the specific need for the net fairness of immediate appellate review.

The significance of the finality test in the federal appealability scheme cannot be denied, as it protects the courts of appeals from a flood of cases. Common-law history and a feeling that a finality rule better serves long-run economy, as well as correctness and rightfulness, have worked to enshrine the finality test. However, the strong arguments on the other side have guaranteed the existence of equitable exceptions. The courts and Congress thereby search for the optimum between the two poles of strict finality and of liberal interlocutory appeal. Thus, in the end, the federal acceptance of a finality rule is less significant than it appears, because it merely means that the search for the optimum departs from the strict finality pole rather than from the opposite pole, and the search therefore proceeds by means of drawing exceptions to finality.

---

213. See Nat'l Union of Marine Cooks & Stewards v. Arnold, 348 U.S. 37, 43 (1954) ("While a statutory review is important and must be exercised without discrimination, such a review is not a requirement of due process."); Harlon Leigh Dalton, Taking the Right to Appeal (More or Less) Seriously, 95 Yale L.J. 62 (1985).

214. See Liberty Mut. Ins. Co. v. Wetzel, 424 U.S. 737 (1976) (appellate "jurisdiction"); supra § 1.2(A)(2)(c) (history).

Some of the judicial and legislative exceptions aim at the rigid definition of a category of orders appealable as of right, while other exceptions surrender to the discretionary definition of an ad hoc approach. It seems that, in defining an exception to the finality standard, one is inevitably forced to choose between the certainty (ensuring predictability and workability) of a rigid definition and the accuracy (permitting appeal if and only if needed) of a discretionary definition, unless one wants nothing more than the drawbacks of both.

Appealability is an intensely practical subject for the competent litigator, who works with the possibility of review by the court of appeals constantly in mind. It is of immense theoretical importance too, because appealability proves to be the determinative feature of the federal appellate system. It is also the area most desperately in need of reform, as the system has managed to craft an incredible appealability scheme comprising complicated exceptions that in number have no logical limit, that are created by both the courts and Congress, that may be unclearly limited in scope or limited by discretion or both, that mesh in foggy ways, and that raise countless subsidiary procedural problems.[215]

a. Final Decisions

The final decision rule finds expression in 28 U.S.C. § 1291: "The courts of appeals * * * shall have jurisdiction of appeals from all final decisions of the district courts * * *." If the district court has fully treated the case, except for award of costs and enforcement of judgment, then its judgment is appealable.[216] If not, as where the district court orders discovery or finds liability but still needs to assess damages or has granted a new trial, there is normally no immediate appeal.[217]

However, the courts have played with this meaning of "final decision." That is, although the courts are stuck with the final decision statute, they can effectively create exceptions to it by redefining final decision. They have done this in three different ways.

First, there are several judge-made doctrines that treat certain categories of orders in the course of an action as final decisions under § 1291. For one example, consider the appealability of con-

---

215. See, e.g., Joan Steinman, The Scope of Appellate Jurisdiction: Pendent Appellate Jurisdiction Before and After Swint, 49 Hastings L.J. 1337 (1998) (examining extent to which the appellate court can consider matters that go beyond the appealable interlocutory order).

216. See generally Wright & Kane, supra note 3, § 101.

217. See, e.g., Dilly v. S.S. Kresge, 606 F.2d 62 (4th Cir. 1979); Apex Hosiery Co. v. Leader, 102 F.2d 702 (3d Cir. 1939).

tempt orders: essentially, all definitive contempt sanctions, except an order sanctioning a *party* adjudged to be in purely *civil* contempt, are considered final and hence appealable.[218] But the most important and illustrative example of the judge-made doctrines is the collateral order doctrine recognized in *Cohen v. Beneficial Industrial Loan Corp.*[219] For a type of order to be appealable thereunder, (1) it must conclusively determine an issue, (2) that issue must be separate from the merits of the action, and (3) the order must be effectively unreviewable on later appeal from a final judgment and thus impose the risk of important and irreparable injury.

Any attempt at rigidly defining a category, such as the contempt doctrine, is inevitably *inaccurate* in that it allows some unnecessary appeals and fails to reach other needy cases. For example, no appeal is ordinarily allowed a party who has been jailed for contempt until she complies with a discovery order requiring surrender of material she claims to be privileged.[220]

The collateral order category additionally proves *uncertain* in application. *Cohen*'s definitional boundaries cannot be maintained, because the appellate courts will play with such a category and deform it to avoid paying the unacceptably high price of inaccuracy, and because the limits of the human mind and language and the variety of the human experience make hard and fast lines an impossibility here. First, we are not sure if all of *Cohen*'s numbered requirements are still applicable. Second, even if they are all applicable, we are not sure what each means. Third, even if their meanings are ascertainable, the definition of each must be in terms of a continuum. Fourth, the requirements interlock, and a strong showing on one tends to satisfy others. Such complexity has to lead to mushy thinking and a mushy exception, so that almost all

---

218. See Wright & Miller, supra note 6, § 3917; see also id. § 3910 ("Hardship: Orders Transferring Property"), § 3912 ("Death Knell Orders"); cf. Quackenbush v. Allstate Ins. Co., 517 U.S. 706 (1996) (holding that an order that effectively puts the litigants out of court is final).

219. 337 U.S. 541 (1949) (allowing appeal from denial of the defendant's motion to require security for bringing suit; also imposing a fourth requirement, which has since fallen by the wayside, that the order involve a serious and unsettled question); see Digital Equip. Corp. v. Desktop Direct, Inc., 511 U.S. 863, 868 (1994) ("we have also repeatedly stressed that the 'narrow' exception should stay that way and never be allowed to swallow the general rule"); cf.

Will v. Hallock, 546 U.S. 345 (2006) (refusal to dismiss for claim preclusion not appealable); Cunningham v. Hamilton Co., Ohio, 527 U.S. 198 (1999) (discovery sanction against an attorney not appealable); Lauro Lines s.r.l. v. Chasser, 490 U.S. 495 (1989) (order refusing to enforce a forum selection clause not appealable); Richardson–Merrell, Inc. v. Koller, 472 U.S. 424 (1985) (order granting a motion to disqualify counsel not appealable); Firestone Tire & Rubber Co. v. Risjord, 449 U.S. 368 (1981) (order denying a motion to disqualify counsel not appealable).

220. See Thomas J. André, Jr., The Final Judgment Rule and Party Appeals of Civil Contempt Orders: Time for a Change, 55 N.Y.U. L. Rev. 1041 (1980).

advantages of rigidity are gone. The bottom line is that we have an uncertain exception (i.e., unpredictable and unworkable), which breeds wasteful disputes at the threshold of the court of appeals and which is hard to apply for the appellate court unfamiliar with the details of the case and unfamiliar with the arguments about allowing an immediate appeal for that case. Moreover, although as a result of the mushiness we have a somewhat accurate exception to finality (i.e., permitting appeal if and only if needed), the lingering effects of rigidity preclude a high degree of accuracy. Thus, attempts at rigidity seem likely to deliver both inaccuracy and uncertainty—which renders the pursuit of accuracy alone, by some more flexible approach, look desirable.

Second, there is conceivable such a flexible approach, namely, the ad hoc cost-benefit approach epitomized by *Gillespie v. United States Steel Corp.*[221] Very rarely, the court of appeals thereby treats an appealed order as a final decision under § 1291 simply because the needs for immediate appellate review are deemed strong relative to the reasons behind the final decision rule.

Obviously, this free-form approach multiplies wasteful threshold disputes on appealability. Instead of screening out the filing of appeals taken from interlocutory orders, this ad hoc approach invites appeals by any aggrieved party willing to take a shot or to harass. Its difficult cost-benefit analysis then necessitates much squabbling on appealability, in a court that comes at the dispute cold. *Gillespie* indeed makes accuracy look like a very costly luxury. These effects will result in squandering the appellate court's resources and undermining its effective functioning, as well as diminishing the trial court's sense of responsibility and image of legitimacy. Once one has *Gillespie*, one realizes anew the need for certainty, and rigid exceptions begin to look good again. Naturally, the appellate courts will yearn to reduce the *Gillespie* approach to a narrowly defined category, and they have succeeded in limiting the case almost to its facts.[222]

In sum, the courts seem destined to swing from rigid exceptions through mushy exceptions to ad hoc exceptions back to rigid exceptions. And nowhere in that oscillation do they appear any closer to that optimum that must lie somewhere between strict finality and liberal interlocutory appeal. What the courts need are exceptions that are both certain and finely tuned.

---

221. 379 U.S. 148 (1964) (allowing appeal from dismissal of some claims for relief).

222. Compare Coopers & Lybrand v. Livesay, 437 U.S. 463, 477 n.30 (1978) ("If Gillespie were extended beyond the unique facts of that case, § 1291 would be stripped of all significance."), with Am. Exp. Lines v. Alvez, 446 U.S. 274, 279 (1980) (allowing Gillespie-type appeal on facts similar to Gillespie's).

Third, there is Federal Rule 54(b), which is indeed fairly certain and finely tuned.[223] In multiclaim and multiparty litigation, the district court may render an appealable ruling that disposes of fewer than all of the claims or parties by directing entry of final judgment on that part of the case "if the court expressly determines that there is no just reason for delay":

> When an action presents more than one claim for relief— whether as a claim, counterclaim, crossclaim, or third-party claim—or when multiple parties are involved, the court may direct entry of a final judgment as to one or more, but fewer than all, claims or parties only if the court expressly determines that there is no just reason for delay. Otherwise, any order or other decision, however designated, that adjudicates fewer than all the claims or the rights and liabilities of fewer than all the parties does not end the action as to any of the claims or parties and may be revised at any time before the entry of a judgment adjudicating all the claims and all the parties' rights and liabilities.

The trial judge acts under Rule 54(b) as a sort of dispatching agent who can refuse to allow an appeal or, within the specified guidelines, can decide to allow an appeal. That is, within the Rule's limits, the district court can authorize appeal of certain decisions under § 1291, thus readily picking out appropriate rulings for appeal and labeling them clearly as being appealable. This approach promises accuracy by relying on the informed discretion of the trial judge, who is familiar with the case and the desirability of an immediate appeal; this approach also promises certainty, as the trial judge can readily pick out appropriate rulings and clearly label them for appeal. This approach differs from rigidly defined exceptions to the normal finality standard, in that it relies on discretion; this approach also differs from *Gillespie*, in that it relies on the discretion of the "dispatcher" and not on the discretion of the "receiver."

If the trial judge so certifies an appeal, a litigant is put on notice that the time for appeal has begun to run. Note that here, unlike for the other exceptions, the parties can waive the right to appellate review by failure to take a timely appeal from a Rule 54(b) judgment. Systemically, a risk exists that the lower court will be too willing to send cases up. But appellate review of the Rule 54(b) certification is available, albeit of narrow scope,[224] and this review will result in dismissal of an immediate appeal (1) if there was no final disposition of some but fewer than all of the claims or parties, (2) if only a single claim for relief with two or more variants was involved, or (3) if the trial court abused its discretion

223. See Wright & Miller, supra note 6, §§ 2653–2661.

224. See, e.g., Curtiss–Wright Corp. v. Gen. Elec. Co., 446 U.S. 1 (1980).

under the Rule.[225] Indeed, to ensure attention and to facilitate review, some appellate courts encourage or even require the district judge to articulate the reasons for certification.[226]

If the trial judge refuses to certify an appeal, a litigant is safe not to appeal before termination of the entire action. Any immediate appeal of the underlying order will be dismissed, unless the order is appealable under some other doctrine or provision. Appellate review of the refusal to certify under Rule 54(b) itself should normally be unavailable, although there is some weak authority for forcing a recalcitrant district judge to certify an appeal by use of the mandamus writ discussed below.[227]

b. Interlocutory Decisions

In addition to the above-discussed masked exceptions to the final decision rule created by judges, there are three explicit statutory exceptions that directly allow review of avowedly interlocutory decisions.[228] They too suffer from the same shortcomings as to certainty and accuracy.

First, the statute 28 U.S.C. § 1292(a) carves out a number of categories of interlocutory decisions for immediate appeal, including receivership and admiralty orders. Most importantly, § 1292(a)(1) draws on the tradition of equity to allow immediate appeal of the often critical decisions concerning injunctions: "the courts of appeals shall have jurisdiction of appeals from: (1) Interlocutory orders of the district courts * * *, or of the judges thereof, granting, continuing, modifying, refusing or dissolving injunctions, or refusing to dissolve or modify injunctions * * *." One relatively clear rule from statutory construction is that temporary restraining orders are generally not within the scope of § 1292(a)(1), but preliminary injunctions are within it. But beyond that rule, there remain remarkable disputes about what does and does not fall within this category.[229]

---

225. See, e.g., Liberty Mut. Ins. Co. v. Wetzel, 424 U.S. 737, 742–44 (1976).

226. See, e.g., Stockman's Water Co. v. Vaca Partners, 425 F.3d 1263, 1265 (10th Cir. 2005); In re Se. Banking Corp., 69 F.3d 1539, 1546 (11th Cir. 1995); Anthuis v. Colt Indus. Operating Corp., 971 F.2d 999, 1003 (3d Cir. 1992).

227. See Wright & Miller, supra note 6, §§ 2656, 2658.3 ("there may be instances in which it would be proper to invoke Section 1651 to petition an appellate court to mandamus the district court to make a Rule 54(b) certification").

228. See generally Wright & Kane, supra note 3, § 102.

229. See, e.g., Gulfstream Aerospace Corp. v. Mayacamas Corp., 485 U.S. 271 (1988) (holding that denial of motion to stay or dismiss an action for damages in favor of a similar state suit is not denial of an injunction); Saudi Basic Indus. Corp. v. Exxon Corp., 364 F.3d 106 (3d Cir. 2004) (saying that grants of injunctions are more readily appealable than denials). Compare, e.g., Carson v. Am. Brands, Inc., 450 U.S. 79 (1981) (allowing appeal from order rejecting settlement that would have included immedi-

Relatedly, the statute 28 U.S.C. § 1292(e), added in 1992, authorizes the Supreme Court to prescribe Federal Rules that would allow immediate appeal of types of interlocutory decisions.[230] So far, the Supreme Court in 1998 promulgated Federal Rule of Civil Procedure 23(f), by which the court of appeals in its discretion may permit an immediate appeal from an order granting or denying class certification.

Second, there is the writ of mandamus issued against the trial judge under the authority of 28 U.S.C. § 1651(a).[231] The court of appeals has the power immediately to review and correct the district court's action or inaction by granting a petition for a writ of mandamus (1) if the case ultimately could be within the court of appeals' jurisdiction and (2) if the petition passes the threshold screening test of a clear and indisputable showing that the district court has committed reversible error by usurping power, disregarding a duty to exercise power, or perhaps just abusing its discretion; if so, the court of appeals will discretionarily choose to grant the writ (3) if the cost-benefit analysis favors interlocutory review. Currently, the appellate courts yearn to restrict this irregular and essentially ad hoc means of review—even though already restricted, by history and Supreme Court admonitions, to truly extraordinary cases—to a narrowly defined category.[232]

Third, the statute 28 U.S.C. § 1292(b) permits an immediate appeal of an interlocutory decision (1) if the district court in its discretion has certified that the decision "involves a controlling question of law" on which there exists "substantial ground for difference of opinion" and also that an immediate appeal "may materially advance the ultimate termination of the litigation" and (2) if the court of appeals in its discretion agrees to hear the appeal. Because both the district judge and the court of appeals must agree to allow such an appeal and they emphasize different interests, appeals under § 1292(b) are uncommon, accounting for maybe one such accepted appeal in every three hundred federal civil appeals.[233]

ate injunctive relief), with, e.g., Switz. Cheese Ass'n v. E. Horne's Mkt., Inc., 385 U.S. 23 (1966) (not allowing appeal from denial of summary judgment seeking permanent injunctive relief).

230. 28 U.S.C. § 1292(e) ("The Supreme Court may prescribe rules * * * to provide for an appeal of an interlocutory decision to the courts of appeals that is not otherwise provided for under [section 1292]."); cf. 28 U.S.C. § 2072(c) ("Such rules may define when a ruling of a district court is final for the purposes of appeal under section 1291 of this title.").

231. 28 U.S.C. § 1651(a) ("The Supreme Court and all courts established by Act of Congress may issue all writs necessary or appropriate in aid of their respective jurisdictions and agreeable to the usages and principles of law.").

232. See Wright & Miller, supra note 6, §§ 3932–3935.7.

233. See Michael E. Solimine, Revitalizing Interlocutory Appeals in the Federal Courts, 58 Geo. Wash. L. Rev. 1165, 1174 (1990); see also Kraus v. Bd. of County Road Comm'rs, 364 F.2d 919 (6th Cir. 1966); Atlantic. City Elec. Co.

c. Reform Proposal

Maybe all the foregoing exceptions to the finality standard other than mandamus should be scrapped, and in their place should operate a rule patterned on the "dispatcher" idea of Rule 54(b) but much more broadly applicable: for any nonfinal order, not just orders in multiclaim and multiparty litigation, the trial judge in his discretion, as long as he respects any of the rule's guidelines enforced by the appellate court's oversight, could decide to allow an immediate appeal by entering judgment upon an express determination that there is no just reason for delay. Otherwise, the interlocutory order should be nonappealable.

This proposal would wipe the appealability slate almost clean.[234] This proposal would use the trial judge's informed discretion to create a combination of certainty and accuracy: the trial judge is familiar with the litigation and the desirability of an interlocutory appeal and, acting cheaply and quickly, can by certification provide certainty. Relying instead on the appellate court's discretion would reintroduce all the problems of *Gillespie*.[235] Moreover, invoking the Court's rulemaking power to introduce this reform holds more promise than relying on the Congress's legislative power, at least based on the congressional track record. Thus, it is the model of Rule 54(b) that holds promise, although using this proposed approach to overhaul appealability would pose some problems.

First, any rule like Rule 54(b) has the inevitable definitional problems, such as the precise meaning of "claim for relief" in the current Rule. But by the proposed rule's being universally applicable to interlocutory orders, at least the unnecessary line-drawing such as "claim for relief" would be eliminated.

Second, under such a broadened Rule 54(b) the trial judge might be too willing to send cases up, either shirking judicial duties or giving inadequate weight to the appellate court's interests. Although the court of appeals could review whether the trial judge had observed the broad guidelines of the revised Rule 54(b), or had abused discretion thereunder, this difficulty would still remain to

---

v. Gen. Elec. Co., 337 F.2d 844 (2d Cir. 1964).

234. Cf. Timothy P. Glynn, Discontent and Indiscretion: Discretionary Review of Interlocutory Orders, 77 Notre Dame L. Rev. 175 (2001) (proposing categories plus dispatcher).

235. Compare Edward H. Cooper, Timing as Jurisdiction: Federal Civil Appeals in Context, Law & Contemp. Probs., Summer 1984, at 157, 163–64 (making a similar proposal based on trial-court discretion), with Maurice Rosenberg, Solving the Federal Finality–Appealability Problem, Law & Contemp. Probs., Summer 1984, at 171, 174–77 (criticizing Cooper's still too heavy reliance on appellate-court discretion).

some extent. But perhaps it would be well to recognize that whoever determines appealability might be wrong occasionally, and it might be better to hear the appeals than to expend energy on second-guessing decisions granting appeals.

Third, if the suggested reform of a broadened Rule 54(b) were promulgated in lieu of all existing exceptions to the finality rule, there would be the problem of handling the arguably rare recalcitrant trial judge who refuses to dispatch a needy case to the appellate court, either because of bad motives or bad judgment. This difficulty is not so easily dismissed. But perhaps the extraordinary writs offer hope of a solution already in existence, although it might need to be loosened up a bit to serve this purpose. Mandamus could prove a sufficiently flexible tool for circumventing the recalcitrant dispatcher, and so mandamus could serve as a useful complement to a revised Rule 54(b). In extraordinary cases, the courts of appeals could reach down and review the refusal to dispatch a challenged interlocutory order. There is then a danger that the appellate courts would use this limited preservation of appellate mandamus to become roving overseers, reviving all the problems of *Gillespie*. But the history of mandamus and the recent words of the Supreme Court would likely restrain the courts of appeals, so that they would stay on the lookout for only the fairly extraordinary case of trial-judge recalcitrance.

2.   Routes to Supreme Court

Under 28 U.S.C. § 1254, there are two routes from a court of appeals to the Supreme Court, namely, certiorari and certification:[236]

Cases in the courts of appeals may be reviewed by the Supreme Court by the following methods:

(1) By writ of certiorari granted upon the petition of any party to any civil or criminal case, before or after rendition of judgment or decree;

(2) By certification at any time by a court of appeals of any question of law in any civil or criminal case as to which instructions are desired, and upon such certification the Supreme Court may give binding instructions or require the entire record to be sent up for decision of the entire matter in controversy.

The usual route is a petition for a writ of certiorari under § 1254(1). Any party can so petition at any time after the case

---

236. See generally Wright & Kane, supra note 3, § 106. On direct review of district-court decisions by Supreme Court in special circumstances, see id. § 105.

reaches the court of appeals. Granting a petition means only that the Supreme Court will review the case. Review by certiorari is a matter of discretion, not right, and "will be granted only for compelling reasons."[237] The Court grants a petition only where there are special and important systemic reasons for review. A showing of a conflict in decisions of the courts of appeals on a point involved in the case is likely to weigh strongly with the Court as a factor favoring review, but the fact that it is strongly arguable that the decision below was wrong is not in itself a compelling reason for review. So a denial of certiorari, theoretically, says nothing as to the merits of the case.

The court of appeals under § 1254(2) theoretically may, but very rarely does, certify at any time any question of law as to which instructions are desired. Review by this sort of certification occurs about once a decade.

B. Reviewability

A "reviewable" issue is one that the appellate court will consider on an appeal from a trial judge's decision, whenever that appeal occurs under the appealability scheme. Ordinarily, to be reviewable an act by the trial judge that supposedly infects the decision must have been objected to at the time of the act, must appear on the record, and must be asserted on appeal. Finally, the appeal will fail if the error alleged or shown by the appellant was harmless,[238] which the opponent can establish by showing the noneffect of error to be highly probable.[239]

Those are the general requirements for reviewability. But there are some special features of reviewability too, some of which further limit review while others broaden review.

On the one hand, the appellate court simply will not review certain issues. Recall, for example, that the midtrial state of the evidence is not reviewable, so that on an appeal from final judgment the appellate court will not examine the denial of the defendant's motion for judgment as a matter of law at the close of the plaintiff's case if the defendant "waived" the point by proceeding with her own evidence.[240]

---

237. Sup. Ct. R. 10.

238. See 28 U.S.C. § 2111 ("On the hearing of any appeal or writ of certiorari in any case, the court shall give judgment after an examination of the record without regard to errors or defects which do not affect the substantial rights of the parties.").

239. See, e.g., McQueeney v. Wilmington Trust Co., 779 F.2d 916, 928 (3d Cir. 1985); cf. Yates v. Evatt, 500 U.S. 391 (1991) (for constitutional errors on habeas corpus review, applying higher standard of noneffect beyond a reasonable doubt).

240. See Wells v. State Farm Fire & Cas. Co., 993 F.2d 510 (5th Cir. 1993); cf. Donovan v. Penn Shipping Co., 429 U.S. 648, 650 (1977) ("we now reaffirm the longstanding rule that a plaintiff in

On the other hand, although the general rule, subject to certain exceptions, is that a party cannot introduce new issues or even change its theories on appeal,[241] the appellate court may invoke the plain error rule to reach some issues not raised below. This plain error power is very sparingly exercised and normally will be invoked only to prevent a miscarriage of justice caused by an obvious error. Of course, any such power could reflect appellate whim and so is difficult to restrain, but the cases suggest that properly the plain error doctrine requires a clear and convincing showing of reversible error as well as of the error's net harm to the public interest if left uncorrected.[242]

As to appellants, only a party, and indeed only a party aggrieved by an error, can appeal. Usually, then, only the party who lost the decision below can appeal. But even the decision's victor can very occasionally appeal, if an error resulted in a decision somehow adverse to his interests.[243]

As to appellees, such a party can defend the decision below even on grounds rejected by the lower court. But to attack the decision in order to improve its position thereunder, the appellee must file a formal cross-appeal.[244]

federal court, whether prosecuting a state or federal cause of action, may not appeal from a remittitur order he has accepted").

241. See, e.g., Altman v. Altman, 653 F.2d 755, 758 (3d Cir. 1981) (applying "the rule barring a party from raising new issues on appeal," but recognizing exceptional circumstances could exist "when the public interest requires that the issue be heard or when manifest injustice would result from the failure to consider the new issue" or "when the new theory was advanced to affirm the district court and prejudice would not result to the other party"); Wratchford v. S.J. Groves & Sons Co., 405 F.2d 1061 (4th Cir. 1969); Apex Smelting Co. v. Burns, 175 F.2d 978 (7th Cir. 1949); see also Robert J. Martineau, Considering New Issues on Appeal: The General Rule and the Gorilla Rule, 40 Vand. L. Rev. 1023 (1987) (also discussing subject-matter jurisdiction exception); Rhett R. Dennerline, Note, Pushing Aside the General Rule in Order to Raise New Issues on Appeal, 64 Ind. L.J. 985 (1989); cf. Barry A. Miller, Sua Sponte Appellate Rulings: When Courts Deprive Litigants of an Opportunity to Be Heard, 39 San Diego L. Rev. 1253 (2002).

242. See Fed. R. Civ. P. 51(d)(2); Kevin M. Clermont, Procedure's Magical Number Three: Psychological Bases for Standards of Decision, 72 Cornell L. Rev. 1115, 1129 n.60 (1987). Compare Nimrod v. Sylvester, 369 F.2d 870 (1st Cir. 1966), with City of Newport v. Fact Concerts, Inc., 453 U.S. 247 (1981).

243. See Deposit Guaranty Nat'l Bank, Jackson, Miss. v. Roper, 445 U.S. 326, 333 (1980) (victorious plaintiffs can appeal the denial of class certification); Elec. Fittings Corp. v. Thomas & Betts Co., 307 U.S. 241 (1939) (defendant who was actually decreed not to have infringed plaintiff's valid patent can appeal the decree as to validity, because that decree could have adverse practical effects on defendant's business); Aetna Cas. & Sur. Co. v. Cunningham, 224 F.2d 478 (5th Cir. 1955) (if plaintiff "was denied judgment of the quality to which it laid claim, it is a party aggrieved on appeal"); cf. In re DES Litig., 7 F.3d 20 (2d Cir. 1993) (dismissing victor's appeal for lack of adverse effect); Watson v. City of Newark, 746 F.2d 1008 (3d Cir. 1984) (victorious plaintiffs cannot appeal unfavorable dictum); Midland–Guardian of Pensacola, Inc. v. Carr, 425 F.2d 793 (5th Cir. 1970) (in any event, appellate court still needs the contestedness of a real case or controversy).

1. Standards of Review

Unavoidably, the appellate court must apply a standard of review.[245] Such a standard specifies how certain the reviewer must be of error by the original decisionmaker in order to overturn the original decision. This degree of scrutiny is the most important feature of reviewability. Accordingly, the parties must specifically state in their briefs the applicable standard of review for each issue on appeal.[246]

The applicable standard is fixed by a complex balancing of the needs for appellate review of the issue (such as controlling possible abuses of power by the trial judge and maintaining uniformity of the law) against the policies that favor limited review (such as conserving judicial resources and enhancing the appellate court's effective functioning, as well as augmenting the trial court's sense of responsibility and image of legitimacy). The available choices among standards of review conceivably constitute a sliding scale of infinite gradations. However, like standards of proof, the prevailing standards of review have actually coalesced around three degrees of scrutiny that the appellate court can apply in reviewing the trial judge's different kinds of decisions.[247]

First, there is nondeferential, or plenary, review. The appellate court makes a virtually de novo, or fresh, determination of questions of law, although it reverses only if it disagrees with the trial judge's resolution and so thinks error in ascertainment of the correct law to be more likely than not. As always, the law/fact distinction is fuzzy and chameleonic.[248] But legal questions here include allegedly erroneous instructions on the law to the jury and also the trial judge's decision on a motion for judgment as a matter of law at the close of all the evidence. Society cares about getting the answers to these questions of law right.

---

244. See Standard Accident Ins. Co. v. Roberts, 132 F.2d 794 (8th Cir. 1942) (questionably applying the cross-appeal rule).

245. See generally Steven Alan Childress & Martha S. Davis, Federal Standards of Review (3d ed. 1999).

246. See Fed. R. App. P. 28(a)(9)(B), (b)(5).

247. See infra § 7.1(A)(2) (law-and-psychology explanation).

248. See Pullman–Standard v. Swint, 456 U.S. 273 (1982) (drawing law/fact line, and saying discriminatory intent under civil rights statute is ques-tion of fact entitled to deferential review); 1 Childress & Davis, supra note 245, § 3.09 (fact/law distinction for appellate review); Evan Tsen Lee, Principled Decision Making and the Proper Role of Federal Appellate Courts: The Mixed Questions Conflict, 64 S. Cal. L. Rev. 235 (1991); cf. Ronald J. Allen & Michael S. Pardo, The Myth of the Law–Fact Distinction, 97 Nw. U. L. Rev. 1769, 1771 (2003) ("the decision to label an issue 'law' or 'fact' is a functional one based on who should decide it under what standard, and is not based on the nature of the issue").

Second, there is middle-tier review. The appellate court shows deference on most determinations for which presence on the trial-court scene, hearing the evidence and such, was important. The appellate court does not disturb such a determination unless it is clearly convinced there was error. Middle-tier review includes the clearly erroneous test, by which a judge's factfindings in a nonjury trial stand "unless clearly erroneous, and the reviewing court must give due regard to the trial court's opportunity to judge the witnesses' credibility."[249] On issues of judge-found fact, then, the appellate court normally defers to the trial court's view, reversing only if that view generates "the definite and firm conviction that a mistake has been committed."[250]

Third, there is highly restricted review. The appellate court intrudes on certain determinations only in the most extreme situations. Thus, a denial of a new-trial motion based on the weight of the evidence—where the court of appeals is reviewing the trial judge's approving review of the sacrosanct jury's verdict—should very rarely be disturbed.[251] For another instance, the appellate court will grant a petition for mandamus only if the trial judge has clearly and indisputably committed reversible error; now if the trial error alleged is abuse of discretion, then this threshold test means at least "clear abuse of discretion," which seems to be equivalent to almost certain error.[252]

Appellate courts do employ other formulations, such as an abuse of discretion standard of review for certain applications of law to fact. To illustrate, the core decision on a motion for a new trial on the ground of misconduct of counsel lies within the trial judge's discretion, and the appellate court will reverse only if there was an abuse of that discretion.[253] How such a standard correlates with the tripartite scale of the three preceding paragraphs is not immediately apparent. "Abuse of discretion is thus a nebulous concept which remains essentially undefined."[254] In the illustrative situation, however, most observers would invoke middle-tier review

---

249. Fed. R. Civ. P. 52(a)(6); see Anderson v. City of Bessemer City, N.C., 470 U.S. 564 (1985).

250. United States v. U.S. Gypsum Co., 333 U.S. 364, 395 (1948).

251. See supra note 166 and accompanying text.

252. See Allied Chem. Corp. v. Daiflon, Inc., 449 U.S. 33, 36 (1980) (per curiam) (summarily reversing the court of appeals' issuance of a writ of mandamus to overturn the trial judge's discretionary grant of a new trial on the ground of erroneous evidentiary rulings: "In short, our cases have answered the question as to the availability of manda-

mus in situations such as this with the refrain: 'What never? Well, *hardly ever!*' "); Will v. Calvert Fire Ins. Co., 437 U.S. 655, 665 n.7 (1978) (plurality opinion); id. at 676 (Brennan, J., dissenting).

253. See Pettingill v. Fuller, 107 F.2d 933, 936 (2d Cir. 1939) (after retrial, reversing original grant of new trial on ground of misconduct of counsel).

254. Federal Civil Appellate Jurisdiction: An Interlocutory Restatement, Law & Contemp. Probs., Spring 1984, at 13, 62.

and say that only if an appellate court is convinced that the court below was clearly wrong will it reverse.[255] In other situations, however, the appellate court might be more willing or more reluctant to intercede, given stronger or weaker reasons for review rather than deference. This variety of meanings justifies a generalization: "Discretionary decisions fall into three categories, with corresponding limitations on appellate review."[256] Thus, review of discretionary decisions seems to replicate in parallel the traditional triunity of standards of appellate review.

What Is the Affirmance Rate?

The striking feature about federal civil appeals, when looking at published and unpublished decisions, is the high rate of affirmance, which is the percentage of decided appeals that result in either dismissal of the appeal on the merits or affirmance of the decision below. That rate is about 80%. While win rates in the trial court can be high or low in particular case categories, affirmance rates in the appellate court remain elevated for all kinds of cases.

This affirmance rate might seem unsurprising to you. One might expect a high affirmance rate because of appellate deference to the district court's result. One might even expect a high affirmance rate when review is nondeferential, because of the tendency of experts to agree at about a 75% rate. Combining the two expectations based on appellate deference and expert agreement would push one's expected affirmance rate even higher toward 80%. Appellate judges should and do lean toward affirmance as the usual course.

However, if the high affirmance rate is owing to those deference and expertise factors, why do the parties not take them into account and settle all but the close appeals, thereby whittling down that high affirmance rate? Appeals that clearly favor either the appellant or the appellee should tend to be settled readily, because both sides could save costs by so acting in light of their knowledge of all aspects of the case. Difficult appeals falling close to the applicable standard of review should tend not to settle, because the parties would be more likely to disagree substantially with respect to their predicted outcomes. These unsettled, difficult appeals entailing divergent expectations should fall more or less equally on either side of the standard of review, regardless of both the standard's degree of scrutiny and the underlying distribution of appealed cases. Case selection, then, should leave for appellate adjudication a residue of appeals exhibiting some nonextreme affirmance rate. Indeed, under simplifying assumptions, and as a limiting implication, such case-selection theorizing would predict a 50% affirmance rate. That is clearly wrong, as the data prove.

Thus, the persistently elevated affirmance rate suggests at least that settlement is not very effective at the appellate stage in weeding out clear cases. After all, if every litigated judgment underwent appeal, one would expect about an 80% affirmance rate because of reviewer's deference and

---

255. Cf. Cooter & Gell v. Hartmarx Corp., 496 U.S. 384, 401 (1990) ("When an appellate court reviews a district court's factual findings, the abuse-of-discretion and clearly erroneous standards are indistinguishable: A court of appeals would be justified in concluding that a district court had abused its discretion in making a factual finding only if the finding were clearly erroneous.").

256. Federal Civil Appellate Jurisdiction, supra note 254, at 62; see Am. Hosp. Supply Corp. v. Hosp. Prods. Ltd., 780 F.2d 589, 594 (7th Cir. 1986) (describing three standards of review of discretionary decisions: simple disagreement, strong conviction of error, and virtually complete deference).

because of experts' agreement. In fact, only a fraction of litigated judgments undergo appeal—maybe a fifth, and only half of those reach a decisive appellate outcome—and yet one nevertheless still sees an 80% affirmance rate. It seems as if the parties have chosen to pursue on appeal, by whatever selection method they employ, a set of cases that functions, at least with regard to overall affirmance, as if it were a random sampling. In sum, case selection apparently has a very limited effect in systematically filtering the cases for adjudication on appeal.

Why would that be? Perhaps the failure to filter out clear appeals is owing to appeals' not being very costly, in relative terms. After slogging through the trial court, the parties must see the small cost and effort in appealing as comparatively insignificant. Judgment below leaves the winner feeling vindicated and the aggrieved loser wanting justice at long last. Something telling emerges in the countless scenes on the evening news in which losers immediately proclaim on the courthouse steps their intention to appeal. These losing parties decide that they might as well stagger to the finish line, pretty much regardless of the chances on appeal. Simply put, an 80% affirmance rate suggests that the law should consider reform aimed at the efficiency of forcing the would-be appellant to pause. A possible reform proposal would involve shifting attorney's fees on appeal to a losing appellant, which would seem a fair condition of access to a second court for a party already found to be in the wrong. See generally Kevin M. Clermont & Theodore Eisenberg, Litigation Realities, 88 Cornell L. Rev. 119, 150–52 (2002).

2. Appellate Procedure

Appeal does not entail a retrial of the case, but a rather academic reconsideration of the reviewable issues in search of error.

Procedure in the federal courts of appeals is largely governed by the Federal Rules of Appellate Procedure and local circuit rules.[257] Speaking generally, the party challenging an appealable decision must timely file a simple notice of appeal with the clerk of the district court—note that this is the sole jurisdictional step, but remember that the right to appeal may be waived by failure to complete this step. With the help of the parties' counsel, that clerk then assembles and transmits the record to the court of appeals, where the clerk of the court of appeals files the record. A panel of three judges hears the appeal on that record and on the briefs of counsel; usually there is also oral argument. The panel then affirms, reverses, or modifies the decision by majority vote. If it follows from the view of the case adopted by the appellate court that further testimony should be taken, this will not be done by the appellate court, but rather by the lower court on remand.[258] Cur-

257. See generally Gregory A. Castanias & Robert H. Klonoff, Federal Appellate Practice and Procedure in a Nutshell (2008): Robert L. Stern, Appellate Practice in the United States (2d ed. 1989); Michael E. Tigar & Jane B. Tigar, Federal Appeals (3d ed. 1999); Wright & Kane, supra note 3, § 104.

258. See 28 U.S.C. § 2106 ("The Supreme Court or any other court of appellate jurisdiction may affirm, modify, vacate, set aside or reverse any judgment, decree, or order of a court lawfully brought before it for review, and may remand the cause and direct the entry of

rently, about 20% of federal courts of appeals' decisions are published in the Federal Reporter (only a very small percentage of district-court decisions are published in any form, while all of the Supreme Court's decisions appear in the reporters).[259]

Procedure in the Supreme Court is largely governed by the Rules of the Supreme Court of the United States.[260] Speaking generally, the Court decides, on the basis of a first round of papers timely submitted, whether to consider fully the issues presented. More particularly as to review on certiorari, the petition for a writ of certiorari must contain the questions presented for review, a concise statement of the case, and an argument regarding the reasons relied on for allowance of the writ. Certiorari is granted or denied by the Supreme Court upon consideration of the petition and any brief in opposition and reply brief; there is no oral argument at this stage. If the petition is granted, which requires the vote of only four of the nine Justices, the Court has thereby agreed to consider the merits. The case is normally then briefed on the merits and heard on oral argument. Finally, the Supreme Court—by majority vote, with six Justices constituting a quorum—affirms, reverses, or modifies the decision being reviewed, possibly remanding to a court below for further proceedings.

The pendency of an appeal usually stays further judicial proceedings in the court below. Also, there are complex provisions for staying the victor's enforcement of a judgment prior to the conclusion of the appeal stage.[261] Some such stays of enforcement are automatic, but many rest successively in the discretion of the district court, the court of appeals or a judge thereof, and a Justice of the Supreme Court or the whole Court. Usually, such a stay is conditioned upon the applicant's giving a bond.

---

such appropriate judgment, decree, or order, or require such further proceedings to be had as may be just under the circumstances.'').

259. See Kevin M. Clermont & Theodore Eisenberg, CAFA Judicata: A Tale of Waste and Politics, 156 U. Pa. L. Rev. 1553, 1558–60 (2008).

260. See generally Robert L. Stern, Eugene Gressman, Stephen M. Shapiro & Kenneth S. Geller, Supreme Court Practice (8th ed. 2002); Wright & Kane, supra note 3, § 108.

261. See Fed. R. Civ. P. 62; Fed. R. App. P. 8; 28 U.S.C. § 1651(a).

Chapter 3

GOVERNING LAW

Table of Sections

---

§ 3.1   Choice of Law

A pervasive problem in litigation that involves nondomestic elements is choosing which sovereign's law to apply. Generally, it is the forum court's task to choose the governing law under some technique for choice of law.

A.   Constitutional Limits

The Supreme Court has interpreted the Federal Constitution in a way that gives American courts a very free hand in choosing the governing law and, in particular, in choosing to apply their own law. Here is the Court's most expressive summary of the constitutional restriction:

> In deciding constitutional choice-of-law questions, whether under the Due Process Clause or the Full Faith and Credit Clause, this Court has traditionally examined the contacts of the State, whose law was applied, with the parties and with the occurrence or transaction giving rise to the litigation. In order to ensure that the choice of law is neither arbitrary nor fundamentally unfair, the Court has invalidated the choice of law of a State which has had no significant contact or significant aggregation of contacts, creating state interests, with the parties and the occurrence or transaction.[1]

1. Allstate Ins. Co. v. Hague, 449 U.S. 302, 308 (1981) (plurality opinion) (citations and footnotes omitted).

B.   Techniques for Choice

The technique for choice of law followed in any particular jurisdiction has typically evolved from (1) a traditional set of wooden and crude rules that pointed with relative certainty to the law of a particular place where some particular event occurred (e.g., the rule of lex loci delicti, or the law of the place of the wrong, controlled the choice for substantive issues in tort cases; but the lex fori, or the law of the forum, applied on all issues that the forum court characterized as procedural) to (2) a very flexible and sensitive but quite uncertain approach of comparing as to each issue the interests of the involved sovereigns in having their own law applied and then applying the law of the sovereign whose policies would be more impaired by nonapplication (so-called interest analysis).

Nevertheless, this is a subject dominated today by competing subtheories that elaborate or alter interest analysis, and these subtheories conflict sharply at least on the verbal level. Many of these modern differences of opinion have arisen as theorists have worked to reinject some degree of practical certainty into the theoretical precision of interest analysis. For example, one might use interest analysis to create a new series of general rules to cover common situations.[2] Such matters are the subject of study in the upperclass course of Conflict of Laws.[3]

§ 3.2   Choice Between State and Federal Law

The subject here is extraordinarily important. It concerns the special choice-of-law problem ubiquitously encountered in our federal system: the choice between state and federal law. This situation involves a "choice of law" in the sense that the federal authority is deciding whether federal law should be generated to apply to a given issue or state law should be left to govern. The decision on this "vertical" choice of law is often reached by a process similar to that employed for the "horizontal" choice of law examined above.[4]

Why this subject is so important is initially a bit mysterious. Many of the major cases involve merely a judicial application of

---

2. See Symeon C. Symeonides, The American Choice–of–Law Revolution: Past, Present and Future 423–37 (2006).

3. See generally Luther L. McDougal, III, Robert L. Felix & Ralph U. Whitten, American Conflicts Law (5th ed. 2001); William M. Richman & William L. Reynolds, Understanding Conflict of Laws (3d ed. 2002); Eugene F. Scoles, Peter Hay, Patrick J. Borchers &

Symeon C. Symeonides, Conflict of Laws (4th ed. 2004); David D. Siegel & Patrick J. Borchers, Conflicts in a Nutshell (3d ed. 2005); Russell J. Weintraub, Commentary on the Conflict of Laws (5th ed. 2006).

4. See Joseph P. Bauer, The Erie Doctrine Revisited: How a Conflicts Perspective Can Aid the Analysis, 74 Notre Dame L. Rev. 1235 (1999).

quasi-procedural state law in federal diversity cases. Consequently, some people view this subject as technical or arcane. They could not be more wrong. Those cases are the tail of a humongous dog. We study only those tough major cases because they arose where the battle is being waged, but the outcome of those cases controls across-the-board in the infinitude of more obvious cases too.

The choice-of-law problem arises not only in diversity cases but in all other federal cases. It also arises in all state cases. But that makes it sound like a problem only for the judiciary. Instead, it arises in all matters of lawmaking and law-applying faced by the legislature and the executive, as well as in their administrative agencies. And this problem was the main concern of the Framers of the Constitution, which is really a choice-of-law document, in their task of creating a federation. But all that makes it sound like solely a governmental problem. Instead, our legal system imposes on all persons living under it and trying to apply the law, whether as lawyers or other citizens, the problem of divining whether the government allocates a matter to state or federal law.

The government performs this allocation task in its ordinary manner, acting by its hierarchy of lawmakers: Constitution, Congress (or its authorized administrative delegate), and the courts. If the Constitution makes the choice between state and federal law, its choice is binding of course. If it does not choose, then Congress, subject to the existing constitutional constraints discussed below, can make the binding choice. Only if the Constitution and Congress have not chosen, then the courts, as junior partners in this endeavor, get to make the choice, acting by a judicially developed choice-of-law technique that today operates well inside the outer constitutional constraints.

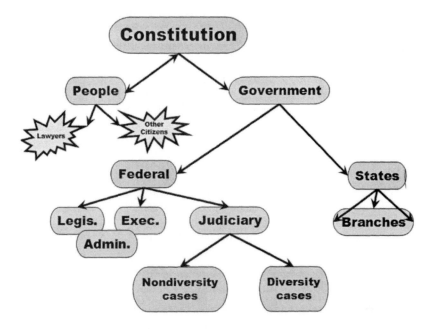

Consequently, the simple fact is that every question of law in a federal system such as ours is preceded by the choice-of-law problem of whether the legal question is a matter of state or federal law. "Every question of law" means all tasks of making or applying law, whether by public or private actors. If a police officer or a car driver is trying to determine the speed limit, that person needs first to resolve whether state or federal law governs by determining the choice that the Constitution, Congress, or courts have made or would make. Most often, the resolution of such a choice-of-law problem is very easy and so has a clear, intuitive answer. Closer to the dividing line between state and federal law, however, the resolution can be exquisitely difficult. Either way, the choice-of-law problem is literally ubiquitous: the first step in any legal act in our federal system is vertical choice of law.

In sum, the subject under study is far from technical or arcane. Instead, it implicates a megadoctrine that seeks the optimal relationship between state and federal law in our country. It is the profound key to understanding federalism and hence our governmental and legal system.

A.   State Law in Federal Court

More specifically, the concern addressed initially here is the solution of that problem of choosing between state and federal law *in actions litigated in federal court.*

If the Constitution or Congress expressly or impliedly makes the choice of law, that choice is binding on the federal courts. In the absence of such a constitutional or congressional directive, the federal courts must decide whether state or federal law applies. This latter situation gets all the attention in casebooks, but it represents only part of the big picture. So we should consider first the constitutional and congressional limits imposed on judicial choice of law.

1. Constitutional Limits on Choice

The Federal Constitution can dictate a choice in favor of federal law, and of course this is binding. An example is the Seventh Amendment's guarantee of trial by jury: the constitutional jury right governs in all federal cases. But most often the Constitution does not so dictate. Then the Constitution must confront the greater danger of the other federal authorities' choosing to apply too much federal law.

In many circumstances Congress can validly make a choice by statute in favor of federal law, and that choice will bind the federal courts. In the absence of such a congressional directive, the federal courts can sometimes validly choose to apply federal law. This recurrent stress on "validly" raises the difficult threshold question: To what extent does the Constitution limit the powers of the federal government—either Congress or the federal courts—to choose to apply federal law in federal court? In other words, when does the Constitution dictate a choice in favor of state law? The Supreme Court has gone from a constitutional interpretation giving the federal government wide powers to choose federal law to a slightly more restrictive view.

In *Swift v. Tyson*,[5] Justice Story, for the Court, ruled that in a diversity contract case, federal law effectively governed the issue of whether satisfaction of a pre-existing debt constituted proper consideration.

First, the Court asked whether Congress had already made the choice of law in the Rules of Decision Act of 1789 ("RDA")—now with slight changes 28 U.S.C. § 1652, which in its present form reads:

> The laws of the several states, except where the Constitution or treaties of the United States or Acts of Congress otherwise require or provide, shall be regarded as rules of decision in civil actions in the courts of the United States, in cases where they apply.

5. 41 U.S. (16 Pet.) 1 (1842).

But the Court answered that only state constitutions and statutes (and state judicial construction thereof) and local usages (such as state decisional law on real estate and other immovable and intra-territorial matters), and not the state's general common law, constituted binding "laws of the several states" within the statute: "In the ordinary use of language, it will hardly be contended, that the decisions of courts constitute laws. They are, at most, only evidence of what the laws are, and are not, of themselves, laws. They are often re-examined, reversed and qualified by the courts themselves, whenever they are found to be either defective, or ill-founded, or otherwise incorrect. The laws of a state are more usually understood to mean the rules and enactments promulgated by the legislative authority thereof, or long-established local customs having the force of laws."[6] This construction of the RDA was debatable, but far from indefensible.

Second, the Court explained that the federal courts, in the absence of any applicable congressional directive, were constitutionally free to depart from the general common law declared by the state courts and should make their own rulings thereon. That is, the federal courts had the power to come to an independent conclusion as to the "true" general common law.

By so construing the RDA narrowly and the Constitution loosely, the Court freed the federal courts to create a broad federal common law. In the *Swift* case itself, a federal version of common law, which would treat satisfaction of a pre-existing debt as proper consideration, governed the point of commercial law in issue. *Swift* rested (1) somewhat on jurisprudential arguments linked to the belief in a transcendental body of natural law and to the declaratory theory of law by which judges apply law but do not create it, (2) more on a dream of the federal courts' leading the state courts to uniformity of law, and (3) mainly on other instrumentalist policies motivating the decision, such as asserting the nascent federal authority and ensuring a better commercial law.

The ensuing century saw (1) a change in jurisprudence toward positivism and realism, (2) the partial failure of Story's dream of uniformity, and (3), given the considerable achievement of Story's other instrumentalist policies, an ascendancy of competing policies to counter the evils generated by the persisting gap between state and federal precedents: forum-shopping between federal and state courts, problems of an equal-protection nature caused by the favored position of the person (often a corporation) who has access to two sets of courts with differing laws, and the federal invasion of the states' authority.

6. Id. at 18.

Accordingly, the Court, by Justice Brandeis, overruled *Swift* in *Erie Railroad Co. v. Tompkins*.[7] The *Erie* Court held that the federal judiciary lacks the power to declare and apply its own brand of general common law. In reaching this conclusion, Justice Brandeis discussed *Swift's* supposed mistake in statutory construction and the considerable mischief consequently engendered by that decision, but he ultimately judged those flaws insufficient to overcome the dictates of stare decisis. Instead, he argued that it was the unconstitutionality of the course pursued by the federal courts under *Swift* that compelled its overruling.

Nonetheless, the actual basis for overruling was a fairly tiny constitutional one. The *Erie* Court held that the power to make general common law that the federal court system had appropriated under the *Swift* doctrine would occasionally take those courts into areas constitutionally prohibited or, more properly phrased, take those courts beyond the powers constitutionally bestowed on the federal courts. The Constitution gave the federal government only enumerated, and hence limited, powers. The constitutional holding of *Erie* was that the federal courts did not have the power under the Constitution to create federal common law with respect to *all* nonlocal matters for which there was no state statute in point. It was the across-the-board nature of this power assumed by the Court in *Swift* that was invalid. Although the federal courts have significant lawmaking power under the Constitution, there is a boundary beyond which the federal courts' lawmaking power cannot extend consistently with the Constitution. Because *Swift* would permit occasional extension beyond that boundary, *Swift* had to fall.

With *Erie* on the books and *Swift* off, we can venture a fairly confident answer to that threshold question: To what extent does the Constitution limit the powers of the federal government—either the federal courts or Congress—to choose to apply federal law in federal court?

a.   Constitutional Limit on Federal Courts

Article III's reference to the "judicial power" extending to cases within federal jurisdiction signifies the federal courts' constitutional power to create some law in the limited areas of high federal interest (e.g., admiralty). But the federal courts would unconstitutionally exceed their power by lawmaking in areas of very high state interest (e.g., immunity of charities from tort

---

7.   304 U.S. 64 (1938). For the story of this case, see Edward A. Purcell, Jr., The Story of Erie: How Litigants, Lawyers, Judges, Politics, and Social Change   Reshape the Law, in Civil Procedure Stories 21 (Kevin M. Clermont ed., 2d ed. 2008).

liability), whether the state interest finds expression in state statutory law or in state decisional law. In other words, the constitutional power implicit in Article III's reference to the "judicial power" has a constitutional limit. *Erie* so held, while leaving that limit vague. It is helpful to envisage this scheme as having a core of high federal interest and around the core a roughly circular boundary, albeit one inevitably ill-defined, beyond which lie matters that the federal courts' lawmaking power cannot constitutionally reach.

Equivalently conceived, this boundary represents the constitutional limit on the federal courts' power to choose on their own to apply federal law. This formulation in terms of choosing federal law is equivalent to the prior paragraph's formulation of the judicial lawmaking power because, whenever the federal courts so choose to apply federal law, they are extending and hence making federal law.

b.   *Constitutional Limit on Congress*

The *Erie* case concerned only the power appropriated by the federal court system in the realm of general common law. In *Swift*, Justice Story had construed the RDA to be inapplicable by a narrow reading of "laws of the several states." Then, in the vacuum beyond such "laws," Justice Story had claimed for the courts the power to create federal common law. In *Erie*, Justice Brandeis really addressed and condemned only this judicially assumed power. Thus, *Erie* did not hold anything with respect to the scope of the *power of Congress*. More to the immediate point, *Erie* never even mentioned the power of Congress to mandate federal law *applicable only in federal court*. Justice Brandeis does speak at one point of Congress's power to declare substantive law applicable in all courts, but not specifically of its power to declare law for application only in the federal courts.[8]

Nevertheless, it is clear that under Articles I and III, including the Necessary and Proper Clause, Congress has broad power so to lawmake for application only in the federal courts (e.g., Federal Rules of Evidence, which was enacted as a statute).[9] The limit on that lawmaking power remains largely unexplored in any authoritative way, but presumably Congress would exceed its constitutional power by so legislating in areas of extremely high state interest (e.g., title to real estate). That is to say, Congress cannot unreasonably affect those primary decisions concerning human conduct that the Constitution did not subject to federal legislation and so reserved to the states. This limit is implicit in the very structure of the Constitution.

---

8. 304 U.S. at 78.

9. See Stewart Org., Inc. v. Ricoh Corp., 487 U.S. 22, 27 (1988); Prima

Paint Corp. v. Flood & Conklin Mfg. Co., 388 U.S. 395, 404–06 (1967).

Again, this boundary demarking the legislative lawmaking power equivalently represents the limit on the congressional power to choose to apply federal law in federal court.

c. Comparison of Constitutional Limits

Because the *Erie* Court treated the limit on judicial power, but not the limit on congressional power, the relation between the two limits remained unstated. Nonetheless, it would seem that the boundary demarking constitutionally permissible matters for the federal courts is more restrictive than the boundary applicable to federal legislators. The idea is that, in addition to the Court's emphasis on *federalism*, the constitutional structure of *separation of powers* limits the federal courts' power to lawmake on their own. Congress may validly make federal law more often than the federal courts can, because under our constitutional structure Congress should be the more active articulator of federal interests, while the courts must steer clear of blatantly formulating policies. The lawmaking function of Congress is thus more expansive, permitting greater intrusion into matters of state interest. In other words, the circular boundary on congressional reach lies outside the boundary on the judiciary.

Incidentally, specific constitutional provisions, most importantly the Due Process Clause of the Fifth Amendment along with its equal protection ingredient, might further limit slightly the powers of the federal courts and Congress to choose to create a distinctive federal law solely for use in federal court.

d. Role of Constitutional Limits in Erie Doctrine

Beware of overemphasizing the constitutional aspects of the *Erie* doctrine. First, both constitutional limits, on the federal courts and on Congress, permit significant lawmaking activity by the federal government. Second, the *Erie* case used the Constitution merely to overturn *Swift*. *Erie* did not use the Constitution to solve the actual choice-of-law problem before the Court. That is, *Erie* did not suggest that henceforth in practice the line between federal and state law applied in federal court should lie at either of the outer constitutional limits on choosing federal law. Instead, *Erie* suggested that the line would lie inside those outer boundaries. Later cases confirm that the line lies far inside those boundaries. Accordingly, those later cases did not have to face the question, or provide better definition, of the constitutional limits on making or choosing federal law.

Thus, in federal court today state law will apply in many situations where such application is not constitutionally compelled, the federal government so deferring to state law and declining to exercise the full extent of its constitutional powers, as a matter of comity. Consider in particular the range of cases in which the federal courts must make the choice of law:

(1) Easy Cases. Whenever an issue entails such high state interest as to raise a question of the federal courts' constitutional power to choose federal law, state law will almost invariably apply on that issue as a matter of federal deference. There is no practical difference whether state law governs the issue by constitutional compulsion or it governs as a result of federal deference. Therefore, such an issue presents an easy case with respect to choice of law, and the court need not face any constitutional question.

(2) Hard Cases. A hard case arises when the issue falls farther inside the constitutional boundary applicable to the federal courts, because of either lower state interest or heightened federal interest. An example would be a procedural issue in a diversity case. It then becomes critical to locate the line that marks the choice, as a matter of deference, between federal and state law. For such an issue that falls close to this line, the Constitution is a distant consideration and does not directly affect the decisional process. It is this line of deference that has great practical significance. It is locating this line that the *Erie* cases are all about: the line that marks the choice of law as a matter of judicial deference rather than as a matter of constitutional compulsion. Therefore, this line defines for federal actions the actual realms for federal law and for state law.

(3) More Easy Cases. Whenever an issue entails such high federal interest as to raise a question of the federal courts' constitutional obligation to choose federal law, we are back where we began this constitutional discussion. Albeit rarely, sometimes the Constitution actually dictates a choice in favor of federal law, and of course this is binding. But federal law will almost invariably apply on that issue anyway, by virtue of the federal choice-of-law process. Therefore, such an issue presents another easy case, and the court need not face any constitutional question.

In this sense, it can be concluded that the Constitution does not enter into solving the usual choice-of-law problem under the *Erie* doctrine. Any doubts in the hard cases under current doctrine could be resolved in favor of either the federal law or the state law— resolved either by Congress or by the federal courts—without substantial fear of *unconstitutional* usurpation or derogation of state or federal powers. This leaves Congress and the federal courts largely free, as far as constitutional powers go, to rationalize and rework the *Erie* doctrine.

2. Legislative Limits on Choice

After relegating the Constitution to its proper background role, we face the next question. To what extent can Congress, either directly or through an authorized administrative delegate, limit the power of the federal courts to choose the applicable law in federal court?

a. Theory

As already suggested, within constitutional limits Congress can expressly or impliedly make the *choice of law between state and federal law* for actions litigated in federal court, and its choice will bind the federal courts.[10] If Congress chooses the applicable law, the only choice-of-law question remaining for the courts is whether that choice was constitutionally valid, because the Constitution imposes the only bounds on the congressional power. And those bounds are very loose.

If Congress chooses federal law, it can also specify the *content of that federal law*,[11] although it sometimes delegates to the federal courts the task of generating part or all of that federal law.[12] It now becomes important to keep clear in one's mind the distinction between choosing the applicable law and specifying its content.

b. Practice

Congress has made this choice of law, choosing either federal or state law, in countless specific statutes. Antitrust law is federal because Congress says it is, for example. For the antitrust area, Congress chose federal law and also specified its substantive content.

Conceivably, the above-quoted RDA broadly made a choice in favor of state law. However, neither the development of the *Erie* doctrine nor its current condition is consistent with a view that the RDA actively affects the choice-of-law process. That is, the judicial interpretation of the RDA has significantly softened the impact of its words. A question is how the courts have done this.

"Laws of the Several States." It is possible to argue that these words of the RDA retain a narrow meaning. *Swift* read them

---

10. Compare, e.g., Fed. R. Evid. 302 (state law governs some presumptions in federal court), with, e.g., id. 407 (federal law governs admissibility in federal court of subsequent remedial measures).

11. E.g., id. 601 (competency).

12. E.g., id. 501 (privilege).

to mean state legislation and local usages but not general common law. *Swift* went on to claim for the federal courts a broad lawmaking power with respect to general common law. The *Erie* case stated its view that as a matter of statutory construction this narrow reading of "laws of the several states" had been erroneous, but under the dictates of stare decisis it left that construction intact. In the realm of general common law outside the RDA, *Erie* invoked the Constitution to strike down the judicial practice under *Swift* and then began the process of shaping a new judicial practice under the *Erie* regime.

Thus, *Erie* arguably left undisturbed *Swift*'s narrow reading of the RDA. However, any such narrowness possibly still implicit in the term "laws of the several states" is without practical significance in applying the RDA. The reason is that when *Erie* addressed the federal courts' power outside the statute, *Erie* observed that the RDA was merely declarative of the rule that would exist in its absence.[13] Therefore, the inherent restrictions on the federal courts' power in the realm of general common law would henceforth be equivalent to the congressionally imposed restrictions on their power in the realm of state legislation and local usages covered by the RDA. That is, the courts' power in the common-law realm is the same as their power in the realm covered by 28 U.S.C. § 1652. So, no matter how broadly or narrowly one has decided to read the RDA, today nothing turns on whether the relevant state law is statutory law or decisional law.

Nevertheless, this realization that the old statutory reading of "laws of the several states" could be left undisturbed helps to clarify the *Erie* decision itself. This key insight—that *Erie* faced a judicially assumed power that could be struck down without declaring unconstitutional the plain or construed meaning of any congressional directive—explains how Justice Brandeis (much to Justice Butler's distress) was able to avoid compliance with the statute requiring certification to the Attorney General when the constitutionality of an act of Congress is drawn in question.[14] It also explains Justice Brandeis's qualification in closing: "In disapproving that [*Swift*] doctrine we do not hold unconstitutional [the RDA] or any other act of Congress. We merely declare that in applying the doctrine this Court and the lower courts have invaded rights which in our opinion are reserved by the Constitution to the several states."[15] In other words, Congress had not enacted the federal

---

13. See Mason v. United States, 260 U.S. 545, 559 (1923) ("The statute, however, is merely declarative of the rule which would exist in the absence of the statute.").

14. 28 U.S.C. § 2403(a).

15. 304 U.S. at 79–80.

common law, nor had Congress told the federal courts to create it, so *Erie* did not pass on Congress's power to do either such thing.

"In Cases Where They Apply." This language is not significant either. It seems merely to make the obvious point that state law should apply only where relevant. Thus, for example, state tort law would apply only in tort cases.

"Except Where the Constitution or Treaties of the United States or Acts of Congress Otherwise Require or Provide." This clause is the RDA's key exception, allowing the federal courts to apply federal law where the Constitution, treaties, or federal statutes "otherwise require or provide." There are various ways this exception could be read. However, the federal courts now seem to read it sensibly as not only accommodating express federal constitutional and statutory directives but also preserving a judicial choice-of-law power otherwise required or provided by the whole federal constitutional and statutory scheme. Thus, the RDA, when applicable, provides that *state law presumptively applies* in federal court—applying except when the Constitution, a treaty or federal statute, or the judicially developed choice-of-law technique displaces it.

In this sense, the RDA declares the status quo and incorporates the *Erie* jurisprudence by reference. So, if Congress has not made the choice of law by a more specific statute, then the RDA leaves the courts to make the choice under the *Erie* doctrine.

3. Judicial Techniques for Choice

The remaining basic question is how a federal court should choose between state and federal law for application to a particular issue in a case before it, in those circumstances where the federal courts are free under the Constitution and federal legislation to go either way. That is, when neither the Constitution nor Congress has determined the law applicable to a particular situation, how should a federal court exercise its residual choice-of-law power (and hence its potential lawmaking power)?

The federal court is not determining whether pre-existing federal law *already* covers the question, because if the law did, the court would not be dealing with a situation of silence by the lawmakers above the court in the lawmaking hierarchy. Instead, the situation is one where the court is free to choose, and therefore it truly is choosing. It must look at federalism policies somehow to decide if federal law *should* govern. If so, and because that federal law does not already exist, the court then must create the federal law, most often by analogy or adoption. That is, once the court chooses federal law, it must extend and hence make federal law, which thereafter exists and applies by stare decisis.

Since 1938 the Supreme Court, with the lower federal courts in tow, has progressed through a sequence of choice-of-law techniques for judicially handling the *Erie* problem. But the Court has not yet arrived at any truly clear or optimal solution.

a. Erie

On its facts, *Erie* ruled that in a diversity tort case, state law governed the issue of the plaintiff's status as trespasser or licensee. The Court did make clear that nothing turned on whether the state law was statutory law or decisional law. But *Erie* did not further explain its technique for choosing between state and federal law. Apparently, Justice Brandeis saw the choice in the case before the Court as a relatively easy one, treating it by assumption. Clearly this case presented an issue appropriate for state law (even though the case involved a railroad in interstate commerce). The Court's implicit treatment seemed to be that if anything in federal court was to be governed by state law, this issue would be.

That is, Justice Brandeis made no real effort to provide any comprehensible formula for solution of this choice-of-law problem that he had just imposed on the federal courts. All he offered on the problem was an exposition on the undesirability of applying federal law in federal court to issues of state concern like the issue before the Court: differences in applicable law between federal and state courts (1) fostered forum-shopping between the two court systems, (2) put the person who had a choice between the two systems in an unfairly favored position, and (3) infringed on the states' authority. The only guidance, then, was that these considerations would be relevant in resolving future state-federal conflicts.

Thus, the *Erie* case was surely a fountainhead, but not an especially voluble or eloquent one. By rediscovering the essence of federalism *Erie* may have worked a revolution, but it displayed little interest in the details of establishing a new government. The latter task was left to the progeny of *Erie*.

b. Substance/Procedure Test

Despite the marked absence of any formula in *Erie*'s majority opinion—of any "endeavor to formulate scientific legal terminology"[16]—the federal courts in the late 1930s and early 1940s seized upon a substance/procedure dichotomy as the test for choosing between state and federal law. Interestingly enough, Justice Brandeis's opinion in *Erie* makes no mention of the substance/procedure distinction that one sees in later cases; in fact, the word "proce-

---

16. Guaranty Trust Co. v. York, 326 U.S. 99, 109 (1945).

dure" never appears, and the word "substantive" appears only once in a somewhat different context.[17] Instead, the substance/procedure test seems to have been taken from the concurring opinion of Justice Reed, particularly from his statement that the "line between procedural and substantive law is hazy but no one doubts federal power over procedure";[18] indeed, several of the problems of subsequent misinterpretation of *Erie* seem to stem from Justice Reed's restatement of the majority's position.

In any event, seeking refuge from the difficulties of the choice-of-law problem imposed by *Erie*, the later courts succumbed to the attractions of apparent certainty in the crude and mechanical method of adjudication suggested by the familiar but deceptive dichotomy between substance and procedure. If the issue was one of substantive law, then state law applied; if procedural, then federal law governed. Although the deficiencies of such a test did not go completely unnoticed at the time, this simplistic technique came to be accepted by the lower courts and, quite possibly, by the Supreme Court itself in *Cities Service Oil Co. v. Dunlap*.[19]

This mechanical jurisprudence was not to continue indefinitely, as we shall see. Today the substance/procedure test is dead. Courts still use those terms in the *Erie* context, but they use them in a very different way. Under the old substance/procedure test, if the issue was deemed one of substantive law, then state law applied, and if procedural, then federal law governed. Today, if state law applies, the court will label the issue as substantive, and if federal law governs, the court will label the issue as procedural. But now these are merely conclusory labels. That is, modern courts do not look to the substance/procedure divide to decide the *Erie* question. Instead, courts use some later-developed methodology to decide the *Erie* question, and then use these handy labels to encapsulate their conclusion.

c. *Outcome-determinative Test*

In *Guaranty Trust Co. v. York*,[20] the pendulum swung back toward a more sensitive and flexible choice-of-law methodology. The issue was whether a state statute of limitations barring recovery on a state-created claim was binding in federal court. Although the applicability of a statute of limitations had traditionally been thought a procedural question in many contexts, Justice Frankfurter refused to apply federal law and emphatically rejected as dys-

---

17. 304 U.S. at 78.

18. Id. at 92.

19. 308 U.S. 208 (1939) (state law governs burden of proof on matter gov-erned by state law); see also Palmer v. Hoffman, 318 U.S. 109 (1943).

20. 326 U.S. 99 (1945) (state statute of limitations applies to state-created claim).

functional the prior method of *Erie* decisionmaking. Abstract characterization of rules as procedural or substantive, he argued, is immaterial. A court should instead examine the context within which the characterization issue arose and weigh the relevant policies within that context. Within the *Erie* domain, an important policy is that "the outcome of the litigation in the federal court should be substantially the same, so far as legal rules determine the outcome of a litigation, as it would be if tried in a State court."[21] Frankfurter did not go on to catalogue all the possibly relevant policies in an *Erie*-type situation, but instead focused on this "outcome-determinative" notion, perhaps because that seemed to constitute a statement of relevant policy sufficient for deciding in favor of state law in the case before the Court. Nevertheless, *Guaranty Trust Co. v. York* had considerable significance in that it eliminated the crude and mechanical substance/procedure test and installed in its place an analysis more responsive to what the Court perceived to be the aims of *Erie*.

Although " '[o]utcome-determination' analysis was never intended to serve as a talisman,"[22] it surely was susceptible to being so transformed. The elaboration in *Guaranty Trust Co. v. York* of a major policy behind *Erie* could very well be interpreted as a statement of the only policy behind *Erie*. The seeming certainty of a crude and mechanical rule that dictated the choice of state law whenever federal law would "significantly affect the result"[23] provided a tempting alternative to the dreary task of examining each issue, identifying the particular policies involved, and weighing them in some ill-defined manner. And so, in later cases, the new approach sank back into oversimplification.

The Supreme Court yielded to the temptation of the simplistic outcome-determinative test in three different cases decided on the same day—*Ragan v. Merchants Transfer & Warehouse Co.*,[24] *Woods v. Interstate Realty Co.*,[25] and *Cohen v. Beneficial Industrial Loan Corp.*[26]—and again later in *Bernhardt v. Polygraphic Co. of America*.[27] In all four of these diversity cases, the Court held under the outcome-determinative test that state law must be applied, saying in *Cohen* that "in diversity cases the federal court administers the state system of law in all except details related to its own conduct

---

21. Id. at 109.

22. Hanna v. Plumer, 380 U.S. 460, 466–67 (1965).

23. Guaranty Trust Co. v. York, 326 U.S. 99, 109 (1945).

24. 337 U.S. 530 (1949) (state statute governs when action is deemed commenced for statute-of-limitations purposes).

25. 337 U.S. 535 (1949) (state statute closing courthouse doors to nonqualifying foreign corporations applies).

26. 337 U.S. 541 (1949) (state security-for-suit statute applies).

27. 350 U.S. 198 (1956) (state law applies on enforceability of agreements to arbitrate).

of business."[28] Although the actual results in those cases are arguably correct under more recent decisions, the narrow focus of the Court's opinions in those cases indicated that the outcome-determinative principle had no discernible limit and that the federal courts were on the path toward blind deference to any conflicting state law. This outcome-determinative stage of mechanical jurisprudence was soon to come to an end, however.

d. Interest Analysis

In *Byrd v. Blue Ridge Rural Electric Cooperative*,[29] the *Erie* pendulum swung back again to sensitive and flexible balancing of interests. The aim of the new approach was to interpret the competing laws by balancing state interests against federal interests, in order to see how far federal law should extend in light of its purposes. *Byrd* was a diversity action for damages brought by an injured workman, who met a defense that he was a statutory employee under South Carolina law and was therefore obliged to accept statutory compensation benefits as his exclusive remedy. The case's *Erie* issue was whether a certain fact-based element of this state-created defense should be decided by a judge, in accordance with South Carolina law, or by a jury, in accordance with federal practice. Bypassing a possible route along Seventh Amendment lines, the Court elaborated a more general threefold analysis that led to its choosing federal law.

First, the Court looked at the interests of the state, in light of all legitimate policies reflected by the content of its law, in having its legal rule applied in federal court on this particular issue. Here, South Carolina singled this defense out for decision by the judge, while all other factual issues in such cases went to the jury; but the state's interests in so doing were weak, as the state rule appeared to be primarily the result of historical accident. *Second*, the Court examined the federal interests in having federal law govern, calling these interests "affirmative countervailing considerations." Here those interests were considerable, there being a federal interest in uniformly controlling the judge-jury relationship in the federal courts and also a federal policy in favor of having the jury decide contestable fact questions. *Third*, the Court acknowledged an off-setting federal interest in uniform enforcement of state-created rights and duties. Here the outcome-determinative effect of granting a jury trial as opposed to a bench trial was not too weighty, however, as the likelihood of a different result seemed not great. Finally, using this complex approach—(1) the state's interests balanced against the difference of (2) affirmative countervailing con-

---

28. 337 U.S. at 555.   **29.** 356 U.S. 525 (1958).

siderations less (3) outcome-determinative effect—the Court concluded that the federal jury practice should apply.

Justice Brennan's sensitive and flexible approach in *Byrd* rejected simplistic tests and represented a hearty embrace of all the goals implicit in *Erie*. It still stands as the clearest and most complete exposition of the interest-analysis approach to the *Erie* problem. But it seemed unpredictably malleable, and it imposed on the courts the heavy practical burden of carefully discerning and delicately weighing all competing state and federal interests involved in the particular issue. The lower courts after *Byrd* did their struggling best to apply the new approach.

e. Hanna

In *Hanna v. Plumer*,[30] the Court attempted to afford a degree of relief by reinjecting some certainty. The issue there, as framed by the Court, was whether in a diversity case service of process shall be made in the manner prescribed by state law or in the manner set forth in Federal Rule of Civil Procedure 4. In holding that federal law controlled, Chief Justice Warren distinguished these situations in which the state law in question conflicted with a Federal Rule from those situations in which no Federal Rule was in point.

First, the *Hanna* Court held that whenever a valid Federal Rule is in point, as the service-of-process Rule supposedly was in that case, the Rule applies. The Court declared, for somewhat unclear reasons, the whole *Erie* line of cases inapposite when a Rule is in point. The Rule need only be valid under the Constitution, as very broadly read in *Hanna*, and under the Rules Enabling Act, as very permissively interpreted in *Sibbach v. Wilson & Co.*[31] This "*Hanna-Sibbach*" test effectively insulates the Federal Rules from attack. At any rate, Rule 4 clearly passed muster under the validity test, and it was therefore to govern in the case at hand.

Second, in extended dicta, the *Hanna* Court considered the application of *Erie* when no Federal Rule is in point. Here *Erie* was to govern still. There is some play in how the Court's dicta should be read. On the surface, at least, the Court formulated a *refined* version of the outcome-determinative test. Under this "*Hanna-Erie*" test, the federal courts should not look to mere differences in outcome, but look only to differences in law that would undermine "the twin aims of the *Erie* rule: discouragement of forum-shopping and avoidance of inequitable administration of the laws."[32] By this phrase, the Court apparently referred to the federal interest in

30. 380 U.S. 460 (1965).   **32.** 380 U.S. at 468.
31. 312 U.S. 1 (1941).

avoiding those differences in the laws applied in the federal court and in the forum state court that (1) would inflict the systemic costs of forum-shopping by plaintiff or defendant between federal and state courts or (2) would cause the unfairness of treating similarly situated persons differently given that certain classes of people have a choice of court systems. Thus, the federal courts should apply state law when necessary to avoid differences that are significant in such ways.

Hanna signaled a major retreat from *Byrd* balancing toward mechanical jurisprudence, which would now entail two mechanical rules. And the signal was received, as the lower courts came to apply mechanically the *Hanna* holding as to the Federal Rules and, albeit somewhat less mechanically, the *Hanna* dicta redefining the outcome-determinative test for the legal world beyond the Federal Rules.

Nevertheless the courts had some difficulty in following *Hanna*. In gross terms, *Hanna-Sibbach* ignored relevant state interests, and *Hanna-Erie* ignored relevant federal interests. Furthermore, the *Hanna* opinion failed to reject definitively the more precise *Byrd* approach of interest analysis. Consequently, some lower courts launched significant rebellions against both *Hanna-Sibbach* and *Hanna-Erie*, with the rebels resorting to ad hoc balancing of state and federal interests in cases where the simplistic *Hanna* formulations yielded a result that seemed to conflict with the broader aim of *Erie* and *Byrd* to reconcile state and federal interests. All this left the *Erie* doctrine in considerable confusion.

For example, a circuit court case, which was decided right after *Hanna*, demonstrated the inadequacy of *Hanna*'s refined outcome-determinative test.[33] The court faced a state door-closing statute, in an airplane crash case with out-of-state plaintiffs litigating an out-of-state cause of action against an out-of-state corporation as well as against an in-state defendant. Under *Hanna* and *Woods*, the outcome-determinative effect, or primarily the policy against intrastate forum-shopping, would have seemed to call for application of the state law. However, a closer examination of the interests involved showed that no state interests were at stake, this state statute apparently expressing only the desire to keep such a claim between nonresidents off the state-court docket, a desire akin to that of forum non conveniens; on the other hand, significant federal interests in nondiscriminatorily providing a forum for joined multistate parties would have been defeated by application of the state law. Hence, the federal court refused to apply the state door-closing

---

33. Szantay v. Beech Aircraft Corp., 349 F.2d 60 (4th Cir. 1965); see also, e.g., Masino v. Outboard Marine Corp., 652 F.2d 330 (3d Cir. 1981) (expressly applying Byrd); Davis v. Piper Aircraft Corp., 615 F.2d 606, 612 (4th Cir. 1980); Miller v. Davis, 507 F.2d 308, 314 (6th Cir. 1974).

statute. The court's refusal can be explained most easily by its attention to those affirmative countervailing federal considerations, an attention authorized not by *Hanna* but by *Byrd*. Thus, *Hanna* was put under attack, as this court and others shifted away from its dual mechanical rules toward a more flexible approach reminiscent of *Byrd*, an approach that might have been called *Hanna-Byrd*.[34]

f. Gasperini

In *Gasperini v. Center for Humanities, Inc.*,[35] the Court, by Justice Ginsburg, uttered its most recent major words on *Erie*, but failed miserably to make them clear ones. The case held in a diversity case, first, that New York's tort-reform interests called for applying its intrusive new-trial standard for setting aside a jury verdict in the federal district court, but, second, that federal interests called for applying the deferential federal standard of appellate review in the federal court of appeals. Thus, the Court's compromise applied state law on one of the case's *Erie* issues and federal law on the other.

However, the Court's holding required a crabbed reading of Federal Rule of Civil Procedure 59, to the effect that the Rule does not cover the standard for the trial judge's review of jury decision-making. This approach implies that *Hanna-Sibbach* will henceforth be applied narrowly,[36] thus rejecting earlier cases that had suggested a willingness to read the Federal Rules' reach more broadly.[37]

Moreover, the case undercut *Hanna-Erie* by reimposing an ad hoc approach to balancing. This approach surprisingly allowed the Court to apply state law to the trial judge's scrutiny of the jury decision, a matter that lies in the heartland of the judge-jury relationship and that by *Byrd*'s holding had been seemingly confided to federal law. As the different result on the appellate *Erie* issue in *Gasperini* proved, the courts must balance interests issue-by-issue: only this approach will allow state law to apply on one issue, while federal law governs another. On each issue, the courts must now weigh the very specific state and federal interests at stake in the particular case, leaving little room for applying stare decisis:

---

34. For developments on the Hanna–Sibbach front analogous to these on the Hanna–Erie front, compare Marshall v. Mulrenin, 508 F.2d 39, 44–45 (1st Cir. 1974) (applying more permissive state law in the face of the conflicting Fed. R. Civ. P. 15(c), which has since been amended), with Welch v. La. Power & Light Co., 466 F.2d 1344 (5th Cir. 1972) (declining to apply state law less permissive than 15(c)).

35. 518 U.S. 415 (1996), criticized in C. Douglas Floyd, Erie Awry: A Com-

ment on Gasperini v. Center for Humanities, Inc., 1997 BYU L. Rev. 267, 290–305.

36. See also Semtek Int'l Inc. v. Lockheed Martin Corp., 531 U.S. 497, 503–04 (2001) (narrowly reading Fed. R. Civ. P. 41).

37. See, e.g., Burlington N.R.R. v. Woods, 480 U.S. 1 (1987) (broadly reading Fed. R. App. P. 38).

only this approach will allow federal judge-jury law to prevail over South Carolina's weak interests in a *Byrd*-type case, while subjugating it to New York's stronger tort-reform interests in a *Gasperini*-type case.

In sum, *Gasperini* preserves *Hanna-Sibbach*, but only in a narrowed realm for the Federal Rules. Outside the Rules, *Gasperini* seems to embrace modern interest analysis as the appropriate *Erie* methodology—(1) the state's interests balanced against the net sum of (2) affirmative countervailing considerations less (3) the forum-shopping and inequality effects of any outcome-determinative difference between state and federal law—this formula basically being the *Byrd* formula but with its outcome-determinative element replaced by *Hanna-Erie*'s quite proper refinement of that element.

Certainly, *Gasperini* is neither the final word nor the correct word on this subject, but it is an important word. Nothing very solid can be said about today's *Erie* doctrine without accounting for *Gasperini*.

g. Precepts for Applying Judicial Technique

Regardless of the choice-of-law technique adopted, certain precepts are observed by the federal courts.

What Is the Role of the Type of Jurisdiction? The type of subject-matter jurisdiction, such as diversity of citizenship or federal question, is not determinative on the *Erie* problem. The choice-of-law technique applies issue-by-issue in each case, not case-by-case.

So, in a diversity case, certain issues will be governed by federal law.[38] And although heightened federal interests will call for federal law on most issues in a federal question case, some issues of great state concern may be governed by state law, as for example an issue of mortgage law arising in bankruptcy proceedings.[39]

Which State Supplies the Governing Law? This was yet another one of those points left open by the *Erie* case. Justice Brandeis assumed the law of the place of the wrong governed, but did not explain why. The Supreme Court has since rejected his assumption, instead adopting the so-called *Klaxon* rule that, in connection with matters governed by state law under *Erie*, the forum state's law governs horizontal choice of law.[40]

---

38. See, e.g., Bank of Am. Nat'l Trust & Sav. Ass'n v. Parnell, 352 U.S. 29 (1956) (overdueness of U.S. bonds in diversity case).

39. See, e.g., United States v. Yazell, 382 U.S. 341 (1966) (family law issue in federal loan case).

40. Klaxon Co. v. Stentor Elec. Mfg. Co., 313 U.S. 487 (1941).

Klaxon's holding—that a federal court in this diversity case, in order to avoid intrastate differences in result, must apply the forum state's conflicts rules—has been subject to vigorous and continuous criticism by distinguished commentators, almost from the very day of its decision. Arguments are made that the advantage of *Klaxon* in eliminating intrastate forum-shopping are offset by the consequent availability of opportunities for interstate forum-shopping. Moreover, *Klaxon* absorbs parochial state choice-of-law doctrine into the potentially neutral federal forum, while preventing the federal judiciary from developing rational and equitable horizontal choice-of-law rules—despite the unique capacity of the federal courts for exactly that task and despite the essentially federal nature of those choice-of-law problems. Nevertheless, *Klaxon* has enjoyed almost undeviating support in the courts and has enlisted its own group of eminent defenders among the commentators. The arguments on this side are that state conflicts rules embody significant state interests and that, after all, intrastate forum-shopping is a more serious danger than shopping among states' laws.

Although the *Klaxon* rule certainly entails many complexities not even hinted at here, it can safely be said that its wisdom remains a close question.[41] Yet, *Klaxon* is the clearly established law.[42] So, to find the potentially applicable nonfederal law for any matter in a case, federal law tells the federal courts to look to the forum state's choice-of-law doctrine. That state doctrine will tell which state's (or country's) law would govern that matter if nonfederal law were to be applied.

How Is the Content of State Law Determined? Sometimes there is no clear state law on a particular matter to be governed under *Erie* by state law. Justice Brandeis in *Erie* bobbled this one too. Today, when facing unclear state law, the federal trial or appellate court should fabricate whatever state law governs as if it were then sitting as the forum state's highest court, taking into account all the latest precedent and other data that court would.[43]

---

41. Compare Henry M. Hart, Jr., The Relations Between State and Federal Law, 54 Colum. L. Rev. 489, 513–15, 541–42 (1954) (critical), with David F. Cavers, The Choice-of-Law Process 216–24 (1965) (supportive).

42. See Day & Zimmermann, Inc. v. Challoner, 423 U.S. 3 (1975) (Klaxon applies without exceptions, no matter how appealing the facts—even when U.S. servicemen, maimed and killed in an unpopular war far from home, are left without recovery by Texas's seemingly purposeless application of a very foreign and rather regressive Cambodian

law); Griffin v. McCoach, 313 U.S. 498 (1941) (Klaxon applies even when the forum state court could not have entertained the action, such as a statutory interpleader case).

43. See Comm'r v. Estate of Bosch, 387 U.S. 456, 465 (1967); DeWeerth v. Baldinger, 38 F.3d 1266 (2d Cir. 1994); cf. Webber v. Sobba, 322 F.3d 1032 (8th Cir. 20003) (arguably overactive interpretation of state law); see also Salve Regina College v. Russell, 499 U.S. 225 (1991) (ordering nondeferential review by the courts of appeals of the district court's Erie guess, because such review

Alternatively, the federal court may use the potentially burdensome and troublesome procedure of certifying an unsettled question concerning a state's law directly to that state's highest court, if that state has made provision for responding to such certified questions.[44] Although certification does sometimes offer a neat means of avoiding the anomaly of different answers to the same question of law from a state and a federal court, this neat solution comes at a stiff price. First, certification inevitably causes some delay and increased expense for the parties. At the least, this requires the federal court to balance the equities involved, taking into account the type of question and the circumstances of the particular case. Second, certification imposes a burden on the state court. The unavoidably abstract nature of the question may make it difficult to answer; indeed, certification may run aground if the state has a constitutional prohibition against giving advisory opinions. Third, certification poses a possible threat to the judicial function of the federal courts in diversity cases. The effect may be to diminish their authority and their sense of responsibility.

When Does Federal Law Apply in Federal Court? Obviously, federal law very often applies in federal question cases and often even in diversity cases, as a consequence either of a constitutional or congressional choice or of a judicial choice-of-law decision. Oftentimes when federal law governs by nonjudicial choice, the Constitution or Congress formulates the content of the applicable federal law, which of course is then binding on the federal courts.

In all situations when federal law governs, but the Constitution and Congress have not formulated the applicable federal law, the federal courts must step in by formulating *federal common law*. This is occasionally termed "specialized federal common law," to distinguish it from the general common law that the federal courts formerly created under *Swift*.

Realm of Federal Common Law. The Constitution or Congress may have chosen federal law, but neither has formulated that law's content. In that situation, the courts must formulate the law. For example, the federal courts might have to formulate federal common law pursuant to a congressional delegation of power that chose federal law but left it to the courts to formulate it.[45]

Or the federal courts might on their own choose federal law, and thus also have to formulate its content. A prime example of such federal common law lies in *Clearfield Trust Co. v. United*

"best serves the dual goals of doctrinal coherence and economy of judicial administration," even in the Erie setting).

44. See Lehman Bros. v. Schein, 416 U.S. 386 (1974); Clay v. Sun Ins. Office Ltd., 363 U.S. 207 (1960).

45. See, e.g., Fed. R. Evid. 501 (privilege).

States,[46] where, perhaps questionably, the Court chose and created federal law to govern rights and duties of the United States on its commercial paper. When will the federal courts on their own choose federal law? This problem, sometimes called the *Clearfield* problem, is little more than a facet of the *Erie* problem. If the judicial choice-of-law technique developed under *Erie* ends up pointing to federal law rather than state law, then the federal courts must choose and then formulate the chosen federal law, as was done in *Clearfield.*

Adopting State Law as Federal Common Law. In formulating the content of federal common law, federal courts sometimes purely create common law and sometimes simply extend some closely related or analogous federal statutory provision.[47] But often federal courts opt to adopt the appropriate state's law concerning the point in issue, which law is already formulated (although it may vary from state to state).[48]

Adoption of state law is a simple route to take, tends to reduce the federal courts' involvement in lawmaking, and might also serve to accommodate any state interests that may be involved. Indeed, whenever unformulated federal law governs by virtue of the *Clearfield* balance, there is a rebuttable presumption in favor of adopting state law as the federal common law. That is, federal courts should so adopt state law, unless there is a relatively significant federal interest in uniformity of the federal law throughout the nation or there are relatively important federal interests calling for a particular content to the federal law or for particular limits on the content.[49]

Such optional adoption of state law as the federal law is distinguishable from the binding application of state law in federal court under *Erie* in two big ways. First, when adopting a state's law as the federal common law, federal courts can adopt the appropri-

46. 318 U.S. 363 (1943) (effect of United States' delay in notifying check's endorser of forgery); see also Boyle v. United Techs. Corp., 487 U.S. 500 (1988) (military contractors' liability).

47. See, e.g., Agency Holding Corp. v. Malley–Duff & Assocs., 483 U.S. 143 (1987) (civil RICO action subjected to Clayton Act's four-year limitations period).

48. See, e.g., Owens v. Okure, 488 U.S. 235 (1989) (in absence of federal statute of limitations for federally created claim, federal courts ordinarily should adopt the basic aspects of the forum state's statute of limitations for the most closely analogous general type of state cause of action). But cf. 28 U.S.C. § 1658 (statute enacted in 1990

and providing a limitations period for future federal enactments); Jones v. R.R. Donnelley & Sons Co., 541 U.S. 369 (2004) (§ 1658 applicable if the claim was made possible by a post–1990 statutory amendment). See generally Mitchell A. Lowenthal et al., Special Project, Time Bars in Specialized Federal Common Law: Federal Rights of Action and State Statutes of Limitations, 65 Cornell L. Rev. 1011 (1980).

49. See United States v. Kimbell Foods, Inc., 440 U.S. 715 (1979) (in absence of federal statute treating priority of liens in connection with federal loans, federal courts should adopt the priority scheme of the appropriate state as long as that scheme is nondiscriminatory).

ate state's law, rather than the law that the forum state would apply. Second, federal courts can reject state law that impinges on federal interests, so that a federal court may alter or ignore part or all of the relevant state law in the particular case at bar.[50]

h. Summary

In clearly "substantive" areas of great state concern, state law rather surely governs in federal court, sometimes even by constitutional necessity. As one moves into more "procedural" areas of some state concern, the hard *Erie* cases arise—and so do the hot disputes over the proper methodology. Finally, as one moves into areas of strong federal concern, such as clearly "substantive" areas of great federal interest, federal law surely applies, sometimes even by constitutional command. The following diagram suggests this scheme. The relative intensity of state interests in having state law applied in federal court increases with distance from the center of the diagram:

50. See, e.g., Holmberg v. Armbrecht, 327 U.S. 392 (1946) (federal tolling notion read into state statute of limitations for particular federal suit on federally created claim).

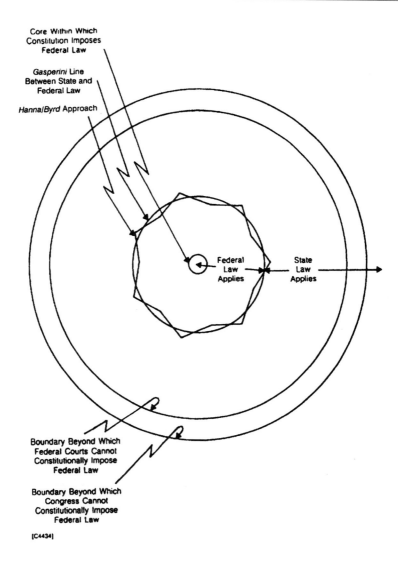

Core Within Which
Constitution Imposes
Federal Law

Gasperini Line
Between State and
Federal Law

Hanna/Byrd Approach

Federal
Law
Applies

State
Law
Applies

Boundary Beyond Which
Federal Courts Cannot
Constitutionally Impose
Federal Law

Boundary Beyond Which
Congress Cannot
Constitutionally Impose
Federal Law

[C4434]

Looking back over the history of the attempts to draw the *Erie* line between state and federal law, one can see that the courts have been regularly oscillating from some certain but inaccurate fixed test to a precise but uncertain ad hoc balancing approach, back to a certain but inaccurate test, and so on. The following diagram depicts and evaluates the history of judicial choice-of-law techniques that tried to answer the *Erie* problem (not the cases' specific results), with the passage of time progressing down the page:

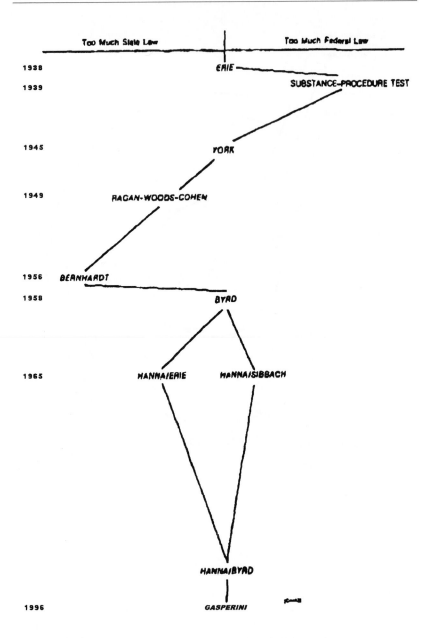

At any rate, the law today seems to be that the Constitution or Congress may make a definitive choice of law, and also that federal law prevails if a Federal Rule covers the matter. Otherwise, when the choice of law is left to the courts, they evaluate (1) the state's interests, in light of all legitimate purposes or policies reflected by the content of its law, in having its legal rule applied in federal court on this particular issue, in order to see if they equal or outweigh the net sum of (2) the federal interests in having federal law govern, which are called affirmative countervailing considerations, and (3) the negative federal interest in avoiding the forum-shopping and inequality effects of any outcome-determinative difference between state and federal law.

Despite the sound of that, this methodology does not in fact leave the question of governing law terribly unclear. In federal court today, state law will routinely apply in many situations. And federal law very often applies in federal question cases and often even in diversity cases, as a consequence either of a constitutional or congressional choice or of an already decided or relatively predictable judicial choice-of-law decision. The lack of clarity on vertical choice of law extends only to a relatively small group of hard cases, and therein lies the explanation of how our system can live with the lack of clarity.

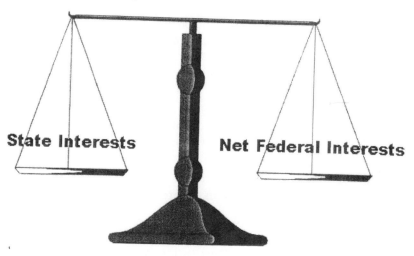

State Interests   **Net Federal Interests**

B. Federal Law in State Court

In determining the applicable law *in state court*, we have a slightly different problem. In this so-called reverse-*Erie* setting, unlike in the *Erie* setting of federal courts, the relevant federal law will always be essentially pre-existing. This fact brings the Supremacy Clause into play. Accordingly, reverse-*Erie* and *Erie* do not strictly involve the same task for courts: *Erie* is telling the federal court when to create federal law, while reverse-*Erie* is telling the state court when to apply existing federal law under the command of the Supremacy Clause.

This reverse-*Erie* question—whether federal law should displace state law under the Supremacy Clause—is a simple one if the

Constitution or Congress, the latter acting within constitutional limits, actually chose to displace state law in state court, expressly or impliedly. If so, that choice is binding on the state courts under the Supremacy Clause. But in the absence of such a constitutional or congressional directive, the state courts and ultimately the U.S. Supreme Court must decide whether the existing federal law applies in state court.

The courts do so by employing a choice-of-law technique mandated by the Supreme Court and similar to the *Erie* technique. If that technique yields a choice in favor of federal law, that choice is binding on the state courts under the Supremacy Clause. Thus, *Hinderlider v. La Plata River & Cherry Creek Ditch Co.*,[51] an interstate water case decided in an opinion by Justice Brandeis on the same day as *Erie*, held that substantive federal common law, which would govern in the federal courts,[52] also binds the state courts. But if that technique yields a choice in favor of state law, the state is left free to create and apply it. Thus, *Oregon ex rel. State Land Board v. Corvallis Sand & Gravel Co.*,[53] on review of the Oregon Supreme Court, held that state law solely governed the disputed ownership of lands along a navigable river inside the state, after the lands had become riverbed because of avulsive changes in the river's course.

The fact is that a great amount of federal law—be it constitutional, statutory, or common law—flows down to apply in state courts.

1. Constitutional Limits on Choice

Not unlike the *Erie* scheme, there are constitutional limits on the powers of Congress and the Supreme Court to choose the applicable law. The Federal Constitution itself made some binding choices of federal law for state courts. The Due Process Clause of the Fourteenth Amendment provides a nice example.

Conversely, the constitutional limits on imposing federal law on the state courts are quite significant. The federal government cannot extend federal law beyond the relevant boundary demarking the matters constitutionally reserved to the states.

2. Legislative Limits on Choice

Just as for *Erie*, Congress can expressly or impliedly make the choice between state and federal law for application in state court,

---

51.   304 U.S. 92 (1938).

52.   See id. at 110; Illinois v. City of Milwaukee, 406 U.S. 91, 103 (1972).

53.   429 U.S. 363 (1977).

but of course only within constitutional limits. A valid congressional choice will bind the state courts.

Congress frequently makes an express choice for federal law. For example, in some areas, such as patents, Congress can decide to regulate and then specify substantive laws that will apply in federal and state courts henceforth. When it does so act, analysts frequently draw on the terminology of the preemption doctrine.[54] They look to preemption because it is a Supremacy Clause doctrine related to the task of determining the reach of federal law.

Preemption, in brief, is an ill-bounded constitutional doctrine that invalidates state law if it interferes with federal law. Although preemption tends to focus on displacement of state substantive law by congressional statute, it can occur by constitutional command or federal administrative act or even by the effect of federal common law, and it can extend its effect beyond substantive law to state procedural law. Moreover, preemption can not only be express but also be implied; and implied preemption can trump a state provision that conflicts by discrimination against or contradiction to federal law or stands as an obstacle to federal law, or it can authorize federal law to occupy exclusively a whole field, although of course all these categories are blurry.

Preemption obviously constitutes an important but hitherto unmentioned part of *Erie* in federal court, calling for the application of much federal law in federal court without any resort to judicial balancing. Even more obviously, it is at work in state court too. It rejects any state law that impermissibly collides with federal law, and does so regardless of the outcome of any balancing methodology.

3. Judicial Techniques for Choice

Analogously to *Erie*, the courts must use some technique for choosing between state and federal law for application in state court, whenever they may under the Constitution and federal statutes, and in the absence of preemption, go either way.

a. *Methodology*

There is no clearly developed choice-of-law technique here. However, the developments on the *Erie* front shed some light. The courts employ a federally mandated choice-of-law technique seemingly similar to the one worked out by the *Erie* line of cases down through *Gasperini*.

---

54. See Erwin Chemerinsky, Constitutional Law: Principles and Policies § 5.2 (2d ed. 2002); Christopher R. Dra- hozal, The Supremacy Clause 84–86, 89–125 (2004).

Thus, courts facing the reverse-*Erie* problem generally appear to balance state interests in having state law applied in state court against federal interests in having federal law displace the rule of this particular state, while trying to avoid difference in outcome.[55] Note, however, that here the outcome-determinative effect now *adds* to the other federal interests in having federal law applied in state court, because applying federal law would avoid any outcome-determinative difference between federal and state courts.

If the state court thereby determines that federal law governs, then the state court applies it. That is, the state court will decide in accordance with "existing" federal law. The federal law might be constitutional, statutory, or common law; it might be purely federal, or it might involve state law adopted as federal common law; it might be fully formulated or more incipient. The state court may have to envisage a federal court's *Erie* analysis to determine the reach of federal law, but the state court is merely a federal-law-applier and will never act as a federal lawmaker in the true sense. Sometimes the state court has to be the very first to enunciate the federal law. It has authority to enunciate federal law, if it decides in accordance with other existing federal law by trying to discern what the federal courts would decide is the law—and not by undertaking to formulate federal law either in pursuit of strictly forward-looking policies that might guide a legislature or in accordance with general nonpositivist principles that might guide a law-creating court. That is, the state court should act as federal courts do when applying state law under *Erie*. In both the *Erie* setting and the reverse-*Erie* setting, the court's job is to apply the other sovereign's existing law, not to create law for it.

If the content of the governing federal law is really unclear, how should the state court determine what the federal law says? No undisputed answer exists to this pervasive and fundamental question, illustrating how unexplored all reverse-*Erie* matters remain. Specifically, the question of whether state courts are bound by lower federal courts on the federal law's content remains open. The better view—mainly trying to effectuate the constitutional status of state courts, while accepting some local disuniformity in the short term—is that the state court should try to determine what the U.S. Supreme Court would rule.[56] On the one hand, the state court

---

55. See Dice v. Akron, C. & Y.R.R., 342 U.S. 359 (1952) (in state-court FELA case, federal law governs jury right); Norfolk & W. Ry. v. Liepelt, 444 U.S. 490 (1980) (in state-court FELA case, federal law governs jury instruction).

56. See United States ex rel. Lawrence v. Woods, 432 F.2d 1072 (7th Cir.

1970); Hall v. Pa. Bd. of Prob. & Parole, 851 A.2d 859 (Pa. 2004). But see Yniguez v. Arizona, 939 F.2d 727 (9th Cir. 1991). See generally Donald H. Zeigler, Gazing into the Crystal Ball: Reflections on the Standards State Judges Should Use to Ascertain Federal Law, 40 Wm. & Mary L. Rev. 1143 (1999).

should not consider itself actually bound, rather than merely informed, by the local federal courts' rulings. On the other hand, the state court would naturally be bound under stare decisis by decisions within that state's hierarchy of courts as to the federal law's content. Note the profound implication of this view: it makes the state courts into judicial hierarchies that can independently enunciate federal law, parallel to the lower federal courts and the other states' courts, and subject only to rare U.S. Supreme Court review.

In practice, judicial choice of law works together with preemption. If the state and federal laws directly collide, then the state court must recognize that federal law preempts; if not, then the state court must perform the federally mandated accommodation of interests to choose the applicable law.[57] This judicial choice-of-law methodology complementarily smooths, while it explains, the outer reaches of preemption. On the one hand, in the setting that involves a matter more of inference by judge than of implication by statute, when state law would merely frustrate federal law, those *Erie*-like ideas provide refinement of how obstacle and field preemption should work: whenever federal interests outweigh state interests in an *Erie* sense, there should be preemption. On the other hand, as one gets into more independent judicial choice of law under reverse-*Erie*, the direct application of *Erie*-like ideas makes the precise location of the outer boundary of preemption unimportant, as that boundary becomes merely a transitional zone in the middle of the broad subject of reverse-*Erie*.

b. Summary

The reverse-*Erie* doctrine, comprising both preemption and judicial choice of law, tells the state court when to apply existing federal law to displace state law under the command of the Supremacy Clause. This, then, is the reverse-*Erie* doctrine: federal law—be it constitutional, statutory, or common law—will apply pursuant to the Supremacy Clause in state court, subject to the Constitution or Congress having already chosen the applicable law, whenever it preempts state law *or* whenever it prevails by an *Erie*-like judicial choice of law.

The end-product is that in areas of strong state concern, such as clearly "substantive" areas of great state interest, state law naturally governs in state court, often by constitutional necessity. As one moves into questions of access to state court on federally created claims and other more "procedural" areas of federal con-

---

57. Compare Felder v. Casey, 487 U.S. 131 (1988) (preempting state's notice-of-claim statute, for federal civil rights case in state court), with Johnson v. Fankell, 520 U.S. 911 (1997) (refusing to preempt state's appealability doctrine, for federal civil rights case in state court).

cern, the hard reverse-*Erie* cases arise. Finally, as one moves into clearly "substantive" areas of great federal concern, federal law more surely applies, sometimes even by direct constitutional command.

Reverse-*Erie* for state courts and *Erie* for federal courts are therefore nicely symmetric. However, the reverse-*Erie* scheme is not simply the mirror image of *Erie*. One major difference is that reverse-*Erie* seems to be the slightly more intrusive doctrine: in the middle and more-procedural area, state courts must apply federal law to federally created claims more extensively than federal courts must apply state law to state-created claims. Take the *Brown* case as an example, in which a plaintiff brought a Federal Employers' Liability Act case in a Georgia state court, and the defendant demurred; contrary to federal practice, a Georgia rule would have construed allegations most strongly against the pleader and so resulted in dismissal of the plaintiff's complaint with prejudice; but here in the state court the Georgia pleading rule had to bow to the more lenient federal practice.[58] In the analogous *Erie* setting of a diversity case, a federal court would never bow to such a state pleading practice.

The explanation for this discrepancy between reverse-*Erie* and *Erie* is that in state court the Supremacy Clause plays an additional role through conflict preemption, which works in favor of federal law by rejecting any state law that imposes unnecessary burdens upon federal rights. In the FELA pleading example, because the state's anti-plaintiff pleading rule conflicted with the pro-plaintiff FELA, it fell, regardless of any state interests. In the analogous *Erie* setting, where the question would be whether a state pro-plaintiff procedural provision must apply in a diversity case, the Supremacy Clause has no role to play, and the *Erie* balance manages to tilt in favor of federal procedural interests and hence call for applying federal pleading law under *Hanna-Sibbach*. That is, in *Brown* the Supremacy Clause causes federal procedure to preempt state procedure, but in converse-*Brown* the Supremacy Clause plays no comparable role to cause the state sovereign's law to trump any conflicting procedural rules of the home court. Thus, reverse-*Erie* for state courts and *Erie* for federal courts are not and should not be perfect mirror images.

C. Reform Proposal

To summarize the big picture of our federal system, in areas of clear state "substantive" concern, state law governs in both state and federal courts. As one moves into "procedural" areas, state law

58. Brown v. W. Ry., 338 U.S. 294 (1949).

tends to govern in state court and federal law tends to govern in federal court. Finally, as one moves into areas of clear federal "substantive" concern, federal law governs in both state and federal courts. So the interlocking *Erie* and reverse-*Erie* doctrines ultimately form a logical pattern. And that is not surprising, because both these situations involve similar problems of determining the appropriate reach of state and federal laws under a system of cooperative federalism, and any such problem has an accommodation of interests, against a background consciousness of federal supremacy, as its proper answer.[59]

Still, this area of law appears messy. Admittedly, there are profound complexities lurking here, necessarily imposed by the complications of federalism itself. However, there must be a better way for courts to make the choice of law. For clarity, let me speak about a better way specifically in the *Erie* context of federal courts, rather than expressly extending the discussion into reverse-*Erie* terms.

To blaze a better way, one must begin at the beginning. A classic theme in law is the clash between the demand for rule-based certainty and the desire for individualized precision—that is, between decisionmaking by mechanical rules and a sensitive approach based upon an ad hoc and flexible balancing of competing interests.[60] Each of the two polar approaches possesses its own distinct virtues and vices, so that over time courts tend to oscillate between those poles—that is, each time the courts embrace one particular polar approach, they recognize its imperfections and surrender to the allures of the other, and so the pendulum shortly thereafter swings back.[61] Looking back over the history of attempts to draw

59. See generally Kevin M. Clermont, Reverse–Erie, 82 Notre Dame L. Rev. 1 (2006).

60. See Frederic R. Coudert, Certainty and Justice 1 (1913) ("There is in all modern states to-day a general conflict between certainty in the law and concrete justice in its application to particular cases; in other words, between the effort to have a general rule everywhere equally applicable to all cases at all times and the effort to reach what may seem to be concrete right dealing between the parties at bar upon the particular facts in each case."); Paul Heinrich Neuhaus, Legal Certainty Versus Equity in the Conflict of Laws, 28 Law & Contemp. Probs. 795, 795 (1963) ("The struggle between legal certainty and equity is as old as the law itself. * * * One is the public interest in clear, equal, and foreseeable rules of law

* * *. The other is the need for deciding current, concrete disputes adequately, by giving due weight to the special and perhaps unique circumstances of each case.").

61. See Coudert, supra note 60, at 1, 12 ("In actual practice the pendulum swings first one way and then the other. * * * The truth is that the courts are constantly oscillating between a desire for certainty on the one hand and a desire for flexibility * * * upon the other."); Neuhaus, supra note 60, at 796 ("But the conflict between legal certainty and justice (equity) will never come to an end. In different countries and at different times, the one or the other of these twin objectives of the law will dominate; there is no permanent solution. Especially neither goal can replace the other.").

the *Erie* line between state and federal law, one can see that the courts have been regularly oscillating from some certain but inaccurate fixed test to an uncertain but precise balancing approach, back to a certain but inaccurate test, and so on.

The jurisprudential task is to still this pendulum by compromise, but at a point close to the right place.[62] The right line of division between state and federal law should lie at the point around which *Erie*'s judicial oscillation is dampening. The history also reveals that the lower courts have long perceived the need for some compromise between the sophisticated but uncertain interest analysis of *Byrd* and *Gasperini* and the somewhat more certain but simplistic tests such as the substance/procedure, outcome-determinative, and *Hanna* approaches. In recent years, during the *Hanna-Byrd* era, the lower courts were indeed meeting some success in stilling the pendulum at the right place by striking such a compromise.

The desirable compromise apparent in that case law was to create a series of fairly general rules that soundly made the choice between state and federal law for all the common situations, allocating one subject to federal law and another subject to state law and so on. For example, under *Hanna* federal law governs if a Federal Rule is in point, while under *Klaxon* state law governs horizontal choice of law. The long-term product of this compromise approach would be an extensive series of fairly workable and predictable general rules that, when laid end-to-end, approximate the line between state and federal law ideally mandated by the goals of *Erie*.[63]

A practical way to create and apply this series of general rules, and a way that had support in actual lower-court practice, was *initially* to apply a sophisticated interest-analysis approach to resolve the vertical choice-of-law problem for a broad area or "pocket" of the law, and *then* to rely on a tough stare decisis approach to prevent the resultant general rule from later being eaten up by exceptions in appealing cases.

First, the process of initially creating a general rule by balancing the interests involved across a broad pocket of the law actually entails two substeps:

---

62. See H.L.A. Hart, The Concept of Law 127 (1961); Roscoe Pound, Jurisprudence, in The History and Prospects of the Social Sciences 472–73 (Harry Elmer Barnes ed., 1925) ("Much of the administration of justice is a compromise between the tendency to treat each case as one of a generalized type of case, and the tendency to treat each case as unique. * * * One of the chief problems of jurisprudence is to adjust these tendencies * * *.").

63. Cf. Cavers, supra note 41, at 121–22, 139–203 (analogous approach of "principles of preference" for horizontal choice of law).

(1) Defining the Pocket. The initial difficulty obviously is to define the pocket. The solution for the court is to extend out from the instant case as far as the relevant state and federal interests remain substantially constant. But if the proper bounds of the pocket are not evident, as is likely, the court should resort to certain canons: (a) the court should opt for a pocket that can be described in a communicable form (this fosters the application of stare decisis); and (b) the court, if still in doubt, should lean toward defining the pocket broadly, even sweeping up narrow situations with aberrational state and federal interests (this fosters certainty in the application of the *Erie* doctrine). An example of a communicable pocket is the pocket comprising the Federal Rules; however, that pocket may be too broad, there being some doubt whether the relevant state and federal interests remain sufficiently constant throughout the pocket.

(2) Balancing the Interests. Next the court should establish the general rule that state law governs in the pocket, unless the state interests are overcome by the federal interests involved across the whole pocket. More precisely, the court should functionally weigh (a) the interests of the states generally in having state law applied in federal court to this particular pocket against the net federal interests, which are (b) the federal interests in having federal law govern in the pocket less (c) the federal interest in avoiding differences in the laws applied in the federal court and in the forum state court that would inflict the systemic costs of forum-shopping by plaintiff or defendant between federal and state courts or would cause the unfairness of treating similarly situated persons differently given that certain classes of people have a choice of court systems.

To make this process work well, the rule-establishing court's opinion should be maximally explanatory as to performance of these two substeps.

Second, once one of these general rules has been formulated, as many have been, it should normally be binding under stare decisis in the same court and lower courts. Those courts should resolve an *Erie* question otherwise of first impression by deduction from the relevant general rule. That general rule would resolve all future cases within its scope, even when a narrow and aberrational case involves state and federal interests that support a contrary resolution. That is, the later court could not create an explicit exception to the general rule, as that would be inconsistent with the proposed approach. Moreover, the later court should be very hesitant to escape the general rule by narrowly redefining the established pocket, because that in effect creates an exception and leads back down the road to ad hoc balancing. Only rarely, when the later court perceives such a stark imbalance of the relevant state and federal interests as almost to demand the contrary rule, should that court entertain the possibility of narrowly redefining the established pocket in order to treat the case before it as an uncovered *Erie* question (or entertain the less promising possibility of rebalancing with respect to the established pocket). In sum, resolving most *Erie* questions would entail only identifying the predefined pocket that embraces the particular question and then applying the established choice-of-law rule for that pocket.

This proposed methodology sounds more complicated than it is. After all, the lower courts in recent years were intuitively operating it. Moreover, two additional Supreme Court cases illuminated and thereby ameliorated the methodological difficulties, while also exhibiting a helpfully strong affection for stare decisis:

(1) Scope of Pockets. Difficulties in determining the scope of the pockets are inevitable. Guidance from above is sometimes necessary. The Supreme Court accordingly stepped in to settle that the issue of when an action is deemed commenced for statute-of-limitations purposes is indeed still in the statute-of-limitations pocket rather than the Federal Rules pocket, at least for state-created claims.[64]

(2) Exceptions to Rules. There have also been predictable instances of lower courts' undermining general rules by creating exceptions. Such sensitivity is here undesirable. Accordingly, the Supreme Court slapped down, perhaps even too zealously, such an attempt to create an exception on appealing facts to the state-law rule for the horizontal choice-of-law pocket.[65]

As for the role of Congress, it is the senior partner in the cooperative venture of drawing the line between state and federal law in federal court. Ideally, Congress would use a similar technique when it legislates a choice between state and federal law. It too would define a pocket and, after considering state and federal interests, dictate the applicable law. However, Congress may properly opt for federal law more often than the federal courts would, because under our constitutional structure Congress should be the more active articulator of federal interests. And, of course, in practice Congress can be less systematic and rational than the courts. Whatever the congressional choice, as long as the choice is constitutionally valid, it would thenceforth bind the federal courts without exception.

---

64. Walker v. Armco Steel Corp., 446 U.S. 740 (1980) (reaffirming Ragan); cf. West v. Conrail, 481 U.S. 35 (1987) (federal law governs commencement for federally created claims).

65. Day & Zimmermann, Inc. v. Challoner, 423 U.S. 3 (1975) (reaffirming Klaxon).

Admittedly, even if practical for use by courts and Congress, and even if not that different from many lawmaking acts, this proposed approach still sounds a little bizarre. However, such oddity is a small price to pay for its benefits.

In the first place, this compromise approach avoids the disadvantages, without sacrificing the advantages, of the two polar approaches. Through adoption of a series of rules, it avoids the crudeness and inaccuracy of any all-encompassing mechanical rule; it at least approximates the sensitivity and precision of an ad hoc approach. Meanwhile, it does not sacrifice the aim of certainty as an individualized approach does; it has as much predictability and workability as the various mechanical rules of the past have managed to deliver. In other words, this compromise approach thus would obtain considerable accuracy as well as certainty. It might be thought of as either "gross balancing" or "sensitive rulemaking."

Moreover, the compromise approach seems to explicate and rationalize what the federal courts have in fact been doing over the years, and also why casual commentators tend to discuss *Erie* in terms of rules for various areas of the law. In creative retrospect, a generous selection of general rules has already evolved, most of which rules are sound and all of which rules act to remove much of the uncertainty from the *Erie* doctrine. For example, state law governs countless clearly "substantive" pockets of state concern, and also:

(1) statutes of limitations on state-created claims;

(2) territorial jurisdiction on state-created claims, a result now codified in Federal Rule 4;

(3) door-closing statutes of the *Woods*-type, but not of the forum-non-conveniens-type, on state-created claims;

(4) horizontal choice of law on matters governed by state law under *Erie*; and

(5) burden and standard of proof on matters governed by state law under *Erie*.

But, for example, federal law governs countless clearly "substantive" pockets of federal concern. It governs countless "procedural" pockets in connection with federal question cases, and also governs even in diversity cases such pockets as:

(1) judge-jury relations;

(2) order of trial;

(3) the pocket of law occupied by the Federal Rules of Civil and Appellate Procedure;

(4) venue and forum selection; and

(5) joinder of claims and parties.

Finally, the compromise approach offers an intellectually defensible means to reconcile and preserve as "good law" all the cases thus far discussed, and almost all lower-court cases heretofore decided. What is striking about the *Erie* cases, in the Supreme Court and the lower courts, is that they almost all came to the right result on their facts. They did so by an intuitive sense of the compromise that federalism requires. It is true that many lower-court opinions mouthed the prevailing Supreme Court formula. But the opinions might have been doing so only to invoke a convenient and approved route to a predetermined result. As long as the intuitive methodology and the prevailing formula pointed the same way, the courts would simply quote the formula. When intuition and formula diverged, however, the lower courts began to sound more like interest-balancers. The Supreme Court's cases appear similarly result-driven.

Passing from these good results to the officially blessed methodology, I see the progress of Supreme Court decisions, except for *Gasperini*'s insistent ad-hocism, as supporting the compromise approach. *Gasperini*, at least for the time being, seems to have reactivated the *Erie* pendulum, as the Court embraced anew individualized precision in demarking the *Erie* line. The future will prove, once again, the need to still the pendulum by optimal compromise. It is this need that the proposed approach tries to address.

Chapter 4

AUTHORITY TO ADJUDICATE

Table of Sections

---

§ 4.1   Jurisdiction over Subject Matter

A.   Introduction

For a court properly to undertake a civil adjudication, the court must have jurisdiction over the subject matter. That is, it must have, under applicable constitutional and statutory provisions, *authority to adjudicate the type of controversy before the court.*

Each legal system gives a lot of attention to its law of subject-matter jurisdiction. What are the systems' ends in delineating subject-matter jurisdiction? The systems use it to divide functions among their organs of government, thus accommodating federal and state authority, separating courts from the other governmental branches, and differentiating one court from another. Accordingly,

175

the requirement of jurisdiction over the subject matter is taken very seriously, generating the commonly repeated rules that (1) the parties cannot confer subject-matter jurisdiction by consent, collusion, waiver, or estoppel and (2) the court must ever be ready to question its own subject-matter jurisdiction.

As to the systems' means in delineating subject-matter jurisdiction, their constitutions and statutes specify the scope of the courts' subject-matter jurisdiction in various terms. For example, a particular court might be empowered to hear patent cases or be excluded from hearing cases against the government involving more than $10,000. However, unlike territorial authority to adjudicate, subject-matter jurisdiction is defined in essentially nongeographic terms.

Because we live in a federal system, we need to give separate attention to the subject-matter jurisdiction of state and federal courts, as the succeeding pages do. Given our particular brand of federalism, state courts enjoy broad and general authority to adjudicate all sorts of cases. The federal courts have a sharply limited, and rather complicated, authority to adjudicate.

Why Is Forum Such a Big Deal?

The existence of federal jurisdiction often gives a litigant's lawyer a choice between federal and state court. According to empirical studies of attorneys' preferences, there are many considerations that might affect the choice. Most of these considerations may be grouped under four general headings: expected bias against a litigant, logistical and practical concerns, perceived disparity between federal and state judges and juries in such characteristics as quality, and the different procedures offered by one or the other court system. Which of these considerations will be most important can vary with the situation.

First, an out-of-state defendant insurance company, for example, would expect to face more bias in an action brought by a resident individual plaintiff in state court than would an out-of-state individual defendant being sued by a resident insurance company. A resident litigant from a city sued in a rural county court could conceivably expect as much bias as a litigant from another state. Whether or not all these kinds of prejudices still exist, many litigants think they do.

Second, logistical concerns include the parties' relative distances from the courthouse or from the place where most of the legal action will take place. Sometimes a litigant's lawyer may choose a court far from the opponent's residence to increase leverage in settlement. Very importantly, a litigant's lawyer may be more familiar with the practices of the local state court, where also there may be less expense involved. Also, one's purposes would likely be served by a longer or shorter docket.

Third, federal judges often are seen as being of higher quality and greater independence than are state judges. Federal juries are drawn from a wider geographical area than are state juries.

Fourth, the different procedures offered by the court systems require a lawyer to consider many other variables when choosing a court. Many preferences regarding federal court turn on its pleading practices, discovery devices, summary judgment, and judicial activism in procedural matters.

> The state courts' trial rules of evidence might differ. The two systems' effectiveness of appellate review might affect choice.
>
> Whatever lawyers' reasons might be, and no matter how intangible those reasons might seem, the choice of forum apparently makes a significant difference. In recent years, the plaintiffs' win rate in nonprisoner federal question cases brought as original actions in federal court has been 52%; for such cases removed to federal court, the plaintiffs' win rate was only 25%. In diversity jurisdiction, the plaintiffs' win rate in original actions has been 71%; for removed cases, it was 34%. One must be wary in analyzing win rates because the groups of compared cases do comprise different cases, which may differ in many respects. But here when the statistician controls for as many variables as possible, this robust result survives: removal seems seriously to affect case outcome—just as it should in accordance with removal's purpose of protecting defendants. See generally Kevin M. Clermont & Theodore Eisenberg, Do Case Outcomes Really Reveal Anything About the Legal System? Win Rates and Removal Jurisdiction, 83 Cornell L. Rev. 581, 599 (1998).

B. State Courts

1. Structure of State Courts

A state may organize its judicial branch as it wishes. There are courts of *original jurisdiction*, where an action may be initiated— and one to three levels of courts of *appellate jurisdiction*, where a judgment of a lower court may be reviewed. The state constitution and statutes prescribe the subject-matter jurisdiction of these courts, although federal statutes do impose certain limits described below.

Among the courts of original jurisdiction in the typical state, there will be one set of courts of *general jurisdiction*, with courthouses all over the state. Such a court can hear any type of action, unless specifically prohibited by constitution or statute. There will also be several sets of courts of *limited jurisdiction*. These inferior courts can hear only those types of actions that are specifically consigned to them, such as small claims or probate matters.

2. Heads of State Jurisdiction

The states' authority is comprehensive, so that the states can prescribe the substantive rules of law to govern the people's ordinary life, that is, their primary conduct in the private and public life that transpires essentially outside the courtroom. True, the states' authority is subject to any limitations specified in the Federal Constitution and subject to the possibly superseding effect of federal law. But still the states' lawmaking authority is very wide.

Moreover, the states can provide for the enforcement of constitutional, federal, and state law in the state courts. True, subject to some vague but slight constitutional limitations, a state may choose not to exert its full judicial power, that is, a state may by provisions in its constitution or statutes restrict the kinds of disputes that its courts will handle. But still the state courts' jurisdiction is very wide.

Accordingly, state courts entertain most, by far, of this nation's judicial business. A great deal of this business can indeed be handled only by state courts, because the subject-matter jurisdiction of the federal courts is sharply limited. So, for example, if someone wishes to sue a person from the same state, alleging serious injuries incurred in a traffic accident, that plaintiff must sue in a state court.

Among the relatively few cases that the federal courts can hear, most can also be heard in state courts. The federal and state courts have *concurrent jurisdiction* in these cases. So, if a plaintiff wishes to sue someone from another state, alleging serious injuries incurred in a traffic accident, that plaintiff may choose between a state's general jurisdiction and a federal court's diversity jurisdiction.

Among the cases that the federal courts can hear, a very few are restricted by federal statute to the federal courts. Congress has the power so to limit state courts' subject-matter jurisdiction under the powers bestowed upon it by Articles I and III of the Federal Constitution, soon to be described. Such a statute means that the federal courts have *exclusive jurisdiction* in these cases. So, if *P* wishes to sue *D* for patent infringement, *P* must sue in a federal court by virtue of 28 U.S.C. § 1338(a).

C.   Federal Courts

1.   Structure of Federal Courts

Article III, Section 1 of the Federal Constitution establishes the Supreme Court of the United States ("The judicial Power of the United States, shall be vested in one supreme Court, and in such inferior Courts as the Congress may from time to time ordain and establish. * * * "), and Article I, Section 8 further gives Congress the power to establish lower federal tribunals as it sees fit ("The Congress shall have Power * * * To constitute Tribunals inferior to the supreme Court; * * *—And To make all Laws which shall be necessary and proper for carrying into Execution the foregoing Powers * * * ").[1]

Congress has established certain Article III courts of specialized jurisdiction, currently including most significantly the United

---

1. See generally Charles Alan Wright & Mary Kay Kane, Law of Federal   Courts §§ 2–5, 11 (6th ed. 2002).

States Court of International Trade, which handles certain civil actions relating to import transactions. Distinguishably, Congress has established certain Article I bodies that are called legislative courts and are not part of the judicial branch, such as the United States Court of Federal Claims, the United States Tax Court, and the bankruptcy court in each federal district, as well as the territorial courts for the Virgin Islands, Guam, and the Northern Mariana Islands.

In addition to these specialized federal courts, there is the main part of the federal system, which today comprises a three-tiered pyramid of Article III courts: the district courts, the courts of appeals, and the Supreme Court.

The United States District Courts are the principal federal courts of original jurisdiction, with almost 700 active district judges. There is such a district court for each of 91 districts, there being one to four districts within each state, the District of Columbia, and Puerto Rico. The judges of each district normally sit singly. The district court exercises subject-matter jurisdiction to be described below.

The United States Courts of Appeals are at the next higher level, with about 180 active judges. There is such a court of appeals for each of 12 regional circuits, as shown on the following map. The judges of each circuit normally sit in panels of three. The court of appeals, as its foremost duty, exercises appellate jurisdiction over the district courts in the circuit.[2] Additionally, there is a thirteenth court of appeals named the United States Court of Appeals for the Federal Circuit, which similarly hears appeals from a number of specialized tribunals and also hears appeals from all district courts in cases involving certain special areas such as patents or certain claims against the United States.[3]

The Supreme Court is at the summit. There is one Supreme Court in Washington, D.C. Its nine Justices normally sit as a group. The Supreme Court, most significantly, exercises a small original jurisdiction,[4] appellate jurisdiction for important cases coming up from the federal courts of appeals,[5] and appellate jurisdiction for important federal questions decided by the highest state courts.[6]

2. 28 U.S.C. §§ 1291–1292; see supra § 2.6(A)(1).

3. 28 U.S.C. § 1295.

4. 28 U.S.C. § 1251.

5. 28 U.S.C. § 1254; see supra § 2.6(A)(2).

6. 28 U.S.C. § 1257.

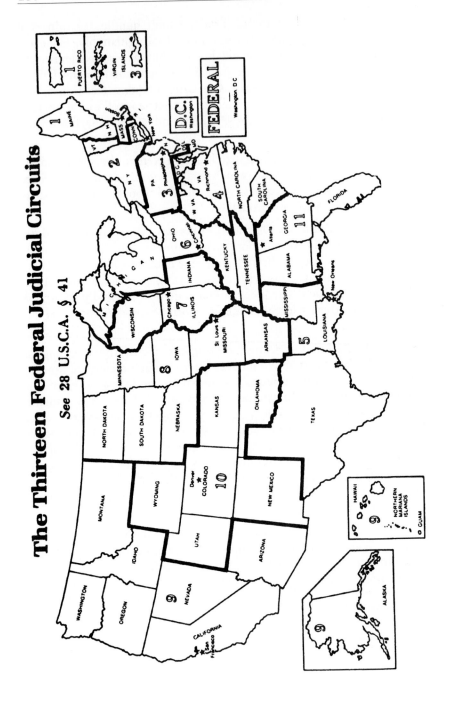

The Thirteen Federal Judicial Circuits

See 28 U.S.C.A. § 41

2. Heads of Federal Jurisdiction

Section 2 of the Constitution's Article III (as modified by the Eleventh Amendment[7]) marks the outer boundary of federal subject-matter jurisdiction:

> The judicial Power shall extend to all Cases, in Law and Equity, arising under this Constitution, the Laws of the United States, and Treaties made, or which shall be made, under their Authority;—to all Cases affecting Ambassadors, other public Ministers and Consuls;—to all Cases of admiralty and maritime Jurisdiction;—to Controversies to which the United States shall be a Party;—to Controversies between two or more States;—between a State and Citizens of another State;—between Citizens of different States;—between Citizens of the same State claiming Lands under Grants of different States, and between a State, or the Citizens thereof, and foreign States, Citizens or Subjects.

> In all Cases affecting Ambassadors, other public Ministers and Consuls, and those in which a State shall be Party, the supreme Court shall have original Jurisdiction. In all the other Cases before mentioned, the supreme Court shall have appellate Jurisdiction, both as to Law and Fact, with such Exceptions, and under such Regulations as the Congress shall make.

> * * * *

It thus extends the federal judicial power to certain types of cases defined in terms of the nature of the claim (e.g., admiralty jurisdiction) or the status of the parties (e.g., jurisdiction for controversies to which the United States is a party).[8]

Moreover, Articles I and III give Congress a fairly free hand in allocating to the federal courts or withholding from them the jurisdiction delimited by Article III.[9] Congress has invoked this authority through a whole series of jurisdictional statutes,[10] although these statutes fall far short of bestowing all of the federal judicial power under the Constitution.

In sum, for a case to come within the jurisdiction of a federal court, the case normally must fall (1) within some congressional authorization[11] and (2) within the bounds of the Constitution.[12] In

---

7. "The Judicial power of the United States shall not be construed to extend to any suit in law or equity, commenced or prosecuted against one of the United States by Citizens of another State, or by Citizens or Subjects of any Foreign State."

8. See generally Wright & Kane, supra note 1, § 8.

9. See generally id. § 10.

10. See, e.g., 28 U.S.C. § 1333 (admiralty), §§ 1345–1346 (controversies to which the United States is a party).

11. See, e.g., Ex parte McCardle, 74 U.S. (7 Wall.) 506 (1869) (upholding a congressional statute repealing a portion of otherwise constitutional jurisdiction).

12. See, e.g., Marbury v. Madison, 5 U.S. (1 Cranch) 137 (1803) (Marshall,

this sense, the federal courts are courts of limited jurisdiction, according with the basic principle of American federalism whereby the federal government is a government of limited powers.[13]

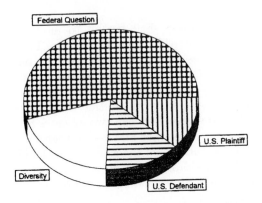

To get an idea of the actual caseload of the federal courts, we can look at the 259,637 federal civil cases terminated during fiscal year 2000. Of these, 12.2% involved the United States as plaintiff, and 13.7% involved the United States as defendant; 54.2% were based on all other kinds of federal questions; and 19.8% were based on diversity of citizenship.

a. Federal Questions

Most importantly, Article III extends the federal judicial power to cases "arising under" the Constitution, federal statutory or common law, or treaties. Congress has acted thereunder to vest original jurisdiction for such cases in the district courts, both by the general provision in 28 U.S.C. § 1331 and by a string of special statutes.

Constitutional Provision. The constitutional phrase of "arising under" sweepingly embraces all cases that include a federal "ingredient."[14] This broad reading of the Constitution means that Congress has wide power to bestow federal question jurisdiction on the federal courts, even where the federal element in a case is slight

C.J.) (invalidating a congressional statute granting jurisdiction beyond constitutional bounds).

13. See generally Wright & Kane, supra note 1, § 7.

14. See Osborn v. Bank of the United States, 22 U.S. 738 (1824) (Marshall, C.J.) (holding that the "arising under"

language of Article III authorized a then-existing statute that bestowed jurisdiction on the federal courts over all actions brought by the federally chartered bank, because any such action would at the least have as an ingredient the minor federal question of whether the bank under its charter had the power to sue).

and not really in issue. But remember, for a case to come within district-court jurisdiction, it does not suffice to come within the Constitution: Congress must also have exercised its jurisdiction-bestowing power in an applicable jurisdictional statute.

General Statutory Provision. 28 U.S.C. § 1331 is the basic statute:

> The district courts shall have original jurisdiction of all civil actions arising under the Constitution, laws, or treaties of the United States.

This statute uses almost the same language as the Constitution, but it has been read much more narrowly. In order to keep themselves from being overwhelmed by a flood of cases having a mere federal ingredient, the federal courts have read three major restrictions into the statutory phrase of "arising under" that do not apply to the constitutional phrase of "arising under."

Adequate Federal Element. One critical restriction deals with the relationship of the case to its federal element. It is clear that to satisfy the statute, the federal element must be more than a mere ingredient. But it is difficult to be precise about how much more, and no single definition that would encompass all the decided cases is evident.

Justice Holmes famously argued: "A suit arises under the law that creates the cause of action."[15] This test yields many correct answers: for an important example, an action for patent infringement arises under federal law, but an action to recover contractual royalties for use of the patent does not.[16] However, there are relatively rare problem cases, where state-created causes of action nevertheless arise under federal law and federally created causes do not. *Smith v. Kansas City Title & Trust Co.*[17] found federal jurisdiction to exist for a suit by a trust company shareholder to enjoin the trust from investing in certain federal bonds, where state law limited investment to legal securities but where the plaintiff claimed that the federal statute authorizing the bonds' issuance was unconstitutional. Conversely, *Shoshone Mining Co. v. Rutter*[18] held that federal jurisdiction did not exist for a suit to determine the right to possession of a mining claim, where a federal statute authorized this type of suit but directed that local law should govern the rights involved.

---

15. Am. Well Works Co. v. Layne & Bowler Co., 241 U.S. 257, 260 (1916).

16. See T.B. Harms Co. v. Eliscu, 339 F.2d 823, 827 (2nd Cir. 1964) (holding there was no federal question jurisdiction for state-law controversy over copyright transfer, even though copyright infringement is a federal claim).

17. 255 U.S. 180 (1921).

18. 177 U.S. 505 (1900).

Therefore, a more accurate formulation of the federal element's adequacy, in cases resting upon both federal and state law, is necessarily fuzzier than the Holmes formulation. The leading article on the subject formulates the test as requiring a "claim founded 'directly' upon federal law."[19] It has also been argued that this absence of a precise definition is an advantage, because it frees the courts to determine the jurisdictional point on the basis of pragmatic considerations, such as "the extent of the caseload increase for federal trial courts if jurisdiction is recognized; the extent to which cases of this class will, in practice, turn on issues of state or federal law; the extent of the necessity for an expert federal tribunal to handle issues of federal law that do arise; the extent of the necessity for a sympathetic federal tribunal in cases of this class."[20]

The Supreme Court now seems receptive to this pragmatic argument. In *Merrell Dow Pharmaceuticals Inc. v. Thompson*,[21] an action for birth defects against the manufacturer of Bendectin, the Court found that state-law negligence claims that incorporate a violation of federal drug-branding law contain an insufficiently "substantial" federal element to confer federal jurisdiction. The Court still attempted to reconcile this case with its past decisions in which a federal element had been present in a state cause of action by saying that the nature of the federal interest at stake influences the outcome of the arising-under analysis: if the federal element does not change the state-law character of the action, there is no federal question jurisdiction. Then in *Grable & Sons Metal Products, Inc. v. Darue Engineering & Manufacturing*,[22] a state-law quiet title action that turned on whether the IRS's failure to follow precisely a federal notice statute invalidated title obtained at a tax sale, the Court upheld federal jurisdiction. The Court explained that the circumstances, such as the involvement of a fairly pure issue of federal tax law and the small risk of opening the federal courthouse doors to a flood of cases, justified "resort to the experience, solicitude, and hope of uniformity that a federal forum offers" on a disputed and significant federal issue when the case could be heard without disturbing any "congressional judgment about the sound division of labor between state and federal courts."

19. Paul J. Mishkin, The Federal "Question" in the District Courts, 53 Colum. L. Rev. 157, 168 (1953); cf. ALI Study of the Division of Jurisdiction Between State and Federal Courts § 1311(a) commentary at 178–79 (1969) (faced with the jumble of cases, the ALI did not attempt definition but instead retained the "arising under" term).

20. William Cohen, The Broken Compass: The Requirement That a Case Arise "Directly" Under Federal Law, 115 U. Pa. L. Rev. 890, 916 (1967); see David L. Shapiro, Jurisdiction and Discretion, 60 N.Y.U. L. Rev. 543, 568–70 (1985).

21. 478 U.S. 804, 814 & n.12 (1986).

22. 545 U.S. 308, 312–13 (2005).

In somewhat indefinite conclusion, then, the adequate federal element restriction means that an *important* element of the plaintiff's claim must be of federal origin.[23]

Well-Pleaded Complaint Rule. The federal element must also be such as would appear on the face of a properly pleaded complaint.[24] This well-pleaded complaint rule drags in the difficulties of applying overly nice pleading rules, serves to prevent federal questions raised by the defendant from receiving the expert, sympathetic, and uniform treatment otherwise available in the federal courts, and also opens the door wider to artful pleading by the plaintiff who is desirous of staying in state court.[25] What are the policies that explain adopting this difficult and obstructive rule, rather than waiting to see if the defendant indeed raises a federal question? Those policies are not overwhelming, but they run something like this: first, the well-pleaded complaint rule is consistent with the general policy of "first things first," that is, a rule making jurisdiction determinable at the very outset of the proceeding, rather than dependent on future contingencies, saves the time and money that would be wasted in litigating a case ultimately dismissed on jurisdictional grounds; second, the well-pleaded complaint rule gives the plaintiff certainty as to jurisdiction, because it avoids the situation where the defendant could veto jurisdiction by omitting the expected federal question from the answer; and, third, the rule ensures that conceptually the court has the power to require a response from the defendant.[26]

The prime example of the rule in action comes from *Louisville & Nashville R.R. v. Mottley*.[27] Plaintiffs sued a railroad for specific performance of an agreement to issue free passes, which the railroad allegedly refused to issue because a subsequent federal statute prohibited the giving of free passes. Plaintiffs further alleged that

---

23. Compare City of Chicago v. Int'l College of Surgeons, 522 U.S. 156, 164 (1997) (important federal element in state-law claim creates federal question jurisdiction, as in this action to review city's administrative action on historic buildings by raising federal constitutional challenges), with Moore v. Chesapeake & Ohio Ry., 291 U.S. 205, 211–17 (1934) (no federal question jurisdiction for action on state tort statute, even though that statute imposed a duty of care that was defined by federal law). See generally Wright & Kane, supra note 1, § 17.

24. See generally Wright & Kane, supra note 1, § 18.

25. Compare Caterpillar Inc. v. Williams, 482 U.S. 386 (1987) (plaintiff

can prevent removal based on federal question by stating a claim solely in terms of state law), with Metro. Life Ins. Co. v. Taylor, 481 U.S. 58 (1987) (removal permissible if federal law completely preempts state law in the subject area), and Avco Corp. v. Aero Lodge No. 735, 390 U.S. 557 (1968) (same).

26. See ALI Study, supra note 19, at 190–91; Donald L. Doernberg, There's No Reason for It; It's Just Our Policy: Why the Well–Pleaded Complaint Rule Sabotages the Purposes of Federal Question Jurisdiction, 38 Hastings L.J. 597 (1987).

27. 211 U.S. 149 (1908); see also Bracken v. Matgouranis, 296 F.3d 160 (3d Cir. 2002) (applying rule to removed case).

the statute was inapplicable or unconstitutional. The Court held there was no federal question jurisdiction, because the federal questions appeared only in relation to an improperly anticipated defense and not as part of a properly pleaded contract complaint.

Suppose the *Mottley* action were instead structured as one for a declaratory judgment under the present Declaratory Judgment Act ("DJA"),[28] with the railroad as plaintiff seeking a declaration of its obligation in light of the statute prohibiting free passes. The Supreme Court has held that the DJA granted no new jurisdiction, and therefore one must test jurisdiction by applying the well-pleaded complaint rule to the coercive action that would have been brought in the absence of the declaratory judgment procedure.[29] This authority supports the view that federal jurisdiction would not exist for the railroad's suit, because for the underlying coercive action (the Mottleys' suit against the railroad for specific performance) the federal questions would appear only in relation to an improperly anticipated defense and not on the face of a well-pleaded complaint. For a contrasting example, federal jurisdiction would exist if a potential patent infringer were to sue the patent holder for a declaration of patent invalidity, with the reasoning that the unscrambled coercive action would be one by the patent holder for infringement.

However, a different approach, one that would test jurisdiction by applying the well-pleaded complaint rule directly to the actual complaint even in a declaratory judgment action, seems preferable. First, this is a simpler approach to follow. No unscrambling is required. Second, this approach better serves the supposed policies behind the well-pleaded complaint rule of making jurisdiction determinable at the outset independently of the content of the defendant's answer. Often the prevailing approach of unscrambling the declaratory judgment action effectively requires applying the rule to the answer in the declaratory judgment suit, which makes no policy sense at all. Third, the existing requirement of an adequate federal element suffices to ensure that only appropriate cases will come into federal court. Any federal question case must involve an important federal question. Fourth, the question of which of these two approaches creates new jurisdiction is largely semantic and hence indeterminate. In the patent example, the DJA has in one sense created federal jurisdiction because the potential infringer, who as plaintiff is not asserting a federal right but is instead asserting that the defendant has no federal right, could not have

---

28. 28 U.S.C. §§ 2201–2202; see supra § 2.5(B).

29. Skelly Oil Co. v. Phillips Petroleum Co., 339 U.S. 667 (1950); see ALI Study, supra note 19, at 170–72; Wright & Kane, supra note 1, § 18, at 112–14; cf. Franchise Tax Bd. v. Constr. Laborers Vacation Trust, 463 U.S. 1, 16 (1983) (endorsing Skelly Oil view).

invoked federal jurisdiction before the DJA. Fifth, congressional intent in the DJA on this point was by no means explicit. The legislators were focused on the Article III dangers of reaching less ripe controversies, while giving no attention whatsoever to possibly expanding statutory jurisdiction by affecting the application of the well-pleaded complaint rule.[30]

Substantiality Rule. The basis of the federal claim must be substantial, that is, sufficiently meritorious, to avoid dismissal on jurisdictional grounds.[31] This restriction requires little. It means that the federal element must not be factually immaterial, in the sense of being without significance and tacked on only to get into federal court. It also means that the federal claim cannot be legally frivolous, in the sense of being laughably weak but asserted to establish federal jurisdiction.[32]

The mystery for the student here is why this restriction exists, because an insubstantial claim will lose on the merits, even if the claim survives threshold jurisdictional tests. The reason for the substantiality restriction lies in keeping the plaintiff from using an insubstantial claim to get a foot in the federal courthouse door, a foot that would allow the plaintiff to inject supplemental state claims into the federal court.

Special Statutory Provisions. Note that § 1331 neither covers the whole range of the federal question clause in the Constitution, because of those three statutory restrictions, nor makes the federal jurisdiction exclusive, because the statute says no such thing.

However, if applicable, one of the special federal question statutes might avoid some of the restrictions read into § 1331, or might impose other restrictions such as a jurisdictional amount requirement, or might make the jurisdiction exclusive. Many of these special statutes are found in title 28 of U.S.C., such as § 1338 (patents and the like). Others are scattered elsewhere, such as 15 U.S.C. §§ 15 and 26 (antitrust actions).

In addition, special jurisdictional statutes invoke Article III's clauses related to the arising-under clause, such as the clauses extending the federal judicial power to "all Cases of admiralty and maritime Jurisdiction" and "to Controversies to which the United

---

30. See Donald L. Doernberg & Michael B. Mushlin, The Trojan Horse: How the Declaratory Judgment Act Created a Cause of Action and Expanded Federal Jurisdiction While the Supreme Court Wasn't Looking, 36 UCLA L. Rev. 529 (1989).

31. See generally Charles Alan Wright, Arthur R. Miller & Edward H.

Cooper, Federal Practice and Procedure § 3564 (2d ed. 1984).

32. See Bell v. Hood, 327 U.S. 678 (1946) (finding a weak claim to be nevertheless substantial enough); Levering & Garrigues Co. v. Morrin, 289 U.S. 103 (1933) (granting dismissal).

States shall be a Party." These statutes, which give the federal courts jurisdiction over cases where federal interests are strong, also come under the head of federal question jurisdiction.[33]

b. Diversity of Citizenship

Article III extends the federal judicial power to controversies "between Citizens of different States" (so-called diversity jurisdiction) and those between state citizens and foreign citizens (so-called alienage jurisdiction). Congress has acted thereunder to vest original jurisdiction for such cases in the district courts, both by the general provision in 28 U.S.C. § 1332(a) and by special statutes such as the interpleader statute in 28 U.S.C. § 1335. However, Congress has restricted the federal jurisdiction by imposing jurisdictional amount requirements on most such cases, as will be discussed later.[34]

Constitutional Provision. The Supreme Court has read these constitutional clauses to require only "partial (or minimal) diversity," which is satisfied in any action that involves a state citizen as a party when any opposing party is of different citizenship.[35] Thus, Congress has broad power to bestow diversity and alienage jurisdiction on the federal courts. But again remember, for a case to come within district-court jurisdiction, it does not suffice to come within the Constitution: Congress must also have exercised its jurisdiction-bestowing power in an applicable jurisdictional statute.

General Statutory Provision. The basic statute is 28 U.S.C. § 1332:

> (a) The district courts shall have original jurisdiction of all civil actions where the matter in controversy exceeds the sum or value of $75,000, exclusive of interest and costs, and is between—
>
> > (1) citizens of different States;
> >
> > (2) citizens of a State and citizens or subjects of a foreign state;
> >
> > (3) citizens of different States and in which citizens or subjects of a foreign state are additional parties; and
> >
> > (4) a foreign state, defined in section 1603(a) of this title, as plaintiff and citizens of a State or of different States.
>
> For the purposes of this section, section 1335 [interpleader], and section 1441 [removal], an alien admitted to the United States for

---

33. See, e.g., 28 U.S.C. § 1333 (admiralty); cf. 28 U.S.C. §§ 1345–1346 (controversies to which the United States is a party).

34. See infra § 4.1(C)(3)(f).

35. State Farm Fire & Cas. Co. v. Tashire, 386 U.S. 523 (1967) (interpleader).

permanent residence shall be deemed a citizen of the State in which such alien is domiciled.

(b) Except when express provision therefor is otherwise made in a statute of the United States, where the plaintiff who files the case originally in the Federal courts is finally adjudged to be entitled to recover less than the sum or value of $75,000, computed without regard to any setoff or counterclaim to which the defendant may be adjudged to be entitled, and exclusive of interest and costs, the district court may deny costs to the plaintiff and, in addition, may impose costs on the plaintiff.

(c) For the purposes of this section and section 1441 of this title—

(1) a corporation shall be deemed to be a citizen of any State by which it has been incorporated and of the State where it has its principal place of business, except that in any direct action against the insurer of a policy or contract of liability insurance, whether incorporated or unincorporated, to which action the insured is not joined as a party-defendant, such insurer shall be deemed a citizen of the State of which the insured is a citizen, as well as of any State by which the insurer has been incorporated and of the State where it has its principal place of business; and

(2) the legal representative of the estate of a decedent shall be deemed to be a citizen only of the same State as the decedent, and the legal representative of an infant or incompetent shall be deemed to be a citizen only of the same State as the infant or incompetent.

* * * *

This statute most importantly bestows federal jurisdiction, where the matter in controversy exceeds $75,000, for actions (1) between citizens of different states, with or without foreign citizens as additional parties on either or both sides, and (2) between state citizens and foreign citizens. This general statute is much criticized, largely on the ground that it has outlived its traditional justification of providing a federal forum to avoid state-court bias against litigants from other states.[36]

Complete Diversity. Reading the statutory language of "citizens of different States" more narrowly than the almost identical constitutional language, the Supreme Court has held that the statute requires "complete diversity"—that is, no two opposing parties can be citizens of the same state.[37] So if *P–1* of New York and *P–2* of California sue *D–1* of New Mexico and *D–2* of California, there is no diversity jurisdiction, because citizens of California are on opposing

---

36. See generally Wright & Kane, supra note 1, § 23.

37. Strawbridge v. Curtiss, 7 U.S. (3 Cranch) 267 (1806) (Marshall, C.J.).

sides of the action; although there is partial diversity that would satisfy the constitutional requirement, there is no complete diversity to satisfy the more demanding statutory requirement.

The statute, with its complete-diversity gloss, works out this way in the two main types of cases:

(1) Actions Between Citizens of Different States. Any such cast of characters is fine jurisdictionally, as long as no two opposing parties are citizens of the same state.[38] Indeed, foreign citizens can be tossed into the mix in any combination, as long as two opposing parties are citizens of different states (and no two opposing parties are citizens of the same state).[39]

(2) Actions Between a State Citizen and a Foreign Citizen. Whether it is state citizen versus foreign citizen or foreign citizen versus state citizen, this situation too is fine jurisdictionally and, indeed, you can add other state citizens in any combination on the one side and other foreign citizens in any combination on the opposing side.[40] But in the absence of any state citizens, aliens cannot sue aliens under diversity or alienage jurisdiction, because the Constitution's language simply does not extend to that situation.[41] And the courts have held that § 1332(a) does not extend to a suit between, on one side, a state citizen and a foreign citizen and, on the other side, a foreign citizen, because this suit literally is neither a suit between merely a state citizen and a foreign citizen nor a suit between state citizens with foreign citizens as additional parties.[42]

Meaning of Citizenship. This head of jurisdiction turns on the definition of citizenship, which turns out to be quite tricky:[43]

(1) Individual. For an individual, state citizenship requires the person (a) to be a U.S. citizen (or have the equivalent status of permanent resident alien) and (b) to be domiciled in the state.

---

38. 28 U.S.C. § 1332(a)(1).

39. 28 U.S.C. § 1332(a)(3); see Nancy M. Berkley, Note, Federal Jurisdiction over Suits Between Diverse United States Citizens with Aliens Joined to Both Sides of the Controversy Under 28 U.S.C. § 1332(a)(3), 38 Rutgers L. Rev. 71 (1985).

40. 28 U.S.C. § 1332(a)(2); see Iraola & CIA, S.A. v. Kimberly–Clark Corp., 232 F.3d 854, 857–60 (11th Cir. 2000) ("citizens of a State" includes citizens of different states).

41. See Hodgson v. Bowerbank, 9 U.S. (5 Cranch) 303 (1809) (Marshall, C.J.); cf. Saadeh v. Farouki, 107 F.3d 52

(D.C. Cir. 1997) (foreign citizen versus U.S. permanent resident alien falls outside § 1332(a) bound, because statutory amendment regarding permanent resident aliens was intended to narrow diversity jurisdiction).

42. See, e.g., Iraola & CIA, S.A. v. Kimberly–Clark Corp., 232 F.3d 854, 860 (11th Cir. 2000); Faysound Ltd. v. United Coconut Chems., Inc., 878 F.2d 290, 294–95 (9th Cir. 1989); Eze v. Yellow Cab Co., 782 F.2d 1064 (D.C. Cir. 1986).

43. See generally Wright & Kane, supra note 1, §§ 24, 26–27.

Foreign citizenship requires the person only to be a citizen of the foreign country under its laws (or have the equivalent status of subject under a monarchy). Accordingly, an American domiciled abroad[44] or a person without any national citizenship status[45] does not come within the crudely written jurisdictional statute, and so cannot sue or be sued in federal court based on the diversity statute. As to the meaning of domicile, a person has only one such domicile at a time; to acquire a new domicile, a person must (a) be physically present in the new place (b) with the intention to make his home there indefinitely.[46] As to a person with foreign and state citizenship, who is involved in a lawsuit against either a foreign citizen or a state citizen, the treatment for diversity purposes is not clear, but the leading approach concludes that the required diversity exists unless the dual citizen's opponent is a citizen of the same U.S. state.[47]

(2) Corporation. For a corporation, the usual reading of the definition in § 1332(c)(1) makes an American corporation a citizen (a) of every state by which it has been incorporated and also (b) of the one state in which it has its principal place of business, if its principal place of business is in the United States.[48] Courts used to read the statute so as to treat a foreign corporation as a citizen only of the country of incorporation, but they are today shifting toward treating it as a citizen of the country of incorporation and also as a citizen of its principal place of business.[49] Determining the principal place of business is a factual question that requires looking at the locale of both the corporate management and the corporation's activities,

---

44. See Hammerstein v. Lyne, 200 F. 165 (W.D. Mo. 1912) (expatriate not within jurisdictional statute, although possibly within Article III bound); Redner v. Sanders, No. 99 CIV 9306, 2000 WL 1161080 (S.D.N.Y. Aug. 16, 2000) (same).

45. See Blair Holdings Corp. v. Rubinstein, 133 F. Supp. 496 (S.D.N.Y. 1955) (stateless person not within jurisdictional statute, although possibly within Article III bound); Medvedieff v. Cities Serv. Oil Co., 35 F. Supp. 999 (S.D.N.Y. 1940) (same). But see Blanco v. Pan–Am. Life Ins. Co., 221 F. Supp. 219, 228 (S.D. Fla. 1963), modified on other grounds, 362 F.2d 167 (5th Cir. 1966).

46. See Sheehan v. Gustafson, 967 F.2d 1214 (8th Cir. 1992); Lundquist v. Precision Valley Aviation, Inc., 946 F.2d 8 (1st Cir. 1991); Mas v. Perry, 489 F.2d 1396 (5th Cir. 1974) (plaintiff, although residing in Louisiana, was not a Louisiana domiciliary because she intended to move after her husband finished graduate school); cf. Baker v. Keck, 13 F. Supp. 486 (E.D. Ill. 1936) (plaintiff can establish new domicile, even with purpose of creating diversity jurisdiction).

47. See, e.g., Coury v. Prot, 85 F.3d 244 (5th Cir. 1996); Action S.A. v. Marc Rich & Co., 951 F.2d 504, 507 (2d Cir. 1991).

48. See Randazzo v. Eagle–Picher Indus., Inc., 117 F.R.D. 557 (E.D. Pa. 1987) (to establish diversity jurisdiction against a defendant U.S. corporation, plaintiff's pleading must allege both the state of incorporation and the principal place of business).

49. See Wright & Miller, supra note 31, § 3628.

although giving somewhat more weight to the latter factor.[50]

(3) Unincorporated Association. For an unincorporated association, the courts treat it like a group of individuals and so
deem it a citizen of every state and country of which one of its
members is a citizen.[51] Such a rule sharply diminishes the
chance that complete diversity will exist. However, a class
action covering the association's members may offer an avenue
into federal court, because only the citizenships of the named
parties are considered and not the citizenships of all class
members.[52]

Realignment of Parties. In determining jurisdiction, the court
does not treat as conclusive the pleadings' alignment of the parties
as plaintiffs and defendants. Instead, the court will realign the
parties for jurisdictional purposes according to the ultimate interest
of each.[53] Realignment may either create or defeat jurisdiction.

Exceptions to 28 U.S.C. § 1332. Neither domestic relations
cases nor probate proceedings come within the statute. These
exceptions, which judges carved out long ago and which they
preserve because of a desire not to interfere in matters better left to
state courts, give rise to difficult definitional problems.[54]

Special Statutory Provisions. Congress has neither bestowed on the federal courts the whole constitutional range of
diversity and alienage jurisdiction nor made the federal jurisdiction
exclusive. But it has enacted a couple of other statutes that expand
this head of jurisdiction.

28 U.S.C. § 1335. This statute bestows federal jurisdiction,
where the amount in controversy equals or exceeds $500, for
interpleader actions involving claimants that include a state citizen
and someone of different citizenship. That is, the statute requires
only minimal diversity. Using the federal courts to adjudicate
special kinds of cases involving dispersed parties, such as inter-

---

50. See J.A. Olson Co. v. City of Wi-
nona, Miss., 818 F.2d 401 (5th Cir. 1987)
(constructing "total activity" test that
implements purpose of § 1332(c)(1) by
fully and flexibly considering both
nerve-center factor and, somewhat more
heavily, place-of-activity factor); cf. Pe-
terson v. Cooley, 142 F.3d 181 (4th Cir.
1998) (emphasizing nerve-center factor
for corporation with few physical assets).

51. See United Steelworkers v. R.H.
Bouligny, Inc., 382 U.S. 145 (1965).

52. See infra § 6.3(B)(3)(d).

53. See City of Indianapolis v. Chase
Nat'l Bank, 314 U.S. 63 (1941). See gen-

erally Wright & Kane, supra note 1,
§ 30.

54. See Marshall v. Marshall, 547
U.S. 293 (2006) (Anna Nicole Smith
case); Ankenbrandt v. Richards, 504
U.S. 689 (1992) (domestic relations exception prevents courts from assuming
diversity jurisdiction to issue divorce, alimony, and child custody decrees, but
does not prevent jurisdiction over tort
suits between family members). See generally Wright & Kane, supra note 1,
§ 25.

pleader actions, represents a good use of the constitutional authorization of diversity and alienage jurisdiction.[55]

28 U.S.C. § 1369. A less well-executed attempt to handle complex litigation in federal court came in the Multiparty, Multiforum Trial Jurisdiction Act of 2002, which now appears in 28 U.S.C. § 1369 ("original jurisdiction of any civil action involving minimal diversity between adverse parties that arises from a single accident, where at least 75 natural persons have died in the accident at a discrete location" with dispersed defendants or events), § 1391(g) (venue "in any district in which any defendant resides or in which a substantial part of the accident giving rise to the action took place"), § 1441(e) (removal), § 1697 (nationwide process), and § 1785 (nationwide subpoenas).

28 U.S.C. § 1332(d). An important extension of jurisdiction came in the Class Action Fairness Act of 2005, which covers interstate class actions, with the expressed intent of defeating plaintiff lawyers' manipulation of state courts by funneling more class actions away from the state courts and into the federal courts. Congress bestowed original jurisdiction on the federal district courts for sizable multistate class actions, generally if there is minimal diversity between any plaintiff member of the class and any defendant and if the plaintiff class contains at least 100 members and their claims aggregated together exceed $5 million. By 28 U.S.C. § 1453, Congress further provided that any defendant alone can remove such a class action from state court to the local federal district court.[56]

c. *Supplemental Jurisdiction*

Although the Constitution and the jurisdictional statutes did not expressly authorize the federal district courts to hear claims merely related to pending claims within the federal jurisdiction, the courts generally read Article III and those statutes to permit so hearing whole cases when desirable. Because these doctrines of pendent and ancillary jurisdiction allowed a federal court to hear a claim that would otherwise be a state claim, they constituted a head of federal jurisdiction, but they did require as a hook some related claim that came within a more traditional head of federal jurisdiction.

In 1990, Congress codified the pendent and ancillary doctrines in 28 U.S.C. § 1367, which is entitled Supplemental Jurisdiction:

> (a) Except as provided in subsections (b) and (c) or as expressly provided otherwise by Federal statute, in any civil action of

---

55. See infra § 6.3(B)(3)(c).   **56.** See infra § 6.3(B)(3)(d).

which the district courts have original jurisdiction, the district courts shall have supplemental jurisdiction over all other claims that are so related to claims in the action within such original jurisdiction that they form part of the same case or controversy under Article III of the United States Constitution. Such supplemental jurisdiction shall include claims that involve the joinder or intervention of additional parties.

(b) In any civil action of which the district courts have original jurisdiction founded solely on section 1332 of this title, the district courts shall not have supplemental jurisdiction under subsection (a) over claims by plaintiffs against persons made parties under Rule 14, 19, 20, or 24 of the Federal Rules of Civil Procedure, or over claims by persons proposed to be joined as plaintiffs under Rule 19 of such rules, or seeking to intervene as plaintiffs under Rule 24 of such rules, when exercising supplemental jurisdiction over such claims would be inconsistent with the jurisdictional requirements of section 1332.

(c) The district courts may decline to exercise supplemental jurisdiction over a claim under subsection (a) if—

(1) the claim raises a novel or complex issue of State law,

(2) the claim substantially predominates over the claim or claims over which the district court has original jurisdiction,

(3) the district court has dismissed all claims over which it has original jurisdiction, or

(4) in exceptional circumstances, there are other compelling reasons for declining jurisdiction.

(d) The period of limitations for any claim asserted under subsection (a), and for any other claim in the same action that is voluntarily dismissed at the same time as or after the dismissal of the claim under subsection (a), shall be tolled while the claim is pending and for a period of 30 days after it is dismissed unless State law provides for a longer tolling period.

(e) As used in this section, the term "State" includes the District of Columbia, the Commonwealth of Puerto Rico, and any territory or possession of the United States.

Pendent Jurisdiction. This doctrine evolved from an ancient core of practical necessity: a court of original jurisdiction must have the power to entertain all of a claim's elements that need to be resolved in order to render judgment on the claim. Such power for the district courts exists, whether those elements are federal or state in nature, with theoretical justification for this and related powers lying in the constitutional reference to jurisdiction over "cases," rather than merely over certain federal issues, and also in the statutory references to "civil actions."[57]

57. See Osborn v. Bank of the United States, 22 U.S. 738 (1824) (Marshall,

However, after "pendent jurisdiction" developed as a judge-made doctrine around that core of necessity, the district courts began reaching much farther into the states' domain in pursuit of fairness, convenience, and efficiency. Given subject-matter jurisdiction over a federal question or nondiversity claim, and in order to facilitate access to the federal forum, the district court could entertain certain of the plaintiff's state claims that did not independently satisfy federal jurisdictional requirements.[58]

In specifying the reach of pendent jurisdiction, an early decision came in *Hurn v. Oursler*,[59] where *P*'s claims against *D* in district court included (1) a federal claim for infringement of the copyright in a play and (2) a state claim for unfair competition in unauthorized use of the play. The holding was that the federal court could exercise jurisdiction over the pendent state claim because the two claims constituted "a single cause of action."[60] Later, *United Mine Workers v. Gibbs*[61] generalized and expanded that test, thereby setting out the modern law of pendent jurisdiction by imposing tests of both power and discretion.

Today, for the district court to have the *power* to entertain the state claim, the federal claim and the state claim must be closely enough related to constitute one "case" in the constitutional sense. *Gibbs* seemingly defined a constitutional case as requiring that (1) the two "claims must derive from a common nucleus of operative fact" and (2) they must be such that the plaintiff "would ordinarily be expected to try them * * * in one judicial proceeding."[62] And *Aldinger v. Howard*[63] expressed the further point that the district court's power can be constricted by Congress. Pendent jurisdiction is impermissible if expressly prohibited by statute, although in fact Congress generally has not chosen to prohibit it. Instead, § 1367(a) now broadly codifies this judicial power.[64]

Under *Gibbs*' treatment of *discretion*, the district court will not exercise this power to hear pendent claims when "considerations of judicial economy, convenience and fairness to litigants" and "of comity" between federal and state courts argue, on balance, against

---

C.J.) (although a federal question case might include only a federal ingredient, the federal court was empowered to decide all state-law questions it ran into in disposing of the federal claim); cf. Siler v. Louisville & Nashville R.R., 213 U.S. 175 (1909) (the federal court could decide the state-law questions in a way that resulted in the court's never reaching the federal-law questions).

58. See generally Wright & Kane, supra note 1, § 19.

59. 289 U.S. 238 (1933), which case's particular result is now codified in 28 U.S.C. § 1338(b).

60. 289 U.S. at 246.

61. 383 U.S. 715 (1966).

62. Id. at 725.

63. 427 U.S. 1 (1976).

64. See, e.g., Jin v. Ministry of State Sec., 254 F. Supp. 2d 61 (D.D.C. 2003) (allowing supplemental jurisdiction over state-law defamation claims joined in federal civil rights and RICO action).

federal jurisdiction.[65] The court in its discretion will decline to exercise pendent jurisdiction, for example, when state issues substantially predominate or sometimes when the federal claim is dismissed at an early stage.[66] That is, the federal court may dismiss the state claim, or remand it if the case arrived via removal.[67] So, the court's discretion cuts back on its broad power. Now § 1367(c) codifies this discretion; however, in codifying discretion, the statute appears to have cabined the courts' discretionary range, limiting it to the reach of the statutory words of § 1367(c).[68]

Pendent Parties. Pendent jurisdiction extends to a state claim against a different party, subject as always to the court's discretion. So if *P* sues *D–1* in district court on a nondiversity claim, the court can exercise pendent jurisdiction in that action over a closely related state claim that *P* has against *D–2*.[69]

Territorial Jurisdiction and Venue. The normal rules of territorial jurisdiction and venue apply. But note that one such rule gives personal jurisdiction with respect to any related claim added to a pending action, if the defendant has already appeared in the action and if determining the additional claim concurrently with that action would not be unreasonable.[70] And another such rule sometimes extends a long-arm statute for a certain claim to cover similar claims, regardless of whether the defendant has appeared in the action.[71]

Ancillary Jurisdiction. This doctrine drew on a related notion of necessity: a court of original jurisdiction should have the power to entertain certain matters incidental to the main claim, such as conflicting claims to property under the court's control. The district courts should be able to deal with a whole case, including some claims not by themselves within the courts' jurisdiction.[72]

---

65. 383 U.S. at 726.

66. See Palmer v. Hosp. Auth., 22 F.3d 1559 (11th Cir. 1994) (discretionarily retaining supplemental jurisdiction after dismissal of federal claim). But cf. Estate of Harshman v. Jackson Hole Mountain Resort Corp., 379 F.3d 1161 (10th Cir. 2004) (mandatorily declining supplemental jurisdiction after dismissal of all federal claims for lack of subject-matter jurisdiction).

67. See Carnegie–Mellon Univ. v. Cohill, 484 U.S. 343 (1988) (remand); Borough of W. Mifflin v. Lancaster, 45 F.3d 780 (3d Cir. 1995).

68. See Executive Software N. Am., Inc. v. U.S. Dist. Court, 24 F.3d 1545 (9th Cir. 1994); Jon D. Corey, Comment, The Discretionary Exercise of Supplemental Jurisdiction Under the Supplemental Jurisdiction Statute, 1995 BYU L. Rev. 1263.

69. See 28 U.S.C. § 1367(a), which overturned Finley v. United States, 490 U.S. 545 (1989).

70. See infra § 4.2(B)(1)(e).

71. See infra § 4.2(C)(1)(a).

72. See Freeman v. Howe, 65 U.S. (24 How.) 450 (1861) (holding that a federal court had jurisdiction over a claim by mortgagees to the mortgaged property—where that property had previously been brought under the court's control by attachment in a diversity action to which the mortgagees were not parties—even though there was no independent jurisdictional ground for the mortgagees' claim).

However, after "ancillary jurisdiction" developed as a judge-made doctrine around this notion of necessity, the district courts began reaching much farther in pursuit of fairness, convenience, and efficiency. Given subject-matter jurisdiction over the main claim, and in order to protect defendants by not splitting up cases, the district court could entertain certain counterclaims, cross-claims, and other additional claims that did not independently satisfy federal jurisdictional requirements.[73]

In specifying the reach of ancillary jurisdiction, an early step came in *Moore v. New York Cotton Exchange*,[74] where *P* sued *D* in district court on a federal antitrust claim, and *D* asserted a related state counterclaim. The Court held that the federal court could exercise jurisdiction over the ancillary state counterclaim, provided that the incidental claim bore a "logical relationship" to the main claim.[75] Later, in *Owen Equipment & Erection Co. v. Kroger*,[76] the Supreme Court became less vague, thereby suggesting the modern law of ancillary jurisdiction.

Seemingly like *Gibbs*, *Owen* required *power* to exist under the Constitution (claims must arise from "a common nucleus of operative fact") and not be negated by statute. Although § 1367(a) now codifies this judicial power, § 1367(b) broadly, but very ambiguously, negates that power in diversity cases with respect to claims added by plaintiffs, as opposed to additional claims asserted by those in a defensive posture. *Owen* also allowed the district court in its *discretion* to decline to exercise ancillary jurisdiction, an option now codified in § 1367(c).

In practice, however, the lower courts refused these invitations to flexibility and instead adopted an unfortunately rigid approach, working out wooden rules to decide the propriety of ancillary jurisdiction for each kind of claim.[77] They continue to do so under § 1367. Today, the following claims come within ancillary jurisdiction:

(1) compulsory counterclaims under Federal Rule 13(a);

(2) crossclaims under Rule 13(g);

(3) intervention of right under Rule 24(a), unless the intervenor is intervening as a plaintiff in a diversity case or unless the intervenor would have been an indispensable party under Rule 19(b);

---

73. See generally Wright & Kane, supra note 1, § 9.

74. 270 U.S. 593 (1926).

75. Id. at 610.

76. 437 U.S. 365 (1978). For the story of this case, see John B. Oakley, The Story of Owen Equipment v. Kroger: A Change in the Weather of Federal Jurisdiction, in Civil Procedure Stories 81 (Kevin M. Clermont ed., 2d ed. 2008).

77. See infra §§ 6.2–6.3.

(4) impleader claims under Rule 14(a)(1); and

(5) third-party defendants' claims against plaintiffs under Rule 14(a)(2)(D).[78]

The doctrine of ancillary jurisdiction does not cover:

(1) permissive counterclaims under Rule 13(b);

(2) permissive intervention under Rule 24(b), unless the intervenor is a class member intervening in a class action; or

(3) plaintiffs' claims against third-party defendants under Rule 14(a)(3), when the main claim rests on diversity jurisdiction.[79]

Ancillary Parties. Ancillary jurisdiction permits a defendant to assert a compulsory counterclaim or a crossclaim that involves new parties under Rule 13(h). However, ancillary jurisdiction does not permit a plaintiff suing in diversity to join a claim against a different defendant that would otherwise be beyond the federal jurisdiction. So if *P* of New York, invoking diversity jurisdiction, sues *D–1* of Vermont for $160,000, the district court cannot exercise ancillary jurisdiction in that action over a closely related state claim that *P* has against *D–2* of New York for $170,000, because 28 U.S.C. § 1332(a) and its requirement of complete diversity implicitly prohibit ancillary jurisdiction here.

Again, such wooden rules are likely either too broad or too narrow from the viewpoint of desirable policy, which would counsel looking more closely at both relatedness and the discretionary factors. Nevertheless, in the Supreme Court's sole foray into supplemental jurisdiction, it chose to read § 1367(b)'s prohibition rigidly.[80] Rejecting clear legislative intent in favor of explicit statutory wording, it held that the statute did not prohibit the use of supplemental jurisdiction to satisfy the jurisdictional amount requirement for multiple plaintiffs joined under Federal Rule 20 or 23 who are suing a single defendant. Still, supplemental jurisdiction does not exist if the case does not satisfy the complete diversity rule or if the multiple plaintiffs are suing multiple defendants.

Territorial Jurisdiction and Venue. On the one hand, the normal rules of territorial jurisdiction apply. On the other hand, if the district court exercises ancillary jurisdiction over the subject matter, then the doctrine of "ancillary venue" steps in to overcome any defense of improper venue.[81]

---

78. See Revere Copper & Brass Inc. v. Aetna Cas. & Sur. Co., 426 F.2d 709 (5th Cir. 1970).

79. Compare Owen Equip. & Erection Co. v. Kroger, 437 U.S. 365 (1978), with Ortiz v. U.S. Gov't, 595 F.2d 65 (1st Cir. 1979).

80. Exxon Mobil Corp. v. Allapattah Servs., Inc., 545 U.S. 546 (2005), overruling Zahn v. Int'l Paper Co., 414 U.S. 291 (1973).

81. See Wright & Miller, supra note 31, § 3808.

Synthesis: Supplemental Jurisdiction. The doctrines of pendent and ancillary jurisdiction exhibited a similar evolution and theory. They shared a common ancient origin, although later American courts came to speak of them separately. Then their realms began to overlap, and their precedents were becoming interchangeable. Now Congress has combined them in its statutory brand of "supplemental jurisdiction."[82]

The future should see them truly merge into a doctrine giving the federal courts broad constitutional and statutory power over the whole "case" and relying on the judicial exercise of discretion in accord with good policy to restrain that broad power. Of course, in order to serve the strong systemic interests underlying nondiversity jurisdiction, there will be a generally wider scope of supplemental jurisdiction in the classic pendent areas (involving a plaintiff's state claim against a defendant additional to a nondiversity main claim) than in the classic ancillary areas (involving supplemental jurisdiction in nonpendent situations), but this follows from the realization that good policy calls for different degrees of extension and restraint in different situations.

3. Jurisdictional Incidents

a. Role of Discretion in Jurisdiction

I have just described how the federal courts, in connection with supplemental jurisdiction, have discretion to define their own jurisdiction within broad bounds of power. This is not atypical.[83] After all, the judicial branch in effect has discretion regarding the scope of federal question jurisdiction too: as previously described, the Supreme Court reads the Constitution broadly as requiring only a federal ingredient, but reads the statutes more narrowly as imposing such fluid limits as almost to free itself to define the scope of federal question jurisdiction on the basis of pragmatic considerations. Moreover, judicial discretion plays a large role in the doctrines of limitation that have grown up from the constitutional requirement of "case or controversy," including such doctrines as ripeness and standing.[84] Also, the doctrine of "abstention" calls sometimes for the federal courts, usually in deference to a state's interests, discretionarily to decline federal jurisdiction.[85] Such matters are the subject of study in upperclass courses like Federal Courts.

---

82. For a proposed further revision, see ALI Federal Judicial Code Revision Project pt. I (2004).

83. See generally Gene R. Shreve, Pragmatism Without Politics—A Half Measure of Authority for Jurisdictional Common Law, 1991 BYU L. Rev. 767.

84. See generally Wright & Kane, supra note 1, §§ 12–15.

85. See generally id. §§ 52–52A.

b. Hypothetical Jurisdiction

Federal courts should decide subject-matter jurisdiction at the outset of the case.[86] But if the defendant challenges the existence of some other threshold jurisdiction-like requirement, and if this challenge is more easily resolved than subject-matter jurisdiction, the court has discretion to act as if it has subject-matter jurisdiction and can dismiss on the basis of that other defect. Thus, relying on this so-called hypothetical jurisdiction over the subject matter, the court can dismiss after rendering a binding determination of the lack of, say, personal jurisdiction.[87]

c. Time as of Which to Determine Jurisdiction

Federal jurisdiction is generally determined as of the time it was invoked, by complaint or upon removal.[88] It is not ordinarily ousted by subsequent events.[89] It can, however, be saved by certain corrective steps, which comprise the amendment of defective jurisdictional allegations under 28 U.S.C. § 1653 or the dropping of misjoined parties under Federal Rule 21.[90]

Thus, citizenship is determined as of the time when jurisdiction was invoked. So if P, a citizen of New York, wishes to sue D, a citizen of New York, for $160,000 in damages from an automobile accident, P may create diversity jurisdiction by first validly changing his domicile to New Jersey. If subsequent to instituting suit, P moves again, establishing a new domicile back in New York, diversity jurisdiction is not ousted.

d. Removal

Although the Constitution makes no mention of removal of cases from state court to federal court, Congress from the very beginning has used its powers under Articles I and III to provide

---

86. See Steel Co. v. Citizens for a Better Environment, 523 U.S. 83 (1998) (holding that the court must determine subject-matter jurisdiction before dismissing for failure to state a claim, even when the latter question is easier to resolve).

87. See Ruhrgas AG v. Marathon Oil Co., 526 U.S. 574 (1999), criticized in Scott C. Idleman, The Emergence of Jurisdictional Resequencing in the Federal Courts, 87 Cornell L. Rev. 1 (2001); cf. Sinochem Int'l Co. v. Malay. Int'l Shipping Corp., 549 U.S. 422 (2007) (same for determination of forum non conveniens).

88. See Grupo Dataflux v. Atlas Global Group, L.P., 541 U.S. 567 (2004).

89. But cf. Am. Fiber & Finishing, Inc. v. Tyco Healthcare Group, LP, 362 F.3d 136 (1st Cir. 2004) (holding that substitution of correct but nondiverse defendant, for diverse but wrong defendant, will oust jurisdiction).

90. See Iraola & CIA, S.A. v. Kimberly–Clark Corp., 232 F.3d 854, 860–61 (11th Cir. 2000); cf. Caterpillar Inc. v. Lewis, 519 U.S. 61 (1996) (holding that federal judgment in improperly removed case was saved by earlier dismissal of the nondiverse party who had settled).

for such removal from state trial courts to the district courts of specified cases within the federal judicial power. I did not include removal under the heads of jurisdiction, because removal jurisdiction is only a defendant's route into federal court, analogous to original jurisdiction as a plaintiff's route. Moreover, normally some other head of jurisdiction, such as federal question or diversity, must exist for the defendant to invoke the removal route, as reflected by the basic removal statute in 28 U.S.C. § 1441:

> (a) Except as otherwise expressly provided by Act of Congress, any civil action brought in a State court of which the district courts of the United States have original jurisdiction, may be removed by the defendant or the defendants, to the district court of the United States for the district and division embracing the place where such action is pending. For purposes of removal under this chapter, the citizenship of defendants sued under fictitious names shall be disregarded.

> (b) Any civil action of which the district courts have original jurisdiction founded on a claim or right arising under the Constitution, treaties or laws of the United States shall be removable without regard to the citizenship or residence of the parties. Any other such action shall be removable only if none of the parties in interest properly joined and served as defendants is a citizen of the State in which such action is brought.

> (c) Whenever a separate and independent claim or cause of action within the jurisdiction conferred by section 1331 of this title is joined with one or more otherwise non-removable claims or causes of action, the entire case may be removed and the district court may determine all issues therein, or, in its discretion, may remand all matters in which State law predominates.

> * * * *

Under § 1441(a), only a *defendant* can remove. *Shamrock Oil & Gas Corp. v. Sheets*[91] so held in circumstances where P sued D in state court, D asserted a counterclaim that would have been within the federal original jurisdiction, and P sought to remove; despite facing that counterclaim, P could not remove, because P was not formally a defendant in the case as a whole.

Moreover, a defendant can remove only on the basis of the federal jurisdictional attributes of the claims *against* her, and not on the basis of any counterclaims asserted by her. But upon removal, the whole case, with all its claims including counterclaims, goes to the federal court.

Finally, *all* served defendants must seek removal together under § 1441(a). So if P joins and serves $D-1$ and $D-2$ as joint tortfeasors in a state-court case, $D-1$ alone cannot remove, even if

---

91.   313 U.S. 100 (1941).

the case would have been within the district courts' original jurisdiction.

Removable Actions. All defendants can remove from state court (1) pursuant to § 1441 any civil action against them that is within the district courts' original jurisdiction, subject to the exceptions noted immediately below, and (2) certain other cases that are outside said original jurisdiction, although within the bounds of Article III, such as those cases specified in 28 U.S.C. § 1442 (federal officers sued) and § 1443 (certain civil rights matters).

Nonremovability Statutes. Certain cases that might be within the district courts' original jurisdiction are nevertheless declared by various statutes to be nonremovable, thus protecting plaintiffs' choice of a state forum. Examples include 28 U.S.C. § 1445(a) (Federal Employers' Liability Act cases) and § 1445(c) (workmen's compensation cases).

An important exception to the removability of cases *not founded on a federal question* appears in § 1441(b), whereby defendants cannot remove a case under § 1441(a) *if any served defendant is a citizen of the forum state.* The idea here is that such defendants have no need to escape from local bias in the state court. So if *P*, a citizen of New York, joins *D–1*, a citizen of New Jersey, and *D–2*, a citizen of Pennsylvania, as defendants in a New Jersey state court, asking $160,000 from each, and if the defendants seek to remove, they cannot remove (unless the case is founded on a federal question) because *D–1* is from the forum state. Strangely, no comparable limitation restricts local plaintiffs when they are invoking the federal courts' original diversity jurisdiction, so that a plaintiff can use diversity to sue even in the federal court at home.

Separate and Independent Claims. Some slim hope for circumventing the restrictions on removal appears to lie in § 1441(c).[92] This narrow and difficult statute provides for defendants' removal of a federal question claim when joined by plaintiffs with a separate and independent claim that would otherwise be nonremovable. That is, the defendants to the original plaintiffs' federal question claim can remove if that claim would have been removable when sued upon alone, even though the plaintiffs have joined a completely unrelated claim that those defendants could not have removed if it stood by itself. "Separate and independent" means completely unrelated on the facts.[93]

Given such joinder, the entire case becomes removable. Once the entire case comes before the federal district court via § 1441(c),

---

92. See generally Wright & Kane, supra note 1, § 39.

93. See Am. Fire & Cas. Co. v. Finn, 341 U.S. 6, 14 (1951); Borough of W.

Mifflin v. Lancaster, 45 F.3d 780 (3d Cir. 1995).

it may remand those matters as to which state law predominates.[94] Indeed, in the usual situation of a completely unrelated state claim not within the court's original jurisdiction, the district court must remand that claim and thus avoid any constitutional problem of entertaining a claim otherwise outside Article III.[95]

Removal Procedure. Congress has specified the mechanics of removal in 28 U.S.C. §§ 1446–1450.

Defendants' Steps. To avoid waiver, defendants must seek removal promptly, normally within 30 days of receipt of the complaint by service.[96] Defendants file in the local federal district court a notice of removal, subject to Federal Rule 11 and setting forth the grounds that justify removal; note that the proper federal court is the district court for the district in which the particular state courthouse is located. Next, defendants give notification of the filing to plaintiffs and to the state court. Removal is then complete.

Judicial Steps. After this activity solely on the part of defendants, the state court can proceed no further. The action is now in the federal court, and under Federal Rule 81(c) the action will be treated henceforth like a normal federal action.[97] If the action has been improperly removed, the federal court will "remand" it to the state court. Such a remand order is generally not appealable or reviewable, so the case would then resume in the state court.[98]

---

94. Compare Kabealo v. Davis, 829 F. Supp. 923 (S.D. Ohio 1993) (construing "matters" to mean claims), aff'd on other grounds, 72 F.3d 129 (6th Cir. 1995), with Burnett v. Birmingham Bd. of Educ., 861 F. Supp. 1036 (N.D. Ala. 1994) (construing "matters" to permit remand of entire case).

95. See Fullin v. Martin, 34 F. Supp. 2d 726, 729–35 (E.D. Wis. 1999).

96. See Murphy Bros. v. Michetti Pipe Stringing, Inc., 526 U.S. 344 (1999) (specifying when period starts to run); Noble v. Bradford Marine, Inc., 789 F. Supp. 395 (S.D. Fla. 1992) (finding waiver).

97. See also 28 U.S.C. § 1448 (treating service of process).

98. Compare 28 U.S.C. § 1447(d), with Thermtron Prods., Inc. v. Hermansdorfer, 423 U.S. 336 (1976) (finding exception to statute).

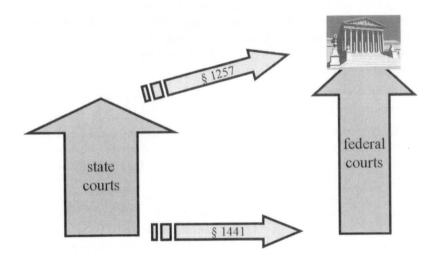

e. Devices to Manipulate Jurisdiction

Devices to Create Jurisdiction. In order to get a case into federal court, a potential plaintiff will sometimes assign his claim to someone whose citizenship is different from the defendant's, or use some analogous tactic such as naming a diverse representative for a potential party. However, such tactics will often fail. First, courts ignore the citizenship of any named party whose interest at stake is strictly nominal, such as a purely formal obligee; motive in naming the party has no effect. The diversity statute itself was amended to prevent manipulation by appointment of legal representatives of infants, incompetents, and decedents.[99] Second, 28 U.S.C. § 1359 says to ignore the citizenship of any party "improperly or collusively" named. In applying § 1359, courts look for a motive to manufacture federal jurisdiction; but as the named party's interest at stake becomes more substantial, the motive necessary for triggering § 1359 must increasingly be a blatant one.[100] Indeed, if the named party has a very real or even exclusive interest, and bears no resemblance whatsoever to a straw party, then his or her citizenship is considered, as motive in naming the party again becomes irrelevant. A complete and absolute transfer of interest will thus affect jurisdiction.[101]

Devices to Defeat Jurisdiction. In order to prevent the defendant from removing the action to federal court, a potential

---

99. 28 U.S.C. § 1332(c)(2).

100. See Kramer v. Caribbean Mills, Inc., 394 U.S. 823 (1969).

101. Cf. Baker v. Keck, 13 F. Supp. 486 (E.D. Ill. 1936) (holding that plain-

tiff could establish new domicile, even with purpose of creating diversity jurisdiction).

plaintiff will sometimes try to destroy complete diversity by joining a party whose state citizenship is the same as an opposing party's. If the joined party is not nominal, this device will often work, because there is no general equivalent of 28 U.S.C. § 1359 that would prohibit obstruction of federal jurisdiction.[102] Nevertheless, some courts of late have invoked a power supposedly inherent in the judiciary to reject artificial devices that would defeat jurisdiction, shaping the so-called fraudulent joinder doctrine into a kind of converse § 1359.[103]

f. Jurisdictional Amount

Various statutes impose a jurisdictional amount requirement, but by far the most important is the requirement in 28 U.S.C. § 1332(a) that "the matter in controversy exceeds the sum or value of $75,000, exclusive of interest and costs." The purpose of such a requirement is to keep petty controversies out of the federal courts. However, what it seems to do best is to create litigation over how it should be applied.[104]

Test Applied. The amount in controversy is measured under the state of affairs that existed when the action was commenced in or removed to federal court.[105] To satisfy the requirement, if the plaintiff pleads a claim for more than $75,000 against the defendant, the party invoking federal jurisdiction must be able to show that the plaintiff's judgment could legally exceed $75,000 under the applicable law. This test is called the legal-certainty test, because an allegation in excess of $75,000 survives challenge unless there is *legal* certainty that damages will not exceed $75,000.[106]

So, for example, imagine that P invokes diversity jurisdiction by suing D on a $75,000 interest-free promissory note, seeking the $75,000 debt plus $500,000 in punitive damages. D challenges jurisdiction. There will be a dismissal if punitive damages in such a contract action are not recoverable under the applicable law, because then the award of damages could not legally exceed $75,000.

The legal-certainty test is very easily passed, especially in unliquidated tort cases, because jurisdiction exists even though a

102. See Mecom v. Fitzsimmons Drilling Co., 284 U.S. 183 (1931).

103. See, e.g., Rose v. Giamatti, 721 F. Supp. 906 (S.D. Ohio 1989). See generally Wright & Kane, supra note 1, § 31.

104. See Wright & Miller, supra note 31, § 3701.

105. See generally Wright & Kane, supra note 1, §§ 33–35; Kevin M. Clermont & Theodore Eisenberg, CAFA Ju-

dicata: A Tale of Waste and Politics, 156 U. Pa. L. Rev. 1553, 1569–79 (2008) (discussing application of test upon removal).

106. See Saint Paul Mercury Indem. Co. v. Red Cab Co., 303 U.S. 283 (1938). Compare Drach v. Am. Kennel Club, Inc., 53 F.3d 338 (9th Cir. 1995) (no jurisdiction), with A.F.A. Tours, Inc. v. Whitchurch, 937 F.2d 82 (2d Cir. 1991) (jurisdiction).

recovery over $75,000 is on the *facts* highly unlikely. Some courts will at an early stage nevertheless dismiss occasional cases in which requested damages are very flagrantly exaggerated, but all tests routinely more rigorous than the legal-certainty test have proved impractical.[107]

Interest and Costs. In applying this jurisdictional amount requirement, the court will not include any interest on the underlying claim or any court costs expected to be awarded in the instant suit. However, problem cases exist here. For example, if *P* sues *D* for $76,000 in interest owing on *P*'s loan to *D*, the jurisdictional amount exists, because the claim is for interest, rather than merely seeking interest on a claim.[108]

Injunctive and Declaratory Relief. When the plaintiff seeks relief other than money damages, the court must look to some dollar valuation of the objective of the suit, there being no amount that will be awarded by judgment. For example, if the plaintiff sues to overturn a statute regulating his business, the amount in controversy would be the difference between the business's value regulated and its value unregulated.[109]

Collateral and Future Effects. In applying this jurisdictional amount requirement, the court will include only the *direct* value of judgment *on the claim* before the court.[110] The court will not include side effects of the judgment sought, such as possible penalties for noncompliance with the judgment or even the value of collateral estoppel effects when the judgment could be used in other actions. To measure the direct value within these bounds of the claim, the court will value requested relief establishing future rights or dispelling future duties by roughly subjecting the relief to usual valuation techniques, which take into account time and probabilities. So if *P* sues *D* to establish a contractual right to a life annuity, the expected present value of which is $76,000, the jurisdictional amount exists. However, on such matters the courts do demonstrate unlimited confusion.

Viewpoint for Valuation. The courts show more confusion on how to apply the test when the value of the requested relief to the plaintiff is apparently different from the cost to the defendant of complying with the requested relief, as where a shipowner sues to remove the defendant's bridge.[111] Among the possible solutions,

107. See, e.g., Nelson v. Keefer, 451 F.2d 289 (3d Cir. 1971); cf. Kevin M. Clermont, Jurisdictional Fact, 91 Cornell L. Rev. 973, 1008–11 (2006) (discussing standard of decision).

108. See Brown v. Webster, 156 U.S. 328 (1895) (holding that plaintiff could count any interest that was sought as part of the claim for damages, but not "interest as such").

109. See McNutt v. Gen. Motors Acceptance Corp., 298 U.S. 178 (1936).

110. See Healy v. Ratta, 292 U.S. 263 (1934).

111. See Miss. & Mo. R.R. v. Ward, 67 U.S. (2 Black) 485 (1863).

most courts seem to choose the "plaintiff-viewpoint rule," looking only at the value to the plaintiff.[112] Perhaps a more logical approach would look to the smaller of the plaintiff's value and the defendant's cost, with the idea being that the parties could theoretically strike a bargain with one party paying the other's smaller price and that therefore this smaller amount is what is really in controversy; but this approach has no case support.

Costs Sanction. In 1958 Congress authorized a costs sanction in 28 U.S.C. § 1332(b), giving the courts discretionary power to impose court costs on any plaintiff who has invoked diversity jurisdiction but has recovered less than the jurisdictional amount. This has proved ineffective, because the courts use the power rarely and because court costs as opposed to attorney's fees are usually minuscule.

Aggregation of Claims. Consider now this problem: When can the amounts in controversy on two or more joined claims be added together to satisfy this jurisdictional amount requirement?[113]

Claims Between Same Parties. All claims asserted by one plaintiff against the same defendant may be aggregated, regardless of the relation among the claims. So if P sues D for $36,000 on a contract claim, and P joins an unrelated tort claim against D for $40,000, the jurisdictional amount exists.

Claims Involving Different Parties. Separate and distinct claims asserted by multiple plaintiffs against the same defendant, or asserted by the same plaintiff against multiple defendants, cannot be aggregated. So if P–1 and P–2, invoking diversity jurisdiction, sue D for $51,000 and $58,000 respectively, on claims arising out of the same automobile accident, and someone challenges jurisdiction, then there will be a dismissal, because P–1 and P–2 cannot aggregate.[114]

The same rule applies to class actions. So, for a plaintiff-class action based on diversity jurisdiction, class members with separate and distinct claims cannot aggregate to satisfy the jurisdictional amount requirement.[115] Strangely, while the citizenships of only the named parties enter into determining the existence of diversity of

---

112. See Glenwood Light & Water Co. v. Mut. Light, Heat & Power Co., 239 U.S. 121 (1915) (upholding jurisdiction). But cf. Ronzio v. Denver & Rio Grande W.R.R., 116 F.2d 604, 606–07 (10th Cir. 1940) (holding that jurisdiction exists if either plaintiff's value or defendant's cost exceeds jurisdictional amount); McCarty v. Amoco Pipeline Co., 595 F.2d 389, 391–93 (7th Cir. 1979) (same in removal case).

113. See generally Wright & Kane, supra note 1, § 36.

114. On the application of supplemental jurisdiction, as distinguished from aggregation, where one of the claims alone satisfies the jurisdictional amount, see supra § 4.1(C)(2)(c).

115. See Snyder v. Harris, 394 U.S. 332 (1969).

citizenship, the jurisdictional amount requirement applies to every class member's claim.

But an exception to the rule allows aggregation of claims that assert a "common and undivided interest," which represents a small category of ancient lineage that is virtually undefinable and can only be delineated by example (e.g., an estate's distributees suing a defendant who allegedly converted the estate). Suffice it to say that this exception requires much more than relatedness among the claims.[116]

A Better Approach. Both of the established rules above are undesirable. A more sensible rule, at least outside the class-action context, would allow aggregation if and only if the claims are related. This rule would better conform to the congressional purpose to keep petty controversies out of the federal courts and let the others in.

Counterclaims. Consider finally the problem of whether the amount in controversy on a counterclaim can be considered in applying this jurisdictional amount requirement to the main claim. The courts show yet more confusion in approaching this question in its varied factual settings, leaving it unsettled.[117]

Marginally, the best approach under the current statutory scheme and case law is to ignore the counterclaim in applying the jurisdictional amount requirement to the main claim, whether it is a permissive or compulsory counterclaim.[118] So if *P*, invoking diversity jurisdiction, sues *D* for $35,000 for damages from an automobile accident, and if *D*, alleging damages from the same automobile accident, counterclaims for $108,000, then there should be a dismissal. Nevertheless, if the counterclaim falls into that small category of "common-law compulsory counterclaims,"[119] then the counterclaim is actually part of the main claim and should be considered—not as a counterclaim but as a component in measuring the main claim.[120]

§ 4.2   Territorial Authority to Adjudicate

A.   Introduction

1.   Definitions of Concepts

116. See Wright & Miller, *supra* note 31, § 3704.

117. See generally Wright & Kane, *supra* note 1, § 37.

118. See, e.g., Cont'l Carriers, Inc. v. Goodpasture, 169 F. Supp. 602 (M.D. Ga. 1959) (noting need for remedial legislation).

119. See infra § 5.2(C).

120. See Horton v. Liberty Mut. Ins. Co., 367 U.S. 348 (1961) (jurisdictional amount, then $10,000, exists where workers' compensation insurer sues to set aside administrative award of $1050 and claims no liability, and workman counterclaims for his full claim of $14,035).

For a court properly to undertake a civil adjudication, the court must have territorial authority to adjudicate.[121] This requirement confines the *place of litigation*, putting restrictions on the court's authority to entertain litigation with nonlocal elements. The scope of territorial authority to adjudicate is defined in terms of the geographic relationship among the parties, the forum, and the litigation. Territorial authority to adjudicate comprises both territorial jurisdiction and venue.

The concept of *territorial jurisdiction*, sometimes termed "judicial jurisdiction," "amenability," or "nexus," comprises the more important rules of territorial authority to adjudicate. Indeed, territorial jurisdiction rests heavily on the Federal Constitution. Accordingly, those territorial restrictions deriving from the Due Process Clause will be first considered below. Then consideration will be given to all the other territorial restrictions on jurisdiction.

Any study of territorial authority to adjudicate would be incomplete without next considering its subset of law on *venue*, which specifies the place of suit. The choice of venue nay be restricted by the applicable law or by the parties' agreement. Nonetheless, the definition of venue is frustratingly murky, this lesser but related concept being sometimes difficult to distinguish from territorial jurisdiction.

What Is the Ultimate Difference Between Territorial Jurisdiction and Venue?

State venue restrictions are most often defined as those rules of territorial authority to adjudicate that specify as proper forums only certain courts within a state that has territorial jurisdiction, so that state-court territorial jurisdiction comprises interstate rules while state-court venue is intrastate. This accepted interstate/intrastate distinction on the state level is, however, not very meaningful. A sounder and more fruitful doctrinal distinction would view territorial jurisdiction as those mandatory limits flowing from the Federal Constitution, while considering venue to encompass all the other limitations both interstate and intrastate in nature. In this view, venue appears as a scheme that aims in an integrated fashion at the convenient, efficient, and otherwise desirable distribution of judicial business among and within the states, and also appears as a scheme that is not immune to reform by legislative or judicial reworking or refinement.

Federal venue restrictions most often are rather arbitrarily defined as those rules of territorial authority to adjudicate that are not linked to service provisions but instead are separately and statutorily prescribed. Yet, both Federal Rule 4's service provisions and 28 U.S.C. § 1391 perform, albeit crudely, their common mission of distributing judicial business within the federal system in a convenient, efficient, and otherwise desirable manner. Classifying the former as jurisdiction and the latter as venue can be dangerous to the extent practical consequences ride on the distinction, and this misleading line also leaves the doctrines in-between as difficult to classify. So, just as for state courts, a sounder and more fruitful doctrinal

---

121. See generally Kevin M. Clermont, Civil Procedure: Territorial Jurisdiction and Venue (1999).

distinction would view territorial jurisdiction as those mandatory limits flowing from the Federal Constitution, while considering venue to include all the lesser limitations. This might induce a reform whereby Congress would extend service to those constitutional limits with the sole purpose of providing notice, while Congress would simplify, narrow, and rationalize the whole venue scheme with the purpose of optimally distributing judicial business.

In sum, venue naturally includes so-called venue statutes and doctrines, but it also abuts and should include forum non conveniens, transfer provisions, and forum selection clauses, as well as restrictions on serving process and other of the sovereign's self-imposed limitations such as door-closing statutes and local-action doctrines. Best defined, venue comprises all the subconstitutional doctrines that work to site litigation in particular and presumably appropriate courts, among the several of the sovereign's courts that have constitutional authority—or, conceivably, work to oust all those courts of authority. See generally Kevin M. Clermont, Restating Territorial Jurisdiction and Venue for State and Federal Courts, 66 Cornell L. Rev. 411 (1981).

2. Summary of Law

The basic U.S. law on the subject of territorial authority to adjudicate is, in a nutshell, this: the forum acquires adjudicatory authority in civil cases through *power* over the target of the action (be it a person or a thing), unless litigating the action there is *unreasonable* (that is, fundamentally unfair)—although the sovereign can choose *self-restraint* (exercising less than its full adjudicatory authority).

I shall elaborate this basic statement of the law in the state and federal court settings, then apply the learning to international litigation, and finally suggest how I think the current law should be reformed.

Once Again, Why Is Forum Such a Big Deal?

No doubt about it, lawyers in the United States expend significant time, energy, and other resources on the process of forum selection. The name of the game is forum-shopping. Few cases reach trial in the civil litigation system today; after perhaps some initial skirmishing, most cases settle. Yet all cases entail forum selection, be it choosing between state and federal court, or selecting local venue, or interstate shopping, or international shopping. First, consider the individual case. The plaintiff's opening moves include selecting the most favorable forum. Then, the defendant's parries and thrusts might include some forum-shopping in return, possibly by a motion for transfer of venue. Forum is worth fighting over because outcome is thought often to turn on forum. When the dust settles, the case does too—but on terms that reflect the results of the skirmishing over forum. Thus, the fight over forum can be the most critical dispute in the case. Second, cumulate these tendencies systemically. Forum selection is very important not only to the litigator, but also to the office lawyer who is drafting contracts with an eye toward possible future litigation arising from the contracts. Not surprising, then, there exist entire treatises devoted to the subject. Once in litigation, the parties frequently dispute forum. Courts deal with many more transfer-of-venue motions than trials. Thus, forum selection should be a critical concern of those in charge of the legal system as a whole. If the choice of forum in fact has an impact on the chance of winning and hence on the value of settlement, then basic fairness would be at stake, and accordingly lawmakers should worry about the law of territorial authority to adjudicate.

Are all those lawyers out there wasting their clients' money on forum fights? What is the actual effect of forum selection on the outcome of cases? Practitioners and policymakers share an obvious interest in these questions.

Consider transfer of venue from one federal district court to another. The plaintiffs' win rate drops markedly after transfer of venue, from 58% in cases in which there is no transfer to 29% in transferred cases. The loss of a favorable forum seems, after detailed analysis, to be the primary explanation. The transferred plaintiffs all lost a big forum advantage and thus litigated less successfully in the unfavorable forum, so the win rate dropped. Indeed, because neither the court system nor the applicable law changes after transfer, one is seeing only the effects of a strongly shifted balance of inconveniences and a shift of local biases. See generally Kevin M. Clermont & Theodore Eisenberg, Exorcising the Evil of Forum-Shopping, 80 Cornell L. Rev. 1507 (1995); Kevin M. Clermont & Theodore Eisenberg, Simplifying the Choice of Forum: A Reply, 75 Wash. U. L.Q. 1551 (1997).

When one starts thinking about shopping among states, differences in substantive and procedural law enter the equation. The fact is that choice-of-law doctrines, as applied, fail to eliminate differences in governing law.

In international litigation, the choice of forum becomes even more important. Shifting inconveniences and changing biases from one forum to a foreign forum become staggeringly effective, as does the change in cultural and institutional context. Moreover, the differences in substantive and procedural law—as well as the matters of remedies and expenses—dwarf the small variations within American law. What is the forum's law on antitrust, will there be a jury, how big will the damages be fixed and will they be trebled, and can the plaintiff's lawyer proceed on a contingent fee and will the loser have to pay the winner's expenses?

Forum matters.

B. State Courts

1. Federal Limitations on State Reach

The plaintiff brings an action in state court, thus implicitly asserting that the state has territorial jurisdiction. If the defendant challenges this assertion, the courts must pass on jurisdiction, ultimately subjecting it to constitutional scrutiny.

The U.S. Supreme Court has formulated the principal limitations on a court's territorial authority from the opaque few words of the Due Process Clauses of the U.S. Constitution. The Constitution's Fourteenth Amendment provides: "nor shall any State deprive any person of life, liberty, or property, without due process of law." As the Supreme Court finally clarified its earlier landmark cases' implications in *World-Wide Volkswagen Corp. v. Woodson*,[122]

122. 444 U.S. 286, 291–92 (1980) (The Due Process Clause "can be seen to perform two related, but distinguishable, functions. It protects the defendant against the burdens of litigating in a distant or inconvenient forum. And it acts to ensure that the States, through their courts, do not reach out beyond the limits imposed on them by their status as coequal sovereigns in a federal system."). For the story behind this case, see Charles W. Adams, World–Wide Volkswagen v. Woodson—The Rest of the Story, 72 Neb. L. Rev. 1122 (1993);

due process dictates both that the forum must have *power* over the target of the action *and* that litigating the action there must be *reasonable*. And then the Supreme Court, in *Burger King Corp. v. Rudzewicz,*[123] further instructed that while the plaintiff has the burden of persuasion as to power, it is up to the defendant to show unreasonableness—thus changing a natural-sounding reasonableness test into a more grammatically challenging unreasonableness test, as the shifted burden causes the unreasonableness test to operate more as a counterpoint to the power test.

Verbal gymnastics aside, there is nothing bizarre about federal authority exerting control over state reach. It is true that a full sovereign can do whatever it wants, having the raw force to adjudicate any dispute when, and how, it pleases, as well as the capability to enforce its adjudication on persons and things over which it eventually acquires physical control. Nevertheless, international law envisages some limit on that raw force, a requirement of an adequate connection between the sovereign and the target of the action. Moreover, any suprasovereign authority, such as the federal government that exists above the states, can impose further limits.

The Constitution envisages the states as independent sovereigns for many purposes, but it also imposes a higher federal authority that limits the states' authority in some regards. In particular, the Due Process Clause of the Fourteenth Amendment limits how far the states' authority to adjudicate can reach, as first established by *Pennoyer v. Neff*[124] with its reliance on international law. This crucial sacrifice of sovereignty accepted by the states in the current Constitution enables them to realize fully the benefits of the judicially unified nation, as delivered by the modern implementation of the Full Faith and Credit Clause. That is, the states can confidently give, and thereby get in return, largely automatic recognition and enforcement of sister-state judgments, because the states know that the due process requirements restrict all the other states to appropriate territorial authority to adjudicate, as well as to basically fair procedure.

In sum, no debate persists as to whether the federal authority can or should control state reach through the Constitution, but

Hipolito R. Corella, Tucsonans Lose Battle Against Audi, Ariz. Daily Star, Jan. 9, 1996, at 1A, available at 1996 WL 4979662. See also Ins. Corp. of Ir. v. Compagnie des Bauxites de Guinee, 456 U.S. 694, 702 & n.10 (1982) (The jurisdictional requirement "represents a restriction on judicial power not as a matter of sovereignty, but as a matter of individual liberty.").

123.   471 U.S. 462, 476–78 (1985).

124.   95 U.S. 714 (1878). For the story behind this case, see Wendy C. Perdue, Sin, Scandal, and Substantive Due Process: Personal Jurisdiction and Pennoyer Reconsidered, 62 Wash. L. Rev. 479 (1987).

there remains plenty of difficulty in specifying precisely what the Due Process Clause's words mean in this regard.

a. Categorization

The very image of "power" inevitably raises the question of power over whom or what, despite the undeniable fact that all actions really affect the interests of people. That is, to measure the strength of the power relation between the sovereign and the target of the action, the law has to specify the target of the action. In still other words, the action must initially be categorized in terms of the target of the action so that the jurisdictional tests may be appropriately applied. Thus arose the American categorization of territorial jurisdiction into jurisdiction over persons and things. In the *Pennoyer* case, the Supreme Court laid the theoretical foundation: under the Due Process Clause, the basic **categories** of jurisdiction are personal jurisdiction and the nonpersonal categories of in rem and quasi in rem jurisdiction.

Jurisdiction *in personam*, or "personal jurisdiction," can result in a judgment imposing a personal liability or obligation upon the defendant in favor of the plaintiff or, more generally, diminishing the personal rights of a party in favor of another party. This is the most common kind of territorial jurisdiction. For example, a successful tort action resting on personal jurisdiction subjects all of the defendant's nonexempt assets to execution. For another example, a successful suit for an injunction requires jurisdiction in personam and subjects the defendant to the court's contempt sanctions.

Jurisdiction *in rem* usually involves an action against a thing, but can be stretched to cases treating status as a thing. First, jurisdiction in rem can result in a judgment affecting the interests of *all* persons in a designated thing. Theoretically and formally, the action is against the thing. No personal liability or obligation results. Examples of proceedings in rem include actions to register title to land and forfeiture actions. Second, jurisdiction over status, which is best classified as a subtype of in rem jurisdiction, can result in a judgment establishing or terminating a status, such as a family relationship or citizenship. By so treating the status as a thing, the state may determine status. For example, the state where the plaintiff spouse is domiciled may grant a divorce, but note that the state could not impose support obligations without personal jurisdiction over the defendant spouse.

Jurisdiction *quasi in rem* can result in a judgment affecting only the interests of *particular* persons in a designated thing. The difference between in rem jurisdiction and this category is that here state law does not authorize a judgment affecting the interests of all persons in the world. Although a proceeding quasi in rem is formally brought against the named defendants, only their interests in the thing are at stake. There are two distinct varieties of proceedings quasi in rem. First, in subtype one, the plaintiff seeks to establish an interest in the thing, an interest allegedly pre-existing the lawsuit that is now to be established against the defendant's interest. Examples include actions to partition land, to quiet title, and to foreclose a mortgage. Second, in subtype two, the plaintiff seeks to apply the defendant's property to the satisfaction of a claim against the defendant that is *unrelated* to the property. For example, the plaintiff might seek attachment jurisdiction in a New York state court for a tort claim arising from an auto accident elsewhere, by garnishing the defendant's New York bank account. Thus, because of this unrelatedness feature, subtype two of quasi in rem jurisdiction, sometimes termed "attachment jurisdiction," fundamentally differs from in rem and subtype one of quasi in rem.

b. Power

Prompted by the tensions among states in a federation of sovereigns, the United States early applied a theory of exclusive power based on territoriality: each state sovereign had jurisdiction, exclusive of all other sovereigns' jurisdiction, to bind persons and things present within its territorial boundaries. This power test is of unknown origin,[125] but the Supreme Court adopted it in the *Pennoyer* case, and subsequently pronounced: "The foundation of jurisdiction is physical power * * *."[126]

Although the power test initially rested on this notion that each state had exclusive authority over persons and things present within its territorial boundaries at the time the state acted against them, later changes in society doomed such a wooden approach. The Court so explained in *International Shoe Co. v. Washington*,[127] when it transformed the test into its elastic new phrase of "minimum contacts." *Hanson v. Denckla*[128] fleshed out the metaphor of minimum contacts by generalizing that power exists over a defendant who has purposefully availed itself "of the privilege of con-

---

125. Compare James Weinstein, The Dutch Influence on the Conception of Judicial Jurisdiction in 19th Century America, 38 Am. J. Comp. L. 73 (1990) (crediting its genesis to the seventeenth-century Dutch theorist Ulric Huber's De Conflictu Legum of 1684), with Harold L. Korn, The Development of Judicial Jurisdiction in the United States (pt. 1), 65 Brook. L. Rev. 935 (1999) (more credibly stressing originality of the American heresy).

126. McDonald v. Mabee, 243 U.S. 90, 91 (1917) (Holmes, J.).

127. 326 U.S. 310 (1945) (replacing physical-power approach with "minimum contacts" formulation). For the story behind this case, see Christopher D. Cameron & Kevin R. Johnson, Death of a Salesman? Forum Shopping and Outcome Determination Under International Shoe, 28 U.C. Davis L. Rev. 769 (1995).

128. 357 U.S. 235, 253 (1958).

ducting activities within the forum State, thus invoking the benefits and protections of its laws," a phrase that would come to include acts intentionally directed toward the forum state with knowledge that effects would result there.[129] Accordingly, today there are several **bases** of power other than physical presence (i.e., domicile, consent, and state-directed acts), which represent power only in the metaphorical sense.

This evolution of the common law of territorial jurisdiction has come largely in response to socio-economic-political pressures, as well as changes in technology and even philosophy. Evolving societies, intermeshing economies, and shifting politics have compelled the courts not only to increase the categories and bases of power, but also to stretch them—and to contract them as well. All sorts of factors from life's complexities have affected the evolution of territorial jurisdiction. Think of the arrival of simple automobile accidents: the basis of presence at the time of service of process was useless against the out-of-state driver who had returned home, but the state could reach the driver by claiming that the driver by driving in the state had somehow consented to its jurisdiction or, more aptly, had purposefully availed herself of the privilege of conducting activities within the state. The development of the business corporation, acting only through agents and often outside its home state, had an earthshaking impact on jurisdiction. Of course, the revolution in transportation and communication has increased the occurrence of long-distance disputes, but it has also decreased the burden of long-distance litigating. The twentieth century's shift from a laissez-faire to a social-welfare philosophy favored plaintiffs' desire for long jurisdictional reach, but a more recent pro-business outlook has produced cutbacks to protect defendants from litigiousness. The only constant is change.

Still, the old requirement of power remains very much a part of U.S. law today. The common element in specifying the current bases of power, and the defining feature of the power test, is the narrow focus on the defendant's interests—asking whether the relation of the target of the action to the sovereign constitutes minimum contacts—as opposed to a broader inquiry that would take account of the plaintiff's and the public's interests. Neverthe-

---

129. See Calder v. Jones, 465 U.S. 783, 788–90 (1984) (allowing the entertainer Shirley Jones to sue for libel in her home state of California against the National Enquirer's writer and editor living and working in Florida, the Court stressed that the defendants had "intentionally directed" their Florida acts at California while knowing that their conduct would have "effects" there); C. Douglas Floyd & Shima Baradaran–Robison, Toward a Unified Test of Personal Jurisdiction in an Era of Widely Diffused Wrongs: The Relevance of Purpose and Effects, 81 Ind. L.J. 601 (2006).

less, the rationale for still making this separate narrow inquiry, that is, for retaining the current power test, has become foggy.[130]

c. Unreasonableness

The *International Shoe* case not only expanded the old notion of power, but also gave birth to an additional test by its reference to the requirement of "fair play and substantial justice." Thus, another product of the judicial elaboration of due process has been the overlaying of a reasonableness test onto the power test, now with the burden on the defendant to show unreasonableness.

World-Wide Volkswagen and *Burger King* explained that the flexible test of unreasonableness balances the opposing parties' interests, along with the public's interests in the litigation. It also takes into account a diverse and complete set of relevant considerations, such as the actualities of the choice-of-law process. Other examples of relevant interests include the convenience of litigating in the forum state, the availability of an alternative forum, and the state's interest in adjudicating the dispute. The application of the unreasonableness test is amorphous, with the courts resorting to a sort of gut check.[131] Although rather uncertain in application, this party-neutral and all-things-considered test directly measures jurisdiction by the pertinent standard of fundamental unfairness in the broadest sense. The chosen forum need not be the ideal forum, but the forum, even if it has power, must not be an unreasonable one in light of all these interests in the litigation.

It might not be unreasonable to allow a poor and oppressed plaintiff to sue at home, even when the defendant has had no contacts with the plaintiff's home state (the power test would, however, block such suit). But this is not to say that the defendant's interests are ignored in applying the unreasonableness test. Thus, it might be unreasonable to assert jurisdiction over an out-of-state mom-and-pop business, despite its in-state minimum contacts and even if it would not be unreasonable to drag in Wal–Mart in similar circumstances.

The essential defining feature of the unreasonableness test is that it takes account of all interests in deciding whether jurisdiction would be fundamentally unfair—unlike the power test's narrow

130. See infra § 4.2(E)(1)(a) (further developing the proposition that the power test has lost its rationale).

131. See Nowak v. Tak How Invs., Ltd., 94 F.3d 708, 717 (1st Cir. 1996) ("These 'gestalt factors' are as follows: (1) the defendant's burden of appearing, (2) the forum state's interest in adjudicating the dispute, (3) the plaintiff's interest in obtaining convenient and effective relief, (4) the judicial system's interest in obtaining the most effective resolution of the controversy, and (5) the common interests of all sovereigns in promoting substantive social policies.").

focus on the defendant's interests. In fact, a fairness, or reasonableness, test inherently must be unbounded in factors to weigh.

d. Other Federal Limitations

Looking beyond the Due Process Clause, restrictions on the territorial jurisdiction of state courts may be found in other federal law or in state law. In the interests of orderly restraint, any jurisdictional inquiry by a court should proceed in two steps: (1) whether the asserted jurisdiction is permissibly within the restrictions imposed other than by the Federal Constitution and, if so, (2) whether the asserted jurisdiction passes muster under the Federal Constitution. But here I shall continue to sketch first those constitutional limitations.

Other Federal Constitutional Limitations. As already noted, the principal limitations on state-court territorial jurisdiction flow from the Due Process Clause of the Fourteenth Amendment. Some authorities argue that other provisions of the Federal Constitution impose independent restrictions on territorial jurisdiction applicable in certain unusual circumstances. The better view, however, is that the policies behind these other provisions enter into the balance of interests under due process's unreasonableness test, thus only indirectly restricting jurisdiction.[132]

An assertion of state-court jurisdiction might offend the policies underlying our First Amendment freedoms, binding on the states through the Fourteenth Amendment. Jurisdiction over out-of-state newspapers in libel cases is the obvious example. However, the Supreme Court has warned against an activist approach here, ruling that free press policies do not impede jurisdiction for libel actions.[133]

Still, there are other examples of constitutional limitations with at least an indirect role to play. Imagine that the defendant's only contacts with the District of Columbia are its dealings with a federal regulatory agency. An independent contractor employed by the defendant to handle those dealings sues there for fees. Jurisdiction is unconstitutional, in view of the policies behind the First

---

132. See N.Y. Times Co. v. Connor, 365 F.2d 567, 572 (5th Cir. 1966).

133. Calder v. Jones, 465 U.S. 783, 790 (1984) ("We * * * reject the suggestion that First Amendment concerns enter into the jurisdictional analysis. The infusion of such considerations would needlessly complicate an already imprecise inquiry. * * * Moreover, the potential chill on protected First Amendment activity stemming from libel and defamation actions is already taken into account in the constitutional limitations on the substantive law governing such suits."); see Keeton v. Hustler Magazine, Inc., 465 U.S. 770 (1984) (nonresident individual can seek damages suffered throughout the country in a libel action against nondomestic magazine in New Hampshire, where there is a uniquely long statute of limitations but where sales of magazine are only ten to fifteen thousand per month).

Amendment right to petition for redress of grievances. This illustrates the fledgling "government contacts" principle. The idea is that by doing nothing more than dealing with the government, one does not expose oneself to suit at the seat of government.[134]

Similarly, in rare circumstances, an assertion of state-court jurisdiction might similarly offend the policies against burdening interstate and foreign commerce. In *Davis v. Farmers' Co-operative Equity Co.*,[135] a Kansas plaintiff sued a Kansas railroad corporation in a Minnesota state court for a cause of action arising in Kansas. The railroad did not own or operate any lines in Minnesota, but it did maintain an agent there solely for the solicitation of traffic. The transaction was in no way connected with Minnesota or with the soliciting agency located there. Without reaching the due process question, the Supreme Court held that a statute authorizing service on the agent "imposes upon interstate commerce a serious and unreasonable burden which renders the statute obnoxious to the commerce clause." Otherwise, the Commerce Clause has very rarely been invoked for such purpose, and its continuing vitality as an independent limitation on a state's exercise of judicial authority is somewhat in doubt. In any event, it seems unlikely that the Commerce Clause would be invoked so to dismiss in a situation where the current interpretation of the Due Process Clause has been satisfied.

Federal Subconstitutional Limitations. Congress has the constitutional power to regulate state-court territorial jurisdiction, having such authority under the Fourteenth Amendment, Full Faith and Credit Clause, and Commerce Clause, not to mention its powers with respect to foreign relations. It has done so, however, only in a couple of statutes like the National Bank Act, which dictates the locality where certain actions involving a national bank can be brought.[136]

Also, federal jurisdictional law might conceivably apply in state courts under the reverse-*Erie* doctrine.[137]

---

134. Environmental Research Int'l, Inc. v. Lockwood Greene Eng'rs, Inc., 355 A.2d 808 (D.C. 1976); see Lamb v. Turbine Design, Inc., 538 S.E.2d 437 (Ga. 2000) (mere dealings with a federal regulatory agency in Georgia do not expose defendant to a related private tort action brought at the agency's site, in view of First Amendment right to petition for redress of grievances); Hilaire H. Butler, Note, The Government Contacts Exception to the District of Columbia Long–Arm Statute: Portrait of a Legal Morass, 36 Cath. U. L. Rev. 745 (1987).

135. 262 U.S. 312 (1923); see Bryson v. Northlake Hilton, 407 F. Supp. 73 (M.D.N.C. 1976) (alternative holding).

136. 12 U.S.C. § 94; see also Fair Debt Collection Practices Act, 15 U.S.C. § 1692i.

137. See David S. Welkowitz, Beyond Burger King: The Federal Interest in Personal Jurisdiction, 56 Fordham L. Rev. 1, 49–51 (1987); supra § 3.2(B).

e. *Mapping the Outer Limit of State Reach*

To summarize, by far the most significant limitations on a state court's territorial jurisdiction derive from the Due Process Clause of the Fourteenth Amendment to the Federal Constitution. The ever-evolving due process doctrine now requires the categorization of the action and then the application of both the power and the unreasonableness tests. Other federal law may further restrict reach slightly.

So, how do these federal limitations on a state's reach play out? Applying this law more specifically will give a better idea of the reach of state-court territorial jurisdiction. Therefore, I shall now map—category by category, basis by basis—how far a state can reach.

In Personam. In a case of personal jurisdiction, usually the court will apply the power test before the unreasonableness test, power being the higher hurdle for most such cases. If the state has no power over the defendant, there is no jurisdiction and therefore unreasonableness is irrelevant. If there is power, then the court must consider unreasonableness. Note that normally, but not always, reasonableness of personal jurisdiction follows almost a fortiori from a finding of power, because reasonableness involves looking at a broader range of interests and these additional interests most often favor jurisdiction.

Consider these three examples in which, respectively, (1) power is lacking, (2) power and reasonableness both exist, and (3) reasonableness is lacking:

(1) In *World-Wide Volkswagen Corp. v. Woodson*,[138] the plaintiffs had a car accident while passing through Oklahoma on a move from New York to a new home in Arizona. They suffered burns allegedly resulting from their car's defective design. While still hospitalized in Oklahoma, they sued in state court there. They included as defendants the car's regional wholesale distributor for New York, New Jersey, and Connecticut and the retail dealer from whom they had bought the car, both those defendants being incorporated in New York and also having their place of business there. These two defendants' only connection with Oklahoma was selling the car involved in this accident. The U.S. Supreme Court held against jurisdiction over these two defendants. They did not have minimum contacts with Oklahoma, which therefore had no power over them. Admittedly, one could argue that these defendants sell cars predictably to be used in Oklahoma, plaintiffs have an interest

---

138.   444 U.S. 286 (1980); see infra text accompanying note 152.

in litigating at the scene of the accident, and Oklahoma has an interest in enforcing its highway safety laws. And one could further argue that all this makes jurisdiction reasonable. However, reasonableness is irrelevant if there is no power.

(2) The Court did not rule on jurisdiction over two other corporate defendants in *World-Wide Volkswagen*, the car's German manufacturer and its American importer incorporated in New Jersey, because they did not contest jurisdiction. But personal jurisdiction over them was constitutional. By their active purposes to serve the market for cars in Oklahoma, these two defendants subjected themselves to that state's power to adjudicate lawsuits based on Oklahoma accidents. The exercise of jurisdiction over them would also not have been unreasonable.

(3) In *Asahi Metal Industry Co. v. Superior Court*,[139] the Californian plaintiff was severely injured in a motorcycle accident in California, allegedly caused by the explosion of the cycle's defective rear tire. In California state court he sued the Taiwanese manufacturer of the tube, which impleaded the Japanese manufacturer of the tube's valve. The main claim settled, leaving only the ancillary indemnity claim between aliens. The valve manufacturer made valves in Japan and sold some of them in Taiwan to the tube manufacturer, who sold tubes throughout the world including California. In these circumstances, according to the Supreme Court, there was no jurisdiction over the valve manufacturer. Although power might or might not exist, jurisdiction would be unreasonable, considering the severe burdens of defending in a foreign legal system, the slight interests of the third-party plaintiff and California in the exercise of jurisdiction, and the international interests in not subjecting this alien corporation to an indemnification offshoot of a U.S. product liability action.

All of the relationships between the defendant and the forum state that are sufficient to establish the state's power fall into four basic types: presence, domicile, consent, and state-directed acts. These are the primary bases of power. Of course, to survive due process scrutiny, any exercise of jurisdiction must not fail the more free-form test of unreasonableness. Nevertheless, cataloguing the primary bases of power is an expressive means for mapping the bounds on state-court personal jurisdiction.

General Jurisdiction. Two of these bases of power rest on strong contacts between the defendant and the forum state, giving the state power to adjudicate any personal claim whether or not

---

139.   480 U.S. 102 (1987); see infra text accompanying note 153.

related to those contacts. Thus, one says these bases support "general jurisdiction."

(1) Presence. This ancient basis gives the state power to adjudicate any personal claim if the defendant is served with process within the state's territorial limits. Thus, even momentary presence of the defendant creates power to adjudicate a claim totally unrelated to that presence.[140] So imagine that D, a Minnesotan driving to Maine for a vacation, stops at a gas station in Vermont and, while waiting in line there, assaults P, who is a businessman from Ohio. P sues D in an Ohio state court, managing to serve D with process when D stops for the night in Ohio on a later trip to New York. In these circumstances, such "transient jurisdiction," or "tag jurisdiction," is constitutional. Although *Burnham v. Superior Court*[141] seemed to suggest that transient jurisdiction merely by its historical pedigree satisfies any reasonableness test, transient jurisdiction probably is constitutional only where its application is not so outlandish as to be unreasonable in the particular circumstances.[142]

Despite former attempts fictitiously to apply the "presence" concept to corporations, the view today is that this basis meaningfully refers only to jurisdiction over individuals, since only individuals can be physically present. And service on a corporate employee present in the state does not establish personal jurisdiction over the corporation.[143] Even for individuals, the presence basis is not an inevitable one. We could get by without it. Plaintiffs today need it only when the other, more appropriate bases of jurisdiction are unavailing.

(2) Domicile. This basis gives the state power to adjudicate any personal claim if the defendant is domiciled in the state when served anywhere with process. "The state which accords him privileges and affords protection to him and his property by virtue of his domicile may also exact reciprocal duties."[144] So imagine that P sues

---

140. See Darrah v. Watson, 36 Iowa 116 (1873); Grace v. MacArthur, 170 F. Supp. 442 (E.D. Ark. 1959) (valid service on defendant flying over state); Amusement Equip., Inc. v. Mordelt, 779 F.2d 264, 270–71 (5th Cir. 1985) (a Florida corporation achieved in-state in-hand service of process on a German attending a convention in New Orleans: jurisdiction upheld, in this Louisiana action on a contract between them for delivery of German goods to Florida).

141. 495 U.S. 604 (1990) (after a New Jersey couple separated by agreement, and the wife and their two children moved to California, the wife served process on the husband while he briefly visited California on business and

to see his children: jurisdiction upheld, in this California state-court suit seeking divorce and money).

142. See Sarieddine v. Moussa, 820 S.W.2d 837, 840 (Tex. Ct. App. 1991).

143. See Riverside & Dan River Cotton Mills v. Menefee, 237 U.S. 189 (1915).

144. Milliken v. Meyer, 311 U.S. 457, 463 (1940) (a Wyoming state-court suit against a Wyoming domiciliary to recover profits from Colorado oil properties, with service in Colorado: jurisdiction upheld); cf. Blackmer v. United States, 284 U.S. 421 (1932) (federal courts could be given general jurisdic-

D in Minnesota, where *D* is domiciled, for a battery that occurred in Vermont. Note that the claim is unrelated to *D*'s contacts with Minnesota. Still, personal jurisdiction is constitutional. Some support indeed exists for stretching this basis of power to reach defendants who were domiciliaries only when the claim arose or to reach defendants who are mere residents as opposed to domiciliaries.[145]

For corporations, the analogy to state of domicile is state of incorporation.

Specific Jurisdiction. Two other bases of power rest on lesser contacts between the defendant and the forum state, giving the state power to adjudicate only those personal claims related to the contacts. Thus, these bases support "specific jurisdiction."

The due process tests for specific jurisdiction over individuals and corporations historically come from different lines of cases, but today are essentially the same.

(1) Consent. An individual or corporate defendant may consent to personal jurisdiction, thereby creating a basis of power defined by the terms of the consent. The possibility of the defendant's limiting the consent justifies classifying the consent basis under the label of specific jurisdiction.

The defendant may express actual consent in a number of ways. The defendant may consent *before* suit is brought, as in the common provision in business contracts consenting to a particular state's jurisdiction, or as pursuant to the common statutory requirement that anyone seeking a license to do business in a state must appoint a local agent to accept service of process. Alternatively, the defendant may consent *after* suit is brought, as by accepting or waiving service of process, or as by choosing not to object to personal jurisdiction.

In *National Equipment Rental, Ltd. v. Szukhent*,[146] Michigan farmers leased equipment from a New York corporation under a standard printed lease. By one of the lease's terms, the farmers appointed a New York woman, whom they did not know personally, as their agent to accept service in connection with any litigation under the lease. A dispute arose, the corporation sued in New York by serving the woman, and she forwarded the process to the farmers. Personal jurisdiction for the lease dispute was constitutional.

tion based on the defendant's U.S. nationality).

145. See Restatement (Second) of Conflict of Laws §§ 29–30 (1971).

146. 375 U.S. 311 (1964) (suit in federal court, but same principle applies in state court).

In the past, the courts stretched the "consent" basis into various *fictitious* forms, in order to uphold jurisdiction where it was highly desirable but where the then-prevailing jurisdictional theory did not yet extend. This is probably no longer necessary or proper. Thus, the better view is that only *actual* consent is a valid basis of power. In *Hess v. Pawloski*,[147] a nonresident motorist had an accident in Massachusetts. He later left the state. The accident then spawned a suit against him in Massachusetts. The Supreme Court upheld jurisdiction under a Massachusetts statute that deemed driving on the state's roads to be "implied consent" to jurisdiction for litigation arising from an accident on those roads. Today the same result would be achieved, but the basis of power would be the "state-directed act" rather than fictitious consent.

(2) State-directed Acts. This relatively new and very vibrant basis of power gives the state power over an individual or corporation that has committed certain acts directed at the state. Although specific jurisdiction extends only to those personal claims arising out of or related to those acts,[148] *International Shoe Co. v. Washington*[149] made the point that as the level of the defendant's state-directed activity increases, the state's constitutional power extends to claims less related to that activity.

(a) Tortious Acts. A plaintiff sued a Wisconsin defendant in Illinois, alleging that the defendant, while unloading his truck in Illinois, had negligently injured the plaintiff. Personal jurisdiction for the negligence action is constitutional.[150]

As by now should be obvious, the four bases of power for personal jurisdiction construct a complicated yet indefinite body of doctrine. To prove that point, consider the line of cases treating the **"stream of commerce."** Consider in particular a safety-valve manufacturer in Ohio that sells a valve to a heater manufacturer in Pennsylvania that sells the heater with the valve to a consumer in Illinois, who is injured there by the product's exploding and who there sues the valvemaker for negligence. A consensus evolved that,

---

147. 274 U.S. 352 (1927).

148. See Ratliff v. Cooper Labs., Inc., 444 F.2d 745 (4th Cir. 1971) (no jurisdiction in South Carolina for *P* of Florida suing *D*, a drug manufacturer incorporated in Delaware with its principal place of business in Connecticut, on account of alleged injuries suffered from drugs manufactured by *D* outside South Carolina, and purchased and consumed in Florida by *P*, when *D*'s activities in South Carolina are limited to solicitation by mail to South Carolina dealers and wholesalers and the mailing of promotional literature to about 650 South Carolina doctors on its mailing lists);

Coastal Video Communications, Corp. v. Staywell Corp., 59 F. Supp. 2d 562, 566–68 (E.D. Va. 1999) (no specific jurisdiction for declaratory judgment that plaintiff's handbook did not violate defendant's copyright, even though defendant sold its publication in the state).

149. 326 U.S. 310 (1945) (a Washington State action against a Delaware corporation to recover employment taxes due on commissions paid to in-state salesmen: jurisdiction upheld).

150. See Nelson v. Miller, 143 N.E.2d 673 (Ill. 1957).

as a constitutional matter, Illinois had personal jurisdiction based on the in-state effect of the out-of-state act, because the valvemaker had put its product into a stream of commerce flowing into Illinois.[151] The Supreme Court seemed to approve that result in *World-Wide Volkswagen Corp. v. Woodson.*[152] In that case, however, the Court refused to follow the stream of commerce to wherever the consumers themselves might take the product before injury: the holding rejected Oklahoma's attempt to extend its power to nonresident automobile dealers in a product liability litigation, when the nonresident plaintiffs had suffered an accident while driving through Oklahoma. Then in *Asahi Metal Industry Co. v. Superior Court,*[153] the Supreme Court split badly on the question of power in the stream of commerce context, with a minority arguing that, to bestow jurisdiction, the manufacturer must have had an active purpose to serve the market in the forum state where the product was sold. That case's actual holding, however, was that regardless of power, jurisdiction in California was unreasonable because of the unusual facts: the state could not inflict on a Japanese valve manufacturer the burden of defending this third-party claim by a Taiwanese tire-tube manufacturer, when the main product liability claim had settled and neither the Taiwanese party nor the forum state had adequate interests in sustaining jurisdiction for the indemnity claim. Given all this ambiguous guidance, the lower courts currently appear to be split, but they do seem to be moving toward a new consensus that only slightly shortens the prior jurisdictional reach down the stream of commerce. More decisions,

151. E.g., Gray v. Am. Radiator & Standard Sanitary Corp., 176 N.E.2d 761 (Ill. 1961); cf. Indianapolis Colts, Inc. v. Metro. Baltimore Football Club Ltd. P'ship, 34 F.3d 410 (7th Cir. 1994) (jurisdiction exists at place of injury in trademark infringement action); Murphy v. Erwin–Wasey, Inc., 460 F.2d 661, 664 (1st Cir. 1972) ("Where a defendant knowingly sends into a state a false statement, intending that it should there be relied upon to the injury of a resident of that state, he has, for jurisdictional purposes, acted within that state."). But cf. IMO Indus., Inc. v. Kiekert AG, 155 F.3d 254 (3d Cir. 1998) (no jurisdiction in action against German corporation for tortiously interfering with New Jersey corporation's attempt to sell Italian subsidiary because defendant did not expressly aim its tortious conduct at New Jersey). On the many similar cases involving interstate or international defamation, compare Calder v. Jones, 465 U.S. 783 (1984) (jurisdiction over newspapermen in plaintiff's state), Hugel v. McNell, 886 F.2d 1 (1st Cir. 1989) (same), and Burt v. Bd. of Regents of Univ. of Neb., 757 F.2d 242 (10th Cir. 1985) (jurisdiction over writer of letter of recommendation), vacated as moot, Connolly v. Burt, 475 U.S. 1063 (1986), with Reynolds v. Int'l Amateur Athletic Fed'n, 23 F.3d 1110 (6th Cir. 1994) (no jurisdiction, under due process test, in track star's suit at home against IAAF in regard to positive drug test), Madara v. Hall, 916 F.2d 1510 (11th Cir. 1990) (no jurisdiction, in action against singer who allegedly defamed plaintiff in magazine interview, in a state simply where magazine circulated), and Nat'l Ass'n of Real Estate Appraisers, Inc. v. Schaeffer, No. CV 88–7774–RJK (TX), 1989 WL 267762 (C.D. Cal. Mar. 23, 1989) (similar).

152. 444 U.S. 286, 297–98 (1980); see supra text accompanying note 138.

153. 480 U.S. 102 (1987); see supra text accompanying note 139.

and the better ones, hold that an in-state purchase gives the state power over a nondirect seller with an actual awareness of its products' being regularly sold there, and that such personal jurisdiction normally will not be unreasonable.[154]

(b) Business Activity. In California, a California woman sued a Texas insurance company to recover on a policy on her son's life, where the defendant's only contacts with California were mailing this solitary insurance contract to the son residing in that state and accepting premiums mailed by him from there. *McGee v. International Life Insurance Co.*[155] held that personal jurisdiction for the recovery action was constitutional. *Henry L. Doherty & Co. v. Goodman*[156] had earlier allowed Iowa to exercise jurisdiction over a person conducting securities business in the state, for a claim arising from a contract made in Iowa for the sale of stock. *Burger King Corp. v. Rudzewicz*[157] later reached the same result for a Florida franchisor's action in Florida against a breaching Michigan franchisee.

As the level of the defendant's state-directed activity increases, the state's constitutional power extends to claims less related in nature and time to that activity. Both the level of activity and the degree of unrelatedness are continua. If state-directed activities are considerable, the activities will bestow power, even though the activities might be considered partial, parallel, or incidental to the activities that the claim actually "arose from," as long as those

---

154. See Russell J. Weintraub, A Map Out of the Personal Jurisdiction Labyrinth, 28 U.C. Davis L. Rev. 531, 533, 554–55 (1995); cf. Larry L. Teply & Ralph U. Whitten, Civil Procedure 254–55 (3d ed. 2004) (saying that jurisdiction would exist if the injured plaintiff were to sue Asahi directly). Compare Bridgestone Corp. v. Superior Court, 121 Cal. Rptr. 2d 673, 680 (Ct. App. 2002) ("We conclude that a manufacturer's placement of goods in the stream of commerce with the expectation that they will be purchased or used by consumers in California indicates an intention to serve the California market * * * and constitutes purposeful availment if the income earned by the manufacturer from sale or use of its product in California is substantial."), and DeMoss v. City Mkt., Inc., 762 F. Supp. 913, 919 (D. Utah 1991) ("personal jurisdiction is proper if a corporation delivers its products into the stream of commerce with the expectation that they will be purchased by consumers in the forum state"), with Parry v. Ernst Home Ctr.

Corp., 779 P.2d 659, 666 (Utah 1989) (no jurisdiction, observing, "They were informed of potential sales to the western United States, but they neither came to Utah nor sent sales representatives to Utah to facilitate the marketing and purchase of their product."), and Lesnick v. Hollingsworth & Vose Co., 35 F.3d 939 (4th Cir. 1994) (no jurisdiction over manufacturer of asbestos-containing filters for cigarettes; must show more than mere expectation of in-state sale; must show purposeful activity on part of manufacturer to establish meaningful contact with forum state).

155. 355 U.S. 220 (1957); see Alchemie Int'l, Inc. v. Metal World, Inc., 523 F. Supp. 1039 (D.N.J. 1981) (jurisdiction for breach of contract action in New Jersey, based on significant mail and telephone contacts with New Jersey plaintiff in solicitation of contract).

156. 294 U.S. 623 (1935).

157. 471 U.S. 462 (1985) (suit in federal court, but same principle applies in state court).

state-directed activities sufficiently "relate to" the claim. Indeed, if a defendant's business activities in the forum state when served with process are extensively continuous and systematic—which is phrased as **"doing business"** rather than merely "transacting business"—the defendant becomes subject to jurisdiction even on claims wholly unrelated to the in-state activities. Thus, *Perkins v. Benguet Consolidated Mining Co.*[158] held that the defendant's activities were so extensive in the forum state as to support jurisdiction in an action unrelated to those activities. In this way, the development of jurisdiction based on state-directed acts has brought into the open the absence of any clear distinction between specific and general jurisdiction—they just comprise the rules for the two ends of the unrelatedness continuum.[159] This general jurisdiction based on doing business, which is peculiar to the United States,[160] entails terrible problems of line-drawing and does not conform to the usual rationale of general jurisdiction.[161] This basis of general jurisdiction arose to provide appropriate jurisdiction when specific jurisdiction was not yet fully available. Because doing-business jurisdiction requires the defendant to be so active in the forum as to seem a native,[162] it is seldom available under its own terms.[163] Today, courts resort to it, albeit usually inappropriately, only when all appropriate bases of personal jurisdiction fail to reach the defendant.[164]

158. 342 U.S. 437 (1952) (upholding jurisdiction in an Ohio state-court suit against a Philippine corporation, which was performing all of its management activities in Ohio while mining was suspended by the effects of war in the Philippines, on a basically unrelated claim); cf. Helicopteros Nacionales de Colombia, S.A. v. Hall, 466 U.S. 408 (1984) (finding no general jurisdiction of Texas over a foreign corporation, but not reaching the difficult issue of more specific jurisdiction).

159. Compare Russo v. Sea World of Fla., Inc., 709 F. Supp. 39 (D.R.I. 1989) (applying due process test and holding that slip-and-fall claims did not "arise out of or relate" to Florida theme park's sale of ticket to plaintiff in Rhode Island and that its other Rhode Island sales activity did not create general jurisdiction), and Weber v. Jolly Hotels, 977 F. Supp. 327 (D.N.J. 1997) (similar), with Nowak v. Tak How Invs., Ltd., 94 F.3d 708 (1st Cir. 1996) (more loosely reading due process's requirement of relating to in-state transaction of business).

160. See Mathias Reimann, Conflict of Laws in Western Europe 77, 82–83 (1995).

161. See Gary B. Born & Peter B. Rutledge, International Civil Litigation

in United States Courts 110–22 (4th ed. 2007).

162. See Charles W. "Rocky" Rhodes, Clarifying General Jurisdiction, 34 Seton Hall L. Rev. 807 (2004).

163. See Helicopteros Nacionales de Colombia, S.A. v. Hall, 466 U.S. 408, 418 (1984) (holding that "mere purchases, even if occurring at regular intervals, are not enough to warrant a State's assertion of in personam jurisdiction over a nonresident corporation in a cause of action not related to those purchase transactions"); Bird v. Parsons, 289 F.3d 865 (6th Cir. 2002). Compare Nichols v. G.D. Searle & Co., 991 F.2d 1195 (4th Cir. 1993) (insufficient activity in Maryland to create general jurisdiction over IUD manufacturer), with Metro. Life Ins. Co. v. Robertson–Ceco Corp., 84 F.3d 560 (2d Cir. 1996) (general jurisdiction over building materials manufacturer was unreasonable in absence of any cognizable interest on part of plaintiff or Vermont in adjudicating claims in Vermont).

164. E.g., Frummer v. Hilton Hotels Int'l, 227 N.E.2d 851, 854 (N.Y. 1967); Bryant v. Finnish Nat'l Airline, 208 N.E.2d 439 (N.Y. 1965) (maintaining a

(c) Property Ownership, Use, or Possession. A plaintiff sued a New Jersey defendant in Pennsylvania for injuries sustained on the defendant's Pennsylvania property. Personal jurisdiction for the tort action is constitutional.[165]

(d) Litigating Acts. A nonresident plaintiff sued a defendant in California. The defendant brought a counterclaim arising out of the same transaction. *Adam v. Saenger*[166] held that personal jurisdiction over the plaintiff for the counterclaim was constitutional. More generally, a state has power over anyone who has appeared as a party in a pending action in a court of the state, and it may exercise that power with respect to an additional claim related to the original action if determining it concurrently would not be unreasonable.[167] The appearance suffices to pass the power test. But still the usual constitutional test of unreasonableness applies, making any appearance "restricted" in the sense that it does not bestow personal jurisdiction on unrelated claims or on claims for which the forum would be unreasonable.[168]

When Can a Court Impute Another's Contacts to the Defendant?

Specific jurisdiction exposes the fundamental problem of when to attribute another's acts to the defendant for jurisdictional purposes. A general proposition is that to justify personal jurisdiction over a principal, the court can attribute the state-directed acts of the principal's agent. To determine whether an agent-principal relationship exists, the court looks to the ordinary law of agency, asking whether the defendant has empowered an agent and whether the agent has acted within the scope of that authority. To establish jurisdiction over the principal based on the agent's acts, then, the plaintiff must make a prima facie showing of the principal's vicarious liability under the applicable substantive law. The rationale is that if the principal would be substantively liable for the agent's acts, then those acts can contribute to a finding of jurisdiction over the principal.

Indeed, that rationale extends to a variety of contexts where a jurisdictional argument exists for attributing another's acts to the defendant. See generally Lea Brilmayer & Kathleen Paisley, Personal Jurisdiction and Substantive Legal Relations: Corporations, Conspiracies, and Agency, 74 Cal. L. Rev. 1 (1986). Of those contexts, the one giving the courts the greatest difficulty is the attribution of state-directed acts by a validly incorporated and formally separate corporation that, along with the defen-

---

small New York office for paperwork and a small New York bank account creates general jurisdiction in New York); see Russell J. Weintraub, How Substantial Is Our Need for a Judgments–Recognition Convention and What Should We Bargain Away to Get It?, 24 Brook. J. Int'l L. 167, 187–89 (1998) (explaining that elimination of doing-business jurisdiction "will block suit in only a few cases in which the United States has a legitimate interest in providing a forum").

165. See Dubin v. City of Philadelphia, 34 Pa. D. & C. 61 (C.P. 1939).

166. 303 U.S. 59 (1938).

167. See Restatement (Second) of Judgments § 9 (1982).

168. See Gibbons v. Brown, 716 So. 2d 868 (Fl. Dist. Ct. App. 1998) (person who brought a now-concluded tort action in Florida is not thereby subject to personal jurisdiction in the same court for an action regarding the same Canadian car accident, filed two years after the first filing but by a person who was not party to the first suit).

> dant, constitutes part of a modern multistate or multinational enterprise. If the affiliate corporation has an agent-principal relationship to the defendant corporation, then the courts will attribute the affiliate's contacts to the defendant. But some courts have gone perceptibly beyond the "agency" standard, coming up with tests that ask, for example, whether the state-directed acts are sufficiently important to the defendant that it would have performed them itself in the affiliate's absence. Such tests, however, seem to be confused stabs at the right standard, one that would conform to the rationale of tying jurisdictional attribution to substantive liability. The proper "alter ego" standard would take the courts into corporate law, asking whether the defendant would be liable for all of the affiliate's activities under the doctrine of piercing the corporate veil, which, in special situations of common control, overcomes the usual limited liability of corporations and merges the corporate entities. If so, then those activities of the affiliate can contribute to a finding of jurisdiction over the defendant.

No Jurisdiction. These examples should not give the idea that anything goes. The Supreme Court has sometimes found the defendant's state-directed activity too slight to bestow power on the state, as in the *World-Wide Volkswagen* case.

Or in *Hanson v. Denckla*,[169] a Delaware trustee had no contact with Florida other than remitting trust income to the trust's settlor after she moved there and receiving her occasional instructions from there. After her death, her legatees sued in Florida to attack the validity of the Delaware trust. There was no jurisdiction over the trustee, because it had not purposefully availed itself of the privilege of conducting activities within the state.

And in *Kulko v. Superior Court*,[170] a New York husband had no contact with California, but his estranged wife and children had moved there with his consent. She sued him in California for child support. Startlingly, the Court held against jurisdiction over the husband for lack of power.

Drawing the line in applying the power test is difficult. However phrased, the test in application turns on a close inspection of the facts and circumstances peculiar to the case. The issue of power "is one in which few answers will be written in 'black and white. The greys are dominant and even among them the shades are innumerable.' "[171] *International Shoe* did the pioneering theoretical work on what would constitute sufficient contacts. *Hanson* equated power to the defendant's purposeful availment. The *Kulko* case sought refinement by rephrasing the power test as "whether the 'quality and nature' of the defendant's activity is such that it is 'reasonable' and 'fair' to require him to conduct his defense in that State."[172]

---

169. 357 U.S. 235, 253 (1958) (power exists over a defendant who has purposefully availed itself "of the privilege of conducting activities within the forum State, thus invoking the benefits and protections of its laws").

170. 436 U.S. 84 (1978).

171. Id. at 92 (quoting Estin v. Estin, 334 U.S. 541, 545 (1948)).

172. Id. (quoting Int'l Shoe Co. v. Washington, 326 U.S. 310, 316–17, 319 (1945)).

Intentional acts therefore have more significance than unintentional acts; a big-time operator is more susceptible to a finding of jurisdiction than is a small-fry defendant. Ultimately, *Kulko* required "a sufficient connection between the defendant and the forum State to make it fair to require defense of the action in the forum."[173] Possibly, "fair" in *Kulko*'s language could be read narrowly to evoke only the defendant's tacit consent to jurisdiction embodied in *Hanson*'s language. But eventually whether it is fair to exercise power over the defendant will come to turn on the interests of others, and so the power test is inevitably eroding into a reasonableness test.

At any rate, the following graph structurally embodies the power rationale of *International Shoe, Hanson, Kulko*, and more recent cases, and further tries to plot the results of the major Supreme Court cases on this subject. Specific jurisdiction is on the left and general jurisdiction on the right. The hatched area represents the zone beyond the due process limit on state-court power. The graph tries to show that for POWER, an increase in unrelatedness requires a higher level of activity.

---

173. Id. at 91; see Burger King Corp. v. Rudzewicz, 471 U.S. 462, 472–76 (1985); Wendy Collins Perdue, Personal Jurisdiction and the Beetle in the Box, 32 B.C. L. Rev. 529, 534–50 (1991); supra text accompanying note 129.

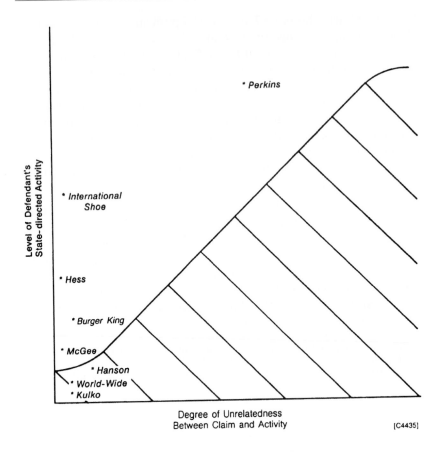

Degree of Unrelatedness
Between Claim and Activity   [C4435]

Internet Jurisdiction. New technologies easing interstate transactions have challenged the courts to adapt the law of personal
jurisdiction, without compromising due process, in deciding whether to reach distant defendants. The internet is not exceptional in
that regard. But it is a social development so earthshakingly
important as to deserve special attention here. The advance sheets
are teeming with cases testing jurisdiction based on internet activity. The most interesting cases involve only internet activity that
has misled, defamed, or infringed the plaintiff, without other activity such as an accompanying sale of a tangible good.

Some radical theorists insist that a whole new approach to
personal jurisdiction for such cases is necessary, one that down-
plays territoriality. They argue that the internet's seamless web is
unique in its indifference to geographic boundaries, while our legal
systems are built on these boundaries. An operator of a website
cannot know or control where its users are located, and users
cannot know with certainty the location of the site. Admittedly, the
radicals make a good observation about cyberspace's boundlessness.

It will require special regulation in many areas of the law.[174] But as to jurisdiction, the radicals forget the other side of the equation: jurisdiction under extant legal systems necessitates a decision as to which of the geographically dispersed courts can entertain a case, and so jurisdiction unavoidably remains a territorially based concept.[175]

Other commentators argue much more persuasively that the problem here is the outmoded power test, because the broad geographic coverage of the internet and the ease of access to it make arbitrary any inference that an internet defendant has purposefully availed itself of any specific forum. They call for a shift to a single test focused on reasonableness.[176] The courts, however, continue applying the traditional minimum-contacts power test to determine personal jurisdiction for controversies arising through this new medium, with unreasonableness as the back-up constitutional test. And recently they seem to be reaching acceptable results.

Zippo Manufacturing Co. v. Zippo Dot Com, Inc.[177] was an early attempt to lay out a special jurisdictional approach to the internet. Perhaps in an overreaction, *Zippo* held that the "likelihood" that personal jurisdiction met constitutional standards was "directly proportionate to the nature and quality of commercial activity that an entity conducts over the Internet." Thus, commercial activity was to be measured on a special sliding scale—with proactive sites used for repeated in-state business transactions likely subject to jurisdiction, interactive sites' jurisdictional status dependent on the nature of the interactions enabled by the site, and passive sites merely displaying information likely not subject to jurisdiction.

More recent cases place less significance on the technological medium and instead evaluate whether the defendant's internet activities support jurisdiction in the terms of the traditional and malleable analysis. Power is more likely to be found for websites that generate income from the forum state, are designed to serve people there, or are posted with the knowledge that they will cause damage there. Sites are less likely to constitute purposeful availment when they are not much used by residents of the forum state

---

174. See Arthur R. Miller, The Emerging Law of the Internet, 38 Ga. L. Rev. 991 (2004).

175. See generally Symposium, Personal Jurisdiction in the Internet Age, 98 Nw. U. L. Rev. 409 (2004).

176. See, e.g., Danielle Keats Citron, Minimum Contacts in a Borderless World: Voice over Internet Protocol and the Coming Implosion of Personal Jurisdiction Theory, 39 U.C. Davis L. Rev.

1481 (2006); Martin H. Redish, Of New Wine and Old Bottles: Personal Jurisdiction, the Internet, and the Nature of Constitutional Evolution, 38 Jurimetrics J. 575, 580 (1998).

177. 952 F. Supp. 1119, 1124 (W.D. Pa. 1997) (in trademark action by Pennsylvania company, jurisdiction exists over California internet news service that has 3000 Pennsylvania subscribers).

or when their content and design indicate they are intended to serve a different place.[178]

Defendants who by their internet conduct purposely avail themselves of the forum state's laws, or target residents of the forum state, are, on the one hand, subject to that state's specific jurisdiction for causes of action arising from that conduct. For example, personal jurisdiction was constitutional in an action to declare noninfringement by a resident software distributor against a nonresident software designer who had electronically entered a contract with the distributor and repeatedly transmitted software to be sold on the distributor's site.[179] For a different example, a court in a trademark action exercised personal jurisdiction over a nonresident defendant who aimed his conduct at a resident company by registering its trademark as a domain name for the purpose of extracting money by selling the domain name to the company.[180] On the other hand, despite a few much-criticized decisions to the contrary,[181] informational websites viewable from the forum state as well as everywhere else usually do not support personal jurisdiction,[182] unless they target the plaintiff for fraud, defamation, or

---

178. See Wright & Miller, supra note 31, § 1073.1; David M. Fritch, Beyond Zippo's "Sliding Scale"—The Third Circuit Clarifies Internet-based Personal Jurisdiction Analysis, 49 Vill. L. Rev. 931 (2004).

179. CompuServe, Inc. v. Patterson, 89 F.3d 1257 (6th Cir. 1996) (after a Texan software designer, over several years, transmitted thirty-two shareware programs to his internet service provider as part of the programs' marketing plan and advertised that shareware on the provider's system, and then the designer accused the provider of infringing the programs in developing its own software, the provider could sue at its Ohio home for a declaratory judgment of noninfringement).

180. Panavision Int'l, L.P. v. Toeppen, 141 F.3d 1316 (9th Cir. 1998) (suit in California against Illinois defendant concerning Panavision.com).

181. See, e.g., Inset Sys., Inc. v. Instruction Set, Inc., 937 F. Supp. 161 (D. Conn. 1996) (a Connecticut corporation can sue in Connecticut a Massachusetts corporation for trademark infringement, when defendant had a website on a Massachusetts computer advertising its software products under the domain name of inset.com).

182. See, e.g., Cybersell, Inc. v. Cybersell, Inc., 130 F.3d 414 (9th Cir.

1997) (an Arizonan corporation named Cybersell cannot sue in Arizona a Floridian corporation for trademark infringement, when defendant had a home page on a Florida computer offering its webpage construction services under the business name of Cybersell); Bensusan Rest. Corp. v. King, 126 F.3d 25 (2d Cir. 1997) (its website does not render Missouri's Blue Note cabaret owner subject to New York's jurisdiction for trademark suit by New York's famous Blue Note jazz club); Millennium Enters., Inc. v. Millennium Music, LP, 33 F. Supp. 2d 907 (D. Or. 1999) (in trademark infringement action by Oregon company, South Carolina company's website allowing customers to purchase merchandise did not constitute minimum contacts with Oregon because site sold tiny amount of merchandise and site primarily aimed at getting viewers to visit South Carolina retail locations); Pavlovich v. Superior Court, 58 P.3d 2 (Cal. 2002) (no jurisdiction over website operator from Texas who allegedly posted a computer program to enable the decryption and copying of DVDs containing motion pictures); cf. ALS Scan, Inc. v. Digital Serv. Consultants, Inc., 293 F.3d 707 (4th Cir. 2002) (Georgia-based internet service provider lacked sufficient contacts with Maryland in copyright infringement action brought by Maryland

infringement in that state.[183]

In sum, the courts now consider a range of contacts with the forum, including internet activity, in their constitutional analysis. They have not chosen to follow some formula like the *Zippo* sliding scale or otherwise to revamp the law of personal jurisdiction in the internet context.[184]

In Rem. Jurisdiction in rem brings us into the realm of nonpersonal jurisdiction. Consider separately the subtypes of pure in rem and jurisdiction over status.

Pure In Rem. Recall that jurisdiction in rem can result in a judgment affecting the interests of all persons in a designated thing (or "res"). Theoretically and formally, the action is against the thing. No personal liability or obligation results. Examples of proceedings in rem include actions to register title to land, forfeiture actions, admiralty proceedings to enforce a maritime lien upon a vessel, and probate proceedings to settle an estate.

To satisfy the power test, a proceeding in rem normally must be brought where the thing is. Bases of power for nonpersonal jurisdiction have not multiplied beyond presence the way they have for personal jurisdiction. Unreasonableness will thus be the key test under the modern law for in rem proceedings brought where the thing is.

Jurisdiction in rem, if exercised at the thing's location (or "situs"), will not be unreasonable when litigating there is fair to the persons whose property interests in the thing are to be affected and when the state has an interest in adjudicating the dispute. Since an in rem action involves conflicting claims to the property itself, most likely reasonableness follows because those claims indicate that the claimants expected to benefit from the situs state's protection of their property interests, because important records and witnesses are in the state, and because the state has an interest in maintaining the marketability of property within its borders and in peacefully resolving disputes concerning that property.

owner of photographs against provider and its customer who allegedly published photographs on customer's website, because providing bandwidth to Georgia customer was merely passive).

183. See, e.g., Bellino v. Simon, No. Civ. A. 99–2208, 1999 WL 1059753 (E.D. La. Nov. 22, 1999) (nonresident defendant does not establish minimum contacts with the forum state by libeling nonresident plaintiff during an unsolicited phone call initiated from that state, but a different nonresident defendant who sends libelous e-mails into the state establishes minimum contacts with that state).

184. See, e.g., A. Benjamin Spencer, Jurisdiction and the Internet: Returning to Traditional Principles to Analyze Network-mediated Contacts, 2006 U. Ill. L. Rev. 71; Dennis T. Yokoyama, You Can't Always Use the Zippo Code: The Fallacy of a Uniform Theory of Internet Personal Jurisdiction, 54 DePaul L. Rev. 1147 (2005).

For example, Massachusetts provided by statute for a proceeding to register title to any land within the state. The proceeding would determine the interests in that land of all persons in the world. Jurisdiction so to clear title against all the world is constitutional, because such jurisdiction in rem is fair and highly desirable.[185]

Must There Be Seizure?

A pervasive problem concerning nonpersonal jurisdiction is the threshold necessity of officially seizing the thing, as by attachment. Despite some cases' intimations to the contrary, the better view is that there is no constitutional requirement of actual seizure.

It is true that in superficial consistency with its power theory, Pennoyer might have implied in some of its dicta that seizure was necessary, at least for jurisdiction quasi in rem of the second subtype. However, later authorities clarify that for nonpersonal jurisdiction the Constitution requires no more than the plaintiff's directing the action at its outset clearly against the specific in-state thing, as by a statement in the complaint. Seizure is properly of significance only as to security for enforcement of judgment, which concerns solely the plaintiff, and very rarely nowadays as to notice, which normally requires more direct means.

Seizure may very well be statutorily required by a state as a prerequisite to the exercise of nonpersonal jurisdiction—and state statutes in fact usually do so, although apparently for reasons more of tradition than of policy. But seizure is not constitutionally required. See Heidritter v. Elizabeth Oil-Cloth Co., 112 U.S. 294, 301–02 (1884) (dictum); Avery v. Bender, 204 A.2d 314 (Vt. 1964); Closson v. Chase, 149 N.W. 26 (Wis. 1914); Linda J. Silberman, Shaffer v. Heitner: The End of an Era, 53 N.Y.U. L. Rev. 33, 45–47 (1978).

Jurisdiction over Status. Recall that this kind of jurisdiction can result in a judgment establishing, terminating, or changing a status, such as a family relationship, citizenship, or mental capacity. By so treating the status as a thing, the state may determine status.

To satisfy the power test, jurisdiction over status must be exercised where the status is located; a status can be sited in any state to which one party in the relationship has a significant connection. The exercise of jurisdiction must not be unreasonable.

For example, the state of the plaintiff spouse's domicile may grant a divorce. Imagine that a husband leaves the marital home in New York and goes to Idaho, which has more permissive grounds for divorce. Having established his domicile in Idaho, he sues there for divorce. The wife defaults. Jurisdiction for divorce in Idaho is constitutional.[186] But Idaho could not impose support obligations without personal jurisdiction over the rich wife.

---

185. See Tyler v. Judges of the Court of Registration, 55 N.E. 812 (Mass.), writ of error dismissed, 179 U.S. 405 (1900).

186. See Williams v. North Carolina, 317 U.S. 287 (1942).

Quasi In Rem. Jurisdiction quasi in rem can result in a judgment affecting only the interests of particular persons in a designated thing, with the proceeding formally brought against the named defendants and with their interests in the thing alone at stake. Consider separately its two subtypes.

Subtype One. Recall that in subtype one, the plaintiff seeks to establish a pre-existing interest in the thing as against the defendant's interest. Examples include actions to partition land, to quiet title, and to foreclose a mortgage, as well as suits to foreclose other liens on things or to remove a cloud on title to property. These kinds of actions are by no means uncommon.

To satisfy the power test, this kind of jurisdiction normally must be exercised where the thing is. Unreasonableness will then be the key test. Subtype one of jurisdiction quasi in rem, if exercised at the situs, will not be unreasonable when the balance of interests of defendant, of plaintiff, and of the public favors jurisdiction.

Imagine that a plaintiff sues a nonresident defendant in New York to partition New York real estate, which the plaintiff and the defendant own jointly. Jurisdiction over the land is constitutional, because such jurisdiction in New York is not unreasonable.[187]

How Does the Process of Reification Work?

Another pervasive problem concerning nonpersonal jurisdiction is the play in the process of identifying the thing in dispute and of attributing an in-state situs to it. This "reification process" is especially elastic when the res is an intangible, such as a domain name in cyberspace, a marital status, or a debt evidenced by a writing. See generally Michael P. Allen, In Rem Jurisdiction from Pennoyer to Shaffer to the Anticybersquatting Consumer Protection Act, 11 Geo. Mason L. Rev. 243 (2002). In passing on its own jurisdiction over a debt, say, a state might deem the res to be either the writing or the debt itself, and might consider the latter to be located where the debtor is present, where the debtor is domiciled, or elsewhere. There must be some limit, even if ill-defined, on the state's ability to expand its own jurisdiction by stretching reification. The current approach would apparently ask, as a special aspect of the jurisdictional inquiry's unreasonableness test, whether the state unreasonably performed this reification process.

Subtype Two. Recall that in subtype two, or attachment jurisdiction, the plaintiff seeks to apply the defendant's property to the satisfaction of a claim against the defendant that is unrelated to the property. By this unrelatedness, subtype two of quasi in rem jurisdiction fundamentally differs from in rem jurisdiction and subtype one of quasi in rem jurisdiction. It comprises cases where the plaintiff has a personal claim against the defendant and seeks to satisfy it through attachment of unrelated property of the defendant—or by garnishment of an unrelated obligation owed the defendant by a third party—without obtaining personal jurisdiction

---

187. See Garfein v. McInnis, 162 N.E. 73 (N.Y. 1928).

over the defendant. Despite their uniqueness, cases of this second subtype are traditionally referred to as actions quasi in rem, because they technically concern the interests of particular persons in a designated thing.

To satisfy the power test, this kind of jurisdiction normally must be exercised where the thing is. Unreasonableness will then be the key test. But here the unreasonableness test is particularly difficult to satisfy.

Subtype two of jurisdiction quasi in rem was always quite useful. If the plaintiff had any claim against the defendant but failed to acquire personal jurisdiction, the plaintiff could proceed against any of the defendant's property within the state, such as a bank account. The defendant usually defaulted, and the resulting judgment allowed the plaintiff to apply the property to satisfy the claim. A successful plaintiff would apply the property to awarded court costs and then to satisfaction of the claim itself. Anything extra would go back to the defendant. However, on such attachment jurisdiction, the plaintiff's recovery is limited to the particular property.[188] The defendant is not liable for any deficiency. The plaintiff could later sue on any unsatisfied portion of the claim, either in personam or again by this subtype of quasi in rem against other property belonging to the defendant.

Also, subtype two was formerly quite appropriate. Consider its origin. In the infant American colonies, a tremendous trade deficit with the mother country led to a severe shortage of cash. This in turn induced a risky reliance on credit. And this precipitated, in part, the Depression of 1640. Bad economic times and lessened social cohesiveness encouraged debtors to abscond or at least to evade payment. The inadequacy of rudimentary personal jurisdiction to remedy the politically powerful creditors' consequent collection needs motivated the legislative and judicial invention of attachment jurisdiction around 1650. Henceforth, the creditor could attach any local property of the missing debtor, and then satisfy any resulting judgment out of that property.[189]

Three hundred and fifty years later, attachment jurisdiction is still with us. In the course of history, it facilitated the industrialization of America. But today the needs that generated it are much less intense, because personal jurisdiction has much expanded. Nevertheless, the courts must continue wastefully to work out the doctrinal implications and complications and critically to control the abuses that this ancient form of jurisdiction has allowed.

---

188. See CME Media Enters. B.V. v. Zelezny, No. 01 CIV. 1733 (DC), 2001 WL 1035138 (S.D.N.Y. 2001) (bank account contained one nickel).

189. See Joseph J. Kalo, Jurisdiction as an Evolutionary Process: The Development of Quasi In Rem and In Personam Principles, 1978 Duke L.J. 1147, 1150–62.

For example, in *Harris v. Balk*,[190] the Supreme Court held that the plaintiff could invoke this subtype of jurisdiction by garnishment of a debt owing from a third person to the defendant, in order to pursue the plaintiff's unrelated claim against the out-of-state defendant. The debt was the res, and the forum state deemed the debt present within the state because the third person was temporarily present in that state. However, in *Shaffer v. Heitner*,[191] the Court overturned *Harris* by making clear that nonpersonal jurisdiction must pass the reasonableness test. Mere presence of some bit of the defendant's property is not enough to render reasonable the state's entertaining of a totally unrelated claim, even if the defendant's liability were limited to the value of that property. Something more—an adequate relation of the forum, the parties, and the litigation—has to exist before a court will, in its subjective opinion, deem an adjudication to be fundamentally fair.

The result of *Shaffer* is that subtype two of quasi in rem jurisdiction is now available only[192] in these rather special situations described by hypotheticals:

(1) Ohio plaintiff sues by attaching Iowa defendant's land in New York in order to *secure* a judgment being sought by plaintiff in California for personal injuries stemming from a traffic accident with defendant in California. Attachment jurisdiction in New York is constitutional.[193]

(2) Ohio plaintiff sues by attaching Iowa defendant's land in New York in order to *enforce* a judgment already rendered for plaintiff in California for personal injuries stemming from a traffic accident with defendant in California. Attachment jurisdiction in New York is constitutional.[194]

(3) Ohio plaintiff sues by attaching Iowa defendant's land in New York in order to *recover* for his personal injuries stemming from a traffic accident with defendant in New York. Attachment jurisdiction in New York is constitutional. If a state *could constitutionally exercise personal jurisdiction*, it may choose to allow plaintiff instead to cast his suit in the form

190. 198 U.S. 215 (1905).

191. 433 U.S. 186 (1977). For the story of this case, see Wendy Collins Perdue, The Story of Shaffer: Allocating Jurisdictional Authority Among the States, in Civil Procedure Stories 135 (Kevin M. Clermont ed., 2d ed. 2008).

192. But see Rhoades v. Wright, 622 P.2d 343, 345–48 (Utah 1980) (allowing jurisdiction when based on attachment of real estate).

193. See Shaffer, 433 U.S. at 210; Carolina Power & Light Co. v. Uranex,

451 F. Supp. 1044, 1048–49 (N.D. Cal. 1977). In particular, New York might require legislative authorization of any form of jurisdiction, and its legislature has not in fact authorized this sort of anticipatory attachment. See David D. Siegel, New York Practice § 104 (4th ed. 2005).

194. See Shaffer, 433 U.S. at 210 n.36; Biel v. Boehm, 406 N.Y.S.2d 231 (Sup. Ct. 1978).

of this subtype of quasi in rem jurisdiction,[195] although arguably the Constitution prohibits actual seizure solely for this unnecessary formalism.[196]

(4) Ohio plaintiff sues by attaching French defendant's land in New York in order to *recover* for his personal injuries stemming from a traffic accident with defendant in Japan. Attachment jurisdiction in New York is thought to be constitutional, assuming personal jurisdiction is not available in any other American forum.[197] This is an example of so-called jurisdiction by necessity, in which the *unavailability of an alternative American forum* arguably allows jurisdiction to squeak by the unreasonableness test. Other factors could help to rebut unreasonableness, such as the neediness of the plaintiff or some link between the cause of action and the attached property. Power is no problem, because the property is present in New York.

How Does the Process of Categorization Work?

Still another pervasive problem concerning nonpersonal jurisdiction is the play in the process of categorizing an action as the preliminary step in applying the appropriate constitutional standard. A state could avoid the jurisdictional tests for personal jurisdiction by considering the suit to be quasi in rem. Conversely, a state could avoid the jurisdictional tests for jurisdiction over things by proceeding in personam. There must be some limit, even if ill-defined, on the state's ability to expand its own jurisdiction by distorting the categorization process. The current approach would apparently ask, as a special aspect of the jurisdictional inquiry's unreasonableness test, whether the state unreasonably categorized the action.

This is a key to understanding Shaffer v. Heitner, 433 U.S. 186 (1977). The plaintiff sought to assert in Delaware a shareholders' derivative suit against nonresident officers and directors of a Delaware corporation by going after their shares in the corporation. The plaintiff alleged mismanagement occurring in Oregon. Delaware authorized suit as an exercise of subtype two of quasi in rem jurisdiction. The U.S. Supreme Court held jurisdiction in Delaware unconstitutional. The state's only apparent purpose in categorizing the suit as attachment jurisdiction was to evade the restrictions on personal jurisdiction, and this purpose was not a reasonable one. Accordingly, in applying the constitutional standard, the state had to categorize the suit as personal jurisdiction, which was unavailable in the circumstances because Delaware had no power over the defendants. Similarly, Rush v. Savchuk, 444 U.S. 320 (1980), struck down Minnesota's categorization of an action as subtype two of quasi in rem jurisdiction, where the resident plaintiff injured in an out-of-state auto accident sought to garnish

---

195. See Shaffer, 433 U.S. at 208 & n.29; Lawrence W. Newman & David Zaslowsky, Litigating International Commercial Disputes 35 (1996).

196. See Richard W. Bourne, The Demise of Foreign Attachment, 21 Creighton L. Rev. 141, 185–95 (1987) (invoking the Privileges and Immunities Clause of the Constitution).

197. See Feder v. Turkish Airlines, 441 F. Supp. 1273 (S.D.N.Y. 1977) (a

post-Shaffer federal case, allowing New York plaintiffs to obtain attachment jurisdiction in a New York state court for a tort claim arising from a plane crash in Turkey, simply by garnishing a New York bank account belonging to the defendant Turkish Airlines); cf. Shaffer, 433 U.S. at 211 n.37 (leaving the constitutional question open).

the nonresident defendant's liability insurance on the ground that the insurer did business in Minnesota.

A state could also act unreasonably in categorizing an action as in personam. For example, imagine that a plaintiff sues a Connecticut defendant in Connecticut to partition land in New York. Jurisdiction in Connecticut is unconstitutional. This action must meet the jurisdictional tests for subtype one of quasi in rem, and there is no power over the land.

The existence of such limitations on categorization implies that the categories are susceptible to definition. So, what is the defining feature of personal and nonpersonal jurisdiction? It is the remedy, not the nature of the dispute. If the remedy sought acts against the person, the plaintiff must have personal jurisdiction. If the remedy sought affects a specific thing directly, the plaintiff needs nonpersonal jurisdiction. See Austin Wakeman Scott, Fundamentals of Procedure in Actions at Law 31 (1922). The state does have some capacity for shifting a cause of action between personal and nonpersonal jurisdiction, but only if the state changes the remedy it affords.

Categorization is important to the parties too. For a nonpersonal remedy, such as partition of real estate that parties own jointly, the court must have nonpersonal jurisdiction over the thing. For a personal remedy, the court must have jurisdiction over the person. Often, however, in a court without jurisdiction over the thing, the plaintiff can accomplish the equivalent of the nonpersonal remedy by casting the action to seek instead a certain personal remedy addressed to the defendant and based on personal jurisdiction, such as seeking an order that commands the defendant to convey title to the land. The nature of the dispute is similar in that both kinds of action would determine interests in the land, but the former action for partition would yield a nonpersonal judgment and the latter action for an order to convey would yield a personal judgment.

2.   State Limitations on State Reach

The state sovereigns have in fact chosen to exercise somewhat less than their full adjudicatory authority under the U.S. Constitution. These choices find expression in a variety of provisions and doctrines of self-restraint. Most prominent among them is the law of venue. But venue, at least as traditionally defined, does not exhaust these subconstitutional restrictions on geographic selection of forum. For an obvious example, forum non conveniens is a doctrine of self-limitation, whereby a court may discretionarily decline existing territorial authority to adjudicate if the court is a seriously inappropriate forum and if a substantially more appropriate forum is available to the plaintiff. Sovereigns have developed other provisions and doctrines that decline, albeit usually in minor ways, constitutionally permissible territorial authority to adjudicate with respect to certain nonlocal cases. For example, a state's statute might close its courthouse doors to any action between nonresidents on a claim arising outside the state. Therefore, all of these self-imposed limitations form part of the law of territorial authority to adjudicate, properly conceived.

In a nutshell, then, the story of state-court territorial authority to adjudicate comes in two major parts: the active federal restraint in the name of due process and this somewhat less active self-

restraint through a smorgasbord of state-law provisions and doctrines.

In fact, due process's unreasonableness test and this exercise of
self-restraint are similar in theory. The former embodies the most
basic aspects of fairness, and so the Supreme Court has forced it on
the states by means of constitutional interpretation. The latter
restraints are those that the state governments have additionally
chosen to adopt as restrictions on their courts.

a.   State Constitutions and Statutes

State Constitutions. Some restriction on state-court territorial jurisdiction might occasionally be found inserted in a state
constitution.

Jurisdictional Statutes. For separation-of-powers reasons,
the states generally hold that a state court must be authorized by
state statute to exercise the various bases of jurisdictional power,
except for the bases of presence and consent which were recognized
at common law. Accordingly, once *International Shoe* and its immediate progeny suggested the possible extent of state reach, all the
states enacted statutes, often called **long-arm statutes**, to extend
their territorial jurisdiction.[198]

However, a state is certainly not required to extend its jurisdiction all the way to constitutionally permissible limits. Of great
practical importance is the fact that to the extent these state
statutes fall short of authorizing all the jurisdiction permitted by
the Constitution, these statutes serve in effect to restrict state-
court jurisdiction.[199] Many assertions of jurisdiction fail because the
situation in suit does not come within the statute.[200]

As to the content of these state long-arm statutes, there exist
two variations on two basic types:

(1) One basic type of state statutory scheme culminates in a
long-arm provision extending jurisdiction over the defendant

---

198.   See generally Robert C. Casad
& William B. Richman, Jurisdiction in
Civil Actions (3d ed. 1998) (two volumes,
with supplements).

199.   See Flint v. Gust, 351 S.E.2d 95
(Ga. Ct. App. 1986), rev'd, 356 S.E.2d
513, 514 (Ga.) ("The rule that controls
is our statute, which requires that an
out-of-state defendant must do certain
acts within the State of Georgia before
he can be subjected to personal jurisdiction."), on remand, 361 S.E.2d 722 (Ga.
Ct. App. 1987).

200.   Compare Crocker v. Hilton Int'l
Barbados, Ltd., 976 F.2d 797 (1st Cir.
1992) (guest's action against Barbados
hotel for damages resulting from rape on
hotel grounds during trip booked
through travel agency located in Massachusetts neither arose out of hotel's
transaction of business in Massachusetts
nor involved tortious injury in Massachusetts), with Nowak v. Tak How Invs.,
Ltd., 94 F.3d 708 (1st Cir. 1996) (more
loosely reading Massachusetts statute's
requirement of arising from in-state
transaction of business).

far enough to permit suit on claims arising from certain listed activities by the defendant within the state, such as committing a tortious act, transacting business, and owning, using, or possessing real property.[201] There is no jurisdiction unless the long-arm-type case falls within the enumerated-acts statutory provision, and unless the provision so construed is within the Due Process Clause.

(2) A variation on this basic type of statutory scheme reads just the same, but the state courts have so stretched the statutory wording that jurisdiction actually extends to the limits imposed by the Due Process Clause.[202]

(3) A second basic type expressly authorizes jurisdiction wherever consistent with the Due Process Clause.[203] This candid and conceptually straightforward approach maximizes reach, and also simplifies legislative drafting and ensures that the statutory scheme keeps in step with evolving notions of due process. But this vague type of statute is relatively difficult to apply, and also converts every jurisdictional issue into a constitutional question and squanders the legislative opportunity to rationalize jurisdiction.

(4) A variation on this second basic type of statutory scheme contains a catch-all due process provision, but also, in an attempt to provide some suggestive guidance to the courts, includes as alternatives an enumerated-acts list of jurisdiction-bestowing activities.[204]

Taking a closer look at an example of the last-described statute, from Illinois, manages in one shot to illustrate the enumerated-acts and catch-all kinds of long-arm statutes. This statute also concretizes a sense of the outer limit on specific and general jurisdiction (indeed, a state representative speaking in opposition to the 1989 enactment had this to say, "As I understand it, a law school professor sat down in his dusty room one night and thought about all the potential things he could do to enhance his career as a law professor. And he came up with expanding the concept of long arm jurisdiction to coincide with the constitutional limitations on that jurisdiction."):

201. E.g., N.Y.C.P.L.R. § 302; see Longines–Wittnauer Watch Co. v. Barnes & Reinecke, Inc. (Feathers v. McLucas), 209 N.E.2d 68 (N.Y. 1965).

202. E.g., Tex. Civ. Prac. & Rem. Code Ann. §§ 17.041–.069; see U–Anchor Advertising, Inc. v. Burt, 553 S.W.2d 760 (Tex. 1977).

203. E.g., Cal. Civ. Proc. Code § 410.10; see Cornelison v. Chaney, 545 P.2d 264 (Cal. 1976).

204. E.g., Ill. Comp. Stat. ch. 735, § 5/2–209 (the somewhat redundant clauses (a)(6) and (a)(8) derived from separate but simultaneous bills); see Keith H. Beyler, The Illinois Long Arm Statute: Background, Meaning, and Needed Repairs, 12 S. Ill. U. L.J. 293 (1988).

(a) Any person, whether or not a citizen or resident of this State, who in person or through an agent does any of the acts hereinafter enumerated, thereby submits such person, and, if an individual, his or her personal representative, to the jurisdiction of the courts of this State as to any cause of action arising from the doing of any of such acts:

(1) The transaction of any business within this State;

(2) The commission of a tortious act within this State;

(3) The ownership, use, or possession of any real estate situated in this State;

(4) Contracting to insure any person, property or risk located within this State at the time of contracting;

(5) With respect to actions of dissolution of marriage, declaration of invalidity of marriage and legal separation, the maintenance in this State of a matrimonial domicile at the time this cause of action arose or the commission in this State of any act giving rise to the cause of action;

(6) With respect to actions brought under the Illinois Parentage Act of 1984, as now or hereafter amended, the performance of an act of sexual intercourse within this State during the possible period of conception;

(7) The making or performance of any contract or promise substantially connected with this State;

(8) The performance of sexual intercourse within this State which is claimed to have resulted in the conception of a child who resides in this State;

(9) The failure to support a child, spouse or former spouse who has continued to reside in this State since the person either formerly resided with them in this State or directed them to reside in this State;

(10) The acquisition of ownership, possession or control of any asset or thing of value present within this State when ownership, possession or control was acquired;

(11) The breach of any fiduciary duty within this State;

(12) The performance of duties as a director or officer of a corporation organized under the laws of this State or having its principal place of business within this State;

(13) The ownership of an interest in any trust administered within this State; or

(14) The exercise of powers granted under the authority of this State as a fiduciary.

(b) A court may exercise jurisdiction in any action arising within or without this State against any person who:

(1) Is a natural person present within this State when served;

(2) Is a natural person domiciled or resident within this State when the cause of action arose, the action was commenced, or process was served;

(3) Is a corporation organized under the laws of this State; or

(4) Is a natural person or corporation doing business within this State.

(c) A court may also exercise jurisdiction on any other basis now or hereafter permitted by the Illinois Constitution and the Constitution of the United States.

* * * *

Certain state statutes denying court access are closely related to jurisdictional statutes. For example, to conserve resources, a statute might close the state's courthouse doors to any suit between nonresidents on a claim arising outside the state. These would be called **door-closing statutes**.

b. Judicial Doctrines of Self–Restraint

State courts have developed a number of doctrines that further restrict their exercise of territorial jurisdiction. In some instances, these doctrines are now embodied in state statutes. Note that as reasonableness has developed into a constitutional requirement, some of these doctrines of self-restraint may have acquired a constitutional underpinning.

Fraud or Force. In most states, a court will not exercise power over a person or thing if that power has been acquired by fraud or unlawful force. So if the plaintiff lures the defendant into Florida with fraudulent promises of a candlelit dinner and more, and then serves the defendant with process at the Miami airport, the Florida court will not exercise jurisdiction, at least in the absence of some basis other than this presence.[205] Today the unreasonableness test would most likely mandate the same result that is achieved under the older fraud and force rules.

Immunity. Many states grant immunity from service of process to witnesses, counsel, and parties when present in the state for attendance at litigation and during a reasonable time coming and going. Similarly, a state will not exercise power over a chattel sent into the state for use as evidence. Granting immunity facilitates judicial administration. For example, it encourages the attendance of witnesses. So if a witness comes to Florida to testify at a criminal trial, and during the trial is served with process in an unrelated

---

205. See Wyman v. Newhouse, 93 F.2d 313 (2d Cir. 1937) (suit in federal court, but same principle applies in state court).

civil action, the Florida court will not exercise jurisdiction, at least in the absence of some basis other than this presence.

Some states have extended immunity to presence for the purpose of settlement negotiations.[206] Other states have rejected the immunity doctrine altogether for being ineffective.[207] In any one state, the doctrine will present line-drawing problems.[208]

Forum Non Conveniens. The doctrine of forum non conveniens is relatively recent in origin, mainly Anglo–American in adoption, and quite troublesome in application. By it, a state court may discretionarily decline existing territorial jurisdiction if the court is a seriously inappropriate forum and if a substantially more appropriate forum is available to the plaintiff. Most states have adopted this important doctrine, usually by court decision but sometimes by statute.

Principal Rules. In practice, the doctrine of forum non conveniens entails four significant precepts.[209] *First,* forum non conveniens may be invoked on the defendant's motion or on the court's own motion. The plaintiff obviously would oppose forum non conveniens. The burden of proof does not rest on the plaintiff. *Second,* in passing on the motion, the court balances the interests of both the private parties and the public for and against litigating elsewhere. Examples of relevant private factors include residence of the parties, relative ease of access to sources of proof, and problems of judgment enforcement; examples of relevant public factors include which sovereign's law will apply, relative burdens on the court system from hearing the case, and benefits to the polity from deciding the case. All these incommensurable factors go onto the balance to see, by a very imprecise process, in which direction it tilts. Critically, however, the plaintiff's choice of forum receives great deference, especially when the plaintiff is a local, so that the court will decline to hear a case only in an extreme situation, when the balance tilts strongly toward the alternative forum. *Third,* if the court grants the motion, the remedy is ultimately dismissal, either outright or conditional upon defendant's waiving defenses (such as personal jurisdiction or the statute of limitations) that would impede suit in the more appropriate forum. *Fourth,* once the

---

206. See Olean St. Ry. v. Fairmount Constr. Co., 67 N.Y.S. 165 (App. Div. 1900); Sunshine Kitchens, Inc. v. Alanthus Corp., 65 F.R.D. 4 (S.D. Fla. 1974).

207. See Arthur J. Keeffe & John J. Roscia, Immunity and Sentimentality, 32 Cornell L.Q. 471 (1947).

208. E.g., State ex rel. Sivnksty v. Duffield, 71 S.E.2d 113 (W. Va. 1952) (man in jail awaiting criminal trial for reckless driving not immune from service of process for civil suit regarding same incident because his initial entry into state was voluntary).

209. See generally Born & Rutledge, supra note 161, at 347–433; Michael Karayanni, Forum Non Conveniens in the Modern Age (2004); Wright & Miller, supra note 31, §§ 3828–3828.5; Martin Davies, Time to Change the Federal Forum Non Conveniens Analysis, 77 Tul. L. Rev. 309 (2002).

trial judge has muddled through these rules and declared a result of balancing, the appellate court supposedly subjects that result only to deferential review, under an abuse of discretion standard of review.[210]

For example, in *Gulf Oil Corp. v. Gilbert*,[211] a Virginia plaintiff brought suit in New York against a Pennsylvania corporation qualified to do business in both New York and Virginia, alleging negligence that caused the plaintiff's warehouse in Virginia to burn. The defendant moved for dismissal, arguing that Virginia was the appropriate place for trial. The result was dismissal.

In *Piper Aircraft Co. v. Reyno*,[212] Scottish survivors of five Scottish passengers killed in a crash in Scotland arranged to appoint a U.S. administratrix, who brought a product liability suit in the United States against the U.S. manufacturers of the aircraft and the propeller. The defendants moved for dismissal, arguing that Scotland was the appropriate place for trial. The result was dismissal, with the Court declaring that "the central focus of the forum non conveniens inquiry is convenience." Even if the difference in substantive law between the United States and Scotland was what this whole procedural fight really was about, with Scottish law disfavoring the plaintiffs, the Court held that an unfavorable change in law was not a determinative factor in defeating a forum non conveniens dismissal.

Alternative Forum. One way that courts nonetheless still take changing law into account is the supposed rule that a prerequisite to dismissal is the existence of an alternative forum. Courts say that another court must be available, and it must be able to offer a real remedy. Obviously, this standard proves obscure and even illogical in meaning. It is hard to discern when a poor remedy deteriorates into a lack of remedy. But apparently dismissal to a less generous law such as Scotland's can reduce a $10 million claim to $100 thousand,[213] while courts will not allow forum non conve-

---

210. Compare Creative Tech., Ltd. v. Aztech Sys. Pte, Ltd., 61 F.3d 696 (9th Cir. 1995) (affirming dismissal in favor of Singaporean courts of action between two Singaporean corporations over copyright violation in the United States, because it was action between two foreigners), with Guidi v. Inter–Continental Hotels Corp., 224 F.3d 142 (2d Cir. 2000) (reversing dismissal of action brought by U.S. victims of shooting in Egyptian hotel against hotel operator, because inconvenience and emotional burden of dismissal on plaintiffs outweighed greater convenience of litigating in Egypt). But see Karayanni, supra note 209, at 46–48 (arguing that de novo

review applies in practice, and that this would be the better standard).

211. 330 U.S. 501 (1947) (suit in federal court); see, e.g., MacLeod v. MacLeod, 383 A.2d 39 (Me. 1978) (suit in Maine state court dismissed in favor of Virginia state proceeding).

212. 454 U.S. 235, 249 (1981) (suit in federal court). For the story of this case, see Kevin M. Clermont, The Story of Piper: Forum Matters, in Civil Procedure Stories 199 (Kevin M. Clermont ed., 2d ed. 2008).

213. See Gonzalez v. Chrysler Corp., 301 F.3d 377 (5th Cir. 2002) (dismissal despite fact that alternative forum of

niens to reduce a $100 thousand claim to a legal worth of zero because of there being no forum or remedy at all.[214]

The prerequisite of an alternative forum might be more of a useful verbiage than a working rule, consequently. When courts today apply the prerequisite in denying dismissal, they do so as a shorthand expression in extreme cases, to sum up the obvious conclusion that the balance of factors indicates that dismissal would be very unjust. Other than in that situation, courts invoke the prerequisite merely in the course of conditioning dismissal on the defendant's waiving the defenses of personal jurisdiction and the statute of limitations. Indeed, an alternative forum turns out not to be an absolute prerequisite, its absence being overlooked rarely when the tilt of the factors toward dismissal is utterly overwhelming.[215] In the end, the prerequisite of an alternative forum is not really a rule.

Conditioned Dismissal. Courts take changing law into account more globally by that technique of conditioned dismissal. Here *Piper* was particularly obscure. The Court said that consideration of changes in law was ordinarily off the table, but it seemed to approve conditioning dismissal on the defendants' waiving jurisdictional and limitations defenses—two aspects of the alternative forum's quasi-substantive law strikingly unfavorable to the plaintiff. Indeed, the Court suggested a possible condition that the defendants agree to discovery along U.S. lines—a condition that would temper unfavorable procedural law in the foreign court. The Court never explained why courts should so consider foreign law, or when they should force such concessions from the moving party.

No rule on conditions exists, consequently. Today courts in some cases impose quite a variety of conditions, ranging from a substantive condition that the defendant waive the right to contest liability in exchange for escaping U.S. damages law[216] to the ill-advised procedural condition that the defendant consent to U.S.-style discovery in the new court.[217] Although the lower courts' standard for imposing conditions is understandably unarticulated,

---

Mexico caps damages below cost of litigating).

214. See Born & Rutledge, supra note 161, at 370, 404–06, 415–25.

215. See, e.g., Islamic Republic of Iran v. Pahlavi, 467 N.E.2d 245, 57 A.L.R.4th 955 (N.Y. 1984) (dismissal of case against former Shah of Iran), discussed in Ann Alexander, Note, Forum Non Conveniens in the Absence of an Alternative Forum, 86 Colum. L. Rev. 1000 (1986).

216. See, e.g., Myers v. Boeing, 794 P.2d 1272 (Wash. 1990).

217. See, e.g., In re Union Carbide Corp. Gas Plant Disaster at Bhopal, India in Dec., 1984, 809 F.2d 195 (2d Cir. 1987) (dismissing in favor of India's courts, but reversing this condition), discussed in John Bies, Comment, Conditioning Forum Non Conveniens, 67 U. Chi. L. Rev. 489 (2000); cf. Gross v. British Broad. Corp., 386 F.3d 224, 234–35 (2d Cir. 2004) (disapproving conditions of waiving UK fee rules).

it appears that they impose a condition whenever necessary to offset an unfair change in substantive or procedural law sufficiently to keep the dismissal from being its own miscarriage of justice.

Summary. Forum non conveniens most often applies when the preferred court is foreign. In actual practice, it is almost always fatal to the plaintiff's case.[218] With such a stark effect of forum non conveniens on outcome, is it fair then for the court both to ignore an unfavorable change in applicable law and to dismiss readily on the basis of mere inconvenience? The *Piper* Court seemed to think so. But, simply put, that is not a fair approach. Forum non conveniens should not have expanded into a doctrine to mitigate inconvenience of forum but instead should have remained a doctrine to curb forum-shopping abuse—with dismissal only when the plaintiff has so abused the privilege of forum-selection, maybe by exploiting loose jurisdictional law and malleable choice-of-law doctrine in an unrelated forum, that going forward here rather than there would be a miscarriage of justice, all things considered. If there has been such abuse by the plaintiff, albeit a plaintiff who has sued in a technically proper court, it becomes fair to inflict the change in law on that plaintiff.

Fortunately, if one holds this view, what most trial judges seem in fact to be doing is balancing all interests, and then dismissing relatively seldom and only when in their subjective opinion the balance tilts beyond a tough standard for dismissal: something like whether the plaintiff has so abused the privilege of forum-selection that going forward would be a miscarriage of justice.[219] Furthermore, the judge commonly conditions any such dismissal on the defendant's varied concessions so as to keep the dismissal from being its own miscarriage of justice.

Yet, if forum non conveniens is becoming once again only a doctrine of abuse, what does it contribute beyond the unreasonable-

---

218. See David W. Robertson, Forum Non Conveniens in America and England: "A Rather Fantastic Fiction," 103 Law Q. Rev. 398, 418–20 (1987); see also David W. Robertson, The Federal Doctrine of Forum Non Conveniens: "An Object Lesson in Uncontrolled Discretion," 29 Tex. Int'l L.J. 353 (1994) (arguing for reliable rules to temper judicial discretion and otherwise to narrow forum non conveniens).

219. See, e.g., Tuazon v. R.J. Reynolds Tobacco Co., 433 F.3d 1163 (9th Cir. 2006) (affirming the Western District of Washington's finding of general jurisdiction over tobacco company and denying of forum non conveniens dismissal, in a product-liability action brought by a Philippine smoker); Bhatnagar v. Surrendra Overseas Ltd., 52 F.3d 1220 (3d Cir. 1995) (affirming denial of dismissal, because alternative forum of India had backlog of cases greatly delaying resolution in that system); cf. Wiwa v. Royal Dutch Petroleum Co., 226 F.3d 88 (2d Cir. 2000) (reversing dismissal in favor of UK courts of action initiated by Nigerian émigrés against foreign corporations for human rights abuses abroad). But see, e.g., In re Factor VIII or IX Concentrate Blood Prods. Litig., 531 F. Supp. 2d 957 (N.D. Ill. 2008) (dismissing case in favor of Argentine courts).

ness test for territorial jurisdiction, a test discovered by the Supreme Court in the Due Process Clauses soon after the birth of forum non conveniens? Not much, besides (1) multiplying costs, (2) increasing uncertainty, and (3) facilitating discrimination against foreigners. First, forum non conveniens often raises intricate questions, requiring extensive investigation and research. Second, the judicial decision involved is blatantly discretionary and hence unpredictable. Third, the *Piper* Court's ambiguous blessing of various rules and presumptions, such as a strong presumption in favor of a plaintiff who is a U.S. citizen or resident, can skew that discretion away from fairness. In brief, although some judicial flexibility in rejecting jurisdiction might be desirable, the Constitution's unreasonableness test provides it, while subjecting it to nondeferential appellate review.

Nevertheless, does not forum non conveniens tend to narrow the currently overbroad law of territorial authority to adjudicate? Yes, but the desirable course of narrowing territorial reach should be approached openly and directly by legislative reform of jurisdiction and venue, rather than surreptitiously and dangerously by a judicial embrace of forum non conveniens. For example, the very substantive decision on whether U.S. and multinational corporations should be amenable to foreigners' suits here should not be delegated to the haphazard quilt work of trial judges' discretion and biases. In short, a decent jurisdiction and venue statute would eliminate the need for a doctrine of forum non conveniens, by narrowing in advance the plaintiff's choice of forum to a smaller list of appropriate courts.[220]

Parallel Proceedings. The pendency of a lawsuit in one court is normally no impediment to bringing a related suit in a different court, or indeed in the same court. Although the first suit to go to judgment should be res judicata in the other, otherwise the pendency of parallel proceedings is a commonplace with no ready cure.

A minor doctrine of some relevance is the affirmative defense called **other action pending**, or prior pending action.[221] It will result in dismissal without prejudice if another action on the same claim between the same parties was pending in the same state when the instant action was commenced and if that other action is still pending. It tries to stop repetitive litigation in its tracks, well before any troublesome rendition of judgment. Although this approach seems a sensible way to reduce repetitive litigation, the defense is only narrowly applicable. Thus, its very limited scope of application serves powerfully to underscore that the usual approach

220. See Kevin M. Clermont, The Story of Piper: Forum Matters, in Civil Procedure Stories 199 (Kevin M. Clermont ed., 2d ed. 2008).

221. See 1 C.J.S. Abatement and Revival §§ 19–86 (2005).

is to allow a second court to proceed toward judgment despite earlier-instituted litigation.

Besides other action pending, other inroads on the usual approach exist, but they too are minor. One court, usually the first to acquire jurisdiction, might enjoin proceedings in the other court. Alternatively, one court, usually the second, might stay its own hand in deference to the other court. A little more detail on these two approaches is appropriate.[222]

An **antisuit injunction** by one court against proceedings in another court within the United States is generally prohibited by statute or at least will be discretionarily refused. On the international level, however, some American courts are slightly more willing to enjoin a party subject to its personal jurisdiction from participating in specified foreign proceedings, equitably balancing interests but still in the name of comity weighting the balance against interference.

Under the vague doctrine called lis alibi pendens ("suit elsewhere pending"), or just **lis pendens**, one court may stay its own proceedings in deference to another court's, if the related proceedings are in a more appropriate forum. This discretionary power has been judicially created as an incident to the courts' inherent power to control their own dockets. But here too the American case law is split, as precedent either emphasizes the court's obligation to proceed with the case by narrowly limiting the court's power to stay its proceedings or gives the court considerable discretion to decide on an all-things-considered basis whether to stay its proceedings. When a court so stays itself, it is exercising self-restraint with respect to its territorial jurisdiction. Indeed, this doctrine is very similar to forum non conveniens, albeit where applicable a bit more readily invoked, the differences being that this doctrine requires a pending alternative and that stayed proceedings are more easily revived if necessary than dismissed proceedings.

c.   Venue Restrictions

Related to all these limits on state-court territorial jurisdiction are state venue restrictions, which most often are defined as those rules of territorial authority to adjudicate that specify as proper forums only certain courts within a state having territorial jurisdiction. Thus, state-court territorial jurisdiction comprises interstate rules, while state-court venue is intrastate.

---

222. See, e.g., Csohan v. United Benefit Life Ins. Co., 200 N.E.2d 345 (Ohio Ct. App. 1964) (injunction denied). See generally Edward Dumbauld, Judicial Interference with Litigation in Other Courts, 74 Dick. L. Rev. 369 (1970); James P. George, Parallel Litigation, 51 Baylor L. Rev. 769 (1999).

Venue Statutes. The state legislature distributes judicial business among the counties or other state subdivisions by means of a statutory venue scheme. This scheme turns on such grounds as where the claim arose or where the defendant or the plaintiff resides or does business. The venue scheme varies from state to state, but is seldom a monument to good policy or intelligent drafting.[223]

Local Actions. Most states perpetuate an ancient, confusing, and unsound judge-made doctrine that overrides the usual venue statutes and requires any of a rather arbitrary group of actions to be brought in the county or other subdivision where the subject of the action is located. These "local actions" contrast with "transitory actions," which can be brought anywhere the usual rules of territorial jurisdiction and venue are satisfied. Local actions involve claims that supposedly could take place only in one locale, which usually means that local actions include proceedings in rem and those within subtype one of quasi in rem, as well as certain personal actions such as trespass to land, negligent damage to land, and abatement of nuisance. Note that if the subject of a local action is not located within the state, this venue doctrine restricts territorial authority to adjudicate on an interstate level. Indeed, there is some dispute about whether the local-action doctrine falls within the realm of territorial jurisdiction or even subject-matter jurisdiction, but the better view would classify it as a venue rule.

In the classic case of *Livingston v. Jefferson,*[224] Edward Livingston of New York sued Thomas Jefferson of Virginia in a Virginia court, alleging trespass to land in New Orleans by the President. The case was dismissed for improper venue. Venue lay only where the land was, even though in those old days Jefferson was not amenable to service of process issuing from there.

d. Agreements Among Parties

The parties may consent in advance to state-court territorial jurisdiction not otherwise existing, and they may waive in advance the restrictions of state-court venue and the other doctrines of self-

---

223. See George N. Stevens, Venue Statutes: Diagnosis and Proposed Cure, 49 Mich. L. Rev. 307 (1951) (criticizing the confused situation and proposing a model venue code).

224. 15 F. Cas. 660 (C.C.D. Va. 1811) (No. 8411) (suit in federal court). But see Reasor–Hill Corp. v. Harrison, 249 S.W.2d 994 (Ark. 1952) (abolishing local-action doctrine in Arkansas); cf. Raphael J. Musicus, Inc. v. Safeway Stores, Inc., 743 F.2d 503 (7th Cir. 1984) (deciding suit by lessor against lessee to void subleases and renewal options and to enjoin breach of lease, and secondarily seeking damages for trespass, is transitory). For the story behind the Livingston case, see George Dargo, Public Power and Privatization 114–70 (1980), revised in George Dargo, Law in the New Republic 107–36 (1983); Ronan E. Degnan, Livingston v. Jefferson—A Freestanding Footnote, 75 Cal. L. Rev. 115 (1987).

restraint. Most states under modern law will usually give effect to such "prorogation" agreements, apparently subject to ordinary contract law and the requirement that the forum not be an unconscionable one.

Conversely, the parties generally may, by a "derogation" agreement, restrict any potential litigation to one or more courts among the forums otherwise permissible under the law of state-court territorial authority to adjudicate. That is, state law, in a further show of self-restraint, allows the parties themselves to restrict territorial authority to adjudicate.

In *The Bremen v. Zapata Off-Shore Co.*,[225] there was a contract providing that a German corporation (*G*) would tow from Louisiana to Italy an oil rig belonging to a Delaware corporation (*T*) based in Texas, and further providing that any dispute would be heard in a London court known for its neutrality and expertise in such matters. After a storm damaged the rig under tow, *G* put into port in Florida. *T* sued *G* in Florida, but *G* invoked the "forum selection clause." The result was dismissal, with the Supreme Court shifting from a jurisdictional to a contractual paradigm and thereby generally approving forum selection clauses. In *Carnival Cruise Lines v. Shute*,[226] the Court shifted further toward the contract paradigm, even more expansively enforcing such agreements and seemingly narrowing exceptions to either fraud in inclusion of the clause or an unreasonably chosen (or unconscionable) forum. Consequently, the Court there enforced the choice of Florida courts printed on the ticket, against a Washington State passenger injured on a West Coast cruise.

Thus, American courts have shifted with time from a view that territorial authority to adjudicate is largely a matter for the sovereign and not the parties to decide, through a grudging acceptance of party agreements, and toward a perhaps overly enthusiastic embrace of freedom of contract even in the face of uneven bargaining capabilities and powers. Where the optimum lies and where American law will end up are still matters of debate and evolution.

In any event, forum selection clauses are becoming more and more important. Good lawyers try increasingly by agreement to contract their clients' way around the morass of the law on territorial authority to adjudicate, and to do so in a way that advantages their clients. Lots of litigated cases, however, turn on how to interpret these clauses, most often as a result of the lawyers' failings. Office lawyers need to know a lot of law, including choice of law, to negotiate and write a forum selection clause effectively and clearly.

225.   407 U.S. 1 (1972) (suit in federal court).

226.   499 U.S. 585 (1991) (suit in federal court).

C. Federal Courts

1. Federal Limitations on Federal Reach

a. Federal Constitution, Statutes, and Rules

Federal Constitution. The principal constitutional limitations on a federal court's territorial jurisdiction come from the Due Process Clause of the Fifth Amendment. Although clear case law is very scanty, it seems that this Clause operates analogously to the Fourteenth Amendment's Due Process Clause. Thus, here due process requires the categorization of the action and then the application of both the power and the unreasonableness tests.[227]

The federal court must have power over the target of the action. But here power requires only "minimum contacts" *with the United States*. Thus, this power test is a constitutional impediment only in international cases.

The particular district must not be fundamentally unfair in light of all the interests of the defendant, the plaintiff, and the public concerning the litigation. This is the same test of "fair play and substantial justice" that applies to state courts, although very rarely results could differ because suit in a federal *district* court affects the relevant interests practically in a marginally different way than does suit in the *state* court.

Other constitutional provisions can play a role. Most prominently, just as for state courts, the First Amendment possibly may affect federal-court territorial jurisdiction.

Jurisdictional Statutes and Rules. Federal courts generally exercise territorial jurisdiction only where authorized by Congress or its rulemaker. Congress and the Supreme Court, the latter acting as Congress's rulemaker, have implicitly or explicitly authorized varying degrees of federal-court territorial jurisdiction in a confusing complex of statutes and Rules treating service of process.

The rules of service concern the means of officially notifying the interested persons that the plaintiff has brought an action and of formally asserting power over the target of the action. Federal Rule 4(a) specifies the form of the summons. Rule 4(b) dictates that upon or after the plaintiff's filing a complaint, the court clerk must issue the summons. Rule 4(c) says that the summons must be served with a copy of the complaint, and then describes the persons authorized to effect service. Rule 4(e)-(j) deals with the "manner of

---

227. See generally Maryellen Fullerton, Constitutional Limits on Nationwide Jurisdiction in the Federal Courts, 79 Nw. U. L. Rev. 1 (1984); Robert A. Lusardi, Nationwide Service of Process: Due Process Limitations on the Power of the Sovereign, 33 Vill. L. Rev. 1 (1988).

service," i.e., the mechanics of delivering original process to different kinds of defendants.[228] Also, Rule 4(*l*) treats proof of service, and Rule 4(m) sets a time limit for service. Since 1993, Rule 4(d) provides that a plaintiff suing an individual (who is neither a minor nor an incompetent), a corporation, or an unincorporated association can mail a notice to a defendant requesting a waiver of service: if the defendant complies, the suit can proceed without the need for the rather expensive formality of service; if the defendant fails to comply, the plaintiff needs to arrange for service of process, but the defendant normally will have to pay the expenses of that service.

Rule 4 goes on to deal with a variety of service situations. The key provision is Rule 4(k) and (n):

(k) Territorial Limits of Effective Service.

(1) *In General.* Serving a summons or filing a waiver of service establishes personal jurisdiction over a defendant:

(A) who is subject to the jurisdiction of a court of general jurisdiction in the state where the district court is located;

(B) who is a party joined under Rule 14 or 19 and is served within a judicial district of the United States and not more than 100 miles from where the summons was issued;

(C) when authorized by a federal statute.

(2) *Federal Claim Outside State–Court Jurisdiction.* For a claim that arises under federal law, serving a summons or filing a waiver of service establishes personal jurisdiction over a defendant if:

(A) the defendant is not subject to jurisdiction in any state's courts of general jurisdiction; and

(B) exercising jurisdiction is consistent with the United States Constitution and laws.

(n) Asserting Jurisdiction over Property or Assets.

(1) *Federal Law.* The court may assert jurisdiction over property if authorized by a federal statute. Notice to claimants of the property must be given as provided in the statute or by serving a summons under this rule.

(2) *State Law.* On a showing that personal jurisdiction over a defendant cannot be obtained in the district where the action is brought by reasonable efforts to serve a summons under this rule, the court may assert jurisdiction over the defendant's assets found in the district. Jurisdiction is acquired by seizing the assets under the circumstances and in the manner provided by state law in that district.

---

228. See infra § 4.3(C).

This Rule so creates six service provisions, for each of which the law specifies the "circumstances of service," i.e., where service will be effective in asserting territorial jurisdiction. In the following descriptions of the circumstances of service under the six provisions, note the source of the governing law. On the one hand, for service under some of these provisions, federal law exclusively governs territorial jurisdiction. That federal law usually comprises only the Fifth Amendment due process standard, although the service provision may impose additional restrictions. On the other hand, for service under the remaining provisions, the provision itself adopts state jurisdictional law.[229] This means that the circumstances must be such that the local state would have to be able to exercise jurisdiction under its long-arm statutes and under the Fourteenth Amendment.[230]

(1) Rule 4(k)(1)(A) is read to cover all ordinary situations of service. This Rule itself specifies that state law governs the circumstances of service thereunder, whether the claim is federally created or state-created. Thus, the federal court ordinarily can reach only as far as the forum state could under its long-arm statutes and under the Fourteenth Amendment.

(2) Rule 4(k)(1)(B) is a special alternative treating service within the United States and within a 100–mile radius of the particular federal courthouse. Note that it *applies only to additional parties being brought in under Rules 14 and 19.* This "100–mile bulge" provision facilitates complex litigation in metropolitan areas. Currently, there are numerous possible views on how to read this Rule with respect to federal-court reach. The best but disputed view is that if the additional party is served within the bulge, then the only restrictions on reach are the Fifth Amendment limits on the federal court.[231] For illustration, if a third-party defendant in an action in the Southern District of New York is personally served in Hackensack, New Jersey, the only questions will be whether she has minimum contacts with the United States and whether it is unreasonable to hear the impleader claim in the Southern District.

(3) Rule 4(k)(1)(C) incorporates by reference any special federal service statute, such as the securities long-arm statute in 15 U.S.C. § 22. Federal-court reach turns on the particular federal service statute. The reach extends to the Fifth Amendment limits,

---

229. See DeJames v. Magnificence Carriers, 491 F. Supp. 1276 (D.N.J. 1980), aff'd, 654 F.2d 280 (3d Cir. 1981).

230. See Cofield v. Randolph County Comm'n, 844 F. Supp. 1499 (M.D. Ala. 1994).

231. See Benjamin Kaplan, Amendments of the Federal Rules of Civil Procedure, 1961–1963 (I), 77 Harv. L. Rev. 601, 632–33 (1964). But see Hollerbach & Andrews Equip. Co. v. S. Concrete Pumping, Inc., Civ. A. No. HAR 95–826, 1995 WL 604706 (D. Md. Sept. 29, 1995) (requiring minimum contacts with forum state plus bulge).

unless the statute otherwise indicates. For example, under the provision for nationwide service in 28 U.S.C. § 2361, a claimant in a statutory interpleader suit may be served anywhere in the United States, but not by service abroad.

(4) Rule 4(k)(2) is a narrow alternative applying in *federal law* actions, but *only to defendants who are beyond the jurisdiction of every single state.* Federal-court reach here extends to the Fifth Amendment limits, so that the defendant must have minimum contacts with the United States, and the particular district must not be an unreasonable forum.[232]

(5) Rule 4(n)(1) implicitly refers to 28 U.S.C. § 1655, which provides for service in federal proceedings in rem and those within subtype one of quasi in rem. That statute requires the res to be in the district where the federal court sits.

(6) Rule 4(n)(2) treats service in all categories of nonpersonal proceedings, thus sometimes offering an alternative to 28 U.S.C. § 1655. Rule 4(n)(2) incorporates by reference the forum state's service provisions for proceedings in rem and quasi in rem. This Rule requires the res to be in the district where the federal court sits, and provides that state law (subject to constitutional limits) further governs the circumstances of service thereunder.

Obviously, each of the six service provisions presents problems of interpretation. Consider as an example the situation in which a nonfrivolous federal claim and a state claim are joined in a federal action, with service being made under Rule 4(k)(1)(C) in accordance with a federal statute providing nationwide service for the federal claim. Assuming that subject-matter jurisdiction exists for the state claim, but that the nationwide-service provision is the sole basis for exercising jurisdiction over the defendant, is there personal jurisdiction for the purposes of the state claim? A careful reading of the applicable statutes reveals no congressional intent to extend nationwide service of process to state claims. However, the policies of

---

232. See United States v. Swiss Am. Bank, Ltd., 191 F.3d 30, 41 (1st Cir. 1999) ("We hold that a plaintiff who seeks to invoke Rule 4(k)(2) must make a prima facie case for the applicability of the rule. This includes a tripartite showing (1) that the claim asserted arises under federal law, (2) that personal jurisdiction is not available under any situation-specific federal statute, and (3) that the putative defendant's contacts with the nation as a whole suffice to satisfy the applicable constitutional requirements. The plaintiff, moreover, must certify that, based on the information that is readily available to the plaintiff and his counsel, the defendant is not subject to suit in the courts of general jurisdiction of any state. If the plaintiff makes out his prima facie case, the burden shifts to the defendant to produce evidence which, if credited, would show either that one or more specific states exist in which it would be subject to suit or that its contacts with the United States are constitutionally insufficient."), on remand, 116 F. Supp. 2d 217 (D. Mass. 2000), aff'd, 274 F.3d 610 (1st Cir. 2001) (no jurisdiction because of lack of sufficient contacts with the United States); Graduate Mgmt. Admission Council v. Raju, 241 F. Supp. 2d 589 (E.D. Va. 2003).

judicial economy, convenience, and fairness underlying the exercise of supplemental subject-matter jurisdiction suggest that some degree of "supplemental service" should exist. The courts over time have split on this problem, but the trend toward the supplemental-service view is accelerating.[233]

Of great practical importance is the fact that to the considerable extent these service provisions are written or construed to fall short of authorizing all the jurisdiction permitted by the Federal Constitution, as is the most important Rule 4(k)(1)(A), these provisions serve in effect to restrict federal-court jurisdiction.

b. Judicial Doctrines of Self–Restraint

Just as state courts have done, federal courts have developed a number of doctrines that further restrict their exercise of territorial jurisdiction. These doctrines are basically similar to their state-court analogues, so their detailed description above will not be repeated here.

Fraud or Force. A federal court will not exercise jurisdiction acquired through fraud or unlawful force.[234]

Immunity. Federal courts grant immunity from service of process to witnesses, counsel, and parties when in attendance at litigation and during a reasonable time coming and going.[235] A similar rule exists for chattels used as evidence.

Forum Non Conveniens. A federal district court, without any statutory authority, may discretionarily decline existing authority to adjudicate by dismissing the case if the court is a seriously inappropriate forum, if a substantially more appropriate forum (normally foreign but conceivably state) is available to the plaintiff, and if transfer of venue to a more convenient federal forum (a statutory procedure described below) is not an adequate remedy.

Although the *Erie* question here is not settled, the prevailing and better view is that federal law governs forum non conveniens in federal court.[236] Application of federal law here conforms with the

---

233. See Linda Sandstrom Simard, Exploring the Limits of Specific Personal Jurisdiction, 62 Ohio St. L.J. 1619 (2001); ESAB Group, Inc. v. Centricut, Inc., 126 F.3d 617 (4th Cir. 1997); cf. Action Embroidery Corp. v. Atl. Embroidery, Inc., 368 F.3d 1174, 1180–81 (9th Cir. 2004) (seeming questionably to equate scope of supplemental service to that of pendent subject-matter jurisdiction, rather than merely to analogize).

234. See May Dep't Stores Co. v. Wilansky, 900 F. Supp. 1154 (E.D. Mo. 1995) (arguably overbroad application).

235. See Fun–Damental Too, Ltd. v. Hwung, No. 97 CIV. 0866 (MBM), 1997 WL 289712 (S.D.N.Y. May 30, 1997) (arguably overbroad application).

236. See Kevin M. Clermont, The Story of Piper: Forum Matters, in Civil Procedure Stories 199, 221 (Kevin M. Clermont ed., 2d ed. 2008).

general rule that federal courts do not look to state law concerning the other doctrines of self-restraint and venue.

Indeed, as a general rule of choice of law, all aspects of territorial authority to adjudicate are controlled by the forum's law, subject to due process's limits. The sovereign has decided how much authority its courts will exercise, and so the court should look to its sovereign's law. Therefore, *Erie* questions in this area are seldom intense. The authorities agree rather effortlessly that state law governs state venue, and federal law governs federal venue. On the other aspects of territorial authority to adjudicate, more hesitation precedes what is normally the same resolution.[237]

Parallel Proceedings. The minor affirmative defense called other action pending will result in dismissal without prejudice if another action on the same claim between the same parties was pending in the same federal district when the instant action was commenced and if that other action is still pending.[238]

An antisuit injunction by a federal court against proceedings in another jurisdiction is generally prohibited by statute[239] or at least will be discretionarily refused.

Likewise, a vague federal lis pendens doctrine exists, allowing the court discretionarily to stay its own proceedings in deference to another court's, if the related proceedings are in a more appropriate forum.

c. Venue Restrictions

Related to all these limits on federal-court territorial jurisdiction are federal venue restrictions, which most often are rather arbitrarily defined as those rules of territorial authority to adjudicate that are not linked to service provisions but instead are separately and statutorily prescribed.

General Venue Statute. Under the historically independent but equivalent subsections of 28 U.S.C. § 1391(a) and (b), venue today lies in a district where (1) any defendant resides, if all defendants reside in the same state, or (2) where a substantial part of the events or omissions giving rise to the claim occurred or a substantial part of property that is the subject of the action is situated;[240] however, the statute, by its varying but still equivalent

---

237. See, e.g., Am. Dredging Co. v. Miller, 510 U.S. 443 (1994) (state law governs forum non conveniens in state-court admiralty case); infra text accompanying notes 255–56.

238. See Sutcliffe Storage & Warehouse Co. v. United States, 162 F.2d 849 (1st Cir. 1947).

239. See 28 U.S.C. § 2283; Chick Kam Choo v. Exxon Corp., 486 U.S. 140, 148 (1988).

240. Compare First of Mich. Corp. v.

language in subsections (a)(3) and (b)(3), effectively waives this venue requirement in the rare circumstance when it would block suit in every federal court:

(a) A civil action wherein jurisdiction is founded only on diversity of citizenship may, except as otherwise provided by law, be brought only in (1) a judicial district where any defendant resides, if all defendants reside in the same State, (2) a judicial district in which a substantial part of the events or omissions giving rise to the claim occurred, or a substantial part of property that is the subject of the action is situated, or (3) a judicial district in which any defendant is subject to personal jurisdiction at the time the action is commenced, if there is no district in which the action may otherwise be brought.

(b) A civil action wherein jurisdiction is not founded solely on diversity of citizenship may, except as otherwise provided by law, be brought only in (1) a judicial district where any defendant resides, if all defendants reside in the same State, (2) a judicial district in which a substantial part of the events or omissions giving rise to the claim occurred, or a substantial part of property that is the subject of the action is situated, or (3) a judicial district in which any defendant may be found, if there is no district in which the action may otherwise be brought.

(c) For purposes of venue under this chapter, a defendant that is a corporation shall be deemed to reside in any judicial district in which it is subject to personal jurisdiction at the time the action is commenced. In a State which has more than one judicial district and in which a defendant that is a corporation is subject to personal jurisdiction at the time an action is commenced, such corporation shall be deemed to reside in any district in that State within which its contacts would be sufficient to subject it to personal jurisdiction if that district were a separate State, and, if there is no such district, the corporation shall be deemed to reside in the district within which it has the most significant contacts.

(d) An alien may be sued in any district.

* * * *

Bramlet, 141 F.3d 260 (6th Cir. 1998) (clarifying that more than one district can host "a substantial part"), and Bates v. C & S Adjusters, Inc., 980 F.2d 865, 868 (2d Cir. 1992) (finding venue proper for suit against a bill collector in the district where plaintiff resides and received a forwarded demand for payment, because "receipt of a collection notice is a substantial part of the events giving rise to a claim under the Fair Debt Collection Practices Act"), with Database Am., Inc. v. Bellsouth Adver. & Publ'g Corp., 825 F. Supp. 1216 (D.N.J. 1993) (in action for declaration of nonliability, a letter ordering plaintiff to cease and desist copyright infringement does not constitute the necessary substantial activity, because it is not an element of copyright infringement or ownership), and Magic Toyota, Inc. v. Se. Toyota Distribs., Inc., 784 F. Supp. 306 (D.S.C. 1992) (venue is improper when events giving rise to the claim were directed at the forum but occurred elsewhere).

For an example, imagine that in the Federal District of Utah, *P–1* of North Dakota and *P–2* of South Dakota sue *D–1* of Wyoming and *D–2* of Utah, based on a traffic accident in Salt Lake City. Then, federal venue lies in Utah, but nowhere else.

For an *individual,* the cases equate residence with the district in which the individual is domiciled as a U.S. citizen, so that individuals have only one residence. But for any alien defendant, § 1391(d) virtually eliminates the venue requirement.[241] For a *corporate defendant,* § 1391(c) expands residence to include any district where the corporation would be subject to personal jurisdiction.[242] For an *unincorporated association,* the courts apply the rules that they had developed for corporations.[243]

Note that unlike most service provisions, which emphasize state boundaries, venue rules distribute judicial business on a district-by-district level.[244] Incidentally, many districts are subdivided into divisions, but these divisions have significance only for local judicial administration.[245]

Special Venue Statutes. There are many federal statutes prescribing special rules for particular kinds of cases. They form a hopelessly complex pattern and raise countless interpretive problems. Most are read to supplement the choice of venue under 28 U.S.C. § 1391, but some are read as overriding § 1391.

For *shareholders' derivative actions,* 28 U.S.C. § 1401 adds, as a permissible venue, "any judicial district where the corporation might have sued the same defendants." For *interpleader actions,* 28 U.S.C. § 1397 provides that statutory interpleader suits may be brought only in a district wherein any claimant resides, thus overriding § 1391(a) and (b). For *removed actions,* 28 U.S.C. § 1441(a), which provides that the venue for a removed action is the district in which the particular state courthouse is located, overrides the rest of federal venue law.

Local Actions. The federal courts perpetuate this mysterious and ill-advised doctrine, which was described above for state courts. The doctrine requires local actions to be brought in the district where the subject matter of the action is located. The federal doctrine derives from case law, although it is now mentioned in 28

---

241. See Dee–K Enters., Inc. v. Heveafil Sdn. Bhd., 982 F. Supp. 1138 (E.D. Va. 1997) (§ 1391(d) overrides special venue provision).

242. See Tranor v. Brown, 913 F. Supp. 388 (E.D. Pa. 1996) (holding that a corporation does not "reside" in a district of a multidistrict state simply because it incorporated or licensed to do business in that state).

243. See Denver & R.G.W.R.R. v. Bhd. of R.R. Trainmen, 387 U.S. 556 (1967).

244. See generally Wright & Kane, supra note 1, § 42.

245. See generally Wright & Miller, supra note 31, § 3809.

U.S.C. § 1392. The doctrine overrides the rest of federal venue law, except the removal statute.

Transfer of Venue. Preempting most of forum non conveniens, Congress in 1948 authorized the discretionary transfer of a federal case to another federal district.[246] The statute, 28 U.S.C. § 1404(a), provides:

> For the convenience of parties and witnesses, in the interest of justice, a district court may transfer any civil action to any other district or division where it might have been brought.

An action properly commenced in or removed to a district court may be transferred to a more convenient district. There are several important rules here. *First*, such transfer may be invoked on any party's motion or on the court's own motion. *Second*, in passing on the motion, the court considers all relevant interests, but will grant it on a lesser showing of relative convenience than is required under forum non conveniens. *Third*, if the court grants the motion, the remedy is transfer rather than dismissal. *Fourth*, and most importantly, under § 1404(a) transfer can be ordered only to a federal forum where the case "might have been brought." This provision has unfortunately been read to mean a district where the plaintiff could originally have satisfied the federal requirements of territorial jurisdiction and venue over the defendant's objection.[247]

There is another important, but quite different, transfer statute in 28 U.S.C. § 1406(a):

> The district court of a district in which is filed a case laying venue in the wrong division or district shall dismiss, or if it be in the interest of justice, transfer such case to any district or division in which it could have been brought.

Under § 1406(a) as construed, if a federal action fails to meet the requirements of either territorial jurisdiction or venue, or both, the court may "in the interest of justice" transfer the case to a proper federal district. Thus, a misguided plaintiff might avoid dismissal after the statute of limitations has run.[248]

---

246. See generally Wright & Kane, supra note 1, § 44. On transfer of venue in multidistrict litigation under 28 U.S.C. § 1407, see infra § 6.1(C)(2).

247. See Hoffman v. Blaski, 363 U.S. 335 (1960); cf. A.J. Indus., Inc. v. U.S. Dist. Court, 503 F.2d 384, 387 (9th Cir. 1974) ("ability to raise the subject matter of a suit in the transferor district by counterclaim in the transferee district will, as a general proposition, satisfy the 'where it might have been brought' requirement").

248. See Goldlawr, Inc. v. Heiman, 369 U.S. 463 (1962); cf. Nichols v. G.D. Searle & Co., 991 F.2d 1195, 1201 (4th Cir. 1993) ("district court acts within its discretion when it finds that the interest of justice is not served by allowing a plaintiff whose attorney committed an obvious error in filing the plaintiff's action in the wrong court, and thereby imposed substantial unnecessary costs on both the defendant and the judicial system, simply to transfer").

Somewhat similarly, 28 U.S.C. § 1631 authorizes transfer from one federal court to another in order to cure a defect of subject-matter jurisdiction:

> Whenever a civil action is filed in a court as defined in section 610 of this title or an appeal, including a petition for review of administrative action, is noticed for or filed with such a court and that court finds that there is a want of jurisdiction, the court shall, if it is in the interest of justice, transfer such action or appeal to any other such court in which the action or appeal could have been brought at the time it was filed or noticed, and the action or appeal shall proceed as if it had been filed in or noticed for the court to which it is transferred on the date upon which it was actually filed in or noticed for the court from which it is transferred.[249]

Choice of Law. After transfer under § 1404(a), the transferee court applies the law that the transferor court would have. Thus, if plaintiffs sued in the Eastern District of Pennsylvania for wrongful deaths in an air crash in Boston, and the defendants moved successfully to transfer under § 1404(a) to the District of Massachusetts, the Massachusetts federal court would have to apply the law that the Pennsylvania federal court would have, which in this case would have been Pennsylvania state tort law.[250]

After transfer under § 1406(a) or § 1631 from an improper court to a proper court, however, the transferee court applies transferee law—except that the transferee's statute of limitations will be tolled by the initial filing if within the transferor's as well as the transferee's limitations period.[251] After all, the plaintiff could hardly become generally entitled to transferor law by suing in an improper court.

d. Agreements Among Parties

Just as was described above in connection with state-court litigation, the parties generally may, by agreement, expand or restrict the choice among federal forums.

Ultimately, however, 28 U.S.C. § 1404(a) or forum non conveniens can override such an agreement, allowing the agreed court to transfer to a court where the case might have been brought absent

---

249. See generally Jeffrey W. Tayon, The Federal Transfer Statute: 28 U.S.C. § 1631, 29 S. Tex. L. Rev. 189 (1987).

250. Van Dusen v. Barrack, 376 U.S. 612, 639 (1964) (such transfer is "but a change of courtrooms," not of law); see Ferens v. John Deere Co., 494 U.S. 516 (1990) (applying same approach even on plaintiff's motion).

251. See John D. Currivan, Note, Choice of Law in Federal Court After Transfer of Venue, 63 Cornell L. Rev. 149 (1977); Roberto Finzi, Note, The 28 U.S.C. § 1406(a) Transfer of Time-barred Claims, 79 Cornell L. Rev. 975 (1994).

the agreement.[252] If, conversely, the plaintiff lays venue in violation of the forum selection clause and the defendant protests under Federal Rule 12(b)(3), the court can transfer under 28 U.S.C. § 1406(a), making transferee law applicable.[253]

2. State Limitations on Federal Reach

As already noted, state jurisdictional law embodied in long-arm statutes and the Fourteenth Amendment frequently applies in federal court, because the applicable federal statute or Rule adopts that state law, the prime example being Rule 4(k)(1)(A). The bottom line is this: as a result of such self-restraint by the federal government, a federal court usually reaches no farther than the forum state does, despite the constitutional authority to reach considerably farther.

However, also as already noted, federal courts would not apply most of the other state law limiting state reach. For example, state forum non conveniens law and state venue law do not carry over into federal court.[254] On the one hand, a state's statute aimed at conserving resources might close the courthouse doors to any action between nonresidents on a claim arising outside the state, but the federal court would not apply this statute.[255] On the other hand, a state's statute might close the courthouse doors to any action brought by a foreign corporation that had failed to comply with a requirement to register before transacting business in the state. Because this policy is more substantive than the desirable distribution among courts of judicial business, a state door-closing statute of the latter type would apply in federal court under the *Erie* doctrine.[256]

D. International Litigation

1. Suits in the United States

The U.S. Supreme Court has largely elaborated the U.S. law of territorial jurisdiction by deciding cases that arose on the interstate level, and in fact it has decided only four international jurisdiction cases.[257] The United States has no general treaties on international jurisdiction.

252. See Stewart Org. v. Ricoh Corp., 487 U.S. 22 (1988).

253. See Jackson v. W. Telemarketing Corp. Outbound, 245 F.3d 518 (5th Cir. 2001).

254. See supra text accompanying notes 236–37.

255. See Szantay v. Beech Aircraft Corp., 349 F.2d 60 (4th Cir. 1965).

256. See Woods v. Interstate Realty Co., 337 U.S. 535 (1949).

257. Asahi Metal Indus. Co. v. Superior Court, 480 U.S. 102 (1987); Helicopteros Nacionales de Colombia, S.A. v. Hall, 466 U.S. 408 (1984); Perkins v.

Consider a suit against a Frenchwoman in a court here. In the absence of a specific treaty, international law imposes no significant restrictions on state-court territorial jurisdiction beyond those restrictions already imposed by the Due Process Clause of the Fourteenth Amendment. Likewise, in the absence of a specific treaty, international law imposes no significant restrictions on federal-court territorial authority to adjudicate beyond those restrictions already imposed by the Due Process Clause of the Fifth Amendment.[258]

Thus, the Frenchwoman is treated just like anyone else, with no special international protections.[259] Indeed, one might instead wonder why she can even invoke the U.S. constitutional protections.[260] But the U.S. Supreme Court has always assumed that a person subject to suit in our courts can demand treatment in accord with the Constitution. Accordingly, the lower courts extend to foreign defendants all the jurisdictional protections given to U.S. defendants.[261]

2. Suits in Foreign Courts

A quick look at the European[262] approach to territorial jurisdiction serves to show how differently the law can work out, given different origins.[263]

Roman law, enjoying unlimited power, embraced the idea of restraint imposed in a spirit of fairness. *Actor sequitur forum rei*, or the plaintiff follows the defendant's forum. Generally, then, the plaintiff had to go to the defendant's domicile, although that forum could entertain any cause of action against the defendant. Eventually, there was additional provision for long-arm-like jurisdiction in

Benguet Consol. Mining Co., 342 U.S. 437 (1952); *cf.* Omni Capital Int'l v. Rudolf Wolff & Co., 484 U.S. 97 (1987) (construing Federal Rules of Civil Procedure's implementation of international jurisdiction).

258. See generally Robert C. Casad, Jurisdiction and Forum Selection (2d ed. 1999).

259. See Kadic v. Karadzic, 70 F.3d 232 (2d Cir. 1995) (holding that an invitee of the United Nations is not immune from personal service of process).

260. See Afram Export Co. v. Metallurgiki Halyps, S.A., 772 F.2d 1358, 1362 (7th Cir. 1985) (Posner, J.) (raising, without addressing, this question).

261. See Gary B. Born, Reflections on Judicial Jurisdiction in International Cases, 17 Ga. J. Int'l & Comp. L. 1, 21–22 (1987). But see Austen L. Parrish,

Sovereignty, Not Due Process: Personal Jurisdiction over Nonresident Alien Defendants, 41 Wake Forest L. Rev. 1 (2006). On the treatment of foreigners in U.S. courts, see Kevin M. Clermont & Theodore Eisenberg, Xenophilia or Xenophobia in U.S. Courts? Before and After 9/11, 4 J. Empirical Legal Stud. 441 (2007); Kevin M. Clermont & Theodore Eisenberg, Xenophilia in American Courts, 109 Harv. L. Rev. 1120 (1996).

262. See also Kevin M. Clermont, A Global Law of Jurisdiction and Judgments: Views from the United States and Japan, 37 Cornell Int'l L.J. 1, 24–26 (2004).

263. See generally Andrew S. Bell, Forum Shopping and Venue in Transnational Litigation (2003).

actions of tort, contract, and property, so that, for example, a plaintiff could sue for a tort at the place of wrongful conduct. In other words, the Roman law and its direct descendant, the civil law, avoided the problems of the U.S. territorial dogma exalting power.[264]

Modern French law, for example, builds on the Roman restraint idea. Domicile is thus the foundation of French jurisdiction. But socio-economic-political pressures similar to those prevailing in the United States, as well as the usual procedural policies of accuracy, fairness, and efficiency, have pushed France to reach defendants whose acts have caused harm in France. The territorial power idea, not being inevitable, was absent from France, with telling implications. On the one hand, without the impulses of that power idea, France has not produced such excesses as tag or attachment jurisdiction. On the other hand, without the restraints of that power idea, France has succumbed even more blatantly to parochial impulses, so that as construed Article 14 of its Civil Code authorizes territorial jurisdiction over virtually any action brought by a plaintiff of French nationality. Thus, a French person can sue at home on any cause of action, whether or not the events in suit related to France and regardless of the defendant's connections and interests. This French approach to jurisdiction has emigrated with French law to other countries. The forum-shopping potential of jurisdiction based on the plaintiff's nationality is evident, even though in practice this exorbitant jurisdiction is not abused all that often.[265]

A different example from the German system further shows that foreign is not always better than American when it comes to jurisdiction. Germany follows the usual civil-law approach, which makes no distinction between jurisdiction over things and jurisdiction over persons but instead gets to a similar result through the notion of exclusive jurisdiction for certain kinds of suits that intrinsically involve things. Nevertheless, Article 23 of Germany's Code of Civil Procedure authorizes ordinary *personal jurisdiction* given only the presence in Germany of a tangible or intangible thing belonging to the defendant, thus going considerably further than the U.S. authorization in certain circumstances of *jurisdiction over a thing* based upon presence of the thing. Recovery in a German case founded on presence of goods is not limited to the

---

264. See generally Rudolf B. Schlesinger, Hans W. Baade, Peter E. Herzog & Edward M. Wise, Comparative Law 379–80, 405, 413–34 (6th ed. 1998); Friedrich Juenger, Judicial Jurisdiction in the United States and in the European Communities: A Comparison, 82 Mich. L. Rev. 1195, 1203–12 (1984).

265. See Kevin M. Clermont & John R.B. Palmer, French Article 14 Jurisdiction, Viewed from the United States, in De tous horizons 473 (Société de Législation Comparée 2005).

value of the goods, although obviously the plaintiff might have trouble enforcing the judgment outside Germany. Traditionally, the cause of action did not have to relate to the thing or even to Germany, but the German Supreme Court has recently invented a vague requirement that the cause of action be linked to Germany. The forum-shopping potential here too is frightening, as many enterprises have assets in countries with German-based law.

Still, when all is said and done, the civil law of today is not so different from the common law of territorial jurisdiction, at least if one ignores the described exorbitant bases of jurisdiction on both sides. This evolution demonstrates how different legal systems tend toward so-called convergence, given similar influences.

Even in the doctrinal details of exorbitant jurisdiction, where national peculiarities peak, the differences are smaller than they appear in the mirror. French nationality-based jurisdiction or German property-based jurisdiction may not look much like U.S. tag or attachment jurisdiction, but in fact they share a common core: all nations tend to give their own people a way to sue at home, at least when the home country will be able to enforce the resulting judgment.[266]

3. Treaty Possibilities

The European countries also appear ahead of the United States on the treatment of foreign judgments. The European Union has an enlightened, albeit far from perfect, treaty dating from 1968. That treaty is the Brussels Convention on Jurisdiction and the Enforcement of Judgments in Civil and Commercial Matters, which morphed into a European Union regulation on March 1, 2002.[267]

By the Brussels Convention, the member states agreed to provide virtually automatic recognition and enforcement of the judgments of the other member states. This provision was like the Full Faith and Credit Clause of the U.S. Constitution. In order to make this judgments agreement acceptable, the Brussels Convention was a "double convention" that also defined the bases of territorial jurisdiction—jurisdiction being the doctrine that must, in any judgment-respecting agreement, serve almost alone in ensuring adjudicative restraint. The European member states could give respect to the others' judgments because they knew that the Brussels Convention restricted the others to appropriately limited jurisdictional reach. This latter restriction worked as the Due Process Clause does in the United States.

---

266. See Kevin M. Clermont & John R.B. Palmer, Exorbitant Jurisdiction, 58 Me. L. Rev. 473 (2006).

267. No. 44/2001, 2001 O.J. (L 12) 1, as amended by 2002 O.J. (L 225) 13.

Today, the Brussels Regulation's jurisdictional bases follow the civil-law approach. The defendant's domicile is the usual place for suit, although there is additionally long-arm-like jurisdiction for tort and contract actions. Certain disadvantaged plaintiffs, such as consumers, can often sue at home. Moreover, there is authorization for forum selection clauses, and there is exclusive local jurisdiction in actions concerning real property and the like.

Further on the prohibited side, each member state gave up its exorbitant jurisdiction, so that for example France gave up its personal jurisdiction based on the plaintiff's French nationality, and Germany gave up its exorbitant jurisdiction. England gave up tag jurisdiction and attachment jurisdiction. Additionally, the Brussels Regulation not only prohibits exorbitant jurisdiction, but also makes mandatory the permissible bases of jurisdiction. So, England abandoned its judicial practice of sometimes declining jurisdiction on expressly discretionary grounds such as forum non conveniens.

Europe does not appear superior in all regards, however. The Brussels Regulation applies only to defendants domiciled in a member state. Indeed, the Brussels Regulation openly discriminates against outsiders. Accordingly, although France cannot use its exorbitant jurisdiction in a suit by a French domiciliary against an English person, it can still use it when the defendant is an American instead. Moreover, the resulting French judgment gets recognition and enforcement in England, Germany, and elsewhere in the European Union against the American or the American's assets there. Admittedly, this example is an extreme one, without much actual use in practice to date, but it works to illustrate the theoretical context.

Similarly, the virtually automatic recognition and enforcement under the Brussels Regulation does not extend to judgments rendered by countries that are not member states. The European countries, in fact, have traditionally been and continue to be rather stingy in extending respect to foreign judgments not covered by treaty, such as U.S. judgments.

In short, Americans are being whipsawed by the European approach. Not only are they still subject (in theory) to the far-reaching jurisdiction of European courts and the wide recognition and enforceability of the resulting European judgments, but also U.S. judgments tend (in practice) to receive short shrift in European courts.

The overall international situation, as exacerbated by the Brussels Regulation, is untenable in the long run for the United States. Therefore, in 1992 the United States initiated a push to conclude a worldwide convention on jurisdiction and judgments, naturally choosing to work through the Hague Conference on Private International Law. Drafting and agreeing on a multilateral convention could yield great returns for the United States. A convention would resolve the whipsawing predicament in which Americans today find themselves regarding exercise of jurisdiction as well as treatment of judgments. A convention would rationalize both jurisdiction law and judgments law on an international level. In the specific matter of treatment of foreign judgments, a convention would unarguably be desirable for the United States. It would mean that the United States could get returns for the respect the United States is already according other nations' judgments. As to the jurisdictional side, a convention would cause other nations to renounce their own exorbitant jurisdiction. It also could improve the content of U.S. jurisdiction law in international cases.

Will such a convention come into existence, as opposed to some sort of narrow convention treating a special problem area such as choice-of-court agreements in business-to-business contracts that select forums for disputes to the exclusion of other forums?[268] Not in the near future.[269] The United States has little bargaining power under the current regime. It needs a convention, while the Europeans have little to gain over their presently favorable situation. Because of this imbalance of power, the expectation is that any convention of general scope, if ever agreed upon, would be very similar to the Brussels Regulation. This prediction means that the United States would abandon—on the international level, but not necessarily with respect to its courts' actions against its own habitual residents—attachment jurisdiction (other than for security or enforcement), tag jurisdiction (a relic of the power theory), even doing business (as a basis for general jurisdiction), and much of forum non conveniens (too discretionary). The Europeans' objection is to the U.S. proclivity to base general jurisdiction on rather thin contacts, namely, allowing any and all causes of action to be brought on the basis of the defendant's property ownership, physical presence, or doing business in the forum. They do not object to specific jurisdiction, as long as a rules-based approach controls its nondiscretionary application. Thus, jurisdiction under a general convention would exist at the unconsenting defendant's habitual residence or where a specific part of the events in suit occurred, but would not extend to the broader bases of jurisdiction now authorized by U.S. law. In sum, a general convention would agree on certain bases of territorial jurisdiction, but chiefly those palatable to the Europeans—and judgments based thereon would receive

268. On this type of narrow proposed convention that did emerge from the negotiations, see Ronald A. Brand & Paul M. Herrup, The 2005 Hague Convention on Choice of Court Agreements : Commentary and Documents (2008).

269. See Kevin M. Clermont, An Introduction to the Hague Convention, in A Global Law of Jurisdiction and Judgments: Lessons from The Hague 3 (John J. Barceló III & Kevin M. Clermont eds., 2002).

virtually automatic recognition and enforcement in other signatory countries (except those judgments that the Europeans consider too generous or punitive).

Negotiations have broken off for now. Nevertheless, the negotiations were definitely worth the effort. Merely trying to draft a convention taught all sides a lot about jurisdiction.[270] For example, exorbitant jurisdiction looks different when viewed through foreign eyes. Such new vision has opened an opportunity for the United States on its own to untangle its law in domestic cases, a project I next consider.

E. Reform Proposal

Any legal system's task is to site litigation in a fashion that puts appropriate constraints on the litigators' gaming and the system's overreaching. The aim should be optimal constraints. Our current law does not achieve this aim. By this point, you would surely agree that this law is overly complicated and uncertain. Indeed, commentators like to sum up all of the preceding discussion by simply concluding that the U.S. law on territorial authority is a "mess."[271] Moreover, its content is deficient. It gives the litigants too much room for forum-shopping and allows sovereigns to reach too far, while at the same time the power test occasionally defeats appropriate exercises of jurisdiction.

What, then, would an optimized U.S. law look like? My preceding discussion established that this inquiry should proceed on both constitutional and subconstitutional levels. The Constitution puts an outer limit on the list of available forums with territorial authority to adjudicate a litigation with nonlocal elements, but it produces a list of forums that is generally too long to be optimal, or even to be acceptable, as the sole limit. The U.S. legal systems therefore must utilize the various strands of subconstitutional law

---

270. See Kevin M. Clermont, Jurisdictional Salvation and the Hague Treaty, 85 Cornell L. Rev. 89 (1999); Kevin M. Clermont & Kuo–Chang Huang, Converting the Draft Hague Treaty into Domestic Jurisdictional Law, in A Global Law of Jurisdiction and Judgments: Lessons from The Hague 191 (John J. Barceló III & Kevin M. Clermont eds., 2002).

271. E.g., Patrick J. Borchers, Comparing Personal Jurisdiction in the United States and the European Community: Lessons for American Reform, 40 Am. J. Comp. L. 121, 143 (1992); John M. Brumbaugh & William L. Reynolds, The Straight–Line Method of De-

termining Personal Jurisdiction, 44 J. Legal Educ. 130, 130 (1994); Kevin M. Clermont, Jurisdictional Salvation and the Hague Treaty, 85 Cornell L. Rev. 89, 89 (1999); Friedrich K. Juenger, A Shoe Unfit for Globetrotting, 28 U.C. Davis L. Rev. 1027, 1027 (1995) ("American jurisdictional law is a mess."); Russell J. Weintraub, supra note 154, at 547; cf. Stephen B. Burbank, Jurisdiction to Adjudicate: End of the Century or Beginning of the Millennium?, 7 Tul. J. Int'l & Comp. L. 111, 123 (1999) ("[T]he American house of jurisdiction to adjudicate is not a place where any sensible person other than a lawyer (if that is not redundant) wants to live.").

to narrow the list, producing a shorter listing of appropriate forums. Concomitantly, an overhaul of the subconstitutional law could deliver a degree of certainty long lacking in this realm.[272]

1. Constitutional Limit

The Due Process Clauses impose the outer limit, currently comprising power and unreasonableness tests but more ideally contracting to a reasonableness test. Even though change over time is a certainty, constitutional reform normally must be expressed more as a hope than as a proposal. So here it would be advisable to pass quickly to the shaping of an optimal jurisdiction and venue scheme on the subconstitutional level. Nevertheless, before doing so, a few more observations on the constitutional scheme are in order.

a. Power

Admittedly, the U.S. jurisdictional doctrine's founding on a power theory is a significant marker.[273] This beginning still affects the law in many ways, although the effects are diluted because the scope of power has expanded so far beyond the original basis of physical presence.

But is a jurisdictional law's foundation on power, rather than on some more "enlightened" concept, an essential feature of the law of the United States? No, I do not think so, based on two general arguments.

First, power no longer has a reason for continued existence as part of our law. Power is far from being some essential authorization of governmental authority under a peculiar U.S. theory built on Hobbesian premises, as some have suggested. In fact, we do not really know where the power test came from. The Supreme Court has never even settled on the function it is to serve. As traced in the next three paragraphs, its rationale in the Court's view has changed with time, from an arid sovereignty theory to an instrumentalist jurisdictional allocation and then to a redundant fairness concern.

The principal thrust of America's power theory was in fact never an authorization that justified extensions of reach, but was instead a limiting delineation of the outer bounds of existing sovereign authority. It is true that U.S. courts have sometimes used

---

272. See generally Kevin M. Clermont, The Role of Private International Law in the United States: Beating the Not–Quite–Dead Horse of Jurisdiction, 2 CILE Studies: Private Law, Private International Law & Judicial Cooperation in the EU–US Relationship 75 (2005).

273. See supra § 4.2(B)(1)(b).

the theory to justify nonrecognition of judgments of foreign courts for lack of jurisdiction. More significantly, though, U.S. courts used the theory to impose self-limitation, to specify when the sovereign should choose not to exercise its existing authority. After all, any full sovereign had the raw force to adjudicate any dispute when, and how, it pleased, as well as the capability to enforce its adjudication on persons and things over which it eventually acquired physical control. Yet, use of all that raw force was not how sovereigns acted. They used jurisdictional law as a limit on how far to reach in exercising their existing authority, a limit imposed not only in the hope that other sovereigns would restrain themselves similarly but also increasingly with the intuition that such restraint was fair. In other words, the power theory never linked to raw power, but served merely as a metaphorical label for jurisdictional actualities of restraint. Accordingly, raw power was never the true rationale of U.S. jurisdiction in any realistic sense. The true rationale instinctively was always the desirable allocation of jurisdictional authority.[274]

With time, U.S. courts came to think openly of power as a label, albeit an odd one, for the rough pursuit of some unclear notion of reciprocal sovereignty: State *1* would not reach far into State *2*'s domain in exchange for State *2*'s restraint in analogous cases. The rationale thus became more instrumentalist, aimed directly at a desirable allocation of jurisdiction.[275] The Supreme Court, with instrumentalist motives, was forcing this allocation on the states.

Eventually, however, the Supreme Court explicitly abandoned this instrumentalist rationale of jurisdictional allocation, ruling that sovereigns' interests do not reside in the Due Process Clauses or in jurisdictional doctrine, which after all the defendant might elect not to raise. Instead, the Court shifted the due process power test onto the defendant's liberty interest in not being subject to the illegitimate power of a sovereign foreign to the defendant.[276] But the

---

274. See Andrew L. Strauss, Where America Ends and the International Order Begins: Interpreting the Jurisdictional Reach of the U.S. Constitution in Light of a Proposed Hague Convention on Jurisdiction and Satisfaction of Judgments, 61 Alb. L. Rev. 1237, 1250–63 (1998); James Weinstein, The Federal Common Law Origins of Judicial Jurisdiction: Implications for Modern Doctrine, 90 Va. L. Rev. 169 (2004).

275. See World–Wide Volkswagen Corp. v. Woodson, 444 U.S. 286, 291–94 (1980) (The Due Process Clause "can be seen to perform two related, but distinguishable, functions. It protects the de-

fendant against the burdens of litigating in a distant or inconvenient forum. And it acts to ensure that the States, through their courts, do not reach out beyond the limits imposed on them by their status as coequal sovereigns in a federal system.").

276. See Ins. Corp. of Ir., Ltd. v. Compagnie des Bauxites de Guinee, 456 U.S. 694, 702 & n.10 (1982) (The jurisdictional requirement "represents a restriction on judicial power not as a matter of sovereignty, but as a matter of individual liberty.").

continuing difficulty is that the power test as now applied does not try to determine and enforce the liberty interest's limits on that sovereign power over the defendant, whatever those limits might be. Instead, the power test's purposeful-availment formulation of minimum contacts searches for the defendant's tacit consent to jurisdiction, and then the cases confusingly tend to find this consent where fair. Yet, any power test seems ill designed to serve such a fairness rationale, and a reasonableness test would serve it much more clearly. In this course of evolution toward becoming merely a clumsy and redundant fairness test, the power test has lost its raison d'être, and so the time is ripe for jettisoning it.

Second, and more briefly, the difficulties inherent in the power test's application are evident and numerous, including its highly conceptual nature and inflexible application.[277] Most prominently, the power test remains undefinable and hence difficult to apply. It never succeeded in fulfilling *Pennoyer*'s promise of exclusive jurisdiction for each sovereign. As the power test became increasingly metaphorical after *International Shoe*, one state's jurisdiction more evidently came to overlap other states' jurisdiction. Instead of looking only to physical presence, courts looked to the in-state effects of the defendant's acts or even to the quality and nature of the acts. Ultimately, the Supreme Court has come to require "a sufficient connection between the defendant and the forum State to make it fair to require defense of the action in the forum."[278] Whether it is "fair" to exercise power over the defendant will come to turn on the interests of others, and so even the verbal formulation of the power test is eroding into a reasonableness test.

In sum, the power test remains a complicated way station on the road to a better law of jurisdiction for the United States. It is not an essential feature. Accordingly, a good number of commentators have argued that the due process doctrine should speedily evolve into a much simpler formulation that merely asks whether the state court's exercise of territorial jurisdiction is reasonable. Any valid concerns underlying the power test could still be taken into account as part of a multifactored reasonableness test. And this could be done without the arguably undesirable denials of jurisdiction that the power test now yields, as in the *World-Wide Volkswagen* case. Accordingly, these reformers call for the demise of the power test and the triumph of reasonableness as the sole due process test for territorial jurisdiction.

Such reform would have a side benefit. The traditional categorization of proceedings in terms of the target of the action is

---

277. See Kevin M. Clermont, Jurisdictional Salvation and the Hague Treaty, 85 Cornell L. Rev. 89, 99–104 (1999).

278. Kulko v. Superior Court, 436 U.S. 84, 91 (1978); see supra text accompanying note 173.

necessary for the power test, because that test translates as power over whom or what. However, categorization is unnecessary for determining reasonableness. A reasonableness test is the same for all types of proceedings, although the varying effects of the different kinds of judgment naturally enter into the wide-ranging consideration of reasonableness. Thus, there might be circumstances where it would be reasonable to cut off a nonresident's interest in local land, but where it would not be reasonable to render a money judgment against her. Yet there is no need to call the former in rem and the latter in personam. In sum, eliminating the power test in favor of a reasonableness test would obviate the need for categorization too.

The Supreme Court actually adopted this law of the future in *Mullane v. Central Hanover Bank & Trust Co.*[279] At issue was New York's territorial jurisdiction to conduct a judicial settlement of accounts by the trustee of a New York common trust fund, a routine statutory proceeding that would cut off all resident and nonresident beneficiaries' rights against the trustee for improper management during the period covered by the accounting. Because neither in personam jurisdiction existed nor in rem jurisdiction sufficed to cut off the nonresident beneficiaries' rights against the person of the trustee, the Court refused to categorize, acting in the belief that due process did "not depend upon a classification for which the standards are so elusive and confused generally." And the Court then found jurisdiction to be reasonable, especially in light of New York's interest in providing a means to regulate New York trusts. However, in subsequent years the Court abandoned this futuristic approach of category-less reasonableness, leaving the *Mullane* case in uncertain health under the currently prevailing power test. Nonetheless, someday the Supreme Court may go back to the future represented by *Mullane*.

b. Unreasonableness

As just suggested, the unreasonableness test embodies the readily justified rationale of fundamental fairness. Moreover, the unreasonableness test remains conceptually straightforward. Additionally, flexible application is the hallmark of the unreasonableness test, as it readily relaxes or tightens in response to socio-economic-political pressures and technological and philosophical changes. This free-form test can adjust effortlessly to changing times and changing needs. In brief, doctrinal baggage is not its problem.

Why, then, has the power test not withered away, leaving in its place some sort of reasonableness test? The explanation is that

279. 339 U.S. 306, 312 (1950).

courts continue to hope that the power test will mitigate the uncertainty of a case-specific fairness test. Courts strangely remain hopeful, despite the experience of centuries proving that the power test itself has always been uncertain in application, and despite the evident instability of the current jurisdictional doctrine.

It is indeed a common criticism that the constitutional law in this area is too vague, and that nothing can be done about that flaw. So, a few more words on the supposed unclarity of this constitutional law are appropriate. Is the constitutional law on jurisdiction—future or even current—fatally infected by the evil of uncertainty? No.

First, we should always bear in mind that complete certainty in law is unachievable. And we should remember that certainty is never the only goal of a legal provision.

Second, we should acknowledge that the uncertainty of this constitutional law is not all that severe. The courts through their many decisions on territorial authority have given it definite meaning in all but unusual cases.

Third, and most importantly, we should recognize the Constitution's restricted role here, a role that does not require certainty. It is a *constitutional* limitation, after all. Its role is to serve as an outer limit preventing jurisdictional excess in special and unforeseeable circumstances. Its real function is as a backup test to block jurisdiction when, in a particular case, the ordinary rules in place would permit a fundamentally unfair exercise of jurisdiction. It thereby protects outsiders from truly exorbitant jurisdiction, and so in theory should be needed only rarely. It is an outer limit also in the sense that courts should not in theory be routinely exercising a reach all the way to the limit of due process, just as they do not punish to the very limit of cruel and unusual punishment. The law should operate within and safely distant from outer limits. Thus, the constitutional tests should not be in routine use.

Fourth, I might go so far as to argue that certainty in this constitutional limit on territorial jurisdiction is not even desirable. It should be a flexible outer limit. Flexible application should be its hallmark, as it must apply to cases in-between general and specific jurisdiction, apply across a range of defendants' state-directed activities, and apply in light of the effects of a particular lawsuit on the defendant. Also, it has to apply in unforeseeable circumstances, and it needs to relax or tighten in response to socio-economic-political pressures and technological and philosophical changes.

In short, the Constitution is not the place to seek certainty. We should seek certainty—and provide the necessary and appropriate degree of fair warning and predictability—by subconstitutional regulation inside the constitutional outer limit. In concrete terms, lawmakers should specify that venue lies only in the more convenient, efficient, and otherwise desirable of all the forums not fundamentally unfair.

2. Subconstitutional Limits

a. Lessening the Effects of Constitutionalization

A distinctive feature of U.S. jurisdictional law is the prominence of the Constitution in the development and content of that law. Ever since the *Pennoyer* Court anchored the limit on the states' reach in the Due Process Clause of the Fourteenth Amendment, the Constitution has reigned in the foreground. Currently, the Due Process Clauses put an outer limit on the list of state and federal forums with territorial authority to adjudicate a litigation with nonlocal elements. This outer limit ensures that the forum is not wildly inappropriate, indeed, that it is not fundamentally unfair.

Again, however, this prominence is not a determinative feature of the law of the United States. First, the outer limit imposed by the Constitution is a generous one, and it is an evolving one. It would become even more generous with the abolition of the power test. Second, the extensive set of statutes and doctrines of self-restraint reflects the unquestionable propriety of subconstitutional law on jurisdiction. Thus, there is no impediment to the lawmakers' reasserting themselves by making jurisdictional law inside the currently generous constitutional limit. In fact, such reassertion is the only path open to improving the jurisdictional law.

The well-known failures of the current law flow from the Supreme Court's trying to do too much in shaping that law out of the few bare words of the Constitution. Nothing in the Court's raw materials—the constitutional language, subject to judicial interpretation—can generate a set of jurisdictional criteria that would be both certain and sensible. The Supreme Court should therefore recognize its own limitations. The Court should continue playing its role in policing the subordinate systems' excesses in extending their reach, but should withdraw from the task of actually allocating jurisdictional authority by case law. The former of these two roles conforms to the traditional and proper one for the Court in applying the Due Process Clauses, while the latter task seems more legislative in nature and in need of the legislatures' capabilities. In other words, the Court should leave to other lawmakers the task of narrowing the choice among reasonable forums.

If these other lawmakers stepped up to perform this task, then the constitutional limit could fade into the background, becoming not only a nonessential feature but also a less important one. We could thereby achieve the optimal law on territorial authority to adjudicate: a law under which the constitutional limit fades into the background and subconstitutional provisions move to the fore.

b. Lessening the Primacy of Judiciary

U.S. courts have been active in shaping jurisdictional law. This contextual feature has had significant effects on that law's development and content. The reason is that judges tend to expand their focus beyond any rules in place, looking both up toward first principles and also down toward messy facts.

Still, a large judicial role does not amount to a determinative feature of the U.S. approach to jurisdiction. Consider the reasons that this feature is not an ineradicable one.

First, the active role of courts would naturally diminish as the constitutional tests retreated into the background and as subconstitutional law emerged in their place, as proposed above. Courts would no longer have to play on a daily basis their key role of constitutional interpretation.

Second, the subconstitutional law should come by legislation, not by judicial action. Traditionally, legislatures have played the dominant role in writing the subconstitutional jurisdictional and venue law, utilizing their superior capabilities to investigate social problems and then draft comprehensive and detailed provisions. Case-by-case adjudication is obviously a mechanism unsuited to generating the basic law, and normally courts cannot or do not use even their rulemaking power to treat this subject. Legislative action therefore is the preferred route to reform.

Third, after such reform the courts must cooperate, by treating the statutes' words as if they meant something. Courts must avoid destroying rules by ad-hoc and result-oriented stretching that would undo those legislative moves toward certainty and restraint.

It is true that legislatures and courts have not done a good job in the past. Legislatures have mainly abdicated, relying on the Constitution and on the courts to supply the bulk of the law on territorial jurisdiction. For example, many long-arm statutes expressly incorporate by reference the constitutional tests. The other long-arm statutes require active judicial interpretation, and most often the courts have managed to strip them of any specific guidance they might have provided. By default, all too often, constitutional law is almost the sole jurisdictional law.[280]

---

280. See generally Douglas D. McFarland, Dictum Run Wild: How Long–Arm Statutes Extended to the Limits of Due Process, 84 B.U. L. Rev. 491 (2004) (criticizing this approach).

But legislatures, on both the state and the federal level, could undertake a much more serious effort expressly to site cases in convenient, efficient, and otherwise desirable courts than they have hitherto. If the state legislatures prove reluctant to rein in their own courts, then Congress could, but unlikely would, intercede by utilizing its constitutional powers to legislate general limits on the states' interstate and international reach.[281] Moreover, courts are capable of sticking to the subsidiary role of rule-applying, as they do in many areas of the law. Some state courts behave even in regard to jurisdiction; for example, New York courts have respected their long-arm statute, even while other states' courts have freely reworked theirs.[282]

c. Increasing the Role of Rules

Relatively speaking, the United States emphasizes the role of fact-specific inquiry in matters of jurisdiction:

> The civil law system simply attempts to identify in advance an appropriate nexus for asserting jurisdiction in *most* cases, but with full awareness that such nexus may be less proper in some cases. This is a deliberate policy choice in favor of legal certainty and the speedy resolution of preliminary jurisdictional issues, at the expense perhaps of individual equity.
>
> Compared to this clear, yet flat and non-distinguishing Continental attitude, the elaborate American search for sufficient contacts appears as an overwhelming concern for individualized justice, even at the expense of certainty and predictability. * * * American notions of establishing adjudicatory jurisdiction invite a scrutiny of defendants and causes of action on a case-by-case basis and in a manner not disassociated from a contemplation of the merits.[283]

281. See supra text accompanying note 136; Kevin M. Clermont & Kuo–Chang Huang, Converting the Draft Hague Treaty into Domestic Jurisdictional Law, in A Global Law of Jurisdiction and Judgments: Lessons from The Hague 191 (John J. Barceló III & Kevin M. Clermont eds., 2002) (attempting to draft such a statute); cf. ALI Recognition and Enforcement of Foreign Judgments: Analysis and Proposed Federal Statute (2006) (advocating a federal statute to govern the recognition and enforcement of foreign judgments in the United States). Indeed, the Supreme Court would possibly accept a congressional articulation of the constitutional tests, even one that supplants the moribund power test. See Kevin M. Cler-

mont, Jurisdictional Salvation and the Hague Treaty, 85 Cornell L. Rev. 89, 124–27 (1999); cf. Ayelet Ben–Ezer & Ariel L. Bendor, The Constitution and Conflict–of–Laws Treaties: Upgrading the International Comity, 29 N.C. J. Int'l L. & Com. Reg. 1 (2003) (more general treatment).

282. Compare Longines–Wittnauer Watch Co. v. Barnes & Reinecke, Inc. (Feathers v. McLucas), 209 N.E.2d 68 (N.Y. 1965), with, e.g., Gray v. Am. Radiator & Standard Sanitary Corp., 176 N.E.2d 761 (Ill. 1961).

283. Konstantinos D. Kerameus, A Civilian Lawyer Looks at Common Law Procedure, 47 La. L. Rev. 493, 497 (1987); see Tapio Puurunen, The Judicial Jurisdiction of States over Interna-

Another way to phrase this difference is that the United States has handled jurisprudence's fundamental, and unavoidable, tension between certainty and precision in a way that unduly favors precision.[284] This difference between U.S. and European approaches to jurisdiction is indeed a big one.

Yet there is nothing inevitable about the route chosen by the United States. Its law strikes the certainty/precision balance differently in areas other than jurisdiction. Its chosen route for jurisdiction could undergo rethinking, while the legislatures undertake the task of constructing subconstitutional jurisdictional law. The rethinking's focal issue might be phrased in terms of whether the legislatures should act by rules or by a standard. That is, should they accomplish the limiting of forum-choice by a set of preconceived legislative rules that would rigidly treat categories of cases or instead by a delegation to the courts via a standard with a list of factors that would permit fact-specific analysis individualized to the case?

The latter route can be more precise, leading to a tiny list of available forums, but at the considerable cost of difficult judicial decision in many cases. The expense of so seeking the best forums does not seem like a socially productive way to expend resources, at least when compared to other possible reforms regarding choice of forum and choice of law. In contrast, the rule route seems more efficient in that it can offer some certainty, and it seems more neutral in application by the crafting of general rules in advance. In short, Europeans have rightly opted to take the rule route.

d. Decreasing the Role of Discretion

Finally, further showing their allegiance to case-specific fairness, U.S. courts see nothing particularly troubling in discretionarily declining jurisdiction, in order to shift the litigation to a more appropriate forum and thereby fine-tune an otherwise overbroad choice of forum. Europeans, by contrast, very much view jurisdictional provisions as mandatory, detesting discretion in their general provisions on territorial authority.[285] "The approaches of the civil-

---

tional Business-to-Consumer Electronic Commerce from the Perspective of Certainty, 8 U.C. Davis J. Int'l L. & Pol'y 133, 241–49 (2002).

284. See Arthur Taylor von Mehren, Theory and Practice of Adjudicatory Authority in Private International Law: A Comparative Study of the Doctrine, Policies and Practices of Common– and Civil–Law Systems, 295 Recueil des cours 9, 68 (2002) ("two sets of basic policies

control the design of jurisdictional provisions applicable to multistate litigation: ease of administration and predictability, on the one hand; litigational fairness, on the other").

285. See Reimann, supra note 160, at 82–85 (discussing Continental law's rejection of forum non conveniens); Burbank, supra note 271, at 117–18; Weintraub, supra note 164, at 210–11; cf. Joachim Zekoll, The Role and Status of

and common-law worlds to fine tuning are indeed 'the fruit of a distinctive legal history, and also reflect to some extent cultural differences.' ''[286]

Of course, Europeans may detest explicit discretion in jurisdiction, but they implicitly exercise discretion through creative judicial construction of code provisions, "a little like Monsieur Jourdain in *Le Bourgeois Gentilhomme* who spoke prose without knowing it."[287] The United States is no purist either. Refusing to choose, U.S. legal systems take both routes. The federal courts, by way of illustration, mainly rely on rules affirmatively siting litigation, which range from the basic venue statute (which generally sites litigation where the defendant resides or "a substantial part of the events or omissions giving rise to the claim occurred") to the judicially created and obscure local-action doctrine (involving claims that supposedly could take place only in one locale); but the federal system also expressly gives a role to discretionary declination via the transfer-of-venue provision and the forum non conveniens doctrine.

Thus, the legal systems do not really differ on fundamentals, and indeed both European and U.S. instincts are probably correct. Legislative rules should be the dominant motif. But there will irresistibly be a small residual role for judicial discretion to decline jurisdiction, in adjusting the rigid rules to the demands of the rare case. That residual role should be an express one, as the Americans would argue, because openness allows control. But the role should be a small one, as the Europeans would argue. For the United States, the role could shrink ever smaller when its rules, as proposed below, became more restrained, giving plaintiffs less jurisdictional excess to play with.

e.   *Formulating the Subconstitutional Law*

A good law of territorial authority to adjudicate, then, would have subconstitutional provisions actively restricting forum selection inside the constitutional limit—or, in other words, it would have a rational scheme that incorporates and revamps today's subconstitutional jurisdiction law as well as all the statutory and doctrinal strands traditionally considered to be more venue-like. What form and content should the legal system give to this subconstitutional law?

American Law in the Hague Judgments Convention Project, 61 Alb. L. Rev. 1283, 1297–98 (1998) (discussing Continental law's taste for a rule-based lis pendens, with a strict preference for the court first seised).

286. von Mehren, supra note 284, at 400 (quoting Airbus Industrie G.I.E. v.

Patel, [1999] 1 A.C. 119, 131 (Eng. H.L. 1998)).

287. Catherine Kessedjian, Judicial Regulation of Improper Forum Selections, in International Dispute Resolution: The Regulation of Forum Selection 273, 290 (Jack L. Goldsmith ed., 1997).

As explained above, legislative action is the preferred route to domestic reform, and general rules should be the dominant motif, although there will irresistibly be a small residual role for discretion in adjusting the demands of the rare case to the rigid rules. Preferably after wiping the jurisdiction and venue slate clean of its current mélange—discarding, for example, the patchwork of special venue statutes and the local-action doctrine—the replacement statutes should set out rules expressly phrased in the language of venue.

Such new statutes should site cases usually at the defendant's habitual residence or where a specific part of the events in suit occurred. In settling on these terms, the lawmakers should engage the policy battles that must precede optimizing this law, be they fought along plaintiff/defendant, individual/business, or liberal/conservative axes. The statutes should state their resolutions in forms that embrace a rules-based approach to territorial authority to adjudicate, resisting the allure of individualized fact-specific analysis. The statutes should thus nudge the law along the spectrum toward certainty, giving outsiders clearer guidance on what activities will and will not subject them to local suit. If the United States, on both the state and the federal level, were to undertake the other parts of the reform that I have suggested—eliminate the power test, push the constitutional reasonableness test into the background, rely less on the judiciary, and downplay the role of discretion—its jurisdictional law could indeed become somewhat more certain.

Furthermore, the new legislation should move toward greater restraint as well as greater certainty. Because the choice of forum importantly affects a case's outcome and because currently the plaintiff has a wide choice and in fact has too much opportunity to shop for a favorable forum or a forum oppressive to the defendant, the lawmakers should take a more restrictive approach to territorial authority to adjudicate. This resolution reflects a policy that Professor von Mehren calls proportionality, which "seeks to ensure not only that the forums in which claims can be pursued are appropriate and sufficient in number but also, in order to deter unjustified forum-shopping, no more numerous than is required to give the plaintiff, absent exceptional circumstances, a fair opportunity to litigate his cause."[288]

Now, the question remains whether the system should aim for a short list of appropriate forums or instead aim for allocating the case to the very best forum. It is conceivable that some sort of "law of *forum conveniens*"[289] could be developed to route cases to the one

---

288. von Mehren, supra note 284, at 68.

289. See Albert A. Ehrenzweig, The Transient Rule of Personal Jurisdiction:

right court, probably where the case primarily arose, which would then apply local law.[290] But shooting for precision is terribly costly.[291] And given the current state-federal-international institutional structure, this approach is simply not feasible. Therefore, the system should settle for the efficiency of a short list.

To be more explicit, I am suggesting legislation along these lines:

§ 1. General Jurisdiction

(a) A state has personal jurisdiction, as to any claim, over a natural person whose habitual residence is in that state. "Habitual residence" means the place where a natural person dwells in the ordinary course of his or her life or a new place to which the person moves with the intention to dwell for an indefinite period.

(b) A state has personal jurisdiction, as to any claim, over an incorporated organization organized under the law of, or having its principal place of business activity in, that state.

(c) A state has personal jurisdiction, as to any claim, over an unincorporated association or other legal person having its principal place of business activity, or for a nonbusiness entity the principal place of administration, in that state.

§ 2. Specific Jurisdiction

(a) Contract

(1) A state has personal jurisdiction over a defendant as to a claim in contract if the claim arose from the defendant's transacting business in that state.

(2) A state has personal jurisdiction over a merchant as to a claim on a consumer contract by a consumer if the consumer habitually resides in that state and the claim arose from or related to the merchant's transacting business in, or purposefully directing other commercial activities to, that state.

(3) A state has personal jurisdiction over an employer as to a claim on an individual employment contract by an employee if the employee was to perform his or her principal obligation in that state.

(b) Tort

A state has personal jurisdiction over a defendant as to a claim in tort if:

The "Power" Myth and Forum Conveniens, 65 Yale L.J. 289, 292, 312 (1956).

290. See Kalo, supra note 189, at 1194 ("Instead, the focus should be on which forum is best qualified to adjudicate the parties' claims.").

291. See David P. Currie, The Federal Courts and the American Law Institute (pt. 2), 36 U. Chi. L. Rev. 268, 307 (1969) ("It would be mellow to try every action in the most convenient forum. But deciding where that forum is costs altogether too much time and money.").

(1) the act or omission causing injury occurred in that state; or

(2) the injury occurred in that state and the defendant purposefully directed other activities relating to the tortious injury to that state.

(c) Real Property

A state has personal jurisdiction over a defendant as to a claim arising from the defendant's owning, using, or possessing real property in that state.

(d) Appearance

(1) A state has personal jurisdiction over a defendant if the defendant appears without objection to jurisdiction asserted in accordance with applicable procedure rules. A defendant's appearance does not affect any codefendant's right to object to jurisdiction.

(2) A state having jurisdiction as to a claim also has personal jurisdiction over an appearing party as to the claimant's additional claim, the defending party's counterclaim, a crossclaim, or an additional claim interposed by or against an intervening party if the additional claim, counterclaim, or crossclaim arose from the same transaction or occurrence as the primary claim.[292]

As for fine-tuning the selection of forum within these confines, legislatures could retain a role for courts by authorizing them to transfer a particular case's venue in the interest of justice. For example, an excellent argument can be made in favor of the current scheme of transfer of venue between federal courts, as it efficiently and fairly works to remove unjust forum advantage while leaving unchanged the applicable law.[293] But forum non conveniens is quite a different doctrine, and it would not fit in a newly rationalized scheme.[294] Its valid function could be played by a largely mandatory rule of lis pendens, whereby the second-seised court would normally

---

292. See Kevin M. Clermont & Kuo-Chang Huang, Converting the Draft Hague Treaty into Domestic Jurisdictional Law, in A Global Law of Jurisdiction and Judgments: Lessons from The Hague 191 (John J. Barceló III & Kevin M. Clermont eds., 2002) (suggesting, and explaining, such legislation in the form of a comprehensive federal statute limiting state reach, but appending this section: "In accordance with a state's own law, within the limits of the Due Process Clause of the Fourteenth Amendment to the Constitution of the United States, that state may, but need not, exercise specific jurisdiction as to a claim regarding one of the following matters: (a) domestic relations; (b) electronic commerce or tort; or (c) international human rights.").

293. See Kevin M. Clermont & Theodore Eisenberg, Exorcising the Evil of Forum–Shopping, 80 Cornell L. Rev. 1507 (1995); Kevin M. Clermont & Theodore Eisenberg, Simplifying the Choice of Forum: A Reply, 75 Wash. U. L.Q. 1551 (1997).

294. See Kevin M. Clermont, The Story of Piper: Forum Matters, in Civil Procedure Stories 199, 230–31 (Kevin M. Clermont ed., 2d ed. 2008).

have to stay its own proceedings in favor of the first-seised court.[295] In brief, the rules of territorial authority to adjudicate should normally be mandatory in application.

Finally, what is the likelihood of such reform proceeding on the constitutional, judicial, and legislative levels in the United States? It is not completely a pipe dream, given recent international developments. First, the experiences at The Hague have had a profound educational effect on U.S. academics and policymakers. Second, global changes and the pressures toward convergence are accelerating yearly. Third, if a general treaty on jurisdiction or judgments were ever achieved, the need for implementing legislation by the United States Congress would provide a realistic and tempting opportunity for domestic reform along the proposed lines.

§ 4.3 Notice and Opportunity to Be Heard

A. Introduction

For a court properly to undertake a civil adjudication, the persons whose property or liberty interests are to be significantly affected must receive *adequate notice*, which in turn most importantly ensures an opportunity to be heard. If any such person duly challenges the adequacy of notice, the courts must pass on whether the notice satisfied constitutional and other requirements.

B. Constitutional Requirement

State and federal courts can be treated together here, because the same requirement of notice and opportunity to be heard applies to the state courts under the Due Process Clause of the Fourteenth Amendment to the Federal Constitution as applies to the federal courts under the Fifth Amendment. Moreover, the same constitutional requirement applies regardless of the category of territorial jurisdiction, be it jurisdiction in personam, in rem, or quasi in rem.

The uniformly applicable test for constitutional notice is the following: for adjudication that will significantly affect a person's property or liberty interests, due process requires fair notice of the pendency of the action to the affected person or that person's representative. The notice must be more than a feint, although it need not be perfect: (1) fair notice must be suitably formal in tenor and informative in content; (2) fair notice must be either (a) actual notice or (b) notice that is reasonably calculated to result in actual

---

295. See Kevin M. Clermont, A Global Law of Jurisdiction and Judgments: Views from the United States and Japan, 37 Cornell Int'l L.J. 1, 22–24 (2004).

notice; and (3) fair notice must afford a reasonable opportunity to be heard.[296]

If the person entitled to notice and opportunity to be heard duly challenges their adequacy, the court passes on the constitutional requirement. The most typical setting where such a challenge might succeed is the defendant's attack after a default judgment. Here the Constitution generally requires the courts to provide relief from judgment if there was a violation of procedural due process, whether or not the defendant has a meritorious defense on the merits.[297]

The leading case on notice is *Mullane v. Central Hanover Bank & Trust Co.*[298] There, a trustee of a common trust fund sued to get a judicial settlement of accounts. In accordance with the governing statute, notice to the numerous trust beneficiaries was by publication in a newspaper. Upon special appearance by a court-appointed guardian of nonappearing beneficiaries, this notice was held insufficient under the Due Process Clause. Due diligence must be used in identifying and locating affected persons, and in these circumstances they then must be informed at least by ordinary mail. For those who cannot be identified or located, "constructive service" in the form of notice by publication suffices.[299]

For illumination of the constitutional test, consider the special situation where the plaintiff seeks seizure of the defendant's property as security for an eventual judgment, as by attachment, garnishment, replevin, or sequestration under Federal Rule 64. In the old days, these procedures were freely available to the plaintiff. According to fairly recent decisions by a divided Supreme Court, however, due process now actively constrains these procedures because they involve governmental action. The Supreme Court struck down the procedure employed in *Sniadach v. Family Finance Corp.*,[300] *Fuentes v. Shevin*,[301] and *North Georgia Finishing, Inc. v. Di–Chem, Inc.*,[302] and required pre-seizure notice and hearing

---

296. See Restatement (Second) of Judgments § 2 (1982).

297. See Peralta v. Heights Med. Ctr., Inc., 485 U.S. 80 (1988).

298. 339 U.S. 306, 314–15 (1950) (notice must be "reasonably calculated, under all the circumstances, to apprise interested parties of the pendency of the action," and the "means employed must be such as one desirous of actually informing the absentee might reasonably adopt to accomplish it"); see Roller v. Holly, 176 U.S. 398 (1900) (opportunity to be heard).

299. See also Mennonite Bd. of Missions v. Adams, 462 U.S. 791 (1983)

(expressing more of a blanket hostility to constructive service when personal service or mailed notice is possible).

300. 395 U.S. 337 (1969) (garnishment of wages).

301. 407 U.S. 67 (1972) (replevin of stove and stereo). For the story behind this case, see C. Michael Abbott & Donald C. Peters, Fuentes v. Shevin: A Narrative of Federal Test Litigation in the Legal Services Program, 57 Iowa L. Rev. 955 (1972).

302. 419 U.S. 601 (1975) (garnishment of corporation's bank account).

on the propriety of the seizure and the likelihood of success on the claim. Nevertheless, in *Mitchell v. W.T. Grant Co.*,[303] the Court approved much less protection by upholding a state sequestration procedure under which:

(1) the plaintiff must state specific facts by affidavit supporting issuance of the writ of sequestration;

(2) the plaintiff must file a bond sufficient to protect the defendant against any damage resulting from wrongful issuance;

(3) a judge issues the writ;

(4) the defendant is able immediately to seek dissolution of the writ, which must then be ordered unless the plaintiff proves the grounds upon which the writ was issued; and

(5) the defendant is able to regain possession simply upon posting a bond for 125% of the lesser of the value of the property or the amount of the claim.

Then in *Connecticut v. Doehr*,[304] the Supreme Court again struck down a state procedure, and thereby restricted *Mitchell*'s application to special circumstances: there must be pre-seizure notice and hearing except where the plaintiff has a pre-existing interest in the property or where exigent circumstances endanger security. Moreover, in its opinion, the *Doehr* Court rationalized and generalized from the prior cases' bare holdings the proposition that due process requires a procedural safeguard whenever the risk of harm without the safeguard substantially exceeds the cost of the safeguard.[305]

This cost-benefit rule—this definition of due process—has direct implications ranging far beyond pre-judgment seizures of property for security. Broadly speaking, those implications extend to the many other ways in which the government may temporarily alter legal rights.[306] More specifically, they extend to seizures of property for purposes other than security. The rule for pre-judgment seizures of property for security should also apply when property is seized to provide power for the exercise of territorial jurisdiction, as in nonpersonal jurisdiction under Federal Rule 4(n)(2).[307] Apparent-

---

303. 416 U.S. 600 (1974) (sequestration of household goods in which plaintiff had pre-existing lien).

304. 501 U.S. 1 (1991) (attachment of real estate). For the story of this case, see Robert G. Bone, The Story of Connecticut v. Doehr: Balancing Costs and Benefits in Defining Procedural Rights, in Civil Procedure Stories 159 (Kevin M. Clermont ed., 2d ed. 2008).

305. See infra § 7.1(A)(1) (law-and-economics formulation).

306. See, e.g., Goldberg v. Kelly, 397 U.S. 254 (1970) (cutting off welfare benefits). For the story of this case, see Judith Resnik, The Story of Goldberg: Why This Case Is Our Shorthand, in Civil Procedure Stories 473 (Kevin M. Clermont ed., 2d ed. 2008).

307. See United States v. James Daniel Good Real Prop., 510 U.S. 43 (1993) (seizure of drug dealer's house to provide jurisdiction for in rem forfeiture proceedings is invalid without showing

ly, however, the defendant is entitled to less procedural protection if property is seized to enforce an already rendered judgment, as by execution under Federal Rule 69, when perhaps the only requirement is fair and prompt post-execution notice and opportunity to be heard.[308]

To sum up today's constitutional picture, fair notice and opportunity to be heard must be given before governmental action may unduly impair a person's property or liberty interest (or at least the procedure of a *Mitchell*-like statute must be followed in the case of a pre-judgment seizure of property where the plaintiff has a pre-existing lien on the property or where exigent circumstances exist). The required level of procedural protection in theory depends on a balancing of the various interests involved and thus on the costs and benefits entailed (so, for example, the Constitution requires no more than the procedure of a *Mitchell*-like statute when the creditor's interest is relatively substantial, as where a pre-existing lien or exigent circumstances exist). But in practice the courts seem to be developing a series of wooden constitutional rules, such as: at a minimum under *Mullane*, mailed notice of a hearing must be sent to anyone significantly affected whose identity and whereabouts are reasonably knowable; or under *Doehr*, the notice and hearing must come before any pre-judgment seizure, unless a pre-existing lien or exigent circumstances exist, and even in these two exceptional circumstances the seizure must conform to a procedure that tracks *Mitchell*'s five provisions at least.

C. Subconstitutional Requirements

The provisions for service of process further specify the manner of giving notice to parties. Here the manner of service will be elaborated primarily by drawing examples from the federal procedure for service on defendants in personal actions.[309]

For serving *individuals*, under Federal Rule 4(e)(2) a process server may serve an individual defendant by handing her a copy of the summons and the complaint (so-called personal delivery), or by leaving these papers at her dwelling house or usual place of abode with some person of suitable age and discretion who resides there[310]

---

of "exigent circumstances"); Karen Nelson Moore, Procedural Due Process in Quasi In Rem Actions After Shaffer v. Heitner, 20 Wm. & Mary L. Rev. 157 (1978).

308. See Finberg v. Sullivan, 634 F.2d 50 (3d Cir. 1980) (en banc); Virginia C. Patterson, Commentary, Due Process and Postjudgment Enforcement

Procedures: Where Do We Stand?, 37 Ala. L. Rev. 759 (1986).

309. See generally Wright & Kane, supra note 1, §§ 64–65.

310. See Nat'l Dev. Co. v. Triad Holding Corp., 930 F.2d 253, 257 (2d Cir. 1991) (because of mobility of twentieth-century population, service of process at one of many residences is valid

or by delivering these papers to her agent authorized by appointment or by law to receive service of process (examples of so-called substituted service, i.e., service other than by personal delivery). A special rule for minors and incompetents appears in Rule 4(g).

For serving *corporations and unincorporated associations*, under Rule 4(h)(1)(B) a process server may serve such a defendant by delivering a copy of the summons and the complaint to one of its officers or to its agent.

For serving *other defendants*, Rule 4(i) and (j) makes special provision for serving governmental defendants. The many other service provisions cover other special cases, such as Rule 4(f) treating service in a foreign country. However, some of the other provisions merely add options to the manner of service for the ordinary cases, such as Rule 4(e)(1) allowing service under state law. Sometimes no service technique has been specified or no usual technique can be employed, as where a defendant has completely disappeared. The court can then permit so-called expedient service, which is service in such manner as the court directs.

Process servers must sometimes be very ingenious or devious to serve a defendant. They can effect service by fraud, provided that the fraud does not undermine the notice-giving function of service and does not supply the only basis for territorial jurisdiction. Thus, they can gain access to the defendant by disguising their identity,[311] but they cannot in July serve process hidden in a gift-box with a do-not-open-until-Christmas note[312] and they cannot establish jurisdiction by fraudulently luring the defendant into the state.[313] Moreover, use of unlawful force in serving process is held to invalidate that service.[314]

Local law may strictly enforce some of the subconstitutional requirements for giving notice. For example, the defendant may

provided that the residence "contains sufficient indicia of permanence").

311. See Gumperz v. Hofmann, 283 N.Y.S. 823 (App. Div. 1935), aff'd, 2 N.E.2d 687 (N.Y. 1936) (defendant, an Argentine doctor sojourning in a New York City hotel, was telephoned by a process server who falsely represented himself to be a Dr. Goldman with a letter from the president of the New York County Medical Society to be personally delivered; they arranged to meet in the hotel lobby, where service was made; motion to vacate service denied).

312. See Bulkley v. Bulkley, 6 Abb. Pr. 307 (N.Y. Sup. Ct. 1858) (husband, an attorney, accompanied his wife to a New York dockside, whence she was to sail to California to visit her mother;

during an affectionate farewell, he gave her a wrapped box, telling her it contained a present for her mother, but in reality it contained process for a divorce action; she sailed without opening it, and she consequently defaulted; service invalidated).

313. See Terlizzi v. Brodie, 329 N.Y.S.2d 589 (App. Div. 1972) (New Jersey defendants were telephoned at home and falsely told that they had been chosen to receive two Broadway tickets as a promotional venture to get their opinion of the new 7:30 p.m. curtain time; they were served in the theater by the man sitting behind them; motion to vacate service granted).

314. See supra § 4.2(B)(2)(b), (C)(1)(b).

succeed in attacking notice if the summons inaccurately named her or if the manner of service did not precisely comply with the statutes and rules.[315] However, the trend is away from an overly strict approach, with courts now tending to ignore such irregularities (1) where the party actually received suitably formal and informative notice or (2) where the form of the notice and the manner of transmitting it substantially complied with the prescribed procedure.[316]

Indeed, local law may dispense altogether with the requirement of formal service of process, as is done for example in connection with jurisdiction over plaintiffs for counterclaims. Moreover, a person may waive service of process.[317]

D.   Contractual Waiver of Protections

Surprisingly enough, a person may indeed waive in advance all of these procedural protections. However, the waiver of the due process rights must be voluntary, intelligent, and knowing.

In *D.H. Overmyer Co. v. Frick Co.*,[318] as part of a business deal, a corporation for consideration and on advice of counsel signed a "cognovit note" or confession of judgment, a device whereby a debtor consents that upon breach its creditor may obtain a judgment without the debtor's getting notice or hearing and without any showing by the creditor. An Ohio court entered judgment on the cognovit note. Under Ohio law, the court did have discretionary power to open the judgment later, if there were a showing of a valid defense on the merits. The Supreme Court held that entry of judgment here comports with due process—while noting the possibility of a different result in a consumer setting, and noting that cognovit notes are in many situations prohibited or restricted by statute.

§ 4.4   Procedural Incidents

A.   Procedure for Raising

The procedural treatment of subject-matter jurisdiction significantly differs from that of territorial authority to adjudicate and of notice.

---

315. See, e.g., Md. State Firemen's Ass'n v. Chaves, 166 F.R.D. 353 (D. Md. 1996) (default judgment set aside because of invalid service of process sent by first-class mail, even though actually received).

316. See Restatement (Second) of Judgments §§ 2–3 (1982).

317. See Fed. R. Civ. P. 4(d), 12(h)(1).

318. 405 U.S. 174 (1972); see Underwood Farmers Elevator v. Leidholm, 460 N.W.2d 711 (N.D. 1990).

1. Subject–Matter Jurisdiction

This requirement is considered so fundamental that its satisfaction is open to question throughout the ordinary course of the initial action including appeal. Being courts of limited jurisdiction, the federal courts apply this requirement somewhat more strictly than do most state courts.[319]

The party invoking federal jurisdiction must affirmatively allege the grounds upon which subject-matter jurisdiction depends.[320] If challenged, the party relying on federal jurisdiction bears the burden of showing that such jurisdiction exists. Any party may challenge federal jurisdiction at any time in the ordinary course of the initial action including appeal, and the trial or appellate court should on its own motion dismiss for lack of subject-matter jurisdiction whenever perceived.[321] Thus, even the party who invoked jurisdiction may, on his appeal from a judgment against him, challenge such jurisdiction.

2. Territorial Authority to Adjudicate and Notice

By bringing an action, the plaintiff implicitly asserts that the court has territorial jurisdiction and is a proper venue, and that the plaintiff has properly notified the defendant. Several states, however, require specific pleading of the basis for long-arm jurisdiction.

If the defendant challenges these implicit or explicit assertions early in the ordinary course of the initial action, the court must pass on territorial authority to adjudicate and notice. But the defendant must raise these personal defenses in a way that avoids waiver.

a. Special Appearance

In the initial action the key for the defendant is thus to raise these personal defenses in a way that avoids waiving them. The special appearance is the basic technique by which the defendant raises these threshold defenses. There have been four significant judicial approaches to the availability of a special appearance:

(1) Appearance Treated as Waiver. According to old case law, a state can constitutionally treat *any* appearance as waiving

---

319. See generally Wright & Kane, supra note 1, §§ 7, 69; Restatement (Second) of Judgments § 11 cmt. d (1982).

320. See Fed. R. Civ. P. 8(a)(1) (complaint); 28 U.S.C. § 1446(a) (notice of removal).

321. See Fed. R. Civ. P. 12(h)(3).

these threshold defenses.[322] Thus, the defendant would have to choose between (a) appearing in order to defend on the merits and (b) defaulting in order to preserve the important threshold defenses as grounds for relief from judgment. However, today all states have removed this wrenching dilemma by permitting some manner of special appearance.

(2) Defense on Merits Treated as Waiver. Although allowing a special appearance, a few states rule that if the trial judge rejects such challenge, the defendant must then choose between (a) defending on the merits and (b) appealing only on the basis of those threshold defenses.[323] In other words, these states treat a defense on the merits as a waiver of any right to pursue further those threshold defenses, including on appeal.

(3) Interlocutory Appeal Allowed. Some states mitigate this later dilemma by permitting the defendant to appeal an unsuccessful special appearance before defending on the merits.

(4) Defense on Merits and Final Appeal Allowed. Most states, and the federal courts,[324] permit some fashion of special appearance. If that fails, the defendant may proceed to defend on the merits. If that too fails, the defendant may appeal both on those threshold defenses and on the merits.

The defendant must be very careful to follow precisely the procedural steps of the special appearance, making immediately clear that she is appearing specially to challenge territorial authority to adjudicate or notice, or both, and that she is not appearing generally. The correct steps vary from state to state.[325] In federal court the "special appearance" is less formalistic, instead coming in the form of a Federal Rule 12(b) defense:

(1) "lack of personal jurisdiction" under Rule 12(b)(2), which is read to cover all of the defense of lack of territorial jurisdiction;

(2) "improper venue" under Rule 12(b)(3);

(3) "insufficient process" under Rule 12(b)(4), which covers defects in the form of the summons; and

(4) "insufficient service of process" under Rule 12(b)(5), which covers defects in the manner of transmitting notice.

The federal defendant must raise any such available defenses at the very outset, either in a Rule 12(b) motion or in her answer, whichever comes first. With some risk, the defendant may first

---

322. See York v. Texas, 137 U.S. 15 (1890).

323. See Western Life Indem. Co. v. Rupp, 235 U.S. 261 (1914).

324. See Harkness v. Hyde, 98 U.S. 476 (1878) (federal approach).

325. See generally Restatement (Second) of Judgments § 10 cmt. b (1982).

engage in certain preliminary procedural maneuvers, such as moving for an extension of time to respond. But if the defendant first does anything more substantive, she waives those threshold defenses, according to Rule 12(h)(1). Indeed, even after properly asserting such defenses, the defendant may waive them by inconsistent activity, such as by asserting a permissive counterclaim.[326]

b. Limited Appearance

To be sharply distinguished from a special appearance are restricted appearances, or the techniques by which someone restricts his appearance in an action so as not to confer jurisdiction over his person for additional claims. The most frequently discussed example of restricted appearances is the so-called limited appearance, whereby a defendant may limit her appearance in a nonpersonal proceeding to defending on the merits her interests in the thing without submitting to personal jurisdiction for, say, money damages. Note that given the existence of proper nonpersonal jurisdiction, but in the absence of the limited-appearance option, the defendant would have to choose between (1) losing her property or other such interests by default and (2) making a general appearance that subjects her to personal liability. So the defendant's desire for the fairness of a limited-appearance option is obvious.

However, confusion shrouds the availability of the limited appearance.[327] The answer lies in scattered case law. In that case law, the best view is that a limited appearance should be available if it is constitutionally unreasonable for the forum to exercise personal jurisdiction with respect to the additional claim concurrently with hearing the nonpersonal action. Since *Shaffer v. Heitner*[328] prohibited unreasonable nonpersonal jurisdiction, there are few occasions to permit a limited appearance consistently with that view.[329] That is, if the nonpersonal jurisdiction is reasonable, then most likely the requisite personal jurisdiction will be reasonable too, making a limited appearance unavailable. Nevertheless, there may be situations where liability limited to the property is reasonable but unlimited personal liability would be unreasonable, as in certain instances of jurisdiction by necessity exercised in an action quasi in rem subtype two. Therefore, limited appearances, although rare, are still sometimes available.

326. See Dragor Shipping Corp. v. Union Tank Car Co., 378 F.2d 241 (9th Cir. 1967).

327. See I. Daniel Stewart, Jr., Note, Limited Appearances, 7 Utah L. Rev. 369 (1961).

328. 433 U.S. 186 (1977).

329. See Restatement (Second) of Judgments § 8 cmt. g (1982).

For example, if in order to recover for personal injuries from a traffic accident in Japan, a New York plaintiff sues quasi in rem subtype two in New York for $60,000 by attaching the French defendant's land in New York worth $30,000, and if the defendant wishes to defend her property by contesting negligence, but without submitting to personal jurisdiction, then she can do so, because procedural fairness especially counsels that the defendant should be able to make a limited appearance. A New York forum cannot reasonably exercise personal jurisdiction with respect to the associated claim for tort against the appearing defendant.[330] For a contrary example, if in order to foreclose a mortgage on a French defendant's land in New York that secures a debt, a New York plaintiff sues quasi in rem subtype one in New York by attaching the land, and if the defendant wishes to defend her property on the merits without submitting to personal jurisdiction for any excess amount owing on the underlying debt, then she cannot do so, because judicial efficiency especially counsels that the defendant should not be able to make a limited appearance. A New York forum may reasonably exercise personal jurisdiction with respect to the associated claim for debt against the appearing defendant.[331]

Such subtleties explain the confusion existing on the availability of the limited appearance. It is also unclear whether state law on limited appearances ever applies in federal court under the *Erie* doctrine.[332] The marginally better view is that this matter, just like the other procedural incidents, is governed by federal law in federal court.

In any event, if the applicable law permits limited appearances, the defendant must make express at the very outset her intention to limit her appearance. If the court then permits that limited appearance, the defendant can participate in the action fully. If the defense on the merits succeeds, the defendant gets to keep the property. If the defense on the merits fails, the property is gone, but the defendant will not be personally liable on the resulting judgment. That is, the property will go to satisfy the plaintiff's judgment, but the defendant is not liable for any deficiency.

Even after a limited appearance, the plaintiff can sue the defendant again in a separate action—either in personam or quasi in rem based on other property. Even though the parties have vigorously and thoroughly contested the claim, the first judgment does not have merger or bar effect on the claim. It purports only to determine the plaintiff's interest in the property. Although there is disagreement, the better view is that adjudication pursuant to such

---

330. See, e.g., Salmon Falls Mfg. Co. v. Midland Tire & Rubber Co., 285 F. 214 (6th Cir. 1922); Cheshire Nat'l Bank v. Jaynes, 112 N.E. 500 (Mass. 1916).

331. See, e.g., Campbell v. Murdock, 90 F. Supp. 297 (N.D. Ohio 1950).

332. See Wright & Miller, supra note 31, § 1123.

a limited appearance should have no res judicata effects other than determining interests in the property, because giving any wider preclusion would be inconsistent with the notion that a defendant's litigating pursuant to a limited appearance risks nothing more than the property itself.[333] This obvious inefficiency leads plaintiffs and courts to resist the limited-appearance option.

Note that the defendant who makes a limited appearance might also make a special appearance to challenge the court's jurisdiction over the property, as for example to dispute the situs of an intangible. Note also that the defendant may choose instead to make a general appearance, which would permit a personal judgment on any additional personal claim asserted by the plaintiff, but which also gives the defendant the opportunity to dispose of the whole dispute between the parties in one case.

In sum, the limited appearance in its strict usage in nonpersonal jurisdiction is no longer common enough to be important as a practical matter. However, in a broader sense, the limited appearance will live on. It will persist as a general idea that jurisdiction over a party who has appeared in any kind of action extends only to those additional claims related to the original action that do not lack a reasonable relationship to the forum state. Other claims cannot be sprung on the appearing party. The appearance is "limited" or "restricted" in that it does not bestow personal jurisdiction on unrelated claims or on claims for which the forum would be unreasonable.[334]

B. Consequences of Raising

1. Method of Deciding

If any of these forum-authority defenses is raised in the ordinary course of the initial action, the judge (1) may, on the application of any party, hear and determine the defense in a pretrial proceeding or (2) may choose to defer the issue until trial.[335] Additionally, in the post-trial period, a defense of lack of subject-matter jurisdiction will be determined whenever raised in the ordinary course of the initial action including appeal.[336]

In the initial action, the burden of persuasion is on the plaintiff, except as to the unreasonableness test for territorial jurisdiction. What kind of factual showing must the person make in order to establish forum-authority? In theory, the standard is the usual one of preponderance of the evidence. But there are difficulties in

---

333. See infra § 5.5(A).

334. See Restatement (Second) of Judgments § 9 (1982); supra text accompanying notes 167–68.

335. See, e.g., Fed. R. Civ. P. 12(i).

336. See, e.g., id. 12(h).

this regard when there is a similarity of the facts involved in the jurisdictional determination and on the merits. Imagine a paternity suit, brought against an absent man on allegations of in-state impregnation. We know that the plaintiff need not *prove* her cause of action in order to establish personal jurisdiction, because that standard would obviously have all sorts of illogical consequences. But what if the defendant denies the allegation that he "is the author of acts or omissions within the state"? Surely the plaintiff must do more than *allege* that the defendant is the author. After all, we would probably want to allow a defaulting defendant when seeking relief from judgment to raise, say, mistaken identity. So the answer must lie in requiring something between proof and allegation. Apparently the cases' solution is to require the plaintiff, upon challenge, to make a "prima facie" showing, that is, establish some sort of reasonable likelihood that the jurisdictional facts exist. And what that malleable term more precisely means should turn on which particular fact the defendant wishes to contest (identity, intercourse, location, impregnation, or failure to support).[337]

The parties have opportunity for discovery on the issue of forum-authority. The judge determines the issue on documentary proof and affidavits and, if necessary, an evidentiary hearing. The judge decides without the intervention of a jury. If the judge sustains the defense, the remedy is normally dismissal of the action. But if there is a reasonable prospect that the plaintiff could cure the defect by serving process anew in a proper manner, then the judge may instead merely quash service. Or if transfer of venue would cure the defect, the court may order transfer in the interest of justice, as under 28 U.S.C. § 1406(a).

2. Jurisdiction to Determine Jurisdiction

After determination of a forum-authority defense, there may arise the question of its res judicata effects. The normal rules of res judicata apply. For example, if the question of a party's domicile is actually litigated and determined to uphold jurisdiction, and if that question of domicile arises as part of the merits of another claim,

---

337. See Kevin M. Clermont, Jurisdictional Fact, 91 Cornell L. Rev. 973, 998 (2006) ("The legal system would apply a high standard of proof to identity for jurisdictional purposes, requiring the plaintiff to achieve at least equipoise on that issue. Meanwhile, it would require the plaintiff merely to *allege* failure to support, and not to *prove* it at all for jurisdictional purposes, leaving the parties to litigate legal liability on the merits. It would then apply the prima facie standard of proof to the facts in between, but prima facie would imply a different rigor for the different facts: the system might require the 'slightest possibility' for the result of impregnation, meaning little more than good-faith allegation; 'reasonable possibility' for the location of the act, implying that reasonable fact finders could differ; and the higher showing of a 'substantial possibility' for the fact of intercourse.").

the prior finding could have issue preclusion effect. For a quite different example, if a defendant loses a post-judgment attack made on the ground of inadequate notice, that loss will preclude further attacks on that ground, under the normal doctrine of issue preclusion.[338]

But there is the important additional question of the effect that a determination rejecting such a defense in the ordinary course of litigation has on a later attack on the resultant judgment, an attack not in the ordinary course of review in the trial and appellate courts but in subsequent litigation. Assume that in subsequent litigation a defendant tries to get relief from judgment by establishing the rendering court's lack of jurisdiction or failure to give adequate notice, doing so perhaps in the course of a collateral attack.[339] By way of definition, a collateral attack by a party occurs when another litigant tries to use a prior judgment in a new action as the basis for a claim (as when, in enforcing a judgment, the plaintiff brings an action upon the judgment in another state) or as the basis for a defense (as when the defendant pleads res judicata), and then the party attacks the prior judgment to prevent its use. The general rule is that a collateral attack will succeed only if the prior judgment contains certain, very serious errors: lack of subject-matter jurisdiction, territorial jurisdiction, or adequate notice. The question then is: does losing on the defense in the first place prevent attack in the second place?

This additional question is a kind of question different from the normal application of res judicata: it does not involve preclusive use of determinations embedded in a valid judgment, but instead involves preclusive use of prior determinations in order to establish validity. Here the desire for finality generally outweighs the concern for validity, giving the determination preclusive effect and thus generating a special variety of res judicata labeled "jurisdiction to determine jurisdiction." That is to say, affirmative rulings on jurisdiction or notice can preclude the parties from attacking the resultant judgment on that ground in subsequent litigation.[340]

The thrust of the jurisdiction to determine jurisdiction doctrine is a bit shocking upon first impression. After all, seemingly implicit in the concept of due process embodied in the Fifth and Fourteenth Amendments to the U.S. Constitution is the principle that one cannot be bound by a judgment of a court that lacked jurisdiction or failed to give notice. This principle would seem to imply not only

---

338. See, e.g., Arecibo Radio Corp. v. Puerto Rico, 825 F.2d 589 (1st Cir. 1987).

339. See infra § 5.1(B)(1) (describing methods for seeking relief from judgment).

340. See infra § 5.1(A)(3) (distinguishing other doctrines of res judicata).

that such a judgment cannot be entered against the person or the person's property, but also that the judgment will not be enforced or recognized as valid judgments would. The fact is, however, that such a validity principle does not exist.

It is true that if a defendant is sued in a court that lacks jurisdiction or fails to give notice, ordinarily the defendant is not obliged to respond in any way. If the defendant takes no action of any kind in response to the suit, the court may enter a default judgment, but such a judgment is said to be invalid. If the plaintiff should attempt to assert rights based on that judgment in a later suit against the same defendant, the defendant will ordinarily be permitted to avoid the effects of the judgment by showing that it was entered without jurisdiction or notice. The defendant is entitled to a day in court on the question of the authority of the court that rendered the earlier judgment.

The defendant may, instead, choose to raise the jurisdiction or notice issue in the initial action before the challenged court itself. Then, a court that otherwise lacks authority could conceivably have jurisdiction to determine whether it has jurisdiction and whether its notice was good, and its rulings on such questions could be binding on the parties and preclude relitigation of the same questions. The defendant's appearance in the challenged court would then be the defendant's only day in court.

Our law in fact accepts this so-called bootstrap principle, and so allows a court lacking fundamental authority to issue a judgment that will nevertheless be immune from late attack. Because the issue of jurisdiction or notice was actually litigated and determined, even if erroneously, the parties are precluded from relitigating the same issue in subsequent litigation. The erroneous ruling can be reviewed on appeal from the judgment, of course, but it cannot be challenged in seeking relief from judgment.

Indeed, our law accepts the bootstrap principle's value of finality with enthusiasm, despite its conflict with the intuitive value of validity. Our law sometimes applies the principle even more broadly than the foregoing illustration of actually litigated and determined forum-authority defenses, as the rest of this chapter details.

a.   *Subject–Matter Jurisdiction*

In subsequent litigation, then, the bootstrap principle can operate in connection with affirmative rulings by the rendering court on the question of its own subject-matter jurisdiction, in spite of the seeming conflict between that result and the traditional lore about subject-matter jurisdiction's fundamental importance. The bald theory underlying the application of the principle to questions of subject-matter jurisdiction is simply that a court has jurisdiction to decide whether it has subject-matter jurisdiction over a case presented to it. Its final ruling on that question, even if erroneous, will be binding unless set aside on appeal and will have preclusive effect on a later attack.

Nevertheless, sometimes the interests inherent in subject-matter jurisdiction are just too important to ignore. Consequently, a finding of the existence of subject-matter jurisdiction will not preclude the parties from attacking the resultant judgment on that ground in special circumstances, such as where (1) the court *plainly* lacked subject-matter jurisdiction or (2) the judgment *substantially* infringes on the authority of another court or agency.[341]

b. *Territorial Authority to Adjudicate and Notice*

A finding of the existence of territorial authority to adjudicate or of adequate notice precludes the appearing parties from attacking the resultant judgment on either ground in subsequent litigation. That is, if the court rules that the requisites of territorial authority to adjudicate and adequate notice are present, the defendant will be bound by that ruling and hence by the judgment ultimately rendered in the action, whether the defendant participates further or not. If the judgment is not set aside on appeal, it will be binding, and the territorial jurisdiction and adequate notice issues cannot again be litigated. Indeed, upon a challenge to the existence of *either* territorial jurisdiction *or* adequate notice, an affirmative ruling precludes the defendant from attacking the resultant judgment on either ground in subsequent litigation.[342]

The basic lesson, then, is that once a defendant starts litigating in Action #1, the defendant must stay there and correct any errors by appeal, because the threshold forum-authority issues will be foreclosed in Action #2. In *Baldwin v. Iowa State Traveling Men's Association*,[343] an erroneous determination by a Missouri federal court, after a special appearance, of the existence of personal jurisdiction was held to preclude a later attack by the defendant. In *Durfee v. Duke*,[344] a determination by a Nebraska state court, after active litigation of the quiet-title action, of the issue of jurisdiction over the land, a determination that rested on an erroneous finding that the land on the banks of the shifting river was in Nebraska rather than Missouri, was held to preclude a later attack by the

---

341. See Restatement (Second) of Judgments § 12 cmts. c, e (1982); infra text accompanying notes 349–50.

342. See Restatement (Second) of Judgments § 10 cmt. d (1982).

343. 283 U.S. 522 (1931).

344. 375 U.S. 106 (1963); cf. Johnson v. Muelberger, 340 U.S. 581 (1951) (jurisdiction over status).

defendant. Although the Supreme Court referred to the issue in *Durfee v. Duke* as one of "jurisdiction over the subject matter," its characterization was sloppy. The issue there was conceptually one of quasi in rem jurisdiction over particular land, not one of general competence to hear suits to quiet title. Moreover, the policies at stake were those of territorial jurisdiction, not those of subject-matter jurisdiction.[345]

3. Jurisdiction to Determine No Jurisdiction

Passing beyond the res judicata effects of affirmative rulings on forum-authority, what if the initial court decides that it lacks jurisdiction or failed to give notice? That is, can a court, which is admittedly without authority to enter a valid judgment, make any rulings that have preclusive effect? Yes.

The initial court's ruling that it lacks authority will prevent a second try that presents exactly the same issue. Common sense supports preclusion on the threshold issue, in order to prevent the plaintiff from suing repetitively. Thus, the court had authority to determine its lack of authority. For such purposes, the prior judgment is a valid one.[346]

Of course, the dismissal of the initial action on a threshold defense does not generate a bar to a second action in an appropriate court. Moreover, the initial court's ruling probably should have no res judicata effects in such later action, whether to establish the jurisdiction of the other court or to preclude an issue on the merits of the same or any other claim. For these purposes, the prior judgment is an invalid one.

What Does "Jurisdiction to Determine Jurisdiction" Mean?

This term embodies the idea that a court can issue orders necessary to determine its own jurisdiction. An example would be a discovery order probing the existence of jurisdiction. See Insurance Corp. of Ireland v. Compagnie des Bauxites de Guinee, 456 U.S. 694 (1982). From this basic idea, however, have come two quite different doctrines that confusingly share the same name.

First, as the text describes, this is the name of a special branch of res judicata that, upon an attack on a judgment in subsequent litigation, may foreclose relitigation of a prior determination of the existence of subject-matter jurisdiction, territorial jurisdiction, or adequate notice.

Second, a different doctrine, going by this name or sometimes by "collateral bar rule," authorizes punishment by criminal contempt for the violation of a court order even though that order is judicially determined to have been improper (no matter how serious the error, and even for lack of subject-matter jurisdiction), although this doctrine authorizes such punish-

---

345. See Restatement (Second) of Judgments §§ 10, 11 cmt. b, 12 (1982).

346. See Ruhrgas AG v. Marathon Oil Co., 526 U.S. 574, 585 (1999); Michael J. Edney, Comment, Preclusive Abstention: Issue Preclusion and Jurisdictional Dismissals After Ruhrgas, 68 U. Chi. L. Rev. 193 (2001).

> ment only if the violator was personally bound and had an opportunity to
> pursue full review of the order without incurring destruction of a significant
> right in question. The chief precedents are United States v. United Mine
> Workers, 330 U.S. 258 (1947), and Walker v. City of Birmingham, 388 U.S.
> 307 (1967).

C. Consequences of Not Raising

Consider finally the question of what happens if any of these forum-authority defenses is not raised at all in the ordinary course of the initial action, but the aggrieved party subsequently seeks relief from judgment by trying to establish the rendering court's lack of jurisdiction or failure to give adequate notice. As to the grounds that actually remain open on such attack, the law makes a basic distinction between litigated actions and complete defaults.

1. Litigated Action

a. Subject–Matter Jurisdiction

Subject-matter jurisdiction, unlike territorial authority to adjudicate and notice, cannot be conferred by the defendant's consent, collusion, waiver, or estoppel.[347] Nevertheless, because the court supposedly always implicitly determines unraised subject-matter jurisdiction to exist in any action litigated to judgment by contesting parties, the implicit determination has the res judicata consequences of an actually litigated determination of the existence of subject-matter jurisdiction, insofar as foreclosing attack on the judgment goes. The court in subsequent litigation may, however, be more likely in practice to find applicable an exception to res judicata when the determination was implicit rather than actually litigated.[348]

In *Chicot County Drainage District v. Baxter State Bank*,[349] the Supreme Court precluded even a defaulting party from attacking an earlier illegal exercise of subject-matter jurisdiction, because other defendants had contested the initial action, although they had not questioned the court's subject-matter jurisdiction. In this and other less extreme cases, the Court has recognized the propriety of giving preclusive effect to a court's determination of its own subject-matter jurisdiction. But on the same day, in *Kalb v. Feuerstein*,[350] the Supreme Court held that a state court's foreclosure judgment, rendered illegally during the pendency of federal bankruptcy pro-

---

347. See, e.g., Thompson v. Whitman, 85 U.S. (18 Wall.) 457 (1874).

348. See Restatement (Second) of Judgments § 12 cmt. d (1982); Dan B. Dobbs, Beyond Bootstrap: Foreclosing the Issue of Subject–Matter Jurisdiction

Before Final Judgment, 51 Minn. L. Rev. 491 (1967).

349. 308 U.S. 371 (1940).

350. 308 U.S. 433 (1940); see Restatement (Second) of Judgments § 12 cmt. e (1982).

ceedings, was subject to collateral attack, even though rendered after proceedings contested by the later attackers. The Court thereby acknowledged that sometimes the illegal exercise of subject-matter jurisdiction really can undermine the authority of other courts, or truly can be blatant, and so subject-matter jurisdiction must remain open to collateral attack in such circumstances.

b. Territorial Authority to Adjudicate and Notice

By failing properly to raise any such threshold defense, an appearing defendant waives it.[351] That is, by effective consent, the defendant creates territorial authority to adjudicate and waives notice. This prevents the appearing parties from attacking the resultant judgment on either ground in subsequent litigation, obviating the need to reach any question of res judicata.

Nonetheless, defaulting defendants retain the right to challenge later territorial authority to adjudicate and notice, there having been neither waiver nor prior adjudication of these personal defenses. But note that in any proceeding for relief from judgment, if the attacker had notice of the original action, the burden of production regarding invalidity shifts to the attacker.[352]

2. Complete Default

a. Subject–Matter Jurisdiction

There being no res judicata on this point in this situation, a party may later obtain relief from judgment on the ground of lack of subject-matter jurisdiction, provided that he has not induced another person's substantial reliance on the default judgment.[353]

The bottom line is that relief from judgment on the ground of subject-matter jurisdiction is readily available only in cases where *all* defendants defaulted, given the operation of jurisdiction to determine jurisdiction in all other settings.

b. Territorial Authority to Adjudicate and Notice

There being no res judicata or waiver on this point in this situation, an aggrieved party may later obtain relief from judgment on the ground of a constitutional defect in territorial authority to adjudicate or notice, provided that he has not induced another person's substantial reliance on the default judgment. The law of

---

351. See, e.g., Fed. R. Civ. P. 12(h)(1).

352. See infra § 5.7(B) (describing procedure applied upon seeking relief from judgment).

353. See generally Restatement (Second) of Judgments §§ 65–66 (1982).

the court that rendered the judgment normally will treat as additional grounds for relief from a default judgment any violations of the subconstitutional requirements of territorial jurisdiction and the more important subconstitutional requirements of notice, although the list of available grounds might contract as the mode, place, and time of the attack on the judgment become more distant from the initial action.[354]

Thus, relief from judgment on the ground of territorial authority to adjudicate or adequate notice can lie from a judgment entered after the attacker defaulted. Here is a key example: *P* sues *D* in the United States District Court for the District of Maine. Personal jurisdiction over *D* is questionable. What may *D* do? *Either D may suffer a default foreclosing the merits and then later attack the judgment on the jurisdictional ground when *P* attempts to enforce it *or* D may appear in Maine's federal court to litigate fully the jurisdictional point and the merits, *but not both appear now and attack later.*

Under a radical view of some commentators, most or all of territorial authority to adjudicate (and even subject-matter jurisdiction too) should be simply removed from the list of available grounds for relief from judgment in subsequent litigation, because today a party can fairly be required either to raise the point in the initial action or to forfeit the point. That reform would go too far, however. For the near future, the optimum, with an eye to international as well as to domestic cases, would be to allow a defaulting party to obtain relief from a default judgment for a defect in territorial jurisdiction or notice, but only if the defect rose to the level of a due process violation.

354.   See generally id.

Chapter 5

FORMER ADJUDICATION

Table of Sections

§ 5.1 Preliminary Considerations

This chapter's subject is a previously rendered adjudication's impact in subsequent litigation. The most important doctrine within this subject is res judicata or, as it used to be called, res adjudicata.

Res judicata tends to be discussed only when a litigant goes wrong in a way that causes repetitive litigation, and therefore res judicata tends to be envisaged as a bunch of technical provisions to handle this peculiar problem. But it has much greater significance. Because res judicata specifies what a judgment, which is the climactic objective of most adjudicative proceedings, has and has not adjudicated with binding effect, this doctrine is of universal importance both systemic and practical. It is certainly key to understanding and implementing civil procedure, both before and after judgment. From composing pleadings in an initial lawsuit to settling or otherwise ending that case and then to attacking the judgment in a second lawsuit, the litigant must bear res judicata in mind.

The basic idea behind res judicata is that at some point the pursuit of truth must and should cease: justice demands that there be an end to litigation. Consequently, around the world every legal system, from its beginnings, generates a common core of res judicata law to make decisions final. The prime example of this common core of res judicata is that, in order for any nascent judicial system to operate, a decision must have at least some minimal bindingness. This essence of res judicata—its mission of defining "judgment" through its binding effects—is nonoptional for the system. If disputants could just reopen their adjudicated disputes, there would be neither an end to litigation, nor any beginning of judicial authority. Finality is not just an efficient policy, it is a necessary condition for the existence of a judiciary.

Legal systems must accept this impulse, and then formulate law to implement it. At that stage, res judicata law gets uglier, but in different ways in different systems. Systems may differ (1) in how far the bindingness of res judicata law reaches, as the legal system pursues its more refined notions of justice, or merely (2) in how the lawmakers have shaped the doctrine as a matter of form. The most influential components of justice here are procedural efficiency and fairness, although various substantive policies, which range from optimizing market conditions to regulating attorney-client relations, can play a role too.

Under the heading of procedural efficiency, as it underlies res judicata law, comes society's interest in avoiding the expenditure of time and money in repetitive litigation. Society also has an interest in avoiding any increase of uncertainty in primary conduct or of instability in the judicial branch of our legal system. Society has an interest in avoiding possibly inconsistent adjudications, which at the least would erode faith in our system of justice. An important efficiency consideration is the long-run deterrent effect of res judicata: a harsh result in the case at hand might encourage many future litigants to dispose of their disputes in a single lawsuit, which they will take and litigate seriously.

Procedural fairness supports the use of res judicata to avoid the burdens of repetitive litigation on the party invoking the doctrine, to avoid infringing on reliance and equality interests, and to avoid the possibility of the other party's profiting from sneaky or otherwise undesirable litigation tactics. A litigant is entitled to a day in court, but not to inflict a repetition of it.

Contrary considerations, especially those resting on fairness in the individual case, support exceptions to res judicata's principle of finality. One readily perceives that some applications of the doctrine do seem outrageously unfair, and litigating about whether to relitigate can be seriously inefficient. After all, by res judicata, courts are just trying to pursue those policies that weigh against repetitive litigation. Clearly, other policies will often point in the other direction and sometimes overwhelm. Iron-clad rules of preclusion hardly seem the appropriate resolution, and so exceptions abound.

Such policy tensions dictate the *scope* of res judicata. The *form* of res judicata law, also reflecting the pursuit of justice, turns on the jurisprudential interplay of rules and exceptions. Here, "rules" mean the series of statements constituting a general formulation of inclusion that establishes the prima facie reach of the doctrine, and "exceptions" remain exceptional in excluding only certain special situations from the doctrine's application. What is the optimal form? Clear, simple, and rigid rules should approximate the outcome of the balance of the efficiency, fairness, and substantive policies behind res judicata. Flexible or even ad hoc exceptions should then work to remedy any remaining overinclusion of res judicata in particular circumstances, but the exceptions should be small in scope even if necessarily considerable in number. Finally, there should be no exceptions to exceptions, because so extending preclusion is costly with few benefits.

Indeed, the grand trend in the development of the modern doctrine of res judicata has been expanding the theoretical applicability of the finality principle while at the same time recognizing more and more exceptions of some scope and discretionary nature. On the one hand, even the many existing exceptions do not remove all the bite from the sometimes harsh doctrine of res judicata. On the other hand, as exceptions continue to grow in significance, the question arises whether a now marginally narrowing and increasingly discretionary doctrine of res judicata is really preferable to a bare but clearer minimum of preclusion, perhaps a doctrine that would keep judgments from being reopened but not preclude any underlying issues. It must therefore be recognized that if instead a fuller doctrine of res judicata is deemed worth preserving, it must be applied with some woodenness in order not to defeat its purposes.

A. Summary of Doctrines

Res judicata is a classic common-law doctrine. Each jurisdiction generates its own distinctive body of rules and exceptions, almost entirely judge-made and heavily policy-driven. In this chapter, although there will be occasional references where appropriate to contrasting older practice and to local variations, the primary focus will be on the modern approach to res judicata. That modern approach is best exemplified by the federal doctrine or by the similar Second Restatement of Judgments.[1]

The Second Restatement is a highly significant work. It sets out the modern approach to res judicata in the United States. It is not perfect, and leaves some parts of the law unsettled, but it is unarguably a work of the highest quality. Of course, the American Law Institute's Restatements and the country's courts interact. The Second Restatement of Judgments tried to express and refine the recent efforts of the federal courts and the progressive state courts. Today those courts tend to use the Second Restatement in further developing the doctrine of res judicata. As a consequence, a coherent modern law of res judicata has become perceptible and accepted, with the United States today enjoying a semi-codification of most of res judicata law that is fairly uniform albeit unofficial. In fact, at one point Justice Rehnquist felt obliged to remind the other Justices that this Restatement was not binding on the Supreme Court.[2] Even if not binding, and even if the courts are currently putting a gloss on it, the Second Restatement merits careful study because it has managed to bring much order to the field and because it has so influenced the courts.

The place to begin in summarizing res judicata is to describe the context in which it applies. Parties can invoke res judicata only outside the initial action, that is, outside the first-instance process and any direct review such as appeal. So, the usual discussion of res judicata contemplates the context of two actions, presuming an Action #1 that led to judgment and then addressing the judgment's effect on a pending Action #2, which may have begun before or after Action #1. For example, the plaintiff in Action #2 who is suing upon a judgment rendered in Action #1 might invoke res judicata to preclude the defendant from defending in Action #2 on the underlying merits, or during some other kind of Action #2 the

---

1. Restatement (Second) of Judgments (1982).

2. Montana v. United States, 440 U.S. 147, 164 (1979) (concurring in "the Court's opinion on the customary understanding that its references to * * * drafts or finally adopted versions of the Restatement of Judgments are not intended to bind the Court to the views expressed therein on issues not presented by the facts of this case").

plaintiff might invoke res judicata to foreclose relitigation of certain issues decided in Action #1. Similarly, the defendant in some subsequent action might invoke res judicata as a defense by using a prior judgment to defeat a claim or to preclude an issue.

For the moment, consider only the effects of Action #1 in an Action #2 that constitutes civil litigation (1) where the parties to the subsequent litigation are the same as those to the initial action, (2) where the initial action produced a personal judgment for coercive relief from a civil court, and (3) where the subsequent litigation is in the same court system as the initial action. Special situations will be covered later, when consideration will be given to (1) the effects on nonparties, (2) the effects of less ordinary kinds of judgment, and (3) the effects of nondomestic judgments.

With that focus, I shall next sketch the general scheme.[3] Admittedly, authorities categorize and label the rules of res judicata in various ways. But the modern approach is first to divide the doctrine into claim preclusion and issue preclusion, and then to subdivide and supplement this complex doctrine.[4]

1.　Claim Preclusion

Imagine an Action #1 for damages resulting in a valid and final personal judgment, and then an Action #2 in the same civil court between the same parties. As to claim preclusion, if the plaintiff won Action #1, generally his claim is extinguished by, or merged in, the judgment. He cannot maintain Action #2 on the same claim. Similarly, if the plaintiff lost Action #1, generally his claim is extinguished, or barred, by the judgment. If he brings Action #2 to try again, the defendant may plead res judicata and thereby stop him in his tracks.

Thus, outside the context of the initial action, a party may not relitigate a claim decided therein by a valid and final judgment, subject to certain exceptions of course. The judgment extinguishes the whole claim, precluding all matters within the claim that were or could have been litigated in that initial action. The claim is defined transactionally, so as to include all rights arising out of the set of connected facts.

This doctrine of claim preclusion subdivides into "merger" and "bar." On the one hand, if the judgment in the initial action was in the *plaintiff's favor*, the plaintiff's claim is said to merge in the

3. See Restatement (Second) of Judgments § 17 (1982) (laying out general scheme).

4. See Baker v. Gen. Motors Corp., 522 U.S. 222, 233 & n.5 (1998); Charles Alan Wright, Arthur R. Miller & Edward H. Cooper, Federal Practice and Procedure § 4402 (2d ed. 2002) (terminology).

judgment. The plaintiff cannot bring a second action on the claim in the hope of winning a more favorable judgment. However, the plaintiff can seek to enforce the judgment, and the defendant cannot then raise defenses that were or could have been interposed in that initial action. On the other hand, if the judgment in the initial action was in the *defendant's favor*, the plaintiff's claim is said to be barred by the judgment. The plaintiff cannot bring a second action on the claim in the hope of winning this time.

2. Issue Preclusion

What happens if, by virtue of some exception to claim preclusion, the plaintiff can maintain Action #2 on the same claim? Or what happens in the more common situation where the plaintiff and the defendant are involved in an Action #2 on a different claim, but that claim involves some issues common to Action #1? These situations entail the effect in Action #2 of decisions on issues in Action #1. Generally, any such decision is conclusive on the same issue in Action #2 if it was actually litigated and determined in Action #1 and if its determination was essential to the judgment in Action #1. For example, if the judge in Action #1 found the plaintiff negligent in causing an accident, the former defendant normally could use that finding against him to preclude the issue's relitigation in Action #2, which was brought by the former defendant for her own injuries in the accident.

Thus, outside the context of the initial action, a party may not relitigate the same issue of fact or law actually litigated and determined therein if the determination was essential to a valid and final judgment, subject to many exceptions of course. Issue preclusion applies only when claim preclusion does not. Unlike claim preclusion, which reaches even matters that could have been but were not litigated, issue preclusion reaches only matters that were actually litigated and determined.

This doctrine of issue preclusion subdivides into "direct estoppel" and "collateral estoppel." On the one hand, if the second action is on the *same claim* as the initial action, then the applicable variety of issue preclusion is direct estoppel. On the other hand, if the second action is on a *different claim*, then the applicable variety of issue preclusion is collateral estoppel.

3. Jurisdiction to Determine Jurisdiction

It is important to remember that res judicata can apply to an attack on a judgment, not in the ordinary course of review in the trial and appellate courts but in subsequent litigation. One question on attack may be the effect that the rendering court's determination rejecting a defense of subject-matter jurisdiction, territorial jurisdiction, or adequate notice has on the attack. This is a different kind of question from those posed by claim and issue preclusion: it does not involve preclusive use of a valid judgment, but instead involves preclusive use of prior determinations in order to establish validity.

In this setting, the desire for finality generally outweighs the concern for validity, giving the determination preclusive effect and thus generating a special variety of res judicata called jurisdiction to determine jurisdiction, earlier treated in detail.[5] That is to say, an affirmative ruling on jurisdiction or notice can foreclose relitigation of that prior determination of the existence of subject-matter jurisdiction, territorial jurisdiction, or adequate notice and so preclude the parties from attacking the resultant judgment by raising that ground in subsequent litigation.

The doctrine of jurisdiction to determine jurisdiction is a third body of res judicata law, separate from claim and issue preclusion. It is obviously similar to issue preclusion, but it differs in several respects. First, issue preclusion requires a valid prior judgment. Jurisdiction to determine jurisdiction does not require validity, but instead works to make invulnerable what could otherwise be an invalid judgment. Second, issue preclusion applies only in a subsequent action, and so does not apply on a motion for relief from judgment, which is technically a continuation of the initial action.[6] Jurisdiction to determine jurisdiction, however, does apply to preclude a validity attack by such a motion, as well as by the other methods for relief from judgment.[7] Third, issue preclusion usually does not work to bind the party prevailing on the issue. Jurisdiction to determine jurisdiction will preclude the successful plaintiff if the unsuccessful defendant would be precluded on the jurisdiction or notice issue.[8] Fourth, issue preclusion applies only to issues actually litigated and determined. Jurisdiction to determine jurisdiction sometimes applies to issues of subject-matter jurisdiction that were not litigated at all, and even against a defaulting party. Fifth, and most importantly, special policies and concerns are at work with respect to the jurisdiction and notice defenses, so the law needs to develop special rules and exceptions for jurisdiction to determine jurisdiction.

---

5. See supra § 4.4(B)(2).

6. See, e.g., Harduvel v. Gen. Dynamics Corp., 801 F. Supp. 597, 601 (M.D. Fla. 1992) (involving Fed. R. Civ. P. 60(b)).

7. See, e.g., Nemaizer v. Baker, 793 F.2d 58, 64–66 (2d Cir. 1986) (involving Fed. R. Civ. P. 60(b)).

8. Cf. McDonald v. Mabee, 243 U.S. 90 (1917) (holding that plaintiff can collaterally attack default judgment, as could defendant).

4. Related Doctrines

To understand res judicata, one must distinguish it from numerous related doctrines that fall under the rubric of former adjudication.[9] Together they reflect the determination that courts do not and should not proceed as if writing on a blank slate, because former adjudication does and should affect future adjudication.

a. Stare Decisis

Intended to give stability to the law and to improve judicial performance, this doctrine provides that a court's holding on a legal question will normally be followed without serious reconsideration, by the same court and any lower courts in that judicial hierarchy, in future cases presenting undistinguishable facts.

Contrasted with res judicata, stare decisis (1) permits courts to handle precedent more flexibly, (2) applies only to issues of law, as well as only to holdings and not to dicta, and (3) governs even in cases involving wholly new parties on both sides.

b. Law of the Case

Intended to foster judicial economy, this doctrine provides that a court, and any coordinate or lower courts as well, will normally adhere to a ruling it has declared in a particular action if a party later raises the point again in the same action. It means that a question once resolved in the course of litigation will not lightly be reconsidered, except by a higher court.

Contrasted with res judicata, law of the case (1) applies very flexibly, so that the rendering court and coordinate courts can revisit the ruling if convinced it was wrong, (2) applies traditionally to issues of law, although it can apply to mixed issues or issues of fact, and (3) applies only in the one case at hand, even before res judicata kicks in.

c. Former Adjudication as Evidence

When a judgment does not receive conclusive effect in a subsequent action pursuant to res judicata, one might wonder whether it is admissible therein as probative evidence on a common issue. It is not. It is normally inadmissible on hearsay grounds, being a prior

---

9. See generally Robert C. Casad & Kevin M. Clermont, Res Judicata: A Handbook on Its Theory, Doctrine, and Practice 13–27 (2001) (citing sources; also distinguishing double jeopardy, in the course of discussing a previously rendered adjudication's impact in subsequent criminal litigation).

statement offered for its truth. Generally, then, a judgment either has conclusive effect under the rules of res judicata or has no effect at all.

However, the hearsay rule is relaxed in certain circumstances to allow introduction of a judgment into evidence. The main statutory and judicial exceptions involve certain administrative findings, antitrust judgments, findings of patent validity, and criminal convictions. For example, a felony conviction is usually admissible in a subsequent civil action.[10]

Civil-law countries heavily employ this evidential use rather than expand their doctrine of res judicata. U.S. res judicata is distinctively a good deal more expansive than res judicata law in other countries. One could argue that the United States should have taken the same route as the civilians. Such a practice would give to all rulings an effect similar to the effect that stare decisis gives to legal rulings. The arguments against extending evidential weight to factual findings are that combining a past decision with new evidence, especially new oral evidence, is a bit like combining apples and oranges; that our jury system especially might have trouble in weighing a past decision; and that the evidential approach lacks res judicata's advantage of altogether avoiding trial, which is a more burdensome procedural stage in our system. Therefore, the United States has in the main rejected this route.

d.　Former Recovery

Intended to prevent double recovery, this distinctive doctrine provides in accord with common sense that an award by judgment will be diminished by the amount recovered on any earlier judgments for the same injury.

e.　Estoppel

This doctrine, in its most important subdoctrine named "equitable estoppel," provides that a party generally may not take a position in litigation when that position is inconsistent with earlier conduct and the change would unfairly burden another party who has detrimentally relied. For an example of when this many-faceted and ill-bounded subdoctrine might apply, consider the situation of a party having recovered worker's compensation for an accident and then in subsequent tort litigation unfairly trying to deny that she was an employee.

Contrasted with res judicata, the flexible subdoctrine of equitable estoppel looks to the party's earlier out-of-court or in-court

---

10.　See infra § 5.5(C).

conduct, rather than to a prior judgment. Thus, equitable estoppel can usefully complement res judicata.

Another subdoctrine that some people confuse with res judicata is "judicial estoppel." This controversial subdoctrine, which varies widely from jurisdiction to jurisdiction and which is even rejected outright in a good number of states and federal circuits, holds that a person generally may not take factual positions in litigation that are directly inconsistent with positions previously taken by the person in a prior proceeding. Usually the subdoctrine applies only to statements made under oath. Abuse of the court by violation of the oath seems to be the main justification for the subdoctrine, although sometimes courts give different rationales, some courts apply it to statements that were not verified under oath, and a few courts use the term indiscriminately. The law might be better off without the subdoctrine, while allowing use of the inconsistent prior statements, whether or not under oath, as evidence in the later action under the normal rules of evidence.

Judicial estoppel differs from equitable estoppel in that it does not require detrimental reliance. It differs from the issue-precluding effect of res judicata in that it does not require the prior rendering of a judgment.

f. Election of Remedies

Also focusing on party-conduct, this doctrine provides that a party who ordinarily would have a choice among alternative remedies can disentitle himself to one or more of those remedies by engaging in conduct deemed inconsistent therewith. For example, alteration of a purchased chattel may foreclose rescission as a remedy for fraud, leaving damages as the only available remedy.

For another example, one that represents an increasingly outmoded view, mere commencement of an action seeking a particular remedy may foreclose other "inconsistent" remedies for the same wrong. This more "procedural" example of election of remedies represents the kind that people sometimes confuse with res judicata. But in today's legal systems, this old branch of election of remedies has no proper role to play.

g. Other Action Pending

Another doctrine provides the minor affirmative defense called other action pending, or prior pending action. It will result in dismissal without prejudice if another action on the same claim between the same parties was pending in the same state, or in the same federal district, when the instant action was commenced and if that other action is still pending. This doctrine tries to stop repetitive litigation in its tracks, well before any troublesome rendition of judgment. Although this approach seems a sensible way to reduce repetitive litigation, the defense is only narrowly applicable.

Thus, this doctrine's limited scope of application serves powerfully to underscore that the usual approach to redundant litigation is to allow a second case to proceed toward judgment despite earlier-instituted litigation. Although the action to go first to judgment should be res judicata in the other, the mere pendency of parallel proceedings is a commonplace with no ready general cure.[11]

B. Conditions for Applying Res Judicata: Validity and Finality

1. Validity

As the above summary of the doctrine indicated, for a judgment to have res judicata effects, it must be "valid." To be treated as valid, the judgment must be of sufficient quality to withstand an attack in the form of a request for relief from judgment. That formulation may sound circular, but it is not, as I shall explain.

Relief from judgment refers to procedural techniques, other than in the ordinary course of review in the trial and appellate courts, for avoiding the effects of the judgment. Relief from judgment encompasses three major techniques: motion for relief, independent suit, and collateral attack.

First, a party may attack a judgment in the rendering court by a motion for relief from judgment.[12] This extraordinary motion is technically considered a continuation of the initial action. This is the preferred means of overturning a judgment, being the most direct and orderly technique.

Second, if adequate relief from judgment is unavailable by motion because of any applicable procedural limitations on use of such motion, a person may bring an independent suit against the judgment-holder to nullify or enjoin the enforcement of the judgment.[13] The essence here is a separate claim in equity, but one aimed directly at the prior judgment. This suit is preferably, but not necessarily, brought in the rendering court, which can exercise continuing jurisdiction.

---

11. See supra § 4.2(B)(2)(b), (C)(1)(b).

12. Compare, e.g., Bank of Montreal v. Olafsson, 648 F.2d 1078 (6th Cir. 1981) (applying Fed. R. Civ. P. 60(b) to give relief), with, e.g., Brandon v. Chica-go Bd. of Educ., 143 F.3d 293 (7th Cir. 1998) (denying relief).

13. See, e.g., Britton v. Gannon, 285 P.2d 407 (Okla. 1955) (entailing direct attack asserted as equitable counterclaim or defense).

Third, if someone in a subsequent action relies on a prior judgment as a basis for claim or defense, as in a subsequent action where the plaintiff sues upon the judgment to enforce it or where the defendant pleads res judicata, the opponent may in that subsequent action attack the judgment to prevent its use.[14] The court will entertain this attack if adequate relief by another procedural technique is not available and more convenient. This is most often called a collateral attack, in distinction to a direct attack that comes as a challenge to a judgment in a proceeding brought specially for that purpose. Because invocation of res judicata tends to provoke collateral attack, the study of res judicata frequently involves problems of collateral attack.

Grounds for attack by these techniques have changed with time, evolving from a fairly rigid listing of grounds to a fluid approach.

Traditionally, motions and independent suits for relief from judgment have been limited to cases of extraordinary harm, being designedly not cures for carelessness. Vulnerable were judgments involving lack of subject-matter or territorial jurisdiction or lack of adequate notice, and in addition judgments resting on severe equitable flaws like fraud.[15] Collateral attacks have been even more limited. The traditional and useful rule of thumb there has been that a collateral attack will succeed on the ground that the rendering court failed to satisfy the requirement of (1) subject-matter jurisdiction, (2) territorial jurisdiction, or (3) adequate notice. Indeed, such an attack will succeed *only* on one of those three grounds and not on the ground of any other error, which should have been corrected on appeal or direct attack.[16] Therefore, a judgment can be valid and so have res judicata effects even though other errors were committed that would have warranted reversal on appeal.

The ultramodern view is that courts should, and to some extent apparently do, approach relief from judgment as a discretionary balancing of equities. Various factors determine the availability of relief:

(1) the nature and importance of the judgment's alleged infirmity;

(2) the technique of relief from judgment employed, this being based on the view that such techniques form a spectrum and that the list of available grounds for relief should contract as

---

14. See, e.g., Marshall v. Lockhead, 245 S.W.2d 307 (Tex. Civ. App. 1952) (entailing collateral attack on prior judgment in course of action to recover land).

15. See Restatement of Judgments ch. 5 (1942).

16. See id. § 4.

the mode, place, and time of attack become more distant from the initial action;

(3) the impact of the relief requested; and

(4) the position of the parties, including diligence in seeking relief and reliance on the judgment.

Under this fluid approach, it can still be said that judgments usually are treated as valid for res judicata purposes if and only if they meet the requirements of subject-matter jurisdiction, territorial jurisdiction, and adequate notice. But there are exceptions. Sometimes and for some purposes judgments not meeting those three requirements have effect,[17] and other judgments meeting those three requirements do not have effect when all the above factors are taken into account.[18]

Probably both traditional and ultramodern approaches are appropriate, but for different purposes. First, litigants and courts need a working sense of validity, especially prospectively. The traditional approach gives one by providing that a judgment would ordinarily prove valid if and only if the rendering court satisfied the requirements of subject-matter jurisdiction, territorial jurisdiction, and adequate notice. Using this rough definition, litigants and courts routinely defer to valid judgments, while disregarding the rare invalid judgment. Second, in the unusual and fuzzier situation of an actual subsequent attack on validity, the subsequent court will take account of a broad range of considerations. It can do so only by a discretionary balancing. So in fact courts will apply some version of the ultramodern view upon attack.

The law expresses this reality in its seemingly circular but actually retrospective definition of validity. It cannot define the prerequisite of validity except as the outcome of a process: to be valid, a judgment must be of sufficient quality to withstand an attack in the form of a request for relief from judgment.

2. Finality

For a judgment to have res judicata effects, it must also be "final." The rendering court must have uttered its last word on the decided claim or issue to qualify the ruling as final. The law does not want to preclude on the basis of the tentative, contingent, or provisional. The effective date of the judgment is its date of

---

17. See, e.g., Gschwind v. Cessna Aircraft Co., 232 F.3d 1342 (10th Cir. 2000) (subject-matter jurisdiction lacking); Marshall v. Lockhead, 245 S.W.2d 307 (Tex. Civ. App. 1952) (personal jurisdiction lacking); Restatement (Second) of Judgments §§ 65–66 (1982).

18. See, e.g., Lee v. Carroll, 146 So. 2d 242 (La. Ct. App. 1962) (collateral attack on fraud ground); Restatement (Second) of Judgments §§ 67–68, 70–74, 82 (1982).

rendition, having nothing to do with the date of the action's commencement. The judgment is final upon its rendering, and it stays final unless and until it is actually overturned. Under modern law, finality does not await execution on the judgment or expiration of the time to seek review, and finality remains unaffected by the taking of an appeal. Nevertheless, finality has a meaning slightly variable as between claim preclusion and issue preclusion.[19]

For the purposes of claim preclusion, a judgment becomes final when the trial court has concluded all regular proceedings on the claim other than award of costs and enforcement of judgment. A judgment is final even though a motion for new trial or an appeal is pending. But a determination of liability is not final if the trial court still has to determine damages, or if some other issue of law or fact involved in the merits stays open.

For issue preclusion, an adjudication is sometimes treated as a final judgment at an earlier stage. According to some recent authorities, the court in the second action has discretion cautiously to treat a prior determination as final if the initial court made a firm decision on the issue after adequate hearing and full deliberation, even though in that initial action there is as yet no final judgment on the whole claim.[20] But this fuzzy extension of issue preclusion in pursuit of rather small benefits can cause some major complications when later decisions come in the initial action, and so the better view is that the prerequisite for issue preclusion should return to the same strict standard of finality that applies for claim preclusion.[21]

More generally, according finality before appeal naturally raises concerns about the impact of an appellate overturning. If a judgment is modified (or reversed) by appeal (or otherwise), its preclusive effects will henceforth be in accordance with its modified terms.[22] If in the meantime some other judgment has relied on that prior judgment before the modification, then relief from the later judgment normally may be had by appropriate proceedings. Federal Rule of Civil Procedure 60(b)(5) authorizes, on motion to the court that granted the later judgment, the granting of relief from that judgment if, inter alia, "it is based on an earlier judgment that has been reversed or vacated." In states not having a comparable rule, the proper procedure to remedy the later judgment might be an

---

19. See Restatement (Second) of Judgments §§ 13–14 (1982).

20. See, e.g., Lummus Co. v. Commonwealth Oil Ref. Co., 297 F.2d 80, 89 (2d Cir. 1961) (this case, however, involved a situation particularly appropriate for early preclusion, because the prior ruling on an issue of fact had been definitively made by a court of appeals on interlocutory reversal of a preliminary injunction); Restatement (Second) of Judgments § 13 (1982).

21. See Avondale Shipyards v. Insured Lloyd's, 786 F.2d 1265, 1269–71 (5th Cir. 1986).

22. See Restatement (Second) of Judgments § 16 (1982).

independent suit to enjoin its enforcement. Restitution, if necessary, would also be available.

If by failure to invoke or apply res judicata two **inconsistent judgments** are rendered, then the judgment later rendered has the controlling preclusive effects.[23] This somewhat arbitrary provision is called the last-in-time rule. The rationale of the last-in-time rule may not be overwhelming, but does exist. The initial supporting argument is that one of the inconsistent judgments must prevail in order to avoid theoretically endless relitigation. Perhaps the second judgment is more apt to be right, as it resulted from relitigation and redetermination. At any rate, the party entitled to the benefit of res judicata in the second action was in a position to avoid the possibility of inconsistent judgments: if he failed to avail himself of the opportunity to invoke res judicata, and so allowed the matter to be relitigated, he is usually not entitled to complain when the second determination is treated as conclusive in a third action; if he did assert his right, but the second court erroneously denied it, he should have sought correction of the error by appeal from the second court, as with any other error by a trial court.[24]

Some authorities have suggested exceptions to the last-in-time rule. A plausible one relates to the case in which the second action is brought in a different state from the state of the first judgment's rendition; the court in the second action erroneously refuses to accord preclusive effect to the first judgment, in contravention of the Full Faith and Credit Clause and statute; and the appellate courts of the second state affirm, and then the U.S. Supreme Court denies certiorari. Should the last-in-time rule still govern when the matter is presented in a third action? It is arguable that the party claiming the benefit of the first judgment should not be bound by the preclusive effect of the second judgment, because the party could have done nothing more to avoid an inconsistent judgment.[25] But res judicata frequently enshrines erroneous judgments, including those to which the Supreme Court has denied certiorari: to be consistent, res judicata should protect the second judgment here by the usual last-in-time rule. Moreover, although this hypothetical scenario works well to expose, on peculiarly wrenching facts, the somewhat arbitrary nature of the last-in-time rule, the remaining reasons behind the rule push toward its application even in this

23. See, e.g., Treinies v. Sunshine Mining Co., 308 U.S. 66 (1939); Donald v. J.J. White Lumber Co., 68 F.2d 441 (5th Cir. 1934).

24. See Restatement (Second) of Judgments § 15 (1982).

25. See Ruth B. Ginsburg, Judgments in Search of Full Faith and Credit: The Last–in–Time Rule for Conflicting Judgments, 82 Harv. L. Rev. 798 (1969); cf. Restatement (Second) of Conflict of Laws § 114 cmt. b (1971) (raising the problem without taking a position).

extreme scenario: one judgment should prevail, and the second is more apt to be right on the merits.[26]

A more plausible candidate for an exception to the last-in-time rule arises if the second court in the hypothetical is not that of a sister state but instead is that of a foreign nation whose law differs from American law by denying preclusive effect to the first judgment. Now in the third court, an American court, the balance of policies might tip.[27] The effect of the foreign judgment falls outside the reach of the Full Faith and Credit Clause and statute. There was no possibility at all of getting a supranational court to "correct" the second court's denial of preclusion. Finally, the third court feels little motivation to honor the judgment of a foreign nation that refuses to honor American judgments.

§ 5.2   Claim Preclusion

A.   Rule

Outside the context of the initial action, a party (or his privy) generally may not relitigate a claim decided therein by a valid and final judgment, whether that judgment came about through litigation, default, dismissal, or consent. The judgment extinguishes the whole claim, precluding all matters within the claim that were or could have been litigated in that initial action. This doctrine of claim preclusion subdivides into merger and bar.

If the judgment in the initial action was in the plaintiff's favor, the plaintiff's claim is said to merge in the judgment. The plaintiff cannot bring a second action on the claim in the hope of winning a more favorable judgment. However, the plaintiff can seek to enforce the judgment, as by an action upon the judgment, and the defendant cannot then raise defenses that were or could have been interposed in that initial action.[28]

If the judgment in the initial action was in the defendant's favor, the plaintiff's claim is said to be barred by the judgment. The plaintiff cannot bring a second action on the claim in the hope of winning this time.[29]

In brief, claim preclusion prohibits repetitive litigation of the same claim once adjudged. The key requirement, then, is identity of claim. This requirement necessitates definition of a "claim."

---

26. See Wright & Miller, supra note 4, § 4404, at 65–75; cf. Parsons Steel, Inc. v. First Ala. Bank, 474 U.S. 518 (1986) (providing strong support for the last-in-time rule in the federal-state setting).

27. See Byblos Bank Europe, S.A. v. Sekerbank Turk Anonym Syrketi, 885 N.E.2d 191 (N.Y. 2008) (denying recognition of Belgian judgment).

28. See Restatement (Second) of Judgments § 18 (1982).

29. See id. § 19.

The old view, to which some jurisdictions still adhere, defined claim narrowly but foggily in terms of a single legal theory or a single substantive right or remedy of the plaintiff. Indeed, the courts used the term "cause of action" rather than claim.[30]

The modern, or "transactional," view is that a claim includes all rights of the plaintiff to remedies against the defendant with respect to the transaction from which the action arose. Whether particular facts constitute a single "transaction" is a pragmatic question, turning on the efficiency-fairness rationale of res judicata and therefore on such factors "as whether the facts are related in time, space, origin, or motivation, whether they form a convenient trial unit, and whether their treatment as a unit conforms to the parties' expectations or business understanding or usage."[31] Still, a claim will be big enough to include: (1) different harms; (2) different evidence; (3) different legal theories, whether cumulative, alternative, or even inconsistent; (4) different remedies, whether legal or equitable; and (5) a series of related events.[32] So, if P sues D for personal injury resulting from an automobile accident and later, after valid and final judgment, P sues D for property damage in the same accident, D can successfully plead claim preclusion under the transactional view.[33]

Even under the transactional view, however, the typical claim involves only a single plaintiff and a single defendant. That is, multiple parties on either side typically mean multiple claims.

The transactional view rests on the idea that the plaintiff *should* in a single lawsuit fully litigate his grievances arising from a transaction, considering that under the modern and permissive rules of procedure the plaintiff *may* do so. This requirement increases efficiency, with an acceptable burden on fairness. Accordingly, the plaintiff must be careful to put any asserted claim entirely before the court, because judgment will not only preclude actual relitigation but also preclude later pursuit of the claim's unasserted portion, that is, the part that could have been but was

---

30. E.g., Smith v. Kirkpatrick, 111 N.E.2d 209 (N.Y. 1953) (action on contract did not preclude later action off contract in quantum meruit), overruled by O'Brien v. City of Syracuse, 429 N.E.2d 1158, 1160 n.1 (N.Y. 1981) (adopting transactional view for New York).

31. Restatement (Second) of Judgments § 24(2) (1982).

32. See id. § 25.

33. See Rush v. City of Maple Heights, 147 N.E.2d 599 (Ohio 1958); Restatement (Second) of Judgments

§ 24 cmt. c, illus. 1–2 (1982). But see, e.g., Clancey v. McBride, 169 N.E. 729 (Ill. 1929) (second action not precluded under Illinois's old-style definition of claim). See generally Andrea G. Nadel, Annotation, Simultaneous Injury to Person and Property As Giving Rise to Single Cause of Action—Modern Cases, 24 A.L.R.4th 646 (1983). For other specific applications of the transactional view, contrasted with the old view, see Robert C. Casad & Kevin M. Clermont, Res Judicata: A Handbook on Its Theory, Doctrine, and Practice 69–82 (2001).

not litigated. Any plaintiff who asserts only a part of his claim is said to have "split" his claim.

Although in its early years the transactional approach was vigorously criticized as being too vague and leaving too much to the whim of the judge, in recent times it has come to be recognized that much of the certainty of application supposedly exhibited by the older approach was illusory. Judges can and will find ways to ameliorate the rigors of a test when the interests of justice seem to require it. The transactional test has the advantage of recognizing this fact of legal life and of focusing the inquiry upon factors that are really relevant to the administration of justice, rather than masking them under some largely artificial analytical concept. The transactional test maximizes the sum of efficiency and fairness concerns. Also, it clearly is more consonant with present-day legal reasoning than the older tests, as shown by the prevalence of transactional approaches in other contexts such as jurisdiction, joinder, and amendments. Consequently, the trend of decisions is toward ever wider acceptance of it.[34]

B. Exceptions

Predictably, this broad conception of claim preclusion has generated several significant exceptions.[35] As a result, the plaintiff sometimes is permitted to bring a second action on part, or all, of the same claim.

1. Jurisdictional or Procedural Limitation

Whenever the plaintiff is unable in his first action to present his entire claim because a jurisdictional or procedural limitation prohibits asserting a certain legal theory or demanding a certain remedy, he can bring a second action on that theory or for that remedy.

For example, if *P* sues *D* for fraud in state court and later, after judgment, *P* sues *D* on the same transaction in federal court under the Federal Securities Exchange Act, which is an action within the exclusive federal jurisdiction, there will be no claim preclusion.[36] Important to note here is that this exception allows

---

34. E.g., Porn v. Nat'l Grange Mut. Ins. Co., 93 F.3d 31 (1st Cir. 1996); Harrington v. Vandalia–Butler Bd. of Educ., 649 F.2d 434 (6th Cir. 1981); Williamson v. Columbia Gas & Elec. Corp., 186 F.2d 464 (3d Cir. 1950); Hennepin Paper Co. v. Fort Wayne Corrugated Paper Co., 153 F.2d 822 (7th Cir. 1946); O'Brien v. City of Syracuse, 429 N.E.2d 1158 (N.Y. 1981). But see, e.g., Herendeen v. Champion Int'l Corp., 525 F.2d 130 (2d Cir. 1975).

35. See generally Restatement (Second) of Judgments § 26 (1982).

36. See Staats v. County of Sawyer, 220 F.3d 511 (7th Cir. 2000); Cream Top Creamery v. Dean Milk Co., 383 F.2d

the plaintiff to preserve only the part of his claim that would clearly not be entertained by the first court. Thus, if in this example the plaintiff had chosen first to sue in federal court, he would there have had to assert both federal and state grounds in order to avoid losing them to claim preclusion, because the federal court could have invoked its supplemental jurisdiction to hear the state ground.[37] In sum, federal and state grievances resting on the same basic facts constitute a single claim; but if the plaintiff jurisdictionally cannot assert both, an exception applies to allow a later action in the other forum.

This jurisdictional-or-procedural-limitation exception allows the plaintiff to preserve a part of his claim only if he could not have joined it with the rest of his claim by selecting some other court in the same court system.[38] Thus, if the plaintiff voluntarily chooses to sue in an inferior state court of limited jurisdiction on a state-law claim and recovers the maximum amount that the court can award, claim preclusion will prevent his suing for any unrecovered excess in a state court of general jurisdiction. In sum, although res judicata does not force the plaintiff to abandon the state court system for the federal court system, it does effectively force the plaintiff into an appropriate court within the state system.

2. Party Agreement

The parties can agree that the plaintiff may split his claim. For tactical reasons, a defendant may expressly waive the right to avoid a second action on the same claim, that is, the defendant may consent to the splitting of the claim. Such agreement creates an exception to claim preclusion.

Moreover, the defendant might inadvertently acquiesce in splitting. The defendant might fail to assert the defense of res judicata when the second action is brought. Or if the plaintiff brings an action for personal injury and another action for property damage resulting from the same accident simultaneously in the same court, and the defendant defends on the merits without raising in either action the defense of other action pending, there will be no claim

---

358 (6th Cir. 1967); Restatement (Second) of Judgments § 26(1)(c) cmt. c, illus. 2 (1982).

37. See Belliston v. Texaco, Inc., 521 P.2d 379, 382 (Utah 1974) ("Since plaintiffs failed to assert their state claim, when the federal court had the power to adjudicate it with their federal claim, they are barred under the doctrine of res judicata from litigating these issues in the instant action."); Restatement (Sec-

ond) of Judgments § 25 cmt. e, illus. 10 (1982).

38. See Sutcliffe Storage & Warehouse Co. v. United States, 162 F.2d 849 (1st Cir. 1947) (U.S. district-court action jurisdictionally belonging in U.S. Court of Claims); cf. Davis v. Dallas Area Rapid Transit, 383 F.3d 309 (5th Cir. 2004) (holding that avoidable procedural impediment does not inhibit claim preclusion).

preclusion after one of the actions goes to judgment, because at least in these extreme circumstances failure to object to claim-splitting is deemed acquiescence.[39]

3. Judicial Permission

Unless prohibited by statute or rule, the court in the first action can specify that its judgment is "without prejudice" to bringing a second action on a portion or all of the same claim, or so provide in other words to that effect. It will so specify where special circumstances justify a second action, such as where only at the time of the prior trial could the plaintiff's counsel finally perceive the breadth of the claim and he now wants to pursue the omitted part.

The court in the second action will defer to a specification of this sort.[40]

4. Adjudication Not on the Merits

A judgment against the plaintiff may be given for various reasons that may have nothing to do with the substantive validity of the claim. For example, a claim may be dismissed for certain procedural defects in the form or manner of its presentation. A claimant should not be penalized to the extent of losing the right to a fair day in court on the substantive merits of the claim just because of such a technical error.

Formerly, to encapsulate this instinct, claim preclusion operated only if the judgment was rendered "on the merits."[41] Today that requirement has broken down to give preclusion wider application, although still certain truly threshold dismissals are treated as exceptions to claim preclusion.[42] The result is that today a dismissal will produce claim preclusion, unless there is some special policy reason to give the dismissed plaintiff another shot.

Thus, the old phrase of "on the merits" has become a bit misleading as a requirement for bar. A superior formulation would

---

39. See Todd v. Cent. Petroleum Co., 124 P.2d 704, 707 (Kan. 1942) ("If a party to an action seeks the benefit of the rule against splitting a single cause of action, he must claim its benefit on the institution of a second or unnecessary action at an early stage of the proceedings, otherwise he will waive his right to its benefit."); Restatement (Second) of Judgments § 26(1)(a) cmt. a, illus. 1 (1982); Wright & Miller, supra note 4, § 4404, at 52–58, § 4415, at 356; Joseph E. Edwards, Annotation, Waiver of, by Failing to Promptly Raise, Objection to Splitting Cause of Action, 40 A.L.R.3d 108 (1971).

40. See Restatement (Second) of Judgments § 26(1)(b) (1982); Wright & Miller, supra note 4, § 4413.

41. See Restatement of Judgments § 48 (1942).

42. See generally Restatement (Second) of Judgments § 20 (1982).

be to say that dismissal produces bar, subject to certain exceptions. That is, only certain dismissals not on the merits fall within an exception to bar, such as:

(1) most voluntary dismissals, as provided for example in Federal Rule 41(a);

(2) dismissals for lack of subject-matter jurisdiction or territorial jurisdiction, improper venue, inadequate notice, or nonjoinder or misjoinder of parties, as recognized for example in Rule 41(b); and

(3) most dismissals for prematurity of suit[43] or failure to satisfy a precondition to suit,[44] this exception being established by case law (note that Rule 41(b), despite its wording, is not read to be an exhaustive listing of such exceptions to the rule of bar.)[45]

Also, as explained above, the court in the first action can specify that its dismissal is not to act as a bar, and the court in the second action will defer to that specification.

Other dismissals, which are perhaps not in any real sense on the merits but which were preceded by an ample opportunity for the plaintiff to litigate his claim and which call for preclusion in accord with the policies behind res judicata, have of late come to operate as a bar, at least in the view of many courts and legislatures. Examples include:

(1) an involuntary dismissal for failure to prosecute or to obey a court order or rule, as suggested for example in Rule 41(b);

(2) a dismissal for failure to state a claim;[46] and

(3) a summary judgment, judgment on partial findings, or judgment as a matter of law, unless given on one of the above threshold grounds that do not generate bar.[47]

If the court in the first action takes upon itself to specify explicitly that its dismissal is "with prejudice" to an action elsewhere, the court in the second action will ordinarily give that specification great weight in deciding whether bar applies. If, however, the

---

43. See Waterhouse v. Levine, 65 N.E. 822 (Mass. 1903) (no bar when dismissed action brought before debt came due).

44. See Costello v. United States, 365 U.S. 265 (1961) (no bar when dismissal based on failure to file a required affidavit of good cause).

45. See id.; cf. Semtek Int'l Inc. v. Lockheed Martin Corp., 531 U.S. 497, 506 (2001) (reading Fed. R. Civ. P. 41(b) even more narrowly, as prohibiting only refiling the same claim in the same dis-

trict court and so leaving preclusion to the common law of res judicata).

46. See Rinehart v. Locke, 454 F.2d 313 (7th Cir. 1971); Restatement (Second) of Judgments § 19 cmt. d (1982); Wright & Miller, supra note 4, § 4439. But see, e.g., Keidatz v. Albany, 249 P.2d 264 (Cal. 1952) (second action not precluded under California's old-style approach to bar).

47. See Restatement (Second) of Judgments § 19 cmts. g-h (1982); Wright & Miller, supra note 4, § 4444.

earlier judgment was a dismissal inherently off the merits—as for lack of jurisdiction, improper venue, or party problems such as the absence of an indispensable party—then the second court should disregard the specification of prejudice; the first court may actually lack the power to dispose finally of a case not rightly before it, and it likely lacks any good reason to try to do so.[48]

Why Does the Statute of Limitations Get Unique Treatment?

The courts have developed a special rule for dismissals on limitations grounds, which will apply if the plaintiff later recasts his action or brings a new action elsewhere in an attempt to circumvent the statute of limitations: a dismissal on limitations grounds acts as a bar in courts applying the same jurisdiction's statute of limitations, but for reasons difficult to fathom it may not act as a bar to suit elsewhere on the same claim.

Perhaps the way to explain this rule is to resort to issue preclusion rather than claim preclusion. Although the first judgment may not have bar effect, it did determine the broad issue of the particular statute's application to that particular claim, however the claim is repleaded. The expiration of the statutory period for that claim was litigated and determined in dismissing the first suit, and relitigation of that issue should be foreclosed by principles of direct estoppel where but only where that same statute of limitations applies.

Nevertheless, courts persist in speaking in terms of bar or no bar: bar in the same jurisdiction, but usually no bar in another jurisdiction. Restatement (Second) of Judgments § 19 cmt. f, reporter's note (1982) restates this traditional doctrine, while questioning the soundness of the part of the doctrine permitting a second action in another jurisdiction after a judgment of dismissal based on the statute of limitations.

In fact, some courts are willing to accord bar effect to all nondomestic judgments based on the statute of limitations. Their reasons are many. First, the plaintiff has had his day in court, and the defendant should not have to suffer another. Fairness and efficiency are at stake. Second, the limitations defense is indistinguishable in policy from many defenses that are unquestionably on the merits such as the statute of frauds, and especially as the realm of bar has expanded to reach defenses like failure to state a claim. The usual rule is that when a plaintiff has lost under the law of one jurisdiction, that plaintiff faces bar in another jurisdiction even though under its law he would have won. Third, given that the limitations dismissal is a bar in the first jurisdiction, giving a different effect in the second jurisdiction is at least anomalous, if not actually in conflict with the principles of full faith and credit. Seemingly, if the dismissal is a bar in the first jurisdiction, then it should be a bar in the second. It appears, then, that the wave of the future will be to treat dismissals on the basis of the statute of limitations like other dismissals on the merits, that is, as creating a bar. See generally Robert C. Casad & Kevin M. Clermont, Res Judicata: A Handbook on Its Theory, Doctrine, and Practice 93–95 (2001).

---

5.   Generalized Exception

In general, the law is reluctant to recognize exceptions to claim preclusion.[49] But, in treating prior judgments, courts do show a

---

48. See Saylor v. Lindsley, 391 F.2d 965 (2d Cir. 1968); Restatement (Second) of Judgments § 20 cmt. d (1982);

Wright & Miller, supra note 4, § 2373, at 762–66.

49. See Federated Dep't Stores v. Moitie, 452 U.S. 394 (1981) (rejecting

limited amount of flexibility in making case-by-case exceptions to claim preclusion. One example of this generalized exception arises where specific reasons of constitutional, statutory, or other substantive policy counsel that the plaintiff should be allowed to split his claim.[50]

Sometimes the situation simply may be extraordinary. So, if the plaintiff has been misled by representations, concealment, or overreaching by the defendant, and the misleading caused the plaintiff to sue on less than the entire claim in the first action, the defendant will not be able to rely on the defense of claim preclusion when the plaintiff sues later for the part omitted from the first action.[51] However, a party trying to get within this extraordinary-situation exception must not only show an extraordinary need for an exception, but also show it clearly and convincingly. And the party probably should have to make the showing on a direct attack aimed at setting aside the judgment, rather than just suing again and making a collateral attack when the opponent invokes the judgment.[52]

C. Counterclaims

Claim preclusion also applies to claims asserted by the defendant against the plaintiff. The defendant who asserts a counterclaim is generally treated, with respect to that claim, as a plaintiff under the normal rules of claim preclusion.[53] The rarely applicable exception centers on the rule that if the defendant is unable to obtain an award for full recovery because of the court's jurisdictional or procedural limitations (e.g., a ceiling on damages in a court of limited jurisdiction from which the defendant could not transfer to a court of more general jurisdiction in the same court system), claim preclusion does not operate to preclude a subsequent action for the unrecovered excess in a competent court.[54]

The defendant who does not assert a counterclaim is generally unaffected by claim preclusion with respect to that claim. This majority rule is most difficult to justify when the facts forming the basis of the potential but formally unasserted counterclaim also constitute the basis of a defense that the defendant does assert.

---

loose exceptions to claim preclusion, like "simple justice" and "public policy," despite appealing facts).

50. See, e.g., White v. Adler, 43 N.E.2d 798 (N.Y. 1942) (refusing to preclude superintendent of banks for mistaken claim-splitting, where doing so would undermine regulatory scheme); Sopha v. Owens–Corning Fiberglas Corp., 601 N.W.2d 627 (Wis. 1999) (al-

lowing second asbestos action for later-developing cancer).

51. See, e.g., Hyyti v. Smith, 272 N.W. 747 (N.D. 1937).

52. See Restatement (Second) of Judgments § 26(1)(f), (2) (1982).

53. See id. §§ 21(1), 23.

54. See id. § 21(2).

Allowing a new lawsuit would seem to undercut the policy in favor of settling all related matters between the parties in a single action. But the thought is that the majority rule is relatively workable and less of a trap for the unwary, that the defendant's interest in selecting the forum for bringing her claim outweighs the undesirability of possibly duplicative litigation, and that here as elsewhere issue preclusion will apply to retrieve in part the policies behind res judicata.[55] Nevertheless, there are two important kinds of unasserted counterclaims on which claim preclusion does prevail even under the majority rule.[56]

First, a *compulsory counterclaim statute or court rule* might effectively provide that, under certain circumstances, failure to assert an available counterclaim precludes bringing a subsequent action thereon.[57] Note, however, that a compulsory counterclaim provision like Federal Rule of Civil Procedure 13(a) is literally full of exceptions, in both its subdivisions:

(1) *In General.* A pleading must state as a counterclaim any claim that—at the time of its service—the pleader has against an opposing party if the claim:

(A) arises out of the transaction or occurrence that is the subject matter of the opposing party's claim; and

(B) does not require adding another party over whom the court cannot acquire jurisdiction.

(2) *Exceptions.* The pleader need not state the claim if:

(A) when the action was commenced, the claim was the subject of another pending action; or

(B) the opposing party sued on its claim by attachment or other process that did not establish personal jurisdiction over the pleader on that claim, and the pleader does not assert any counterclaim under this rule.

The effect of a prior judgment in barring an unasserted compulsory counterclaim is most often described in res judicata terms.[58] However, rather than invoking the rigid doctrine of res judicata, some courts view this preclusion in the more flexible terms of equitable

---

55. See Schwabe v. Chantilly, Inc., 226 N.W.2d 452 (Wis. 1975) (asserting fraud defense in action for rent does not preclude later action for damages from fraud, in state without compulsory counterclaim provision); Restatement (Second) of Judgments § 22(1) (1982). But see Musco v. Lupi, 164 N.Y.S.2d 84 (Sup. Ct. 1957); Mitchell v. Fed. Intermediate Credit Bank, 164 S.E. 136 (S.C. 1932).

56. See Restatement (Second) of Judgments § 22(2) (1982).

57. See infra § 6.2(A)(2) for more complete discussion of the compulsory counterclaim provision.

58. E.g., Horne v. Woolever, 163 N.E.2d 378 (Ohio 1959); see Austin Wakeman Scott, Collateral Estoppel by Judgment, 56 Harv. L. Rev. 1 (1942).

estoppel or waiver, enabling them to preclude even when the prior action did not produce technically a judgment.[59]

Second, even in the absence of an applicable statute or court rule, failure to assert an available counterclaim precludes bringing a subsequent action thereon if granting relief would nullify the judgment in the initial action.[60] This so-called *common-law compulsory counterclaim rule* emerges from the intuitive principle of claim preclusion that a valid and final judgment generally precludes the defendant from later asserting mere defenses to the claim.[61] The implicit extension of this idea is that once a plaintiff obtains a judgment (whether the judgment was litigated or defaulted), the defendant generally cannot bring a new action to undo the judgment by reopening the plaintiff's claim and pushing those defenses (whether or not a compulsory counterclaim provision appears on the books or applies in the circumstances). The evident rationale is that claim preclusion simply must apply when the effect of the defendant's collaterally asserted defense would be to nullify the earlier judgment for the plaintiff, or otherwise judgments would not be worth obtaining.

This implicit barrier to collateral attack may seem to occupy some arcane corner of the specialty of res judicata. But the common-law compulsory counterclaim rule in fact is critical to any judicial system. That is, although it is intuitive, it is also important. Note first that the rule applies whether or not the prior judgment was by default. The rule indeed is especially important because it works to guarantee that default judgments mean something and cannot normally be undone by later litigation. Note also that the rule applies whether or not a compulsory counterclaim statute or rule of court exists. That fact explains why its very name declares it to be a common-law doctrine.

The common-law compulsory counterclaim rule (1) precludes a defendant seeking to impair the plaintiff's property interest declared by the initial judgment,[62] (2) precludes a defendant seeking restitution for money paid pursuant to the initial judgment,[63] and a fortiori (3) prohibits injunctive[64] or declaratory[65] relief against en-

---

59. E.g., Dindo v. Whitney, 451 F.2d 1 (1st Cir. 1971); see Wright & Miller, supra note 4, § 1417, at 132–38; Charles Alan Wright, Estoppel by Rule: The Compulsory Counterclaim Under Modern Pleading, 38 Minn. L. Rev. 423 (1954).

60. See Menard, Inc. v. Liteway Lighting Prods., 698 N.W.2d 738 (Wis. 2005); Kevin M. Clermont, Common–Law Compulsory Counterclaim Rule: Creating Effective and Elegant Res Judi-

cata Doctrine, 79 Notre Dame L. Rev. 1745 (2004).

61. See generally Wright & Miller, supra note 4, § 4414, at 344–48.

62. See Restatement (Second) of Judgments § 22(2)(b) cmt. f, illus. 10, reporter's note (1982).

63. See id. illus. 9, reporter's note.

64. See, e.g., Aerojet–General Corp. v. Askew, 511 F.2d 710 (5th Cir. 1975).

65. See, e.g., ACLU Found. v. Barr, 952 F.2d 457 (D.C. Cir. 1991).

forcement of the initial judgment. Thus, an uncontested judgment quieting title to real estate in the plaintiff precludes a later action by the defendant to claim title based on facts existing at the time of the earlier judgment. Also, if *P* sues *D* for contract damages, wins, and executes on the valid and final judgment, and if *D* later sues to rescind the contract and obtain restitution of the amount recovered, *D* will run into claim preclusion. Finally, the defendant is precluded from bringing an action for a declaratory judgment of nonliability after the plaintiff has obtained a favorable judgment on the same transaction, regardless of the jurisdiction's compulsory counterclaim provision.

But note that the narrow principle behind the common-law compulsory counterclaim rule applies only where the relief sought in the second action would inherently undo the first judgment. Thus, in the absence of a compulsory counterclaim statute or rule of court, *D* may default in *P*'s personal-injury action and then bring a separate action against *P* for *D*'s injuries sustained in the same accident, the idea being that a judgment for *D* for *D*'s injuries would not nullify *P*'s prior judgment for *P*'s injuries.[66] *D*'s recovery might be logically and practically incompatible, but it does not undo the prior judgment.

So also, although the defendant purchaser of goods should be precluded from suing for restitution after the plaintiff seller had obtained and executed on a default judgment for the contract price,[67] an action by the defendant seeking damages for medical malpractice (as opposed to return of the contract price for medical services paid pursuant to the default judgment) should not be precluded in the absence of a compulsory counterclaim statute or rule of court.[68] These examples also clarify that the defendant loses only the ability to defend anew the first action, not the ability to seek any relief arising from the transaction in question.

Those last few paragraphs expose that the scope of the common-law compulsory counterclaim rule is tricky. The rule applies to prevent a second action only if it seeks to nullify the first. Centrally, what does "nullify" mean precisely? The word has an unavoidable fuzziness that will trouble courts,[69] while both leaving defendants in doubt about their exposure ex ante and also providing

---

66. See Restatement (Second) of Judgments § 22(2)(b) cmt. b, illus. 1 (1982).

67. See Massari v. Einsiedler, 78 A.2d 572 (N.J. 1951).

68. See Gwynn v. Wilhelm, 360 P.2d 312 (Or. 1961). But see Harris v. Stein, 615 N.Y.S.2d 703 (N.Y. App. Div. 1994)

(incorrectly applying collateral estoppel after a default judgment).

69. See, e.g., In re Iannochino, 242 F.3d 36 (1st Cir. 2001) (deciding that allowing a malpractice claim would nullify a bankruptcy judgment that had awarded legal fees, given the peculiarities of bankruptcy procedure).

them room for maneuver in structuring their claims for relief ex post. Nevertheless, the fuzziness does not deserve exaggeration. Taking a wide view of the rule's purposes and of its genesis helps in determining its proper scope. Recall that it emerged as a specific means to effectuate the principle that a valid and final judgment generally precludes the defendant from later asserting mere defenses to the claim. Therefore, the defendant cannot later pursue an action that is essentially a way to defend anew against an already adjudicated claim.

§ 5.3   Issue Preclusion

A.   Rule

Claim preclusion aims at limiting the number of lawsuits that may be brought with respect to the same basic controversy. If claim preclusion applies, a whole second lawsuit on the same claim will terminate, regardless of what issues were or were not litigated in the first lawsuit. By contrast, issue preclusion concerns only repeated litigation of the same issues. Thus, issue preclusion would apply only if claim preclusion was inapplicable, either because an exception applied or because a different claim was in suit.

Outside the context of the initial action, a party (or his privy) generally may not relitigate the same issue of fact or of law, or the same mixed issue of law and fact, that was actually litigated and determined therein if the determination was essential to a valid and final judgment. That is, issue preclusion reaches only matters that were actually litigated and determined, not defaulted, admitted, or stipulated. And issue preclusion reaches only essential determinations, not dicta or other asides.[70]

This doctrine of issue preclusion rests on the premise that one court should be as capable as any other to resolve the issues in dispute. Once a judgment resolves the issues, after the adversary system of adjudication has run its full and fair course, the issues should not again be open to dispute by the same parties in any court. Issue preclusion not only accords with the dictates of fairness but also serves the interests of economy of judicial effort, fosters the certainty and stability of repose, and tends to prevent the anomalous situation, damaging to public faith in the judicial system, of two authoritative but conflicting answers being given to the very same question. Nevertheless, an overly aggressive doctrine of issue preclusion would be unfair to a person who had good reason

---

70. Compare Lumpkin v. Jordan, 57 Cal. Rptr. 2d 303 (Ct. App. 1996) (applying issue preclusion), with Cunningham Outten, No. Civ. A. 97C–10–014WLW, 2001 WL 428687 (Del. Super Ct. Mar. 26, 2001) (finding some new issues in second case). See generally Restatement (Second) of Judgments § 27 (1982).

to limit the scope of the prior litigation, and would instigate overlitigation of that prior litigation in anticipation of possible preclusion.

In brief, when claim preclusion does not apply, issue preclusion acts to prevent relitigation of essential issues. This doctrinal statement implies three requirements for application of issue preclusion: same issue, actually litigated and determined, and essential to judgment.

First, prohibiting relitigation of the same issue critically requires definition of an "issue." As already mentioned, the issue can be factual, legal, or mixed in nature. As to the dimensions of a particular issue, the modern, or "functional," view is that the scope of an issue should be determined in light of the efficiency-fairness rationale of res judicata. Whether a matter to be presented in a subsequent action constitutes the same issue as a matter presented in the initial action is a pragmatic question, turning on such factors as the degree of overlap between the factual evidence and legal argument advanced with respect to the matter in the initial action and that to be advanced with respect to the matter in the subsequent action.

Consider two contrasting illustrations. In a litigated tort action that the allegedly speeding defendant won because of the plaintiff's failure to prove negligence, an issue was the broad matter of the defendant's negligence, thus precluding in a subsequent action between the parties the plaintiff's assertion of a different manner in which the defendant may have been negligent in that incident, such as by drunkenness.[71] It was efficient and fair to require the plaintiff to air all negligence grounds in the first action, because of the heavy overlap of factual evidence and legal argument between grounds of negligence. However, in an installment contract action that the plaintiff won, the sole litigated and determined issue was the narrow defensive matter of the contract's illegality, thereby leaving open the defense of the contract's nonexecution as a different issue in a subsequent action on the different claim for a later installment.[72] In view of the differing factual evidence and legal argument for the two defenses, it was not efficient and fair to require the defendant to air both defenses in the first action.

---

71. See id. § 27 cmt. c, illus. 4 (1982); cf. Little v. Blue Goose Motor Coach Co., 178 N.E. 496 (Ill. 1931) (holding that a finding of due care precludes, by inference, an issue of willful and wanton misconduct).

72. See Jacobson v. Miller, 1 N.W. 1013 (Mich. 1879) (holding that nonoccupancy of premises and nonexecution of lease are different issues). But see Denio v. City of Huntington Beach, 168 P.2d 785 (Cal. Ct. App. 1946) (expanding the definition of issue, in light of foreseeability of future litigation, to be defendant's obligation to pay). For other specific applications of the functional view, see Robert C. Casad & Kevin M. Clermont, Res Judicata: A Handbook on Its Theory, Doctrine, and Practice 117–23 (2001).

Fixing the dimensions of an issue certainly is critical to the reach of issue preclusion. Broadly or narrowly defining "issue" means either a widely applicable doctrine, which starts to overlap with claim preclusion as it reaches matters not really contested, or an insignificant doctrine, which would extend only to absolutely indistinguishable questions. The difficulty is that it is always possible as a logical matter to state an issue in a variety of ways, in ascending levels of generality. Courts certainly do not fix the issue in the narrowest terms possible, nor do they readily resort to the broadest terms possible. Instead, the courts fix the issue in-between, in accordance with the particularistic dictates of efficiency and fairness, and guided primarily by what the parties actually contested unless the former question is evidentially and legally as much a unity as negligence is.

Note finally that if a different legal standard applies in the second action,[73] or if the facts have changed,[74] then the issue is different, so preventing issue preclusion. Changed circumstances do change the issue. If the invoker of issue preclusion makes a prima facie showing in support of the issue preclusion rule but the invokee challenges the identity of issues, the invoker must show that the two cases involve the same issue.

Second, for preclusive effect, the issue must have been actually litigated and determined. The meaning here is that the potentially bound and benefited parties must have submitted the issue for determination (by the pleadings or otherwise) and that their adjudicator must have decided the issue (whether by careful weighing of evidence and arguments or by mechanical application of some rule like the burden of proof). Thus, issue preclusion can result from a motion decided on papers or after full-blown trial, but it does not result from admission or stipulation or from a default or consent judgment. The idea is that a rule of issue preclusion without the actually-litigated-and-determined requirement would unnecessarily and undesirably intensify litigation without sufficient offsetting benefits.

Some cases have departed from this requirement in order to apply issue preclusion to default judgments.[75] The theory of these

73. See Levy v. Kosher Overseers Ass'n of Am., 104 F.3d 38, 43 (2d Cir. 1997) (holding that similarity issue in trademark registration action differs from issue in trademark infringement action); Jim Beam Brands Co. v. Beamish & Crawford Ltd., 937 F.2d 729, 734 (2d Cir. 1991) (holding that required public confusion in trademark cancellation action differs from required public confusion in trademark infringement action, and so is different issue).

74. See Berlitz Schools of Languages of Am. v. Everest House, 619 F.2d 211, 216 (2d Cir. 1980) (dictum) (saying that differences in size of printed disclaimer can produce different issues in trademark actions).

75. See E.H. Schopler, Annotation, Doctrine of Res Judicata As Applied to

cases is that the truth of all the facts alleged by the plaintiff and necessary to the recovery are raised by the plaintiff's pleading, and the defendant should not be able to escape the effect of judgment by waiving the right to contest them. Others have treated consent judgments similarly, in spite of the usual rule.[76] However, these cases' approach is not only unfair and inefficient, but also fictional in treating as established the facts that were never decided. Although a default or consent judgment can have claim preclusion effect, it should not ordinarily generate issue preclusion.[77]

Third, under the majority view, issue preclusion applies only to a determination that was essential to judgment. Thus, a determination not strictly necessary to reaching the court's ultimate result is not binding. Some submitted issues actually determined may have no bearing on the ultimate outcome of the case, and some issues may be decided against the party who ultimately wins the judgment, but such determinations, even though the apparent products of actual and vigorous litigation, do not have issue-preclusive effect. The idea behind this requirement is that a nonessential determination is in the nature of dicta and so may not really have been fully and fairly contested and considered, and also appeal on it may have been unavailable or the parties may have been unmotivated to appeal. Moreover, society wants neither to stimulate the parties to fight further over such asides nor to encourage courts so to make unnecessary pronouncements.

For example, in a state following the common law's contributory-negligence rule, if the court specifically found in an accident case both that the plaintiff had been contributorily negligent and that the defendant had been negligent, the determination of the latter issue would have no issue-preclusive effect, because it was not essential to the judgment rendered.[78] That is, the contributorily negligent plaintiff would have lost the case, whether or not the defendant had been negligent. Therefore, the court's finding on the defendant's negligence should just vaporize. Note, in particular, that no argument that the finding of the defendant's negligence was factually, legally, or logically primary or prior to the finding of

Default Judgments, 77 A.L.R.2d 1410, 1425–30 (1961).

76. See Sheldon R. Shapiro, Annotation, Modern Views of State Courts as to Whether Consent Judgment Is Entitled to Res Judicata or Collateral Estoppel Effect, 91 A.L.R.3d 1170, 1183–91 (1979).

77. See Arizona v. California, 530 U.S. 392, 414 (2000) ("But settlements ordinarily occasion no *issue preclusion* (sometimes called collateral estoppel), unless it is clear, as it is not here, that

the parties intend their agreement to have such an effect.").

78. See Cambria v. Jeffery, 29 N.E.2d 555 (Mass. 1940). But see Home Owners Fed. Sav. & Loan Ass'n v. Northwestern Fire & Marine Ins. Co., 238 N.E.2d 55 (Mass. 1968) (expanding issue preclusion to encompass findings not strictly essential but fully litigated and carefully determined), overruled, Rudow v. Fogel, 382 N.E.2d 1046 (Mass. 1978) (alternative holding).

the plaintiff's contributory negligence would succeed in overcoming the result of nonpreclusion.

As to the precise meaning of essential, one must look again to the policies of res judicata—and especially to whether the issue received active litigation and careful determination and to whether the loser on the issue had the opportunity to appeal—rather than to any literalism of essentiality. The second court does not parse the earlier judgment, seeing whether some ground logically narrower than the first court's ground of decision was possible, in order to get down to the bare essentials. Moreover, some litigated determinations not strictly or surely necessary, such as evidentiary decisions, have issue preclusion effect as long as they were links in the chain leading to judgment. In sum, decisions that led toward the judgment are essential, but not those that standing alone would have led toward the opposite outcome.

B. Exceptions

Courts apply issue preclusion quite flexibly, invoking many exceptions.[79] Efficiency concerns might counsel exceptions, especially the policy against encouraging parties to overlitigate by fighting every conceivable issue to the death. Fairness concerns also might suggest exceptions, as where there has been no full and fair opportunity to litigate. Finally, independent substantive policies might overwhelm the policies behind applying res judicata.

1. Certain Issues of Law

Courts tend not to apply issue preclusion to a relatively *pure* issue of law arising in a claim substantially *unrelated* to the claim in which it was previously determined. Also, courts tend not to apply issue preclusion to any issue of law on which it would create *inequity*, such as where binding someone to a legal ruling outmoded by a later change in the decisional law would cause troublingly different legal treatment of similarly situated people. In cases presenting these two situations, the law relies on the more flexible doctrine of stare decisis to guide the courts' handling of past legal rulings, rather than on issue preclusion.

First, a dispute over the proper legal standard or rule to apply, or what it exactly provides, is a pure issue of law. It could arise in different actions involving the same subject matter, say, successive actions on installment obligations or on repeated infringements. But it instead could arise in a totally unrelated claim; for example, the scope of the sovereign immunity defense could arise between

---

79. See generally Restatement (Second) of Judgments § 28 (1982).

the same parties in two totally separate tort actions, say, a plaintiff's slip-and-fall action against a municipality and then years later the same plaintiff's negligent-driving action against the same municipality. If the second action is substantially unrelated to the first, collateral estoppel effect should not be accorded to the fairly pure issues of law decided in the first action. It would be undesirable to hold the litigants bound for all times and for all purposes by a questionable ruling of law, as this would delay law reform. The interests served by the rule of issue preclusion hardly justify universally binding a party, while not binding other persons, to a possibly incorrect legal ruling—which might even involve the meaning of the Constitution—just because that party once litigated the legal issue in a different kind of case.[80]

Second, when there has been a significant change in the "legal climate" between the time of the earlier ruling and the later suit, issue preclusion effect—but not claim preclusion effect—may be denied to the earlier legal ruling even though the same event is involved in the later suit. An example could involve the tax effects of one business arrangement in successive tax years. The point of this exception to the issue preclusion effect of legal rulings is avoidance of the inequity that might result from perpetuating special treatment for one person, who once litigated the legal issue, when the same law currently prescribes different treatment for others similarly situated. Any significant change in the decisions interpreting the law that causes inequity should result in the denial of issue preclusion effect to issues of law or application of law to fact decided in an earlier case.[81]

This attention to changed legal climate is distinguishable from the changed-circumstances limitation on the rule of issue preclusion: when the governing law or facts involved in the second case differ from those in the first, the issue involved becomes a different issue.[82] Here the issue is exactly the same, the positive law not having changed, although the legal climate has evolved so that a court would now decide the issue differently. If that is so, and if the potential difference among persons' legal treatment is serious

---

80. See Montana v. United States, 440 U.S. 147, 162 (1979) (declining to apply "the exception which obtains for 'unmixed questions of law' in successive actions involving substantially unrelated claims" when two successive actions during the 1970s challenged constitutionality of state tax on public contracts and involved two sets of similar federal contracts); cf. Comm'r v. Sunnen, 333 U.S. 591 (1948) (applying old, and broader, exception exempting all but the most closely related issues of law).

81. See Comm'r v. Sunnen, 333 U.S. 591 (1948) (recognizing change in interpretation of tax law); United States v. Stone & Downer Co., 274 U.S. 225 (1927) (tariffs); Bishop v. City of Fall River, 191 N.E.2d 769 (Mass. 1963) (civil service laws); cf. United States v. Moser, 266 U.S. 236 (1924) (applying issue preclusion in the absence of intervening change).

82. See supra text accompanying notes 73–74.

enough to amount to an inequitable administration of the laws, then this exception to issue preclusion should apply. Because it is an exception, the burden of proof is on the invokee of issue preclusion, that is, the person seeking to avoid issue preclusion.

2. Inferior Rendering Court

Consider a subsequent action that is beyond the jurisdiction of the initial court. The court in the subsequent action will not carry over a determination by an inferior court having very much more informal procedures. Also, a court of special competence will not carry over a determination by a regular court if the jurisdictional scheme indicates a legislative intent against such issue preclusion.

First, if the procedures in the first action were not comparable to the better procedures available in the second action, in terms of quality and extensiveness, then the second court will not carry over the determinations of the first. On the one hand, a small-claims court is set up to render informal, quick, and cheap justice—often with lay judges, without legal counsel, and in the absence of rules of evidence. No one intended its determinations to control a court of general jurisdiction handling a much more serious claim.[83] On the other hand, this exception for informal procedures contemplates differences that cause mistrust of the earlier determinations. The absence of a jury right in the first action is not such a difference in procedure,[84] and merely a limited jurisdiction does not make out an exception.[85] In brief, the test is whether the invokee of issue preclusion had no full and fair opportunity, and motivation, to litigate the issue thoroughly in the first court.

Second, statutes purporting to confer on particular courts exclusive jurisdiction over certain subjects present the problem of whether issue preclusion effect will be given in such courts to judgments of other courts.[86] A common situation putting the problem into play arises when certain issues in a case over which the federal courts have exclusive jurisdiction have previously been litigated and determined in a state-court proceeding on a different claim. The resolution will turn on the legislative purpose in vesting exclusive jurisdiction in the particular courts. Thus, state rulings with regard to patents in licensing actions will carry over to the

---

83. See Sanderson v. Niemann, 110 P.2d 1025, 1030–31 (Cal. 1941) (small-claims court).

84. See Parklane Hosiery Co. v. Shore, 439 U.S. 322, 332 n.19 (1979).

85. See Gollner v. Cram, 102 N.W.2d 521 (Minn. 1960) (county court).

86. See, e.g., Loomis v. Loomis, 42 N.E.2d 495 (N.Y. 1942) (denying preclusive effect in state divorce action to prior state family-court determination of marital status).

exclusive federal jurisdiction for patent infringement actions,[87] but in other areas, where the legislative purpose against issue preclusion has been clearly expressed,[88] the state rulings will not carry over.[89]

3. Different Burden of Persuasion

Courts will not preclude an issue if the burden of persuasion in the subsequent action would be more favorable to the side that initially lost on the issue than it was in that initial action.[90]

For example, if the party who failed to carry the burden of persuasion on the issue in the first action would not have to bear it in the second, that party should not be precluded from relitigating it in the second suit. Similarly, even though the burden may be upon the same party in both actions, issue preclusion should not apply if the invokee of issue preclusion had a significantly heavier burden in the first action, or if the invoker has a significantly heavier burden in the second action. Thus, acquittal of the defendant in a criminal prosecution for theft of public property would not preclude the government in its later civil damage action against the defendant.[91]

4. Inability to Appeal

Courts generally will not bind a party on an issue if as a matter of law that party could not in the initial action have obtained appellate review on that issue. However, this exception would not apply when appeal was legally possible, but the party decided to forgo it because the economic motivation was inadequate or because the parties were settling after judgment.[92] Nor does the exception apply when appeal was legally possible, but the appellate court in its discretion denied review.[93]

What if the party who was *unsuccessful* on an issue nevertheless won the judgment? In this situation, normally the issue was

87. See Becher v. Contoure Labs., 279 U.S. 388 (1929); Syntex Ophthalmics, Inc. v. Novicky, 767 F.2d 901 (Fed. Cir. 1985); Vanderveer v. Erie Malleable Iron Co., 238 F.2d 510 (3d Cir. 1956).

88. See Kremer v. Chem. Constr. Corp., 456 U.S. 461, 468 (1982).

89. See, e.g., Brown v. Felsen, 442 U.S. 127 (1979) (not precluding certain issues in bankruptcy case); Lyons v. Westinghouse Elec. Corp., 222 F.2d 184, 188–89 (2d Cir. 1955) (holding, in this antitrust treble damage action, against issue preclusion by a prior state judgment in an accounting suit that had found the challenged conduct did not violate the antitrust laws).

90. See Wright & Miller, supra note 4, § 4422.

91. See infra § 5.5(C).

92. See U.S. Bancorp Mortgage Co. v. Bonner Mall P'ship, 513 U.S. 18 (1994).

93. See 18 Susan Bandes & Lawrence B. Solum, Moore's Federal Practice § 132.03[4][k] (3d ed. 2008).

not essential to the judgment rendered, so there would be no issue preclusion anyway. But what if the winning party was *successful* on an essential issue, but in a later case that issue's prior determination has become unfavorable to the party's position? Because one can appeal only rulings adverse to one's interests, usually this party could not have appealed. Therefore, the inability-to-appeal exception means that issue preclusion (in distinction to possible equitable estoppel) usually does not work to bind the party who prevailed on an issue.

5. Unforeseeability

In compelling circumstances, a court will not apply issue preclusion if such application was unforeseeable at the time of the initial action and such unforeseeability may have affected the effort therein by the party now sought to be precluded.[94]

The Second Restatement formulates its exception so that "preclusion should not operate to foreclose redetermination of an issue if it was unforeseeable when the first action was litigated that the issue would arise" again and if that the lack of foreseeability "may have contributed to the losing party's failure to litigate the issue fully."[95] In fact, the drafters of the Second Restatement warned that such exceptional cases should be rare and that relitigation should follow only a clear and convincing showing of need. Their examples of where this constrained exception for unforeseeability would apply included a factual determination as to a taxpayer's specific property that acquires tremendously greater financial significance in a second action after an intervening amendment to the tax code.

6. Generalized Exception

In compelling circumstances, a court will not apply issue preclusion when substantive policies overwhelm res judicata,[96] and a

---

94. See Hyman v. Regenstein, 258 F.2d 502, 511 (5th Cir. 1958) (dictum) ("collateral estoppel by judgment is applicable only when it is evident from the pleadings and record that determination of the fact in question was necessary to the final judgment and it was foreseeable that the fact would be of importance in possible future litigation"); cf. Evergreens v. Nunan, 141 F.2d 927, 929 (2d Cir. 1944) (dictum) ("Defeat in one suit might entail results beyond all calculation by either party; a trivial controversy might bring utter disaster in its train.").

95. Restatement (Second) of Judgments § 28(5)(b) cmt. i (1982).

96. See, e.g., United States v. La-Fatch, 565 F.2d 81 (6th Cir. 1977) (holding that application of res judicata based on a corporation's unsuccessful attempt in state court to recover $50,000 would violate public policy embodied in bribery and extortion law, where the corporation had reported to federal government La-Fatch's alleged solicitation of bribe and paid him $50,000 in cooperation with FBI).

court will not bind someone on an issue who for some reason lacked a full and fair opportunity to litigate it.

Indeed, the Second Restatement ends its treatment of issue preclusion by generalizing that the doctrine should not apply when the invokee lacked a full and fair opportunity, or incentive, to litigate the issue.[97] Here the risk that this exception will consume the rule is glaringly obvious. Therefore the drafters again warned that such exceptional cases should be rare and that relitigation should follow only a clear and convincing showing of need. Their examples for this exception made that point: where one party may have concealed from the other party information that would have materially affected the outcome of the case and there was a fiduciary relationship between the parties;[98] or where it is evident from the jury's verdict itself that it was the result of compromise.[99]

C. Multiple Determinations

Some special applications of issue preclusion illuminate how it works. Consider cumulative, ambiguous, and alternative determinations.

First, if several issues in a case were litigated and determined cumulatively, each is precluded provided that its determination was essential to judgment. For illustration, imagine that P sues D for extensive property damage to his car resulting from an automobile accident. D defends by denying both her own negligence and also P's ownership of the car. After trial, there is a valid and final judgment for P. Pursuant to an agreement between P and D permitting claim-splitting, P then sues D for personal injury in the same accident and invokes issue preclusion against D's negligence denial—note that negligence is the only relevant prior finding, because ownership is not an issue as to personal injury. Issue preclusion, or more precisely direct estoppel, will apply on negligence, because the issues of negligence and ownership were cumulatively essential to the earlier judgment. Indeed, a court commonly makes a series of rulings on issues to reach a judgment, and each of them can be a necessary step toward that judgment and so support issue preclusion.[100]

By contrast, if the judge trying the initial action ruled that D had been negligent but that P's nonownership prevented recovery,

---

97. Restatement (Second) of Judgments § 28(5)(c) cmt. j (1982).

98. See Spilker v. Hankin, 188 F.2d 35 (D.C. Cir. 1951) (attorney-client dispute over fees).

99. See Taylor v. Hawkinson, 306 P.2d 797 (Cal. 1957) (minuscule damages for personal injury).

100. See, e.g., Little v. Blue Goose Motor Coach Co., 178 N.E. 496 (Ill. 1931) (finding plaintiff's due care and defendant's negligence, both of which needed to be shown).

there would be no issue preclusion in the subsequent action because the finding of D's negligence was not essential to judgment.

Second, if the invoker of issue preclusion cannot show which of several possible issues was determined in a case, then the ambiguous determinations preclude none of the issues.[101] This is true even though it is clear that *some* issues were actually litigated, determined, and essential, but one cannot tell *which*. In the face of ambiguous determinations, the interest in judicial economy that would be promoted by preclusion is too weak to outweigh the party's interest in a chance to prove his case. So, if in preceding example D won the initial action by a jury's general verdict, and in the subsequent action D pled issue preclusion to refute her negligence, there would be no issue preclusion, because one cannot tell if the jury found nonnegligence or nonownership.

By contrast, if P were suing in the second action for further property damage to his car, pursuant to the claim-splitting agreement, then D could use the general verdict for issue preclusion, because either nonnegligence or nonownership would defeat the second action and the jury must have found at least one of those two in the first action.

Third, suppose instead of not knowing which route the decisionmaker took to judgment, we know that it took multiple and alternative routes to judgment. Whether then to preclude turns out to be a very close question. Some courts rule that if the adjudicator determined several issues in a case, and each of those alternative determinations without the others sufficed to support the judgment, then none by itself is precluded. And such is the "modern" view of the Second Restatement.[102] Returning to the recurring example, if D instead won the initial action by a jury's special verdict finding both nonnegligence and nonownership, and in the subsequent personal-injury action D pled issue preclusion to refute her negligence, there would be no issue preclusion. In such a case, although taking at least one of the alternative routes was essential to the judgment, no particular one was essential. The idea behind not precluding any determination is that any one of the alternative

---

101. See Russell v. Place, 94 U.S. 606, 608 (1876) ("If there be any uncertainty on this head in the record,—as, for example, if it appear that several distinct matters may have been litigated, upon one or more of which the judgment may have passed, without indicating which of them was thus litigated, and upon which the judgment was rendered,—the whole subject-matter of the action will be at large, and open to a new contention, unless this uncertainty be removed by extrinsic evidence showing the precise point involved and determined."); Herrera v. Reicher, 608 S.W.2d 539 (Mo. Ct. App. 1980). But see Kelley v. Curtiss, 108 A.2d 431, 435–36 (N.J. 1954) (rare case holding each of the ambiguous findings to be preclusive).

102. Restatement (Second) of Judgments § 27 cmt. i (1982) (relying on Halpern v. Schwartz, 426 F.2d 102 (2d Cir. 1970)).

determinations may not have been completely contested and carefully considered, and the loser may have been rightly discouraged from appealing by the strength of another alternative determination.

Nevertheless, even under this modern view, if there was an appeal, then any alternative determination that was affirmed is binding.[103] The idea is that the exercise of appellate review swings the balance of conflicting policies toward preclusion. Moreover, even without an appeal, issue preclusion will apply if all the alternative "issues" arise in the subsequent action, as they commonly would, and would in the earlier example of *P*'s bringing a second action for further property damage to his car.[104] The idea here is that the alternative rulings can then be viewed as merely alternative bases for an essential determination of a single issue more broadly defined.

Older authority on this problem of alternative determinations held each determination to be precluded, in order to avoid wasteful relitigation.[105] And now the old view seems to be regaining favor in the courts.[106] A good argument against the Second Restatement's modern rule is that under it *D* is in a worse position after winning on two issues than if she had won just on nonnegligence. That is bizarre. What could her attorney have done to avoid this quandary? Not much, in the usual case. If *D*'s attorney abdicates on the ownership issue and litigates only negligence, this strategy avoids the modern rule for alternative determinations but risks losing the whole case—just imagine trying to explain that losing strategy to the client. *D*'s attorney might instead attempt to get the judge to cooperate in subverting the rule by reaching the nonownership issue only if necessary—but such cooperation is unlikely to be forthcoming and efficacious. Thus, the Second Restatement's rule can put a party in a serious fix for no great reason.

Upon balancing all considerations, it seems that the old rule in favor of preclusion for alternative issues is preferable. In the relatively few cases of inappropriate issue preclusion on alternative issues, such as in a situation of unforeseeability, the law can avoid issue preclusion by means of one of the varied existing exceptions to issue preclusion.

---

103. See id. cmt. o.

104. See id. cmt i, illus. 16.

105. See Restatement of Judgments § 68 cmt. n (1942) ("It seems obvious that it should not be held that neither is material, and hence both should be held to be material.").

106. See Monica Renee Brownewell, Note, Rethinking the Restatement View (Again!): Multiple Independent Holdings and the Doctrine of Issue Preclusion, 37 Val. U. L. Rev. 879 (2003).

§ 5.4   Effects on Nonparties

A.   Privies

The conclusory label of privy is used to describe people who were nonparties to an action but who in certain circumstances are nevertheless subjected to generally the same rules of res judicata as are the former parties, the basis for this treatment being some sort of representational relationship between a former party and the nonparty.

This preclusive treatment does not contravene the Constitution, because all that due process guarantees is a full and fair day in court enjoyed in person *or through a representative*.[107] Due process indeed allows binding many more nonparties than most persons assume. A court's judgment could bind almost all persons whose interests received representation, binding them not only through the flexible doctrine of stare decisis, as it does, but also through the strictures of res judicata, as it could. Society, however, has chosen, as expressed in its res judicata law, to go much less far in binding nonparties by judgment than it constitutionally could. Res judicata will bind only those nonparties closely related to the representative party or, as the law phrases it, those in privity with the party.[108]

So the initial task is to specify which nonparties the law has chosen to consider privies for purposes of res judicata. To induce that choice, some substantial reasons in policy must exist to bind a nonparty, and they must outweigh the social costs of binding a nonparty. Then, for the various kinds of nonparties who thus are potential candidates for binding, the law tries to draw a set of clear, simple, and rigid rules that together approximate that balancing of benefits and costs. To generalize about those rules, there are two basic categories that constitute privity for res judicata purposes: procedural privity and substantive privity.

First, procedural privies include persons who were actually represented in the litigation by a party, thus including beneficiaries represented by a trustee or executor, as well as class-action members adequately represented by their class representative.[109] A similar idea makes privies of persons who assumed control of the prosecution or defense of an action and persons who agreed to abide by an action between others, as a liability insurance company might

---

107. See Robert G. Bone, Rethinking the "Day in Court" Ideal and Nonparty Preclusion, 67 N.Y.U. L. Rev. 193 (1992).

108. See Tice v. Am. Airlines, 162 F.3d 966 (7th Cir. 1998) (holding that adequate representation is not enough to constitute privity).

109. See Restatement (Second) of Judgments §§ 41–42 (1982).

do but as an amicus curiae does not.[110] Yet res judicata does not bind all persons represented by parties. That is, it does not extend to the limits of "virtual representation," as the phrase goes in describing merely common interests shared by party and nonparty;[111] nor does res judicata impose a general duty to intervene.[112] Instead, the required relationship must be closer. It must be representation plus something else. That something might be a relationship sufficiently ensuring alignment and protection of interests, or some sort of affirmative conduct signifying consent to representation.

Second, substantive privies include persons who have or had any one of a wide variety of stronger substantive relationships with a party, where that relationship in a sense created at least a weak representative role, e.g., successors in interest, bailors and bailees, assignors and assignees, indemnitors and indemnitees, family members, co-obligors, co-obligees, associations, and partnerships. For a specific example, a successor in interest to property is a privy with respect to a judgment's determining his predecessor's interest in that property.[113] For a quite different example, a member of a partnership is to a limited extent deemed a privy with respect to a judgment to which her partner was a party: generally, if an injured person sues a partner upon a liability incurred in the course of partnership business and wins, the judgment renders the property of the partnership subject to execution; if instead a partner sues an outsider upon a claim on behalf of the partnership, the judgment extinguishes the partnership's claim, and also gives rise to issue preclusion in any subsequent action concerning rights and duties of the partnership; but otherwise, the nonparty partners are not bound merely by virtue of their partnership.[114]

As just implied by that last example, an additional task is to specify the treatment privies will receive. Generally, a procedural or substantive privy is *bound* by and entitled to the *benefits* of claim and issue preclusion as though the privy stood in the shoes of the related party. But it is obvious that the various kinds of privies differ widely in nature, and especially in the nature of the relationship of privy to party. Where the intensity of the privity relation-

---

110. See Gen. Foods Corp. v. Mass. Dep't of Pub. Health, 648 F.2d 784 (1st Cir. 1981); Restatement (Second) of Judgments §§ 39–40 (1982).

111. See Taylor v. Sturgell, 128 S.Ct. 2161, 2176 (2008) (holding that the federal res judicata law does not bind on the basis of virtual representation, but instead requires, in addition to alignment of interests, "either the party understood herself to be acting in a representative capacity or the original court took care to protect the interests of the nonparty").

112. See Show–World Ctr. v. Walsh, 438 F. Supp. 642 (S.D.N.Y. 1977) (holding that tenant is not in privity with landlord, despite having been virtually represented and having had opportunity to intervene).

113. See Restatement (Second) of Judgments §§ 43–44 (1982).

114. See id. § 60.

ship tails off, as it does in the partnership example, qualifications and exceptions start sprouting up, principally with respect to the binding effects of the judgment. As a result, the only safe generalization here is that this subject is dominated by many complicated rules tailored to particular situations. Indeed, the Second Restatement treats in more than twenty separate sections the specific classes of nonparties falling to some degree within the reach of the claim and issue preclusion rules of res judicata.[115] And as always, each jurisdiction's res judicata law could differ on this subject.

B. Strangers

A person who had little or nothing to do with a judgment might benefit from its res judicata effects without generating intense concern, but the judgment cannot bind such a person who is neither party nor privy. Good policy entitles such a person to a day in court before a judgment has any legally binding effect on that person. That person is called a stranger to the judgment.

Another kind of person treated as a stranger is a party who litigated the initial action in a particular posture that prevented a full and fair opportunity to represent the person's full range of interests. For example, a party might have litigated in one capacity and now appears in a subsequent action in another capacity; the two capacities are deemed two different persons, with the latter capacity being in the position of a stranger; thus, someone who sued as a trustee for others is not precluded in a later action that she brings as an individual. This cautious approach to preclusion supposedly ensures a full and fair opportunity to litigate, while it avoids potential conflicts of interest.[116]

In brief, a stranger to a prior judgment cannot be bound by it. However, the stranger could conceivably benefit from it. The most important form of potential benefit is a stranger's using the prior judgment for collateral estoppel against a former party.[117] This possibility deserves careful consideration, which I shall now attempt.

The old doctrine of mutuality of estoppel held that a person may not benefit from a prior judgment if he would not have been bound by any outcome of that initial action. Because strangers were never bound, they could therefore never benefit. Thus, a judgment's estoppels were mutual. Unless both persons could have been

---

115. Id. §§ 39–63.

116. See id. § 36; cf. id. § 35 (parties under incapacity are treated as strangers), § 38 (same for nonadverse parties). But cf. id. § 37 (treating nominal parties).

117. Cf. Wright & Miller, supra note 4, § 4464.1 (treating nonmutual claim preclusion for secondary-liability situations).

bound, neither was bound as to the other, according to this doctrine of mutuality.

There came to exist, however, substantial extensions of res judicata under the mutuality doctrine, allowing strangers in some compelling circumstances to benefit. The most important extension allowed a person whose liability was secondary to claim the benefit of issues adjudicated successfully by the one primarily liable. So if an injured person sues an employee and loses—the employee having been found not negligent—and if the injured person next sues the employer—who has only vicarious liability for the tort of the employee—then the employer can claim the benefit of the employee's judgment, even though he would not have been precluded had the employee lost.[118] Courts built on this justifiable secondary-liability extension, so as to allow preclusion in a range of facially similar situations involving some sort of derivative liability,[119] even including situations not posing a threat to indemnification rights or any equivalent threat.[120]

Eventually, mutuality of estoppel was rejected wholesale by the influential dicta of *Bernhard v. Bank of America National Trust & Savings Association*.[121] Most jurisdictions have since come to agree in some significant part. Thus, the "modern" view is that a stranger may invoke collateral estoppel against a former party, unless the former party lacked a full and fair opportunity to litigate the issue in the initial action or unless other special circumstances justify relitigation.[122]

Under the modern view, a *defendant in the subsequent action* can invoke collateral estoppel against a former party. Such "defensive use" by a stranger was authorized as part of the federal common law of res judicata by *Blonder-Tongue Laboratories, Inc. v. University of Illinois Foundation*.[123]

118. See Good Health Dairy Prods. Corp. v. Emery, 9 N.E.2d 758 (N.Y. 1937); Pinnix v. Griffin, 20 S.E.2d 366 (N.C. 1942) (preclusion as to maximum damages); Restatement of Judgments § 96(1) (1942).

119. See, e.g., Am. Button Co. v. Warsaw Button Co., 31 N.Y.S.2d 395 (Sup. Ct. 1941) (alternative holding), aff'd mem., 38 N.Y.S.2d 570 (App. Div. 1942) (if *A* sues *B* for breach of contract and loses because no breach was shown to have been committed, *A* is precluded from relitigating the same issue in a suit against *C* for inducing *B*'s breach).

120. See, e.g., Giedrewicz v. Donovan, 179 N.E. 246, 248 (Mass. 1932) (allowing the *indemnitor*, e.g., employee, to rely upon a prior judgment in favor of

the *indemnitee*, e.g., employer, to establish nonliability in a later suit by the same plaintiff). But see Restatement of Judgments §§ 96, 97, 99 (1942) (taking narrower approach than Giedrewicz).

121. 122 P.2d 892 (Cal. 1942) (Bernhard lost litigation against Cook over certain funds he had withdrawn from a bank account, and then in her action against the bank to recover those funds she was precluded on the issue of withdrawal's authorization).

122. See Kaufman v. Eli Lilly & Co., 482 N.E.2d 63 (N.Y. 1985) (DES litigation); Restatement (Second) of Judgments § 29 (1982).

123. 402 U.S. 313 (1971) (alleged infringer as defendant can preclude patentee as plaintiff on issue of patent invalid-

Although some jurisdictions balk at going further,[124] the modern view even permits a *plaintiff in the subsequent action* to invoke collateral estoppel against a former party. Such "offensive use" by a stranger was authorized as part of the federal common law of res judicata by *Parklane Hosiery Co. v. Shore*,[125] an astounding case stretching collateral estoppel to its limits.

Still, in an attempt to avoid real threats to fairness and efficiency, courts apply the modern view with great flexibility. They apply all the usual exceptions to issue preclusion. Additionally, courts exercise discretion to deny preclusion when the former party lacked a full and fair opportunity, or incentive, to litigate in the initial action or when all the circumstances otherwise justify allowing the former party to relitigate the issue. Factors affecting that discretion include among many others:

(1) whether there is some reason to suspect the accuracy of the prior determination, such as where it is inconsistent with some other adjudication of the same issue (a factor partially solving the "multiple-plaintiff anomaly," where a string of potential plaintiffs sue an alleged mass tortfeasor seriatim until one wins and theoretically so triggers collateral estoppel for all the future plaintiffs, thus creating an incentive for the most sympathetic plaintiffs to sue first and no incentive for all plaintiffs to join in a single lawsuit);

(2) whether the stranger could reasonably have been expected to join or intervene in the initial action (although in fact courts have seldom invoked this as a factor[126]); and

(3) whether the former party did not choose the occasion, adversary, and forum for the initial action (so extending needed protection to former defendants).

On the one hand, note that the absence of a jury right in the initial action is not such a factor, according to *Parklane*.[127] On the other hand, courts are creating a couple of blanket exceptions to nonmutuality. The Supreme Court simply declared offensive nonmutual collateral estoppel to be unavailable against the federal govern-

---

ity, using judgment in unsuccessful prior action brought by patentee against another alleged infringer).

124. E.g., Albernaz v. City of Fall River, 191 N.E.2d 771 (Mass. 1963); see Michael Kimmel, Note, The Impacts of Defensive and Offensive Assertion of Collateral Estoppel by a Nonparty, 35 Geo. Wash. L. Rev. 1010 (1967).

125. 439 U.S. 322 (1979) (securities plaintiff can preclude defendants in damages action, using judgment in suc-

cessful prior suit for injunction brought by SEC against same defendants). For the story of this case, see Lewis A. Grossman, The Story of Parklane: The "Litigation Crisis" and the Efficiency Imperative, in Civil Procedure Stories 405 (Kevin M. Clermont ed., 2d ed. 2008).

126. See Jack Ratliff, Offensive Collateral Estoppel and the Option Effect, 67 Tex. L. Rev. 63, 87 (1988).

127. 439 U.S. at 332 n.19.

ment,[128] and this relatively rigid exception probably now extends to defensive use and to state governments;[129] although this exception is highly questionable,[130] it has enormous numerical importance given the volume of governmental litigation. Also, the lower courts are creating an exception that prevents use of preclusion by opters-out from a successful class action.[131]

To summarize, the law faced a basic choice between the rule of mutuality, with a few defined extensions for secondary liability, and the rule of nonmutuality, with lots of mainly fuzzy exceptions. Most jurisdictions chose the latter approach, meaning that today a stranger can widely invoke nonmutual collateral estoppel, subject to full-and-fair-opportunity-like exceptions. Was this choice a good one? No.

The rationale behind modern nonmutuality is that the former party is entitled to only one opportunity to litigate an issue, regardless of any change in adversaries, and should inflict no more litigation. But perhaps this rationale elevates simplistic notions of efficiency over real concerns of fairness and substantive policy. Nonmutuality may inefficiently discourage plaintiffs from joining in a single lawsuit, yet instigate overlitigation during the initial action in anticipation of possible preclusion, as well as impose extra litigation about the application of res judicata in the subsequent action. Fairness argues for treating a decision between specific litigants as a contextual truth with limited effect, rather than as a determinate truth that free-floats to conclusiveness in all other contexts.

Most fundamentally, nonmutuality destroys the equivalence of litigating risk by weighting the scale against the common party, and so changes the most basic of the procedural system's rules, namely, procedure must provide a level playing field. Take the mass tort as an example: the first plaintiff risks losing only the one case, which is all the defendant can win; meanwhile, the defendant risks losing all the cases at once; the first plaintiff thereby acquires tremendous settlement leverage, while in the absence of settlement he will face an opponent willing to litigate down to the scorched

---

128. United States v. Mendoza, 464 U.S. 154 (1984).

129. See Wright & Miller, supra note 4, § 4465; Note, Nonmutual Issue Preclusion Against States, 109 Harv. L. Rev. 792 (1996).

130. See Laura Emily Frossard, Collateral Estoppel of the Government: Striking the Necessary Balance Between the Interests of the Government, the Private Litigant, and Those Similarly Situated, 29 S. Tex. L. Rev. 385 (1987).

131. See, e.g., Premier Elec. Constr. Co. v. Nat'l Elec. Contractors Ass'n, 814 F.2d 358 (7th Cir. 1987); Benjamin Kaplan, Continuing Work of the Civil Committee: 1966 Amendments of the Federal Rules of Civil Procedure (I), 81 Harv. L. Rev. 356, 391 n.136 (1967) ("it would be anomalous to give one who opts out collateral estoppel benefits of the action from which he deliberately removed himself").

earth; and over the series of cases, the odds overwhelmingly disfavor the defendant. This fundamental departure from procedural neutrality will inevitably have many unintended substantive effects.[132]

Interestingly, other ways exist to achieve nonmutuality's aims to eliminate relitigation. The most mainstream alternative would be to expand mandatory joinder of all the concerned persons. This route would efficiently dispose of common matters in one shot, but in a fairer shot. The joined parties would be bound, but only after being heard. Their common opponent would be bound if it lost, but if it won it would win against all the joined parties. By so equating the parties' litigating risk, this procedural technique would restore procedural neutrality. Nevertheless, society has chosen, after balancing benefits and costs, to follow this mandatory joinder route no further than such provisions as Federal Rule of Civil Procedure 19 on compulsory joinder go. Because society has in fact chosen not to pursue this joinder alternative or any other of the alternatives, the choice by the courts to adopt on their own the inferior reform of nonmutuality looks even more questionable.[133]

§ 5.5   Nonordinary Judgments

A.   Nonpersonal Judgments

The question here is what effects of claim and issue preclusion a nonpersonal judgment has in a subsequent civil action, assuming it was a valid and final judgment.

A judgment purely in rem, based on *jurisdiction in rem*, has no claim preclusion effects. Instead, it has only two sorts of res judicata effects. First, conclusively with regard to all persons, it determines the interests of all persons in the thing. Second, any actual litigant is subject to issue preclusion, under the normal rules of that doctrine.[134]

A judgment based on *jurisdiction over status* determines, conclusively with regard to the parties and usually with regard to all other persons as well, the status in question. Also, any actual litigant is subject to issue preclusion, again subject to the normal rules of that doctrine. Thus, jurisdiction over status receives treatment analogous to jurisdiction purely in rem. But in actuality the

---

132. See Note, A Probabilistic Analysis of the Doctrine of Mutuality of Collateral Estoppel, 76 Mich. L. Rev. 612 (1978); Note, Exposing the Extortion Gap: An Economic Analysis of the Rules of Collateral Estoppel, 105 Harv. L. Rev. 1940 (1992).

133. See Elinor P. Schroeder, Relitigation of Common Issues: The Failure of Nonparty Preclusion and an Alternative Proposal, 67 Iowa L. Rev. 917 (1982).

134. See Restatement (Second) of Judgments § 30 (1982).

various statuses that can be adjudicated differ deeply in nature, with their determinations having vastly different impacts on persons' and the public's interests. Therefore, the peculiarities of status judgments lead to some differences of detail. On the one hand, some cases go further in applying res judicata by extending claim preclusion to a status judgment, as a successful action for divorce will preclude a later action for alimony if personal jurisdiction was available in the first action. On the other hand, many courts shy from applying res judicata that would conclusively establish a status against a particular stranger to the status proceeding who would suffer an unjust impact. In short, the res judicata law on jurisdiction over status tends to be rather messy and highly particularized in practice.[135]

As to *jurisdiction quasi in rem, subtype one*, such a judgment determines, conclusively with regard to the named parties, the interests of the named parties in the thing, even if judgment goes by default. Also, any party who actually litigated any issue is subject to normal issue preclusion.[136] Note that a claim targeting the thing (e.g., a claim seeking to foreclose a lien) and any associated claim against the person (e.g., a claim seeking to recover the underlying debt) are treated as different claims. Even if jurisdiction to adjudicate both lien and debt were present in a single court, the traditional view has been that separate actions are permitted. For example, a judgment as to foreclosure does not prevent a later action on the personal obligation, unless the property obtained through the foreclosure was sufficient to satisfy the debt. Collateral estoppel might preclude some issues in the later action, but the claim itself would not be merged or barred.[137]

As to *jurisdiction quasi in rem, subtype two*, such a judgment determines, conclusively between the parties, the plaintiff's right to apply the particular thing to the satisfaction of the unrelated claim against the defendant, but no more than that. Although the parties cannot relitigate their rights to the thing in connection with the same claim, the plaintiff may freely sue again for the unsatisfied portion of that claim, suing either in personam or on attachment of other property belonging to the defendant.[138] The plaintiff can even increase the ad damnum in the follow-up suit. Moreover, although the question is a "close" one according to the authorities,[139] and

---

135. See id. § 31.

136. See id. § 30.

137. See Bank of Okla. v. Fidelity State Bank & Trust Co., Dodge City, Kan., 623 F. Supp. 479, 485 (D. Kan. 1985) (rejecting the Wilson case as "dead wrong"). But see In re Wilson, 390 F. Supp. 1121 (D. Kan. 1975) (holding that a judgment on a note merged

the security claim, so that the claimant was denied secured-creditor status in the debtor's bankruptcy proceedings).

138. See Restatement (Second) of Judgments § 32 (1982).

139. Id. § 32(3) cmt. d; Wright & Miller, supra note 4, § 4431, at 50–51. The First Restatement took seemingly contradictory positions. Compare Re-different courts have expressed somewhat different views on the point,[140] the better view is that determinations litigated on this shaky jurisdictional basis, pursuant to a limited appearance,[141] should have no issue-preclusive effects.[142] So if, on the basis of a traffic accident, the plaintiff sues by means of attachment jurisdiction and the defendant vigorously and thoroughly defends via a limited appearance, the resulting judgment does not preclude a later personal action raising the very same issues of negligence, causation, and injury.

Why Should a Limited Appearance Yield No Issue Preclusion?

A point of vanishing practical importance but still of considerable theoretical interest is whether determinations litigated upon subtype two of jurisdiction quasi in rem, pursuant to a limited appearance, should have no issue-preclusive effects. The question, basically, is whether issue preclusion is seen as inconsistent with the modern notion of a limited appearance or whether issue preclusion requires only that issues essential to the judgment be fully and fairly litigated.

If the latter is the proper view, judgments rendered after a limited appearance should be accorded issue preclusion effect, even if claim preclusion effect is to be denied. Restatement (Second) of Judgments § 32(3) (1982) endorses, without citing any case support, this view that quasi in rem judgments should have issue preclusion effect as to the issues litigated through the defendant's limited appearance. However, as the Second Restatement observes, any unfairness to the defendant in being held to a judgment of a court that could not exercise personal jurisdiction would factor into deciding whether there was a full and fair opportunity to litigate, which, of course, is a general exception to issue preclusion. Litigation over that exception's application would be costly. That exception might, indeed, eat up the rule here, because a limited appearance should be allowed only in a court constitutionally unreasonable for personal jurisdiction, and so the question of issue preclusion would arise only where it would be unfair to the defendant. Ultimately, then, the Second Restatement's position is not very clear in application.

In any event, giving issue preclusion effect would significantly reduce the value of the limited appearance as a means of preventing abuses of the quasi in rem procedure. Indeed, giving issue preclusion effect is basically

---

statement of Judgments § 40 cmt. a (1942) (no collateral estoppel where defendant contests the claim without submitting to personal jurisdiction), with id. § 76(2) cmt. c (collateral estoppel applies to questions actually litigated in such circumstances).

140. Compare Minichiello v. Rosenberg, 410 F.2d 106, 112 (2d Cir. 1968) (suggesting unconstitutionality of preclusion), aff'd on reh'g en banc, 410 F.2d 117 (2d Cir. 1969), and Cheshire Nat'l Bank v. Jaynes, 112 N.E. 500, 502 (Mass. 1916) ("In such case the question of the general liability of the defendant to the plaintiff has not been put in issue, because the defendant has chosen to rely on his strict right by confining his appearance to the protection of the proper-

ty alone and not to submit himself to the general jurisdiction of the court."), with United States v. Balanovski, 236 F.2d 298, 302 (2d Cir. 1956) (dictum) (hypothesizing "further litigation, which the taxpayers will lose on the merits by collateral estoppel or stare decisis," but so opining in what was technically a quasi in rem subtype one case).

141. See supra § 4.4(A)(2)(b).

142. See Arthur T. von Mehren & Donald T. Trautman, Jurisdiction to Adjudicate: A Suggested Analysis, 79 Harv. L. Rev. 1121, 1139 n.38 (1966); Ernest L. Schmider, Note, Limited Appearances and Issue Preclusion: Resetting the Trap?, 66 Cornell L. Rev. 595 (1981).

inconsistent with the essence of a limited appearance. The limited appearance's purpose is to allow litigation without deciding the underlying personal claim, that is, to limit the risk of protecting the property to the value of the property. Because the issues are the same in the attachment claim and the underlying personal claim, the purpose of a limited appearance in this peculiar setting clashes with allowing issue preclusion. On the one hand, the losing defendant would receive little benefit from a limited appearance with issue preclusion effect, as the plaintiff could just sue again and win almost automatically by issue preclusion—the defendant's appearance would, after all, have turned out not to have been limited to the nonpersonal proceeding, as was expected. On the other hand, a limited appearance with issue preclusion effect would give the winning defendant the windfall of foreclosing the whole claim while having immediately risked only the property.

Moreover, recall again that a limited appearance should be available only when it is constitutionally unreasonable for the forum to exercise personal jurisdiction. This means that this whole debate swirls about a pretty rare occurrence, as attested by the total absence of recent cases dealing with the issue preclusion effect of a limited appearance. It also means that applying issue preclusion would most often involve giving personal effect to a judgment of a court that constitutionally could not have entertained the underlying personal claim. Only here, in all of litigation, does a finding that jurisdiction for a claim is unreasonable fail to block litigation of that claim's issues, because the issues on the merits are the same in the proper attachment claim and the improper personal claim—indeed, giving issue preclusion here might even be unconstitutional. Thus, only for a limited appearance in attachment jurisdiction (and not for limited appearances in other nonpersonal jurisdiction), does a special blanket exception to issue preclusion need to apply.

Picture now a case in a state that uses attachment jurisdiction when personal jurisdiction could constitutionally exist and that liberally grants limited appearances. Is relitigation desirable after a limited appearance when personal jurisdiction is reasonable? Of course not. But how should the state head off relitigation? The choice is *either* offering a limited appearance and then in the second action surprising the defendant with issue preclusion that makes the appearance rather unlimited after all *or* denying a limited appearance in the first place in order frankly to indicate what is at stake and to avoid the need for duplicative actions. The better choice is obvious. The cure for the waste of litigating the merits without attaining preclusion is to deny a limited appearance whenever fairness does not demand one—not to apply preclusion illogically and unfairly to a limited appearance. Indeed, most recent cases do take the desirable route of denying a limited appearance in such circumstances.

In summary, although there is disagreement, the preferred view is that adjudication under subtype two of quasi in rem jurisdiction pursuant to a limited appearance should have no res judicata effects other than determining interests in the thing and, hence, no issue preclusion effect. See generally Robert C. Casad & Kevin M. Clermont, Res Judicata: A Handbook on Its Theory, Doctrine, and Practice 198–203 (2001).

B. Noncoercive Judgments

A valid and final judgment in a suit solely for *declaratory relief* has two sorts of effects in a subsequent civil action. It is conclusive between opposing parties as to the matters declared, even if by default, but it has no further claim-preclusive effects and so does not preclude a later action for damages or other coercive relief. Also, an actual litigant is subject to issue preclusion, under the normal rules of that doctrine, on all issues actually litigated and determined that were essential to the judgment rendered.[143]

This approach does seem to open the door a little to claim-splitting by a plaintiff who can seek a declaratory judgment and later sue for coercive relief.[144] However, not applying claim preclusion seems consistent with the Declaratory Judgment Act's purpose of authorizing a preliminary action for lesser relief. Also, the initial court can protect against abuse by invoking its discretion to deny the option of declaratory relief in the first place.

C. Non–Civil–Court Proceedings

The question here is what effects of claim and issue preclusion a nonjudicial or noncivil decision has in a subsequent civil action, assuming that it was a valid and final decision.

An *administrative adjudication* by an administrative tribunal is treated like a court judgment, unless the essential elements of judicial adjudication were not employed, such as notice and opportunity to be heard and the other aspects of basic due process, or unless legislative policies support relitigation.[145] Thus, the Supreme Court has said: "When an administrative agency is acting in a judicial capacity and resolves disputed issues of fact properly before it which the parties have had an adequate opportunity to litigate, the courts have not hesitated to apply res judicata to enforce repose."[146] Basically, avoidance of preclusion depends on whether the party to be bound lacked a full and fair opportunity to present its case, as well as on whether any substantive reason aside from procedural fairness justifies relitigation.

An *arbitration award* is generally treated like a court judgment, usually having claim preclusion effects, and also having issue preclusion effects unless the essential elements of judicial adjudication were not employed or unless legislative policies or contractual provisions support relitigation.[147] The binding effects follow in part from res judicata policies and in part from the parties' intent, but here not from respect for a sovereign act. Claim preclusion is on relatively solid ground, especially because the parties likely agreed to arbitration with the idea that it would work to end the dispute once and for all. Contrariwise, courts are more wary as to issue

---

143. See Restatement (Second) of Judgments § 33 (1982).

144. See Wright & Miller, supra note 4, § 4446.

145. See Restatement (Second) of Judgments § 83 (1982); Wright & Miller, supra note 4, § 4475.

146. United States v. Utah Constr. & Mining Co., 384 U.S. 394, 422 (1966) (describing federal res judicata rule).

147. See Overseas Motors, Inc. v. Import Motors Ltd., 375 F. Supp. 499 (E.D. Mich. 1974), aff'd, 519 F.2d 119 (6th Cir. 1975); Restatement (Second) of Judgments § 84 (1982); Wright & Miller, supra note 4, § 4475.1.

preclusion that might possibly rest on a freewheeling arbitrator's decision, especially when the parties likely were not even thinking about issue preclusion when they agreed to arbitration.

A *criminal judgment* is now widely viewed as giving rise to issue preclusion in a subsequent civil action, even giving rise to nonmutual issue preclusion, but not to claim preclusion because the criminal and civil claims are different.[148] Thus, a convicted defendant will generally be bound on essential issues actually litigated and determined, unless some exception applies as where the criminal offense was of such piddling importance as to remove an adequate incentive for the accused to litigate. So if the government by trial convicts D of arson, and the governmental or third-party owner of the building later sues D civilly for damages, then D is subject to preclusion on the common issues.[149] It is only through the exceptions to issue preclusion that the courts take into account the tactical and procedural disadvantages of being a criminal defendant—including possibly lackadaisical assigned counsel, limited discovery, prejudicial setting, and reluctance to take the stand—which might amount to a lack of a full and fair opportunity to litigate the common issues.[150]

Because a guilty plea means the issues were not actually litigated and determined, the generally accepted view is that a conviction based thereon does not give rise to issue preclusion.[151] However, the plea itself will normally be admissible in evidence as an admission, and it may also later equitably estop the convict from taking an inconsistent position in a subsequent civil action.

Speaking of evidence, if under applicable law a conviction does not have preclusive effect in a subsequent civil action, it should be noted that some jurisdictions have adopted a special exception to their hearsay rule. This exception makes a conviction for a serious offense, by trial or guilty plea, admissible evidence on any issue of fact that had been essential to the conviction.[152]

Incidentally, a plea of nolo contendere and the resultant conviction have none of these preclusive or evidentiary effects in a

---

148. See Restatement (Second) of Judgments § 85 (1982); Wright & Miller, supra note 4, § 4474.

149. See Allen v. McCurry, 449 U.S. 90 (1980) (precluding convict in his civil rights action for illegal search and seizure); Teitelbaum Furs, Inc. v. Dominion Ins. Co., 375 P.2d 439 (Cal. 1962) (third party precluding thief).

150. See Jonathan C. Thau, Collateral Estoppel and the Reliability of Criminal Determinations: Theoretical, Practical, and Strategic Implications for Criminal and Civil Litigation, 70 Geo. L.J. 1079 (1982).

151. See Haring v. Prosise, 462 U.S. 306, 315 (1983) ("Unless an issue was actually litigated and determined in the former judicial proceeding, Virginia law will not treat it as final."); David L. Shapiro, Should a Guilty Plea Have Preclusive Effect?, 70 Iowa L. Rev. 27 (1984).

152. See, e.g., Fed. R. Evid. 803(22).

subsequent civil action. This plea is simply a way of saying "no contest."

Consider finally the effect of an acquittal. The government will almost never be bound by the acquittal, because an exception to issue preclusion (e.g., less favorable burden of persuasion) almost always applies.[153] Nor, of course, would the acquittal bind a third-party stranger to the prosecution, so that O.J. Simpson could not use his acquittal when a victim's family later brought a civil action against him.

§ 5.6   Nondomestic Judgments

A.   General Rules

Within one sovereign's boundaries, the sovereign can do pretty much as it wishes. Its courts can reach as far and act as it pleases, and it then can enforce the resulting judgment on the defendant if present or on any of the defendant's assets that are present. In this sense, the sovereign's power is limitless. Of course, the sovereign can choose to respect limits, whether imposed by its own constitution or by its self-restraint. (By sovereign here, I refer to countries and also to U.S. states, which retain their essentially sovereign status in matters of jurisdiction and judgments. But within the United States, of course, the U.S. Constitution's Due Process Clause of the Fourteenth Amendment imposes significant limitations on the sovereign states' powers to do as they please. That is, the higher authority of federal limits can be imposed as part of the state's law. In New York courts, for example, an out-of-state defendant can raise the Due Process Clause as a defense, and so New York is not free to reach as far as it wishes.)

Outside a sovereign's boundaries, on the international or inter-state stage, the sovereign's reach and behavior is inevitably limited. The acts of a foreign government have no effect within a second government's territory, unless the second government chooses to give them effect. The second sovereign's court is free to choose not to respect the first sovereign's judgment that is the product of overreaching or unfairness. Anticipation of such second-guessing by the second sovereign's court indirectly limits the freedom of the

---

153. See One Lot Emerald Cut Stones v. United States, 409 U.S. 232, 235 (1972) ("The acquittal of the criminal charges may have only represented 'an adjudication that the proof was not sufficient to overcome all reasonable doubt of the guilt of the accused.' Helvering v. Mitchell, 303 U.S. 391, 397 (1938). As to the issues raised, it does not constitute an adjudication on the preponderance-of-the-evidence burden applicable in civil proceedings."); Burns v. United States, 200 F.2d 106 (4th Cir. 1952) (holding that a widow, who had been acquitted of the murder of her husband, could not use preclusion on the issue of whether she had killed her husband, in her later claim for the proceeds of his governmental life insurance policy).

first sovereign's court. (Within the United States, moreover, the Constitution's Full Faith and Credit Clause entails significant limitations on the second sovereign's freedom to ignore an American judgment.)

In this chapter, our concern is the effect of judgments, and not on jurisdiction or conduct of litigation except as they bear on judgments' validity. So, focus now on just the effects of judgments. Judgments rendered in the courts of one state or nation frequently bear on litigation conducted in the courts of another. The task here, then, is to specify what treatment a judgment will receive in a subsequent civil action in another judicial system. This task splits into questions of recognition and enforcement.

A court normally will **recognize**, or in other words give effect under the doctrine of res judicata to, a nondomestic judgment that is valid and final. In the U.S. view, when the second court faces the question of whether the prior judgment is valid and final, it normally should apply the law of the judgment-rendering sovereign (which of course is subject to any applicable external restraints, such as due process and other federal provisions imposed on and becoming part of state law).[154] When the second court faces a question of the extent or reach of res judicata based on the prior judgment, it normally should apply the res judicata law that the rendering court would apply (including any applicable external restraints).[155] The basic approach to judgments thus is retroverse, in the sense of turning backward to look at the rendering court's view of its own judgment: the second court lets the first court's law decide what it conclusively adjudicated.[156]

Note especially that the second court will respect only valid judgments, because it does not want to give effects to a judgment that the rendering court would strike down. To be valid, speaking generally in terms of the U.S. view, the judgment's rendering court must have had territorial jurisdiction, as well as possessing subject-matter jurisdiction and giving adequate notice. The second court should not search for mere error, such as violations of venue and other self-restraint provisions or even errors of substantive law. But it will examine, say, territorial jurisdiction. It will deny effect to judgments that reflect jurisdictional overreach. Thus, to some

---

154. See Restatement (Second) of Conflict of Laws §§ 92–93, 107 (1971); Restatement (Third) of Foreign Relations Law of the United States §§ 481(1), 482 (1987).

155. See Restatement (Second) of Conflict of Laws §§ 94–97 (1971) (amended 1988); Restatement (Third) of Foreign Relations Law of the United States § 481(1) cmt. c (1987).

156. See ALI Recognition and Enforcement of Foreign Judgments: Analysis and Proposed Federal Statute § 4 (2006); Robert C. Casad, Issue Preclusion and Foreign Country Judgments: Whose Law?, 70 Iowa L. Rev. 53, 70–76 (1984).

degree the second court can restrict the effective territorial reach of the rendering court. Accordingly, these restrictions are sometimes called the law of indirect jurisdiction.

Furthermore, the second court normally will **enforce** a judgment entitled to recognition. A local sheriff will not enforce a judgment issued by another sovereign, and a local judge cannot directly enforce a judgment that is not a matter of record in that jurisdiction. Instead, the second sovereign will provide some other enforcement procedure that converts the nondomestic judgment into a domestic record.[157] With respect to the method of enforcement, the second court applies its own law, subject to the proviso that the method should not be so complex or expensive as to burden unduly the enforcement of nondomestic judgments.[158] Even foreign equity decrees are entitled to enforcement.[159] But because the second court's law governs the method of enforcement, it has some freedom to enforce the equitable decree in a manner of its own choosing, as long as the manner is evenhanded.

A usual method of enforcement of nondomestic judgments is for the plaintiff to initiate in the second jurisdiction an action upon the prior judgment and thus obtain a regularly enforceable domestic judgment. Such an action for the judgment debt is a cause of action itself, distinct from the original claim. In an action upon the judgment, none of the issues going to the merits of the original claim that were or might have been presented for decision in the original action can be reexamined. This includes matters of the defendant's defense to the original claim, as well as elements of the plaintiff's claim itself.[160]

There have been attempts to facilitate enforcement of nondomestic judgments by creating alternative methods of enforcement. First, federal law provides for registration in any district court of another district court's judgment for recovery of money or property, thus automatically converting the registered judgment into a regularly enforceable local judgment.[161] The statute thus dispenses with the necessity of an independent action upon the judgment. In this way, in addition to saving time and expense, the statute avoids the jurisdiction, service, and venue requirements for

---

157. See McElmoyle v. Cohen, 38 U.S. (13 Pet.) 312, 325 (1839).

158. See Restatement (Second) of Conflict of Laws §§ 99–102 (1971); Restatement (Third) of Foreign Relations Law of the United States § 481(2) (1987).

159. See Baker v. Gen. Motors Corp., 522 U.S. 222, 234–35 (1998).

160. Cf. Moore v. Justices of the Mun. Court, 197 N.E. 487 (Mass. 1935)

(plaintiff can sue upon the judgment in another jurisdiction and obtain a fresh judgment, and the first judgment is not merged in the second, so that plaintiff can seek to enforce either or both, although of course limited to one satisfaction); Restatement (Second) of Judgments § 18 cmt. j (1982).

161. 28 U.S.C. § 1963.

an independent action upon the judgment. Second, most states have built on this idea by adopting some version of a uniform act that permits registration of federal or sister-state judgments, obviating the need for an action upon the judgment.[162]

The subject under consideration here is only court judgments. Judicially unreviewed administrative determinations and judicially unconfirmed arbitration awards often get respect in the courts of a different jurisdiction. But this recognition and enforcement normally flow from the second sovereign's conflict of laws doctrine, which can choose, as a matter of comity, to give effects to them. There is no general obligation to give full faith and credit to nondomestic nonjudgments.[163]

B. Judgments of U.S. Courts

The above rules for recognizing and enforcing a nondomestic judgment are in large part obligatory on American courts when that judgment comes from another American court. These rules help us to realize the benefits of a unified nation.[164] The rules are basically the same in all four possible settings, as next described.

1. State—State

When the prior judgment was rendered by a state court and the second action is brought in a court of another state, the *Full Faith and Credit Clause* of Article IV, Section 1 of the Federal Constitution ("Full Faith and Credit shall be given in each State to the public Acts, Records, and judicial Proceedings of every other State. And the Congress may by general Laws prescribe the Manner in which such Acts, Records and Proceedings shall be proved, and the Effect thereof.") *and* its implementing legislation in *28 U.S.C. § 1738* (" * * * Such Acts, records and judicial proceedings or copies thereof, so authenticated, shall have the same full faith and credit in every court within the United States and its Territo-

---

162. See Revised Uniform Enforcement of Foreign Judgments Act (1964), 13(pt. I) U.L.A. 155 (2002).

163. Cf. Univ. of Tenn. v. Elliott, 478 U.S. 788 (1986) (suggesting that some state administrative findings might fall within the Full Faith and Credit Clause, although not within 28 U.S.C. § 1738); Bandes & Solum, supra note 93, §§ 130.60–.66 (discussing, inter alia, the 1958 U.N. Convention on the Recognition and Enforcement of Foreign Arbitral Awards).

164. See Baker v. Gen. Motors Corp., 522 U.S. 222, 232 (1998) ("The

animating purpose of the full faith and credit command * * * 'was to alter the status of the several states as independent foreign sovereignties, each free to ignore obligations created under the laws or by the judicial proceedings of the others, and to make them integral parts of a single nation throughout which a remedy upon a just obligation might be demanded as of right, irrespective of the state of its origin.' ") (quoting Milwaukee County v. M.E. White Co., 296 U.S. 268, 277 (1935)).

ries and Possessions as they have by law or usage in the courts of such State, Territory or Possession from which they are taken.") require the second court to give the same binding effect[165] to a valid and final judgment as the judgment would have in the courts of the rendering state.[166] Indeed, the better view is that full faith and credit requires the second court to give neither more effect nor less effect than the rendering state would.[167]

Respect is owing only to valid judgments. Consequently, an American court presented with a nondomestic but American default judgment can inquire into the territorial jurisdiction of the rendering court. In deference to the nation's federal structure, the second court asks only whether territorial jurisdiction existed under the law that the rendering court would have applied. This jurisdictional law includes the Due Process Clause.

The second court must give full faith and credit to a valid judgment even if the judgment is erroneous or against local policy. That is, there is no general exception based on the second state's public policy.[168] Thus, the fact that the underlying claim is contrary to the second state's public policy—for example, a claim on a gambling transaction—is not a valid ground for denying recognition or enforcement to a sister-state judgment on that claim.[169]

However, there are narrow exceptions where some or all of the dictates of full faith and credit do not apply, such as where recognition or enforcement would so grossly and improperly interfere with the second state's important interests as to create a national interest against such recognition or enforcement. Distinguish that national interest against recognition or enforcement from the second state's local distaste for the nature of the underlying claim. Specific examples of a national interest are rare: the rendering state has purported directly to transfer title to land in the second state[170] or has enjoined litigation in the second state's courts.[171] A congressionally created exception lies in the 1996 statute[172] that placed same-sex marriages outside the Full Faith and Credit Clause and statute (which clause, by the way, expressly

---

165. See Mills v. Duryee, 11 U.S. (7 Cranch) 481 (1813) (suggesting that congressional implementation of the constitutional provision was necessary to impose a binding effect, as opposed to a merely evidential effect).

166. See Restatement (Second) of Conflict of Laws §§ 93, 100 (1971).

167. See Robert C. Casad & Kevin M. Clermont, Res Judicata: A Handbook on Its Theory, Doctrine, and Practice 213–17, 222 (2001).

168. See Baker v. Gen. Motors Corp., 522 U.S. 222 (1998).

169. See Fauntleroy v. Lum, 210 U.S. 230 (1908).

170. See Fall v. Eastin, 215 U.S. 1 (1909); Restatement (Second) of Conflict of Laws § 102 cmt. d (1971).

171. See James v. Grand Trunk W.R.R., 152 N.E.2d 858 (Ill. 1958); Restatement (Second) of Conflict of Laws § 103 (1971) (amended 1988).

172. 28 U.S.C. § 1738C.

authorizes congressional exceptions.)[173] But even where full faith and credit does not compel recognition or enforcement, the second court can, unless prohibited by federal statute, still choose as a matter of comity to give the same effect to a valid judgment as the rendering state would.[174]

2. State—Federal

When the second court is instead a federal court, then *28 U.S.C. § 1738* (which dictates "full faith and credit in every court within the United States") likewise compels the second court to give the same effect to a valid and final judgment as the judgment would have in the courts of the rendering state.[175] The federal court must therefore apply the res judicata law that the rendering state would.[176] The same is true even when the claim in federal court is within exclusive federal jurisdiction, so that in considering the preclusive effects of an earlier state judgment rendered on a state claim, the federal court will apply state res judicata law even though a state court could not have heard the federal claim.[177] The same is true even if the party was forced to litigate first in state court.[178]

Of course, the state res judicata law is not free of federal command. Most importantly, due process requires that the state not preclude on the basis of a judgment if the proceedings did not afford a full and fair opportunity to litigate.[179] That is, the state must have a basically fair res judicata law, which will apply in that state's own courts as well as in federal court to specify the effects of that state's judgments.[180] It is still accurate to call this res judicata law a body of state law, even though the state formulates its law within federally imposed limits.

However, that body of state res judicata law does not absolutely always govern in federal court. After all, it governs in federal

---

173. See Brainerd Currie, Full Faith and Credit, Chiefly to Judgments: A Role for Congress, 1964 Sup. Ct. Rev. 89.

174. See Restatement (Second) of Conflict of Laws §§ 102–103 (1971) (amended 1988).

175. See Restatement (Second) of Judgments § 86 (1982).

176. See Kremer v. Chem. Constr. Corp., 456 U.S. 461, 466 (1982).

177. See Matsushita Elec. Indus. Co. v. Epstein, 516 U.S. 367 (1996) (securities case); Marrese v. Am. Acad. of Orthopaedic Surgeons, 470 U.S. 373 (1985) (antitrust case).

178. See San Remo Hotel, L.P. v. City of San Francisco, Cal., 545 U.S. 323 (2005). But cf. England v. La. State Bd. of Med. Exam'rs, 375 U.S. 411 (1964) (after abstention, plaintiff may avoid claim preclusion by explicitly reserving the federal grievance for later determination in federal court).

179. See Kremer v. Chem. Constr. Corp., 456 U.S. 461, 480–83 (1982).

180. See William V. Luneburg, The Opportunity to Be Heard and the Doctrines of Preclusion: Federal Limits on State Law, 31 Vill. L. Rev. 81 (1986).

court by virtue of a federal statute, § 1738, so federal law can make exceptions to that statute.[181] In narrow circumstances grounded on strong federal substantive or procedural policies, federal law may provide against (or conceivably augment by statute) recognition or enforcement, such as where federal courts infrequently construe statutes bestowing exclusive federal jurisdiction so as to permit federal relitigation of certain issues already determined in state court.[182]

3. Federal—State

When the prior judgment was rendered by a federal court and the second action is brought in a state court, the second court must similarly give the same effect to a valid and final judgment as the judgment would have in the rendering court. This result follows in the second court by virtue of the *Supremacy Clause*.[183]

Usually, a uniform federal law of res judicata governs the effects of a federal judgment. Federal law governs because of strong federal interests in defining the scope of its own federal judgments, in adapting that res judicata law to the federal procedural system, and in developing a uniform federal law of res judicata and a simple retroverse approach to judgments in a federal system. This federal res judicata law includes the modern rules described in this chapter.

However, when the basis of federal subject-matter jurisdiction in the first court was diversity, the Supreme Court has pronounced that this federal law will adopt the first court's local state law of res judicata as the federal common law, except when that state law is incompatible with federal interests.[184] Yet, I think a better approach for diversity judgments might be to reverse the Court's presumption, so as normally to apply the uniform federal res judicata law and only sometimes to adopt the state's res judicata law, when

---

181. See Kremer v. Chem. Constr. Corp., 456 U.S. 461, 468 (1982).

182. See, e.g., Brown v. Felsen, 442 U.S. 127 (1979) (not precluding certain issues in bankruptcy case); Lyons v. Westinghouse Elec. Corp., 222 F.2d 184, 188–89 (2d Cir. 1955) (holding, in this antitrust treble damage action, against issue preclusion by a prior state judgment in an accounting suit that had found the challenged conduct did not violate the antitrust laws).

183. See Restatement (Second) of Judgments § 87 (1982).

184. Semtek Int'l Inc. v. Lockheed Martin Corp., 531 U.S. 497, 508–09 (2001) (in reviewing the respect a Maryland state court owed to a statute-of-limitations dismissal by a California federal court in a removed diversity case, the Court said: "In short, federal common law governs the claim-preclusive effect of a dismissal by a federal court sitting in diversity. * * * This is, it seems to us, a classic case for adopting, as the federally prescribed rule of decision, the law that would be applied by state courts in the State in which the federal diversity court sits. * * * This federal reference to state law will not obtain, of course, in situations in which the state law is incompatible with federal interests.").

state substantive policies spike high such as for nonmutual collater-al estoppel.[185]

4. Federal—Federal

When the second court is instead another federal court, still the same precept of looking to treatment in the rendering court prevails, because the two courts are *arms of the same sovereign* and that sovereign respects res judicata.[186] Consistently with the univer-sal retroverse approach to judgments, the subsequent federal court should apply the rendering federal court's view of the federal law of res judicata in case of difference in law between circuits.[187]

C. Judgments of Foreign Nations

International law itself plays no real role in U.S. treatment of foreign judgments, except to the extent that the U.S. approach is already a manifestation of any generally recognized principles that constitute part of international law. The United States has not a single treaty on the subject.[188] So, for foreign judgments, there is no binding law comparable to full faith and credit.

Yet U.S. courts do give respect to foreign judgments, not only because finality is a fair and efficient policy even as to foreign judgments, but also because U.S. courts hope to encourage abroad similar respect for their own judgments. Thus, freed from constitu-tional and statutory obligations but motivated by similar policies, U.S. courts generally respect foreign judgments if valid and final under the foreign law, so that the foreign res judicata law should be applicable and the foreign judgment should be enforceable in the United States.

The United States behaves pretty generously in this regard, compared to most other nations. Most other nations appear to demonstrate a relatively heightened notion of sovereignty in this regard. Even if the U.S. judgment passes the foreign court's juris-dictional reexamination, which very well might involve meeting all the standards of the foreign jurisdictional law, the foreign court tends to reexamine the merits to ensure that the applied law conformed to local policy. And in case of recognition, the foreign court tends to apply its own res judicata law.[189]

---

185. See Patrick Woolley, The Sources of Federal Preclusion Law After Semtek, 72 U. Cin. L. Rev. 527 (2003).

186. See Restatement (Second) of Judgments § 87 (1982).

187. See Wright & Miller, supra note 4, § 4466.

188. See supra § 4.2(D)(3).

189. See Samuel P. Baumgartner, How Well Do U.S. Judgments Fare in ?, 40 Geo. Wash. Int'l L. Rev. 1 (2007).

Nevertheless, a closer look at the actual holdings and opinions suggests that U.S. courts too apply slightly different standards to judgments of foreign nations, as compared to those they apply to domestic, state, or federal judgments. The principal reason for difference is that a U.S. court has no guarantee that a foreign judgment, although comporting with the basic requirements of the foreign nation, is minimally acceptable to Americans. The foreign laws concerning validity vary widely. Moreover, the Due Process Clause and the rest of the U.S. Constitution do not control foreign sovereigns, of course, and so the workings of the foreign legal system could be too foreign to tolerate.

From this realistic insight follow four corollaries. First, while a U.S. court can ask whether jurisdiction existed under the foreign law, the U.S. court more importantly may examine whether the foreign assertion of jurisdiction satisfied the U.S. tests of substantive due process.[190] A U.S. court, for example, would disregard a French judgment for which personal jurisdiction was based solely on the plaintiff's French domicile. Second, a U.S. court will give no respect to a foreign judgment that it views as repugnantly unfair.[191] A U.S. court will not recognize or enforce a foreign judgment resulting from proceedings that failed to meet the basic notions of U.S. procedural due process, such as adequate notice, and so prevented the parties from having a fair day in court. Third, a U.S. court might apply other limitations, such as refusing recognition or enforcement if the prior judgment rested on fraud or if the original claim is directly contrary to strong local public policy.[192] For a procedural example of those limitations, a foreign default judgment rendered contrary to a forum selection clause's derogation might fall within the public policy exception. For a substantive example, a U.S. court would reject an English judgment for defamation that impinges on U.S. principles of free speech, and also judgments of foreign countries imposing tax obligations or penal sanctions generally are not regarded as entitled to recognition or enforcement in U.S. courts. Fourth, in principle but not in general practice, a U.S. court may require reciprocity, so respecting judgments only of foreign nations that respect American judgments.[193]

---

190. See Gary B. Born & Peter B. Rutledge, International Civil Litigation in United States Courts 1050–61 (4th ed. 2007).

191. See Society of Lloyd's v. Ashenden, 233 F.3d 473, 477 (7th Cir. 2000) (applying a restrained "international concept of due process"); Restatement (Third) of Foreign Relations Law of the United States § 482(1) (1987).

192. See De Brimont v. Penniman, 7 F. Cas. 309 (C.C.S.D.N.Y. 1873) (No.

3715); Restatement (Second) of Conflict of Laws § 117 cmt. c (1971); Restatement (Third) of Foreign Relations Law of the United States § 482(2) (1987).

193. See Hilton v. Guyot, 159 U.S. 113, 210–28 (1895); Restatement (Second) of Conflict of Laws § 98 cmt. f (1971) (amended 1988); Restatement (Third) of Foreign Relations Law of the United States § 481 cmt. d (1987). Compare J. Noelle Hicks, Facilitating International Trade: The U.S. Needs Federal

In brief, American courts treat judgments of foreign nations pretty much like American judgments, although their approach to such foreign judgments is more flexible because their respect generally flows from "comity" rather than from legal obligation.[194]

As to the governing law on the treatment of foreign judgments, the matter is regulated by general principles of comity under the law of the second court. Thus, state statutory[195] and common law on comity governs in state court, and federal common law on comity governs on federal claims in federal court. However, in a diversity action the federal court under *Erie* looks to state law on how to treat a foreign judgment.[196] An argument could be made that in all federal cases, and even in all state cases as well, federal law should control because of the federal interest in foreign relations,[197] but that is not how the law has worked out. At any rate, both state and federal law will most often refer to the foreign law for specifying the extent of respect, and so state and federal law are basically similar.

What Is the Status of the Reciprocity Doctrine in the United States?
Perhaps a useful illustration of all this law on foreign judgments is the aforementioned doctrine of reciprocity. In the much-criticized decision of

Legislation Governing the Enforcement of Foreign Judgments, 28 Brook. J. Int'l L. 155, 176–78 (2002) (arguing for legislation that would impose reciprocity in all circumstances), with Katherine R. Miller, Playground Politics: Assessing the Wisdom of Writing a Reciprocity Requirement into U.S. International Recognition and Enforcement Law, 35 Geo. J. Int'l L. 239 (2004) (opposing reciprocity). See generally Michael Whincop, The Recognition Scene: Game Theoretic Issues in the Recognition of Foreign Judgments, 23 Melb. U. L. Rev. 416 (1999) (analyzing recognition as an iterative prisoner's dilemma game).

194. See Hilton v. Guyot, 159 U.S. 113, 163–64 (1895) (" 'Comity,' in the legal sense, is neither a matter of absolute obligation, on the one hand, nor of mere courtesy and good will, upon the other. But it is the recognition which one nation allows within its territory to the legislative, executive or judicial acts of another nation, having due regard both to international duty and convenience, and to the rights of its own citizens or of other persons who are under the protection of its laws."). See generally Joel R. Paul, Comity in International Law, 32 Harv. Int'l L.J. 1 (1991).

195. See, e.g., Uniform Foreign Money–Judgments Recognition Act (1962), 13(pt. II) U.L.A. 39 (2002), revised in Uniform Foreign–Country Money Judgments Recognition Act (2005), id. at 5 (Supp. 2008).

196. See, e.g., Bank of Montreal v. Kough, 612 F.2d 467, 469 (9th Cir. 1980) ("Recognition and enforcement of the British Columbia judgment in this case depends upon the proper construction of the Uniform Foreign Money Judgments Recognition Act * * * adopted by California * * *."); Svenska Handelsbanken v. Carlson, 258 F. Supp. 448, 450 (D. Mass. 1966) ("Although the Massachusetts cases are very old, the Massachusetts rule appears to be that a judgment of a court of a foreign country is only prima facie evidence of the underlying claim, and that defendant is entitled to all the defenses he might have made to the original action."); Restatement (Second) of Conflict of Laws § 98 cmt. c (1971) (amended 1988). But see John D. Brummett, Jr., Note, The Preclusive Effect of Foreign–Country Judgments in the United States and Federal Choice of Law: The Role of the Erie Doctrine Reassessed, 33 N.Y.L. Sch. L. Rev. 83 (1988).

197. See John Norton Moore, Federalism and Foreign Relations, 1965 Duke L.J. 248.

Hilton v. Guyot, 159 U.S. 113 (1895)—involving French plaintiffs trying to enforce in federal court a French money judgment against U.S. citizens—a sharply divided Supreme Court of the United States gave a ringing endorsement of comity in a notably modernistic tone, but at the same time held that a federal court should not accord enforcement without relitigation of the merits to a judgment of a foreign country if the courts of that country would not enforce judgments of U.S. courts rendered under similar circumstances. When this reciprocity exception applies, the foreign judgment can be used only evidentially, as prima facie evidence that the judgment exists, but the merits are open for relitigation. For the story of the Hilton case, see Louise Ellen Teitz, The Story of Hilton: From Gloves to Globalization, in Civil Procedure Stories 445 (Kevin M. Clermont ed., 2d ed. 2008).

Today, this reciprocity exception is said to apply only where a personal judgment was rendered in favor of a plaintiff who was a national of the rendering foreign country and against a U.S. defendant. The Hilton holding is not binding on the states, but merely governs enforcement of judgments in federal courts. And even in federal courts, in view of the later-announced Erie doctrine, the exception does not apply in diversity jurisdiction, which is the usual basis of federal jurisdiction for enforcing judgments, unless the state in which the federal court sits has adopted a reciprocity exception itself, which not many states have done.

One can persuasively argue against the Hilton holding that courts should not be pursuing a role in foreign relations that belongs to the other branches of government, especially when American courts have failed to present a united front on the reciprocity matter; that the Court's unclear albeit narrow exception of reciprocity undermines the fairness and efficiency of res judicata law; that reciprocity seems unlike the other exceptions to comity that rely on due process notions; and that it is unfair to punish a foreign litigant for its government's policy. Still, a feeling lingers that, in the absence of supranational authority, a reciprocity exception is about all that the United States can threaten in order to give foreign courts an incentive to abandon any stinginess in respecting U.S. judgments.

Interestingly, the question of reciprocity moved to the front-burner recently, as the global community unsuccessfully pursued a broad treaty on judgments at The Hague. At home, in response, the American Law Institute drafted a proposed federal statute that would federalize the treatment of foreign judgments—and would statutorily impose a reciprocity exception on this country's courts in order to encourage respect for U.S. judgments abroad. See generally ALI Recognition and Enforcement of Foreign Judgments: Analysis and Proposed Federal Statute § 7 (2006).

§ 5.7 Procedural Incidents

A. Invoking Res Judicata

Res judicata is not self-executing. The person wishing to rely on it must raise it or suffer waiver.[198] This result flows from the premises of the adversary system, coupled with the fact that the policies underlying res judicata are not so essential as to require judicial invocation. Although the court has the power to raise res judicata on its own, it will do so only rarely when its own interests

---

198. See, e.g., Arizona v. California, 530 U.S. 392, 412–13 (2000) ("trial courts must be cautious about raising a preclusion bar sua sponte, thereby eroding the principle of party presentation so basic to our system of adjudication"); Carbonell v. La. Dep't of Health & Human Res., 772 F.2d 185, 189 (5th Cir. 1985).

are endangered.[199]

As to timing, res judicata can be used only after judgment, and outside the context of the initial action (and any direct review such as appeal). Thus, the plaintiff in Action #2 might invoke res judicata to foreclose the underlying merits in an action upon the judgment rendered in Action #1. Similarly, as one more example, the defendant in a subsequent action might invoke issue preclusion as a defense to prevent relitigation of certain issues decided in the initial action. Accordingly, it is normally the court handling the subsequent action that decides the applicability of res judicata.

As to the procedure involved, the plaintiff in the subsequent action usually would raise res judicata by pretrial motion, such as a summary judgment motion. The defendant in the subsequent action usually should plead res judicata as an affirmative defense in the answer or an amendment thereto,[200] and then any party can seek decision by motion for judgment on the pleadings or summary judgment.[201] In practice, however, some courts are fairly lax on this procedure, allowing a party to raise res judicata, especially issue preclusion, without special procedure, even at trial, as long as the opponent received fair notice.[202]

As to proof, the burden of persuasion that res judicata applies is on the party raising it, but then, as explained below, the burden of proof that an exception to res judicata applies is on the other side. In deciding the applicability of res judicata, the usual evidence is the formal record of the prior judgment.[203] If necessary, the court may consider extrinsic evidence, such as a trial transcript, in regard to what the prior judgment really decided.[204] But the former jurors[205] and the former judge[206] cannot testify as to their mental

199. See, e.g., Plaut v. Spendthrift Farm, Inc., 514 U.S. 211, 231 (1995) ("What may follow from our holding that the judicial power unalterably includes the power to render final judgments is not that waivers of res judicata are always impermissible, but rather that, as many Federal Courts of Appeals have held, waivers of res judicata need not always be accepted—that trial courts may in appropriate cases raise the res judicata bar on their own motion."); Disimone v. Browner, 121 F.3d 1262, 1267 (9th Cir. 1997).

200. See, e.g., Fed. R. Civ. P. 8(c), 15(a).

201. See, e.g., id. 12(c), 56.

202. See, e.g., Overseas Motors, Inc. v. Import Motors Ltd., 375 F. Supp. 499, 512–15 (E.D. Mich. 1974), aff'd, 519

F.2d 119 (6th Cir. 1975); Bandes & Solum, supra note 93, § 132.05[8][a].

203. See, e.g., 28 U.S.C. § 1738; Fed. R. Civ. P. 44; Fed. R. Evid. 902.

204. See Restatement (Second) of Judgments § 19 cmt. h, § 27 cmt. f, § 77 (1982).

205. See, e.g., Washington, A. & G. Steam Packet Co. v. Sickles, 72 U.S. (5 Wall.) 580, 593 (1867); Fed. R. Evid. 606.

206. See, e.g., Grip–Pak, Inc. v. Ill. Tool Works, 694 F.2d 466 (7th Cir. 1982); Fleming James, Jr., Civil Procedure 579–80 (1965); Wright & Miller, supra note 4, § 4420, at 529–32. But cf. Timothy E. Travers, Annotation, Judge as Witness in Cause Not on Trial Before Him, 86 A.L.R.3d 633, 665–68 (1978) (citing authorities permitting judge's testimony to explain unclear record).

workings. Problems of proof can be avoided if the parties made an effort in the initial action to ensure the record's accuracy and clarity, as by amending pleadings and utilizing a special verdict.

As to mode of decision and standard of review, the cases are in disarray. The most that can be said is that courts tend to view res judicata as a matter of law. This approach allows judges to decide res judicata issues without a jury, facilitating pretrial decision in accord with the doctrine's purpose of avoiding trial and also encouraging an explicated application of the doctrine.[207] In addition, this approach allows appellate courts to apply a nondeferential standard of review, which in turn permits them to tighten up the res judicata doctrine and to supervise closely its application.[208]

B. Defeating Res Judicata

Imagine one party invoking some aspect of res judicata against the opponent, or invokee. The invokee can defeat the invoker's attempt to establish that a rule of res judicata applies in the first place by overcoming the invoker's support for any of the doctrinal requirements of the rule. For example, the invokee could defeat issue preclusion by overcoming the invoker's showing that the current case involves the same issue as the prior case, that the issue was actually litigated and determined, or that its determination was essential to the prior judgment. Alternatively, to defeat the rule of res judicata, the invokee can raise and prove that one of the exceptions to the rule apply. For example, the invokee-defendant could defeat claim preclusion by showing that the parties had agreed to allow the plaintiff to split the claim.

All that is rather obvious. What is less intuitive is that the invokee can avoid res judicata by raising the absence of res judicata's prerequisites of the prior judgment's being valid and final.[209] That is, a party who seeks to avoid the binding effects of a judgment can make an attack against the judgment itself. Of course, the party may do so on many grounds by immediate post-judgment motion or by appeal. But even outside the ordinary course of review in the trial and appellate courts, the party can attack the judgment, at least for the lack of finality or for the lack of validity.

---

207. See, e.g., Wahl v. Vibranetics, Inc., 474 F.2d 971 (6th Cir. 1973); cf. Markman v. Westview Instruments, Inc., 517 U.S. 370 (1996) (fact/law distinction for jury right); supra § 2.4(B)(2).

208. See, e.g., Blasi v. Williams, 775 F.2d 1017 (9th Cir. 1985); cf. 1 Steven Alan Childress & Martha S. Davis, Federal Standards of Review § 3.09 (3d ed. 1999) (fact/law distinction for appellate review); supra § 2.6(B)(1).

209. See supra § 5.1(B) (discussing these prerequisites of res judicata, as well as the methods for seeking relief from judgment).

The burden of persuasion that res judicata applies—that the situation satisfies the requirements of a rule—is on the party invoking res judicata. But then the burden of proof that an exception to res judicata applies is on the other side. That opponent must raise the exception by appropriate response to however the proponent raised res judicata, and then must persuade the court that the exception applies.

One situation does not fit this simple scheme. Upon an attempt at relief from judgment by attacking its validity, the attacker bears at least the burden of production if the attacker had knowledge of the prior action. That is, in this late post-judgment setting, the presumption should shift in favor of validity. Consequently, the burden of production would be on the attacker to establish invalidity, rather than on the proponent of the judgment to show its validity.[210]

---

210. See Bally Export Corp. v. Balicar, Ltd., 804 F.2d 398, 102 A.L.R. Fed. 797 (7th Cir. 1986); Kevin M. Clermont, Jurisdictional Fact, 91 Cornell L. Rev. 973, 986 & n.53 (2006).

Chapter 6

COMPLEX LITIGATION

Table of Sections

---

§ 6.1   Preliminary Considerations

The subject here is complex litigation, defined as being multiclaim or multiparty litigation. Hence the focus shifts to the restrictions regarding which claims and parties the litigants must or may join in their lawsuit.

A. Historical Note

Historically, there has been a general movement in our legal systems toward more broadly requiring joinder of multiple claims and parties and toward permitting even more extensive joinder. And complex lawsuits have very recently become much more common in practice, as liability law evolved and as social and economic interactions have complexified.

The old common law required and permitted joinder in very limited circumstances. For example, although the plaintiff did not have to, he could join claims against the defendant if the claims fell within the same form of action (such as different acts of trespass), but he could join little else. Compulsory and permissive joinder of parties also was strictly limited at law under a highly conceptual approach. Meanwhile, equity took a broader and more instrumental approach to joinder, with the emphasis on effectuating the ideal

365

remedies for the natural rights involved. Here lie the roots of the modern approach.[1]

The later procedural codes, as interpreted, followed a wooden approach that fell between the legal and equitable traditions of joinder.[2] Accordingly, joinder provisions in states still adhering today to the code approach are relatively narrow in scope.

The widely followed modern pragmatic approach, typified by the Federal Rules, requires and permits the broadest joinder consistent with efficiency and fairness.[3] The joinder Rules, especially since their 1966 amendments, have moreover progressed from a jurisprudence of conceptual categorical labels to a jurisprudence of relevant pragmatic factors. In a sense, some of the key Rules in this area are "nonrules," setting out little more than a structure for the court's discretionary decision. The motivation is a belief that although most areas of law are best treated by rules *stricto sensu*, joinder and other areas are best treated by flexible standards. That is, some legal questions cannot be answered generally, but can only be intelligently and helpfully restated. The draftsman of those 1966 amendments, Professor Benjamin Kaplan, explained that "a rule that came out looking smoother would simply have remitted a series of problems to the courts with fewer guides; and that the purpose of procedural rules of this order of difficulty must be precisely that of asking questions—I mean the right ones."[4]

B.　Federal Focus

In this Chapter Six, the primary focus will be on federal practice, as representative of the modern approach. The critical provisions are found in Federal Rules 13–14, 17–24, and 42. There will be occasional references to contrasting state practice, where appropriate.

In any federal action, including diversity actions, the governing law on joinder is federal. Contrary state joinder provisions, as opposed to state laws establishing the underlying substantive rights, do not apply in federal court under *Erie*.[5]

Each claim against a particular party in federal court must satisfy the federal requirements of subject-matter jurisdiction, terri-

---

1.　See supra § 1.2(A)(2)(c); Geoffrey C. Hazard, Jr., Indispensable Party: The Historical Origin of a Procedural Phantom, 61 Colum. L. Rev. 1254 (1961).

2.　See supra § 1.2(B)(2); John W. Reed, Compulsory Joinder of Parties in Civil Actions (pts. 1–2), 55 Mich. L. Rev. 327, 483 (1957).

3.　See supra § 1.2(C)(2); Robert G. Bone, Mapping the Boundaries of a Dis-

pute: Conceptions of Ideal Lawsuit Structure from the Field Code to the Federal Rules, 89 Colum. L. Rev. 1 (1989).

4.　Charles Alan Wright, Class Actions, 47 F.R.D. 169, 170 n.7 (1970) (quoting letter about Fed. R. Civ. P. 23).

5.　See supra § 3.2(A).

torial jurisdiction, and venue. Especially relevant here, however, are the ameliorating doctrines of supplemental jurisdiction and ancillary venue.[6]

C. Uses and Abuses

On the one hand, the rationale behind the modern approach to joinder is the efficiency and even the fairness in disposing of much in one shot. Hence, there must be techniques to compel and permit joinder. On the other hand, as things get too complex, fairness notions and even efficiency concerns begin to cut the other way. When the balance swings, there must be cures in the form of simplifying measures. Obviously, striking the proper balance as to aggregated treatment raises profound questions of collectivization versus individualization.[7]

1. Parties' Defenses of Nonjoinder and Misjoinder

A party can raise the opposing pleader's violation of the joinder rules in a variety of ways.

If a claim was unasserted in violation of the minimal rules of *compulsory joinder*, the defending party on that claim may raise a defense in the nature of res judicata when that claim is asserted in a later action.[8] If a person is not joined in violation of compulsory joinder rules, there is a defense immediately available under Rule 12(b)(7) and (h)(2), or the court may raise the nonjoinder itself to protect the absentee.

If assertion of a claim exceeds the very liberal bounds on *permissive joinder*, a motion to strike or dismiss lies implicitly in the Federal Rules. If a party is joined in violation of permissive joinder rules, a motion to drop the party lies under Rule 21:

> Misjoinder of parties is not a ground for dismissing an action. On motion or on its own, the court may at any time, on just terms, add or drop a party. The court may also sever any claim against a party.

The Rules are not too systematic on misjoinder and exhibit considerable overlap, so that more specific relief lies in some of the Rules embodying special joinder provisions.[9]

---

6. See supra § 4.1(C)(2)(c).

7. Compare Roger H. Trangsrud, Joinder Alternatives in Mass Tort Litigation, 70 Cornell L. Rev. 779 (1985), with David Rosenberg, Class Actions for Mass Torts: Doing Individual Justice by Collective Means, 62 Ind. L.J. 561 (1987).

8. See supra §§ 5.2, 5.7.

9. See, e.g., Fed. R. Civ. P. 14(a)(4) (court may strike a third-party claim on motion).

2. Judicial Power to Divide and Combine

Even where the pleaders have initially formulated a proper case in that wide area between the limits of compulsory and permissive joinder of claims and parties, one must recognize that they did so in pursuit of their own advantages, and so the court can reshape the litigation for efficient and fair disposition, upon motion or sua sponte.[10] Thus, although under modern joinder rules the procedural restrictions on the parties during the pleading stage are pretty loose, there are considerable judicial powers aimed at facilitating the pretrial and trial stages' operation, with the judge's discretion becoming the essential mechanism in reformulating the litigation unit.

The court may contract the case by ordering a *separate trial* of any separate issue or any claim, under Rule 42(b):

> For convenience, to avoid prejudice, or to expedite and economize, the court may order a separate trial of one or more separate issues, claims, crossclaims, counterclaims, or third-party claims. When ordering a separate trial, the court must preserve any federal right to a jury trial.

Or the court may take the further step of *severance*, whereby individual claims against particular parties are cut off to stand as separate cases, under the already quoted Rule 21.[11] Again, more specific relief lies in some of the special Rules.[12]

Alternatively, the court may expand the case by ordering a *joint trial*, in whole or in part, of separate actions pending before it and involving "a common question of law or fact," or the court may take the further step of *consolidation*, whereby such actions are treated together for most purposes, under Rule 42(a):[13]

> If actions before the court involve a common question of law or fact, the court may:
>
> > (1) join for hearing or trial any or all matters at issue in the actions;

---

10. See Manual for Complex Litigation (Fourth) (2004) (this semi-official guide, which is the product of the drafting and revising efforts over the last few decades of a Federal Judicial Center committee composed mainly of judges, serves as a sort of tracking mechanism by suggesting specialized guidelines for handling complex actions).

11. See, e.g., Bridgeport Music, Inc. v. 11C Music, 202 F.R.D. 229 (M.D. Tenn. 2001) (too many defendants).

12. See, e.g., Fed. R. Civ. P. 14(a)(4) (court may order separate trial or severance of a third-party claim on motion, or

in its discretion may simply strike that claim); Fed. R. Civ. P. 20(b) (treating protective orders and separate trials in relation to permissive joinder of parties).

13. See Charles Alan Wright & Arthur R. Miller, Federal Practice and Procedure § 2382 (3d ed. 2008) (despite the sound of Fed. R. Civ. P. 42(a), consolidation is a ministerial act, so that the consolidated actions do not lose their separate identity or merge into a single case, and the parties to one action do not become parties to the others).

(2) consolidate the actions; or

(3) issue any other orders to avoid unnecessary cost or delay.

Furthermore, when actions "involving one or more common questions of fact" are pending in different federal district courts, the seven-judge *Judicial Panel on Multidistrict Litigation* may transfer them temporarily to any single district for coordinated or consolidated pretrial proceedings, including discovery; the Panel so acts—upon its own initiative or any party's motion, and after notice and hearing—when transfer "will be for the convenience of parties and witnesses and will promote the just and efficient conduct of such actions."[14] Congress enacted this transfer scheme in 1968 to allow the combined handling of dispersed but related claims, such as certain protracted antitrust actions. Although in theory this transfer is only for pretrial proceedings, in reality the judge rarely sends cases back to transferor courts. Under current practice most cases terminate before returning, usually by settlement but sometimes by dispositive pretrial decision. A few go to trial in the transferee court, either with the parties' consent or as a result of a full transfer of venue by the transferor court within the more demanding terms of 28 U.S.C. § 1404(a);[15] any such trial usually follows a consolidation order under Rule 42(a).

§ 6.2 Multiclaim Litigation

The subject here is the adjudication of additional claims between those already parties. The initial pleader (i.e., the plaintiff) has the first say in structuring the lawsuit, but the law places limits on any pleader's choices. Which claims must or may a pleader join? A useful image is of inner and outer limits on pleader autonomy. Between those limits, which comprise the law of compulsory and permissive joinder respectively, the pleader can decide what to assert. Outside those limits, the law does not allow the pleader to go, either by the pleader's splitting up a transaction into separate lawsuits or by the pleader's throwing superfluous claims into the pot.

A. Compulsory Joinder

The immediate concern here is the minimum aspect of initial joinder: What claims *must* be joined in the pleadings? Such compulsory joinder requirements are quite limited. These requirements constitute the inner limits on the claim-structure, limits that tell

---

14. See 28 U.S.C. § 1407; David F. Herr, Multidistrict Litigation (1986).

15. See Lexecon Inc. v. Milberg Weiss Bershad Hynes & Lerach, 523 U.S. 26 (1998) (holding under current statute that transferee court cannot transfer to itself); supra § 4.2(C)(1)(c).

the pleader what claims must be forwarded. These limits are enforceable by the opponent if the claimant later tries to assert the omitted claim.

1. Compulsory Parallel Claims

Res judicata does not require a party (e.g., the plaintiff) to join separate claims against his opponent, but its subdoctrine called claim preclusion generally does in effect require him to put any one asserted claim entirely before the court. The eventual judgment will extinguish that whole claim, precluding matters within the claim that were or could have been litigated in the action.

The doctrine of claim preclusion could be viewed as a common-law rule of compulsory joinder. However, claim preclusion has not traditionally been described in terms of compulsory joinder. The plaintiff is not seen as having several grievances that must be joined now, but rather as having one claim that cannot be split without later suffering consequences.

The problem of determining what must be included in a single lawsuit to avoid later consequences thus becomes a problem of defining the scope of that single claim that cannot be split without suffering res judicata. The modern approach views "claim" for this purpose as including all rights of the plaintiff to remedies against the defendant with respect to the transaction from which the action arose.[16]

For technical pleading purposes, a party need not be concerned with the precise boundaries of his claims, as long as he puts fully before the court any transaction about which he complains. He can formulate this transaction as one claim or as multiple versions. Federal Rule 8(d)(2) allows the party to "set out two or more statements of a claim or defense alternatively or hypothetically, either in a single count or defense or in separate ones."[17]

2. Compulsory Counterclaim Provisions

Analogously, Rule 13(a) generally requires a pleader (e.g., the defendant) to put forward any claim that the pleader has against any opposing party, if it "arises out of the transaction or occurrence that is the subject matter of the opposing party's claim":[18]

> (1) *In General.* A pleading must state as a counterclaim any claim that—at the time of its service—the pleader has against an opposing party if the claim:

---

16. See supra § 5.2(A).

17. See also Fed. R. Civ. P. 18(a) (freedom to join claims); Fed. R. Civ. P. 10(b) (separate counts); supra § 2.1(A)(1)(c).

18. See generally Charles Alan Wright & Mary Kay Kane, Law of Federal Courts § 79 (6th ed. 2002).

(A) arises out of the transaction or occurrence that is the subject matter of the opposing party's claim; and

(B) does not require adding another party over whom the court cannot acquire jurisdiction.

(2) *Exceptions.* The pleader need not state the claim if:

(A) when the action was commenced, the claim was the subject of another pending action; or

(B) the opposing party sued on its claim by attachment or other process that did not establish personal jurisdiction over the pleader on that claim, and the pleader does not assert any counterclaim under this rule.

Failure to assert such a counterclaim will preclude bringing a subsequent action thereon. The effect of a prior judgment in barring an unasserted compulsory counterclaim is most often described in res judicata terms.[19] However, rather than invoking the rigid doctrine of res judicata, some courts view this preclusion in the more flexible terms of equitable estoppel or waiver, enabling them to preclude even when the prior action did not produce technically a judgment.[20] In either event, potential preclusion means that a quick plaintiff can choose the forum for the defendant's claim, which can give the plaintiff a significant advantage.

"Transaction" in the Rule is more inclusive than "occurrence," the latter word serving primarily to clarify that the former is not limited to a business sense. A counterclaim arises from the same transaction when it bears a "logical relationship" to the main claim, according to *Moore v. New York Cotton Exchange.*[21] Subsequent cases have employed this vaguely inclusive test to delimit compulsory counterclaims in a functional albeit uncertain way, looking to factual and legal overlap but also taking account of the Rule's purpose of efficiency and considering the particular circumstances in which the question arises.[22] So, for example, if P brings a diversity action against D, alleging D slandered him by saying that P had sold D worthless goods and thereby caused big damages, and

19. E.g., Horne v. Woolever, 163 N.E.2d 378 (Ohio 1959); see Austin Wakeman Scott, Collateral Estoppel by Judgment, 56 Harv. L. Rev. 1 (1942).

20. E.g., Dindo v. Whitney, 451 F.2d 1 (1st Cir. 1971); see Wright & Miller, supra note 13, § 1417, at 132–38; Charles Alan Wright, Estoppel by Rule: The Compulsory Counterclaim Under Modern Pleading, 38 Minn. L. Rev. 423 (1954).

21. 270 U.S. 593, 610 (1926).

22. See Iglesias v. Mut. Life Ins. Co., 156 F.3d 237 (1st Cir. 1998). Compare Maddox v. Ky. Fin. Co., 736 F.2d 380 (6th Cir. 1984) (when holding in a Truth in Lending Act case that a counterclaim on the underlying debt was not compulsory and hence not within supplemental jurisdiction, the court observed: "It is not clear that the interests of judicial economy and efficiency would be served in the least by requiring that the two claims be heard together."), with Plant v. Blazer Fin. Servs., Inc., 598 F.2d 1357 (5th Cir. 1979) (holding counterclaim compulsory in same situation).

if D counterclaims to recover the $5000 paid for those goods, then, when P moves to dismiss the counterclaim for lack of subject-matter jurisdiction, the counterclaim will be deemed compulsory and so will come within the doctrine of supplemental jurisdiction.[23] However, the counterclaim might have been deemed to have been noncompulsory under Rule 13(a)(1)(A)'s transactional test if the issue had arisen instead in a subsequent state action, when the issue's resolution would determine whether D was now precluded from asserting her omitted counterclaim.[24]

Moreover, the federal courts have commonly been generous in applying Rule 13(f), which provides for getting the counterclaim in late but while the first action is still pending:

> The court may permit a party to amend a pleading to add a counterclaim if it was omitted through oversight, inadvertence, or excusable neglect or if justice so requires.

There are exceptions whereby the defendant is not obligated to assert a counterclaim arising from the same transaction or occurrence. At least six narrow ones have arisen from case law.[25] Rule 13(a) itself suggests five more exceptions:

23. See Albright v. Gates, 362 F.2d 928 (9th Cir. 1966); cf. Painter v. Harvey, 863 F.2d 329 (4th Cir. 1988) (analogous facts). But cf. Harris v. Steinem, 571 F.2d 119 (2d Cir. 1978) (holding no supplemental jurisdiction, where plaintiff sued for securities violation, defendant counterclaimed for defamation in complaint and subsequent to complaint, and main claim was dismissed).

24. See Williams v. Robinson, 1 F.R.D. 211 (D.D.C. 1940) (counterclaim for libel expressed by complaint). But cf. Pochiro v. Prudential Ins. Co. of Am., 827 F.2d 1246 (9th Cir. 1987) (counterclaim for pre-and post-complaint defamatory statements); Grumman Sys. Support Corp. v. Data Gen. Corp., 125 F.R.D. 160 (N.D. Cal. 1988) (first-filed action still pending, so that counterclaim could still be pursued). For yet other settings in which this question of compulsoriness can arise, consider Banque Indosuez v. Trifinery, 817 F. Supp. 386 (S.D.N.Y. 1993) (application of contractual waiver of right to make permissive counterclaim was at stake), or consider Bose Corp. v. Consumers Union of United States, 384 F. Supp. 600 (D. Mass. 1974) (application of statute of limitations was at stake). On the application of the statute of limitations, see also Azada v. Carson, 252 F. Supp. 988 (D. Haw. 1966) (applying majority rule that allows assertion of a counterclaim on which the statute of limitations ran between the filing of the complaint and the filing of the counterclaim, as long as the counterclaim arises out of the same transaction or occurrence as the main claim).

25. For example, a purely declaratory action does not trigger Rule 13(a), says Allan Block Corp. v. County Materials Corp., 512 F.3d 912 (7th Cir. 2008). See Wright & Miller, supra note 13, § 1412 ("a counterclaim for treble damages for unfair competition under the Clayton or Robinson–Patman Acts may not be compulsory in an action for patent infringement"; "when defendant's counterclaim arises out of transactions presented in two pending suits, Rule 13(a) does not compel the assertion of the counterclaim in whichever of the two suits the first responsive pleading is filed [and instead defendant may] elect to interpose it in the second action"; "exception to Rule 13(a) arises when the counterclaim falls within the scope of a collective bargaining agreement and still is subject to arbitration at the time defendant interposes his answer to the complaint"; "when the main claim seeks injunctive or declaratory relief and the hearing on the preliminary injunction is accelerated and consolidated with the

(1) No Pleading. Because Rule 13(a)(1) requires inclusion of counterclaims only in a "pleading," a defendant who wins a dismissal of the main claim by a motion without filing an answer need not assert any counterclaim.[26] More importantly, a defendant who defaults need not worry about the Rule.[27]

(2) Unavailable Counterclaim. Because Rule 13(a)(1) applies only to counterclaims that the pleader has at the time of serving the pleading, a defendant need not assert any counterclaim later matured or acquired.[28]

(3) Additional Party. Rule 13(h) expressly authorizes bringing in additional parties to counterclaims. But Rule 13(a)(1)(B) provides that a defendant need not assert any counterclaim involving a necessary party (as defined below) over whom the court cannot acquire personal jurisdiction.[29]

(4) Another Pending Action. Rule 13(a)(2)(A) provides that a defendant need not assert any counterclaim that "was the subject of another pending action" when the present action was commenced. Thus, the plaintiff cannot force the defendant's claim into a court of the plaintiff's choosing if that claim is already pending elsewhere.

(5) Nonpersonal Action. Rule 13(a)(2)(B) provides that a defendant need not assert any counterclaim in an action commenced other than on personal jurisdiction. If she chooses to assert any of her counterclaims, however, the compulsory counterclaim Rule comes back into normal operation.

As to further pleading, the opposing party responds to any counterclaim in the ordinary fashion by motion and/or answer under Rules 7(a)(3) and 12(a). That answer is seemingly subject to Rule 13 regarding inclusion of further counterclaims.[30]

In an action that involves a counterclaim, the plaintiff may prevail on his claim and the defendant on her counterclaim. If the defendant's recovery is for a smaller sum than the plaintiff's, the result is a judgment in favor of the plaintiff for the difference. If

---

trial on the merits, defendant's transactionally related money damages claim is not compulsory"; and "the need to uphold forum selection clauses alters the impact of the compulsory-counterclaim rule so that a party need not file a compulsory counterclaim in an improper forum to avoid having the claim barred in a proper forum").

26. See Lawhorn v. Atlantic Ref. Co., 299 F.2d 353 (5th Cir. 1962); see also Fed. R. Civ. P. 7 (defining "pleading").

27. But cf. Carteret Sav. & Loan Ass'n v. Jackson, 812 F.2d 36 (1st Cir.

1987) (mistakenly applying Fed. R. Civ. P. 13(a) after default, instead of common-law compulsory counterclaim rule).

28. See also Fed. R. Civ. P. 13(e) ("The court may permit a party to file a supplemental pleading asserting a counterclaim that matured or was acquired by the party after serving an earlier pleading.").

29. See Wright & Miller, supra note 13, § 1411.

30. See id. § 1188.

the defendant's recovery is for a larger amount than the plaintiff's, there will be an affirmative judgment in favor of the defendant for the difference. An affirmative judgment for the defendant will also follow where the plaintiff fails on his claim and the defendant succeeds on her counterclaim.

Some states have counterclaim provisions considerably more narrow than the federal model. Indeed, some states have no compulsory counterclaim statute or rule at all, although there is always, in state or federal court, the small category of common-law compulsory counterclaims.

3. Common–Law Compulsory Counterclaims

Even in the absence of an applicable statute or court rule, failure to assert an available counterclaim precludes bringing a subsequent action thereon if granting relief would nullify the judgment in the initial action.[31] This so-called common-law compulsory counterclaim rule emerges from the intuitive principle of claim preclusion that a valid and final judgment generally precludes the defendant from later asserting mere defenses to the claim. The implicit extension of this idea is that once a plaintiff obtains a judgment (whether the judgment was litigated or defaulted), the defendant generally cannot bring a new action to undo the judgment by reopening the plaintiff's claim and pushing those defenses (whether or not a compulsory counterclaim statute or rule appears on the books or applies in the circumstances). The evident rationale is that claim preclusion simply must apply when the effect of the defendant's collaterally asserted defense would be to nullify the earlier judgment for the plaintiff, or otherwise judgments would not be worth obtaining. Therefore, the defendant cannot later pursue an action that is essentially a way to defend anew against an already adjudicated claim.[32]

B. Permissive Joinder

The concern shifts here to the maximum aspect of initial joinder of additional claims between the parties: What claims *may* be joined in the pleadings? The permissiveness of such joinder is almost unbounded, at least in federal court.

---

31. See Kevin M. Clermont, Common–Law Compulsory Counterclaim Rule: Creating Effective and Elegant Res Judicata Doctrine, 79 Notre Dame L. Rev. 1745 (2004).

32. See supra § 5.2(C) for more complete discussion of common-law compulsory counterclaims.

1. Permissive Parallel Claims

Federal Rule 18(a) permits any party asserting any kind of claim to "join, as independent or alternative claims, as many claims" of any kind "as it has against an opposing party".[33]

> A party asserting a claim, counterclaim, crossclaim, or third-party claim may join, as independent or alternative claims, as many claims as it has against an opposing party.

There is no relatedness requirement. Permissive joinder of parallel claims is thus unbounded, except by the usual requirements such as jurisdiction and venue.

Is There a Taxonomy of Claims?

Yes, there is. Federal Rule 18(a) provides it, by allowing free joinder with any "claim, counterclaim, crossclaim, or third-party claim." Given that the first-mentioned "claim" means an original claim, is this an exhaustive listing, or are there other kinds of claims? For a prime example, what should we call a claim by a third-party defendant against the original plaintiff that arises out of the main claim's transaction or occurrence? The leading treatise, Wright & Miller, supra note 13, § 1458, opines:

> There is some inconsistency in the cases as to the proper way of denominating claims by the third-party defendant against the original plaintiff. Some courts refer to them as cross-claims and other courts call them counterclaims. Technically, neither term is appropriate. Claims [like these] are not counterclaims within the meaning of Rule 13 because the original plaintiff and the third-party defendant are not opposing parties at the time the third-party's claim is interposed. Nor are they cross-claims inasmuch as Rule 13(g) requires cross-claims to be asserted against a coparty, and plaintiff and third-party defendant do not fit that description. The denomination of a claim by a third-party defendant against plaintiff is of no practical import when it clearly is within the scope * * * of Rule 14(a). * * * Nonetheless, it would be better simply to describe the claim than to refer to it as a counterclaim or a cross-claim.

Well, as for practical import, can the third-party defendant join with that unnamed claim an unrelated claim against the original plaintiff under Rule 18(a)? He should be able to, given the purpose of Rule 18(a). Under that Rule, "there is no restriction on the claims that may be joined. *** Technically, there can be no misjoinder of claims." Id. § 1582. After all, the original defendant can freely invoke Rule 18(a) in this three-cornered lawsuit, and the third-party defendant can too for claims against the original defendant. True, the third-party defendant could bring its unrelated claim against the original plaintiff as a separate suit and then seek to join the two suits, but it would be simpler to allow pleading the unrelated claim in the initial suit. Admittedly, the unrelated claim could overly complicate the lawsuit, but if hearing the unrelated claim in that one suit is inefficient or unfair, then it can be separated under Rule 42(b) or Rule 21. In sum, the right way to read the relatedness requirement of Rule 14(a)(2)(D) is to require a related claim for the third-party defendant to launch an offensive against the plaintiff, yet once that claim is asserted the third-party defendant is free to plead any other claim against the plaintiff under Rule 18(a). See Arthur F. Greenbaum, Jacks or Better to Open: Procedural Limitations on Co-Party and Third-Party Claims, 74 Minn. L. Rev. 507, 517, 531–34, 546–47 (1990) ("the Rules require a qualifying claim to get in the game (jacks or better to open), but once that requirement is met the Rules allow the parties to play their hands as they wish"). To get to

---

33. See generally Wright & Kane, supra note 18, § 78.

this desirable result, claims under Rule 14(a)(2)(D) must fall within Rule 18(a). In other words, **Rule 18(a)'s listing of kinds of claims is indeed best read to be exhaustive.**

But how can we reach that reading through the words of Rule 18(a)? We can do so by calling the related claim under Rule 14(a)(2)(D) a cross-claim. But how can that be squared with Rule 13(g)'s definition of cross-claim: "any claim by one party against a coparty if the claim arises out of the transaction or occurrence"? By not leaping to view coparties as those having the same status in the suit, but instead defining coparty as any party who is not yet an opposing party to the other (with opposing parties being parties who formally oppose each other on a pleaded claim and who should therefore resort to the counterclaim provision). The recent cases in fact accept this very definition. See, e.g., Mauney v. Imperial Delivery Servs., Inc., 865 F. Supp. 142, 153 (S.D.N.Y. 1994); Earle M. Jorgenson Co. v. T.I. United States, Ltd., 133 F.R.D. 472, 474 (E.D. Pa. 1991) ("This comports with the structure of the federal rules, which envision three types of claims that may be asserted by defendants: counterclaims, third-party claims, and cross-claims."); Ga. Ports Auth. v. Construzioni Meccaniche Industriali Genovesi, S.P.A., 119 F.R.D. 693, 695 (S.D. Ga. 1988) (construing " 'co-party' to mean *any party that is not an opposing party*"). This definition fits the purpose of the crossclaim provision, which allows but does not compel nonadverse parties to introduce an adverse claim and thus avoid multiple suits, as long as the claim arises from the same transaction or occurrence. Moreover, this definition nicely eliminates any gap between Rule 14(a)(1)'s impleader provision, which is available only against a nonparty, and Rule 13's allowance of impleader-type claims against copar-ties and opposing parties; elimination of the gap authorizes an impleader claim to lie against any person, as the rulemakers intended. See John D. Bessler, Note, Defining "Co-Party" Within Federal Rule of Civil Procedure 13(g): Are Cross-claims Between Original Defendants and Third-Party Defendants Allowable?, 66 Ind. L.J. 549 (1991) (convincingly arguing that the claims described in his title are allowable). So, **a coparty is any party who is not yet an opposing party.**

2. Permissive Counterclaims

Analogously to Rule 18(a)'s free joinder, Rule 13(b) permits a pleader to put forward any counterclaim that she has "against an opposing party":[34]

A pleading may state as a counterclaim against an opposing party any claim that is not compulsory.

The predecessors of the universally available counterclaim were recoupment and setoff, but they were much more limited.

As to recoupment, at common law there were narrowly con-fined situations where a defendant, by asserting a claim in the action, could reduce the recovery to which the plaintiff would otherwise be entitled. A building contractor sued the owner for work done and materials furnished; in that action the owner might seek a recoupment on the ground that the work was not well done; and if the recoupment succeeded, the contractor's recovery would be reduced accordingly. The rationale lay in the idea that "recoup-ment, in its original sense, was a mere right of deduction from the

---

34. See generally id. § 79.

amount of the plaintiff's recovery, on the ground that his damages were not really as high as he alleged,"[35] but in time the sharpness of this definition was lost. For instance, where a plaintiff sued on a promissory note given for the sale of his business, the defendant was allowed to recoup for the plaintiff's breach of an agreement not to compete with the business.[36] Still, a recoupment must have arisen out of the same transaction as the plaintiff's claim. It could reduce the plaintiff's claim but could not result in an affirmative judgment in the action in the defendant's favor. However, to maintain a recoupment it was not necessary that the plaintiff's or the defendant's claim be liquidated or certain in amount.

Where the defendant's claim arose out of a different transaction, recoupment was unavailable. So, at early common law the defendant could secure adjudication of the defendant's claim only by bringing an independent action. Equity, however, borrowed the Roman and civil-law doctrine of *compensatio* and allowed the setoff of mutual debts. In the course of time, and by statutory steps, this principle of equity was taken over by the law courts. This statutory setoff, like recoupment, could not be used as a basis for affirmative relief, and so its only effect was to reduce or defeat the plaintiff's claim. At least classically, the plea of setoff was allowed only where the claims on both sides involved debts that were liquidated or could be readily and without difficulty ascertained.[37]

3. Crossclaims

Rule 13(g) permits, but does not compel, a party to assert related claims for relief "against a coparty".[38]

> A pleading may state as a crossclaim any claim by one party against a coparty if the claim arises out of the transaction or occurrence that is the subject matter of the original action or of a counterclaim, or if the claim relates to any property that is the subject matter of the original action. The crossclaim may include a claim that the coparty is or may be liable to the crossclaimant for all or part of a claim asserted in the action against the crossclaimant.

Coparties for the purposes of such a crossclaim are parties who are not yet in opposing posture, which would justify a counterclaim instead.[39] So, if P sues M and S for S's negligence, where M is S's employer, and if M wishes to assert against S a contingent claim

---

35. 3 Theodore Sedgwick, Damages 2162 (9th ed. 1912).

36. See Stacy v. Kemp, 97 Mass. 166 (1867).

37. See Stooke v. Taylor, 5 Q.B.D. 569 (Eng. 1880).

38. See generally Wright & Kane, supra note 18, § 80.

39. See Rainbow Mgmt. Group, Ltd. v. Atlantis Submarines Haw., L.P., 158 F.R.D. 656 (D. Haw. 1994).

under applicable substantive law for indemnity, then a crossclaim is proper, although *M* could instead elect to bring a separate action against *S*. Rule 13(g) states no time limit for asserting crossclaims, leaving this matter to judicial discretion.

To prevent undue complication by addition of crossclaims in which the main claimant has utterly no interest, a crossclaim must arise "out of the transaction or occurrence that is the subject matter of the original action or of a counterclaim" (a limitation that embodies a transactional test interpreted roughly the same as Rule 13(a)'s test) *or* must relate "to any property that is the subject matter of the original action" (a limitation that permits, for example, crossclaims concerning the stake in an interpleader suit).

Some courts have held, probably incorrectly, that the purpose of the transactional requirement in Rule 13(g) is only to permit a party (whether the defendant or the plaintiff) to assert against a coparty a crossclaim growing out of the transaction or occurrence that is the subject matter of a claim (claim or counterclaim) *against that party*.[40] Under that restrictive view, coplaintiff *A* in accident litigation could not crossclaim against another plaintiff *B* in the absence of some claim, such as a counterclaim, against *A*.

§ 6.3   Multiparty Litigation

The subject here is the adjudication of claims that involve multiple or additional parties.[41] The initial pleader (i.e., the plaintiff) has the first say in structuring the lawsuit, but the law places limits on any pleader's choices. Which persons must or may be joined? The useful image again is of inner and outer limits on pleader autonomy. Between those limits, the pleader can decide whom to join. But the law does not allow the pleader to exceed those limits, either by the pleader's omitting a key player or by the pleader's including a superfluous party.

A.   Compulsory Joinder

The immediate concern becomes the minimum aspect of initial joinder: What persons *must* be joined when any party (e.g., the plaintiff) pleads a claim? There are occasions when the plaintiff must enlist other persons who should have joined him as plaintiffs, and there are also occasions when he must bring in certain additional persons to defend the lawsuit. These requirements constitute the inner limits on the party-structure, limits that tell the plaintiff

---

40. See Danner v. Anskis, 256 F.2d 123 (3d Cir. 1958) (adopting restrictive view). But see Ryan ex rel. Ryan v. Schneider Nat'l Carriers, Inc., 263 F.3d 816 (8th Cir. 2001); Harrison v. M.S. Carriers, Inc., No. CIV.A. 98–3177, 1999 WL 195539 (E.D. La. Apr. 7, 1999).

41. See generally Wright & Kane, supra note 18, §§ 70–71.

who must be joined. These limits are enforceable by the defendant or the court.

Federal Rule 19 is the governing provision, applying even when the pleader is asserting a counterclaim or crossclaim[42] or, presumably, almost any other sort of claim such as a third-party claim.[43] Rule 19(a) refers to parties that should be joined as "persons required to be joined if feasible," these being persons who are so closely connected to an action that they not only could properly be joined but must be joined, unless joinder is not feasible under the requirements of jurisdiction and venue:

(1) *Required Party.* A person who is subject to service of process and whose joinder will not deprive the court of subject-matter jurisdiction must be joined as a party if:

(A) in that person's absence, the court cannot accord complete relief among existing parties; or

(B) that person claims an interest relating to the subject of the action and is so situated that disposing of the action in the person's absence may:

(i) as a practical matter impair or impede the person's ability to protect the interest; or

(ii) leave an existing party subject to a substantial risk of incurring double, multiple, or otherwise inconsistent obligations because of the interest.

(2) *Joinder by Court Order.* If a person has not been joined as required, the court must order that the person be made a party. A person who refuses to join as a plaintiff may be made either a defendant or, in a proper case, an involuntary plaintiff.

(3) *Venue.* If a joined party objects to venue and the joinder would make venue improper, the court must dismiss that party.

Thus, the Rule rather broadly defines this group of "necessary parties" to include anyone whose absence would prevent complete relief among those already parties, *or* anyone who claims an interest relating to the subject of the action if proceeding in that person's absence might either impair that interest practically or subject any of those already parties to a substantial risk of double liability.[44] So, for example, if *P* sues *D* for specific performance on a

42. See Fed. R. Civ. P. 13(h) ("Rules 19 and 20 govern the addition of a person as a party to a counterclaim or crossclaim.").

43. But see Fed. R. Civ. P. 19(d) (excepting class actions and so allowing them to proceed in the absence of class members, by providing: "This rule is subject to Rule 23.").

44. See Janney Montgomery Scott, Inc. v. Shepard Niles, Inc., 11 F.3d 399 (3d Cir. 1993) (using flexible approach in finding joint obligor to be not necessary); Daynard v. Ness, Motley, Loadholt, Richardson & Poole, P.A., 184 F. Supp. 2d 55 (D. Mass. 2001) (same), rev'd on other grounds, 290 F.3d 42 (1st Cir. 2002).

contract, *P*'s joint obligee is a necessary party.[45]

If a necessary party cannot be joined because of the restrictions of jurisdiction and venue, the court must decide between dispensing imperfect justice and not acting at all. Rule 19(b) formulates this problem of "equity and good conscience" in pragmatic terms, listing factors to be considered in the context of the particular case:

> If a person who is required to be joined if feasible cannot be joined, the court must determine whether, in equity and good conscience, the action should proceed among the existing parties or should be dismissed. The factors for the court to consider include:
>
> > (1) the extent to which a judgment rendered in the person's absence might prejudice that person or the existing parties;
> >
> > (2) the extent to which any prejudice could be lessened or avoided by:
> >
> > > (A) protective provisions in the judgment;
> > >
> > > (B) shaping the relief; or
> > >
> > > (C) other measures;
> >
> > (3) whether a judgment rendered in the person's absence would be adequate; and
> >
> > (4) whether the plaintiff would have an adequate remedy if the action were dismissed for nonjoinder.

These factors translate to include the interests of the *absentee* in being included, the *defendant* in not going forward without a complete cast, the *plaintiff* in having a forum, and the *public* in efficiently, fairly, and accurately administering justice; the court should also consider the availability of measures by these persons or the court to protect these interests.[46] In some extreme circumstances, the decision to go forward without the absentee could constitute a denial of due process.[47] Note that upon a judicial decision not to proceed, necessary parties are termed "indispensable parties"; but these terms are merely conclusory labels and so do not play a part in the reasoning process.[48]

---

45. See Makah Indian Tribe v. Verity, 910 F.2d 555 (9th Cir. 1990); Jenkins v. Reneau, 697 F.2d 160 (6th Cir. 1983).

46. Compare Haas v. Jefferson Nat'l Bank, 442 F.2d 394 (5th Cir. 1971) (questionably affirming indispensability of nonparty), with Helzberg's Diamond Shops, Inc. v. Valley West Des Moines Shopping Ctr., Inc., 564 F.2d 816 (8th Cir. 1977) (questionably affirming dispensability of nonparty).

47. See W. Union Tel. Co. v. Pennsylvania, 368 U.S. 71 (1961) (disallowing escheat proceeding in absence of other states with potential claims to property).

48. See Provident Tradesmens Bank & Trust Co. v. Patterson, 390 U.S. 102 (1968) (holding nonparty to be not indispensable, validating Fed. R. Civ. P. 19 as amended, and rejecting the abstract approach of Shields v. Barrow, 58 U.S. (17 How.) 130 (1855)).

Students tend to exaggerate the reach of Rule 19. Rule 19(a) is not so broad, for example, as to cover typical concurrent-tortfeasors or to cover vicarious liability such as employee-employer cases.[49] Joinder of defendants in those cases is not required under Rule 19(a) even if feasible; it is entirely optional with the plaintiff under Rule 20 (as discussed below), so that the plaintiff can select his targets. The explanation is found in the character of the substantive rights and duties of the persons involved. The typical version of that substantive law is often summed up as "joint-and-several" liability, but that term really represents the joinder conclusion that the defendants can be sued together or separately. The better description of the substantive law is "entire" liability, meaning that *each* defendant is liable for *all* of the plaintiff's damages. The plaintiff can recover the whole judgment from any judgment debtor, although the plaintiff of course cannot recover more than the amount of the judgment by going after other of the judgment debtors. The substantive policy is to make the plaintiff whole, and to leave it to the defendants to squabble among themselves about relative overpayment of their shares by invoking whatever law of contribution happens to exist. Accordingly, the absence or presence of other potential defendants has no legal effect on the joined defendants, while the substantive law intends the practical effect of disadvantaging defendants, and so the Rules leave it up to the plaintiff whom to sue. As usual, then, much is left to party autonomy.

If the substantive law were different, the joinder conclusion might differ. For example, Vermont apportions fractions of the total amount of liability according to fault but relative only to those tortfeasors actually joined as defendants, and then Vermont allows no right of contribution against those not joined as defendants.[50] Under that strange liability scheme, where it deeply matters to defendants who else is sued, concurrent tortfeasors would more arguably be necessary parties in federal court, and indeed could be indispensable in appropriate circumstances.

As to the procedural details of compulsory joinder of parties, normally all persons joined pursuant to Rule 19 are brought in as defendants by service of process, including persons who should have been plaintiffs but who refused to join voluntarily.[51] However, for the purpose of determining the existence of diversity jurisdiction,

---

49. See Temple v. Synthes Corp., 498 U.S. 5, 7 (1990) (per curiam) ("it is not necessary for all joint tortfeasors to be named as defendants in a single lawsuit").

50. See Mark Righter, Note, No Contribution Among Joint Tortfeasors: The Rule That Has Fooled the Courts and Foiled the Vermont Legislature, 7 Vt. L. Rev. 337 (1982).

51. See Wright & Miller, supra note 13, § 1605.

joined parties will be realigned according to the ultimate interest of each.[52] Realignment may either create or defeat jurisdiction.

Moreover, in very narrow circumstances, Rule 19(a)(2) allows the absentee to be made an "involuntary plaintiff" in order to circumvent the requirement of service of process that normally applies when a new party is brought into an action. A "proper case" for so doing is one in which the recalcitrant absentee is not subject to service, but equitable considerations require him to accept the burdens of permitting the use of his name as a plaintiff. Beware that in actual practice, however, courts approve this procedure only in the factual setting where an exclusive licensee of a patent or copyright sues for infringement and seeks to join the *recalcitrant owner of the patent or copyright* as a coplaintiff.[53]

B. Permissive Joinder

The concern shifts here to the maximum aspect of initial joinder of multiple or additional parties: What persons *may* be joined when any party (e.g., the plaintiff) pleads a claim? This question is answered as part of the broader subject of who are "proper parties" to a lawsuit, which is bounded by outer limits erected from the three relevant provisions that follow.

1. Real Party in Interest

Rule 17(a) changed the common-law practice by requiring every claim to be prosecuted only in the name of "real parties in interest." Thus, assignees and subrogees must now sue in their own names:

(1) *Designation in General.* An action must be prosecuted in the name of the real party in interest. The following may sue in their own names without joining the person for whose benefit the action is brought:

(A) an executor;

(B) an administrator;

(C) a guardian;

(D) a bailee;

(E) a trustee of an express trust;

(F) a party with whom or in whose name a contract has been made for another's benefit; and

---

52. See Eikel v. States Marine Lines, 473 F.2d 959 (5th Cir. 1973); see also City of Indianapolis v. Chase Nat'l Bank, 314 U.S. 63 (1941). See generally Wright & Kane, supra note 18, § 30.

53. See, e.g., Independent Wireless Tel. Co. v. RCA, 269 U.S. 459 (1926) (patent); Ferrara v. Rodale Press, 54 F.R.D. 3 (E.D. Pa. 1972) (copyright).

(G) a party authorized by statute.

(2) *Action in the Name of the United States for Another's Use or Benefit.* When a federal statute so provides, an action for another's use or benefit must be brought in the name of the United States.

(3) *Joinder of the Real Party in Interest.* The court may not dismiss an action for failure to prosecute in the name of the real party in interest until, after an objection, a reasonable time has been allowed for the real party in interest to ratify, join, or be substituted into the action. After ratification, joinder, or substitution, the action proceeds as if it had been originally commenced by the real party in interest.

Rule 17(a)(1)'s list indicates, only by way of illustration, that certain representatives, including administrators and trustees, are usually but not always the real party in interest. Thus, the real party in interest is not necessarily the beneficiary of the action. Instead, the real party in interest is the *person entitled under applicable substantive law to enforce the right sued upon.*[54]

However, having managed to reform the common-law practice, the poorly drafted Rule 17(a) does create considerable confusion today. Some suggest that if it were abrogated, all that is correct in Rule 17(a) would still follow from the rest of modern procedural and substantive law.[55]

As to procedural details, the defendant has interests in being sued by the right person, including an interest in obtaining the benefits of res judicata. So the defendant may seasonably assert a defense based on Rule 17(a), which would be similar to the defense available under Rule 12(b)(6). If the Rule 17(a) defense succeeds, the defect may be corrected within a reasonable time, as by substitution of the real party in interest. In a case of honest mistake, such substitution relates back to the date of the action's commencement.[56]

2. Capacity

Federal Rule 17(b) and (c) puts a further and separate limitation on who is a proper party:

---

54. See Naghiu v. Inter–Cont'l Hotels Group, Inc., 165 F.R.D. 413 (D. Del. 1996).

55. See Thomas E. Atkinson, The Real Party in Interest Rule: A Plea for Its Abolition, 32 N.Y.U. L. Rev. 926 (1957); John E. Kennedy, Federal Rule 17(a): Will the Real Party in Interest Please Stand?, 51 Minn. L. Rev. 675

(1967); June F. Entman, More Reasons for Abolishing Federal Rule of Civil Procedure 17(a): The Problem of the Proper Plaintiff and Insurance Subrogation, 68 N.C. L. Rev. 893 (1990).

56. See Green v. Daimler Benz, A.G., 157 F.R.D. 340 (E.D. Pa. 1994).

   (b) **Capacity to Sue or Be Sued.** Capacity to sue or be sued is determined as follows:

   (1) for an individual who is not acting in a representative capacity, by the law of the individual's domicile;

   (2) for a corporation, by the law under which it was organized; and

   (3) for all other parties, by the law of the state where the court is located, except that:

   (A) a partnership or other unincorporated association with no such capacity under that state's law may sue or be sued in its common name to enforce a substantive right existing under the United States Constitution or laws; and

   (B) 28 U.S.C. §§ 754 and 959(a) govern the capacity of a receiver appointed by a United States court to sue or be sued in a United States court.

   (c) **Minor or Incompetent Person.**

   (1) *With a Representative.* The following representatives may sue or defend on behalf of a minor or an incompetent person:

   (A) a general guardian;

   (B) a committee;

   (C) a conservator; or

   (D) a like fiduciary.

   (2) *Without a Representative.* A minor or an incompetent person who does not have a duly appointed representative may sue by a next friend or by a guardian ad litem. The court must appoint a guardian ad litem—or issue another appropriate order—to protect a minor or incompetent person who is unrepresented in an action.

This "capacity" to sue or be sued is a fairly narrow concept comprising the personal qualifications legally needed by a person to litigate, and it is usually determined without reference to the person's particular claim or defense. For example, an infant or a mental incompetent lacks capacity to sue, and so must litigate through a representative.

   Rule 17(b) and (c) lays down a few federal capacity rules, and also tells which state's law the federal court will adopt for the bulk of its capacity rules. For example, the capacity of a corporation is determined by the law under which it was incorporated.

   As to procedural details, Rule 9(a)(2) requires that any party desiring to challenge capacity must raise the issue by "specific denial." If it is not so raised during the pleading stage, it is waived.

3. Joinder Rules

Additionally, to be a proper party, a person must be the plaintiff or the defendant or must be joinable under one of the permissive joinder Rules. Rule 20 is the general provision for joinder of multiple parties on any side of a litigation. It applies even when a party is asserting a counterclaim or crossclaim[57] or, presumably, any other sort of claim.

But as elaborated below, there are also five special provisions that expand the scope of permissive joinder beyond Rule 20. They authorize specialized devices for asserting claims that peculiarly entail multiple parties.[58]

a. Multiple Plaintiffs or Defendants

Rule 20(a)(1) permits multiple plaintiffs to join together if they meet two tests:

> Persons may join in one action as plaintiffs if:
>
> (A) they assert any right to relief jointly, severally, or in the alternative with respect to or arising out of the same transaction, occurrence, or series of transactions or occurrences; and
>
> (B) any question of law or fact common to all plaintiffs will arise in the action.

For instance, ten passengers in a bus may join in suing the bus company for personal injuries sustained by them in a collision. On the one hand, such joinder may not only be advantageous to the parties by pooling resources or conserving expenditures, but also serve the public interest by preventing relitigation of the same facts in a succession of actions with the possibility of inconsistent results. On the other hand, if passengers in a series of bus accidents join in a single suit, they could be seeking an unfair advantage by presenting a picture of gross wrongdoing by the defendant, or simply seeking to confuse the factfinder. Overall, the tests for such joinder receive flexible, albeit quite generous, interpretations.[59]

Rule 20(a)(2) permits the plaintiff to join multiple defendants if both those tests are analogously met:

---

57. See Fed. R. Civ. P. 13(h) ("Rules 19 and 20 govern the addition of a person as a party to a counterclaim or crossclaim."); LASA per l'Industria del Marmo Societa per Azioni di Lasa, Italy v. Alexander, 414 F.2d 143 (6th Cir. 1969); Schoot v. United States, 664 F. Supp. 293 (N.D. Ill. 1987).

58. See generally Robert H. Klonoff, Class Actions and Other Multi–Party Litigation in a Nutshell (3d ed. 2007).

59. See, e.g., Alexander v. Fulton County, Ga., 207 F.3d 1303 (11th Cir. 2000) (multiple plaintiffs in discrimination case); Mosley v. Gen. Motors Corp., 497 F.2d 1330 (8th Cir. 1974) (same); Puricelli v. CNA Ins. Co., 185 F.R.D. 139 (N.D.N.Y. 1999) (same); Guedry v. Marino, 164 F.R.D. 181 (E.D. La. 1995) (multiple plaintiffs in civil rights case); Kedra v. City of Philadelphia, 454 F. Supp. 652 (E.D. Pa. 1978) (multiple plaintiffs

Persons—as well as a vessel, cargo, or other property subject to admiralty process in rem—may be joined in one action as defendants if:

> (A) any right to relief is asserted against them jointly, severally, or in the alternative with respect to or arising out of the same transaction, occurrence, or series of transactions or occurrences; and

> (B) any question of law or fact common to all defendants will arise in the action.

Of course, the usual requirements of jurisdiction and venue still apply. So, if a bus passenger sues two concurrent tortfeasors, say, the bus company and the driver of the colliding car, who are jointly and severally liable, then such joinder is proper, although not compulsory.

Rule 20(a) thus allows a bunch of plaintiffs to join in suing one or more defendants against whom they all have claims, whether joint, several, or alternative (*P–1, P–2, P–3,* etc. v. *D*). Or it allows one or more plaintiffs to sue a bunch of defendants against all of whom they have claims (*P* v. *D–1, D–2, D–3,* etc.). But it does not allow joinder of a plaintiff-versus-defendant claim with a different-plaintiff-versus-different-defendant claim (*P–1* v. *D–1; P–2* v. *D–2; P–3* v. *D–3;* etc.), even if the transaction is the same and common questions exist.[60] In other words, Rule 20(a) allows the joinder of parties, but it does not allow the joinder of separate cases. When it is desirable to bring separate cases together, the proper route is not to join under Rule 20(a), but to sue separately and then seek consolidation under Rule 42(a), which requires only a common question.[61]

b. Impleader

Concept. Impleader, or "third-party practice," allows but does not compel a defending party to assert a claim against an outsider who is or may contingently be liable to that party for all or part of a claim already made against that party.[62] Rule 14(a) provides:

in police brutality case). But see Insolia v. Philip Morris Inc., 186 F.R.D. 547 (E.D. Wis. 1999) (smokers must sue separately).

60. See Wynn v. Nat'l Broad. Co., 234 F. Supp. 2d 1067, 1078 (C.D. Cal. 2002) ("As understood from Plaintiffs' complaint, Defendants are 51 separate entities, each with distinct hiring and firing practices, and with a multitude of separate individuals in charge of determining these practices for each of the separate entities. Plaintiffs are 50 individuals, some of whom have worked for a few of the employers, some of whom have barely worked for any of the employers, some of whom have applied to work for many of the employers, and some of whom have not applied to work for any of the employers. The mere assertion that because these employers and talent agencies are members of a common industry is not sufficient * * *.").

61. See Wright & Miller, supra note 13, § 1653, at 408 & n.7, § 2382, at 14–16 & n.16.

62. See generally Wright & Kane, supra note 18, § 76.

(1) *Timing of the Summons and Complaint.* A defending party may, as third-party plaintiff, serve a summons and complaint on a nonparty who is or may be liable to it for all or part of the claim against it. But the third-party plaintiff must, by motion, obtain the court's leave if it files the third-party complaint more than 10 days after serving its original answer.

(2) *Third-Party Defendant's Claims and Defenses.* The person served with the summons and third-party complaint—the "third-party defendant":

(A) must assert any defense against the third-party plaintiff's claim under Rule 12;

(B) must assert any counterclaim against the third-party plaintiff under Rule 13(a), and may assert any counterclaim against the third-party plaintiff under Rule 13(b) or any crossclaim against another third-party defendant under Rule 13(g);

(C) may assert against the plaintiff any defense that the third-party plaintiff has to the plaintiff's claim; and

(D) may also assert against the plaintiff any claim arising out of the transaction or occurrence that is the subject matter of the plaintiff's claim against the third-party plaintiff.

(3) *Plaintiff's Claims Against a Third–Party Defendant.* The plaintiff may assert against the third-party defendant any claim arising out of the transaction or occurrence that is the subject matter of the plaintiff's claim against the third-party plaintiff. The third-party defendant must then assert any defense under Rule 12 and any counterclaim under Rule 13(a), and may assert any counterclaim under Rule 13(b) or any crossclaim under Rule 13(g).

(4) *Motion to Strike, Sever, or Try Separately.* Any party may move to strike the third-party claim, to sever it, or to try it separately.

(5) *Third-Party Defendant's Claim Against a Nonparty.* A third-party defendant may proceed under this rule against a nonparty who is or may be liable to the third-party defendant for all or part of any claim against it.

(6) *Third-Party Complaint In Rem.* If it is within the admiralty or maritime jurisdiction, a third-party complaint may be in rem. In that event, a reference in this rule to the "summons" includes the warrant of arrest, and a reference to the defendant or third-party plaintiff includes, when appropriate, a person who asserts a right under Supplemental Rule C(6)(a)(i) in the property arrested.

Take as an important example the master-servant situation: *P* sues *D* for *T*'s negligence. *D* is *T*'s employer. Assume that under applicable (and typical) substantive law, T is liable over to D for any such recovery by P. Thus, D, as a third-party plaintiff, may implead T, as a third-party defendant.[63]

Impleader's advantage for the third-party plaintiff is to get the third-party defendant right into the case as an additional party, thus avoiding the waste of a separate suit against the third-party defendant and ensuring that the third-party defendant is bound under the judgment in the initial suit. A key feature of Rule 14(a)(1)'s phrasing of "may be liable" is its allowing assertion of contingent liability, and so enabling acceleration of a determination of liability.[64]

Impleader claims are not uncommon at all. But beware that the third-party plaintiff may use impleader only to assert the third-party defendant's obligation to cover the third-party plaintiff's liability to the original plaintiff, *not to assert any liability that the third-party defendant might have directly to the original plaintiff.*[65] So the central focus in litigating the third-party claim will be on whether, under the substantive law and the facts, such secondary liability of the third-party defendant to the third-party plaintiff exists. The legal theory of the third-party claim might be indemnity, contribution, subrogation, warranty, or some such theory.[66]

The original defendant is usually the third-party plaintiff, but any defending party can implead. Rule 14(b) specifically authorizes a plaintiff defending against a counterclaim to bring in a third-party defendant.

Moreover, Rule 14(a)(5) authorizes the third-party defendant to bring in a "fourth-party defendant," and so on. This might sound outlandish, but in our modern complex economy, a fourth-party defendant may very well be obligated to cover the liability of someone who is obligated to cover the liability of the original defending party.[67] The business of reinsurance is only the most

63. See, e.g., Clark v. Assocs. Commercial Corp., 149 F.R.D. 629 (D. Kan. 1993) (involving action against creditor for forceful repossession of property, with impleader by creditor against its agents).

64. See, e.g., Jeub v. B/G Foods, Inc., 2 F.R.D. 238 (D. Minn. 1942) (ignoring state law that required an independent action to be brought later).

65. See, e.g., Allstate Ins. Co. v. Hugh Cole Builder, Inc., 187 F.R.D. 671 (M.D. Ala. 1999) (striking third-party complaint); Wallkill 5 Assocs. II v. Tectonic Eng'g, P.C., No. CIV. A. 95–5984, 1997 WL 452252 (D.N.J. July 25, 1997)

(denying leave to file third-party complaint).

66. See, e.g., Price v. CTB, Inc., 168 F. Supp. 2d 1299 (M.D. Ala. 2001) (applying state substantive law on indemnity); Markvicka v. Brodhead–Garrett Co., 76 F.R.D. 205 (D. Neb. 1977) (applying state substantive law on contribution); cf. Banks v. City of Emeryville, 109 F.R.D. 535 (N.D. Cal. 1985) (dismissing claim in the absence of secondary liability).

67. See, e.g., Schutter Candy Co. v. Stein Bros. Paper Box Co., 371 F.2d 340 (7th Cir. 1966) (fourth-party defendant); Bevemet Metais, Ltda. v. Gallie Corp., 3

obvious example. Nevertheless, Rule 14(a) does not expressly cover the pleading of a fourth-party case or a fifth-party case or so on, but instead leaves four-or-more-sided pleading to be done by analogy to Rule 14(a)'s scheme for three-sided pleading.

Incidentally, the third-party defendant, or fourth-party defendant and so on, must be a nonparty to be subject to Rule 14(a). If instead the person liable over is already a coparty, the proper procedure for the defending party to follow is to assert a crossclaim under the second sentence of Rule 13(g).[68] The unusual situation where the person liable over is already an opposing party exposes a discontinuity in the Rules: the technically proper procedure involves severing the particular claim asserted against the defending party, so that she can utilize Rule 14(a) against the person who had been an opposing party.[69]

Pleading. Pleading becomes very complex in third-party practice, even in the simple situation of a plaintiff (*P*) suing a defendant (*D*) who impleads a nonparty (*T*). As to the initial third-party pleading by the third-party plaintiff, *D* institutes impleader as if she were originally bringing an action, serving summons and complaint on *T*.[70] However, if *D* files that complaint more than ten days after serving her original answer, she must obtain leave of court to make service on *T*k.[71] And the court can strike even a prompt impleader under Rule 14(a)(4).[72]

The third-party defendant responds to the third-party complaint in the usual manner prescribed by Rules 12 and 13, with the central focus being the existence of his alleged duty to cover *D*'s liability to *P*.[73] In his third-party answer, *T* may also assert against

F.R.D. 352 (S.D.N.Y. 1942) (fifth-and sixth-party defendants); Kohl's Dep't Stores, Inc. v. Target Stores, Inc., 214 F.R.D. 406 (E.D. Va. 2003) (seventh-party defendant).

68. Fed. R. Civ. P. 13(g) (" * * * The crossclaim may include a claim that the coparty is or may be liable to the crossclaimant for all or part of a claim asserted in the action against the crossclaimant.").

69. See Sporia v. Pa. Greyhound Lines, Inc., 143 F.2d 105, 108 (3d Cir. 1944) (also envisaging eventual consolidation of the claims); Wright & Miller, supra note 13, § 1446, at 375 ("Moreover, although a counterclaim may be asserted against an opposing party, it must involve a mature claim; thus, Rule 13(a) may not be employed."). But see United States ex rel. Westinghouse Elec. Supply Co. v. Nicholas, 28 F.R.D. 8 (D.

Minn. 1961) (reading Rules more loosely).

70. See Fed. Form 16.

71. See id. 41; Gross v. Hanover Ins. Co., 138 F.R.D. 53 (S.D.N.Y. 1991) (allowing impleader on motion).

72. See Goodhart v. U.S. Lines, 26 F.R.D. 163 (S.D.N.Y. 1960) (denying a defendant employer, who had been sued for damages stemming from the negligence of its employee, the right to implead the employee on the ground that the effect might be unfairly to prejudice the plaintiff by encouraging in the jury the false supposition that the employee would actually pay the judgment when, although the employee was legally bound to indemnify the employer in such a case, this employee in fact was essentially judgment-proof).

73. See Wright & Miller, supra note 13, §§ 1455–1456.

P any defenses that *D* has to *P*'s claim (other than *D*'s personal defenses like personal jurisdiction and venue), and so may protect himself against any failure by *D* to defend the merits vigorously.[74] Moreover, Rule 14(a)(2)(D) permits *T* in his third-party answer to assert against *P* any claim "arising out of the transaction or occurrence" that is the subject matter of *P*'s claim against *D*.[75] Often this last kind of claim is considered to be technically neither a counterclaim nor a crossclaim, but as already explained it is better considered a kind of crossclaim against a coparty.

The original plaintiff responds to any claim under Rule 14(a)(2)(D) in the usual manner prescribed by Rules 12 and 13, which response may or must include permissive and compulsory counterclaims. In the absence of such a claim by *T*, Rule 14(a)(3) analogously permits *P* to assert against *T* any claim "arising out of the transaction or occurrence" that is the subject matter of *P*'s claim against *D*; *P* may assert such a claim at any reasonable time by amending his complaint or by serving a new pleading. Why would *P* want to take the offensive against *T*? The original plaintiff may have had a related claim of his own against *T*, but originally elected not to press it. The original defendant's injection of the third-party defendant into the case cannot of itself force the plaintiff to sue an unwanted adversary. Nevertheless, a plaintiff who finds a potential adversary injected into the case may well change his mind.[76]

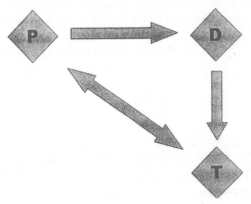

Vouching In. Instead of impleading, a defending party can "vouch in" someone obliged by indemnity or warranty law to cover that party's liability on a claim already made against that party. Under this still-available common-law device, the defending party gives the vouchee simple notice of the action and offers control of

74. See id. § 1457.

75. See id. § 1458.

76. See id. § 1459.

the defense; whether or not the vouchee accepts control, that person normally will be bound by the judgment on the questions of the voucher's liability, although the vouchee normally remains free later to contest the vouchee's obligation under indemnity or warranty law to cover that established liability.[77] This device is especially useful where the restrictions of territorial jurisdiction prevent the use of impleader.[78]

If the defending party neither vouches in nor impleads the nonparty, she does not thereby lose her right to indemnity or warranty. She must, however, establish her claim all over again without reference to the prior judgment, unless a contract with the nonparty provides otherwise. In a second action, the original defendant would have to establish her liability to the original plaintiff and thus have to offer practically the same proof earlier relied upon by the original plaintiff to establish his case. This may leave the original defendant the loser because of differing views of the evidence by the two factfinders, and in any event it is a needless expense to her.

c. Interpleader

Interpleader allows a person to avoid the risk of multiple liability by requiring two or more persons with actual or prospective claims against him to assert their respective adverse claims in a single action.[79] So, if Bank A risks double liability by holding a deposit to which B and C have potential, conflicting claims, then Bank A, as stakeholder, may bring interpleader against B and C, as claimants.[80] There are two kinds of federal interpleader: rule interpleader and statutory interpleader.

First, as to **rule interpleader**, Rule 22(a) descends directly from the old equitable roots of interpleader, although it liberalizes the classic limitations on the equitable remedy. The normal restrictions of subject-matter jurisdiction, territorial jurisdiction, and ven-

---

77. See Restatement (Second) of Judgments §§ 57–58 (1982); Benjamin Hinman, Note, Development of the Common Law Rule Making a Judgment Conclusive Against Warrantors and Indemnitors, 34 Va. L. Rev. 321 (1948).

78. See First Nat'l Bank v. City Nat'l Bank, 65 N.E. 24 (Mass. 1902) (for vouching in, no need for personal jurisdiction); Ronan E. Degnan & Alan J. Barton, Vouching to Quality Warranty: Case Law and Commercial Code, 51 Cal. L. Rev. 471, 477–80 (1963); Paul Stephen Ware, Note, Vouching: In or Out?,

42 Wash. & Lee L. Rev. 121 (1985). But see Peter A. Gross, Comment, Constitutional Limits on Vouching, 118 U. Pa. L. Rev. 237 (1969).

79. See Indianapolis Colts v. Mayor of Baltimore, 741 F.2d 954 (7th Cir. 1984) (finding absence of adverse claims that risk multiple liability). See generally Wright & Kane, supra note 18, § 74.

80. See, e.g., Commonwealth Fed. Sav. & Loan Ass'n v. First Nat'l Bank, 513 F. Supp. 296 (E.D. Pa. 1979) (bank's interpleader of fifteen claimants).

ue apply to such rule interpleader.[81] In particular, if such interpleader rests on diversity jurisdiction, then (1) there must be complete diversity of citizenship between the stakeholder on one side and the adverse claimants on the other and (2) the stake must exceed $75,000. Unless the stake is some tangible thing, there must be personal jurisdiction over the claimants under Rule 4's usual territorial limits. Venue is also governed by the usual provisions.

Second, there is **statutory interpleader**. In order to provide a remedy in cases formerly beyond federal and state judicial power,[82] congressional reform from 1917 onward introduced this important alternative route to interpleader, now found scattered in 28 U.S.C. § 1335 (subject-matter jurisdiction), § 2361 (service of process), and § 1397 (venue). If and only if (1) the parties laying conflicting claims to the stake (an interested stakeholder should be considered to be such a party)[83] include both a state citizen and someone of different citizenship and (2) the stake is $500 or more, subject-matter jurisdiction for statutory interpleader exists.[84] Personal jurisdiction over the claimants can then be obtained by effective service of process in any district of the United States, but claimants can be personally brought into the action only by such service and not by service abroad. Venue for such an interpleader action initiated by the stakeholder lies in, and only in, any district wherein resides any party claiming the stake.

As to **procedural incidents**, § 1335(a)(2) requires the stakeholder to deposit the stake into the court's registry or to post bond, and § 2361 expressly authorizes the court to enjoin the claimants from otherwise judicially pursuing their claims. These statutory provisions do not extend to interpleader under Rule 22(a), although the court could order deposit under Rule 67 and has some power to enjoin other proceedings under 28 U.S.C. § 2283.

For either statutory or rule interpleader, the stakeholder can commence interpleader as an original action;[85] or if the stakeholder has already been sued, he can institute interpleader by counterclaim or crossclaim.[86] The stakeholder need not be a "disinterested" party who admits full liability to someone, but can claim even the whole stake by contending that he owes nothing to every claimant.

---

81. See supra §§ 4.1–4.2.

82. See, e.g., New York Life Ins. Co. v. Dunlevy, 241 U.S. 518 (1916) (emphasizing the narrow limits on the territorial jurisdiction of state courts).

83. Cf. N.J. Sports Prods., Inc. v. Don King Prods., Inc., 15 F. Supp. 2d 534, 541 (D.N.J. 1998) ("The Court concludes that 'claimant' as used in Section 1397 includes plaintiff-stakeholders who assert a claim on the stake. The Court's conclusion is based on a plain textual reading of the statute * * *.").

84. See State Farm Fire & Cas. Co. v. Tashire, 386 U.S. 523 (1967) (upholding such minimal diversity).

85. See Fed. Form 20.

86. See id. 31.

The "first stage" of interpleader embraces the steps involved in properly invoking interpleader. If the stakeholder is disinterested and if he deposits the stake into the court's registry or posts bond, the court will discharge him from the interpleader action.

The "second stage" involves the determination of the parties' interests in the stake. The usual right to jury trial applies, because when a party uses some procedural device previously available only in equity—such as interpleader, class action, shareholders' derivative action, or intervention—a federal court will simply look through the device for jury purposes and give a jury right on legal issues in the underlying claim.[87] The burden of proof on claims to the stake is put on each claimant.[88] The second stage may also include adjudication of additional sorts of claims asserted between the parties within the bounds of joinder, jurisdiction, and venue rules.

d. Class Action

Concept. A class action allows one or more members of a class of similarly situated persons to sue, or be sued, as representative parties litigating on behalf of the other class members without actually bringing them into court.[89] An example might lie where numerous buyers and sellers of securities have allegedly been harmed by brokerage firms' trading practices in violation of the antitrust laws, and a typical investor wishes to bring suit as the representative of the class of investors against the brokerage firms.[90] A class action with its binding effect avoids the risk of inconsistent results and the often prohibitive cost of separate actions, while affording some hope of a manageable format for joinder. Class actions are efficient.

Yet allowing lawsuits to be brought and conducted in situations and in a way not previously possible gives the device undeniable substantive effects. Therefore, in interpreting a class-action provision adopted by judicial rulemaking, courts should attempt to limit the substantive impact to generalized or across-the-board effects, as opposed to particularized effects consciously tailored to special substantive realms.[91]

---

87. See Ross v. Bernhard, 396 U.S. 531, 542 n.15 (1970) (opining on jury right in federal court); supra § 2.4(B)(2).

88. See Phoenix Mut. Life Ins. Co. v. Reich, 75 F. Supp. 886 (W.D. Pa. 1948).

89. See generally Herbert B. Newberg & Alba Conte, Newberg on Class Actions (4th ed. 2002); Wright & Kane, supra note 18, § 72.

90. See Eisen v. Carlisle & Jacquelin, 391 F.2d 555 (2d Cir. 1968) (suit against two brokerage firms that dominated "odd-lot" trading).

91. See Developments in the Law— Class Actions, 89 Harv. L. Rev. 1318, 1353 (1976) ("Class action procedures assist courts in giving full realization to substantive policies in two ways. First, to the extent that they open courts to

Such efficiency and substantive goals can generally be pursued consistently with the fairness notion of having one's day in court, as long as the essential due process requirement of adequate representation is met. Binding absentees does not contravene the Constitution, because all that due process guarantees is a full and fair day in court enjoyed in person *or through a representative*:[92] in the class-action context, the represented person must have been in actual agreement, generally although not necessarily as to all details, with the objectives on the merits of the representative, who vigorously and competently pursued those objectives.[93] Therefore, the always reasonable and realistic due process test allows binding many more nonparties than most people assume: constitutionally, a judicial judgment could bind all persons whose interests received adequate representation, binding them not only through the flexible doctrine of stare decisis, as a judgment already does, but also through the strictures of res judicata, as a judgment could. The Supreme Court's seemingly more demanding decisions that have expressed the day-in-court theme were interpreting statutes or rules or subconstitutional doctrine, not the Due Process Clause itself.

Nonetheless, society has chosen, as expressed in its class-action provisions and its res judicata law, to go much less far in binding nonparties by judgment than it constitutionally could. That is, society tolerates only certain class actions. Federal Rule 23 imposes this additional screen on class actions, and res judicata's definition of privity respects that screen. (States have their own class-action provisions, possibly of lesser or greater scope and detail; these may

---

claims not ordinarily litigated, class actions enable courts to enforce policies underlying causes of action in circumstances where those policies might not otherwise be effectuated. Second, to the extent that they enable courts to see the full implications of recognizing rights or remedies, class action procedures assist courts in judging precisely what outcomes of litigation would best serve the policies underlying causes of action."). On the Rules' possibly shifting the law's aim from compensating injured plaintiffs to sanctioning transgressive defendants, compare Kenneth E. Scott, Two Models of the Civil Process, 27 Stan. L. Rev. 937 (1975), with Kenneth W. Dam, Class Actions: Efficiency, Compensation, Deterrence, and Conflict of Interest, 4 J. Legal Stud. 47 (1975). For an argument in favor of reading the Rules in each case with some attention to the particularized effect on substantive policies, see Robert M. Cover, For James Wm.

Moore: Some Reflections on a Reading of the Rules, 84 Yale L.J. 718, 732–39 (1975). Cf. JoEllen Lind, "Procedural Swift": Complex Litigation Reform, State Tort Law, and Democratic Values, 37 Akron L. Rev. 717 (2004) (discussing not these Rules Enabling Act concerns but instead the Erie concerns of displacing state law by federal procedure that has substantive effects).

92. See Robert G. Bone, Rethinking the "Day in Court" Ideal and Nonparty Preclusion, 67 N.Y.U. L. Rev. 193 (1992).

93. See Hansberry v. Lee, 311 U.S. 32 (1940); see also Martin v. Wilks, 490 U.S. 755 (1989); Richards v. Jefferson County, Ala., 517 U.S. 793 (1996). For the story of the Hansberry case, see Jay Tidmarsh, The Story of Hansberry: The Foundation for Modern Class Actions, in Civil Procedure Stories 233 (Kevin M. Clermont ed., 2d ed. 2008).

offer the opportunity to avoid some of the barriers to and protections of the federal device, but may be subject to their own peculiar limitations as well as possible judicial hostility.[94] In any event, state laws represent a similar decision to go less far in binding nonparties by judgment than the states constitutionally could.)

How far as society chosen to go? What cases will get by the tests of Constitution and statute or rule? The helpful image here is of a due process hurdle that is quite low. Above it, however, in Rule 23(a) and (b) the rulemakers have built a screen that allows through only a select set of cases that satisfy society's policy desires. That is, Rule 23 and its related case law attempt to create a pragmatic screening device, which lets through all the cases clearly appropriate for class-action treatment—those cases that generously realize the goal of efficiency or the rulemakers' rather limited substantive goals and that also amply satisfy fairness concerns—but only those cases. So, more specifically, which cases get through?

First, to be bound consistently with due process, the represented persons in the class must have been in actual agreement with the objectives on the merits of some party, who vigorously and competently pursued those objectives. But the law goes further. It tries to comfortably ensure adequacy of representation at the outset of a class action by a demanding class-certification process. Furthermore, it allows *constitutional* adequacy to be tested after the conclusion of a class action when determining the res judicata effect of the class-judgment (some of the considerations relevant to application of Rule 23—such as class certification, typicality, notice, and consent, as well as the attention given to the procedural activities of all litigants, attorneys, and judges and the substantive interests at stake—should be deemed to be *constitutional* requirements only insofar as needed to provide basic adequacy of representation).

Second, society has chosen to allow class actions to include only those designated nonparties who are related to the representative party in certain ways. The extra relationship required by Rule 23 is either that the absentees share common and thus aligned substantive interests with their representatives or that the former somehow consented to representation by the latter. Rule 23, acting as this sort of screen, strikes a balance between collectivization and individualization. In deciding how strictly to read the Rule in this regard, a lot is left to the judges' judgment.

Third, the obvious dangers of overwhelming the court and the parties and of disadvantaging the absent class members demand some other limits and protections applicable in the class action, which Rule 23 also imposes. But even when those bounds and

94. See generally Thomas A. Dickerson, Class Actions: The Law of 50 States (1988); Mary Kay Kane, Civil Procedure in a Nutshell § 8–2 (6th ed. 2007).

regulations are observed, a class action may pose major management problems.

On balance, the class-action device is a salutary one, with room for incremental improvement. In interpreting Rule 23, a provision promulgated under the Rules Enabling Act but one that has grown way beyond expectations, the Supreme Court may have been right in most of the cases where it adopted a restrictive reading and downplayed substantive goals. Small reforms can come from further amendments by the rulemakers, but any more radical change should probably be left to Congress.

Requirements. The pleader by complaint must propose class-action treatment, as there is no such thing as an unpleaded class action or a compulsory class action forced on the pleader.[95] Normally, the party pleading a class action is the plaintiff on an original claim, although it is conceivable albeit problematic that a class action could be asserted via some other claim such as a counter-claim.[96]

Most class actions brought by a plaintiff involve a class of plaintiffs, but defendant-class actions are possible. The latter merit a few extra words. In appropriate cases, the plaintiff could sue adequate representatives of the defendant class, which might for example comprise the members of a labor union. Rule 23 expressly authorizes such defendant-class actions, but it fails to think them all the way through. So Rule 23 must here be applied with particular sensitivity to the dangers of unfairness to the involuntary representatives and to the absent class members.[97]

To obtain class-action treatment, the case must get through the screen built by Rule 23. There are four initial requirements in Rule 23(a) that must all be met:

> (1) the class must be "so numerous that joinder of all members is impracticable" (this test aiming at efficiency is not simply numerical, but classes usually involve far more than twenty-five members);

---

95. See, e.g., Nance v. Union Carbide Corp. Consumer Prods. Div., 540 F.2d 718, 722–25 (4th Cir. 1976), vacated on other grounds, 431 U.S. 952 (1977); Wright & Miller, supra note 13, § 1785, at 363–64 & n.7; see also Julie A. Shapiro, Note, Class or Individual Action: The Multiple Plaintiffs' Choice of Litigation Form, 3 Rev. Litig. 397 (1983) (reviewing factors that influence the pleader's choice). But see In re Joint E. & S. Dist. Asbestos Litig., 134 F.R.D. 32, 36 (E. & S.D.N.Y. 1990) (forcing a 23(b)(1)(B) action on plaintiff); Argo v. Hills, 425 F. Supp. 151, 159 (E.D.N.Y. 1977), aff'd mem., 578 F.2d 1366 (2d Cir. 1978) (forcing a 23(b)(3) action on plaintiff). To go beyond coordination or consolidation of separate actions and really force joinder on an unwilling plaintiff, one must apply Fed. R. Civ. P. 19, with the issue being whether the absentees are necessary parties to the non-class action (and perhaps thus indirectly forcing the plaintiff to bring a class action).

96. See Newberg & Conte, supra note 89, § 3:2.

97. See Note, Defendant Class Actions, 91 Harv. L. Rev. 630 (1978).

(2) there must be "questions of law or fact common to the class" (this requirement, which aims at ensuring some overlap of substantive interests, will normally be met if the below-described Rule 23(b) is met);

(3) the claims or defenses of the representatives must be "typical" of the class (this is largely ensured by the required commonality and adequacy of representation);[98] *and*

(4) "the representative parties will fairly and adequately protect the interests of the class" (this is a key requirement serving in part to uncover collusion and conflicts of interest, and also involving an inquiry into whether the particular representatives will vigorously champion class objectives through qualified counsel).[99]

The first and fourth requirements are the most important, with the first trying to ensure that class-action treatment will yield considerable benefits and the fourth trying to ensure that such treatment will impose only acceptable costs.

The proposed class action must also fall into one of three situations set out in Rule 23(b), a requirement of linkage between class members, which tries further to ensure very favorable costs and benefits from class-action treatment:

(1) the situation under Rule 23(b)(1) where bringing separate actions would create a risk of establishing incompatible standards of conduct for the class opponent (e.g., a taxpayers' suit against a town to declare a bond issue invalid) or of substantially impairing the other class members' interests as a practical matter (e.g., a suit involving numerous persons claiming against a fund insufficient to satisfy all those claims);[100]

(2) the situation where the defendant has allegedly based her conduct on the characteristics of the plaintiff class, thereby

---

98. See General Tel. Co. v. Falcon, 457 U.S. 147, 157 n.13 (1982) (while holding, in racial discrimination case, that person not promoted cannot represent persons not hired, the Court observed: "The commonality and typicality requirements of Rule 23(a) tend to merge. Both serve as guideposts for determining whether under the particular circumstances maintenance of a class action is economical and whether the named plaintiff's claim and the class claims are so interrelated that the interests of the class members will be fairly and adequately protected in their absence. Those requirements therefore also tend to merge with the adequacy-of-representation requirement, although

the latter requirement also raises concerns about the competency of class counsel and conflicts of interest.").

99. See Fed. R. Civ. P. 23(g) (regulating appointment of class counsel); cf. Amchem Prods., Inc. v. Windsor, 521 U.S. 591, 625–26 (1997) (applying Fed. R. Civ. P. 23 to a settlement class).

100. See Ortiz v. Fibreboard Corp., 527 U.S. 815, 841 (1999) (presumptively, "a limited fund theory was justified [only] with reference to a 'fund' with a definitely ascertained limit, all of which would be distributed to satisfy all those with liquidated claims based on a common theory of liability, by an equitable, pro rata distribution").

making appropriate the award of class-wide final injunctive relief or equivalent declaratory relief, perhaps with a monetary component incidental to or as an element of the equitable remedy, but not relief consisting exclusively or predominantly of money damages (Rule 23(b)(2) would thus include a desegregation case brought by a plaintiff class, but probably has no application to defendant-class actions);[101] *or*

(3) the situation where the potential class action does not fall into the narrowly read categories (1) or (2), but where "the questions of law or fact common to class members predominate over any questions affecting only individual members"[102] and "a class action is superior to other available methods for fairly and efficiently adjudicating the controversy,"[103] with this issue of the desirability of class-action treatment entailing such factors as manageability (Rule 23(b)(3) would thus include an antitrust action by investors in securities, but would less likely include an action arising from a mass tort, especially of the product liability sort).[104]

The third category, embodied in Rule 23(b)(3), has presented most of the problems and controversy associated with the complicated class-action device.

Important additional limitations on the availability of the class-action device lie in the rules of jurisdiction and venue. In applying the federal provisions regarding diversity of citizenship, service of process, and venue, only the named parties (not all the class members) are considered. If all the members were considered, the federal court would of course more often be unavailable. However, the Supreme Court unfortunately ruled that every separate and distinct claim across the whole class must satisfy any federal jurisdictional amount requirement.[105] Yet supplemental jurisdiction

---

101. See, e.g., Communities for Equity v. Mich. High School Athletic Ass'n, 192 F.R.D. 568 (W.D. Mich. 1999) (Title IX discrimination case); Holland v. Steele, 92 F.R.D. 58 (N.D. Ga. 1981) (prisoners' rights case).

102. See Amchem Prods., Inc. v. Windsor, 521 U.S. 591, 624 (1997) (observing, in asbestos litigation, that "the predominance criterion is far more demanding" than the commonality requirement).

103. See Heaven v. Trust Co. Bank, 118 F.3d 735 (11th Cir. 1997) (holding that defendant's counterclaims against class members defeated superiority).

104. See, e.g., Castano v. Am. Tobacco Co., 84 F.3d 734 (5th Cir. 1996) (decertifying class of smokers); In re

Rhone–Poulenc Rorer Inc., 51 F.3d 1293 (7th Cir. 1995) (decertifying class of persons with hemophilia who were infected with AIDS by blood products); Hubler Chevrolet, Inc. v. Gen. Motors Corp., 193 F.R.D. 574 (S.D. Ind. 2000) (certifying class of car dealers who alleged franchising wrongs); Chandler v. Sw. Jeep-Eagle, Inc., 162 F.R.D. 302 (N.D. Ill. 1995) (certifying class of car buyers on credit). Compare Wright & Miller, supra note 13, § 1781 ("Antitrust Actions"), with id. § 1783 ("Mass–Accident Cases"), § 1805 ("Products–Liability Class Actions").

105. Snyder v. Harris, 394 U.S. 332 (1969); see supra § 4.1(C)(3)(f).

under 28 U.S.C. § 1367 can sometimes relieve this serious impediment to federal diversity jurisdiction.[106]

Another way around jurisdictional limitations came in the Class Action Fairness Act of 2005,[107] which covered interstate class actions and had the expressed intent of defeating plaintiff lawyers' manipulation of state courts by funneling more class actions away from the state courts and into the federal courts. In new 28 U.S.C. § 1332(d), Congress bestowed original jurisdiction on the federal district courts for sizable multistate class actions, generally if there is minimal diversity between any plaintiff member of the class and any defendant and if the plaintiff class contains at least 100 members and their claims aggregated together exceed $5 million. By a complicated qualification, this jurisdiction does not extend to a class action in which two-thirds or more of the plaintiff members are citizens of the state where the action was filed and the primary defendants are also local citizens, or the case has certain other markers of a local controversy. If that fraction falls between one-third and two-thirds, and if the primary defendants are citizens of the state where the action was filed, the district court may discretionarily decline jurisdiction over what it sees as an essentially local case. In new 28 U.S.C. § 1453, Congress further provided that any defendant can remove a class action from state court to the local federal district court—only if the action would be within the original federal jurisdiction of § 1332(d), as one presumes in accordance with the clear legislative history but not with the statute's wording.[108] The statute went on to provide that the removing defendant can be a local citizen and need not seek the consent of the other defendants.

On a different matter, a less expansive tone had earlier sounded in an opinion with unclear implications, *Phillips Petroleum Co. v. Shutts*.[109] The Supreme Court there held that in a state plaintiff-class action for money damages, personal jurisdiction over absent members need not otherwise exist, if they received notice and had a right to participate and a right to opt out. But if with respect to an absent plaintiff-class member the constitutional power and reasonableness tests are met without any such resorting to implied

106. See Exxon Mobil Corp. v. Allapattah Servs., Inc., 545 U.S. 546 (2005); supra § 4.1(C)(2)(c).

107. Pub. L. No. 109–2, 119 Stat. 4 (codified in scattered sections of 28 U.S.C.); see Kevin M. Clermont & Theodore Eisenberg, CAFA Judicata: A Tale of Waste and Politics, 156 U. Pa. L. Rev. 1553 (2008). The Act contained a few minor regulatory provisions aimed at curbing certain class-action abuses. Notably, in what is now 28 U.S.C. § 1712, Congress ratcheted up the judicial scrutiny applicable to a federal CAFA or non-CAFA class action's settlement terms that provide for recovery of discount coupons by class members.

108. Se, e.g., Preston v. Tenet Healthsys. Mem'l Med. Ctr., Inc., 485 F.3d 804 (5th Cir. 2007) (remanding case to state court).

109. 472 U.S. 797 (1985).

consent, as normally would be true in federal court, neither territorial jurisdiction nor this *Phillips* holding should in the author's view be of further concern with respect to that member.

Unincorporated associations, such as labor unions, can usually sue or be sued as an entity.[110] But sometimes they may sue or be sued through representatives instead of as an entity. This class-action procedure is especially useful in avoiding the restrictions of diversity jurisdiction and capacity and in easing the requirements of service and venue. Because of these special reasons for utilizing the class-action device here, Rule 23.2 deals separately with such actions.

Mechanics. Class actions pose major management problems for the courts. Rule 23(c)(1) provides that soon after commencement of a proposed class action, the court must determine whether the above requirements are met and then enter an order either granting or denying certification as a class action. Rule 23(c)(4) and (5) provides that the court may limit class treatment to certain issues or divide the proposed class into independently treated subclasses.[111] By the recent addition of Rule 23(f), the court of appeals in its discretion may permit an immediate appeal from an order granting or denying class certification.

As to the statute of limitations, the rule is roughly that commencement of a federal plaintiff-class action tolls for all members of the proposed class the applicable statute of limitations until any denial of class treatment during the class action.[112]

Rule 23(d) authorizes a variety of appropriate "management" orders, thus confirming the court's authority to take an active role in running the case. In particular, Rule 23(d)(1)(B) authorizes the court in any class action discretionarily to order notice to class members advising them of any step in the action or any right they may have.

There are also special provisions on the three matters of notice of class action, appearance through counsel, and opting-out. Rule 23(c)(2)(B) contains these provisions that apply only to actions under Rule 23(b)(3), not to the naturally more cohesive or even necessary classes falling within Rule 23(b)(1) or (2).[113] Discussion of these special provisions follows.

---

110. See Int'l Union, UAW v. Brock, 477 U.S. 274 (1986) (discussing associational standing).

111. See Wright & Miller, supra note 13, § 1790; Scott Dodson, Subclassing, 27 Cardozo L. Rev. 2351 (2006); Note, Certifying Classes and Subclasses in Title VII Suits, 99 Harv. L. Rev. 619 (1986).

112. See Am. Pipe & Constr. Co. v. Utah, 414 U.S. 538 (1974); Wright & Miller, supra note 13, § 1800; William A. Jonason, Note, The American Pipe Dream: Class Actions and Statutes of Limitations, 67 Iowa L. Rev. 743 (1982).

113. See Wetzel v. Liberty Mut. Ins. Co., 508 F.2d 239 (3d Cir. 1975).

First, procedural due process itself seemingly requires notice to absent class members only in the relatively rare circumstances where such notice is necessary to provide an assurance of adequate representation. Apparently going way beyond that standard, however, the Rule requires giving (b)(3) class members "the best notice that is practicable under the circumstances, including individual notice to all members who can be identified through reasonable effort." The Supreme Court has held both that this Rule actually does require individual notice of the class action to all class members identifiable with reasonable effort, even though the cost of individual notice is prohibitive, and also that the named plaintiffs must initially bear all costs of such notice.[114] The Court thus erected another ill-designed barrier to the use of the class-action device.

Second, the (b)(3) class member has the right to enter an appearance through counsel, which would ensure his being kept currently informed about the case. This right is in addition to the possibility in any class action of a class member's intervening under Rule 24, which would allow much greater participation in the conduct of the case.

Third, the (b)(3) class member also has the right to withdraw from the class, and thus escape the burdens (and lose the benefits) of the eventual judgment. He can do this by simply informing the court, in response to the notice, of his desire to opt out. If he does not, he remains tied to the class. Incidentally, although there persists some dispute, Rule 23 does not appear to authorize the court to require absentees instead to "opt in" by taking some affirmative step for inclusion in the class.[115]

Termination. Most class actions are settled rather than adjudicated, but settlement may mark just the beginning of the procedural struggles. Rule 23(e) on dismissal or compromise regulates the settlement stage of a certified class action in an attempt to protect the interests of the class members, whom the named parties or the class counsel may be abandoning in favor of self-interest. Accordingly, reasonable notice of the proposed settlement must be given to all class members who would be bound, and the court must pass on the fairness, reasonableness, and adequacy of the proposed settlement. This process involves a hearing where disgruntled class members may speak and where a very big issue is attorney's fees.[116]

---

114. Eisen v. Carlisle & Jacquelin, 417 U.S. 156 (1974); cf. Oppenheimer Fund, Inc. v. Sanders, 437 U.S. 340 (1978) (holding that a court ordinarily cannot alleviate notice burden by utilizing management orders under Fed. R. Civ. P. 23(d)).

115. See, e.g., In re Crazy Eddie Sec. Litig., 135 F.R.D. 39, 42 (E.D.N.Y. 1991).

116. See, e.g., Hanlon v. Chrysler Corp., 150 F.3d 1011 (9th Cir. 1998); Grunin v. IHOP, 513 F.2d 114 (8th Cir. 1975); see also Fed. R. Civ. P. 23(h) (regulating award of attorney's fees;

Rule 23(c)(3) specifies that any class-action judgment, whether favorable or unfavorable to the class, must describe all class members, excluding those who opted out. Administering the judgment may be a heavy task. The propriety of "fluid recovery," which involves indirectly distributing the residue of a money judgment (as by the defendant's lowering its future prices in an amount equal to any part of the recovery unclaimed by members' filings of proof of claim), has sometimes been questioned.[117]

Normally, the class-action judgment will bind those described therein.[118] (Class members can benefit of course from a successful class action, except for those class members who opted out.)[119] The design is that the judgment will be respected according to its terms as res judicata in subsequent litigation, but that result cannot be assured until the subsequent litigation occurs and a plea of res judicata is made and decided.

When the class-action judgment is invoked in subsequent litigation, it is subject to attack on the usual limited grounds of jurisdiction and procedural due process. An absent class member should also be able to attack its binding effect on him by raising the question of inadequate representation of his interests. This ground falls under the heading of procedural due process, as well as within its spirit of undoing fundamental defects in fairness but only those defects. The absentee should not be able to collaterally attack on the ground of erroneous class-certification, as opposed to the ground of constitutionally inadequate representation. Allowing attacks beyond due process would permit absentees to escape a basically fair judgment, by a sort of post-judgment opt-out that would be unfair to the class's opponent and that would discourage settlement. Of course, taking such a narrow view of the grounds for collateral attack suggests that the courts must be serious in observ-

Wright & Miller, supra note 13, § 1803.2. Compare Gisbrecht v. Barnhart, 535 U.S. 789 (2002) (giving percentage of recovery as fees in Social Security action), with City of Burlington v. Dague, 505 U.S. 557 (1992) (giving lodestar—reasonable hours of work times reasonable hourly fee—for fee-shifting environmental statutes, with lodestar unenhanced by any multiplier for risk or quality of representation).

117. See Wright & Miller, supra note 13, § 1784.

118. See Restatement (Second) of Judgments §§ 41–42 (1982); see also supra § 5.4(A) (binding nonparties); cf. Cooper v. Fed. Reserve Bank, 467 U.S. 867 (1984) (holding that unfavorable judgment on class claim for a pattern of discrimination does not bar class member's individual discrimination claim later).

119. See Premier Elec. Constr. Co. v. Nat'l Elec. Contractors Ass'n, 814 F.2d 358 (7th Cir. 1987); Benjamin Kaplan, Continuing Work of the Civil Committee: 1966 Amendments of the Federal Rules of Civil Procedure (I), 81 Harv. L. Rev. 356, 391 n.136 (1967) ("it would be anomalous to give one who opts out collateral estoppel benefits of the action from which he deliberately removed himself"); see also supra § 5.4(B) (benefiting nonparties).

ance of Rule 23's limits and protections during the class action itself.[120]

e. Shareholders' Derivative Action

A derivative action allows one or more persons to sue for the benefit of similarly situated persons on a claim that their common fiduciary refuses to assert. Rule 23.1 deals specifically with derivative actions by shareholders of a corporation (or by members of an unincorporated association).[121] For example, if a minority shareholder believes that his corporation should be asserting a claim against a third person (either an outsider or a wrongdoing corporate official), but the corporation refuses to sue, then the shareholder may institute a shareholders' derivative action upon the corporation's claim.

Although a shareholders' derivative action has its place even when there are few shareholders, any shareholders' derivative action is basically similar to a class action. Thus, the plaintiff must appear to be a fair and adequate representative of those similarly situated. Also, termination procedure is similar to that for a class action.

The plaintiff must file a verified complaint[122] alleging, among other things, (1) that he was a shareholder at the *time of the transaction* sued upon (or that he later became such by a nonconsensual transfer), as well as at the *time of suit*, and (2) that he made an unsuccessful demand on the *directors* to sue, unless such a demand would have been futile, as well as on the *shareholders* if so required by applicable law. The corporation must be named as a defendant along with the alleged wrongdoer, even though the relief sought is a judgment running in its favor. Any recovery goes into the treasury of the corporation and is shared (in a manner of speaking) by all the shareholders.

The usual rules of jurisdiction and venue generally apply to a shareholders' derivative action. But in particular for diversity jurisdiction, the defendant corporation is rarely realigned as a plaintiff,

---

120. See Dow Chem. Co. v. Stephenson, 539 U.S. 111 (2003) (4–4, affirming Second Circuit); Gonzales v. Cassidy, 474 F.2d 67 (5th Cir. 1973); Note, Collateral Attack on the Binding Effect of Class Action Judgments, 87 Harv. L. Rev. 589 (1974). But compare Epstein v. MCA, Inc., 179 F.3d 641 (9th Cir.1999) (foreclosing attack on judgment even for a constitutional defect, at least if the due process point was fully and fairly litigated in the course of the settled class action), with Restatement (Second) of Judgments § 42 (1982) (reflecting other case law that sometimes allows attack on broader ground of failure to comply with class-action rule). See generally supra §§ 5.1(B), 5.7(B) (obtaining relief from judgment).

121. See generally Wright & Kane, supra note 18, § 73.

122. See Surowitz v. Hilton Hotels Corp., 383 U.S. 363 (1966).

even though the jurisdictional amount requirement is applied to the whole claim of the corporation. For territorial jurisdiction and venue, 28 U.S.C. §§ 1695 and 1401 respectively provide an additional service weapon and additional places for suit. The former nonexclusive statute says:

> Process in a stockholder's action in behalf of his corporation may be served upon such corporation in any district where it is organized or licensed to do business or is doing business.

The latter nonexclusive statute on venue says:

> Any civil action by a stockholder on behalf of his corporation may be prosecuted in any judicial district where the corporation might have sued the same defendants.

f. Intervention

In addition to all these ways of joining parties or litigating on behalf of nonparties, there is the possibility that an outsider might want to join himself to a pending lawsuit. Intervention allows but again does not compel certain persons not named as a party to enter an existing lawsuit, coming in on the appropriate side of the litigation.[123] But which persons should be able so to complicate or even commandeer a lawsuit of others? Alternatively viewed, when should those already litigants be allowed to litigate in the absence of persons who could be affected? Under Rule 24, there are two kinds of intervention: by right and by leave of court.

As to **intervention of right**, either of two circumstances bestows the right to intervene, according to Rule 24(a):

> On timely motion, the court must permit anyone to intervene who:
>> (1) is given an unconditional right to intervene by a federal statute; or
>> (2) claims an interest relating to the property or transaction that is the subject of the action, and is so situated that disposing of the action may as a practical matter impair or impede the movant's ability to protect its interest, unless existing parties adequately represent that interest.

Rule 24(a)(1) notes that a federal statute may confer this right. The most significant of the few such existing statutes is 28 U.S.C. § 2403, which gives the United States or a state the right to intervene in a federal action wherein the constitutionality of one of its statutes is questioned.

More importantly, under Rule 24(a)(2) a person has the right to intervene if she claims an interest relating to the subject of the

123. See generally Wright & Kane, supra note 18, § 75.

action and if the action might practically impair her interest, unless her interest is adequately represented by existing parties. First, the courts have not yet succeeded in defining the *requisite interest*,[124] but probably should approach this term flexibly in light of the functions of intervention and in conjunction with the impairment and representation requirements.[125] Second, the cases have applied the *practical impairment* requirement rather leniently and, for example, would allow intervention of right by an unrepresented person concerned with only the stare decisis effect on a very direct economic interest.[126] Third, as to *adequate representation*, it is unclear who has the burden of proof on this point, but it appears that this test is not too high a hurdle. The would-be intervenor need at most show only that her interest may be inadequately represented.[127] Better viewed, it is up to her opponent to show clearly that her interest is adequately represented.[128] Thus, a member of a class, feeling inadequately represented by the named parties and wishing to intervene in a class action, normally may intervene.[129]

124. Compare Cascade Natural Gas Corp. v. El Paso Natural Gas Co., 386 U.S. 129 (1967) (allowing gas company to intervene with objection to settlement of government antitrust action involving company's sole supplier), with Donaldson v. United States, 400 U.S. 517 (1971) (not allowing taxpayer being investigated by the IRS to intervene in enforcement proceedings regarding subpoenas against his former employer and its accountant).

125. See Coalition of Ariz./N.M. Counties for Stable Econ. Growth v. Dep't of the Interior, 100 F.3d 837 (10th Cir. 1996) (approving intervention of right by photographer coming in on side of government in a suit challenging the protection of the spotted owl); Smuck v. Hobson, 408 F.2d 175, 180 (D.C. Cir. 1969) ("If barriers are needed to limit extension of the right to intervene, the criteria of practical harm to the applicant and the adequacy of representation by others are better suited to the task. If those requirements are met, the nature of his 'interest' may play a role in determining the sort of intervention which should be allowed—whether, for example, he should be permitted to contest all issues, and whether he should enjoy all the prerogatives of a party litigant."). But cf. United States v. 36.96 Acres of Land, More or Less, Situate in the County of LaPorte, Ind., 100 F.R.D. 78 (N.D. Ind. 1983) (denying intervention to public interest group by saying that

interest must be significant, direct, and based on right belonging to intervenor), aff'd, 754 F.2d 855 (7th Cir. 1985) (holding that aesthetic and environmental interest is insufficient to intervene in a condemnation action).

126. See Atlantis Dev. Corp. v. United States, 379 F.2d 818, 828 (5th Cir. 1967) ("We are dealing here with a conjunction of a claim to and interest in the very property and the very transaction which is the subject of the main action.").

127. See Trbovich v. United Mine Workers, 404 U.S. 528, 538 n.10 (1972) ("The requirement of the Rule is satisfied if the applicant shows that representation of his interest 'may be' inadequate; and the burden of making that showing should be treated as minimal."); Grutter v. Bollinger, 188 F.3d 394 (6th Cir. 1999).

128. See Natural Resources Def. Council, Inc. v. U.S. Nuclear Regulatory Comm'n, 578 F.2d 1341, 1346 (10th Cir. 1978) (quoting Wright & Miller, supra note 13, § 1909 with approval: "he ordinarily should be allowed to intervene unless it is clear that the party will provide adequate representation for the absentee").

129. Cf. Cohen v. Republic of the Philippines, 146 F.R.D. 90 (S.D.N.Y. 1993) (allowing intervention by Imelda

As to **permissive intervention**, according to Rule 24(b)(1), either of two circumstances may prompt a court discretionarily to give leave to intervene, after taking into account the burdens that intervention would impose on those already parties:

> On timely motion, the court may permit anyone to intervene who:

>> (A) is given a conditional right to intervene by a federal statute; or

>> (B) has a claim or defense that shares with the main action a common question of law or fact.

Rule 24(b)(1)(A) notes that a federal statute may confer "a conditional right to intervene." Relatedly, Rule 24(b) itself goes on to provide that if a party relies for claim or defense upon any statute, order, or regulation administered by a federal or state officer or agency, then the officer or agency may be permitted to intervene.

More importantly, under Rule 24(b)(1)(B) anyone may be permitted to intervene when her claim or defense "shares with the main action a common question of law." Availability of this broad route would seem to justify a narrower reading of Rule 24(a)(2).

As to the **procedural incidents** for intervention of any type, Rule 24(c) prescribes:

> A motion to intervene must be served on the parties as provided in Rule 5. The motion must state the grounds for intervention and be accompanied by a pleading that sets out the claim or defense for which intervention is sought.

Any person seeking to intervene must make timely application, with the timeliness standard being left to judicial discretion and thus making all of intervention to some degree discretionary. The application consists of a motion stating the grounds for intervention, which must be accompanied by a pleading setting forth the applicant's claim or defense and must be served upon the parties like an ordinary motion.[130]

The intervenor comes in as a full party, being able freely to participate, seemingly even to the extent of asserting additional claims within the court's jurisdiction—unless the court imposes restrictive conditions on its granting of the application to intervene, either when it grants that application or later. The court has undoubted power to impose conditions in the case of permissive intervention, but seems to have at most only limited power to do so for intervention of right.[131]

Marcos as claimant in interpleader action).

130. See Fed. Form 42.

131. See David L. Shapiro, Some Thoughts on Intervention Before

Courts, Agencies, and Arbitrators, 81 Harv. L. Rev. 721 (1968).

    It is helpful to picture the relationship of intervention to the other joinder Rules. The following diagram suggests the relationship of Rules 19, 20, and 24. The connection of the extra party to the litigation diminishes with distance from the center of the diagram.

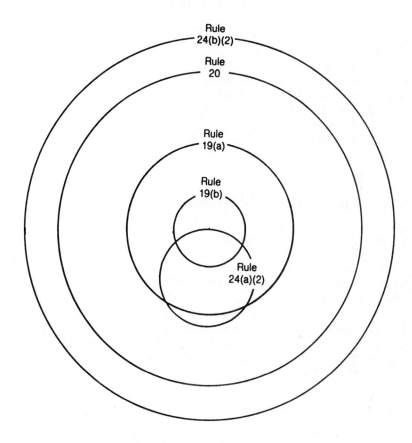

Chapter 7

CONCLUSION

Table of Sections

§ 7.1 Future of Civil Procedure

A. Perspectives on Subject

Envisaging the future of civil procedure, I see as an inevitable development the broadening of perspectives from which to view the subject. Instead of thrashing about within the traditional confines of the subject, with a principal reliance on the pointillist case method, proceduralists will more often have to step back and view a part or the whole from some new angle. The three most promising perspectives so far are law and economics, law and psychology, and empirical legal studies.

1. Law and Economics

To compare and choose among competing procedures, an analytic framework is necessary. A framework that has come to enjoy wide acceptance is cost-minimization. Here is a description from the pioneering civil-procedure-and-economics article by then Professor and now Judge Richard Posner:

> An important purpose of substantive legal rules (such as the rules of tort and criminal law) is to increase economic efficiency [in the sense of maximizing economic value]. It follows * * * that mistaken imposition of legal liability, or mistaken failure to impose liability, will reduce efficiency. Judicial error is therefore a source of social costs and the reduction of error is a goal of the procedural system. * * *

Even when the legal process works flawlessly, it involves costs—the time of lawyers, litigants, witnesses, jurors, judges, and other people, plus paper and ink, law office and court house maintenance, telephone service, etc. These costs are just as real as the costs resulting from error: in general we would not want to increase the direct costs of the legal process by one dollar in order to reduce error costs by 50 (or 99) cents. The economic goal is thus to minimize the sum of error and direct costs.

Despite its generality, this formulation provides a useful framework in which to analyze the problems and objectives of legal procedure. It is usable even when the purpose of the substantive law is to transfer wealth or to bring about some other noneconomic goal, rather than to improve efficiency. All that is necessary is that it be possible, in principle, to place a price tag on the consequences of failing to apply the substantive law in all cases in which it was intended to apply, so that our two variables, error cost and direct cost, remain commensurable.

* * * The cost inquiries required by the economic approach are not simple and will rarely yield better than crude approximations, but at the very least they serve to place questions of legal policy in a framework of rational inquiry.[1]

This framework for minimizing the sum of error and direct costs owes its success to its usefulness. To illustrate how well his approach worked, Posner considered the question whether to entitle the defendant to a trial-type hearing in an administrative action such as deportation or license revocation.[2] He contrasted the traditional legal approach, which tended "to invoke either a purely visceral sense of fairness or a purely formal distinction between penal and nonpenal sanctions," with his economic approach:

We begin by asking, what is the cost of withholding a trial-type hearing in a particular type of case? This inquiry has two branches: first, how is the probability of an error likely to be affected by a trial-type hearing? If the legally dispositive issues are factual issues of the kind most reliably determined in trial-type hearings, the probability of error if such a hearing is denied may be high. Second, what is the cost of an error if one occurs? As a first approximation, if the stakes in the case are large, the cost of error in an individual case will be large, so if in addition the probability of error is high, total error costs will

---

1. Richard A. Posner, An Economic Approach to Legal Procedure and Judicial Administration, 2 J. Legal Stud. 399, 400–02 (1973).

2. See supra § 4.3(B) (discussion of relevant constitutional doctrine).

be very high. Having established the costs of error, we then inquire into the costs of measures—a trial-type hearing or whatever—that would reduce the error costs. If those direct costs are low * * * then adoption can be expected to reduce the sum of error and direct costs and thus increase efficiency.[3]

A similar question that you have probably come across is whether due process requires appointment of counsel in situations such as when the state tries to terminate an indigent's parental rights. In such a case, the Supreme Court reached an ad hoc negative answer by comparing, albeit in an opaque and nonrigorous way, the expected error cost (the product of the probability of error without counsel times the cost of error if it occurs) with the direct cost of the state's providing a lawyer to the indigent parent.[4] Presumably, the expected error cost would have to considerably exceed the direct cost before amounting to a constitutional violation, as opposed to merely bad policy. That is, due process requires counsel if and only if:

$$P_e \, C_e >> C_d \, .$$

Another familiar formula, which employs the same basic idea, governs the law of preliminary injunctions, at least according to some authorities.[5] To minimize costs, the court should grant relief when the expected costs of wrongfully denying it exceed the expected costs of wrongfully granting it. The first factor equals the product of the probability that the plaintiff is in the right, in the sense of winning the case ultimately, times the irreparable harms to the plaintiff and others in the absence of a preliminary injunc-

---

3. Although his 1973 article contained basically the same illustration, this last quotation comes from Richard A. Posner, Economic Analysis of Law 430 (2d ed. 1977), which here appended this footnote: "The Supreme Court has recently adopted essentially this approach as the standard guiding scrutiny of administrative hearing procedures for conformity with the requirements of due process. See Mathews v. Eldridge, 424 U.S. 319, 96 S.Ct. 893 (1976), and, for criticism of the Court's approach, Jerry L. Mashaw, The Supreme Court's Due Process Calculus for Administrative Adjudication in Mathews v. Eldridge: Three Factors in Search of a Theory of Value, 44 U. Chi. L. Rev. 28, 47–49 (1976)."

4. Lassiter v. Dep't of Soc. Servs., 452 U.S. 18 (1981). For the story of this case, see Elizabeth G. Thornburg, The Story of Lassiter: The Importance of Counsel in an Adversary System, in Civil Procedure Stories 509 (Kevin M. Clermont ed., 2d ed. 2008).

5. See Am. Hosp. Supply Corp. v. Hosp. Prods. Ltd., 780 F.2d 589 (7th Cir. 1986) (Posner, J.); John Leubsdorf, The Standard for Preliminary Injunctions, 91 Harv. L. Rev. 525, 542 (1978) ("The court, in theory, should assess the probable irreparable loss of rights an injunction would cause by multiplying the probability that the defendant will prevail by the amount of the irreparable loss that the defendant would suffer if enjoined from exercising what turns out to be his legal right. It should then make a similar calculation of the probable irreparable loss of rights to the plaintiff from denying the injunction. Whichever course promises the smaller probable loss should be adopted."); cf. supra § 2.2(E)(1) (discussion of the law on provisional remedies).

tion (with the substantive law determining which harms count). The second factor equals the product of the probability that the defendant will win the case times the irreparable harms to the defendant and others that would be imposed by a preliminary injunction. To put it algebraically, grant the preliminary injunction if and only if:

$$P H_p > (1 - P) H_d .$$

This formula does serve to discipline somewhat the judge's function by specifying the relevant factors and showing how they interact; and imposing this discipline seems preferable to the sometimes lazy or whimsical and always hidden exercise of equitable power. In other words, this formula serves the important purpose of the law to reduce the realm of subjective decisionmaking's unobservable black box, although that realm can never be completely eliminated.

The cost-minimization framework is indeed so useful that it, all by itself, suggests consideration of its own costs. Among other drawbacks, it tends to distort analysis by ignoring or devaluing certain values, such as the right to participate and other process values that are hard to quantify, while injecting or at least exaggerating others, such as efficiency as opposed even to outcome values.[6] These real drawbacks (rather than such common and simplistic attacks as pointing out the obvious difficulty of putting a dollar amount on certain factors) place in question the framework's utility.[7]

The resulting controversy was only part of a bigger controversy around a much bigger subject: the law-and-economics movement. Around 1960, academics came to apply economic analysis broadly to the legal system, in contrast to an earlier application of economics that was limited to those parts of the law actually regulating economic relationships, such as antitrust law. These new academics, accepting as a premise that people are rational maximizers of their own ends, used existing economic tools to explain much of the law and to propose reforms. The initial but unsuccessful reaction of the traditional academy was across-the-board resistance. Today the intelligent approach is to recognize that law and economics is here to stay, and that therefore one should try to understand its strengths and its weaknesses. A first step in that direction is to

---

6. See Robert S. Summers, Kevin M. Clermont, Robert A. Hillman, Sheri L. Johnson, John J. Barceló III & Doris M. Provine, Law: Its Nature, Functions, and Limits 112, 147–48 (3d ed. 1986) ("We shall use the phrase *process values* to refer to values by which we can judge a legal process to be good as a process, apart from any good outcomes it may yield.").

7. See, e.g., Robert A. Baruch Bush, Dispute Resolution Alternatives and the Goals of Civil Justice: Jurisdictional Principles for Process Choice, 1984 Wis. L. Rev. 893, 929–32.

separate, to the extent possible, law and economics' positive program from its normative agenda.[8]

Law and economics' normative use, as illustrated in the above discussion of cost-minimization, attempts to reform the law—most often in accord with the aim of promoting efficiency, that is, maximizing society's wealth or, equivalently, minimizing social costs. This use, as already suggested, remains highly controversial. But it delivers some undeniable lessons, for example, that you cannot reasonably overlook the price of pursuing justice, no matter how you wish to define justice. And its biggest problem—that its focus on aggregative efficiency tends to obscure process-based and outcome-based considerations of individualized fairness—can be partially overcome by defining wealth, or welfare, and costs more inclusively. In sum, on normative questions, economic analysis can, at the least, inform by illuminating value conflicts and evaluating choices among values, regardless of the prevailing value system.

Economic analysis's positive use is descriptive, explanatory, and predictive as to law, and hence a little less controversial. However, its biggest problem—that its rational-choice premise departs from the reality of humankind's "bounded rationality," as indisputably demonstrated by law-and-psychology scholars[9]—is hard to overcome without destroying the effectiveness of simplified economic modeling. Still, economic analysis retains some descriptive, explanatory, and predictive power.

An example of this positive usefulness is a simple explanatory model of the disputants' settlement/litigation decision.[10] The aim would be to construct the condition for litigation in place of settlement under a number of simplifying assumptions, including known recovery, equal costs, risk neutrality, and rational decision-making by lawyers acting in their clients' best interests. Settlement negotiations will collapse, and litigation will proceed, if the minimum amount that the potential plaintiff will accept in settlement exceeds the maximum amount that the potential defendant will pay. The plaintiff's minimum price is the eventually recoverable judgment (J) discounted by his estimated probability of winning (P_p), minus his future cost of litigating (L) which he would save by settling, plus his transaction cost of settling (S) which he would incur in arranging a settlement. The defendant will pay a maximum of the eventual judgment times her estimate of the probabili-

---

8. See generally Robert G. Bone, Civil Procedure: The Economics of Civil Procedure (2003).

9. See Christine Jolls, Cass R. Sunstein & Richard Thaler, A Behavioral Approach to Law and Economics, 50 Stan. L. Rev. 1471 (1998); Russell B. Korobkin & Thomas S. Ulen, Law and Behavioral Science: Removing the Rationality Assumption from Law and Economics, 88 Cal. L. Rev. 1051 (2000).

10. See supra § 2.3 (discussion of settlement stage).

ty of the plaintiff's winning (P_d), plus litigation cost, minus settlement cost. That is, the sufficient condition for litigation is:

$$P_p J - L + S > P_d J + L - S .$$

The lessons become clearer upon rewriting the inequality as:

$$(P_p - P_d) J > 2 (L - S) .$$

Thus, if the two disputants agree on the probability of the outcome, and given that litigation is normally more expensive than settlement, then the condition for litigation will never be met, because the left side of the second inequality is zero and the right side is positive; in other words, a settlement range between the plaintiff's minimum demand and the defendant's maximum offer will always exist, and the parties will negotiate a settlement amount that divides the range between themselves somehow. Changes in J, L, and S will affect predictably the size of the settlement range. Except when impediments to bargaining exist, litigation should ensue only when each disputant persists in viewing his or her chance more favorably than the opponent does.[11]

Economic analysis turns out to be less informative on the subject of reimbursement of attorney's fees.[12] The so-called American rule against such fee-shifting might be better termed the "American exception." In most of the rest of the Western world, including England, the losing party reimburses the attorney's fees of the prevailing party. Under such a regime that requires the loser to pay, in addition to the loser's own counsel fees, the winning side's counsel fees as costs, victory will be more complete, but the risk of loss is greater. In considering the effects on the litigants' economic incentives that would result from any change in this country toward fee-shifting, the theoretical work has been surprisingly inconclusive.[13] First—on the decision to pursue the claim— probably the English rule relatively encourages small meritorious suits, while somewhat discouraging larger dubious suits and nuisance suits; however, risk aversion would discourage the middle class from resorting to litigation under the English rule. Second— on the subsequent decision whether to settle—although the expected effects of implementing the English rule on the likelihood and timing of settlement are rather unclear, strong claims would tend to be settled for more and weak claims for less than under the American rule. Third—on the conduct of litigation—although the English rule might relatively encourage the litigants to escalate

---

11. See Bone, supra note 8, ch. 2; see also id. ch. 1 (frivolous litigation).

12. See supra § 2.5(B) (discussion of award of costs).

13. See James W. Hughes & Edward A. Snyder, Litigation and Settlement Under the English and American Rules: Theory and Evidence, 38 J. Law & Econ. 225 (1995).

expenditures, its expected influence on the overall economic costs of the litigation system is unknown and arguably unknowable. Fourth—on the incentive to comply with substantive law—the comparison between English and American rules gets really complex, because the interaction or interplay of effects on these various incentives can no longer be ignored. In any event, predicting the direction of an effect tells us nothing of the size of the effect or the importance of side effects—which must also be considered in a broad context accounting at least for the presence or absence of contingent fees, legal aid, legal insurance, small-claims courts, other alternative dispute-resolution mechanisms, class actions, and other representative litigation and also the effects of any security-for-costs or offer-of-judgment provisions. The lesson seems to be this: beware of simplistic economic analysis of the English–American dispute. Life and humans are complicated.[14]

How Hard Will an Attorney Work for a Fee?

Consider first the hourly fee, which accrues whether the client wins or loses. Assume that the client has a claim that conceivably has a positive net value. Because the lawyer's fee is proportional to the number of hours devoted to the case, too much work by the lawyer could reduce the client's net recovery to zero or less. Or too little work could result in little or no recovery, likewise reducing the client's net recovery to zero or less. There is a particular number of hours of work between these two extremes that would result in the largest net recovery for the client. However, the lawyer has no direct economic incentive to work that particular number of hours. No matter how many hours the lawyer devotes to the case before he ceases work and shifts his efforts to other cases, his economic position will be unaffected, because he is being paid at his normal hourly rate and his fee is unconditional. If his workload happens to be light, the lawyer would tend to work more than the particular number of hours required to maximize his client's net recovery—a strategy obviously to his client's disadvantage. The overworked attorney would tend to work fewer than that particular number of hours—also to the client's detriment. In short, the lawyer's economic interests do not align with those of his client. At best, if the hourly rate is fixed at opportunity cost, the hourly fee leaves the lawyer indifferent to the client's economic interests. In this absence of a direct economic incentive to make the lawyer work in the client's best interests, our legal system must rely exclusively on noneconomic or indirect restraints to forestall the potential economic conflict of interest between lawyer and client.

In contrast, a frequently cited advantage of the contingent fee, which pays a percentage of recovery only if the client wins, is that the lawyer and the client become partners. Since the attorney gets a percentage of the recovery but nothing else, the client can rely on her for zealous and faithful service in getting the best possible settlement or judgment. This view is simply a misconception. The lawyer's and the client's economic interests align only partially. Although lawyer and client share a common interest in victory, misalignment exists with respect to the number of hours the lawyer should work. Because the client's net recovery varies directly with the gross recovery, and because the client must pay a fixed percentage fee without regard to the number of hours worked, the client's economic interests are best served when the lawyer devotes a very large number of hours to ensure the maximum settlement or judgment. However, as shown in the graph, the lawyer optimizes her own economic position by working a much smaller

---

14. See Bone, supra note 8, ch. 5.

number of hours; direct economic incentive prods her to obtain a respectable settlement with relatively slight effort, thus securing for herself the maximum profit. Here again our legal system must rely on restraints other than direct economic incentive to make the lawyer act in the client's best interests.

To model this graphically, albeit with numerous simplifying assumptions unstated here, let the horizontal axis measure the number of hours (h) worked by the plaintiff's attorney, and the vertical axis represent the dollar amount of the defendant's settlement offer (s). For each number of hours, the height of the s-curve is the settlement amount then obtainable; eventually the s-curve levels out, so that further effort by the plaintiff's attorney will not increase the settlement. The hourly fee is the hours worked multiplied by an hourly rate, which in theory should be set at opportunity cost (o), and at \$50/hour the fee appears as the o-line; the client's net recovery is the difference between the s-curve and the o-line. The contingent fee is a percentage of the settlement, and at 33% the percentage fee appears as the $f_\%$-curve; the client's net recovery is the difference between the s-curve and the $f_\%$-curve.

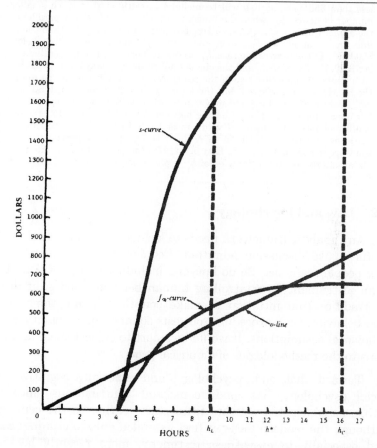

Under the hourly fee, an all-knowing client, wanting the highest possible net recovery, would choose that h for which the s-curve is farthest above the o-line, and that particular number of hours (h^*) occurs when the tangent to the s-curve becomes parallel to the o-line. In the illustrative case,

h^* occurs at 12 hours, when the settlement is $1920, the fee is $600, and the client's net recovery is $1320. No other h would yield a larger net recovery. For any h less than h^*, the *s-curve* rises more rapidly than the *o-line*, so that the hourly increase in the settlement more than covers the $50/hour fee. For any h greater than h^*, the *o-line* climbs more rapidly than the *s-curve*, making the client lose money. Unfortunately, the attorney has no direct economic incentive to work h^*. He receives $50 for each hour worked, an amount that he must forgo in alternative income. Hence, the attorney is economically indifferent. That opens the door to conflict of interest.

Under the contingent fee, the client now would choose that h for which the *s-curve* is farthest above the *f-curve*, and that particular number of hours (h_C) occurs when the tangents to the *s-curve* and the $f_\%$*-curve* become parallel, which is when the *s-curve* reaches its maximum. In the illustrative case, h_C occurs at 16 hours, when the settlement is $2000, the fee is $666, and the client's net recovery is $1334. By contrast, the attorney is recovering a fee of only 33% of the increase in settlement per hour while incurring $50 in opportunity cost per hour. The attorney does not wish to work for less than $50/hour, and so will be inclined to settle at that much smaller number of hours (h_L) when the tangent to the $f_\%$*-curve* becomes parallel to the *o-line*, which is when the $f_\%$*-curve* begins to rise less rapidly than the *o-line* or, in other words, when the attorney's return has fallen below $50/hour. In the illustrative case, h_L occurs at 9 hours, when the settlement is $1620, the fee is $540, and the client's net recovery is way down to $1080. At 9 hours, the absolute size of the fee is less than what it would be under the hourly fee arrangement, but the attorney's profit is maximized. So, she will tend to stop working and move on to other work that will pay at least her opportunity cost. The difference between h_C and h_L makes for a stark conflict of interest, which will work most likely to the client's detriment. See generally Kevin M. Clermont & John D. Currivan, Improving on the Contingent Fee, 63 Cornell L. Rev. 529 (1978) (proposing to align interests via an alternative contingent fee of $h \cdot o$ plus some small percentage, x, of $(s - h \cdot o)$).

2. Law and Psychology

Any analytic framework needs to keep an eye on the real world, as the above discussion admitted. Economists must worry about how people really act. So do lawyers, including proceduralists. Law is an instrument for controlling human behavior, and so it draws on tradition and intuition to make countless assumptions about that behavior. Civil procedure too rests squarely on a gigantic set of behavioral assumptions. It would be smart to subject those assumptions to the methodologies of empirical proof.

Toward that end, psychology, and especially cognitive and social psychology, has made consistent contributions since the 1970s, as contrasted with its fitful starts earlier in the century.[15] Although the modern focus at first extended only to criminal cases and especially to eyewitness testimony, more recently law-and-psychology scholars have expanded their range to cover other legal

---

15. See generally Handbook of Psychology and Law (D.K. Kagehiro & W.S. Laufer eds., 1992).

subjects, including civil procedure.[16] Not only does psychology provide the means to test behavioral assumptions within the law and civil procedure, but also it promises a fruitful "outside perspective" from which to look at law or civil procedure as a whole system operating in a social context.[17]

Some of its lessons are encouraging, such as the pioneering study in which ingenious and cross-cultural experiments tended to prove that an adversary system maximizes satisfaction.[18] It seems that participant and observer appraisal of procedural justice turns most critically on the distribution of control over process, with the ideal being to give process power to opposed litigants under a system of controlled contentiousness and to have a passive judge render decision. Factors such as separate presentations, chosen representatives, and partisan identification of that attorney with the client were important but secondary determinants.

Some of the lessons are no less surprising but much less encouraging. For example, human limits on perception, memory, and communication render some courtroom testimony quite suspect. I need only mention again the path-breaking and downright startling work showing the unreliability of eyewitness testimony.[19]

What Does Psychology Reveal About Standards of Proof?

The principal task of the law's actors is decisionmaking, and decisionmaking takes place in a world of uncertainty. A legal decisionmaker therefore needs to know not only the issue but also how certain one must be to decide it in a particular way. Much of procedure aims at facilitating optimal decisionmaking in the face of uncertainty. A central and critical

---

16. See, e.g., Civil Juries and Civil Justice (Brian H. Bornstein et al. eds., 2008); Reid Hastie, Steven Penrod & Nancy Pennington, Inside the Jury (1983) (modeling decisionmaking as the construction of stories); Chris Guthrie, Panacea or Pandora's Box?: The Costs of Options in Negotiation, 88 Iowa L. Rev. 601 (2003); Chris Guthrie, Framing Frivolous Litigation: A Psychological Theory, 67 U. Chi. L. Rev. 163 (2000); Russell Korobkin & Chris Guthrie, Psychological Barriers to Litigation Settlement: An Experimental Approach, 93 Mich. L. Rev. 107 (1994); George Loewenstein, Samuel Issacharoff, Colin Camerer & Linda Babcock, Self–Serving Assessments of Fairness and Pretrial Bargaining, 22 J. Legal Stud. 135 (1993); Jeffrey J. Rachlinski, Gains, Losses, and the Psychology of Litigation, 70 S. Cal. L. Rev. 113 (1996); cf. Kevin M. Clermont, Teaching Civil Procedure Through Its Top Ten Cases, Plus or Minus Two, 47 St. Louis U. L.J.

111 (2003) (implications of psychology for pedagogy); Kevin M. Clermont, Civil Procedure Archaeology, in Civil Procedure Stories 1 (Kevin M. Clermont ed., 2d ed. 2008) (similar).

17. See Lawrence M. Friedman, The Law and Society Movement, 38 Stan. L. Rev. 763, 777–78 (1986).

18. John W. Thibaut & Laurens Walker, Procedural Justice: A Psychological Analysis 1–2, 118–19 (1975); see E. Allan Lind & Tom R. Tyler, The Social Psychology of Procedural Justice (1988). But see Donna Shestowsky, Procedural Preferences in Alternative Dispute Resolution: A Closer, Modern Look at an Old Idea, 10 Psychol., Pub. Pol'y & L. 211 (2004).

19. Elizabeth F. Loftus, Eyewitness Testimony (1979); see Elizabeth F. Loftus, James M. Doyle & Jennifer E. Dysart, Eyewitness Testimony: Civil and Criminal (4th ed. 2007).

task of procedure, then, is to specify the degree of certainty required to support a particular decision.

Narrow the focus to that procedural task as performed in connection with ordinary legal decisions of a binary nature. This kind of standard of decision comprises the standards of original decision, the standards of review of that decision, and the standards for reviewing the reviewer. The most conspicuous standard of original decision is what is called the standard of proof, or the measure of persuasion or the degree of belief, which specifies the required certainty used by a factfinder in deciding whether a contested fact exists.

The law sets the standard of proof at a level that serves the legal system's aims: in a given circumstance, the law may aim to minimize overall errors, to decrease dangers of deception or bias or to disfavor certain claims, or to avoid a special kind of error such as convicting the innocent. To achieve those aims, the law has settled on three standards that apply in different circumstances: (1) The standard of *preponderance of the evidence* translates into more-likely-than-not. It occupies the bottom end of the usual probability scale that extends upward from equipoise. It is the usual standard in civil litigation, but it appears throughout law. (2) Next comes the intermediate standard or standards, often grouped under the banner of *clear and convincing evidence* and roughly translated as much-more-likely-than-not. These apply to certain issues in special situations, such as when terminating parental rights. Of late, debate has markedly decreased on potential differences among the various distinctive formulations of this intermediate standard. (3) The standard of *proof beyond a reasonable doubt* means proof to a virtual-certainty. It very rarely prevails outside criminal law. There, although debate will continue on the precise practical meaning of this or any standard of proof, everyone accepts the propriety of this standard as the top end of the probability scale in our unavoidably uncertain world.

Most significantly, the law today seems to limit the choice to no more than these three standards from among the infinite range of probabilities stretching from more-likely-than-not to virtual-certainty. The law did not always recognize this limitation, but with time the law acknowledged that the conceivable spectrum of standards had coalesced irresistibly into three. Why?

Well, the cognitive psychology literature suggests that these threefold standards accord with how humans naturally process information. Studies of humans' absolute judgment, short-term memory, and use of biased heuristics all support the "bounded rationality" of humankind. In particular, our cognitive limitations leave us able only weakly to judge probabilities. Judged likelihood usually finds expression in terms of a very limited set of broad and fuzzy categories such as more likely than not, high probability, and almost certainty.

Perhaps the law has optimized by conforming to the coarsely gradated scale of probability already in people's customary use. If so, this legal development represents the law's intuitive but wise reconciliation with humans' cognitive limitations. And then there are some further lessons.

One is that lawmakers in specifying a standard of decision should steadfastly choose from only the customary standards in use and express their choice in familiar language. The available standards will adequately cover the range of underlying policies, and a range of choices limited to quantum leaps will indeed illuminate the policy question. Familiar language will improve comprehension and application by the decisionmakers. Learning and applying this lesson would make for a sounder procedure that better fits humans.

Another lesson is that all other standards of probabilistic decisionmaking, such as new-trial review of jury decisions and appellate review of judicial decisions, do and should follow the same pattern. Thus, the many conceivable standards of review distill into simple disagreement, clear error, and the almost certain error of an irrationality test. See generally Kevin M. Clermont, Procedure's Magical Number Three: Psychological Bases for Standards of Decision, 72 Cornell L. Rev. 1115 (1987).

3. Empirical Legal Studies

One would think that, all theories aside, proceduralists and other lawyers should have always been concerned with how the law works in actuality. But law in fact has long ignored empirical methods. The law's theory, doctrine, and administration sprang from logic and intuition, rather than from scientifically appraised experience.

Today, however, a new era is dawning. Empirical research—empirical studies of the legal system's operation, as distinguished from scientific analyses introduced as evidence in individual legal cases—should have a revolutionary impact on the law. In particular as to civil procedure, a new wave of empirical study is giving a fresh sense of reality to the field. Moreover, there is a growing need for further such study, because in recent years anecdotal evidence has created a frenzy about the current state of litigation and led to a host of ill-conceived reform efforts. Before undertaking reform, one should know whether and to what extent there really is a problem, and then one should realistically assess the proposed reforms.

The social sciences—economics, psychology, and so on—apply a variety of empirical methods. Empirical methods are those that employ means for the systematic observation of experience, in pursuit of inductive ends. The social scientists either create experience by experiment or find experience in records, and then they analyze the experience. In analyzing experience, the social scientists employ a variety of tools. The most powerful of these—and the weapon that has enabled the revolution in legal studies—is statistics. Statistics entails the assembling and organizing of plentiful data, which are almost always in the form of numbers, and then mathematically analyzing the data to reach inductive conclusions. In the arena of legal studies, the statistical research to date divides into three groups, which differ in their assembly of data.

First, there are statistical analyses of published judicial decisions.[20] In a sense, this group of studies represents a systematization of traditional doctrinal research. Instead of reporting the fruits of years of subjective reading of court opinions that had crossed one's desk, the empirical legal scholar turned to selecting randomly, coding tirelessly, and then analyzing hundreds of cases. This new kind of research was a step forward. And it has become much easier

---

20. E.g., Kevin M. Clermont & Theodore Eisenberg, CAFA Judicata: A Tale of Waste and Politics, 156 U. Pa. L. Rev. 1553, 1558–60, 1562–63 (2008).

to do after the development of commercial computerized databases of legal materials. But this research method is a very risky undertaking. On the one hand, judicial decisions represent only the very tip of the mass of grievances. From that highpoint of actual judicial decisions, it is tough to infer truths about the underlying mass of disputes or what lies below disputes. On the other hand, published decisions are a skewed sample of that tip of judicial decisions. A rather small percentage of judicial decisions reach publication by a selection process that is far from random.

Second, the real heroes of empirical research create their own data for their subsequent statistical analysis.[21] They might do this by experimental work or by archival research. That is, they might feed a series of simulated cases to a number of mock juries. Or they might spend months stumbling around in dusty court files, and then go out in the field to uncover each case's real facts to which the file coldly alludes. Such methods have long been possible, and for just as long they have gone rarely employed. And that situation will persist into the future. Basically, the reason is that this kind of work is a drag. It voraciously consumes time and money. Anyway, there is no one to do it. Law-trained persons are unsuited by temperament and training. High opportunity cost and low professional reward also disincline them. Non-law-trained persons are, well, not trained in law. Social scientists have plenty to study that does not require the courage and effort of venturing into the mysterious realm of the law.

Third, the most promising group of statistical studies involves simply analyzing publicly available information, usually governmental databases.[22] One could view this approach as a way to overcome the limits and risks of published-decision research. Or one could view it as a freeriding version of the heroic approach. It is both, as it yields valid results by feasible means. Broad and growing databases are available at no cost. Access is easy, especially given the internet's increasing power. Inexpensive but sophisticated commercial statistical software now exists, facilitating the analysis step. In short, everything is in place for an explosion of empirical work. So it is this group of statistical studies that should have the biggest impact on the law.

---

21. E.g., Harry Kalven, Jr. & Hans Zeisel, The American Jury (2d ed. 1971). This work, first published in 1966, inaugurated the movement of rigorous empirical legal studies, although the movement has only recently exploded in interest. See Valerie P. Hans & Neil Vidmar, The American Jury at Twenty–Five Years, 16 Law & Soc. Inquiry 323 (1991).

22. E.g., Marc Galanter, Contract in Court; or Almost Everything You May or May Not Want to Know About Contract Litigation, 2001 Wis. L. Rev. 577, 577 (describing "a low cost *bricolage* strategy of trying to capture, refine, and juxtapose scattered data already in the public domain").

A principal resource for such research is the data gathered by the Administrative Office of the United States Courts, assembled by the Federal Judicial Center, and disseminated by the Inter-university Consortium for Political and Social Research.[23] These data convey details of all cases terminated in the federal courts since fiscal 1970. When any civil case terminates in a federal district court or court of appeals, the court clerk transmits to the Administrative Office a form containing information about the case. The forms include, inter alia, data regarding the names of the parties, the subject matter category and the jurisdictional basis of the case, the case's origin in the district as original or removed or transferred, the amount demanded, the dates of filing and termination in the district court or the court of appeals, the procedural stage of the case at termination, the procedural method of disposition, and, if the court entered judgment or reached decision, the prevailing party and the relief granted. Thus, the computerized database, compiled from these forms, contains all of the millions of federal civil cases over many years from the whole country.

Now that I have described the range of empirical research, I shall discuss some of what the legal community is just now learning about litigation, thanks to this new use of empirical methods. Mainly using that body of data from the Administrative Office, I shall treat separately the six stages of litigation detailed in Chapter Two: forum selection, pretrial practice, settlement process, trial practice, judgment entry, and appeal practice.[24]

First, as already explained,[25] forum really matters. Study of removal and transfer suggests a consistent "forum effect," whereby the plaintiffs' loss of the forum advantage by removal or transfer reduces their chance of winning by about one-fifth. Here the insight coming from empirical research is no surprise, as it mainly confirms what most lawyers already knew. The name of the game indeed is forum-shopping, and so all those lawyers out there are in fact not wasting their clients' money on forum fights.

Second, the pretrial stage of litigation is the lengthiest stage. Naturally, then, it has been the focus of recent reform efforts to speed up litigation: justice delayed is justice denied, after all. Just as naturally, one would think, the reformers would have demanded empirical groundwork, but they did not. Instead, they have proceed-

---

23. For easy access to this database, see Theodore Eisenberg & Kevin M. Clermont, Judicial Statistical Inquiry, http://empirical.law.cornell.edu, which is discussed in Theodore Eisenberg & Kevin M. Clermont, Courts in Cyberspace, 46 J. Legal Educ. 94 (1996).

24. See generally Kevin M. Clermont & Theodore Eisenberg, Litigation Realities, 88 Cornell L. Rev. 119 (2002); Kevin M. Clermont, Litigation Realities Redux, 84 Notre Dame L. Rev (forthcoming 2009) (including state data on speed of judge-tried and jury-tried cases).

25. See supra §§ 4.1(A), 4.2(A).

ed largely on the basis of logic and intuition—in overhauling pleading and motion practice, while adding disclosure, discovery, and conference mechanisms. There is ample reason, however, to proceed with wariness before accepting the truth either of old maxims about delay or of new proposals for reform based merely on logic and intuition. Both recent theoretical work and recent empirical study argue for such caution: (a) Theoretical work contends that delay is not necessarily an evil.[26] Delay is an unavoidable feature of life, and it is not an evil in itself. The only evil is excessive delay, where excessive means that the costs of delay outweigh its benefits. The costs of figuratively queuing to try a case tend to be exaggerated, because we overlook that the parties can engage in other pursuits while waiting. Queuing in fact has some benefits, such as lowering the demand for expensive trials. (b) Another study, both empirical and theoretical, shows that the many obvious reforms simply have not worked and will not work to reduce delay.[27] The basic insight is that any reduction in delay increases the incentive to litigate and reduces the parties' incentives to settle, with the consequent increase in litigation offsetting the reduction in delay. Most attempts at reform, such as adding judges, will only increase the number of dispositions, rather than decreasing the time to disposition. Adding judges to the system to reduce congestion is similar to expanding the number of freeway lanes, an improvement that would draw traffic off the side streets and from public transportation. More cases might flow into the system, and the lesser burden of litigating might reduce the subsequent incentives to settle, so the increased number of judges would be able to adjudicate basically the same percentage of cases. (c) Empirical work suggests that delay is neither that lengthy nor increasing recently. Moreover, one study used state data to demonstrate that particular processes, such as alternative dispute resolution, do not correlate with shortened disposition times—while the factors that do so correlate, such as forum locale and case category, are simply beyond the reach of process-oriented reform.[28] In short, assumptions about delay are risky, making further empirical study a necessity.

Third, most lawsuits do not make it all the way through the pretrial practice just examined. Indeed, most disputes do not even become lawsuits. Injured persons abandon or settle the overwhelm-

---

26. See Posner, supra note 1, at 445–48.

27. George L. Priest, Private Litigants and the Court Congestion Problem, 69 B.U. L. Rev. 527 (1989) (postulating a "congestion equilibrium hypothesis"); see Tracey E. George & Chris Guthrie, Induced Litigation, 98 Nw. U. L. Rev. 545 (2004); cf. John Leubsdorf, The Myth of Civil Proce-

dure Reform, in Civil Justice in Crisis 53 (Adrian A.S. Zuckerman ed., 1999) (questioning more generally the efficacy of procedural reform).

28. Michael Heise, Justice Delayed?: An Empirical Analysis of Civil Case Disposition Time, 50 Case W. Res. L. Rev. 813 (2000); cf. supra § 2.2(B) (discussion of mandatory disclosure).

ing majority of grievances at some point along the line. A basic truth, then, is that settlement is numerically much more important than actual litigation.[29] Yet empirical research tends to focus on the readily observable, and litigation is much more observable than settlement. Indeed, judgment is the most observable feature of litigation. Therefore, the popular form of recent empirical studies involves examining the parties' success in obtaining judgment after litigation, thus studying the system's output while largely ignoring the variable composition of its input. But doing or interpreting such research demands great caution. The studies can be subjective, difficult, and risky. The danger arises from the unobserved settlement activity, which infects the observable win-rate data with near-fatal ambiguity. The ambiguity arises from the "selection effect" of the settlement process, whereby the parties' selection of the cases to push into and through litigation rather than into settlement produces a biased sample from the mass of underlying disputes.[30] More specifically, disputes and cases that clearly favor either the plaintiff or the defendant tend to settle readily, because both sides can save costs by settling in light of their knowledge of the applicable law and all other aspects of the case. Difficult cases falling close to the applicable decisional criterion tend not to settle, because the parties are more likely to disagree substantially in their predicted outcomes. These unsettled close cases fall more or less equally on either side of the decisional criterion, regardless of the position of that criterion and regardless of the underlying distribution of disputes. Thus, even if, say, the law fixing the criterion highly favors plaintiffs, such as strict liability, one might not observe a plaintiff win rate well above 50%. Instead, case selection will leave for adjudication a residue of unsettled close cases, which consequently exhibit some nonextreme equilibrium win rate. In other words, the case-selection effect means that the win rate reveals something about the set of adjudged cases, a universe dominated by close cases—but, without imaginative and careful study, reveals little about the underlying, variegated mass of disputes and cases, and indeed little about the litigation process's treatment thereof.

Fourth, as caseloads have recently bloomed, the civil trial has all but disappeared. The percentage of filed federal civil cases that see trial is now dropping toward 1%, and state and criminal trials too have dropped off. Interestingly, for federal civil cases, bench trial has fallen much more precipitously than jury trial. The latter development is especially mysterious because both queues for trial pass through the regulation of the same person, namely, the trial

---

29. See supra § 2.3 (discussion of settlement stage).

30. See George L. Priest & Benjamin Klein, The Selection of Disputes for Litigation, 13 J. Legal Stud. 1 (1984).

judge: perhaps the explanation lies in judicial distaste for the time-consuming task of bench trial, or perhaps those litigants who prefer jury trial have proved to be the more determined group as the disincentives to holding any trial have increased.

Which Take Longer, Judge-tried Cases or Jury-tried Cases?

Using the Administrative Office database of federal civil cases, but limiting the study to sizable tort and contract categories that clearly involved a choice between jury and judge trial, one can show that while the actual jury trials themselves may proceed twice as slowly as judge trials, over their lives on the docket judge-tried cases last longer than jury-tried cases: the median judge-tried case spends 619 days on the district court's docket, compared to the median jury-tried case terminating in 566 days. That is, although most commentators have assumed that the wait for decision in the jury queue was longer than the wait for a judge's trial and decision, the reality in the federal courts is the opposite. The explanation is that the press of other duties leads judges to interrupt bench trials and postpone their eventual decisions. Consequently, any reform of restricting jury trials in order to reduce delay is apt to be counterproductive. See generally Theodore Eisenberg & Kevin M. Clermont, Trial by Jury or Judge: Which Is Speedier?, 79 Judicature 176 (1996).

Curiously, data dealing with comparable tort and contract cases in state courts suggest that jury cases do in fact last significantly longer than bench cases: the median disposition time in the state courts of general jurisdiction for a jury-tried case was 21.7 months and for a judge-tried case only 16.1 months. An examination of the underlying state database confirms that state jury trials start almost six months later in a case's life than state bench trials do, while the two modes of trial start about the same time in federal courts. Another important observation is that state judges do not delay nearly as long after the end of bench trial before issuing a decision as do federal judges. It thus seems that the state courts, unlike the federal courts, are imposing waiting costs upon those who wish a jury trial and not on those who agree to a bench trial, with the effect of discouraging jury trials. Not all states follow this practice, as some adopt a more neutral approach or the federal approach. Nonetheless, although ultimately a matter of local culture, most states act in ways that tend to discourage jury trials and federal courts do not.

Fifth, as to judgment, one can cautiously compare outcomes in the stream of cases going through jury trial to outcomes after bench trials.[31] In two of the most controversial areas of modern tort law, product liability and medical malpractice, the federal win rates substantially differ from other categories' win rates and in a surprising way: plaintiffs in these two areas prevail after trial at a much higher rate before judges (48%) than they do before juries (28%). These empirical results proved resistant to all simple explanations, such as differences in the size of award explaining differences in win rates. The explanation must lie in the parties' ability to select which cases reach jury or judge trial. Lawyers entertain longstanding elitist perceptions of the jury as biased and incompetent, relative to the judge. These perceptions have the consequence of a selection of cases reaching jury trial that differs from the case

---

31. See Kevin M. Clermont & Theodore Eisenberg, Trial by Jury or Judge: Transcending Empiricism, 77 Cornell L. Rev. 1124 (1992).

selection reaching judge trial. In particular, in these categories of cases, lawyers view the jury as relatively favorable to plaintiffs. They then settle cases in a way that leaves for trial by jury or judge a residue of what they consider close cases, with juries accordingly seeing on average weaker cases. But the perceptions turn out to be misperceptions, as jury and judge turn out to perform similarly, there being in fact no empirical evidence that juries are relatively biased or incompetent.[32] Thus, the jury produces fewer winners than expected, while the judge produces more winners. More simply put, certain groups of plaintiffs do far better before judges, but the reason likely lies in prevailing misperceptions about juries that produce different trial dockets, rather than in differences between judges and juries, because judges and juries are actually not so different. Practical lessons start to emerge. One could conclude that the jury is less of an advantage for plaintiffs, and the judge less of a disadvantage, than lawyers think. That realization should affect the terms of settlement. Moreover, if only one side comes to that realization, that side could manipulate the jury/judge choice to its bargaining advantage.

Sixth, as to appeal, one striking feature about federal civil appeals, published and unpublished, is the high rate of affirmance at about 80%.[33] More surprisingly, the data show that defendants succeed more than plaintiffs on appeal. For example, defendants appealing their losses after trial obtain reversals at a 33% rate, while losing plaintiffs succeed in only 12% of their appeals after trial. Therefore, defendants emerge from the appellate court in a much better position than when they left the trial court. Why would that be? Both descriptive analyses of the results and more formal regression models tend to dispel explanations based solely on selection of cases. Perhaps the plaintiffs' lower reversal rate stems from real but hitherto unappreciated differences between appellate and trial courts. More precisely, the explanation may lie in appellate judges' attitudes toward trial-level adjudicators, with the appellate judges acting on their perceptions of the trial courts as being pro-plaintiff. The appellate court consequently would be more favorably disposed to the defendant than are the trial judge and the jury. This appellate favoritism would be appropriate if the trial courts were in fact biased in favor of the plaintiff. But as empirical evidence accumulates in refutation of trial-court bias on the plaintiff/defendant axis, any such appellate judges' perceptions appear increasingly to be misperceptions. Or unconscious biases may be at work. Appellate judges' greater distance from the trial process could create an environment in which it is easier to discount harms to the plaintiff. In any event, the data on appellate

---

32. See supra § 2.4(A) (discussion of empirical evidence).

33. See supra § 2.6(B)(1) (discussion of empirical evidence).

leaning in favor of the defendant, an apparent "anti-plaintiff effect," become a cause for concern.[34]

B. Dimensions of Subject

Another future trend, compatible with taking a broader view from many different perspectives, will involve breaking down conceptual and doctrinal boundaries in order to understand civil procedure in a fuller context. The subject of civil procedure is much bigger than its curricular pigeonhole. One should start the more expansive study by pursuing inquiry outward along any of three principal dimensions of the subject.

1. ADR and Complex Litigation

Although this book has emphasized the *ordinary* case, the reader should not let this focus create blinders. Of late, interest in several quarters has shifted toward complex litigation, prototypified by public law litigation such as the desegregation cases and characterized by vastly intensified public concern and participation.[35] Concomitantly, interest has also shifted toward alternatives to litigation—whether by privately negotiated settlement or by other alternative dispute-resolution mechanisms such as arbitration, mediation, and conciliation—whereby almost all grievances conclude short of judicial adjudication.[36] In some significant senses, alternative dispute resolution and complex litigation are both more important than the ordinary case, which falls in the middle of this spectrum. Accordingly, this book has given some attention to those matters at the spectral ends, and the reader should eventually devote advanced study to them.

Nonetheless, an initial focus on ordinary litigation is not nonsensical. One reason is that early mastery of the official procedural

---

34. See Kevin M. Clermont & Theodore Eisenberg, Anti–Plaintiff Bias in the Federal Appellate Courts, 84 Judicature 128 (2000); Kevin M. Clermont & Theodore Eisenberg, Appeal from Jury or Judge Trial: Defendants' Advantage, 3 Am. L. & Econ. Rev. 125 (2001); Kevin M. Clermont & Theodore Eisenberg, Plaintiphobia in the Appellate Courts: Civil Rights Really Do Differ from Negotiable Instruments, 2002 U. Ill. L. Rev. 947; Kevin M. Clermont & Theodore Eisenberg, Judge Harry Edwards: A Case in Point!, 80 Wash. U. L.Q. 1275 (2002); Kevin M. Clermont, Theodore Eisenberg & Stewart J. Schwab, How Employment–Discrimination Plaintiffs Fare in the Federal Courts of Appeals, 7 Employee Rts. & Emp. Pol'y J. 547

(2003); cf. Kevin M. Clermont & Stewart J. Schwab, How Employment Discrimination Plaintiffs Fare in Federal Court, 1 J. Empirical Legal Stud. 429 (2004) (more general empirical treatment of employment discrimination cases); Kevin M. Clermont & Stewart J. Schwab, Employment Discrimination Plaintiffs in Federal Court: From Bad to Worse?, 3 Harv. L. & Pol'y Rev. 1 (2009) (including updated data).

35. For the classic article on this subject, see Abram Chayes, The Role of the Judge in Public Law Litigation, 89 Harv. L. Rev. 1281 (1976).

36. For a broad view of this subject, see Jerome T. Barrett, A History of Alternative Dispute Resolution (2004).

system helps in comprehending the cases read in other law courses. The primary reason, however, is that ordinary litigation provides a better context in which to achieve the purposes of the basic course. Moreover, ordinary litigation is no backwater. It remains extremely important to society and to citizens. The courts thereby act as the default enforcer of law and resolver of disputes. Ordinary litigation not only produces singular decisions that restructure society but also serves as a major vehicle for lawmaking in our government and for articulation of societal values. And the legal system's adjudication enunciates the law that sets the standards under which potential litigants alternatively resolve their disputes by nonlitigation processes, "bargaining in the shadow of the law" to reach outcomes that generally conform to the law and thereby further the law's purposes.[37]

2. Non–Civil–Court and Foreign Comparisons

The typical civil procedure course has a narrow focus along another dimension, as it limits its consideration to *U.S. civil court* procedure. Accordingly, this book too has confined its consideration mainly to procedure in civil court cases in the United States.

However, this narrow focus has costs. It misses a lot of the action, in that a great volume of controversies is adjudicated outside the courts. Furthermore, the stress laid on civil court procedure in the first year of law school sometimes creates an insularity or provincialism among some students. They get the notion that this general style of procedure is the only really viable one for the resolution of controversies and that different styles are necessarily inferior. But students, if they were to examine the other procedures, would find that procedure is related to setting, structure, and purpose. Although it is likely that certain fundamentals must be observed in handling any controversy if the handling is to be accurate and fair and efficient, it is also likely that various rules of procedure appropriate to the regular run of civil court business would be quite unsuitable for resolving a dispute over collective bargaining before the National Labor Relations Board or a question of licensing before the Federal Communications Commission. It may be that the courts have something to learn in the way of procedural finesse from administrative agencies and other bodies that deal with civil controversies. It may also be that the civil courts have something to learn in the way of procedural thoroughness from the criminal courts. Wider study would produce great returns in understanding.[38]

---

37. See Robert H. Mnookin & Lewis Kornhauser, Bargaining in the Shadow of the Law: The Case of Divorce, 88 Yale L.J. 950 (1979).

38. See generally Judith Resnik, Processes of the Law: Understanding

Nevertheless, the modes of operation of administrative agencies and criminal courts are mainly beyond this book's scope, and specialized adjudicative procedures such as those used within corporations, unions, clubs, associations, or churches are completely beyond it. The costs of focusing are necessary, even if lamentable.

Another common misconception is that the particular rules making up the procedure of one's home jurisdiction are the only rules that would really work. A possible corrective for this kind of prejudice lies in realizing that significant differences exist today among federal and various states' procedures. Foreign countries, moreover, have procedures very different from our own, and many of them appear to work fairly well.[39]

Of course, any decrease in parochialism can benefit societies and the individual in myriad ways, as it benefits public thinking, private practice, and ordinary life, but even the more tangibly inclined have to admit that an awareness of comparative law is very practical. Both office lawyers and litigators need some familiarity with the world to function in today's increasingly globalized society, and indeed many lawyers practice across different procedural systems and so need to learn others' procedures, if only to decide where to sue. On a more theoretical level, exposure to comparative aspects of law helps the student to understand the home system's values and rules, while aiding the scholar to evaluate reforms. The great benefit of one's studying other systems of procedure is, however, not the direct instigation of procedural reform but the attainment of a deeper understanding of one's own system.

For such reasons, comparative civil procedure is becoming quite the hot subject.[40] In the study of territorial authority to adjudicate and the effect of judgments, neither a scholar nor this book can still afford to ignore foreign practices.[41] But those subjects offer just the beginning of possibilities for insight. I can give an illustration by returning to the intriguing topic of standards of proof.

Courts and Their Alternatives (2004); David A. Sklansky & Stephen C. Yeazell, Comparative Law Without Leaving Home: What Civil Procedure Can Teach Criminal Procedure, and Vice Versa, 94 Geo. L.J. 683 (2006).

39. International Encyclopaedia of Laws: Civil Procedure (Piet Taelman ed., 2008) nicely collects in five volumes a series of surveys of various countries' civil procedure systems. See also Benjamin Kaplan & Kevin M. Clermont, Ordinary Proceedings in First Instance: Eng-

land and the United States, 16 Int'l Ency. Comp. L. ch. 6 (1984).

40. See Oscar G. Chase et al., Civil Litigation in Comparative Context (2007); Kevin M. Clermont, Foreword: Why Comparative Civil Procedure?, in Kuo–Chang Huang, Introducing Discovery into Civil Law at ix (2003); cf. Kevin M. Clermont, Integrating Transnational Perspectives into Civil Procedure: What Not to Teach, 56 J. Legal Educ. 524 (2007).

41. See supra §§ 4.2(D), 5.1(A)(4)(c), 5.6(C).

In England and the United States, the law treats the standard of proof as centrally important, and its standards of proof are openly probabilistic: civil claims ordinarily must be proved merely by a preponderance of the evidence, that is, the party with the burden of persuasion must prove the fact to be more probable than not. In setting preponderance of the evidence as the civil standard of proof, the common law has overcome the appealing but unsound lay intuition that outcome should not swing from no recovery to full recovery on the basis of a slight shift in the weight of evidence. Instead, the common law pursues an error-minimizing strategy by routinely applying preponderance and not some higher standard. The argument for this approach is strong, because the preponderance standard is optimal given two conditions that are very plausible. The first condition is that an error in favor of the plaintiff is neither more undesirable nor less undesirable than an error in favor of the defendant, or that a dollar mistakenly paid by the defendant (a false positive) is just as costly to society as a dollar mistakenly uncompensated to the plaintiff (a false negative). The second condition is that the goal is to minimize the sum of expected costs from these two types of error, that is, the system wants to keep the amounts suffered mistakenly to a minimum. Under these conditions, which do prevail outside the criminal law, the preponderance standard performs better than any other nonvariable standard of proof. By so deciding in accordance with apparent probabilities, the legal system in the long run makes fewer errors than, for example, the many false negatives that a virtual-certainty standard would impose. Formal proofs indeed show that the preponderance standard minimizes not only the expected number of erroneous decisions but also the expected sum of wrongful amounts of damages, while it optimizes the incentives for primary conduct.

Strangely enough, the non-common-law world, including civil-law countries like France[42] and Japan,[43] rather casually requires the civil litigant with the burden to prove the fact to a much higher probability, identical or similar to the criminal law's virtual-certainty requirement. U.S. lawyers accept their own lower standard of proof as a significant policy choice and an unquestionably proper one, and so they react with disbelief upon learning of the foreign practice. But lessons abound in further consideration. This striking divergence between common and civil law not only entails practical consequences, but also suggests a basic difference in attitudes toward the process of trial and subtle differences between the two

42. See Kevin M. Clermont & Emily Sherwin, A Comparative View of Standards of Proof, 50 Am. J. Comp. L. 243 (2002); Kevin M. Clermont & Emily Sherwin, A Comparative Puzzle: Standards of Proof, in Law and Justice in a Multistate World 629 (James A.R. Nafziger & Symeon C. Symeonides eds., 2002).

43. See Kevin M. Clermont, Standards of Proof in Japan and the United States, 37 Cornell Int'l L.J. 263 (2004).

systems' procedural objectives. The non-common-law systems seek the legitimating benefits of the myth that their courts act only on true facts and not on mere probabilities. Common-law courts seek legitimacy elsewhere, perhaps in other myths, and thus are free to adopt preponderance of the evidence as the standard of proof that more efficiently and fairly captures the real truth of the civil case.

3. History and Reform

Still another common misconception is that the particular rules making up the court procedure of the *current* time are the only rules that would really work in those courts. A possible corrective lies in the realization that procedure has undergone drastic changes without cataclysm in the past, as this book has related by means of the stress it has put on history in its Chapter One. Accordingly, a proposal for future change deserves consideration on its merits without any arbitrary assumption that it will precipitate sudden doom. In other words, expansion of the subject of civil procedure should proceed along the time dimension.

The study of the history of procedure certainly illuminates the current law. After all, given our peculiar legal system, a lot of that old stuff is still good law, and yet that stuff can be fully comprehended only in its old context. Moreover, even the new law has evolved from the old law or has converted the old law in the name of reform, either of which developments requires an understanding of what came before. Today's typical civil procedure course, however, has more and more cut out the history, in the pursuit of greater coverage of current law. The cost comes in less and less understanding of that current law, to say nothing of the cultural loss. The neglect of history needs a cure.

An additional benefit of studying legal history is that it prompts the student to think about the future of law. The law is not going to remain the same during the student's career that is under preparation. But even if the only task were mastering the law of the moment, the student should be reflecting on its problems and hence thinking of and about proposals for reform, or perhaps revolutionary change. As an illustration, some commentators, citing increasing dissatisfaction with the current law, claim that the era of the Federal Rules is in its death throes.[44] Among the radical changes they push is an explicit return to specialized rules tailored to the level of complexity or to particular areas of law, in place of the Federal Rules' transsubstantive approach consisting of very

---

44. E.g., Stephen N. Subrin, David Dudley Field and the Field Code: A Historical Analysis of an Earlier Procedural Vision, 6 Law & Hist. Rev. 311, 311 (1988).

general rules applicable to all sorts of cases.[45] Those who know their history refer to this sort of proposal as the "new forms of action."[46]

In brief, an intelligent understanding of the evolving organism of civil procedure demands a broad take, with a focus willing to extend backward and forward in time.

§ 7.2   Civil Procedure Synthesized

The time has come to start reassembling the subject of civil procedure, to try to understand with a wide view what the shapers of the broadly conceived subject are attempting to accomplish.

A.   Essence of Subject

The basic societal needs and values regarding outcome and process instigate the law of civil procedure for U.S. courts, inducing the lawmakers to generate certain procedural policies and rules. But there are conflicts among these needs and values and also tensions within each. The elusive goal for everyone involved in shaping the law of civil procedure is to strike a sound balance amid these conflicts and tensions.

1.   Policies of Procedure

Policies include the general concerns that underlie the rules of civil procedure. The basic societal needs and values propagate these policies, some fundamental and general but others more arbitrary and associated with a particular place and time. The intelligent study of civil procedure will reveal many policies, such as those in favor of deciding the case on its merits, resolving all disputes concerning the whole transaction in one shot, and forging a cooperative federalism. An individual policy sometimes is in the process of evolution, and one policy often collides with others. Such turmoil is a very important cause of the surprisingly considerable *uncertainty* in the law of civil procedure, and also a very certain indicator of the surprisingly considerable *importance* of that law.

With regard to fundamentals, our society has generally opted to dispense justice by third-party *adjudication* involving an **adversary system** wherein the parties are represented by partisan *advocates*. Archetypically, then, acting through their attorneys active parties combatively formulate a case and also propel it to decision by a passive judge acting merely as an umpire and repre-

---

45. E.g., Judith Resnik, Failing Faith: Adjudicatory Procedure in Decline, 53 U. Chi. L. Rev. 494, 495, 526–27 (1986).

46. See Geoffrey C. Hazard, Jr., Forms of Action Under the Federal Rules of Civil Procedure, 63 Notre Dame L. Rev. 628, 636 (1988).

senting impartially an appropriately disinterested society. The adversary system, implying active and unhindered combatants both formulating and propelling the case with equal but waivable procedural opportunities, is at the heart of this scheme. It reflects a human attempt to maximize the sum total of a number of turbulent justice goals: truth or accuracy, procedural fairness and efficiency, systemic legitimacy, party-satisfaction, and others.

Being but a good compromise in an imperfect world, the adversary system has been subject to frequent and sometimes justifiable criticism. Consequently, the adversary system today exists nowhere in pure form and, indeed, is everywhere to some degree a policy in flux. Further reforms are possible that would not endanger the beneficial essence of the adversary system but that would slightly alter the roles of the participants—with the net effect of ameliorating such shortcomings as excessive combativeness or inequalities between opponents in litigating their cases. More radical restructuring might also be desirable at least for certain cases in these changing times—as perhaps along the lines of the alternative model of public law litigation that gives the judge a greatly more active role in unearthing and solving society's ills.

2. Rules of Procedure

The policies are often partially reduced to concrete rules, appearing in the form of statutes, court rules, or doctrines. A principal focus here has been on the Federal Rules of Civil Procedure. But of course, even in the federal court system, the Federal Rules are the tip of civil procedure's iceberg composed of all its rules. These various rules might be part of an organized and comprehensive set of rules, or they can appear as the holding of a single case on some particular procedural point.

Just for illustration, one set of rules on the boundary of civil procedure comprises those treating **legal ethics**. These rules, which are partially embodied in the ABA's Model Rules of Professional Conduct but which extend into the laws of procedure and of malpractice, specify the lawyer's restricted role in the adversary system. That role is not to "do justice" in accord with the lawyer's personal view of justice, but merely to play a designated role in a system of justice. On the one hand, the lawyer must provide the client with effective representation: working competently; avoiding conflicts of interest; maintaining confidences; and zealously representing the client's interests. On the other hand, the lawyer cannot overzealously harm the opponent or others or overzealously abuse the court system. Those conflicting commands leave a narrow path between them for the lawyer to tread, and admittedly the rules do not always perform wonderfully in delineating and illuminating that path.

Rules are therefore important to the proceduralist. Unfortunately, the untutored usually picture civil procedure as comprising nothing but such rules. It is surely true that technical mastery of these rules is critical. But the focus of the student or lawyer cannot be only on these rules, because some rules are very untrustworthy guides to the highly practical profundities of policy lurking below.

3. Sources for Procedure

Who generates the law of civil procedure that applies in U.S. courts? The federal and/or state *constitution* provides some basics (e.g., the Federal Constitution's Seventh Amendment guarantee of trial by jury, which does not apply to state courts) and also establishes the structure for filling in the rest.

The filled-in pattern of the federal system and for most states is as follows: (1) Within constitutional limits the *legislature* has very broad power to regulate the courts' civil procedure (e.g., Federal Rules of Evidence, which was enacted as a statute by Congress). (2) Within constitutional limits the *courts* themselves have power to regulate their own civil procedure, whether by rulemaking pursuant to a proper delegation of legislative power (e.g., Federal Rules of Civil Procedure, which was promulgated by the Supreme Court under the Rules Enabling Act), or by molding doctrine at the sufferance of and subject to the ultimate control of the legislature (e.g., res judicata), or by rulemaking or molding doctrine within a narrow inherent judicial power to conduct the courts' own business (e.g., discipline of individual attorneys for misconduct before the courts). (3) Finally, *the parties and their attorneys* bear much of the responsibility for running the resultant procedural machinery and hence for giving final content to the law of civil procedure (e.g., litigants' approach to discovery provisions).

4. Motivation for Procedure

Ultimately, why have the constitutions, legislatures, and courts created this complicated law of civil procedure? These are the basic reasons: the inevitability of unsettled disputes over substantive law and the attendant facts, the social necessity of resolving those disputes, and the unavoidability of limits on the resources available for such resolution. Together these mean that there must exist, to some degree, an established way to submit and resolve with finality those disputes.

However, more than such basic needs motivates the lawmakers. Preferably, the resolution should be accurate. In this important sense, civil procedure serves substantive law, as well as equal treatment of individual litigants. Moreover, civil procedure embodies independent values too. The means to the end should, for example, be efficient but fair. Often the values in the procedural arena are latent and subtle, and of course disputable and subjective.

In sum, a *just* law of civil procedure goes beyond responding to felt needs by trying to yield a result that serves outcome values and by embodying independent values concerning process.

5. Justice in Procedure

The key to beginning to understand justice is to realize what it is not. It is not merely truth, nor is it only fairness or efficiency in any narrow sense. Justice is all those, and more. It is the bottom line—it is the conclusion that the sum total of all relevant goals has been maximized.

One can divide the pie of relevant considerations in a variety of ways, such as dividing between outcome and process values, or between error and direct costs. But in the final analysis, the jurisprudential task begins with identifying all of the society's ultimate goals whatever they be (e.g., public order, governmental legitimacy, social equality, and so on), while also admitting that they compete or even conflict with one another. That is, the legal system has multiple goals, which are complicated, debatable, and unavoidably competing. Then, the remaining jurisprudential task is nevertheless to combine those goals. A just law or procedure would maximize the attainment of the ultimate goals or, equivalently, minimize the sum of the costs incurred by failure to attain the different ultimate goals.[47]

Accordingly, as a matter of terminology, the word "justice" should not be thrown about in the course of analysis or discussion in describing or attacking a law or procedure. Instead, its use should await completion of the challenge of balancing all the ultimate goals. The breadth of the meaning of "justice" is of more than terminological importance, however. It signifies that law in general and procedure in particular involve tradeoffs, difficult normative tradeoffs. A very protective process may cost too much, or may even work to undermine accuracy.

Today in society, there is a growing realization of the need for tradeoffs in procedure. But this insight has not calmed the waters. Instead, it has triggered politicized battles in a part of the law that for long stretches of history has been rather pacific. Consequently, procedure is as controversial today as it has ever been, with attacks

---

47. See Bush, supra note 7, at 908–21.

on the basic tenets of the adversary system and the Federal Rules regime as well as on particular procedural points.

B. Definition of Subject

This book opened with a rough definition: the subject of civil procedure concerns the societal processes for handling disputes of a noncriminal sort. This book now closes with the desired end-product of study: a better suggestion of the nature of the subject. Consider separately the two words of "civil procedure."

This sweeping word "civil" distinguishes the subject from the criminal process. "Civil" thus encompasses the particular processes of administrative adjudication, arbitration, and other alternative dispute-resolution formats, as well as court procedure in civil actions.

The word "procedure" distinguishes the subject from substance. That distinction is an especially fuzzy one, and the line is drawn in different spots for different purposes. Speaking roughly, then, "procedure" means the societal process for submitting and resolving factual and legal disputes over the rights and duties recognized by substantive law, which rights and duties concern primary conduct in the private and public life that transpires essentially outside the courthouse or other forum. As the machinery of a legal system, procedure implements substantive law and, in doing so, inevitably affects substantive law in profound ways. But procedure is important in its own right as an integral part of a system of justice.

After this limiting by definition, civil procedure is still a broad subject. But in this book the primary focus was a narrower one, having been on the *current* law governing *U.S. civil court* procedure in *ordinary* actions. For good reasons, most law-school courses in civil procedure are to a considerable extent limited to these same three italicized concerns. Using the three as distinctional dimensions of civil procedure (time, forum, form of action), the following diagram depicts that focus as the diagram's solid portion near the center, while suggesting the full extent of the subject that will eventually deserve your wide-gauged attention:

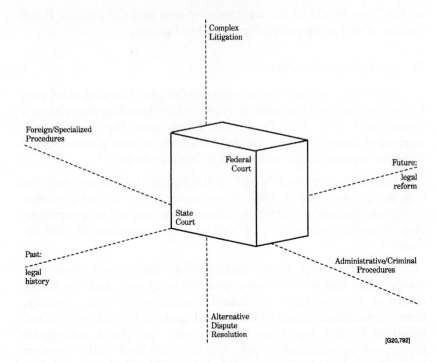

Table of Cases

A

Abbott Laboratories v. Mead Johnson & Co., 971 F.2d 6 (7th Cir.1992)—**§ 2.2, n. 95.**

ACLU Foundation of Southern California v. Barr, 952 F.2d 457, 293 U.S.App.D.C. 101 (D.C.Cir.1991)—**§ 5.2, n. 65.**

Action Embroidery Corp. v. Atlantic Embroidery, Inc., 368 F.3d 1174 (9th Cir.2004)—**§ 4.2, n. 233.**

Action S.A. v. Marc Rich & Co., Inc., 951 F.2d 504 (2nd Cir.1991)—**§ 4.1, n. 47.**

Adam v. Saenger, 303 U.S. 59, 58 S.Ct. 454, 82 L.Ed. 649 (1938)—**§ 4.2, n. 166.**

Aerojet–General Corp. v. Askew, 511 F.2d 710 (5th Cir.1975)—**§ 5.2, n. 64.**

Aetna Cas. & Sur. Co. v. Cunningham, 224 F.2d 478 (5th Cir.1955)—**§ 2.6, n. 243.**

Aetna Cas. & Sur. Co. v. Yeatts, 122 F.2d 350 (4th Cir.1941)—**§ 2.4, n. 153.**

Aetna Life Ins. Co. of Hartford, Conn. v. Haworth, 300 U.S. 227, 57 S.Ct. 461, 81 L.Ed. 617 (1937)—**§ 2.5, n. 207.**

A.F.A. Tours, Inc. v. Whitchurch, 937 F.2d 82 (2nd Cir.1991)—**§ 4.1, n. 106.**

Afram Export Corp. v. Metallurgiki Halyps, S.A., 772 F.2d 1358 (7th Cir.1985)—**§ 4.2, n. 260.**

Agency Holding Corp. v. Malley–Duff & Associates, Inc., 483 U.S. 143, 107 S.Ct. 2759, 97 L.Ed.2d 121 (1987)—**§ 3.2, n. 47.**

Ager v. Jane C. Stormont Hospital and Training School for Nurses, 622 F.2d 496 (10th Cir.1980)—**§ 2.2, n. 63.**

Ahern v. Scholz, 85 F.3d 774 (1st Cir.1996)—**§ 2.4, n. 166.**

A. J. Industries, Inc. v. United States Dist. Court for Central Dist. of California, 503 F.2d 384 (9th Cir.1974)—**§ 4.2, n. 247.**

Albernaz v. City of Fall River, 346 Mass. 336, 191 N.E.2d 771 (Mass.1963)—**§ 5.4, n. 124.**

Albright v. Gates, 362 F.2d 928 (9th Cir.1966)—**§ 6.2, n. 23.**

Alchemie Intern., Inc. v. Metal World, Inc., 523 F.Supp. 1039 (D.N.J. 1981)—**§ 4.2, n. 155.**

Alderman v. Baltimore & O. R. Co., 113 F.Supp. 881 (S.D.W.Va.1953)—**§ 2.2, n. 104.**

Aldinger v. Howard, 427 U.S. 1, 96 S.Ct. 2413, 49 L.Ed.2d 276 (1976)—**§ 4.1, n. 63.**

Alexander v. Fulton County, Ga., 207 F.3d 1303 (11th Cir.2000)—**§ 6.3, n. 59.**

Allen v. McCurry, 449 U.S. 90, 101 S.Ct. 411, 66 L.Ed.2d 308 (1980)—**§ 5.5, n. 149.**

Allied Chemical Corp. v. Daiflon, Inc., 449 U.S. 33, 101 S.Ct. 188, 66 L.Ed.2d 193 (1980)—**§ 2.6, n. 252.**

Allstate Ins. Co. v. Hague, 449 U.S. 302, 101 S.Ct. 633, 66 L.Ed.2d 521 (1981)—**§ 3.1, n. 1.**

Allstate Ins. Co. v. Hugh Cole Builder, Inc., 187 F.R.D. 671 (M.D.Ala. 1999)—**§ 6.3, n. 65.**

ALS Scan, Inc. v. Digital Service Consultants, Inc., 293 F.3d 707 (4th Cir. 2002)—**§ 4.2, n. 182.**

Altman v. Altman, 653 F.2d 755 (3rd Cir.1981)—**§ 2.6, n. 241.**

Alyeska Pipeline Service Co. v. Wilderness Society, 421 U.S. 240, 95 S.Ct. 1612, 44 L.Ed.2d 141 (1975)—**§ 2.5, n. 203.**

Amchem Products, Inc. v. Windsor, 521 U.S. 591, 117 S.Ct. 2231, 138 L.Ed.2d 689 (1997)—**§ 6.3, n. 99, 102.**

American Airlines v. Ulen, 186 F.2d 529, 87 U.S.App.D.C. 307 (D.C.Cir. 1949)—**§ 2.2, n. 99.**

American Button Co. v. Warsaw Button Co., 31 N.Y.S.2d 395 (N.Y.Sup. 1941)—**§ 5.4, n. 119.**

American Dredging Co. v. Miller, 510 U.S. 443, 114 S.Ct. 981, 127 L.Ed.2d 285 (1994)—**§ 4.2, n. 237.**

H

I

N

O

S

T

Y

Z

Table of Statutes and Rules

Index

References are to Pages

†